SPEAK·TRUTH·TO·POWER

COMMANDER
STEVEN HAINES
ROYAL NAVY

INTERNATIONAL LAW AND THE CLASSIFICATION OF CONFLICTS

International Law and
the Classification
of Conflicts

Edited by
ELIZABETH WILMSHURST

Published in association with
the Royal Institute of
International Affairs (Chatham House)

CHATHAM HOUSE

OXFORD
UNIVERSITY PRESS

OXFORD
UNIVERSITY PRESS

Great Clarendon Street, Oxford, OX2 6DP,
United Kingdom

Oxford University Press is a department of the University of Oxford.
It furthers the University's objective of excellence in research, scholarship,
and education by publishing worldwide. Oxford is a registered trade mark of
Oxford University Press in the UK and in certain other countries

First Edition published in 2012
Impression: 3

British Library Cataloguing in Publication Data
Data available

Library of Congress Cataloging in Publication Data
Library of Congress Control Number: 2012938484

ISBN 978–0–19–965775–9

Printed in Great Britain by
CPI Group (UK) Ltd, Croydon, CR0 4YY

Foreword

This is an important book. It brings an empirical discipline and normative rigour to the examination of an issue that has its roots deeply embedded in the structure of international humanitarian law, the differentiation between international armed conflicts and non-international armed conflicts and the distinction between these and other situations of armed violence. Common Article 2 of the 1949 Geneva Conventions provides that the Conventions shall apply to an 'armed conflict which may arise between two or more of the High Contracting Parties'. Common Article 3 provides that '[i]n the case of armed conflict not of an international character . . . each Party to the conflict shall be bound to apply, as a minimum, the following . . .'. Together, these provisions established a framework for the application of the rules of the Conventions which is almost exclusively focused on traditional inter-state conflicts between two sovereigns across an international boundary. This framework was reinforced by the two Additional Protocols of 1977, with their explicit differentiation between international armed conflicts and non-international armed conflicts and the elaboration of detailed rules in respect of the former but a relative paucity of rules in respect of the latter.

From the perspective of a lawyer advising a government that gives weight to its legal obligations, the issue of classification may be important for many reasons. First, it is relevant to an appreciation of the legal framework applicable to conflicts in which the State is itself engaged. Second, it is the normative yardstick for the evaluation of the legality of the conduct of others, both in the case of conflicts in which the State is itself engaged and those in respect of which it is only an observer, but, as with the United Kingdom, an observer with an interest in wider issues of rule of law and of international peace and security. Third, it engages considerations of normative clarity, not simply across the two strands of international humanitarian law but also across international humanitarian law, international human rights law, international criminal law and any relevant and applicable domestic laws of the States involved in the conflict. Fourth, it goes to the optical credibility of the law in an area that is the subject of close public interest and comment. Is it really credible, for example, that the hostilities in Afghanistan, with upwards of 130,000 International Security Assistance Force (ISAF) troops from fifty States, is classified as a non-international armed conflict? Fifth, in the case of hostilities of a multiparty character, it goes to considerations of a common legal framework relevant to conduct that might be undertaken jointly, in cooperation or under common command. Sixth, it is relevant to considerations of the humanitarian imperative that is at the heart of the law. The law applicable to international armed conflicts is both clearer and more developed than the law applicable to non-international armed conflicts. The imperative is, or should be, to proceed by reference to the highest standards of conduct and protection. Seventh, questions of classification may be relevant to an appreciation of the status of the domestic authority of the State in whose territory the hostilities are taking place. Eighth, the classification of a conflict may have a bearing on the appreciation of issues in the context of litigation. Each of these elements may in turn have their own longer tail of further issues.

While issues of detention may be the part of international humanitarian law where the divide between the two strands of law is most sharply defined, the divergence, both qualitative and quantitative, goes much wider. Questions of combatant status and civilian immunity fall to be addressed differently depending on whether the conflict is of an international character or a non-international character. The law relating to fundamental rights and the treatment of persons in the custody of a party is considerably more developed in the Geneva Conventions and Additional Protocol I than it is in Common Article 3 and Additional Protocol II. Questions of accountability, including the repression of breaches and grave breaches, are addressed more fully, and with greater clarity and precision, in the law relating to international armed conflict than they are in the law relating to non-international armed conflict. The list goes on.

One consequence of this divergence has been inclinations and attempts to fill the gap in the law relating to non-international armed conflict by the articulation of principles of customary international law that would apply in all conflicts, regardless of classification. In the nature of things, this approach has extrapolated from conventional principles of law applicable to international armed conflict through customary principles of law applicable to international armed conflict to arrive at principles of customary international law applicable in non-international armed conflicts. Another approach has been to adopt and apply rules of international armed conflict in non-international armed conflict situations either as a matter of discretion or by analogy. A third approach has been to look to rules of international human rights law to inform or supplement international humanitarian law.

While each of these techniques has utility and merit, none is ultimately satisfactory as they leave a residue, in some cases quite substantial, of normative uncertainty about what the law is that applies to non-international armed conflicts. And, as in most circumstances, the strength of the law rests heavily on its clarity, visibility, predictability and formality of application. Analytical techniques that address uncertainty, fill in the gaps and respond to debates about formal application are therefore at best a short-term fix.

The concluding chapter of the book is a notable endeavour to bring together strands of analysis across the disparate case studies that make up the second part of the book and the earlier overarching analyses and commentary in the opening chapters that address broader issues of law. Amongst the conclusions that it notes is that none of the authors recommends a major change in the classification system, concluding that the existing categories of international and non-international armed conflict are sufficient to encompass all existing forms of conflict. In a similar vein, there is no support for the creation of new categories of conflict to address the changing character of hostilities. The point is made that 'the division into non-international and international armed conflict is inevitable so long as the post-Westphalian paradigm of sovereign States remains and as long as the Geneva

Conventions and Protocols are the main body of applicable law, whether as treaties or as customary law'.

This may be correct, and it is undoubtedly the case, as the concluding chapter also notes, that '[i]nternational humanitarian law applicable in the two forms of armed conflict will continue to merge'. The question that remains, however, is whether the time is not right, and ripe, for an initiative to encourage the merger more fully of these two strands into a single body of law that would be applicable in all situations of armed conflict regardless of classification.

The volume concludes with the observation that there is unlikely to be agreement to conclude amending treaties to formalize convergence, whether in a comprehensive treaty or a fusing protocol. It suggests, however, that 'it may be feasible to encourage the making of unilateral commitments by States participating in hostilities with regard to the law they will apply'. Building on this, it may be not simply that States participating in hostilities may be encouraged to make unilateral commitments, whether alone or with others, about the law that they will apply in a particular conflict. There would be merit in States making unilateral declarations of a more general character, away from any issue of application in a particular conflict, that they will henceforth apply the law relevant to international armed conflicts in all situations of armed conflict, whatever their character, save insofar as may be modulated in the unilateral declaration itself to take account of objective distinctions of a practical nature between conflicts of an international and a non-international character. The issue of the classification of conflicts is a distraction from the humanitarian imperative of international humanitarian law, rooted in the edifice of the 1949 Geneva Conventions and the 1977 Additional Protocols. The humanitarian imperative of these instruments can be readily maintained and enhanced while moving past this distinction.

Whether this appreciation is more widely held will be a matter for debate. This volume, with its empirical detail and analytical enquiry, will contribute greatly to this discussion. This is an important, scholarly and timely work that will inform other enquiries in this area that are just getting started. Its authors are to be congratulated.

Sir Daniel Bethlehem QC

20 Essex Street
London WC2
7 February 2012

Preface

This book emerged from a series of meetings held at Chatham House with the participation of a group of international lawyers and representatives of the United Kingdom armed forces, to examine problems arising from the classification of armed violence and their impact on the applicable rules of international law. The authors circulated papers in advance of each meeting; the papers were discussed and then revised, with heated debate sometimes playing a prominent part. Although the book is the product of the whole group, there are some matters on which views remained divided; each chapter is the responsibility of its writer alone and does not necessarily represent the views of all the contributors.

While the main purpose of the book is to discuss classification, it also provides a collection of studies of armed violence viewed through the lens of international humanitarian law, giving historical background, context and an examination of relevant legal issues. As such it is hoped that it will be a valuable resource to all readers interested in international humanitarian law and its applicability and implementation in a wide range of situations.

The book attempts to be consistent in the terminology used by its different writers while recognizing that it is not possible always to succeed. It uses synonymously the 'law of armed conflict' and 'international humanitarian law', while usually preferring the latter. Some terms must be explained. We refer to 'armed conflict' as it is used, but not defined, in the Geneva Conventions and their Protocols; the meaning is discussed more fully in Chapters 3 and 4. Many different terms are used in the literature for hostilities which are of a transnational or extraterritorial nature because a non-international armed conflict in one State spills over into another, or because a State targets a non-state actor in another. We refer to these conflicts as 'extraterritorial' in preference to other terms. In discussing situations where military force is used by a State outside its own country, 'territorial State' describes the State where hostilities take place; 'foreign State' is foreign to the territorial State; 'non-state armed groups' are self-explanatory.

The authors wish to thank the British Red Cross for providing funding for the meetings at Chatham House; the Oxford Institute for Ethics, Law and Armed Conflict, who hosted our final meeting; and Jennifer Wilkinson and Lucy Crittenden who helped with the organization of that meeting. The authors are also indebted to the helpful comments made by those members of the group who discussed the papers on which the book is based although they did not themselves contribute a paper: Lt Col Grant Davies, Lt Col Keith Eble, Charles Garraway, Rupert Hollins and David Kretzmer. The work would not have been brought to a conclusion without the invaluable help with editing and more from Monika Hlavkova; thanks go too to Maria Dogaru for her research assistance.

Table of Contents

Table of Cases

INTERNATIONAL CRIMINAL TRIBUNAL FOR RWANDA

INTERNATIONAL CRIMINAL TRIBUNAL FOR
THE FORMER YUGOSLAVIA

SPECIAL COURT FOR SIERRA LEONE

UN COMMITTEE AGAINST TORTURE

UN HUMAN RIGHTS COMMITTEE

USA

US MILITARY TRIBUNAL AT NUREMBERG

Table of Treaties and Other Instruments

List of Abbreviations

General

1GW	First Generation Warfare
2GW	Second Generation Warfare
3GW	Third Generation Warfare
4GW	Fourth Generation Warfare
AI	Amnesty International
AJIL	American Journal of International Law
CEDAW	Convention on the Elimination of Discrimination against Women
CIA	Central Intelligence Agency (US)
DCDC	Ministry of Defence Development, Concepts and Doctrine Centre
DRC	Democratic Republic of the Congo
ECHR	European Convention on Human Rights
ECtHR	European Court of Human Rights
EJIL	European Journal of International Law
FBI	Federal Bureau of Investigation (US)
FRY	Federal Republic of Yugoslavia
GC	Geneva Conventions
HRC	Human Rights Committee (UN)
HRL	Human rights law
HRW	Human Rights Watch
IAC	International armed conflict
IACHR	Inter-American Commission on Human Rights
ICC	International Criminal Court
ICCPR	International Covenant on Civil and Political Rights
ICG	International Crisis Group
ICJ	International Court of Justice
ICRC	International Committee of the Red Cross
ICTY	International Criminal Tribunal for Former Yugoslavia
IHL	International humanitarian law
ILC	International Law Commission
ILDC	*Oxford Reports on International Law in Domestic Courts*
LOAC	Law of armed conflict
MOD	UK Ministry of Defence
NATO	North Atlantic Treaty Organization
NIAC	Non-international armed conflict
POW	Prisoner of war
ROE	Rules of engagement
SCSL	Special Court for Sierra Leone
SOFA	Status of Forces Agreement
UK	United Kingdom

UKMIL	United Kingdom Materials on International Law
UN	United Nations
UNHCR	United Nations High Commissioner for Refugees
US	United States

5 (Northern Ireland)

BAOR	British Army of the Rhine
INLA	Irish National Liberation Army
IRA	Irish Republican Army
IRSP	Irish Republican Socialist Party
MACA	Military Aid to Civil Authorities
MACP	Military Aid to the Civilian Power
NICRA	Northern Ireland Civil Rights Association
OIRA	The Officials (IRA faction)
PIRA	Provisional Irish Republican Army
PSNI	Police Service of Northern Ireland
RAF	Royal Air Force
RHC	Red Hand Commando
RUC	Royal Ulster Constabulary
SAS	Special Air Service in Northern Ireland
SDLP	Social Democratic Labour Party
SFNI	Security Forces in Northern Ireland
UDA	Ulster Defence Association
UDR	Ulster Defence Regiment
UVF	Ulster Volunteer Force

6 (DRC)

ADF	Allied Democratic Forces
ADP	Democratic Alliance of Peoples
AFDL	Alliance des Forces Démocratiques pour la Libération du Congo-Zaïre
ALC	Armée de libération du Congo
ANC	Armée nationale congolaise
ANT	Armée nationale tchadienne
AZADHO	Association Zaïroise de Défense de Droits de l'Homme
CADDHOM	Collectif des Associations des droits de l'homme
CNDP	Congrès national pour la défense du peuple
CNRD	National Resistance Council for Democracy
DSP	Division Spéciale Présidentielle
FAA	Forças Armadas Angolanas
FAB	Forces Armées Burundaises
FAC	Forces Armées Congolaises
FAPC	People's Armed Forces of Congo
FAR	Forces Armées Rwandaises
FARDC	Forces Armées de la République Démocratique du Congo

FAZ	Forces Armées Zaïroises
FDLR	Democratic Forces for the Liberation of Rwanda
FNI	Front Nationaliste et Intégrationniste
FPLC	Forces Armées pour la Libération du Congo
FRPI	Force de Résistance Patriotique en Ituri
FUNA	Former Uganda National Army
ICD	Inter-Congolese Dialogue
ICGLR	International Conference on the Great Lakes Region
ICOI	International Commission of Inquiry
JMC	Joint Military Command
MAGRIVI	Mutuelle des Agriculteurs et Eleveurs du Virunga
MLC	Mouvement national pour la libération du Congo
MONUC	United Nations Organization Mission in the Democratic Republic of the Congo
MONUSCO	United Nations Organization Stabilization Mission in the Democratic Republic of the Congo
MRLZ	Revolutionary Movement for the Liberation of Zaire
NALU	National Army for the Liberation of Uganda
NCDD-FDD	Conseil National Pour la Défense de la Démocratie-Forces pour la Défense de la Démocratie
NDF	Namibia Defence Force
OAU	Organization of African Unity
PRP	People's Revolutionary Party
PUSIC	Parti pour l'Unité et la Sauvegarde de l'Intégrité du Congo
RCD	Rassemblement Congolais pour la Démocratie
RCD-Goma	RCD, pro-Rwandan wing
RCD-ML	RCD, pro-Ugandan wing
RPA	Rwandan Patriotic Army
RPF	Rwandan Patriotic Front
SADC	Southern African Development Community
SGIT	Secretary-General's Investigative Team
UNITA	União Nacional para a Independência Total de Angola
UNRFII	Uganda National Rescue Front
UPC	Union des Patriotes Congolais
UPDF	Uganda People's Defence Force
WNBF	West Nile Bank Front
ZDF	Zimbabwe Defence Forces

7 (Colombia)

ACCU	Autodefensas Campesinas de Córdoba y Urabá
AUC	Autodefensas Unidas de Colombia
BE	Black Eagles
CTI	Prosecutor General's Corps of Technical Investigators
ELN	Ejército de Liberación National
FARC	Fuerzas Armadas Revolucionarias de Colombia
FARC-EP	FARC-Ejercito del Pueblo

OAS	Organization of American States
ONG	Organización Nueva Generación
UP	Unión Patriótica

8 (Afghanistan)

AIHRC	Afghanistan Independent Human Rights Commission
COIN	US Counter-Insurgency Doctrine
DRB	Detainee Review Board
IED	Improvised explosive device
ISAF	International Security Assistance Force
JSOC	Joint Special Operation Command
OEF	Operation Enduring Freedom
UNAMA	United Nations Assistance Mission in Afghanistan

9 and 12 (Gaza and Lebanon)

EU BAM	European Union Border Assistance Mission
IDF	Israel Defence Forces
OCHA	Office for the Coordination of Humanitarian Affairs (UN)
PA	Palestinian Authority
PLO	Palestine Liberation Organization
UNIFIL	UN Interim Force in Lebanon

10 (South Ossetia)

EUMM	European Union Monitoring Mission
Georgian SSR	Georgian Soviet Socialist Republic
IIFFMCG	Independent International Fact-Finding Mission on the Conflict in Georgia
JCC	Joint Control Commission
OSCE	Organization for Security and Co-operation in Europe
PACE	Parliamentary Assembly of the Council of Europe

11 (Iraq)

CPA	Coalition Provisional Authority
DOD	US Department of Defense
MNF-I	Multinational Force—Iraq
ORHA	Office of Reconstruction and Humanitarian Aid
USF-I	United States Force–Iraq

List of Contributors

Dapo Akande Co-Director of the Oxford Institute for Ethics, Law and Armed Conflict, University Lecturer in Public International Law, University of Oxford and Yamani Fellow, St Peter's College, Oxford.

Louise Arimatsu Associate Fellow, Chatham House

Annie R. Bird London School of Economics

Steven Haines Professor, Faculty Member, Geneva Centre for Security Policy, and Adjunct Faculty Member, Geneva Academy of International Humanitarian Law and Human Rights

Françoise J. Hampson Professor of Law, University of Essex

Philip Leach Professor of Human Rights, London Metropolitan University; Director, European Human Rights Advocacy Centre

Noam Lubell Professor of Law, University of Essex

Jelena Pejic Legal Advisor, Legal Division, International Committee of the Red Cross

Michael N. Schmitt Chairman and Professor, International Law Department, United States Naval War College

Iain Scobbie Sir Joseph Hotung Research Professor, SOAS, University of London

Felicity Szesnat University of Essex

Elizabeth Wilmshurst Associate Fellow, Chatham House

PART I

1

Introduction

Elizabeth Wilmshurst

The debate on the nature and characteristics of contemporary conflict formed the background for the project which led to the present book. A recent publication on the changing character of war refers to 'a deep and widespread feeling that war has entered a new era, significantly different from what we have known in the past'.[1] There are many reasons, it is said, why contemporary conflicts should be described as 'new wars', different from the old in the aims of the belligerents, the methods of warfare and in the manner in which they are being financed and sustained; the economic underpinnings of these new wars include not only mineral and other natural resources of conflict areas but also remittances from the diasporas and humanitarian aid from abroad intended for the victims of the conflict; war has an increasingly criminal element; there is a blurring of distinctions between war and organized crime; civilians, it is said, are increasingly targeted and increasingly involved.[2]

For the international lawyer and the legal adviser to the military, a relevant question is whether such changes as these render the categories used for the purpose of international humanitarian law insufficient and inappropriate to current realities.[3] Among the very first matters the student of international humanitarian law is taught are the distinctions between international and non-international armed conflict and

---

[1] A. Gat, 'The changing character of war' in H. Strachan and S. Scheipers, *The Changing Character of War* (2011) 27.

[2] See M. Kaldor, *New and old wars: Organised violence in the global era* (2006); Mats Berdal 'The "New Wars" thesis revisited' in H. Strachan and S. Scheipers, *The Changing Character of War* (2011) 109 discusses and disagrees with the proposition that the deliberate targeting of civilians is a new feature of the late 20th century; at 114 (Berdal, *The 'New Wars' thesis revisited*).

[3] See e.g. discussion in J. Stewart, 'Towards a single definition of armed conflict in international humanitarian law: A critique of internationalized armed conflict' (2003) 85 *International Review of the Red Cross*; G. Corn, 'Hamdan, Lebanon, and the Regulation of Hostilities: the Need to Recognize a Hybrid Category of Armed Conflict' (2007) 40 *Vanderbilt Journal of Transnational Law*; A. Roberts, 'Transformative Military Occupation: Applying the Laws of War and Human Rights' in M. Schmitt and J. Pejic (eds), *International Law and Armed Conflict: Exploring the Faultlines* (2007). And see K. Watkin, 'Stability Operations: A Guiding Framework for "Small Wars" and Other Conflicts of the Twenty-First Century?' in M. Schmitt (ed), *The War in Afghanistan: A Legal Analysis* (2009) 417: 'it appears that international law has been no more successful than military doctrine in definitively addressing the challenges associated with irregular warfare'.

between an armed conflict on the one hand and situations of internal disturbance, such as riots and isolated and sporadic acts of violence, on the other.[4] The reason why the classification of armed violence into categories is of such significance—why, for example, we need to determine whether the killing by US Seals of Osama bin Laden in 2011 or the killing by US drones of Anwar al-Awlaqi in Yemen in the same year was a part of an international armed conflict, a non-international armed conflict or a law-enforcement operation[5]—is of course because classification provides the signpost to the body of law applicable in each situation. The relevant bodies of law—in particular, international humanitarian law, international human rights law and domestic law—differ according to the classification of the situation.

This book examines how contemporary forms of armed violence are classified in practice. It addresses the question whether the current system of classification is still workable. It considers how contemporary conflicts are reflected in the existing categories for legal classification,[6] and examines the difficulties which are experienced in classifying particular kinds of armed violence. Attention is given to whether problems in identifying and applying the appropriate rules of international law are attributable to difficulties in classifying the kinds of armed violence, or whether problems may be attributable to other causes such as the existence of gaps in the substantive law. In considering the consequences of classification the book focuses on the two issues of international humanitarian law which have caused most controversy in recent years—the use of force within hostilities and the capture of persons and their resultant treatment—to determine in what respects the classification of particular forms of armed violence has an impact on the application of these rules.

There is a need for discussion of the law and practice on classification for three reasons in particular. First, the original categories of hostilities were developed in the 1949 Geneva Conventions at a time when State control of the use of military force was at its greatest; but contemporary forms of hostilities frequently involve non-state armed groups. The initial driver for the debate on the adequacy of the existing categories was the use of military force following 9/11 and the so-called war on terror. The violence used by armed groups and the military responses to it led to proposals that new categories of armed conflict be formulated for legal purposes. 'The war on terror is a new type of war not envisioned when the Geneva Conventions were negotiated and signed', was the view of the first administration of George W. Bush.[7] The issue has generated a huge literature.[8] This book revisits the

---

[4] There is a nice account of this teaching process in A. Duxbury, 'Drawing Lines in the Sand—Characterising Conflicts for the Purposes of Teaching International Humanitarian Law' (2007) 8 *Melbourne Journal of International Law* 259; it also reminds us that while debates about distinctions 'are significant in terms of the legal classification of a particular situation . . . they do little to describe the suffering of those subject to conflict or violence' (at 270).

[5] Osama bin Laden's death is discussed more fully by Noam Lubell in ch. 13, section 5.

[6] It may perhaps go without saying that classification of hostilities for the purpose of national law, e.g. the US War Powers Resolution, is not the subject of this book, which deals only with classification under international law.

[7] War Crimes at Large, Ambassador Richard Prosper Address at Chatham House in London (20 February 2002).

[8] The debate is mentioned in ch. 3, section 9, ch. 13, section 1 and ch. 14, section 3.

question whether there should be a new category of armed conflict to cover military counter-terrorism operations or extraterritorial operations against non-state armed groups more generally. The question is raised against the background of continuing debate as to whether counter-terrorism operations are appropriate to armed conflict or, rather, to a law-enforcement paradigm.

Secondly, this debate is set against the background not only of the contemporary character of armed violence but also of the developing scope of the law. The differences between the rules of international humanitarian law which are applicable in the two categories of armed conflict have in some respects diminished in recent years because of the development of practice—frequently evolving into international customary law—which has extended to non-international armed conflicts some of the law previously applicable only to international armed conflicts.[9] This has led to debate as to whether further merging of international humanitarian law applicable to the different categories of hostilities would be desirable—the so-called 'unification of international humanitarian law'[10]—and consequently whether the continued division into international and non-international armed conflict continues to make sense.

Thirdly, the classification of armed violence is of relevance to the application of international human rights law. The manner in which human rights law applies in armed conflict has become a matter of controversy. Human rights law applies in parallel with international humanitarian law, but the exact relationship between these two branches of international law and the extent of the extraterritorial application of human rights law are given different descriptions by international courts, States and commentators.[11] The matter will not be resolved by changes in classification but issues of classification are relevant to the debate.

These developments provide the context for the book. The *novelty* of all of the 'changing characteristics' of war may not be fully born out by historical examination.[12] Whether there are indeed new wars and old is a matter for debate by scholars of war studies, a debate that is touched on by Steven Haines in chapter 2 of this volume. But those whose task it is to analyse trends in the character of conflict for the purpose of national defence strategy emphasize that modern-day conflicts involve a range of transnational, State, group and individual participants, operating both globally and locally, and adversaries who present hybrid threats, combining conventional, irregular and asymmetric threats in the same time and space.[13] In the same conflict it is possible to see concurrent inter-communal violence, terrorism, pervasive criminality and widespread disorder. Chapter 2 outlines some of the forms of these hostilities and points out: 'Not only are hostilities today rarely as simple as that characterized by set piece battles between opposing States' military forces arrayed on a formalized battlefield (in the manner exemplified by the Battle

---

[9] See ch. 3, section 3; and J.-M. Henckaerts and L. Doswald-Beck, *Customary International Humanitarian Law Study* (2004).
[10] L. Moir, *Towards the unification of international humanitarian law?* (2005) 108–28.
[11] See ch. 4, section 2.
[12] See e.g. Berdal, *The 'New Wars' thesis revisited*, 109.
[13] DCDC, 'Future Character of Conflict' MOD 02/20 c5 (2010).

of Solferino in 1859); they are frequently rendered extremely difficult by the coincidental mix of many of the types of hostilities discussed.'[14] This mix of conflicts has led the UK Ministry of Defence to forecast that 'The distinction between inter-state and intra-state war, and between regular and irregular warfare, will remain blurred and categorising conflicts will often be difficult'.[15]

The legal categories of armed conflict and other situations of violence are described by Dapo Akande in chapter 3, which examines the history of the distinction between the two categories of armed conflict, the consequences of the distinction and whether it still has validity. The author discusses the differences between a non-international armed conflict and other hostilities, as well as extra-territorial hostilities by one State against a non-state armed group, and armed conflicts in which UN 'blue helmets' are engaged. These are all concepts which are necessary to an understanding of the case studies. As will be seen in the concluding chapter, the author's views on some of these concepts are not shared by all authors of the book, and these very differences point up the difficulties experienced in particular instances of classification.

To illustrate the consequences of classification, Jelena Pejic in chapter 4 examines two of the main 'baskets' of rules making up international humanitarian law: those regulating the use of force and those governing the deprivation of liberty of persons, with a view to identifying what the existing law is and where it may be lacking in the face of 'new' conflict situations. The chapter also discusses the difficulties arising from the as yet unsettled relationship between international humanitarian law and human rights law.

The book relies not only on legal analysis but also, and above all, on examination of a number of situations of armed violence which are used as case studies, in order to explore the ways in which classification and its consequences are of significance in practice. Sir Adam Roberts has written that:

> There is little tradition of disciplined and reasoned assessment of how the laws of war have operated in practice. Lawyers, academics, and diplomats have often been better at interpreting the precise legal meaning of existing accords, or at devising new law, than they have been at assessing the performance of existing accords or generalizing about the circumstances in which they can or cannot work. In short, the study of the law of war needs to be integrated with the study of history; if not, it is inadequate.[16]

By giving an overview of recent practice on classification in the context of current military realities, the case studies attempt in part to respond to this challenge. The authors, however, have for the most part been limited to publicly available documents and have thus not been able to provide a *complete* account of the way in which the hostilities were viewed by the participants.

---

[14] Chapter 2, section 4.
[15] DCDC, 'Global Strategic Trends—Out to 2040' MOD 02/10 c30 (2010) and UK Strategic Defence and Security Review 2010.
[16] Sir A. Roberts, 'Land Warfare: From Hague to Nuremberg' in Sir M. Howard, G. J. Andreopoulos and M. Shulman, *The Laws of War: Constraints on Warfare in the Western World* (1994) 117.

The case studies which are chosen to illustrate many of the difficulties of classification can be found in chapters 5 to 14. Together they give examples of characteristics of contemporary conflict, including the 'blurred' nature of different forms of hostilities; motivations for the use of violence which may be criminal rather than political; the changing identity of participants; military operations against non-state armed groups in weaker States; occupations whose beginning, end and geographical extent are difficult to identify and where violence occurring within the occupied country also presents difficulties of classification; proxy conflicts and the attribution of the activities of a non-state armed group to a State; multilateral operations; and the particular characteristics of the 'global war on terror'.

Each of the authors of the studies was asked to follow the same format, outlining the views of the various actors in the armed violence and of outside parties as to the classification of the situation; and then undertaking his or her own analysis of the classification. The case studies test the proposition, which is forcefully made in chapters 3 and 4, that classification is essential to compliance with the law because it provides the appropriate legal framework governing the conduct of hostilities; for this purpose they discuss the application of force and the detention of individuals in hostilities, assessing whether the rules on classification have the expected impact in practice on these two issues.

The first study, in chapter 5, covers the hostilities in Northern Ireland over the years between 1968 and the Good Friday Agreement in 1998, hostilities which spilt over into both mainland United Kingdom and into other States, notably the Irish Republic and parts of western Europe. Since the origins of the hostilities reach back over four centuries, Steven Haines, like the authors of some of the other studies, was faced with the problem of having to condense a very complex history. He had to omit, with reluctance and for reasons of space, the centuries-old causes of the hostilities.

The natural starting point of a study on the hostilities in the Democratic Republic of Congo, with their immense civilian loss of life, would have been the coming of colonialism and the evils of that era. But the last twenty years provide sufficient material for the examination of classification problems. In chapter 6 Louise Arimatsu divides Congo's history of violence into four periods: first, the period from the spring of 1993 until summer 1996; second, the outbreak of the First Congo War in July 1996 until the summer of 1998; third, the Second Congo War until the establishment of the transitional government in July 2003; and fourth, the period since the end of the Second Congo War during which time large-scale fighting has continued to dominate life in the eastern provinces. The classification between international and non-international of the many different armed conflicts in these different periods is rendered extremely difficult by the multiplicity of armed groups and the many forms of intervention by foreign States.

The situation in Colombia faced the authors of the next study, Felicity Szenat and Annie Bird, with the problem of the relationship of crime and armed conflict. Chapter 7 describes the participation in hostilities of non-state armed groups with different objectives, funded by drug trafficking, kidnappings and other crime,

paramilitary groups with strong links with economic and political sectors which
have used them as 'private armies' to protect their interests from the other groups,
and groups whose primary aim is drug trafficking. There have been nearly four
million direct victims of armed violence from 1964 to 2004 alone and huge
numbers of displaced persons. The study deals with the immensely complicated
permutations of the hostilities between these different groups and between them
and the government, as well as the impact of the intervention of foreign States on
their classification. It also covers Operation Phoenix, the Colombian incursion into
Ecuador.

In the case study on Afghanistan in chapter 8, Françoise Hampson discusses a
number of different conflicts occurring in the same country and examines the
extent to which the determination of the law applicable to each was affected by the
classification of the situation. Of course it is not only law which matters; political
direction is also important, and in some circumstances it may be of more consequence than the law itself, allowing less freedom of action than the law. This case
study also provides a particularly useful occasion for the discussion of legal issues
arising from the capture and detention of persons.

In many of the case studies which deal with hostilities between a State and non-
state armed groups, the author had to grapple with the question whether a
particular group considered international humanitarian law to be of any relevance
to it at all. This was a problem in the case study on Gaza in chapter 9. Iain Scobbie
discusses the period following the second *intifada* in September 2000 up to the
present. This period includes Israel's withdrawal from Gaza in September 2005,
Operation Cast Lead in 2008/09 and the Israeli response to the humanitarian aid
flotilla in 2010.

In chapter 10 Philip Leach discusses the 2008 South Ossetian armed conflict
which involved the States of Georgia and Russia and the armed forces of the de
facto authorities of South Ossetia. Among other things, the case study raises the
problem of attribution in the context of classification: the chapter discusses the
extent to which Russia exercised control over the South Ossetian forces, in order to
assess whether the latter can be considered to have been acting as de facto agents of
Russia, thereby rendering the conflict international. The question of attribution is
also a relevant one for Iain Scobbie's study on the conflict in Lebanon in 2006,
because of the relationship between Hezbollah and the Lebanese government.
Chapter 12 examines the armed conflict which was begun by Operation True
Promise (named after a 'promise' by Hezbollah's Secretary General to capture
Israeli soldiers in order to exchange them for Lebanese prisoners in Israeli jail)
and the Israeli response in Operation Change Direction.

Classification is not always a controversial matter. The armed conflict in Iraq,
which began with the military intervention in 2003, changed from what was
universally agreed to be an international armed conflict, through a period of belligerent occupation, to non-international armed conflict. Michael Schmitt discusses in
chapter 11 the relationship between the various forms of armed conflict in the
different periods and how transition occurs between them. A further point of interest
was the role of the Security Council in determining the relevant classification.

The study on 'the war against Al-Qaeda' or 'the global war on terror' is unique in that it deals with 'a war that might not be a war, against an elusive enemy whose existence as an organized entity is sometimes cast in doubt'. Noam Lubell in chapter 13 lists and discusses five different options that have been put forward to classify the hostilities: that it is an international armed conflict between the US and Al-Qaeda; that it is a non-international armed conflict between the same two parties; that it is not a separate armed conflict, but is part of other existing conflicts such as the one in Afghanistan; that it is an armed conflict between the US and Al-Qaeda that requires a new classification since it is neither international nor non-international; and that it is not an armed conflict at all.

The section on case studies ends with chapter 14 on 'the future'. Michael Schmitt considers how 'future visions of conflict may intersect with the contemporary law of armed conflict' and discusses the ways in which law and conflict adjust to each other. At a time when the US Department of Defence has declared that military force can be used in response to cyber attacks, this chapter looks at cyber warfare, as well as extraterritorial conflict and complex battle spaces and considers whether classification of conflicts will be more difficult in the future.

The choice of case studies for this book was a difficult one, not only because of the embarrassment of riches at the time when the list was made but also because, inevitably, once the list had been decided upon new hostilities began which could with benefit have been included. There were two omissions from our list however which we determined in a small way to remedy: the situations in Libya in 2011 and in Mexico in the few years up to and including 2011. Libya in 2011 provides an illustration of two parallel armed conflicts in one space: first, the hostilities between government forces and the opposition which at some point met the definition of a non-international armed conflict such that international humanitarian law was invoked, and second, the international armed conflict between Libya and the NATO-led coalition which took military action under Security Council resolution 1973 (2011) for the protection of civilians. Libya was also a situation where the *ius ad bellum* (the authorization by the Security Council resolution) was the chief constraint on the targeting authorizations. The situation in Mexico is one of massive violence by organized cartels for criminal purposes but with the intention of effectively taking over some organs of State. The UN Security Council has recognized that serious threats to international security can be posed by drug trafficking and transnational organized crime, and has pointed out the increasing link between drug trafficking and the financing of terrorism.[17] In relation to these two situations—Libya and Mexico—there is some description of the hostilities in chapter 2 and brief analysis in chapter 15.

The conclusions reached in chapter 15 distil the findings of the case studies in the light of the discussion earlier in the book of relevant legal concepts and applicable law. The chapter summarizes many of the difficulties experienced in classifying the hostilities covered by the case studies and outlines the consequences

---

[17] Statement by the President of the Security Council, S/PRST/2010/1 (24 February 2010).

of making those classifications. The chapter discusses the picture of classification practice drawn by the case studies and reaches conclusions as to the likely future of the law. It is true that the choice of the case studies has inevitably dictated the conclusions reached. But the choice of studies is intended to be sufficiently representative for generalizations to be made from them.

A word is needed about what the book does not seek to do. The case studies discuss the law which was applied or should have been applied during hostilities; they do not deal with subsequent attempts to bring to justice in international or domestic courts individual violators of the law. The development of international criminal law has had an impact on classification, not least because the list of war crimes within the jurisdiction of the various courts is in most cases divided between the two categories of armed conflict, and a prosecutor may often have to decide, and then prove, which form of conflict prevailed at the time a crime was committed. Classification in international criminal law is a subject in itself; while the case law of the international courts is used liberally in this book, it is not discussed systematically.[18]

The subject of classification is one which can give rise to discussion about almost any issue of international humanitarian law. But this is not a manual of the law applicable to armed forces; nor does it examine the impact of the changing character of war on the substantive rules of international humanitarian law.[19] The contributors restrict themselves chiefly to the issue of classification and its direct consequences. They identify the problems but this book does not seek to resolve them collectively. Further, while it is necessary to deal with situations of internal violence in discussing whether they reach the threshold of non-international armed conflict, the law applicable to 'mere' internal violence is not otherwise examined.

---

[18] It is touched on in ch. 15 (Conclusions), section 3.2.

[19] For discussion of this issue see e.g. R. Pedrozo and D. Wollschlaeger (eds), *International Law and the Changing Character of War* (2011).

2

The Nature of War and the Character of Contemporary Armed Conflict

*Steven Haines**

1. Introduction

While most of this volume is about the law that regulates the conduct of hostilities, this particular chapter is not. It concerns the general nature and characteristics of hostilities, the worst humanitarian effects of which the law exists to mitigate. Contemporary forms of hostilities are less frequently conflicts between States than a variety of armed struggles involving not only States but a growing number of organized armed groups motivated by a wide range of interests. Indeed, the formally constituted armed forces of States may not even be involved directly in such hostilities, especially when different armed groups fight each other within the territory of 'failed' or 'failing' States. The key question the volume as a whole addresses is to do with the extent to which a modern body of law, which first came formally into being when war between States was the principal focus, remains suitably relevant and applicable at a time when it is expected to regulate hostilities in armed conflict between a less distinct range of entities. The aim of this chapter is to provide a brief general context by highlighting the characteristics of contemporary hostilities.

There is a substantial literature on what is variously described as 'war' or 'armed conflict', with important contributions made from a range of disciplines, most notably military history, war studies and law.[1] Historians and war studies specialists tend to use 'war' and 'armed conflict' virtually interchangeably. Lawyers, on the other hand, are conscious of a difference of legal meaning between the two and, since the adoption of the United Nations Charter, prefer 'armed conflict' to 'war'.[2]

* The author thanks Ben Brzezicki for his research assistance in the preparation of this chapter.

[1] The inter-disciplinary approach to the study of war is no better acknowledged than in the context of the University of Oxford's project on the Changing Character of War that ran between 2003 and 2009; see H. Strachan and S. Scheipers (eds), *The Changing Character of War* (2011).

[2] Resort to 'war' as a means of pursuing State policy was prohibited by the 1928 Kellogg-Briand Pact, a key consideration in the prosecutions of major German and Japanese war criminals at the Nuremberg and Tokyo tribunals following the Second World War. (See R. Jackson, 'Nuremberg in Retrospect: Legal Answer to International Lawlessness' in G. Mettraux (ed.), *Perspectives on the*

Although by no means a perfect solution, this chapter (but this chapter alone) refers to the 'nature of war' but to the 'characteristics of armed conflict'. A useful phrase to encapsulate them both will be hostilities.[3] A description of the nature of war tends to be concerned with generalities while the characteristics of armed conflict are more associated with detailed aspects of the conduct of hostilities at the tactical level—the level at which the bulk of the relevant law is applied.

What follows examines the realities of the situations in which the law of armed conflict might apply and how hostilities are viewed by those who spend their time analysing them. It begins by discussing the nature of war as first propounded by Clausewitz, as well as recent criticisms of the Clausewitzian approach. It then considers the characteristics of hostilities as they have developed over time, concentrating ultimately on their current features.

2. Clausewitz and the nature of war

Clausewitz's *On War,* published originally in the 1830s, came to be regarded as the pre-eminent treatment of its subject.[4] Central to the nature of war is Clausewitz's 'remarkable trinity' consisting of war's primordial violence, the interplay of probability and chance within it, and its subordination to politics.[5] The precise manifestation of the nature of war in any particular instance is a product of the relations between these three factors, coupled with a consideration of the other elements of war's enduring nature.

The first enduring feature of war is the presence of armed violence delivered by means of combat resulting in bloodshed. As Clausewitz observed: 'However many forms combat takes, however far it may be removed from the brute discharge of hatred and enmity of a physical encounter, however many forces may intrude which themselves are not part of fighting, it is inherent in the very concept of war that everything that occurs *must originally derive from combat.*'[6]

Not all violence necessarily constitutes armed conflict. Of some importance in the Clausewitzian notion of war is the need for violence delivered through combat to be for a political or policy purpose. 'Politics is the womb in which war develops—where its outlines already exist in their hidden rudimentary form, like the characteristics of living creatures in their embryos.'[7] War is not merely violence for

---

Nuremberg Trial (2008) 369–70.) Since 1945, the term 'war' has fallen further into disuse, the UN Charter having more generally outlawed resort to force. See further, section 5.1 in ch. 3 below. An additional important reason for States to avoid reference to 'war' is that the formal existence of a 'state of war' has significant international and domestic legal effects in relation to a wide range of issues of both a public and a commercial (private) nature. (For a classic treatment of these issues see Lord McNair and A.D. Watts, *The Legal Effects of War* (1966).)

   [3] A word which also encapsulates violence that qualifies as neither, and which is particularly useful when discussing the threshold between such violence and armed conflict.

   [4] C. von Clausewitz, *On War* (ed. and trans. by M. Howard and P. Paret, 1976) (Clausewitz, *On War*).

   [5] Ibid, 89.

   [6] Ibid, 95. Emphasis in original.   [7] Ibid, 149.

its own sake or for a purpose that is not political. Here, the term 'political' may have a broader connotation than is generally understood. It may well include, for example, the pursuit of religious objectives that may be antithetical to the notion of statehood. The State is an objective presence within the modern international system; indeed, it is central to its existence. Fundamentalist religious beliefs and certain political ideologies may well, however, dismiss the essential nature of the State. Those that do are, of course, profoundly subjective in nature. The fact that motivation is related to something as subjective as an idea or a belief rather than to something as objective as a territorially defined State (or potential State) does not necessarily render that motivation non-'political'. Resort to violent combat for such reasons may well constitute a form of war.

Of greater difficulty is the use of violence for purely material gain. A coalition of illicit drug producers may be able to deliver organized violence in a systematic manner and to a level of intensity usually associated with war. Nevertheless, in doing so they are arguably not engaged in 'war' in the Clausewitzian sense.[8] One feature of criminal activity that may mark out the hostile acts of criminal gangs as falling outwith the Clausewitzian understanding of war is related to the criminal's attitude to the termination of conflict. War is traditionally conducted with the aim of achieving a peaceful result favouring the victor. Those engaged in violence for material gain may see that violence as an essential backdrop to their primary endeavour, however. Criminal gangs may actually seek to prolong conflict rather than to bring it to a successful conclusion.[9]

War is always a human, moral and social activity. A conflict 'fought' exclusively by machines against other machines could not constitute a Clausewitzian war. We may fantasize about such a future occurrence because scientific and technological developments increasingly suggest its possibility, but it is a part of the nature of war that all of those engaged in it must be capable of reaching moral judgments about what they are doing and inflicting on others.[10] Violence is applied in order to influence the judgments of those who are affected by it. War is about coercion— either compellence or deterrence. While coercion—especially deterrence—has come to be particularly associated with the strategic level of war, it is emphatically just as essential at the tactical level. A single soldier in combat is doing what he does to coerce his adversaries to acquiesce: to either withdraw or surrender. The threat of death, serious injury or physical destruction is but a means to an end. It is not an end in itself.

War is complex. It is unpredictable and it is non-linear.[11] Information is imperfect: it is often unreliable and it cannot be absolute; even if it were both,

---

[8] Clausewitz makes no reference to the actions of criminal gangs in *On War*.

[9] See discussion in section 3.2 below. On the legal relevance of motivation, see further discussion in ch. 3 section 6.1 below.

[10] There have been some interesting suggestions made about future 'wars' involving robots capable of operating autonomously. See e.g. R. Arkin, *Governing Lethal Behavior in Autonomous Robots* (2009) and P. Singer, *Wired for War: The Robotics Revolution and Conflict in the 21st Century* (2009).

[11] A. Beyerchen, 'Clausewitz, Non-Linearity and the Unpredictability of War' (1992) 17(3) *International Security* 59.

data would be subject to the vagaries and fallibilities of human interpretation. Hostilities are conducted in changing physical circumstances, the effects of which can be assessed, but not to the degree of certainty necessary for accurate prediction. Each move by each protagonist alters the circumstances and demands a new interpretation of its consequences.

The human element renders war at the same time both rational and irrational. The rationality of decisions made by relatively detached strategic and operational commanders applying well-developed doctrine is, for example, countered by the decisions of those fighting at the tactical level whose actions will frequently be rendered irrational by fear of injury and death. By its very nature, courage is irrational. War's complexity demands a rational approach while many of the challenges of actual combat require a determined irrationality. A fundamental dilemma is that the greater the intensity of combat the greater the need for an incompatible combination of both rational and irrational action. It is difficult to identify any human activity that presents such a challenge as a matter of routine.

These features of war—complexity, imperfect information, unpredictability, its mix of the rational and irrational—contribute to the so-called 'fog of war' and result in what Clausewitz termed 'friction'. The devil is in the detail and the complexity and fluidity of war demands a particular genius to command effectively for success over time. The presence of commanding genius cannot, however, be described as part of war's essential nature: very obviously, commanders are frequently found wanting—on both sides. A mere understanding of war's nature and characteristics, backed by a good grasp of sound doctrine may well deliver success.[12] But, as T.E. Lawrence observed: 'Nine tenths of tactics are certain and taught in books; but the irrational tenth is like the kingfisher flashing across the pool, and that is the test of generals.'[13] Possession of that one tenth—of genius—is what marks out a brilliant commander. . . . but he may still fail, even when pitted against the average, if the full range of circumstances confound him.

Finally, war is constantly present as a feature of the human condition. Admittedly, European States have not fought each other for over half a century[14] and there has been no inter-state war in East Asia since the 1970s. Nevertheless, in much of the rest of the world—in the Great Lakes region of Africa, in the Middle East, in the Caucasus, in South Asia, and in Latin America—war continues to be a significant feature. Even in Europe, North America and East Asia, currently the most 'peaceful' of the world's regions, hostilities involving armed groups using terrorist techniques, for example, remain a potent threat to security, especially obvious since the attacks on New York and Washington in 2001.

---

[12] Doctrine is 'that which is taught'. Formally promulgated military doctrine should be a product of operational experience and effective analysis. Many modern armed forces have developed doctrine to guide their commanders at all levels. For a general description of the function of 'doctrine' see UK Ministry of Defence, *British Defence Doctrine* (2001) 1-1 to 1-2 (MOD, *British Defence Doctrine*).

[13] T. Lawrence, 'Evolution of a Revolt' in A. Lawrence (ed.), *Oriental Assembly* (1940) 103–34.

[14] Leaving aside the hostilities in the Balkans that started as a non-international armed conflict, as Yugoslavia began to disintegrate, before becoming a range of conflicts between States once it had.

2.1. Clausewitz and 'New Wars' theory

Clausewitz wrote *On War* in an era in which State-on-State war was the main focus of attention; how does it fare when used to analyse warfare today which is invariably regarded as more complex, including non-state groups as well as States? There has been a significant debate over the last two decades about how hostilities should now be regarded. This debate has been conducted principally by war studies specialists rather than by lawyers. It can be summarized, albeit rather simplistically, as lining up 'Clausewitzians' against so-called 'New Wars' theorists. Beginning as the Cold War ended and prompted by the disintegration of Yugoslavia and the analysis of the hostilities that erupted as a result, the debate has generated a rich literature with important contributions from a distinguished array of writers.[15] A brief resume of the principal opposing themes will be useful background to the discussion of contemporary armed conflict that follows.

The military campaigns with which Clausewitz was familiar consisted of armies of military professionals confronting each other, with civilians largely uninvolved directly in the ensuing hostilities (albeit by no means unaffected by it). War was then regarded as a condition existing between States in pursuit of their political interests and involved formally constituted armies engaged in hostilities with each other. This is what came to be labelled as 'regular war'. Modern warfare, in contrast, frequently affects civilians directly, with the majority of deaths resulting from it often being of non-combatants rather than of those directly engaged in hostilities.[16] Most modern conflicts are not fought between States but are waged principally 'among the peoples'[17] and involve non-state armed groups of varying sorts. Such conflicts are often described as 'irregular'.

For the New Wars theorists, the Clausewitzian hypothesis is too State-centric and too wedded to a concentration of thinking about regular hostilities between States. Hostilities in these circumstances are frequently described as symmetrical as between the protagonists, in contrast to irregular hostilities which are equally

[15] Significant contributions include, for example, M. van Creveld, *On Future War* (1991) (US edition as *The Transformation of War: The Most Radical Reinterpretation of War since Clausewitz* (1991)); M. Kaldor, *New and Old Wars* (1999); J. Keegan, *A History of Warfare* (1993); H. Münkler, *Die Neuen Kriege* (2002), published in English translation as *The New Wars* (2005) (Münkler, *The New Wars*); C. Fleming, 'New or Old Wars?: Debating a Clausewitzian Future' (2009) 32 *Journal of Strategic Studies* 213; W. Lind, K. Nightingale, J. Schmitt, J. Sutton and G. Wilson, 'The Changing Face of War: Into the Fourth Generation' (1989) *Marine Corps Gazette* 22–6 (Lind et al, *The Changing Face of War*), T. Hammes, *The Sling and the Stone: On War in the 21st Century* (2006) (Hammes, *War in the 21st Century*); B. Heuser, *Reading Clausewitz* (2002); H. Strachan, *Carl von Clausewitz's On War: A Biography* (2007); R. Smith, *The Utility of Force: The Art of War in the Modern World* (2005); C. Gray, *Another Bloody Century: Future Warfare* (2005) (Gray, *Another Bloody Century*).

[16] Note however A. Roberts' conclusion that the 'view, that in general civilians are vastly worse off than in earlier periods, is flawed': A. Roberts, 'The Civilian in Modern War' in H. Strachan and S. Scheipers (eds), *The Changing Character of War* (2011) 358.

[17] War 'among the peoples' is a phrase used particularly by General Sir Rupert Smith in *The Utility of Force* (2006).

frequently described as asymmetrical.[18] Clausewitzian thinking is generally regarded as inappropriate in the analysis of contemporary war within States and difficult to apply in relation to armed conflict characterized by rebellion, insurgency, guerilla warfare, terrorism and criminal activities.

Charles Townshend has pointed to an important distinction between regular and irregular warfare, each having a logic directly the reverse of the other:

> Regular armies aim to concentrate force to achieve a decision with maximum speed; guerilla forces disperse and conduct small scale operations over an indefinite period of time. The strength of (irregular) warfare is its resilience; its weakness is the inability of small forces to confront regular armies directly. If guerilla strategy is to achieve victory, this can only happen if it can debilitate the regular force, or if a guerilla force can transform itself into a force capable of defeating the regular force in open battle. The former outcome is unlikely to occur in the physical sense. The arresting metaphor of flies biting a dog to death (alluded to in one of the most popular studies of guerilla war, *The War of the Flea*[19]) cannot be literally applied to human organizations like states and armies. But psychological debilitation is quite possible.[20]

In a sense, however, a regular force is defeated by an irregular force if the irregular force remains undefeated. An irregular force is victorious if its regular opponent fails to overwhelm it. In this way, stalemate represents a form of 'victory' for the irregular and 'defeat' for the regular. This is especially so for those who regard the state of armed conflict as a desirable context for the pursuit of their own purposes.

The Clausewitzian approach is, for example, especially criticized as failing to take into account armed violence motivated by material gain. Since modern internal or civil wars (non-international armed conflicts, in legal parlance) frequently today involve an evil mix of organized crime and other forms of irregular armed violence, the short-comings of the Clausewitzian approach are stressed as so fundamental that a new way of thinking is necessary if such conflicts are to be understood and prosecuted effectively.[21]

A further factor to be considered is that resort to force can no longer be viewed invariably as being in the pursuit purely of national interest. The international community may, for example, be prompted collectively to intervene in States to prevent the worst excesses of internal hostilities, especially in the context of ethnically motivated violence within failed or failing States, during the course of which there is a high risk of mass atrocity crimes being committed. Such interventions for humanitarian motives arguably fall outside the scope of Clausewitzian criteria. One might refer to such armed interventions as 'cosmopolitan action'.[22]

---

[18] This distinction is frequently, if not invariably, erroneous, of course—all wars tend to be asymmetric to some degree. Indeed, all parties in war try to achieve asymmetry in their favour; if there is substantial asymmetry not in their favour they may well resort to irregular warfare against the stronger party.

[19] R. Taber, *The War of the Flea: Guerilla Warfare Theory and Practice* (1970).

[20] C. Townshend, 'Guerilla War' in R. Holmes (ed.), *The Oxford Companion to Military History* (2005) 383 (Townshend, *Guerilla War*).

[21] M. Kaldor, 'Inconclusive Wars: Is Clausewitz Still Relevant in these Global Times?' (2010) 1(3) *Global Policy* 271 (Kaldor, *Inconclusive Wars*).

[22] See e.g. C. Fabre, 'Cosmopolitanism, just war theory and legitimate authority' (2008) 84(5) *International Affairs* 963–76. Fabre is currently preparing a two volume work for Oxford University

Defenders of Clausewitzian thinking counter the New Wars arguments by asserting that none of these considerations have fundamentally changed the nature of war. One important claim is that New Wars theorists have misread Clausewitz and failed fully to understand his true genius. Indeed, they lay stress on the fact that *On War* was an unfinished work that can easily confuse through cursory reading. A more careful analysis that emphasizes the advanced state of Book 1 of *On War* (the only one considered fully worked up) and the advanced drafts of its later books reveals a much deeper understanding than the New Wars theorists give Clausewitz credit for. New Wars thinking relies far too much on Clausewitz's discussion of a theoretically ideal form of war which was an essential part of Clausewitz's dialectical approach. The 'ideal' was not 'real' war. That was the result of an inevitable 'friction' that rendered ideal war unrealizable.

The debate itself represents a dialectic: a Clausewitzian hypothesis came to dominate thinking about armed conflict until it was challenged by the New Wars antithesis. The two theses are rival appreciations of the nature and characteristics of hostilities, neither dominant over the other and each attracting an impressive array of advocates. Should either Clausewitzian or New Wars thinking be dismissed or should each be incorporated in some form of synthesis?[23] In important respects the rival groups of advocates are saying similar things about how they view the character of armed conflict; they simply view it through different lenses, which can lead to differences in their conclusions. On balance, for this author at least, the Clausewitzians' arguments seem to be the more persuasive, although in certain respects the New Wars theorists make important points, especially in relation to two contemporary manifestations of the use of violence—material motive and cosmopolitan action.

While, in order adequately to understand war one needs to be aware of the elements of its enduring nature, it is arguably the constantly shifting characteristics of armed conflict that present us with a particular need not to rely blindly on past assumptions as to what it is we confront. Notwithstanding the importance of war's enduring nature, it is the shifting characteristics of armed conflict that demand regulation, and it is on these that we must focus our attention.

3. The changing characteristics of modern armed conflict

The development of international humanitarian law was initiated largely as a result of Henri Dunant's experience witnessing the prolonged suffering of the injured following the battle of Solferino in 1859.[24] That battle was one of the last of its

Press under the title *A Cosmopolitan Theory of the Just War*, Volume 1 of which will deal with *Cosmopolitan Wars*.

[23] The question was posed by Mary Kaldor most recently in Kaldor, *Inconclusive Wars*.

[24] It initiated the development of that part of international humanitarian law, known as 'Geneva Law', dealing with the treatment of war's victims. 'Hague Law', regulating weapons and methods of warfare, is named for the Hague peace conferences of 1899 and 1907 (see F. Kalshoven and L. Zegveld, *Constraints on the Waging of War: An Introduction to International Humanitarian Law* (2001).

kind and occurred almost half a century after the end of what Russell Weigley has termed the 'Age of Battles'.[25] While Solferino was more akin to Waterloo than to the Western Front battles of the First World War, things were certainly changing by the time it was fought. More revealing of the changing characteristics of armed conflict during the nineteenth century, however, were the American Civil War and the Crimean War. These more than hinted at key aspects of the sort of combat that would become only too familiar to those who experienced warfare in the trenches of the Western Front over half a century later. Today, soldiers rarely dig trenches.

From formal battles with opposing sides lined up in squares and columns on a battlefield with soldiers in brightly coloured uniforms and with flags waving, combat has progressed and involves combatants in camouflage-patterned combat dress (or dressed in no uniform at all) attempting to 'dominate the battlespace' through fluid movement. Soldiers used to be sure who and where their enemy was. Today, this is by no means always the case. How did we get to where we are today and what particular characteristics of hostilities should we identify?

There have been numerous factors affecting the character of armed conflict over the last two centuries and it is tempting to simplify matters when describing them. As already noted, the common means of doing this is to consider the conduct of hostilities as either 'regular' or 'irregular'. But neither of these has been static and predictable. How have they each developed over time? What follows is an attempt to make sense of developments in both, dealing with regular warfare first before going on to deal with the irregular.

3.1. Regular warfare

As already hinted, regular warfare has changed a great deal since the Napoleonic period in Europe, and continues to change as technologies develop. One recently articulated formula for explaining its shifts is Lind's generational construct.[26] He described war in the Napoleonic era as First Generation Warfare (1GW), which he believed was gradually replaced by defensive Second Generation Warfare (2GW) and subsequently by more mobile Third Generation Warfare (3GW).

The essence of 1GW was strategic (or operational) manoeuvre resulting in the confrontation of rival mass armies at a geographical point of tactical decision. The process that produced it was gradual but especially marked by the social changes wrought by the emergence of the nation-State in Europe, by the French Revolution, and by the rise to pre-eminence of Napoleon as military commander. While earlier formations had frequently been composed of mercenary units prepared to fight for the highest bidder,[27] early nineteenth century armies were increasingly a

---

[25] See R. Weigley, *The Age of Battles: The Quest for Decisive Warfare from Breitenfeld to Waterloo* (1991).

[26] See Lind et al, *The Changing Face of War*, 22–6.

[27] With the Swiss cantons and the German States of Hesse, Brunswick and Württemberg regarding war-fighting as a major source of income; see G. Best, *War and Society in Revolutionary Europe, 1770– 1870* (1982) 29.

product of social and political transformations resulting in the mass recruitment of soldiers having a strong national allegiance to the power for which they fought.

The Western Front during the First World War was the ultimate manifestation of 2GW. The machine gun and barbed-wire had rendered the tactics of 1GW obsolete and undermined the ability of commanders to utilize mobility at the higher levels of war.[28] There was no clear point at which one displaced the other although, as already mentioned, the American Civil War and the Crimean War were both indicative of the process of change. In 2GW, wars were fought almost exclusively by national armies made up of citizens of the State for which they fought (both professional soldiers and conscripts), with a still clear distinction between combatants and civilians. There was a degree of stalemate as opposing sides dug in defensively, with offensive action frequently proving far too expensive in manpower to succeed. By 1916 that stalemate on the Western Front had to be broken if any offensive action was to prove feasible. Airpower might have altered the offensive/defensive balance but its full potential was not generally realized at that time. Gas was tried in an attempt to break the deadlock—and, of course, the tank was invented and deployed with some limited success. The key problem was a lack of mobility and manoeuvre on the battlefield. Although things did improve towards the end of the First World War, the overall impression remains one of the bloody slaughter of men vainly attempting to advance in the face of concentrated artillery, machine gun and rifle fire from the opposing side's positions.

Important military thinkers, appalled by this defensive stalemate (soldiers like Fuller, Liddell-Hart, De Gaulle, Rommel and Patton, and airmen like Trenchard and Douhet) were strong proponents of the restoration of the battlefield offensive. They saw new technologies like battlefield armour in the form of the tank, mechanized infantry and aircraft as the obvious answer. The German Panzer commander Guderian and the commanders of the Luftwaffe (the latter being afforded the opportunity to try out their ideas in the Spanish Civil War) took the ideas of mobility, together with the technologies that gave them substance, and operationalized them to profound effect in the development of blitzkrieg during the early stages of the Second World War in Europe.[29]

The result was 3GW. This has survived until today, with the so-called 'manoeuvrist approach' a central feature of doctrine, especially that of land forces. The concept of Air-Land Battle developed in NATO to counter the imbalance of conventional forces on the inner-German border during the later stages of the Cold War, was a particular manifestation of 3GW.[30] In the British Army, the Bagnall reform of operational and tactical doctrine contributed to the development of 3GW and established a clear commitment to manoeuvre warfare within the

---

[28] For a classic account of the impact of the machine gun, for example, see J. Ellis, *The Social History of the Machine Gun* (1993).

[29] R. Holmes, 'Blitzkrieg' in R. Holmes (ed.), *The Oxford Companion to Military History* (2001) 135.

[30] See R. Leonhard, *The Art of Maneuver: Maneuver-Warfare Theory and AirLand Battle* (1991).

British armed forces.[31] Doctrinal developments within NATO led to a mutual compatibility that rendered possible the degree of interoperability used to effect in the coalition operations against Iraq in 1991. Of course, we must also superimpose on the predominantly land-orientated manoeuvrist approach the impact of developing airpower doctrine, with maritime doctrine also contributing through the projection of power from the sea.[32] Contemporary 3GW is joint, high-technology and, given the feasibility of offensive action, potentially decisive.

Lind's 'generations' do provide a narrative of sorts of 200 years of warfare, but they are profoundly simplistic and we need to be wary of them. There were obviously a great many 'generations' predating '1GW'. Generational divisions imply distinctions that are likely to be impossible precisely to identify or define. The suggestion that there were but three generations between the French Revolution and the Second World War is certainly too reductionist. And, of course, it must be stressed that the generations may well exist in parallel; indeed, Clausewitz stressed the non-linearity of war and this is true in terms of its development over time as well as within the conduct of hostilities themselves. One further difficulty is that one is drawn inexorably to ask what it is that follows 3GW—presumably a fourth generation (or 4GW).[33]

3.1.1 A fourth generation of war?

Being the principal focus of major militaries in recent years, 3GW has shaped their development and equipment procurement decisions until today. Operations in Afghanistan in late 2001 employed 3GW principles. Operations against Iraq in 2003 were also high intensity 3GW employing the manoeuvrist approach; their mobility and offensive capacity overwhelmed the Iraqi opposition. But neither operations in Afghanistan from 2002 nor those in Iraq since the invasion in 2003 have been of the same character. Previously, of course, operations in the Balkans (and elsewhere) had already suggested that 3GW was of limited application in the challenging environments characterized by something other than regular inter-state war. The application of the techniques of 3GW proved wholly inappropriate for the armed conflicts that ensued as a result. Was this evidence of another generational shift? Regardless of whether the increase in the frequency of one and reduction in

---

[31] 'The manoeuvrist approach...aims to apply strength against identified vulnerabilities. Significant features are momentum and tempo...shock action and surprise. Emphasis is on defeat and disruption of the enemy by taking the initiative and applying constant and unacceptable pressure at the times and places the enemy least suspects, rather than attempting to seize and hold ground for its own sake.' See Ministry of Defence, *British Defence Doctrine*, 3–5. Field Marshal Sir Nigel Bagnall was, from 1980 to 1985, successively the Commander of First British Corps and Commander of the British Army of the Rhine. He instigated a thorough review of the Army's whole approach to the task of defending against a potential Warsaw Pact offensive, opting for the manoeuvrist approach at the operational and tactical levels, something he saw as essential given the unfavourable balance of conventional forces on the Central Front.

[32] Naval forces have not been so influenced by the generational developments described, which are essentially land orientated. They have, however, developed significantly through technology and are now capable of projecting considerably more power ashore than was ever the case two centuries ago.

[33] B. Schuurman, 'Clausewitz and the "New Wars" Scholars' (2010) 40(1) *Parameters* 89–100.

the frequency of the other is regarded as relative or absolute, there would appear to be at least prima facie evidence of such.

Technology had been the principal reason identified by Hammes for the generational shifts between 1GW and 2GW and also between 2GW and 3GW.[34] But those were also due to economic and sociological factors. For Lind, and subsequently Hammes, a fourth generation had indeed emerged. They argued that those employing 4GW attempt to cause the enemy to collapse internally rather than by actions aimed at physical destruction. While technology remains of some importance, it is the ability of a small force to debilitate a larger force that marks out 4GW. There is a heavy reliance on manoeuvre; more so even than was the case in 3GW. The enemy's centre of gravity—that feature which if attacked and destroyed would cause the enemy to collapse—becomes of paramount importance.

Of course, in 3GW the centre of gravity is also of importance. Arguably, wars in which effort was focused on the centre of gravity to the ultimate degree were the Spanish Civil War and the Second World War. In both, some believed that the centre of gravity was the civilian population. Cities and towns were deliberately targeted for that reason—Guernica in the Spanish instance and numerous others in both the wider European and Japanese theatres. Today, however, politico-legal constraints on attack have come to restrict available targets and have rendered the centre of gravity, by definition, less than paramount. If the centre of gravity of an enemy is something that would be regarded under international humanitarian law as an unlawful target, it should not be attacked.[35]

It is the realm of armed conflict of a non-international character, involving non-state organized armed groups, in which is detected what Lind and Hammes call 4GW. To quote from a recent US Army War College paper that purports to describe it:

> In general, 4GW blurs the lines between war and politics, conflict and peace, soldier and civilian, and battlefield violence and safe zones. This new form of warfare has arisen from the loss of the nation-state's monopoly on violence; from the rise of cultural, ethnic, and religious conflict; and from the spread of globalization, particularly advanced technology. It is conducted in an increasingly decentralized manner, dispersed throughout a region or even the world. It has no defined battlefield; instead, 4GW is conducted simultaneously in population centres, rural areas and virtual networks. It moves constantly to avoid detection and to target its enemy's vulnerabilities. As Lind explains, 'Actions will occur concurrently throughout all participants' depths, including their society as a cultural, not just a physical, entity.' Fourth Generation Warfare's targets are not just soldiers, but also non-combatants, religious ideas, legal frameworks, media outlets, international agencies and agreements, economic activities, political power, and the minds of the people. Accordingly, targets are selected not just for physical destruction but more for their mental and moral impact on an adversary. In the end, 4GW's goal is to exploit an adversary's weaknesses and undermine its strengths in order 'to convince the enemy's political decision-makers that their strategic goals are either unachievable or too costly for the perceived benefit.'[36]

---

[34] Hammes, *War in the 21st Century*.
[35] For further discussion, see ch. 4, section 4 below.
[36] S. Williamson, *From Fourth Generation Warfare to Hybrid War: Strategy Research Project* (2009) 3.

Since the generational approach to describing the characteristics of war introduced the notion of 4GW, there have been two principal criticisms, both of which suggest it is a misnomer.

Firstly it is said that what it describes is nothing more than a contemporary manifestation of irregular warfare. There is, of course, nothing new about irregularity in war. The British experienced it during the Boer War[37] and Lawrence demonstrated its effectiveness in relation to the Arab Revolt which he described in *Seven Pillars of Wisdom*.[38] The great Prussian himself acknowledged this when he referred to the activities of partisans operating against Napoleon's forces in the Iberian Peninsular.[39] To quote David Gates:

> the nature of the Peninsular conflict satisfies all five of the conditions Clausewitz cited for successful partisan warfare: the war must be fought in the country's interior; it must not be decided by a single blow; the theatre of operations must be reasonably large; the terrain must be rough and inaccessible; and the national character must be suited to that manner of warfare.[40]

A second criticism is that those who detect evidence of 4GW rely on a far too optimistic assessment of the extent of the decline in inter-state war. To describe irregular war as of a new generation seems to imply that it will at some point displace previous generations. In that way it presupposes that inter-state war will continue to decline in frequency until logically it peters out altogether.[41] The quality of this sort of thinking simply cannot be conclusively proved or refuted, but it does seem wildly out of kilter with the available evidence. The State system remains healthy and rivalries continue to flare up; the continuing outbreak of inter-state hostilities would appear to be inevitable. Both Benbow and Gray believe this to be the case.[42] So-called 4GW is, therefore, likely to exist in parallel with what is currently termed 3GW. If this is the case, there will be no consequential 'generational shift' out of one and into the other. Indeed, the most likely outcome seems to be the continuing relevance of both. This is certainly the view of one of the more prolific critics of 4GW. Hoffman is convinced that the contemporary manifestation of irregular warfare does nothing to render regular war obsolete.[43] Indeed, irregular warfare, and the methods needed to combat it, have had characteristics running in parallel to the process of regular war's metamorphosis from so-called 1GW to 2GW

---

[37] For the best account of the Boer War see T. Packenham, *The Boer War* (1979).

[38] T. Lawrence, *Seven Pillars of Wisdom* (2003).

[39] Indeed, it is as old as warfare itself. See R. Asprey, *War in the Shadows: A History of Guerilla Warfare from Ancient Persia to the Present* (1994).

[40] D. Gates, *The Spanish Ulcer: A History of the Peninsular War* (1986) 35.

[41] General Sir Rupert Smith has contributed significantly to the growth of this idea in *The Utility of Force* (2006), suggesting that 'war among the peoples' would come to dominate as inter-state war declined, with traditional military force structures and doctrine becoming redundant.

[42] T. Benbow, 'Talking 'Bout our Generation: Assessing the Concept of Fourth Generation Warfare' (2008) 27(2) *Comparative Strategy* 152; and C. Gray, *Another Bloody Century*, 145.

[43] F. Hoffman, *Conflict in the 21st Century: The Rise of Hybrid Wars* (2007) (Hoffman, *The Rise of Hybrid Wars*).

and then on to 3GW. On this basis the label '4GW' is an unnecessary label for what has always been described as irregular war.[44]

3.2. Irregular war

What can we say about the various views of contemporary irregular armed conflict? However we refer to it, it represents the 'messy' end of the spectrum of contemporary hostilities. The proliferation of theories about irregular armed conflict is simply demonstrative and symptomatic of the extent to which the conduct of hostilities today is taxing the finest military minds. While there are clearly differences between the various interpretations of contemporary irregular armed conflict, their significance depends on the perceptions of the individuals doing the analysis. This is not the place to delve into their detailed arguments. Arguably, any attempt to do this would be in vain in any case, since every instance of war has unique characteristics. This point is at the heart of some claims that it is impossible to produce a detailed, valid, effective and universally applicable doctrine for dealing with irregular warfare because each instance of it is *sui generis* and especially demanding of commanding genius.[45] In many instances, predominantly regular military forces are certainly grappling with the complexities of hostilities in which they are finding it almost impossible to prevail.

Certainly there is a variety of labels currently attached to irregular warfare as analysts (both military and academic) attempt to understand its characteristics and arrive at ways of countering it. For lawyers the importance of these terms is not that they have relevance to the classification of conflicts for purposes of international humanitarian law—indeed they describe hostilities in both international and non-international armed conflict—but that they help to explain the factual nature of the hostilities concerned.

Traditional terms associated with irregular warfare are: insurrection, insurgency and guerilla (including urban guerilla) warfare. Prominent recent terms include: complex or advanced irregular war; compound war; hybrid war; and criminal war. The more recent terms are relatively new labels that are products of recent analyses of the latest manifestations of irregular warfare, in the Balkans, in Africa, in Iraq and in Afghanistan, for example. Something needs to be said about each. Finally, although a threat to security for a great many years, terrorism deserves some comment.

3.2.1 Insurrection, insurgency, guerilla (and urban guerilla) warfare

Insurrection, insurgency, guerilla (and urban guerilla) warfare denote the activities of armed movements whose aim is the overthrow of the established regime

---

[44] See also the interesting view that the distinction between 'regular' and 'irregular' forms of war is overstressed, in W.A. Vacca and M. Davidson, 'The Regularity of Irregular Warfare' (2011) 41(1) *Parameters* 18–28.

[45] The author well recalls a debate within the then Joint Doctrine and Concepts Centre at Shrivenham about whether or not the development of doctrine was either wise or feasible when it came to countering insurgency since all insurgencies are arguably *sui generis*.

or government within a State. While they are principally associated with internal or civil campaigns, cross-border activities are often a feature, with armed groups operating out of secure bases in adjacent States from where they launch operations against the target government. According to the US Army definition, an insurgency is 'an organized movement aimed at the overthrow of a constituted government through the use of subversion and armed conflict'.[46] In the main, through force of circumstance, insurgents or guerillas tend to start by engaging in low-intensity armed action against the security forces (police and army) of the State but, if successful, can attract increasing support and eventually engage in more conventional and higher intensity armed conflict. Successful insurrections, insurgencies or guerilla campaigns can certainly defeat conventional forces and result in the seizure of State power. Examples of successful campaigns range from the Bolshevik rising in Russia to Castro's seizure of power in Cuba to the Taliban's eventual domination of much of Afghanistan achieved following the withdrawal of Soviet forces in 1988. Civil wars rarely achieve the degree of symmetry that was evident in the American Civil War (for example) and insurgents are more frequently associated, therefore, with irregular war than regular warfare. Insurgents and guerillas, as Charles Townshend has noted,[47] are unlikely to prevail militarily unless they can develop their campaigns to the extent of confronting conventional forces and defeating them by resort to more conventional methods.

If an insurgency is clearly failing, the groups involved may resort to such techniques as terrorism but, in doing so, they may be inadvertently indicating their ineffectiveness. Successful insurgents and guerillas will not invariably resort to unlawful acts in armed conflict (the deliberate targeting of civilians, for example) because they will need to obtain wide support if they are to prevail. Much will depend, however, on the circumstances, although decisions to constrain their activities within 'lawful' limits are possibly more likely to occur in the context of politically motivated insurgencies than those based on religious differences. The types of irregular warfare we discuss below represent the characteristics of armed conflict employed by insurgents and guerilla groups in many of those contexts described in this volume.

3.2.2 Complex irregular warfare

Complex irregular warfare is a term coined by the London-based International Institute for Strategic Studies.[48] It concluded that:

> the wars that have emerged have been irregular conflicts in which adversaries have deliberately sought to negate Western conventional superiority by retreating

---

[46] Quoted in D. Kilcullen, *Counter Insurgency* (2010) 1. See also, D. Kilcullen, *The Accidental Guerilla: Fighting Small Wars in the Midst of a Big One* (2009).

[47] See Townshend, *Guerilla War*, 383.

[48] International Institute for Strategic Studies, *The Military Balance 2005–2006* (2005) 411–20. See also F. Hoffman, 'Complex Irregular Warfare: The Next Revolution in Military Affairs' (2006) 50(3) *Orbis* 395–411.

into complex terrain and adopting asymmetric approaches to offset technological military power. While airpower played an important supporting role in these conflicts, ground forces have increasingly been required to grapple at close quarters, relatively unsupported with messy and ambiguous conflict situations on the ground . . . the day to day prosecution of these conflicts will be increasingly (conducted) by smaller, more agile mission teams . . . optimised for operations in complex, urbanized, populated areas marked by pervasive media presence and globalised communications.

3.2.3 Advanced irregular warfare

Advanced irregular warfare merely stresses the availability of advanced technology to irregular forces, in particular communications facilities and general global networks, including for the purposes of improving the irregular forces' intelligence picture. In fact, there is no significant difference between it and complex irregular warfare.

3.2.4 Compound warfare

Compound warfare is armed conflict involving a significant degree of strategic coordination between regular and irregular force elements operating simultaneously. The unified command seeks to exploit the strengths of each element of the force, maximizing the threats they each pose to the opposition. The irregular element targets the opposition at its weakest points, forcing it to disperse its forces. The regular element can then force the opposition onto the defensive and prepare the ground for its own decisive offensive operations.[49]

3.2.5 Hybrid warfare

Hybrid warfare, unlike compound warfare which involves a degree of strategic coordination between regular and irregular forces, suggests cooperation and coordination at all levels: strategic, operational and tactical. It is also typified by cooperation between a politically motivated force and other groups engaged in criminal activity, hence the 'hybrid' description of the conflict.[50] It is particularly appropriate to describe such cooperation at the tactical level at which local groups of varying persuasions may deem it convenient to coalesce.

[49] F. Hoffman, 'Hybrid versus Compound War—The Janus Choice: Defining Today's Multifaceted Conflict' (October 2009) *Armed Forces Journal* (Hoffman, *Hybrid versus Compound War*); and L. Jordan, *Hybrid War: Is the US Army Ready for the Face of 21st Century Warfare* (2008).

[50] See Hoffman, *The Rise of Hybrid Wars* and F. Hoffman, 'Hybrid Warfare and Challenges' (2009) 52 *Joint Force Quarterly* 34–48. See also N. Freier, 'The Defense Identity Crisis: It's a Hybrid World' (2009) 39(3) *Parameters* 81–94.

3.2.6 Criminal warfare and insurgency

Criminal warfare and insurgency has been a particularly important development of late (and is clearly related to Hybrid Warfare). It is the resort of criminals intent on material gain through, for example, drug dealing, people smuggling, arms dealing, extortion, kidnapping, theft and the like. It involves groups using violence against State authorities or against rival criminal gangs which seek to dominate the areas in which they operate. In the manner of rival Mafia gangs carving up US cities like Chicago and New York, they may negotiate agreements with each other over their territorial reach. Gangs do not operate in an anarchic fashion but, rather, in a controlled and systematic manner, often imposing effective internal discipline through ruthless action against their own members when necessary. Gangs have little interest in garnering support from the communities within which they operate, but when they do need the cooperation of a community this is usually obtained through fear. Criminal gangs operate largely on the basis of self-interest rather than through dedication to a cause.

When criminal gangs and politically motivated groups each see some strategic value in coalescing with the other in pursuit of their particularly compatible tactical objectives, the result can be a truly evil mix.[51] One can do no better in illustrating what degree of integration can transpire as between criminal gangs and political or military leaders than to quote David Crane, former Chief Prosecutor of the Special Court for Sierra Leone:

> That (international criminal) element formed a joint criminal enterprise in West Africa led by three sitting presidents, Muammar Qadhafi, Charles Taylor and Blaise Compaore of Burkino Faso. Over a period of ten years, these individuals—one indicted, one named and shamed, and the other warned away—led gun runners, diamond dealers, Eastern European mafias, other international thugs and terrorists, including Hezbollah and al Qaeda, in a whirlwind of death and destruction the likes of which the world has never seen . . . The unrest throughout the West African region, particularly in Sierra Leone, the Ivory Coast, and Liberia was started by criminals for their own personal and criminal gain. The civil war in Sierra Leone did not begin on account of the more traditional causes behind warfare, legitimate or otherwise, such as political, religious, cultural, ethnic or social reasons. Rather, the impetus for the civil war was pure criminal avarice and greed. They did it because they could.[52]

Criminal activity is more likely to succeed in situations of instability caused by weak and ineffective government. For that reason, gangs may have a vested interest in maintaining that condition. Criminal warfare is an important addition to the lexicon because the motives behind it differ from those traditionally ascribed to war by Clausewitz and his followers.[53] The presence of criminal motive in war is

---

[51] Hoffman, *The Rise of Hybrid Wars*; Hoffmann, *Hybrid versus Compound War*.
[52] D. Crane, 'Terrorists, Warlords and Thugs' (2005) 21 *American University International Law Review* 515. Crane entitled this phenomenon 'criminal warfare', which seems a suitable label.
[53] M. Clark, 'Does Clausewitz Apply to Criminal-States and Gangs?' in R. Bunker (ed.), *Criminal States and Criminal Soldiers* (2008); S. Metz, *Rethinking Insurgency* (2007).

not new. During the Thirty Years War, for example, entrepreneurs were taking advantage of societal disruption for their own material gain. Wallenstein was to some the archetypal example of a mercenary intent on material gain, but he was not alone—Ernst zu Mansfeld and Christian von Braunschweig, for example, were similarly motivated.[54] Arguably, many of the feudal rulers of a mediaeval Europe, before the advent of the State as a formal political unit, were no more than self-interested opportunists intent on material gain. Hostilities founded on a material motivation may have gone into decline with the development of the nation-State. Now, they seem to be re-emerging.[55]

In Colombia, in Mexico, in Afghanistan and in other conflicts where criminal activity continues alongside other forms of violence, it has become especially significant. The situations in Colombia and Afghanistan are dealt with in chapters 7 and 8 respectively. That in Mexico has not been subjected to detailed analysis in this volume but, nevertheless, deserves some comment. It is of growing concern given the extent of criminal activity and the number of fatalities (almost 40,000 in the four years from 2007). Mexican authorities are dealing with an extreme situation of what Sullivan and Elkus have termed 'criminal insurgency', with a variety of gangs embroiled in hostilities against each other as well as with the security forces.[56] It is estimated that 100,000 former members of the Mexican military have joined the criminal gangs, which are armed with an impressive array of weapons covering the full range of small arms and light weapons. Despite over 32,000 of those weapons and 4 million rounds of ammunition having been seized by the Mexican authorities in the process of making over 60,000 arrests, the insurgency shows no signs of waning.

The principal activity of the gangs is drug smuggling. Over 70 tons of cocaine and 4000 tons of marijuana have been seized but Mexico still supplies about 90 per cent of cocaine entering the US and drug profits remain at roughly 60 billion US dollars per annum. Importantly, the gangs are in effective control of significant

[54] Münkler, *The New Wars*, 2–3. Motives can, of course, be mixed. Wallenstein also had political ambitions, for example and there remains uncertainty as to Mansfeld's precise motives (although his actions were manifestly duplicitous and it is generally assumed he was motivated by even baser instincts). See P. Wilson, *Europe's Tragedy: A History of the Thirty Years War* (2009) 325.

[55] Comparison needs to be made with the role of private military and security companies, which has increased with the 'outsourcing' by governments of activities once regarded as reserved to national armies. These companies must however be distinguished from organized criminal groups in that although, being commercial entities, their motivation is for material gain, their activities are by no means necessarily unlawful. Where they are involved in a situation of hostilities their motivation can be to support 'normal' military activities. (See P. Singer, *Corporate Warriors: The Rise of the Privatized Military Industry* (2003); S. Chesterman and C. Lehnardt (eds), *From Mercenaries to Market: The Rise and Regulation of Private Military Companies* (2007); J. Cockayne et al, *Beyond Market Forces: Regulating the Global Security Industry* (2009)). Employees of private military and security companies may either collectively represent an organized armed group or may individually directly participate in hostilities. As the ICRC's *Interpretive Guidance on Direct Participation in Hostilities* acknowledges: 'Theoretically, private military companies could even become independent non-state parties to a non-international armed conflict.' N. Melzer, 'Interpretive Guidance on the Notion of Direct Participation in Hostilities under International Humanitarian Law' (2009) 39–40.

[56] J. Sullivan and A. Elkus, 'Plazas for Profit: Mexico's Criminal Insurgency' *Small Wars Journal* (26 April 2009), available at: <www.smallwarsjournal.com>.

areas of territory and pursue 'dual sovereignty' over so-called 'plazas' used as trans-shipment routes for drugs. The scale of criminal activity is clearly well in excess of the threshold levels of violence that would qualify it as armed conflict if mounted for political purpose. Combating it, not surprisingly, requires a security response that well exceeds that normally associated with the phrase 'law enforcement'. Whatever the precise theoretical limits of Clausewitzian 'war' and regardless of the regular misuse of the term 'war' in routine domestic political discourse, the Mexican experience certainly justifies serious consideration of the application of armed conflict standards when it comes to the application of force.[57]

In relation to international humanitarian law, which was developed in the context of politically motivated war and armed conflict between States, criminal war has presented something of a dilemma because those involved in mere criminal activity have not generally been regarded as combatants. Rather, they have been assumed to be civilians and not, therefore, ordinarily targetable according to the criteria of international humanitarian law for the application of force. While the idea of a criminal and materialistic motive seems at variance with the Clausewitzian understanding of war, there is nothing in international humanitarian law that would prevent hostilities between rival criminal gangs, or between those gangs and the legitimate authorities of the State, being categorized as armed conflict. Indeed, the term 'organized armed group' in article 1 of Additional Protocol II does not expressly exclude criminal gangs.[58] Nevertheless, the view that the actions of criminal gangs can be regarded as being those of an 'organized armed group', resulting in violent circumstances being categorized as armed conflict, is not uncontroversial.[59] Although the ICRC has been reluctant to describe particular circumstances involving criminally motivated violence as constituting armed conflict, its report to the 31st International Conference of the Red Cross and Red Crescent did accept that it could be an armed conflict, making the point that 'Under IHL the motivation of organized groups involved in armed violence is not a criterion for determining the existence of an armed conflict'.[60]

---

[57] In the event of a spill-over or in relation to transnational organized crime, there may well be what one analyst over two decades ago referred to as 'transnational constabulary warfare'—see J. Shephard, 'On War: Is Clausewitz still Relevant? (1990) 20(3) *Parameters* 85–99. Related issues are dealt with in the case study on Colombia in ch. 7 below.

[58] See ch. 3 section 6.1 below for further discussion of the question of the threshold of organized violence that criminal activity needs to reach for criminal groups to become parties to armed conflict and, therefore, combatants. If criminals are deemed to be civilians, they may only be targeted using minimum use of force standards, in which the individual's actions are the determining factor rather than his or her status. Combatants, or civilians taking a direct part in hostilities, can be targeted by reference to their status.

[59] See e.g. P. Hauck and S. Peterke, 'Organized Crime and Gang Violence in National and International Law' (2010) 92(878) *International Review of the Red Cross* 407–36. I am also grateful to Tom Haeck for sight of his recent thesis that deals with the issue; T. Haeck, 'The Lower Threshold of Non-International Armed Conflict' (2011), unpublished LLM Thesis, Academy of International Humanitarian Law and Human Rights, Geneva. As Haeck points out (see 37–45 and 89–92), the Mexican government does not wish to categorize the situation as a non-international armed conflict.

[60] ICRC, *International Humanitarian Law and the challenges of contemporary armed conflicts*, Report to the 31st International Conference of the Red Cross and Red Crescent (October 2011) 11.

3.2.7 Terrorism

Terrorism is more appropriately regarded as but one method of conducting hostilities rather than as a type of warfare in itself. Attempts to arrive at a generally agreed legal definition have all failed. The late Paul Wilkinson, one of the leading academics studying terrorism from the 1970s to his death in 2011, defined it as: 'the systematic use of coercive intimidation, usually to service political ends. It is used to create and exploit a climate of fear among a wider target group than the immediate victims of the violence, and to publicize a cause as well as to coerce a target to acceding to the terrorists' aims.'[61]

Those employing terrorism, while frequently resorting to indiscriminate attacks on innocent civilians, may distinguish between 'legitimate' targets and others (targeting only off-duty members of the security forces, for example). The more they do distinguish in this way, however, the less their actions can strictly be labeled as 'terrorism' (even though governments faced with such a threat may label it as such). Terrorism is most likely to be the resort of groups who have either not got the necessary support or skill to conduct a more traditional guerilla campaign or insurgency, are not seeking the moral support of communities within which they are operating, or whose attempts at guerilla warfare or general insurgency have been successfully opposed by the forces ranged against them. In that sense, terrorism may be evidence of desperation. Effectively, groups will not resort to terrorism unless they are at a loss to identify other methods of mounting armed opposition in pursuit of their aims.

3.3. Cosmopolitan action

One manifestation of armed conflict that does not fit neatly into Clausewitzian notions of war is cosmopolitan action. This describes a range of uses for military forces by the international community for the protection of individual rights through the establishment of stable and just societies. Although it is not exclusively related to the role of the United Nations, when military forces are used in the context of military sanctions authorized under Chapter VII (article 42) of the UN Charter, for example, we may have a situation that results in an armed conflict but which is not traditional State-on-State war in the Clausewitzian sense. The 2011 NATO action in Libya is a prime example. Security Council resolution 1973 (2011) authorized:

> Member States that have notified the Secretary-General, acting nationally or through regional organizations or arrangements, and acting in cooperation with the Secretary-General, to take all necessary measures . . . to protect civilians and civilian populated areas under threat of attack in the Libyan Arab Jamahiriya, including Benghazi, while excluding a foreign occupation force of any form on any part of Libyan territory.

---

[61] P. Wilkinson, *Terrorism versus Liberal Democracy: The Liberal State Response* (2000) 12–13.

They were also authorized to enforce compliance with the no-fly zone. The bombing by the NATO-led coalition of government targets which were deliberately attacking civilians amounted to an armed conflict as legally understood. Indeed, from a legal point of view, an international armed conflict was being waged by the international community against Libya to prevent humanitarian abuses undertaken in a separate non-international armed conflict between Libyan government forces and armed opposition groups.[62] Interestingly, however, although an international armed conflict was in train between NATO and Libyan forces, the Alliance did not apply force to the limits permitted under international humanitarian law. In this operation, launched specifically to protect civilians under the 'responsibility to protect', NATO's targeting restrictions were significant. Only precision-guided munitions were used and, if an attack on any target was likely to result in any civilian casualties at all, the attack was not mounted or was called off. For this operation, therefore, no proportionality arguments were permitted when targets were being selected. The mandate was defining the limits of the application of force and not the relevant rules of international humanitarian law.[63]

Such cosmopolitan action by the international community is a particular feature of the UN era but has become especially pronounced since the end of the Cold War. The operation in Libya may yet be setting new parameters for the manner in which force is applied in such circumstances. Cosmopolitan uses of force are not justified, except loosely, on grounds of national interest but rather on grounds of humanitarian necessity. The term 'responsibility to protect', which was coined following NATO's campaign in 1999 over Kosovo (but which also reflected concerns generated in the wider Balkan conflicts and by such events as the Rwanda genocide), is becoming an important one in this context.[64]

The significant increase in UN mandated operations following the end of the Cold War resulted in a great deal of analysis about the features of international interventions. This has produced a lengthy list of different types of operations that fall under the rubric of cosmopolitan action, including: enforcement operations; humanitarian intervention; peace enforcement; peace support operations; peace enforcement; peace-keeping; peace-building and humanitarian operations.[65] Military forces are deployed on behalf of the international community in all of these cases. Sometimes the resultant operations take on the appearance of major

---

[62] The operations in Libya constituted interesting conflicts from the point of view of identifying thresholds—when did internal disturbances become sufficiently organized to qualify as non-international armed conflict, and at what point did the rebel forces become the ruling forces within the State, thereby causing NATO forces to cease engagement in an international armed conflict against Libya?

[63] Conversations between the author and senior NATO staff involved in Operation Unified Protector.

[64] The term was coined in International Commission on Intervention and State Sovereignty (ICISS), 'Responsibility to Protect' (December 2001) and achieved formal recognition in the 2005 UN World Summit Outcome Document. Arguably, the first UN mandated operation to rely on R2P (as it is often termed) was that mounted in Libya in response to UN Security Council resolution 1973 (2011).

[65] See e.g. the definitions of many of these in UK Ministry of Defence, *The Military Contribution to Peace Support Operations,* Joint Warfare Publication 3–50 (2004) 1-1 to 1-2.

warfare—as did the enforcement action against Iraq in 1991 following its invasion of Kuwait in 1990. At other times they may involve a combination of uses of force in both the combat and law enforcement senses—as in the case of UN and NATO forces deployed into Bosnia. At yet other times, traditional peacekeeping forces deployed under Chapter VI of the UN Charter may have no mandate to use force (except in the exercise of self-defence)—an example being the UN deployment in Cyprus that has been in place for almost half a century.

4. Conclusions

Contemporary international humanitarian law has to deal with all the circumstances outlined in this chapter. This is far from easy. Not only are hostilities today rarely as simple as those characterized by set piece battles between opposing States' military forces arrayed on a formalized battlefield (in the manner exemplified by the Battle of Solferino in 1859); they are frequently rendered extremely difficult by the coincidental mix of many of the types of hostilities discussed above. As this problematic mix was becoming especially obvious, General Krulak, the then Commandant of the US Marine Corps, coined the term 'three block war' to describe the complexity of an operational theatre in which more than one type of operation would need to be mounted in response to diverse threats and challenges, typically involving a combination of armed combat, internal security and law-enforcement operations, and humanitarian operations.[66] Each has a different legal base governing permissible force and the manner in which individuals are detained or treated while in detention. It requires a particular fluidity of mind at the tactical level, with deployed military personnel having to shift from one mindset to another (appropriate to combat governed by international humanitarian law, to law enforcement constrained by human rights considerations, and to benign aid operations in which the application of force should not be required).

While intervening forces effecting cosmopolitan action are facing such challenges, others against whom they are intervening are themselves engaged in war as Clausewitz understood it—war having both regular and irregular characteristics. A further source of complexity is the tendency for hostilities to spill over State boundaries, with irregular forces often using such boundaries to their advantage through the establishment of relatively secure bases away from the theatres in which they are actually applying force. There are also what amount to stateless networks of individuals engaged in campaigns motivated by a wide range of considerations, including the religious and the purely criminal. With a merging of non-state organized armed groups, whose motive may be largely political or religious, with other groups, whose principal objective may be criminal (drug gangs, people smugglers, armed bandits of varying persuasions), all employing a deliberate policy of confusing the enemy by disguising their fighters as civilians, with a willingness to

---

[66] General C. Krulak, 'The Strategic corporal: Leadership in the Three Block War' (1999) 83(1) *Marine Corps Gazette* 18–23.

target the civilian population for the simple reason that they happen to represent their enemy's centre of gravity, there is an asymmetry in irregular war that goes beyond the simple mismatch of size and technology. This fact can be frustrating for military commanders and incomprehensible to the young soldiers they command who are obliged to comply with the restraining influence of the law.

But what do the developing characteristics of conflict and the trends in hostilities that are in evidence today mean for the future of armed conflict? Speculation is fraught with difficulty, the only certainty being that whatever predictions we come up with are very likely to be proved inadequate over time. Nevertheless, there are certain conclusions we can suggest that will provide some scope for sensible speculation. Central to these is the belief that in general the nature of armed conflict, identified earlier in this chapter, is likely to endure.[67]

It may, however, be the case that Clausewitzian understandings require some modification in relation to criminal motivation and to interventions mounted by the international community for cosmopolitan humanitarian motive. Both seem likely to recur as characteristics of conflict. The experience of criminal insurgency in Mexico is admittedly an extreme example of conflict born of material motive. It would be foolish to suggest, however, that such violence elsewhere will never again reach that level of organization or intensity; it may well do. NATO's intervention in Libya is most unlikely to be the last example of intervention for humanitarian purposes, notwithstanding likely resistance to such from significant States that are traditionally opposed to foreign intervention. Russia and China, in particular, will require some convincing in the Security Council to authorize (or at least refrain from vetoing) the sort of mandate that led to NATO's intervention in Libya. Nevertheless, the indications are that cosmopolitan action will continue to be a feature of the conflict environment. So the future may not be entirely Clausewitzian.

War—or armed conflict—is likely to continue to be messy. It will consist of a mix of the regular and irregular and it is most likely to be markedly asymmetric. Those doing the fighting will find it difficult to distinguish between those fighting on the opposing side and those who are not fighting at all—and those who are only directly participating in hostilities intermittently will be even more difficult to identify. The indications are that armed conflict will involve a hybrid mix of motives, with criminal groups either taking advantage of the conflict circumstances created by others or generating their own conflicts for their own purposes. For some—criminal groups in particular—the aim will probably not be victory but the semi-permanent maintenance of a chaotic or anarchic environment in which criminal gain can be maximized. The Clausewitzian objective of an advantageous peace may well not be a feature. Hostilities will inevitably cross national boundaries without necessarily being formally international.

---

[67] Colin Gray is probably entirely correct in suggesting that almost everything is known about war in general but that we can 'know nothing, literally zero, for certain about the (particular) wars of the future, even in the near term'. C. Gray, 'War—Continuity in Change, and Change in Continuity' (2010) 40(2) *Parameters* 5.

Technologies will inevitably develop. New means and methods of fighting lead to shifts in the characteristics of armed conflict but have done little to alter the underlying nature of war. Having said that, it seems likely that future technologies will lead to the increasing development of remotely controlled platforms and perhaps also pressure for autonomy in decision-making processes. Such developments might challenge the nature of war, leading, as they could, to the removal of moral actors in warfare. Would this even be warfare? Earlier it was suggested that it would not be. Such developments are likely to take some time to materialize in the substantial sense; they are not imminent, but the law will need to cope with them when they enter the battlespace.

In chapter 14 on Future Conflict, Schmitt examines three aspects of conflict he believes will prove especially challenging: the use of cyberspace and the emergence of cyber warfare; the continuation of transnational terrorism; and the increasing complexity of the battlespace. The third and last of these seems the most challenging. Indeed, the first and second seem most likely to contribute to the complexity of the third. It is the make-up of the battlespace that will determine the characteristics of conflict. There are several dimensions to it, the technological being but one. Others include the social and cultural. The case studies in this volume reveal how those dimensions have contributed to the unique sets of circumstances that produced the conflicts examined. They also contribute to our understanding of how those dimensions will shape conflict in the future—conflict that the law will need to be able to regulate over time.

3

Classification of Armed Conflicts: Relevant Legal Concepts

*Dapo Akande**

1. Introduction

International humanitarian law governs the conduct of participants in an armed conflict. In order to determine whether this breach of law applies to situations of violence it is necessary to assess first of all whether the situation amounts to an 'armed conflict'. However, international humanitarian law does not recognize a unitary concept of armed conflict but, rather, recognizes two types of armed conflicts: international and non-international.

This chapter examines the history of the distinction between these two categories of armed conflict, the consequences of the distinction and whether it still has validity. The chapter then discusses legal concepts relevant to the two categories, including the differences between a non-international conflict and other violence, extraterritorial hostilities by one State against a non-state armed group and conflicts in which multinational forces are engaged. All these concepts are relevant to the understanding of the case studies which follow.

2. History of the distinction between international and non-international armed conflicts

This distinction between international and non-international armed conflicts arises out of the history of the regulation of wars and armed conflicts by international law. In the period following the peace of Westphalia and until the end of the Second World War, the international laws of war applied only to wars between States.[1]

* I am grateful to Nicole Urban for assistance with this chapter.

[1] See R. Bartels, 'Timelines, Borderlines and Conflicts: The Historical Evolution of the Legal Divide Between International and Non-International Armed Conflicts' (2009) 91(873) *International Review of the Red Cross* 35, 44–8 (Bartels, *The Historical Evolution*). Cassese defines this period as ending at the time of the Spanish Civil War (1936–39), see A. Cassese, 'Civil War and International Law' in A. Cassese (ed.), *The Human Dimension of International Law: Selected Papers* (2008) 111, 113–14.

This was a consequence of the fact that international law as a whole was concerned only with relations between States[2] and eschewed regulation of matters considered to be within the domestic jurisdiction of States. Internal armed conflicts, or civil wars, were not considered to be 'real war[s] in the strict sense of the term in International Law', since that term was reserved for conflicts between States.[3] It was possible for the laws of war to apply to civil wars but only in cases where there was recognition, either by the State involved in the civil war or by a third State, of the belligerency of the insurgent party.[4] Even in such a case, the application of the rules of international law to what was prima facie an internal situation did not occur automatically but rather because the insurgent party was recognized by the State concerned as having acquired State-like qualities. During the period under consideration, the international laws of war did not distinguish between international and other wars. There was only one body of law which either applied *in toto* to international conflicts between States (or conflicts treated as such) or it did not apply at all.[5]

The extension of international regulation to internal armed conflicts changed decisively after the Second World War. This was, of course, a period in which international law as a discipline began to recognize the possibility of extending rights and, indeed, obligations to individuals and other non-state actors. This recognition was exemplified in that period by the immediate post World War II prosecutions for international crimes and the development of international human rights law, beginning with the Universal Declaration of Human Rights 1948. It is therefore not surprising that around the same time consideration was given to the extension of the laws of war to the regulation of internal armed conflicts. Indeed, the developments in international humanitarian law after World War II were foreshadowed by the practice of some States and of the League of Nations during the Spanish Civil War (1936–1939). Although there was no recognition of belligerency during that conflict, there was an emerging view that international law applied to the conduct of hostilities during a civil war and Antonio Cassese has argued that there was a development, during that conflict, of customary rules applicable to certain internal armed conflicts.[6] In any event, the bifurcation of international humanitarian law into the law of international armed conflicts and that of non-international armed conflicts was established by the Geneva

[2] See L. Oppenheim, *International Law, Vol. I: The Law of Peace* (2nd edn, 1912) 12, para 13: 'States solely and exclusively are the subjects of International Law.'

[3] L. Oppenheim, *International Law, Vol. II: War and Neutrality* (1st edn, 1906) 67.

[4] Ibid, 65; L. Moir, *The Law of Internal Armed Conflict* (2002) 5 et seq. (Moir, *Internal Armed Conflict*).

[5] See Bartels, *The Historical Evolution*, 51; Moir, *Internal Armed Conflict*, 10.

[6] A. Cassese, 'The Spanish Civil War and the Development of Customary Law Concerning Internal Armed Conflicts' in A. Cassese (ed.), *Current Problems of International Law* (1975) 287, reprinted in A. Cassese, *The Human Dimension of International Law: Selected Papers* (2008) 128. See also A. Cassese, 'Civil War and International Law' in A. Cassese, *The Human Dimension of International Law: Selected Papers* (2008) 114–16 (Cassese, *Civil War*). See also Bartels, *The Historical Evolution*, 56; *Prosecutor v Tadić*, IT-94-1-AR72, Decision on Defence Motion for Interlocutory Appeal on Jurisdiction (Appeals Chamber), 2 October 1995, para 63 (*Tadić Jurisdiction*).

Conventions of 1949. As those Conventions apply 'to all cases of declared war or of any other armed conflict which may arise between two or more High Contracting Parties', they apply to international or inter-state armed conflicts. It was proposed by the ICRC to extend the Conventions in their entirety to internal conflicts.[7] However, this proposal was rejected by most States and it was agreed instead to have a single provision—article 3 common to the four Geneva Conventions ('Common Article 3')—which would be applicable '[i]n the case of armed conflict not of an international character occurring in the territory of one of the High Contracting Parties'. Through Common Article 3 international treaty law, for the first time, sought to regulate certain aspects of internal conflicts, even in the absence of a recognition of belligerency. However, it also established a differentiation between the law applicable to inter-state conflicts and those applicable to internal or, more accurately, non-international armed conflicts.

The division of international humanitarian law into rules applicable in international and non-international armed conflicts was further confirmed in 1977 at the time of the adoption of the Protocols Additional to the Geneva Conventions.[8] Additional Protocol I is stated as 'Relating to the Protection of Victims of International Armed Conflicts,' while Additional Protocol II 'relat[es] to the Protection of Victims of Non-International Armed Conflicts'. This division was also recognized in the Statute of the International Criminal Court of 1998, which makes a distinction between war crimes (i.e. serious violations of the laws and customs of war) committed in an international armed conflict[9] and war crimes committed in a non-international armed conflict.[10]

3. Consequences of the distinction between international and non-international armed conflicts

It is essential to distinguish between international and non-international armed conflicts for the purposes of the application of international humanitarian law because differences exist between the content of the law applicable to the different types of armed conflicts. As a matter of treaty law, the differences are vast. The entirety of the Geneva Conventions of 1949, the Hague Conventions which preceded them and Additional Protocol I of 1977 apply to international armed conflicts. These treaties contain many hundreds of articles which establish a fairly detailed body of rules relating to the conduct of hostilities (so called 'Hague Law'), as well as elaborate rules relating to the protection of those who do not take part, or

---

[7] See Cassese, *Civil War*, 116–17; Bartels, *The Historical Evolution*, 57.

[8] The division can also be seen in the relevant provisions of the 1954 Hague Convention for the Protection of Cultural Property in the Event of Armed Conflict. Under art. 18 of that treaty, the entirety of the treaty applies to international armed conflicts while under art. 19 only limited aspects apply to non-international armed conflicts. See R. O'Keefe, *The Protection of Cultural Property in Armed Conflict* (2006) 96–8.

[9] ICC Statute, art. 8(2)(a) and (b).

[10] ICC Statute, art. 8(2)(c) and (e).

who no longer take part, in hostilities (so called 'Geneva Law'). By contrast, the treaty rules applicable specifically to non-international armed conflicts are rather limited. In essence, they are restricted to Common Article 3 of the 1949 Geneva Conventions, the provisions of Additional Protocol II of 1977 and article 8(2)(c) and (e) of the ICC Statute. Common Article 3 is limited to basic protection of those who do not, or who no longer, take part in hostilities and has no rules regulating the conduct of hostilities. Additional Protocol II, which has fewer than twenty substantive provisions, and those parts of the ICC Statute dealing with non-international armed conflicts extend, somewhat, the rules relating to the protection of victims of armed conflict and introduce some modest rules relating to the conduct of hostilities[11] but fall far short of establishing a regime of international humanitarian law close to that established for international armed conflicts.[12]

Notwithstanding this difference in the regulation of international and non-international armed conflicts by the bedrock treaties of international humanitarian law, the distinction between international and non-international armed conflict is being eroded such that there is now greater, though by no means complete, unity in the law applicable to these two forms of conflict.[13]

First of all, there are recent treaties that govern the conduct of participants in an armed conflict which apply to all situations of armed conflict, without distinction. The list of such treaties includes the Biological Weapons Convention 1972, the Chemical Weapons Convention 1993, the Convention Prohibiting Anti-Personnel Land Mines 1997, the Second Protocol to the Hague Convention of 1954 for the Protection of Cultural Property 1999 and the 2001 amendment which extends the Convention on Conventional Weapons and its protocols to non-international armed conflicts.

Secondly, and more importantly, it has been argued that customary international law now provides for a broader set of rules governing non-international armed conflicts and fills the gaps left by treaty law such that the dichotomy between international and non-international armed conflicts is much less significant today. This was the position taken by the Appeals Chamber of the ICTY in the *Tadić (Appeal on Jurisdiction)* case when it stated that:

> Notwithstanding ... limitations, it cannot be denied that customary rules have developed to govern internal strife. These rules ... cover such areas as protection of civilians from hostilities, in particular from indiscriminate attacks, protection of civilian objects, in particular cultural property, protection of all those who do not (or no longer) take active part in hostilities, as well as prohibition of means of warfare proscribed in international armed conflicts and ban of certain methods of conducting hostilities.[14]

---

[11] See further discussion in ch. 4 section 4 below.

[12] See section 6 below for a discussion of the relationship between Common Article 3 and Additional Protocol II.

[13] See L. Moir, 'Towards the Unification of International Humanitarian Law?' in R. Burchill, N. White and J. Morris (eds), *International Conflict and Security Law* (2005) 108.

[14] *Tadić Jurisdiction*, para 127.

The ICTY also held that:

> elementary considerations of humanity and common sense make it preposterous that the use by States of weapons prohibited in armed conflicts between themselves be allowed when States try to put down rebellion by their own nationals on their own territory. What is inhumane, and consequently proscribed, in international wars, cannot but be inhumane and inadmissible in civil strife.[15]

The ICRC, in its comprehensive study of customary international humanitarian law (the Study) published in 2005,[16] has taken a similar approach. It found that nearly all the rules identified in the Study applied to both international and non-international armed conflicts. It went on to state that:

> This study provides evidence that many rules of customary international law apply in both international and non-international armed conflicts and show the extent to which State practice has gone beyond existing treaty law and expanded the rules applicable to non-international armed conflicts. In particular, the gaps in the regulations of the conduct of hostilities in Additional Protocol II have largely been filled through State practice, which has led to the creation of rules parallel to those in Additional Protocol I, but applicable as customary law to non-international armed conflicts.[17]

The suggestion that there are rules of customary international law applicable to non-international armed conflicts which go beyond the rules in Common Article 3 and Additional Protocol II appears to be contrary to the earlier report of the Commission of Experts appointed by the Security Council to investigate violations of humanitarian law in the former Yugoslavia.[18] However, though questions have been raised as to the methodology used by the ICRC study for determining rules of customary international law,[19] there also seems to be acknowledgement, even by States, that customary international law now provides more elaborate rules for non-international armed conflicts than the rules to be found in Common Article 3 and Additional Protocol II. Thus, the provisions of the ICC Statute, which was adopted in 1998, relating to war crimes in non-international armed conflicts, contain rules which go beyond the text of those treaties. However, it also ought to be noted that the provisions of the ICC Statute reflect a reluctance on the part of States to go as far as the ICTY and the ICRC. The Statute was adopted after the *Tadić* decision and incorporated some elements of that decision (e.g. the definition of non-international armed conflicts). However some of the rules identified by the ICTY

---

[15] *Tadić Jurisdiction,* para 119.

[16] J.-M. Henckaerts and L. Doswald-Beck, *Customary International Humanitarian Law Study* (2004).

[17] Ibid, xxix.

[18] See Final Report of the Commission of Experts Established Pursuant to Security Council Resolution 780(1992), S/1994/674 (27 May 1994) 13, para 42.

[19] See D. Bethlehem, 'The Methodological Framework of the Study' and I. Scobbie, 'The Approach to Customary International Law in the Study' in E. Wilmshurst and S. Breau, *Perspectives on the ICRC Study on Customary International Humanitarian Law* (2007) 3, 15; and also J. Bellinger and W. Haynes, 'A US Government Response to the International Committee of the Red Cross Study on *Customary International Humanitarian Law*' (2007) 89 (866) *International Review of the Red Cross* 443.

and ICRC as customary rules applicable in non-international armed conflicts (e.g. the prohibition of attacks on civilian objects) are not included in the war crimes provisions of the ICC Statute. Although it is possible that the drafters of the Statute were simply more reluctant to criminalize violations of international humanitarian law in non-international armed conflicts than in international armed conflicts, it is nonetheless noteworthy that the Statute includes a significantly longer list of war crimes in international than in non-international armed conflicts.[20] In conclusion, the distinction between the law applicable in international and non-international armed conflicts is blurring; however, whenever States have been presented with opportunities to abolish the distinction they seem reluctant to do so. Also, it is undeniable that two key parts of international humanitarian law—the law relating to the status of fighters and the rules relating to detention of combatants and civilians—differ depending on the status of the armed conflict.[21] For these reasons, classification of armed conflicts for the purpose of applying international humanitarian law remains important.

4. Why does the distinction exist and should it be abolished?

As explained above, the distinction between international and non-international armed conflicts can be explained by reference to the history of the development of international law in general and international humanitarian law in particular. However, asserting that international law was, historically, only concerned with inter-state conflicts does not explain why, once it was accepted that international law ought to regulate non-international conflicts as well, it was not extended in its entirety to such conflicts. Nor does it explain why the distinction persists, even if in an attenuated fashion. The main reason for the persistence of the distinction is the view by States, or some of them, that equating non-international and international armed conflicts would undermine State sovereignty and, in particular, national unity and security.[22] States have been concerned that treating non-international armed conflicts in the same way as international armed conflicts would not only encourage secessionist movements, by giving them a status under international law, but it would restrain the hand of the State in seeking to put down rebellions.[23]

[20] Compare art. 8(2)(a) and (b) with art. 8(2)(c) and (e) of the ICC Statute. The Pre-Trial Chamber of the ICC has regarded the difference in criminalization of attacks on civilian objects as reflecting a difference in international humanitarian law. *The Prosecutor v Bahar Idriss Abu Garda*, ICC-02/05-02/09, Confirmation of Charges Decision (Pre-Trial Chamber), 8 February 2010: 'The Majority notes that, while international humanitarian law offers protection to all civilians in both international armed conflict and armed conflict not of an international character, the same cannot be said of all civilian objects, in respect of which protection differs according to the nature of the conflict.'
[21] For further discussion of detention, see ch. 4, section 3 below.
[22] See Cassese, *Civil War*, 116. See also Bartels, *The Historical Evolution*, 61–4. See H.S. Levie (ed.), *The Law of Non-International Armed Conflict: Protocol II to the 1949 Geneva Conventions* (1987) (Levie, *Additional Protocol II*) for statements made, during the drafting of Additional Protocol II, by the representatives of Argentina (30, para 17); the German Democratic Republic (32, para 29); Indonesia (35, para 53); Romania (42, para 33) and Yugoslavia (47, para 6).
[23] F. Bugnion, '*Jus Ad Bellum, Jus in Bello* and Non-International Armed Conflicts' (2003) 6 *Yearbook of International Humanitarian Law* 167, 168.

For example, if the principle of combatants' immunity—which applies to international conflicts and prevents prosecutions of combatants merely for taking part in an armed conflict—were to be applied in non-international armed conflicts, States would be unable to criminalize acts which are traditionally regarded as treasonous.[24]

It was these concerns that led to the inclusion of article 3 in Additional Protocol II stating that nothing in the Protocol restricts the responsibility of the State 'by all legitimate means, to maintain or re-establish law and order'.[25] There has also been concern on the part of States that abolishing the distinction and treating non-international armed conflicts in the same way as international armed conflicts would give international status to non-state groups and might even encourage international intervention in internal conflicts.[26] This concern led to the inclusion of paragraph 4 in Common Article 3 which states that '[t]he application of the preceding provisions shall not affect the legal status of the Parties to the conflict'.

Given that the relevant treaties include provisions which make clear that the issues of concern to States should not be read into the treaties, it is difficult to see why those concerns should persist. Furthermore, these concerns relate primarily to the status of fighters and should not prevent the extension of other norms of international humanitarian law to non-international armed conflicts.[27] Also, the idea that intervention by the international community follows from a classification of a conflict is to some extent erroneous. Firstly, the UN Security Council has in recent years demonstrated its capacity and willingness to intervene in non-international conflicts.[28] Secondly, international law does not permit unilateral 'humanitarian intervention'[29] and therefore does not permit forceful unilateral intervention by States within another State based on the nature of a conflict going on in that other State. However, it is probably fair to recognize that adding to the rules that apply to non-international armed conflicts increases the opportunity for other States to assert that violations of international law are occurring and may also increase opportunity for lawful non-forcible countermeasures (sanctions or other forms of political pressure) taken by other States and directed at addressing violations by the States engaged in the conflict.[30]

---

[24] See D. Fleck, 'The Law of Non-International Armed Conflicts' in D. Fleck (ed.), *The Handbook of International Humanitarian Law* (2008) 611–12 (Fleck, *Non-International Armed Conflicts*); W. Solf, 'Non-International Armed Conflicts: Commentator' (1982) 31 *American University Law Review* 927.

[25] See also ICC Statute, art. 8(3).

[26] See Levie, *Additional Protocol II,* for statement made, during the drafting of Additional Protocol II, by the representatives of Yugoslavia (47, para 6) and Mexico (49, para 14).

[27] See Fleck, *Non-International Armed Conflicts,* 611–12.

[28] E.g. see Security Council resolution 1973 (2011) with respect to Libya which authorizes a no-fly zone and protection of civilians in the context of a non-international armed conflict. See also the World Summit Outcome Document, GA res. 60/1 (2005) para 139, in which the UN General Assembly recognizes the authority of the Security Council to take action in cases of genocide, war crimes and crimes against humanity.

[29] See generally, S. Chesterman, *Just War or Just Peace: Humanitarian Intervention and International Law* (2001).

[30] See art. 54 of the International Law Commission's Articles on Responsibility of States for Internationally Wrongful Acts (2001) (ILC Articles on State Responsibility) and accompanying commentary, in *Yearbook of the International Law Commission,* Vol. II, Part Two (2001). That

Although it has been argued that the humanitarian aims of international humanitarian law are best fulfilled by the abolition of the distinction between international and non-international armed conflicts,[31] the concerns of States regarding sovereignty remain (even if they are misplaced) and are a reason why the law, particularly the law relating to the status of fighters, continues to be different in non-international armed conflicts.

5. The scope of application of international humanitarian law: international armed conflicts

5.1. Inter-state conflict

Article 2 common to the Geneva Conventions of 1949 states that the Conventions 'shall apply to all cases of declared war or of any other armed conflict which may arise between two or more High Contracting Parties, even if the state of war is not recognized by one of them'. It follows from this that an international armed conflict is essentially an inter-state conflict.[32] However, the key question for the application of international humanitarian law is 'when does an armed conflict exist between two States such that this body of law applies?'

5.1.1 War

Before considering what amounts to an armed conflict, it is worth noting that prior to the Geneva Conventions the laws of war applied to 'war'. 'War' was something that came to have a technical meaning in international law. It was a state of relations between States that was opposed to a state of peace.[33] Traditional international law and the 1907 Hague Convention (III) relative to the Opening of Hostilities required a formal declaration of war for the laws of war to apply to the relations between the parties. This meant that where the parties failed to consider themselves

---

commentary refers to sanctions imposed on the former Yugoslavia by a number of States and the European Communities for actions that occurred when armed conflict broke out in that country in 1991. Likewise in 2011, the United States (and others) imposed sanctions on Libya (which went beyond that authorized by SC res. 1970) in response to measures taken by Libya during the violence and conflict that broke out there in 2011. See White House, 'Executive Order: Blocking Property and Prohibiting Certain Transactions Related to Libya' (25 February 2011), available at: <www.whitehouse.gov/sites/default/files/2011libya.eo_.rel_.pdf>.

[31] J.G. Stewart, 'Towards a Single Definition of Armed Conflict in International Humanitarian Law: A Critique of Internationalized Armed Conflict' (2003) 85(850) *International Review of the Red Cross* 313; A. Duxbury, 'Drawing Lines in the Sand—Characterising Conflicts for the Purposes of Teaching International Humanitarian Law' (2007) 8 *Melbourne Journal of International Law* 259; J. Crawford, 'Unequal Before the Law: The Case for the Elimination of the Distinction Between International and Non-International Armed Conflicts' (2007) *Leiden Journal of International Law* 441.

[32] Except in situations covered by art. 1(4) of Additional Protocol I on which see section 5.2 below.

[33] C. Greenwood, 'Scope of Application of Humanitarian Law' in D. Fleck (ed.), *The Handbook of International Humanitarian Law* (2008) 45 (Greenwood, *Scope of Application*).

at war they were able to escape the application of the laws of war.[34] Today, international humanitarian law will apply once an armed conflict exists between States even if the parties do not consider themselves at war. Despite the wording of Common Article 2, which speaks of the application of the Conventions to armed conflicts even if the state of war is not recognized by *one* of the parties, the position generally taken is that international humanitarian law applies to an armed conflict even if *neither* party recognizes a state of war.[35] What is important today is the fact of an armed conflict rather the formal status of war. However, the Geneva Conventions will apply to cases of declared war, even if no fighting or hostilities take place between States and will, for example, govern the status of interned enemy nationals and the exercise of belligerent rights at sea. Greenwood notes that there are no modern cases of a formal declaration of war being delivered through diplomatic channels as was the practice during World War I and World War II.[36] However, there are examples of statements by States to the effect that they are at war with another State.[37] Whether statements referring to a state of war are to be regarded as a declaration of war bringing into effect the application of the Geneva Conventions and other rules of international humanitarian law is essentially a question of intention. For there to be a war in the technical sense, there needs to be an *animus belligerendi*. However, '[t]here is probably a presumption that nations do not intend to create a state of war'[38] and '[s]o serious a matter as the existence of a state of war is not lightly to be implied'.[39]

5.1.2 Armed conflict

In both the *ius ad bellum* and the *ius in bello*, post World War II international law has moved away from conditioning the applicability of the law on the formal or technical concept of war and towards much more factual criteria. Under the *ius ad bellum,* what is prohibited by the UN Charter is the 'use of force' and, under international humanitarian law, the application of the law depends on the existence of an 'armed conflict'. The Geneva Conventions do not define 'armed conflict'. However, it has been defined by the Appeals Chamber of the ICTY in *Tadić (Appeal on Jurisdiction)* case as follows:

> an armed conflict exists whenever there is a resort to armed force between States or protracted armed violence between governmental authorities and organized armed groups or between such groups within a State. International humanitarian law applies from the initiation of such armed conflicts and extends beyond the cessation of hostilities until a general conclusion of peace is reached; or in the case of internal

---

[34] See R. Provost, *International Human Rights and Humanitarian Law* (2002) 249.
[35] See Greenwood, *Scope of Application*, 47; See also J. Pictet (ed.), *Commentary on the Geneva Conventions of 12 August 1949, Vol. IV* (1952) 21 (Pictet, *Commentary on Geneva Convention IV*).
[36] See Greenwood, *Scope of Application*, 49.
[37] See examples cited in C. Greenwood, 'The Concept of War in Modern International Law' (1987) 36 *International and Comparative Law Quarterly* 283.
[38] Greenwood, *Scope of Application*, 49.
[39] Lord McNair and A.D. Watts, *The Legal Effects of War* (1966) 8.

conflicts, a peace settlement is achieved. Until that moment, international humanitarian law continues to apply to the whole territory of the warring States or, in the case of internal conflicts, the whole territory under the control of a party, whether or not actual combat takes place there.[40]

By asserting that an international armed conflict exists *whenever* there is resort to armed force by States, this decision suggests that the threshold for an international armed conflict is very low.[41] As Vité notes, 'it is . . . not necessary for the conflict to extend over time or for it to create a certain number of victims'.[42] Almost any use of armed force by one State against another will bring into effect an international armed conflict,[43] except perhaps in cases where the use of force is unintended (for example arising out of error).[44] The low threshold for international armed conflicts is reflected in the ICRC commentary to the Geneva Conventions which states that:

> Any difference arising between two States and leading to the intervention of members of the armed forces is an armed conflict within the meaning of Article 2, even if one of the Parties denies the existence of a state of war. It makes no difference how long the conflict lasts, how much slaughter takes place, or how numerous are the participating forces; it suffices for the armed forces of one Power to have captured adversaries falling within the scope of Article 4. Even if there has been no fighting, the fact that persons covered by the Conventions are detained is sufficient for its application. The number of persons captured in such circumstances is, of course, immaterial.[45]

The alternative view, which asserts that an international armed conflict only comes into effect when the use of force between States reaches a certain intensity[46] seeks consistency with the definition of non-international armed conflicts, which does have an intensity requirement.[47] However, this analogy is mistaken. To import an intensity requirement into the definition of international armed conflicts is effectively to assert that no law governs the conduct of military operations below that level of intensity, including the opening phase of hostilities. This is different from the position in non-international armed conflicts where domestic law and

---

[40] *Tadić Jurisdiction*, para 70.

[41] S. Vité, 'Typology of Armed Conflicts in International Humanitarian Law: Legal Concepts and Actual Situations' (2009) 91(873) *International Review of the Red Cross* 69, 72 (Vité, *Typology*); W. Fenrick, 'Article 8, War Crimes' in O. Triffterer (ed.), *Commentary on the Rome Statute of the International Criminal Court* (1999).

[42] Vité, *Typology*, 72.

[43] See Greenwood, *Scope of Application*, 46, para 202: 'An international armed conflict exists if one state uses force against another state.'

[44] UK Ministry of Defence, *The Manual of the Law of Armed Conflict* (2004) 29: 'an accidental border incursion by members of the armed forces would not, in itself, amount to an armed conflict, nor would the accidental bombing of another country.'

[45] J. Pictet (ed.), *Commentary on the Geneva Conventions of 12 August 1949, Vol. III* (1960) 23 (Pictet, *Commentary on Geneva Convention III*). In support of this view, see R. Baxter, 'The Duties of Combatants and the Conduct of Hostilities (Law of the Hague)' in *International Dimensions of Humanitarian Law* (Henry Dunant Institute/UNESCO, 1988) 98; M. Cottier, W. Fenrick, P. Sellers and A. Zimmerman, 'Article 8, War Crimes' in O. Triffterer (ed.), *Commentary on the Rome Statute of the International Criminal Court, Observers Notes, Article by Article* (2008) 182.

[46] See International Law Association, 'Final Report of the Meaning of Armed Conflict in International Law' (2010).

[47] See discussion of non-international armed conflicts in section 6 below.

international human rights law will govern tensions and internal disturbances that fall below the intensity of an armed conflict.

It is a question of fact whether or not an armed conflict exists between two States. Where it does, military operations may only be carried out by the parties in the territories of the parties, as well as on the high seas (including the airspace above and the sea floor below) and including the exclusive economic zones of neutral States.[48] In international armed conflicts, international humanitarian law will apply to the activities of the parties across this broad geographical area, and in any other area where military operations are actually carried out.

As the *Tadić* decision indicates,[49] in international armed conflicts international humanitarian law applies until a general conclusion of peace is reached. The clearest example of a general conclusion of peace is the conclusion of a peace treaty between the belligerent parties. However, since the Second World War, such peace treaties have not been common (the 1979 peace treaty between Israel and Egypt being a notable exception[50]). This is probably due, in part, to the fact that peace treaties have in the past been used for the termination of 'wars' and there has been a noticeable decline in declared wars. Therefore questions have arisen as to whether other events might constitute a conclusion of peace, and are therefore to be regarded as bringing to an end an armed conflict between two or more States. In particular, the issue has arisen as to whether a ceasefire or an armistice agreement is to be regarded as bringing an armed conflict to an end or whether, alternatively, the parties are to be regarded as in a state of war and therefore subject to international humanitarian law until a peace treaty is signed. This latter view would mean, for example, that the belligerents remain entitled to continue to use force against one another or that they may continue to exercise belligerent rights at sea, where there is a breach of the armistice or ceasefire agreement.[51] Under the Hague Regulations of 1907, an armistice only suspended military operations and the belligerent parties could resume operations at any time.[52] This was because an armistice was not regarded as bringing the war to an end.

The issue of what is required to bring an armed conflict to an end is of great significance in contemporary international affairs given that there has, as yet, been no peace treaty terminating the Korean conflict of the early 1950s, nor a peace treaty between Israel and some of her Arab neighbours since the 1949 conflict. The better view seems to be that taken by Greenwood that 'since armed conflict is not a technical, legal concept but a recognition of the fact of hostilities, the cessation of active hostilities should be enough to terminate the armed conflict'.[53] A fortiori,

---

[48] See Greenwood, *Scope of Application,* 59, para 216. Note that military operations will be prohibited in certain areas, such as hospital and safety zones, demilitarized zones, and neutralized zones, all of which are established by agreement of the parties. Ibid, paras 219–20.

[49] *Tadić Jurisdiction,* para 70.

[50] Peace Treaty between Egypt and Israel of 1979 (1979) 18 *International Law Materials* 362.

[51] See G. Chang, 'How to Stop North Korea's Weapons Proliferation' *Wall Street Journal* (1 July 2009).

[52] Regulations Respecting the Laws and Customs of War on Land, annexed to Hague Convention IV Respecting the Laws and Customs of War on Land (1907), art. 36.

[53] See Greenwood, *Scope of Application,* 72, para 250.

a ceasefire or armistice agreement will bring an armed conflict to an end where it is intended to bring the hostilities to an end.[54] In any event, the cessation of hostilities will trigger the application of certain duties, such as the duty to release prisoners of war[55] and of persons interned in occupied territory or in the territory of the parties to the conflict.[56] However, certain parts of international humanitarian law will apply beyond the cessation of hostilities, for example the law of occupation,[57] as well as the law applicable to those protected persons who are not released and repatriated.[58]

When the proposition that an armistice or ceasefire which brings hostilities to a close should now be regarded as terminating an armed conflict is combined with the prohibition of the use of force contained in the UN Charter, the effect is that the parties to an armed conflict may no longer exercise belligerent rights at sea and may no longer resort to force after the conflict is terminated, even if there are breaches of the agreement. Resort to force would only be permissible where it constitutes a lawful use of force in self-defence.[59] This was confirmed by the Security Council in resolution 95 (1951) where it rejected Egypt's continued exercise of belligerent rights against shipping, after the armistice which ended hostilities in the 1949 conflict with Israel.[60]

The question whether or not a conflict is an inter-state one may be difficult to answer where one of the parties claims to be a State and the other party rejects that claim—as occurred, for example, during the dissolution of the former Socialist Federal Republic of Yugoslavia. It is possible that what begins as a non-international armed conflict becomes international when an internal rebel movement is successful in creating a new State. However, as Crawford has pointed out, except in the case of entities possessing the right of external self-determination (i.e. colonial or other non-self governing peoples with a right to determine their political status including a right to independence),[61] secession without the consent of the parent State is rarely recognized as successful as a matter of international law.[62] Therefore, where an armed conflict involves an attempt at secession it would be difficult to argue that a rebel group had gained statehood such that the conflict had now become international. Nonetheless, this may be possible in cases of dissolution of the parent State or where the parent State consents to secession but continues to fight (perhaps indirectly by providing support for groups within the new State).

---

[54] Y. Dinstein, *War, Aggression and Self-Defence* (2005) 44.

[55] Geneva Convention III, art. 118.

[56] Geneva Convention IV, art. 133 and 134.

[57] Ibid, art. 6.

[58] Geneva Convention III, art. 5; Geneva Convention IV, art. 6; Additional Protocol I, art. 3.

[59] See Greenwood, *Scope of Application*, 68.

[60] For a general discussion, see D. Akande, 'The Korean War Has Resumed!! (Or so we are told)' *EJIL: Talk!* (22 July 2009).

[61] See GA res. 1514 (1960); GA res. 2625 (1970).

[62] J. Crawford, *The Creation of States in International Law* (2006), ch. 9 (Crawford, *Creation of States*). The main exception to this has been Bangladesh—which was admitted to the UN before consent by Pakistan. Kosovo represents an example of a seceding entity which at the time of writing, in early 2012, had not yet achieved recognition by the majority of States in the face of opposition by Serbia of such recognition.

However, the fact that the armed conflict is ongoing may itself make it more difficult to argue that the criteria for statehood had been met. In *Prosecutor v Milošević*,[63] the ICTY's Trial Chamber had to determine the question of when Croatia became a State (at the time of the dissolution of the former Socialist Federal Republic of Yugoslavia) such that the conflict became an international armed conflict. Applying the criteria for statehood contained in the Montevideo Convention, it determined that Croatia was a State by October 1991; this was before Croatia was recognized by the European Community in January 1992 and admitted to the UN in May 1992.

5.1.3 Occupation

Common Article 2 to the 1949 Geneva Conventions states that the Conventions shall also apply to all cases of partial or total occupation of the territory of a Party, even if the occupation meets with no armed resistance. The last part of that provision (dealing with occupation without armed resistance) is intended to cater for situations like the German annexation of Czechoslovakia prior to World War II. The Geneva Conventions do not themselves define occupation, but occupation is defined under customary international law by article 42 of the 1907 Hague Regulations which states that 'territory is considered occupied when it is actually placed under the authority of the hostile army'.[64] This means that the occupier must exercise effective territorial control, substituting its own authority for the authority of the territorial State,[65] and do so without the consent of the government.[66] Usually this will require the occupying power to deploy troops on the ground in order to impose a degree of stability and to carry out the obligations imposed by international humanitarian law. A brief incursion will probably not amount to occupation under the Hague Regulations.

Alternatively, it may be possible for a State to be in occupation of the territory of another State, or parts of it, not directly but rather through a subordinate (or puppet) administration that it controls. Where the former State exercises such control over the administration, or over a group exercising control over the territory of a State such that the acts of the administration or group are attributable to the State, the State may constitute an occupying power. In the *Armed Activities* case, the International Court of Justice considered the possibility that Uganda was in occupation of parts of the Democratic Republic of the Congo that were controlled by rebel groups outside the Ituri region (where it found a belligerent occupation) but dismissed the possibility on the facts because those groups were not 'under the

---

[63] *Prosecutor v Milošević*, IT-02-54-T, Decision on Motion for Judgment of Acquittal Under Rule 98 bis (Trial Chamber), 16 June 2004 (*Prosecutor v Milošević*).

[64] See *Case Concerning Armed Activities on the Territory of the Congo (Democratic Republic of the Congo v Uganda)* ICJ Rep 2005, 168, paras 172ff (*Armed Activities* case).

[65] *Armed Activities* case, para 173. For the unusual situation in Gaza, and the debate as to whether there can be occupation without 'boots on the ground', see discussion in ch. 9 below.

[66] See generally, A. Roberts, 'What is Military Occupation?' (1984) 55 *British Yearbook of International Law* 249.

control of Uganda'.[67] However it has been asserted that the situation in Nagorno-Karabakh constitutes an example of indirect occupation on the basis that Armenia is in control of the administration that exercises control of the so-called 'Nagorno-Karabakh Republic', which is recognized as a part of Azerbaijan.[68]

The Fourth Geneva Convention imposes particular obligations with regard to occupation and occupied territory. Part III, Section III of that Convention imposes obligations relating to the status and treatment of protected persons in occupied territories. Also, Part III, Section IV details regulations for the treatment of internees in occupied territory (as well as in the territory of the belligerent). However, questions have been raised as to whether 'occupation' and 'occupied territory' under this Convention mean the same thing as 'belligerent occupation' under customary international law and under article 42 of the Hague Regulations. Article 6 of the Fourth Convention states that '[t]he present Convention shall apply from the outset of any conflict or occupation mentioned in Article 2'. The important point here is that the Convention applies from the beginning of the conflict as well as from the beginning of occupation. This has been interpreted to mean that a belligerent occupation, as defined above, does not need to have been established in order for obligations under the Fourth Convention to apply.[69] The ICRC Commentary to article 6 states that:

> the word 'occupation', as used in the Article, has a wider meaning than it has in Article 42 of the Regulations annexed to the Fourth Hague Convention of 1907. So far as individuals are concerned, the application of the Fourth Geneva Convention does not depend upon the existence of a state of occupation within the meaning of the Article 42 referred to above. The relations between the civilian population of a territory and troops advancing into that territory, whether fighting or not, are governed by the present Convention. There is no intermediate period between what might be termed the invasion phase and the inauguration of a stable regime of occupation. Even a patrol which penetrates into enemy territory without any intention of staying there must respect the Conventions in its dealings with the civilians it meets. When it withdraws, for example, it cannot take civilians with it, for that would be contrary to Article 49 which prohibits the deportation or forcible transfer of persons from occupied territory. The same thing is true of raids made into enemy territory or on his coasts. The Convention is quite definite on this point: all persons who find themselves in the hands of a Party to the conflict or an Occupying Power of which they are not nationals are protected persons. No loophole is left.[70]

---

[67] *Armed Activities* case, para 177. The possibility of indirect occupation has also been accepted by the ICTY. See *Prosecutor v Tadić*, IT-94-1-T, Judgment (Trial Chamber), 7 May 1997, para 584 (*Tadić* Trial Judgment). The level of control that will be required for such indirect occupation is the level provided for by the law of State responsibility. However, contrary to the ICTY decisions, the correct test of control under the law of State responsibility will be complete control and dependence under art. 4 of the International Law Commission's Articles on State Responsibility or failing that 'effective control' under art. 8 of those Articles. See further discussion in section 7 below.

[68] See Vité, *Typology*, 74–5. The effective overall control (which Turkey exercises over Northern Cyprus (See *Loizidou v Turkey* (Judgment) App No. 15318/89 (18 December 1996)) may also lead to the conclusion that it is in indirect occupation of that territory.

[69] See discussion by K. Dörmann, 'The Legal Situation of "Unlawful/Unprivileged Combatants"' (2003) 85(849) *International Review of the Red Cross* 45, 61–3 (Dörmann, *Unlawful Combatants*).

[70] See Pictet, *Commentary on Geneva Convention IV*, art. 6. Quoted with approval by the ICTY Trial Chamber in *Prosecutor v Rajić*, IT-95-12, Review of the Indictment (Trial Chamber), 13 September 1996.

Clearly, this interpretation of article 6 provides maximum protection for civilians as it means that even if they are in territory that is not yet under the full administration of the opposing belligerent, they are entitled to the protections of the Fourth Geneva Convention. However, it results in the bifurcation of the law of occupation, with the law deriving from the Hague Regulations applying where occupation is actually established (stable situations of administration) and the law deriving from the Fourth Geneva Convention applying even in areas where stable control is not yet established. The alternative interpretation, which would require that the conditions for the application of article 42 be met, even for the application of the Fourth Geneva Convention,[71] would not only leave significant gaps in the protection of the civilian population but would render redundant that part of article 6 which provides that the Fourth Geneva Convention applies from the outset of an occupation. For these reasons the ICRC interpretation is to be preferred.

In a situation of occupation, the occupying power may be engaged in hostilities with, or otherwise take military action against, a local non-state group, as happened in Iraq after the 2003 invasion by the US and UK and the fall of the regime of Saddam Hussein. In order to determine the law applicable to such action, it must first of all be determined that the situation is not merely an internal disturbance or riot (in which case domestic law will apply) but rather hostilities or combat governed by the law of armed conflict. Questions will arise in such a scenario as to whether or not those actions are governed by the law applicable to international armed conflicts (since the context is one of occupation) or rather by the law applicable to non-international armed conflicts (since the particular contention is between a State and a non-state group).[72] There are two possibilities in this sort of situation. First of all, the non-state group may be fighting on behalf of the occupied State or may be under a command responsible to the occupied State within the meaning of articles 4(A)2 of the Third Geneva Convention or article 43 of Additional Protocol I.[73] Secondly, the non-state group may be independent of the occupied State. In the first case, it is clear that the conflict will be governed by the law applicable to international armed conflicts since the group, though an irregular force, would form part of the armed forces of the State under the provisions mentioned above. The case of other non-state groups is more difficult. The Israeli Supreme Court has taken the view that confrontations between the occupying party and non-state groups in occupied territory are governed by the law applicable to international armed conflicts, even in cases where the non-state group

[71] That interpretation is shared by R. Baxter, 'So-Called "Unprivileged Belligerency": Spies, Guerrillas and Saboteurs' (1951) 28 *British Yearbook of International Law* 325; H.P. Gasser, 'Protection of the Civilian Population' in D. Fleck (ed.), *The Handbook of International Humanitarian Law* (2007) (Gasser, *Civilian Population*), appears to take this view at 276, para 528; Y. Dinstein, *The International Law of Belligerent Occupation* (2009) 41 (Dinstein, *Occupation*).
[72] See A. Paulus and M. Vashakmadze, 'Assymetrical War and the Notion of Armed Conflict—A Tentative Conceptualization' (2009) 91(873) *International Review of the Red Cross* 95, 113–15 (Paulus and Vashakmadze, *Assymetrical War*).
[73] See later discussion in section 7.1 below on how these provisions should be interpreted.

is not fighting on behalf of a State.[74] In the view of this author, this conclusion is correct.[75] The conclusion follows from the fact that the Geneva Conventions, and other rules concerning international armed conflicts (including Additional Protocol I, where applicable), apply to the acts of the occupying power and regulate the relationship between the occupying power and the people in the occupied territory.

The argument that armed conflicts between an occupying power and a non-state group within occupied territory amount to a non-international armed conflict proceeds from the view that every international armed conflict is between two opposing States.[76] However, the relevant question is not what type of conflict exists between the State and the non-state group but what law applies to the acts of an occupying power within occupied territory. It is important to note that the law of occupation is not just about the relationship between two contending States and not just a means of indicating the temporary nature of the authority of the occupier vis-à-vis that of the territorial State. The law of occupation is also a means of regulating what may well be the tense relationship between the occupying power and persons within the occupied territory and a means of providing restraint with regard to how the occupier treats the local population. The tension between the occupier and the local population may well result in acts of hostilities but the fact that the local population has chosen to rise up in arms does not free the occupier from the restraints it otherwise has. Indeed it ought to strengthen those restraints. The law of occupation is no less necessary in those situations. Moreover, the law of occupation is cognizant of the fact that persons who are not combatants (in the sense in which that term is used in international armed conflicts) may well engage in hostilities against the occupier, acts of sabotage, or other acts which imperil the security of the occupier. For example, article 5 of the Fourth Geneva Convention contemplates persons who engage in sabotage and the provisions of that Convention relating to internment deal with persons who may imperil the security of the State. Likewise, article 45(3) of Additional Protocol I contemplates that persons who engage in hostilities in a situation of occupation, and are not entitled to prisoner of war status, are nevertheless entitled to the protections of the Fourth Geneva Convention or of the fundamental guarantees in article 75 of Additional Protocol I (which represents customary law).[77]

Thus, it is the law of occupation and other rules of international armed conflict (including the law of targeting) that conditions how the occupier may respond to an uprising in the foreign territory of which it has temporary occupation. This

---

[74] *The Public Committee against Torture in Israel. The Government of Israel*, High Court of Justice, HCJ 769/02 (13 December 2006) paras 16–23 (*Targeted Killings* case).

[75] See in support, A. Cassese, *International Law* (2005) 420–3; A. Cassese, 'On Some Merits of the Israeli Judgment on Targeted Killings' (2007) 5 *Journal of International Criminal Justice* 339; Dinstein, *Occupation,* 100. For a contrary view, see M. Milanovic, 'Lessons for Human Rights and Humanitarian Law in the War on Terror: Comparing Hamdan and the Israeli Targeted Killings Case' (2007) 89 (866) *International Review of the Red Cross* 373, 383–6 (Milanovic, *Lessons for Human Rights*); Y. Arai-Takahashi, *The Law of Occupation: Continuation and Change of International Humanitarian Law, and its Interaction with International Human Rights Law* (2009) 300–03; see also ch. 6 section 4.2 below.

[76] See Milanovic, *Lessons for Human Rights.*

[77] See generally, Dörmann, *Unlawful Combatants.*

conclusion is also supported by the International Court of Justice's decision in the *Armed Activities* case where the Court applied the law of occupation (derived from the Geneva Conventions and from customary law emerging from the Hague Regulations) and the law of international armed conflicts (as derived from the Geneva Conventions and Additional Protocol I) to Uganda's acts in the Ituri region. This was despite the fact that Uganda was acting primarily against non-state groups in that region.[78] To determine otherwise would be to ignore much of the protections to which occupied people are entitled. However, this is not to suggest that there may never be a non-international armed conflict in occupied territory. There may well be such a conflict between two non-state groups (e.g. Hamas and Fatah in Gaza) with the result that those parties are bound by the rules relating to non-international armed conflict.[79]

Occupation will cease 'with the end of actual control of the territory by the occupying power'.[80] Usually the end of actual control will coincide with the removal of the occupying power's troops from the occupied territory. However, control may extend beyond this removal, for example, in cases where the direct control of the occupier is simply replaced by indirect occupation carried out through a group or administration that is established by the occupier and is under its complete control. More difficult is the situation, such as that in Gaza, where the armed forces of the occupier leave the territory and no longer exercise control over the governance of the territory but continue to exercise control over other aspects of the territory (in the case of Gaza, control over the airspace, over certain borders and over adjacent sea areas). Opinion is divided over whether such a situation constitutes a continuation of occupation.[81] However, it may be argued that, like the criteria for statehood (where the criteria for the creation of statehood are not the same as the criteria for the maintenance or continuation of statehood[82]), the criteria for the establishment of occupation may not be the same as the criteria for the maintenance of occupation. This argument would suggest that even in cases where a former occupying power no longer exercises the level of control that would justify the establishment of occupation, if it exercises such control as to prevent another power from exercising full control, the occupying power remains in occupation.

[78] *Armed Activities* case. For a similar view, see the decision of the ICC Pre-Trial Chamber in *Prosecutor v Lubanga*, ICC-01/04-01/06, Decision on Confirmation of Charges (Pre-Trial Chamber) 29 January 2007, para 220 (*Prosecutor v Lubanga* Pre-Trial Chamber, Confirmation of Charges Decision); also *Prosecutor v Katanga and Chui*, ICC-01/04-02/07, Decision on Confirmation of Charges (Pre-Trial Chamber) 26 September 2008, para 240 (*Prosecutor v Katanga and Chui*).
[79] See *Prosecutor v Thomas Lubanga Dyilo* (Trial Chamber Judgment Pursuant to Article 74, ICC Statute) ICC-01/04-01/06, March 2012, paras: 563–5 (*Prosecutor v Lubanga, Trial Judgment*); Paulus and Vashakmadze, *Asymetrical War*, 115.
[80] Gasser, *Civilian Population*, 282, para 537.
[81] See the discussion by Vité, *Typology*, 83–5 with extensive references to the opposing views, and the discussion in ch. 9 below.
[82] Crawford, *Creation of States*, 667 et seq.

5.2. Self-determination conflicts of national liberation under article 1(4) of Additional Protocol I

Although it is usually the case that an international armed conflict involves two (or more) States in conflict against each other, Additional Protocol I of 1977 also provides for the application of the laws of international armed conflict to a category of internal armed conflict. Under article 1(4), Additional Protocol I (which applies to international armed conflicts) also applies to armed conflicts:

> in which peoples are fighting against colonial domination and alien occupation and against racist regimes in the exercise of their right of self-determination, as enshrined in the Charter of the United Nations and the Declaration on Principles of International Law concerning Friendly Relations and Co-operation among States in accordance with the Charter of the United Nations.

The provision is a reflection of popular concerns of the era in which Additional Protocol I was negotiated as well as a response to the desire, mainly of developing countries, for legitimation of those engaged in liberation struggles. The provision was primarily aimed at the situation regarding Israel's occupation of Palestine, the struggle in South Africa and Rhodesia (as it was then called) and the colonial struggles of the time.[83] However, Additional Protocol I has never been applied in any of those situations. One of the reasons why the provision has not been applied is that the three situations are difficult to define. However, it must be remembered that the key question identified by the provision is whether a movement is fighting in the exercise of the right of self-determination. That is a matter to be determined by reference to general international law.

Most authors consider that article 1(4) has not been accepted as a norm of customary international law.[84]

5.3. Recognition of belligerency[85]

As noted above, even prior to the Second World War, international law provided for one circumstance in which the laws of war would apply to a civil war between a State and a rebel group. This was where an insurgent group was recognized as a belligerent for the purpose of and with the consequence of bringing the laws of war into operation in relation to the conflict. The recognition of belligerency could be granted either by the government against whom the insurgent group was fighting or

---

[83] See G. Aldrich, 'Prospects for United States Ratification of Additional Protocol I to the 1949 Geneva Conventions' (1991) 85 *AJIL* 1, 6.

[84] See eg Y. Dinstein, *The Conduct of Hostilities Under the Law of International Armed Conflict* (2010) 28. However, Cassese has argued that when one takes into account the views of States expressed during the drafting of the provision, together with the General Assembly resolutions on the same topic, the provision ought to be regarded as embodying a customary rule. See A. Cassese, 'Wars of National Liberation and Humanitarian Law' reprinted in A. Cassese (ed.), *The Human Dimension of International Law: Selected Papers* (2008) 99, 106.

[85] See E. Riedel, 'Recognition of Belligerency' in R. Bernhardt (ed.), *Encyclopedia of Public International Law, Vol. 4* (2000) 47 (Riedel, *Recognition of Belligerency*).

alternatively by third States, usually through a declaration of neutrality by that foreign State. According to Oppenheim, 'any State may recognize insurgents as a belligerent Power, provided (1) they are in possession of a certain part of the territory of the legitimate Government; (2) they have set up a Government of their own; and (3) they conduct their armed contention with the legitimate Government according to the laws and usages of war'.[86]

The effect of a recognition of belligerency by the belligerent government was that the entire laws of war were brought into effect between the contending parties. The effects of recognition of belligerency are primarily relative, i.e. they operate between the recognizing State and the belligerent group and do not, in principle, change the relations between other States and the belligerent group.[87]

The practice of recognizing belligerencies appears to have declined since the creation of the concept of non-international armed conflicts and it has been claimed that the doctrine is now either obsolete or has fallen into desuetude. However, though there seem to have been no instances since the Boer War (1899–1902) in which a belligerent government has expressly recognized the belligerency of an insurgent group, there seem to have been instances of third States recognizing belligerency of insurgents operating in other countries.[88] Also it should be remembered that even in the nineteenth century 'most instances of recognition of belligerency . . . concerned implied recognition, usually by declarations of neutrality or acquiescence in confiscation of contraband or in blockade maintained by one of the belligerents'[89] and there have been blockades instituted in non-international armed conflicts since 1949. These blockades may be regarded as implicit recognitions of belligerency and thus internationalizing the conflict.[90] Finally as Professor Scobbie argues, persuasively, with regard to Gaza,[91] non-application of a doctrine of customary international law does not suffice to extinguish it. There is no concept of desuetude with regard to custom.

6. The scope of application of international humanitarian law: non-international armed conflicts

It is not always easy to determine when a situation of violence within a State is to be classified as a non-international armed conflict. Where a situation of violence is regarded merely as one of internal strife or civil disturbance, international law considers that it does not reach the threshold of 'armed conflict' and international

---

[86] L. Oppenheim, *International Law, Vol. II: Disputes, War and Neutrality* (2nd edn, 1912) 92.
[87] L. Oppenheim, *International Law, Vol. II: Disputes, War and Neutrality* (7th edn, 1952) 251.
[88] E.g. recognition of the belligerency of the Nicaraguan Sandinistas by the Andean Group in 1979, cited in N. Navia, 'Hay o no hay conflict armado en Colombia' (2008) 1 *Anuario Colombiano de Derecho International* 139, 147; recognition, in 1981, by France and Mexico of El Salvadoran rebels and recognition by Venezuela of the FARC group in Colombia in January 2008.
[89] Riedel, *Recognition of Belligerency*, 48.
[90] See the discussion on this issue with respect to Gaza in ch. 9 below.
[91] See ch. 9, section 4.4 below.

humanitarian law does not apply. However, where the internal violence does reach this threshold, international humanitarian law will apply to that internal, or more accurately, non-international armed conflict. The relevant question, therefore, is what is considered to be the threshold above which a non-international armed conflict may be said to be taking place.

6.1. Common Article 3

Unfortunately, article 3 Common to all four 1949 Geneva Conventions does not specify precisely when it will apply, referring only to an 'armed conflict not of an international character occurring in the territory of one of the High Contracting Parties'. Whether or not such a conflict is taking place is determined by criteria which have been fleshed out by customary international law. In the *Tadić* case, the Appeals Chamber of the ICTY referred to a non-international armed conflict as a situation of 'protracted armed violence between governmental authorities and organized armed groups or between such groups within a State'.[92] This test is also adopted in article 8(2)(f) of the Statute of the ICC. As the ICC Statute indicates, a non-international armed conflict excludes 'situations of internal disturbances and tensions, such as riots, isolated and sporadic acts of violence or other acts of a similar nature'.[93]

For a non-international armed conflict to exist there must be, firstly, parties to that conflict. What is evident from customary international law is that a non-international armed conflict governed by Common Article 3 may be a conflict between a State and a non-state group or alternatively, may be a conflict arising between non-state groups. It is clear that in all non-international armed conflicts, at least one side must be considered a non-state group and international humanitarian law provides the rules for determining when such a group may be regarded as party to an armed conflict. In order to be a party to an armed conflict a non-state group must have a certain level of organization with a command structure.[94] In short, in the words of the Appeals Chamber in *Tadić*, it must be an 'organized armed group'.[95] The factors relevant to determining whether an armed group is sufficiently organized are as follows: the existence of a command structure and disciplinary rules and mechanisms within the group; the existence of a headquarters; the fact that the group controls a certain territory; the ability of the group to gain access to weapons, other military equipment, recruits and military training; its ability to plan, coordinate and carry out military operations, including troop movements and logistics; its ability to define a unified military strategy and use military tactics; and its ability to speak with one voice and negotiate and conclude agreements such as

[92] *Tadić Jurisdiction*, para 70.
[93] ICC Statute, art. 8(2)(d) and 8(2)(f), following art. 1 of Additional Protocol II.
[94] J. Pejic, 'Status of Armed Conflicts' in E. Wilmshurst and S. Breau (eds), *Perspectives on the ICRC Study on Customary International Humanitarian Law* (2007) 85–6 (Pejic, *Status of Armed Conflicts*).
[95] *Tadić Jurisdiction*, para 70.

ceasefire or peace accords.[96] It is worth noting that these are not minimum factors that must be present but rather indicators of organization.

The question may arise whether violence involving criminal groups which act for private non-political motives may be classified as a non-international armed conflict and therefore subject to the application of international humanitarian law. Although it is usually the case that groups involved in non-international armed conflicts have a political purpose or aim, this is not a requirement under international humanitarian law. The cases in the international criminal tribunals, which set out the criteria for classifying conflicts, do not include reference to the motivation or purpose of the groups in questions. What is important is that the group has a sufficient degree of organization, taking into account the factors indicated above, and that the group is able to and does conduct, or is otherwise involved, in an armed campaign which reaches the required degree of intensity. Factually, it is unlikely that these conditions will be met with criminal gangs but the possibility cannot be ruled out. Indeed, the possibility of the application of international humanitarian law to the fight against piracy has been acknowledged by the United Nations Security Council. In resolution 1851 (2008), the Security Council authorized States and regional organization 'to undertake all necessary measures that are appropriate in Somalia, for the purpose of suppressing acts of piracy and armed robbery at sea, . . . provided, however, that any measures undertaken pursuant to the authority of this paragraph shall be undertaken consistent with applicable international humanitarian and human rights law'. The reference to international humanitarian law appears to be an indication that the use of force against the pirates *may* rise to a level where it amounts to, or is in any event a part of an armed conflict.[97]

The second criterion required for a non-international armed conflict is that the level of violence or fighting must reach a certain degree of intensity.[98] In *Tadić* the ICTY spoke of 'protracted armed violence'.[99] While the word 'protracted' suggests that the criterion relates exclusively to the time over which armed conflict takes place, it has come to be accepted that the key requirement here is the intensity of the force. There are factors, beyond timing, that go to determining whether the violence reaches the 'intensity' that would cause it to be classified as an armed conflict. The requirement for a degree of intensity indicates that the threshold of violence that is required for the application of international humanitarian law in

---

[96] *Prosecutor v Ramush Haradinaj*, IT-04-84-T, Judgment (Trial Chamber), 3 April 2008, para 60 (*Prosecutor v Haradinaj*).

[97] See R. Geiss, 'Armed Violence in Fragile States: Low Intensity Conflicts, Spill Over Conflicts, and Sporadic Law Enforcement Operations by External Actors' (2009) 91(873) *International Review of the Red Cross* 127, 139 et seq; M. Passman, 'Protections Afforded to Captured Pirates Under the Law of War and International Law' (2008) 33 *Tulane Maritime Law Journal* 1. See however D. Guilfoyle, 'The Law of War and the Fight against Somali Piracy: Combatants or Criminals?' (2010) 11 *Melbourne Journal of International Law* 141, pointing out that it is difficult to regard the Somali pirates as participants in an armed conflict, and stating that there is no need to have recourse to international humanitarian law in relation to the fight against piracy.

[98] For a summary of the two criteria, see D. Schindler, 'The Different Types of Armed Conflicts According to the Geneva Conventions and Protocols' (1979) 163 *Recueil des cours* 147.

[99] *Tadić Jurisdiction*, para 70.

non-international armed conflicts is higher than the case of international armed conflicts. Unlike the law regulating international armed conflicts, which applies from the initiation of inter-state violence (and perhaps even before), the situation with respect to non-international armed conflicts is more fluid as often the violence pre-dates the establishment of a non-international armed conflict and the application of international humanitarian law. Thus, the question when the violence crosses the threshold of applicability of international humanitarian law will often need to be answered.

In *Prosecutor v Ramush Haradinaj et al*, which arose out of the conflict in Kosovo between the authorities of the Federal Republic of Yugoslavia and the Kosovo Liberation Army, the ICTY relied on a number of indicative factors for assessing the two criteria of 'intensity' and 'the organization of armed groups'.[100] The factors relevant to intensity include: the number, duration and intensity of individual confrontations; the type of weapons and other military equipment used; the number and calibre of munitions fired; the number of persons and type of forces partaking in the fighting; the number of casualties; the extent of material destruction; and the number of civilians fleeing combat zones. The involvement of the UN Security Council may also be a reflection of the intensity of a conflict.[101] Clearly, these criteria may point in different directions and a complete assessment has to be made of the overall situation without there being any particular formula that can be applied to determining what weight should be given to the different factors. It may well be that violence of relatively short duration amounts to a non-international conflict where the scale of violence and destruction is particularly high. In the *Abella* case the Inter-American Commission of Human Rights held that a confrontation lasting thirty hours between the Argentinian military and a dissident group of soldiers was covered by Common Article 3.[102] Alternatively prolonged violence may suffice even though the individual confrontations do not result in extensive casualties or destruction and are mere 'pin-pricks'. However, in the case of violence implicating State authorities it is to be expected that the violence is of the kind that would be used by the armed forces of a State though what is decisive is the activity rather than the arm of the State that is carrying it out.[103] Thus even operations

---

[100] *Prosecutor v Haradinaj*. See also in *Prosecutor v Milošević*, para 14 et seq. See generally, A. Cullen, *The Concept of Non-International Armed Conflicts in International Humanitarian Law* (2010).

[101] *Prosecutor v Haradinaj*, para 49.

[102] *Abella v Argentina*, Inter-American Commission on Human Rights, Case No. 11.137, Report No. 55/97 (18 November 1997). This case is however criticized in ch. 11 (M. Schmitt) and ch. 13 (N. Lubell) below.

[103] A question that is sometimes posed is whether the threshold of derogation from human rights treaties in case of a 'public emergency threatening the life of the nation' may serve as an indication that the threshold of a Common Article 3 conflict under international humanitarian law has been reached. There is nothing in the treaty texts to suggest such an interpretation and it would appear that such a linkage cannot always be established in practice. The existence of a non-international armed conflict is a question of fact that does not (and should not) require a State declaration, including one derogating from a human rights treaty. Moreover, there are cases in which States declared public emergencies and presumably fulfilled the derogation criteria even though no non-international armed conflict was threatened or ongoing. There are also cases in which non-international armed conflicts have occurred without the State declaring a public emergency and derogating from its human rights obligations,

conducted by law-enforcement agents are not excluded from classification as non-international armed conflicts.

6.2. Additional Protocol II

The threshold for the application of Additional Protocol II to non-international armed conflicts is higher than that for Common Article 3. As is the case with the Common Article 3, Additional Protocol II does not apply to situations of internal disturbance and tensions such as riots, isolated and sporadic acts of violence (the threshold for 'armed conflict'). However, under article 1(1) of Additional Protocol II, the rules contained therein only apply to armed conflicts which take place on the territory of a party 'between its armed forces and dissident armed forces or other organized armed groups which, under responsible command, exercise such control over a part of its territory as to enable them to carry out sustained and concerted military operations and to implement this Protocol'.

This test is similar to that which was historically applied by States in recognizing belligerency in civil wars for the purpose of bringing into effect the law of armed conflict.[104] However, this provision applies only to Additional Protocol II and is a more stringent test of non-international armed conflicts than that which exists in customary international law.[105]

The test is more rigorous than the threshold for the application of Common Article 3 in a number of ways. First of all, it excludes conflicts which arise solely between organized armed groups and applies only if government forces are involved in the armed conflict. Secondly, there is the requirement that the organized armed group exercises control over territory. The test seems designed for a situation in which a rebel group is a contending power, with the government, for authority over the State or a part of it. The requirement of control over territory is linked to an ability to carry out sustained and concerted military operations as well as an ability to implement the protocol. Textually, the words do not seem to require the actual carrying out of such operations but merely the ability to do so. However, in practice

mainly for political reasons. It could also be asked how any linkage between the derogation threshold could trigger the application of international humanitarian law if a State is not a party to the relevant treaty, for instance the ICCPR. Similarly it is not clear how a derogation threshold could be relied on with respect to treaties that make no provision for derogation, such as the African Charter on Human and Peoples' Rights. What is the utility of this proposal for non-international armed conflicts waged only between non-state armed groups? These and other queries suggest that the existing international humanitarian law triggers remain sufficient to enable a determination of when a situation may be classified as a non-international armed conflict, without the need to resort to additional criteria. See Human Rights Committee, 'General Comment 29: States of Emergency (article 4)' CCPR/C/21/ Rev.1/Add.11 (2001).

[104] See eg the criteria set out by L. Oppenheim, *International Law, Vol. II: Disputes, War and Neutrality* (2nd edn, 1912) 92.

[105] It has been suggested that under customary international law there might be two separate thresholds for classifying non-international armed conflict, with these thresholds corresponding to the tests under Common Article 3 and Additional Protocol II. See further discussion in ch. 4, section 4 (n 96) below. However, there seems to be very little, if any evidence that the test contained in Additional Protocol II is regarded as anything other than the test for the application of the rules in that treaty.

it is difficult to conceive of control of territory being achieved and maintained without sustained and concerted military operations being carried out at some stage.

A third differentiation between the application of Additional Protocol II and Common Article 3 is that Additional Protocol II applies to non-international armed conflicts taking place in the territory of a party between '*its* armed forces' and organized armed groups described above. The combination of the requirements that the conflict be (i) in the territory of a party and (ii) between the forces of that party and armed groups is to limit the application of the Protocol in internationalized non-international armed conflicts. As will be discussed below, in situations when a foreign State intervenes in an internal armed conflict with the consent of the State where the conflict is taking place, the armed conflict remains non-international. However, even where both the intervening State and the territorial State are parties to Additional Protocol II, that treaty will not apply to the acts of the intervening State in the conflict. This is because the conflict does not take place in its territory and though it takes place in the territory of another party to the Protocol, the conflict is not between the armed forces of that party and armed groups. Applying this interpretation to the armed conflict in Afghanistan, (since it became a non-international conflict in 2002) would mean that though Afghanistan became party to Additional Protocol II in 2009 and though some of the countries fighting in Afghanistan with its consent are also parties to Additional Protocol II, the Protocol does not apply to the conflict between those intervening countries and armed groups they fight.[106] It is not clear whether this was intended in the drafting of article 1(1) of the Protocol. An alternative interpretation would be to consider the forces of the intervening State to be part of the armed forces of the territorial State.[107] Although this would be desirable in order to extend the humanitarian protections of Additional Protocol II, this test for armed forces does not find support in the rest of international humanitarian law. The forces of a co-belligerent are not usually regarded as part of the armed forces of a party. A State is responsible for all the acts of its own armed forces[108] and it would be a stretch to say that a State is responsible for all acts of the co-belligerent's forces.

A different way of reaching a similar result (i.e. making Additional Protocol II apply to acts of invited foreign forces) is to consider whether the territorial State is legally responsible under the law of State responsibility for violations of Additional Protocol II committed by foreign forces invited by the territorial State. However, for that to occur, the foreign forces would need to be 'placed at the disposal of' the territorial State.[109] This means that those forces must act under the exclusive direction and control of the territorial State and not under the authority of the

---

[106] D. Akande, 'Afghanistan accedes to Additional Protocols to Geneva Conventions: Will AP II govern the conflict in Afghanistan?' *EJIL Talk* (30 June 2009) (Akande, *AP II and the Afghan conflict*).
[107] See Vité, *Typology*, 80.
[108] For international armed conflicts, see Additional Protocol I, art. 91.
[109] ILC Articles on State Responsibility, art. 6. See also discussion in Akande, *AP II and the Afghan conflict*.

sending State.[110] This test would rarely be satisfied and, therefore, the acts of foreign forces will rarely be attributable to the territorial State.

The effect of the different thresholds for the application of Common Article 3 and Additional Protocol II is that there are at least two types of non-international armed conflicts. On the one hand there are those covered by Additional Protocol II (and also by Common Article 3) and on the other hand there are those covered only by Common Article 3.

6.3. A third threshold?

It has been suggested that the provisions of the ICC Statute dealing with war crimes in non-international armed conflicts introduce a third type of non-international armed conflict, or rather, introduce a third threshold at which a different regime of law will apply to certain non-international armed conflicts.[111] This suggestion is based on the fact that article 8(2)(f) of the Statute states that article 8(2)(e), which deals with war crimes in a non-international armed conflict (other than violations of Common Article 3, which are dealt with in article 8(2)(c)), applies where there is 'protracted armed conflict between governmental authorities and organized armed groups or between such groups'. It is said that this threshold falls between those identified by Common Article 3 and Additional Protocol II because it requires a 'protracted conflict'. It is noteworthy that article 8(2)(d), which deals with the applicability of Common Article 3, does not contain wording regarding protracted armed conflict. Despite the different wording of paragraphs (2)(d) and (2)(f) of article 8, it is not at all clear that it was intended to create different thresholds of application. Nor does the wording actually do so. As is obvious, the wording in article 8(2)(f) is taken from the *Tadić* case and in *Tadić* the ICTY was trying to define the sorts of conflicts that would fall within Common Article 3. While it is true that some emphasis is placed on the duration of the conflict and the fact that it must be protracted, ICTY jurisprudence has already indicated that this is one of the factors to be taken into account in applying Common Article 3 and in judging intensity. Article 8(2)(f) is better interpreted as simply stating the intensity test with the protracted nature of the conflict being a factor to be assessed in determining intensity.

7. Foreign intervention in non-international armed conflicts

Despite the significance of the distinction between international and non-international armed conflicts, making the distinction is often difficult. This is particularly so in cases where there is foreign intervention in a non-international armed conflict. It is often noted that since the end of the World War II there have been many more internal rather than inter-state armed conflicts. However, during the

---

[110] See ILC Articles on State Responsibility, commentary to art. 6.
[111] See Vité, *Typology*, 80–3 and also discussion in Pejic, *Status of Armed Conflicts*, 89.

Cold War this trend was coupled with the phenomenon of 'proxy wars' where many internal conflicts were fought through the intervention of foreign States. Similarly, as is demonstrated by some of the case studies in this work (e.g. Iraq, Afghanistan, DRC, South Ossetia), the period after the end of the Cold War has continued to see increased foreign intervention in what would otherwise be internal conflicts between a State and non-state groups.

Since international armed conflicts are essentially inter-state conflicts, whether or not intervention in a non-international armed conflict transforms that conflict into an international armed conflict (or at least grafts an international armed conflict onto an existing, and perhaps continuing, non-international armed conflict) will depend on which side of the conflict the foreign State intervenes. A proposal by the ICRC, at the initiation of the process which led to the conclusion of the Additional Protocols, for all such conflicts to be deemed international armed conflicts was rejected.[112]

7.1. Foreign intervention on the side of a non-state armed group against a State

Where the forces of a foreign State intervene on the side of the rebel or non-state group fighting against a State, there will be two opposing States involved in a conflict and, therefore, an international armed conflict will ensue. In cases where a foreign State intervenes through the introduction of its armed forces on the side of rebels then the situation is hardly any different from that which would exist in the quintessential international armed conflict. However, the fact that there is an international armed conflict between two States does not necessarily affect the classification of the conflict between the territorial State and non-state group. That conflict will remain as a non-international armed conflict in so far as the non-state group does not act on behalf of the foreign intervening State. There will therefore be a mixed conflict with an international armed conflict going on alongside the pre-existing and continuing non-international armed conflict. In the *Nicaragua* case, the International Court of Justice held that the actions of the US in and against Nicaragua were governed by the rules applicable to international armed conflicts but that the conflict between the Nicaraguan forces and the Contra rebels remained a non-international armed conflict.[113]

More difficult is the situation where a foreign State intervenes on the side of a rebel movement not by way of introduction of its forces but rather through support given to rebels or non-state groups in cases where it is the non-state group who actually does the fighting against the territorial State. It is accepted that where a non-state group fighting against a State acts on behalf of a different State, there will

---

[112] ICRC, 'Protection of Victims of Non-International Armed Conflicts' (1971) cited by Vité, *Typology*, fn 31.

[113] *Military and Paramilitary Activities in and against Nicaragua (Nicaragua v United States of America)* ICJ Rep 1986, 14, para 219 *(Nicaragua)*. See section 7.3 below for discussion of 'Mixed conflicts'.

be an international armed conflict. However, there has been much controversy as to the relevant test for determining when a conflict is internationalized in such a situation. The question that arises here is what level of involvement by the State supporting the non-state group is sufficient to internationalize the conflict.[114]

The leading case here is the *Tadić* decision of the ICTY.[115] First of all, the Appeals Chamber of the ICTY held that whether or not State support for a non-state group suffices to turn the conflict into an international armed conflict depends on whether the non-state group belongs to a party to the conflict (within the meaning of article 4 of the Third Geneva Convention). The question whether the non-state group 'belongs' to the State was then interpreted as one of whether the non-state group was to be regarded as a de facto State organ. In other words, the question was whether the acts of the non-state group are attributable to the State under the law of State responsibility. In the view of the ICTY Appeals Chamber, only where the non-state group is to be considered as a de facto organ of the foreign State is there an international armed conflict between the foreign State and the territorial State. Secondly, the Appeals Chamber held that the relevant test of attribution with regard to the responsibility of a State for the acts of non-state organized armed groups is a test of 'overall control'. On this second point, the Appeals Chamber took issue with the test the International Court of Justice had constructed for attribution in the *Nicaragua* case. The ICTY Appeals Chamber was of the view that the International Court of Justice had put forward a test of 'effective control' in order for a non-state group to be regarded as a de facto State organ. In the Appeals Chamber's view this test was too strict and, in cases of organized groups it proposed a test of 'overall control'. The 'overall control' test would be satisfied

> when the State (or, in the context of an armed conflict, the Party to the conflict) *has a role in organizing, coordinating or planning the military actions* of a military group, in addition to financing, training and equipping or providing operational support to the group. Acts performed by the group or members thereof may be regarded as acts of *de facto* State organs regardless of any specific instruction by the controlling State concerning the commission of each of those acts.[116]

On the basis of these holdings, the Appeals Chamber held that because the Bosnian Serbs were under the overall control of the Federal Republic of Yugoslavia, the conflict between that group and the Muslim-led Bosnian government was an international armed conflict. The overall control test put forward by the ICTY has also been approved by the ICC in the *Lubanga* case.[117]

However, though the actual decision on the facts in *Tadić* was probably right, the reasoning by which it reached its conclusion has been the subject of criticism,

---

[114] See generally, C. Byron, 'Armed Conflicts: International or Non-International' (2001) 6 *Journal of Conflict and Security Law* 63.

[115] *Tadić* Trial Judgment.

[116] *Tadić Jurisdiction*, para 139 (emphasis in original).

[117] *Prosecutor v Lubanga (Pre-Trial Chamber, Confirmation of Charges Decision)*, para 210, 211, and *Prosecutor v Lubanga, Trial Judgment*, para 541.

and rightly so, in the view of this author.[118] Both of the points made by the Appeals Chamber regarding the internationalization of armed conflicts on the basis of support to non-state groups are open to dispute. To take the second point first: the ICTY misinterpreted the decision in the *Nicaragua* case regarding the test of attribution of acts of non-state groups to a State. As the International Court of Justice has since confirmed in the *Bosnia Genocide Convention* case,[119] the *Nicaragua* case, customary international law and the International Law Commission's (ILC) Articles on State Responsibility do not contain a single test for attribution of acts of non-state groups. Rather there are at least two tests. First of all, there is the test to determine whether a non-state group is to be considered de facto as a State organ under article 4 of the ILC's Articles. If that test is satisfied, then all the acts of a non-state group would be attributable to a State. In some ways this (attributing all acts of a non-state group to a State) is precisely what the Appeals Chamber was seeking to achieve in *Tadić*. But the test for whether a non-state group is to be regarded as de facto organ of a State is not, in the eyes of the ICJ, a question of 'overall control' but rather a much stricter test of 'complete dependence and control'. As stated in the *Bosnia Genocide Convention* case, 'according to the Court's jurisprudence, persons, groups of persons or entities may, for purposes of international responsibility, be equated with State organs even if that status does not follow from internal law, provided that in fact the persons, groups or entities act in "complete dependence" on the State, of which they are ultimately merely the instrument'.[120]

Secondly, where a group is not completely dependent on a State and is therefore not to be regarded as a de facto State organ under article 4, *specific acts* of a non-state group can be attributed to a State, under article 8 of the ILC's Articles, where the non-state group's specific acts are carried out on that State's instructions or under its direction or 'effective control'.[121] So, in fact, the tests for State

[118] See S. Talmon, 'The Responsibility of Outside Powers for Acts of Secessionist Entities' (2009) 58 *International and Comparative Law Quarterly* 493 (Talmon, *Secessionist Entities*); M. Milanovic, 'State Responsibility for Genocide' (2006) 17 *EJIL* 553 and M. Milanovic, 'State Responsibility for Genocide: A Follow-Up' (2007) 18 *EJIL* 669.

[119] *Case Concerning Application of the Convention on the Prevention and Punishment of the Crime of Genocide (Bosnia and Herzegovina v Serbia and Montenegro)* ICJ Rep 2007, 43, paras 385–95 (*Genocide Convention* case).

[120] *Genocide Convention* case, para 392. See also para 393: 'However, so to equate persons or entities with State organs when they do not have that status under internal law must be exceptional, for it requires proof of a particularly great degree of State control over them, a relationship which the Court's Judgment quoted above expressly described as "complete dependence".'

[121] *Genocide Convention* case, paras 396–402. See in particular, para 400, where the Court stated that: 'The test thus formulated differs in two respects from the test—described above—to determine whether a person or entity may be equated with a State organ even if not having that status under internal law. First, in this context it is not necessary to show that the persons who performed the acts alleged to have violated international law were in general in a relationship of "complete dependence" on the respondent State; it has to be proved that they acted in accordance with that State's instructions or under its "effective control". It must however be shown that this "effective control" was exercised, or that the State's instructions were given, in respect of each operation in which the alleged violations occurred, not generally in respect of the overall actions taken by the persons or groups of persons having committed the violations.'

responsibility are stricter than that put forward by the ICTY and there are good reasons for this.[122] A State should only be held to be legally responsible for acts which are really its own, while (if the relevant primary rules permit), it may be held responsible for its own failure to control others or for creating a situation which permitted particular acts to occur.[123]

Since the test of State responsibility is rather strict, it raises the question whether the internationalization of an armed conflict is actually dependent on rules of attribution in the law of State responsibility. The starting point for answering this is that the ICTY is right, that where a non-state group is indeed a de facto organ of a State (or where it acts on specific instructions from a State), and that non-state group fights against another State, the conflict will be international. This is because, in such a scenario, the acts of the non-state group are to be regarded as that of the State on whose behalf it acts. That State is therefore taken as fighting against the other State. However, this does not exhaust the issue of whether the primary rules of international humanitarian law have a different test for whether a conflict is to be regarded as international or not. As the ICJ stated in the *Bosnian Genocide Convention* case:

> Insofar as the 'overall control' test is employed to determine whether or not an armed conflict is international, which was the sole question which the Appeals Chamber was called upon to decide, it may well be that the test is applicable and suitable; the Court does not however think it appropriate to take a position on the point in the present case, as there is no need to resolve it for purposes of the present Judgment. On the other hand, the ICTY presented the 'overall control' test as equally applicable under the law of State responsibility for the purpose of determining—as the Court is required to do in the present case—when a State is responsible for acts committed by paramilitary units, armed forces which are not among its official organs. In this context, the argument in favour of that test is unpersuasive.
>
> It should first be observed that logic does not require the same test to be adopted in resolving the two issues, which are very different in nature: the degree and nature of a State's involvement in an armed conflict on another State's territory which is required for the conflict to be characterized as international, can very well, and without logical inconsistency, differ from the degree and nature of involvement required to give rise to that State's responsibility for a specific act committed in the course of the conflict.[124]

There are three different views that may be put forward with regard to the test for internationalization of internal armed conflicts as a result of State support for non-state groups. One view would agree with *Tadić* that the key question is whether the non-state group belongs to a foreign State but hold that the answer to this question does not depend on the general law of State responsibility but on specific rules in international humanitarian law. On this view, the specific rules of international humanitarian law (IHL) regarding the test for the internationalization of internal

---

[122] See Talmon, *Secessionist Entities*, 517.

[123] E.g. in the *Genocide Convention* case while the ICJ held that Serbia was not responsible for the genocide that occurred in Bosnia it was held responsible for breaching its duty to prevent and to punish the genocide.

[124] Ibid, paras 404–5. See M. Spinedi, 'On the Non-Attribution of the Bosnian Serbs' conduct to Serbia' (2007) 5(4) *Journal of International Criminal Justice* 829.

armed conflicts would be different from the test of control in State responsibility. Under these rules, an armed group would be regarded as belonging to (and thus fighting on behalf of) a State (in particular under article 4 of the Third Geneva Convention) even if the State does not exercise control over the group but there is a de facto agreement between the State and the group.[125] This test draws from the ICRC commentary to article 4 which states that

> International law has advanced considerably concerning the manner in which th[e] relationship [between a party to a conflict and irregular forces deemed to fight on that party's behalf] shall be established. The drafters of earlier instruments were unanimous in including the requirement of express authorization by the sovereign, usually in writing, and this was still the case at the time of the Franco-German war of 1870–1871. Since the Hague Conferences, however, this condition is no longer considered essential. It is essential that there should be a 'de facto' relationship between the resistance organization and the party to international law which is in a state of war, but the existence of this relationship is sufficient. It may find expression merely by tacit agreement, if the operations are such as to indicate clearly for which side the resistance organization is fighting. But affiliation with a Party to the conflict may also follow an official declaration, for instance by a Government in exile, confirmed by official recognition by the High Command of the forces which are at war with the Occupying Power.[126]

This test of a de facto relationship is probably a looser test even than the 'overall control' test. What this approach does is to accept that there is a *lex specialis* in the regime of State responsibility[127] for breaches of international humanitarian law. A State would, therefore, be responsible for the acts of non-state groups that belong to it[128] but would be identified as responsible using a test that is looser than the general test under the law of State responsibility.

A second approach for achieving internationalization of internal conflicts would be to argue along similar lines to the first but to say that the 'overall control' test is a special test of responsibility, introduced by international humanitarian law. This approach would be different from the approach in *Tadić* in that it would not seek to show (as *Tadić* does) that the 'overall control' test is derived from general international law.

A third approach with respect to the question of internationalization of internal conflicts, and the approach to be preferred, is to adopt the test that was used by Judge Shahabuddeen in his Separate Opinion in the *Tadić* case. In his view, the question to be addressed, in considering whether support by a foreign State for a non-state group transforms the conflict into an international armed conflict, is whether a foreign State can be said to have used force against another State. He set out the relevant question with regard to the Bosnian conflict in this succinct way: '*Ex hypothesi*, an armed conflict involves a use of force. Thus, the question whether

---

[125] See K. del Mar, 'The Requirement of Belonging Under International Humanitarian Law' (2010) 21 *EJIL* 105.

[126] Pictet, *Commentary on Geneva Convention III*, 23.

[127] A possibility contemplated by art. 55 of ILC Articles on State Responsibility.

[128] Additional Protocol I, art. 91.

there was an armed conflict between the FRY [Federal Republic of Yugoslavia] and BH [Bosnia Herzegovina] depended on whether the FRY was using force against BH through the Bosnian Serbian Army of the Republika Srpska ("VRS").'[129]

If a foreign State has used force against another State, albeit indirectly by supporting a non-state group, there is an international armed conflict between the two States. In order to determine whether there is a use of force by one State against another we must turn to those aspects of the *ius ad bellum* that determine this question. Ironically, the leading case here is the *Nicaragua* case[130] but not the parts referred to by the majority in *Tadić*. The case law of the International Court of Justice and customary international law shows that a State is taken to have used force against another State even where it has not intervened with its own troops or, even where it has not used forces that are de facto its own (e.g. by organizing and sending forces) but also where it arms and trains non-state forces.

7.2. Foreign intervention at the invitation (or with consent) of a State against a non-state group

Where there is intervention by a foreign State in an internal armed conflict on the side of the government (or at its invitation) and against a non-state group, such intervention is not sufficient to transform an armed conflict into an international armed conflict and the conflict remains non-international.[131] As noted above, the ICRC's proposal in the 1970s, that all conflicts where there was the intervention of a foreign State are to be regarded as international, was rejected by States. Despite this rejection some distinguished voices, notably George Aldrich,[132] have argued that whenever there is foreign intervention this transforms the conflict fundamentally and it should be regarded as international. Aldrich relies on the experience of the Vietnam War and argues that it would be practically impossible to apply both the rules on international armed conflict and those of non-international armed conflict to what is, in fact, a single armed conflict with two warring sides. These proposals have not met with general approval.

Where a foreign State intervenes initially on the side of rebels, but where those forces then take control of the capital (and perhaps the majority of territory) and a government is established (supported by the foreign State) but where fighting continues with the former government or other forces, questions will arise as to the classification of that continued fighting. In accordance with the analysis above, at the time when the foreign State was supporting what was a non-state group, the conflict would have been an international armed conflict. However, once a new

---

[129] See *Tadić* Trial Judgment, Separate Opinion of Judge Shahabuddeen, para 7.

[130] Now also the *Armed Activities* case.

[131] See Fleck, *Non-International Armed Conflicts*, 605; also *The Prosecutor v Jean-Pierre Bemba Gombo*, ICC-01/05-01/08, Confirmation of Charges Decision (Pre-Trial Chamber), 15 June 2009, para 246 where it was held that the conflict in the Central African Republic (CAR) was non-international despite the presence of foreign troops in the country, as those troops were there to support the government of the CAR.

[132] G. Aldrich, 'The Laws of War on Land' (2000) 94 *AJIL* 42, 62–3.

government takes over and the intervention of foreign forces is at the invitation of that new government, traditional analysis is that the conflict is transformed to a non-international conflict.[133] However, if this position is always taken, and without safeguard, there could be an undermining of the law of occupation by setting up a puppet regime and claiming consent from that regime. What is required is some assurance that the so-called government is indeed the government of the State and has a degree of independence from the foreign forces such that the consent which transforms the conflict is one that genuinely comes from the proper authorities of the State in question. Otherwise, those rules designed for the protection of the population from arbitrary power by the foreign occupier could be swept aside by a supposed transfer of power to an authority that is not in fact independent of the foreign power. In order to assure that the new government that gives consent is indeed the government, one should look at the degree of effectiveness of its control over the territory of the State and also at whether it has achieved a general international recognition.[134]

7.3. Mixed conflicts

International and internal armed conflicts may be going on simultaneously in the same area at the same time. For example in the *Nicaragua* case, the ICJ held that the conflict between the United States and Nicaragua was to be analysed under the law relating to international armed conflicts and the conflict between the Contras and the government of Nicaragua was to be analyzed under the law relating to non-international armed conflicts. Likewise, the ICTY Appeals Chamber held, in the *Tadić Jurisdiction Appeal*,[135] that the conflict in the former Yugoslavia had both internal and international characteristics, thus requiring a determination in each particular case as to what conflict was at issue and what law applied. This approach, which allows for mixed (international and non-international) conflicts in the same factual situation, has been criticized on the ground that it creates 'a crazy quilt of norms that would be applicable in the same conflict, depending on whether it is

---

[133] See the letter to the UK House of Commons by Philip Spoerri, Legal Adviser, International Committee of the Red Cross: 'Following the convening of the Loya Jirga in Kabul in June 2002 and the subsequent establishment of an Afghan transitional government on 19 June 2002 which not only received unanimous recognition by the entire community of States but could also claim broad-based recognition within Afghanistan through the Loya Jirga process the ICRC has changed its initial qualification as follows: The ICRC no longer views the ongoing military operations in Afghanistan directed against suspected Taliban or other armed groups as an international armed conflict.' Available at: <www.publications. parliament.uk/pa/cm200203/cmselect/cmintdev/84/84ap09.htm>. Others have suggested that the nature of the conflict changed from international to non-international at an even earlier date: see Y. Arai-Takahashi, 'Disentangling Legal Quagmires: The Legal Characterisation of the Armed Conflicts in Afghanistan Since 6/7 October 2001 and the Question of Prisoner of War Status' (2002) 5 *Yearbook of International Humanitarian Law* 61, 97 (citing the signature of the Bonn Agreement of 5 December 2001 as the date when the conflict became non-international in nature).

[134] For a similar situation in Libya, see M. Milanovic, 'How to Qualify the Armed Conflict in Libya' *EJIL Talk* (1 September 2011).

[135] *Tadić Jurisdiction*.

characterized as international or non-international'.[136] However, as Greenwood has noted, there is nothing 'intrinsically illogical or novel in characterizing some aspects of a particular set of hostilities as an international armed conflict while others possess an internal character'.[137]

The fact that it is possible for two different types of conflicts to be ongoing simultaneously has made the application of international humanitarian law much more complicated in many recent conflicts. Questions relating to the standards for detention will sometimes depend solely on who happened to capture or to detain a particular person since the Third Geneva Convention dealing with POWs and the Fourth Geneva Convention, which includes provisions on internment, are only applicable if the person is interned by State forces in an international armed conflict, but are not applicable if the conflict in question is non-international.

In cases where there is intervention by foreign State forces on the side of or alongside a non-state group which is fighting the territorial State, whether the conflict is a mixed conflict or is internationalized entirely will depend on whether the non-state group is seen as 'belonging to' the intervening State. Where the foreign intervening State exercises the requisite degree of control over the non-state group or where it is in fact using force through the non-state group,[138] the entire conflict will become an international armed conflict. Therefore even fighting between the non-state group and the territorial State will be governed by the law relating to international armed conflicts.

8. Intervention by multinational forces under UN command or authorized by the UN

Particular problems regarding the classification of conflicts arise when forces authorized by the United Nations (or indeed another international organization, such as the African Union) are involved in, or intervene in, an armed conflict. It is worth bearing in mind that the United Nations does not have any forces of its own and forces authorized by the UN are always composed of national armed forces or contingents from national armed forces. Therefore the key question with regard to classification of conflicts involving UN authorized forces is whether the authorization of force by the UN somehow affects the classification of a conflict such that the result would be different from cases where national armed forces act without that authorization. In order to answer that question, the first issue that needs to be determined is whether any particular UN authorized force is to be regarded simply as a national armed force or whether it is to be regarded instead as a UN force with the UN having responsibility under international law for the acts of those forces.

---

[136] See T. Meron, 'Classification of Armed Conflict in the Former Yugoslavia: *Nicaragua's* Fallout' (1998) 92 *AJIL* 236, 238; see also US Amicus Brief in the *Tadić* case.

[137] C. Greenwood, 'Development of International Humanitarian Law by the ICTY' (1998) 2 *Max Planck Yearbook of UN Law* 98, 117.

[138] See discussion in section 7.1 above regarding the test for internationalization of such conflicts.

Under article 7 of the International Law Commission's (ILC) Draft Articles on Responsibilities of International Organization, an international organization will only be responsible for acts of a State organ, such as a part of its armed forces, which is placed at the disposal of the international organization, for example in a peace-keeping or peace-enforcement operation, where the organization is in effective control of the organ or forces that are placed at its disposal.[139] Although the European Court of Human Rights has held to the contrary,[140] the UN or other international organization will only be in effective control of a contingent from a State's armed forces where the UN has operational control of the force.[141] UN responsibility for the force is not established simply because the UN has ultimate control over the force in that it authorized it and can terminate its mandate. Where there is no UN responsibility for the force because the UN does not have effective control over it, the force is simply a national one, albeit operating by virtue of a UN mandate. In such a case, if the force is involved in an armed conflict, whether the conflict is international or non-international is determined by the principles established above.

In broad terms, when the UN Security Council authorizes the use of force, the armed forces acting under the authorization will be one of three types. Firstly, the Security Council may authorize States, acting individually, in coalition, or through regional arrangements to take enforcement action under Chapter VII of the UN Charter. Examples of this type of authorization include the authorization to remove Iraq from Kuwait in 1990 and to protect civilians in Libya in 2011.[142] In these cases, the forces are not placed under UN command but remain under national command or some other unified command. Since these forces are not under the UN's effective control they are national forces and the principles for classification already discussed apply to those conflicts that these forces are involved in.

Secondly the UN may create and authorize a peace-keeping mission of the classic or traditional mode where the force is under UN command, operates with consent, in a neutral manner and uses force only in self-defence. Often these peace-keeping forces are established as buffer forces overseeing ceasefires that have suspended or

---

[139] See International Law Commission, Draft Articles on Responsibility of International Organizations (adopted on 2nd reading in June 2011) A/CN.4/L.778, art. 7.

[140] In *Behrami and Saramati v France and others* (Decision) App No. 71412/01 and 78166/01 (2 May 2007), the European Court of Human Rights held that despite the fact that the UN had no operational control over forces authorized to act in Kosovo, it was the UN and not the States whose force was at issue, that was responsible for the acts of the force. But see *Al Jedda v The United Kingdom* (Judgment) App No. 27021/08 (7 July 2011) para 84 where the ECHR mentioned effective control together with ultimate control.

[141] In its commentary to art. 6 (now art. 7) of the Draft Articles on the Responsibility of International Organizations, the ILC has pointed out that the ECHR's decision in *Behrami and Saramati*, though reliant on art. 6, misunderstood the scope of art. 6. See International Law Commission, 'Report on the work of its 61st session' A/64/10 (2009), ch. IV: Responsibility of International Organizations, 67. The ECHR decision has been criticized by many scholars. See e.g. M. Milanovic and T. Papic, 'As Bad as it Gets: The European Court of Human Rights Behrami and Saramati Decision and General International Law' (2009) 58 *International and Comparative Law Quarterly* 267, and other works cited by the ILC in its commentary to art. 6 of the Draft Articles.

[142] See SC res. 678 (1990) and SC res. 1973 (2011) respectively.

terminated hostilities in an international armed conflict.[143] Thirdly, the UN may create and authorize what has come to be known as a robust peace-keeping force where the national contingents operate under UN command but where the force is authorized to use all necessary means (i.e. to use military force) to achieve certain objectives such as protecting civilians or facilitating humanitarian deliveries. Very often, these forces are deployed in internal conflicts and sometimes in situations where the armed conflict is ongoing or where peace is not secure.[144] In the second and third categories, the fact that the forces are under UN command will mean that they act, in principle, as organs of the United Nations. Indeed the UN accepts that peace-keeping forces constitute a subsidiary organ of the UN.[145] However, where a force is not in fact under the effective control of the UN but is acting primarily under national control, the UN will not be responsible for its acts. It is in the case of these peace-keeping missions including 'robust peacekeeping forces' where one needs to address particular issues regarding the classification of the conflict.

In the early years of the UN there was much debate and discussion about the application of international humanitarian law to UN forces.[146] The matter has since been resolved by universal acceptance of the position that UN forces are bound by international humanitarian law where they are engaged in an armed conflict.[147] Although the UN is not bound by the relevant treaties, it is bound by customary international humanitarian law. In order to promote observance of international humanitarian law by UN Forces, the UN, by the 1990s, began to include in Status of Forces Agreements with host States, as well as agreements with troop-contributing countries, provisions which required respect for the 'principles and spirit of the general conventions applicable to the conduct of military personnel'. The provision went on to state that these conventions include the Geneva Conventions and their Additional Protocols.[148] Moreover, in 1999, the UN Secretary-General issued a Bulletin on Observance by United Nations Forces of International Humanitarian Law which asserts that the fundamental principles and

---

[143] Examples include the United Nations Emergency Force I and II deployed in the Middle East after the conflicts in 1956 and 1973. More recent is the United Nations Mission in Ethiopia and Eritrea. For details on these operations, see <www.un.org/en/peacekeeping/operations/past.shtml>.

[144] See e.g. ch. 6 below on the DRC.

[145] See Letter of 3 February 2004 by the United Nations Legal Counsel to the Director of the Codification Division, A/CN.4/545 (2004), section II.G: 'As a subsidiary organ of the United Nations, an act of a peacekeeping force is, in principle, imputable to the Organization, and if committed in violation of an international obligation entails the international responsibility of the Organization and its liability in compensation.'

[146] For an overview of this debate, see H. McCoubrey and N.D. White, *The Blue Helmets: Legal Regulation of United Nations Military Operations* (1996) and P. Szasz, 'UN Forces and International Humanitarian Law' in M. Schmitt, *International Law Across the Spectrum of Conflict: Essays in Honour of Professor L.C. Cohen on the Occasion of His Eightieth Birthday* (2000) 507.

[147] See C. Greenwood, 'International Humanitarian Law and United Nations Military Operations' (1998) 1 *Yearbook of International Humanitarian Law* 3 (Greenwood, *UN Operations*); Resolution on the Conditions of Application of Humanitarian Rules of Armed Conflict to Hostilities in which United Nations Forces may be Engaged, adopted at Zagreb in 1971 ('the Zagreb Resolution') (1971) 54 (II) *Annuaire de l'institut de droit international* 465. See also the 1994 Convention on the Safety of United Nations and Associated Personnel, art. 2(2).

[148] See agreements cited in Greenwood, *UN Operations,* 21.

rules of international humanitarian law as set out in the bulletin are applicable to UN forces when in situations of armed conflict they are actively engaged as combatants.[149]

It is not easy to determine when peacekeepers become direct participants in hostilities such that they are engaged in armed conflict with another party. The fact that peacekeepers are present in a situation where an armed conflict is ongoing does not mean that they are a party to it. Also the fact that peacekeepers use force in exercise of their right of personal and individual self-defence will not mean that they are combatants involved in the armed conflict. As the Trial Chamber of the Special Court for Sierra Leone put it in *Prosecutor v Sesay, Kallon and Gbao (RUF Judgment)*:[150] 'Where peacekeepers become combatants, they can be legitimate targets for the extent of their participation in accordance with international humanitarian law. As with all civilians their protection would not cease if the personnel use armed force only in exercising their right to individual self-defence.'

The holding that peacekeepers will not be involved in an armed conflict simply because they act in individual self-defence was echoed by a Pre-Trial Chamber of the ICC in *The Prosecutor v Bahar Idriss Abu Garda*.[151] More complicated is the scenario where a peace-keeping force is authorized to use force beyond self-defence but also to execute a particular mandate. In such scenarios, the peace-keeping force may initiate the use of force in the context of an ongoing armed conflict or even where there is no longer an armed conflict, if the force deems this to be necessary to carry out its mandate. The Special Court for Sierra Leone (SCSL) held, immediately following the text just quoted, that: 'Likewise, the Chamber opines that the use of force by peacekeepers in self-defence in the discharge of their mandate, provided that it is limited to such use, would not alter or diminish the protection afforded to peacekeepers.'[152]

The view that when peacekeepers act in defence of their mandate they will, in most cases, not be participating directly in hostilities and thus are to be regarded as entitled to civilian protection has received some scholarly support.[153] However, it is interesting to observe that though the ICC Pre-Trial Chamber 'noted' this part of the decision of the SCSL (and only in a footnote), it pointedly did not endorse this part of the SCSL decision and confined itself to holding that peacekeepers who act in self-defence do not engage in hostilities. It is difficult to see why the fact that peacekeepers are acting to enforce their mandate will mean that they are not

[149] 'Secretary-General's Bulletin: Observance by United Nations Forces of International Humanitarian Law' ST/SGB/1999/13 (6 August 1999). For a discussion of the issues raised by the Bulletin, see D. Shraga, 'The Secretary-General's Bulletin on the Observance by United Nations Forces of International Humanitarian Law—A Decade Later' (2009) *39 Israel Yearbook on Human Rights* 357.

[150] *Prosecutor v Sesay, Kallon and Gbao (RUF case)*, SCSL-04-15-T, Judgment (Trial Chamber), 2 March 2009, para 233 (*RUF Judgment*).

[151] *The Prosecutor v Bahar Idriss Abu Garda*, ICC-02/05-02/09, Confirmation of Charges Decision (Pre-Trial Chamber), 8 February 2010, para 83.

[152] *RUF Judgment*, para 233.

[153] S. Sivakumaran, 'War Crimes before the Special Court for Sierra Leone: Child Soldiers, Hostages, Peacekeepers and Collective Punishments' (2010) 8 *Journal of International Criminal Justice* 1009, 1028–9.

engaged in an armed conflict. Such an approach appears to condition the application of international humanitarian law on the legality of the use of force by the UN force and seems to be a throwback to the idea that UN forces are not subject to its rules because of the high mission they fulfil. Where the force used by UN forces is of a nature and intensity as would otherwise bring into effect an armed conflict, it ought to be recognized that they are involved in one, despite the fact that they act lawfully (in terms of the *ius ad bellum*) in using such force. That legality under the *ius ad bellum* ought not to free the force from the constraints that international humanitarian law would impose.

Another way of getting to the result sought by the SCSL (a high threshold for the application of international humanitarian law to UN forces) is indicated by Christopher Greenwood, who has pointed out that the UN Convention on the Safety of United Nations and Associated Personnel 1994 makes the threshold for the application of international humanitarian law, the ceiling for the application of the Convention (i.e. peacekeepers lose the protection of the Convention once the law of international armed conflict applies). He surmises that troop-contributing countries to UN operations will be reluctant to accept the Convention if there is intense fighting and this leads him to the conclusion that 'a United Nations force and national units operating in association with it but under national command will be regarded as parties to an armed conflict only when they have engaged in hostilities on a scale comparable to those of a force established for the purpose of enforcement action. That scale will be considerably higher than that which is used to define an armed conflict for other purposes.'[154] However, although UN forces have an important function and despite the merits of granting them protection from attack, it is difficult to see why the normal rules for determining whether an armed conflict is taking place should not apply. In the first place, international humanitarian law is based on the equality of the parties and this is so despite the fact that one side will usually be acting lawfully under the *ius ad bellum*. Secondly, the view that UN forces should be subject to the same constraints of international humanitarian law, in the similar ways to national forces, is one which takes into account the protection that the population of the territory ought to be entitled to.

However, holding that UN peacekeepers may be involved in an armed conflict with another entity when acting to carry out their mandate but are not involved in an armed conflict when acting in exercise of the individual right of self-defence leads to an imbalance in the application of IHL to UN forces. The position appears to be that UN forces are engaged in an armed conflict with another entity when the UN force uses force against that entity but are not involved in an armed conflict when it is the other entity that has engaged in hostile acts against the UN force. In that latter scenario, the UN force is not involved in an armed conflict and its members are protected as civilians. Thus, UN forces gain an advantage as they may carry out initial acts of targeting which would be lawful if they comply with international humanitarian law principles, but by contrast other forces may not

---

[154] See Greenwood, *UN Operations*, 25.

initiate attacks on UN forces as there would be no armed conflict at that point and those other forces would even be committing a war crime.[155] This result appears. on one level, to be contrary to the principle of equal application of international humanitarian law. However, from a formal perspective it is not, given the fact that once an armed conflict is initiated between the UN forces and others both sides are equal. All that the result being discussed here leads to is an imbalance as to who may start an armed conflict when UN forces are involved. In this way, the UN's special role does seem to have an impact on the application of international humanitarian law. An alternative approach is to say that acts of individual self-defence by peace-keepers do not make them direct participants in an armed conflict, but where there is a sustained attack on such peace-keeping forces which would normally pass the intensity threshold for an armed conflict one ought to take the view that there is an armed conflict between the UN forces and the attackers (albeit one initiated by other forces). The difficulty with this approach is that it would mean that those attacks on UN peacekeepers would be made lawful (in terms of international humanitarian law) if they are sustained and draw the UN into a conflict, while lower level attacks would not be lawful since there would be no armed conflict with the UN, and the peacekeepers would remain protected as civilians.

Where multinational forces are involved in an armed conflict, it may need to be determined whether that conflict is international or non-international. Where they are engaged in hostilities against the armed forces of a State (as happened, for example with MONUC in the Congo in the 1960s), it would appear that the conflict is an international armed conflict.[156] However, the basis of this assumption is not so easy to justify since the conflict is not between two States but between an international organization and a State. It may be argued that the conflict is international because the actual fighting is carried out by State forces though acting under the umbrella of the UN. However, it has already been established that when those State forces are under the effective control of the UN, they are an organ of the UN and it is the UN that is responsible for them. In those circumstances, there is no armed conflict between the State from which those troops are drawn and the State whose forces they engage.[157] Either there is a customary rule that broadens international armed conflicts to include conflicts involving international organiza-tions and States or alternatively it could be said that the conflict is international because the States providing contingents remain bound by the treaties to which they are party since they have an obligation not only to respect them but also to

---

[155] ICC Statute, art. 8(2)(b)(iii) and (2)(e)(iii).

[156] See Vité, *Typology,* 88. See also Greenwood, *UN Operations,* 27; H. McCoubrey and N.D. White, *The Blue Helmets: Legal Regulation of United Nations Military Operations* (1996), ch. 8 of which seems to assume that when UN forces act it is the law of international armed conflict that is applicable. See also art. 2 of the 1971 Zagreb Resolution of the Institute of International Law on Conditions of Application of Humanitarian Rules of Armed Conflict to Hostilities in which the United Nations Forces May be Engaged.

[157] Unless the view is taken that attribution of the acts of the forces to the UN does not also preclude attribution to the State.

'ensure respect' for the conventions in circumstances where their troops act, even if for someone else.[158]

Where the UN engages in an armed conflict with a non-state group within a State and the UN's presence in the State is with the consent of the host State, the conflict ought to be regarded as a non-international armed conflict in line with the analysis above regarding foreign intervention. Where the UN's presence is without consent and solely on the basis of a Security Council resolution, the matter is more difficult and opinion is divided. There are those who would argue that conflicts of this sort are to be regarded as non-international conflicts.[159] However, the sovereignty concerns which led to the establishment of a diminished law with regard to non-international armed conflicts are clearly absent in this sort of case. Others take the view that whenever the UN is involved in an armed conflict, 'these situations are to be equated with international armed conflicts. To the extent that the operations concerned are decided, defined and carried out by international organizations, they are by nature, included in that category. It is of little relevance in that case whether the opposing party is a State or a non-governmental group.'[160]

The temporal and geographical scope of armed conflicts involving UN peace-keepers is unclear. Does the fact that one contingent of peacekeepers is involved, in one part of the country, in hostilities that are of such intensity as to qualify as an armed conflict, mean that all UN peace-keeping forces in the country are engaged in an armed conflict with that group? It is difficult to think why the answer should be different from that which one would give with regard to State forces (a positive answer). However, the effect of that answer would be to deprive all UN peace-keepers of the protected status they ordinarily enjoy. The matter is made more complicated by the lack of a definite answer as to when the hostilities phase or armed conflict phase ceases. May peacekeepers move from armed conflict to non-conflict depending on whether they are using force? Or once an armed conflict kicks in does it continue until there is some general conclusion of peace? To require a general conclusion of peace in terms of a ceasefire seems artificial as UN peace-keepers with robust enforcement mandates use force in order to achieve a result that is authorized and ought not to be compelled to negotiate a peace in order to regain their civilian protection.

9. Extraterritorial conflicts with non-state armed groups

There are many situations in which a State (the foreign State) will use force on the territory of another State (the territorial State) but where that force is not primarily directed at the territorial State but rather is directed at a non-state armed group based in that State. Examples drawn from the case studies considered in this work include the use of force by Israel in Lebanon in 2006, acts by Uganda and Rwanda

---

[158] See UK Ministry of Defence, *The Manual of the Law of Armed Conflict* (2004) 376.
[159] See Vité, *Typology*, 88 who asserts this is also the ICRC position.
[160] See Vité, *Typology*, and the extensive literature referred to in fn. 70 of that article.

in the Democratic Republic of the Congo, Columbia attacks on the FARC in Ecuador in 2008 and US targeting of persons connected with Al-Qaeda in countries such as Yemen, Somalia and Pakistan. Several other examples may be given, such as the Turkish use of force directed at PKK targets in Northern Iraq. In most of these cases, the attack by the State on a non-state group abroad represents an extension of a pre-existing conflict taking place within the foreign State, between the foreign State and the non-state group. It may be that the foreign State is pursuing the non-state group across an international border in order to deny the group cross-border refuge. In other cases, though more rarely, the non-state group is primarily based within the territorial State but has engaged in cross-border attacks on the foreign State or is otherwise deemed to be a threat to the security of the foreign State.

It is possible that despite the use of force by a State against a non-state group, the level of violence does not cross the threshold of an armed conflict.[161] However, where it does, one question that arises in all of these situations is how the distinction between international and non-international armed conflicts applies to these transnational or transborder conflicts. At one level, the distinction appears to be an imperfect fit. The hostilities in question do not engage the armed forces of two States and are thus factually different from the quintessential international armed conflicts (which are, of course, inter-state conflicts). On the other hand, though the hostilities and other acts are between a State and a non-state group they are not internal to the foreign State or to any particular State. There is, as a matter of fact, an international element to the conflict. Furthermore, both Common Article 3 and Additional Protocol II, dealing with non-international armed conflict, appear, on their face, to confine such conflicts to the territory of one Contracting Party. Common Article 3 speaks of an 'armed conflict not of an international character occurring in the territory *of one* of the High Contracting Parties' (emphasis added) and article 1(1) of Additional Protocol II refers to an armed conflict 'which take[s] place in the territory of a High Contracting Party'.

As a result of these apparent incongruities between the facts and the law, some have suggested that international humanitarian law ought to recognize a new and different form of armed conflict which takes account of the transnational aspects of these conflicts but which also recognizes that the conflicts in question are conflicts between States and non-state groups.[162] These new approaches have not found much favour and have been rejected by other scholars who have sought to apply international humanitarian law, as it exists, to the conflict between the State and the non-state group. This traditional approach requires, first, examining whether the violence between a State and a non-state group is an 'armed conflict' and

---

[161] See further discussion in ch. 13 on Al-Qaeda below.

[162] See G. Corn, 'Hamdan, Lebanon, and the Regulation of Armed Hostilities: The Need to Recognize a Hybrid Category of Armed Conflict' (2006) 40 *Vanderbilt Transnational Law Journal* 295; R. Schöndorf, 'Extra-State Armed Conflicts: Is There a Need for a New Legal Regime?' (2004) 37 *New York University Journal of International Law and Politics* 26.

secondly, making a determination as to how to fit it into the international or non-international dichotomy.[163]

Some writers who take this latter approach have come to the conclusion that conflicts involving the use of force by a State against a non-state group on the territory of another State are non-international armed conflicts where the force is directed solely at that non-state group.[164] This is also the view of the majority of contributors to the present book. These writers argue, correctly, that the wording of Common Article 3, referred to above, does not prevent a non-international armed conflict from straddling more than one State. Indeed those who take this view note that the reference to *one* of the High Contracting Parties was simply a reference to the fact that this provision in the Conventions only applies where fighting occurs in the territory of, at least, one party to the Conventions, without an intention to confine the application of Common Article 3 to situations where fighting occurs solely within the territory of only one of the parties.[165] It is further argued that the classification of the conflict as non-international follows from the fact that the opposing parties are not two States but rather a State and a non-state group. It is said that classifying such a conflict as international would not only be contrary to the party structure of international armed conflicts, but also that 'non-state actors would be unable to comply with many of the international armed conflict provisions, and States would be unwilling to grant non-state actors immunities from prosecution granted to prisoners of war in conflicts of this type. The rules of non-international armed conflict are precisely designed for conflicts in which one of the parties is a non-state actor'.[166]

It may well be that a conflict between a State and a non-state group is not to be regarded as an international armed conflict in and of itself. However, that contention does not itself resolve the matter under consideration. It is important to recall that the purpose of classification of conflicts is so that one can determine the law which applies to the actions of participants in the conflict. Therefore, the essential question in such a case is which law applies to the conflicts between a foreign State and a non-state group that occurs in the territorial State. Where the conflict between the foreign State and the non-state group is inextricably bound up with another conflict (notably a conflict between two States) such that acts under the

---

[163] M. Sassoli, 'Transnational Armed Groups and International Humanitarian Law' Harvard University Program on Humanitarian Policy and Conflict Research, Occasional Paper Series, No. 6 (Winter 2006) 5 (Sassoli, *Transnational Armed Groups*); Paulus and Vashakmadze, *Asymmetrical War* 111; N. Lubell, *Extraterritorial Use of Force Against Non-State Actors* (2010) (Lubell, *Extraterritorial Use of Force*), part II (particularly ch. 4) and also N. Lubell, ch. 13 below; C. Kreβ, 'Some Reflections on the International Legal Framework Governing Transnational Armed Conflicts' (2010) *15 Journal of Conflict and Security Law* 245.

[164] See the writers cited in the previous note (with the exception of Sassoli). See also T. Hoffman, 'Squaring the Circle?—International Humanitarian Law and Transnational Armed Conflicts' in M.J. Matheson and D. Momtaz (eds), *Rules and Institutions of International Humanitarian Law Put to the Test of Recent Armed Conflicts* (2008).

[165] See Vité, *Typology*; Lubell, *Extraterritorial Use of Force*, ch. 4 and Lubell, ch. 13 below; Sassoli, *Transnational Armed Groups*. See also *Hamdan v Rumsfeld*, 548 U.S. 557, 126 S.Ct. 2749 (29 June 2006) (*Hamdan v Rumsfeld*).

[166] See discussion in ch. 13, secion 4.2 below.

two conflicts (to the extent the conflicts can be distinguished) cannot be separated, the participants will, in reality, be bound to observe the law of international armed conflicts.

In the view of this author, the law that governs transnational conflicts between a State and a non-state group will depend, in the first place, on whether the territorial State in which the non-state group is based has given its consent to the foreign State using force against that group. Where such consent exists, then the conflict will be governed by the law of non-international armed conflicts. The situation here will be no different from a situation in which the territorial State is itself fighting the non-state group and invites the foreign State to intervene. The consent of the territorial State has the effect that there are not two opposing States involved in the conflict.[167]

Irrespective of the consent of the territorial State, there are at least two situations where, applying our earlier analysis, a transnational conflict between a State and a non-state group will be governed by the law of international armed conflicts. First of all, where the non-state group belongs to, or acts on behalf of a State (other than the intervening foreign State) a conflict between that non-state group and the foreign State will be an international armed conflict because there will be two opposing States. Therefore, it may be considered whether Hezbollah was to be regarded as belonging to Lebanon (or indeed to a third State) in the 2006 conflict with Israel. If it was,[168] then the conflict was international. Secondly, where a State occupies a foreign State, in order to act against a non-state group, or as a result of a conflict with a non-state group, then the actions of the occupying State during the period of occupation will be governed by the law of occupation and other rules relating to international armed conflicts. This follows from our earlier analysis[169] and was the position adopted by the International Court of Justice and the International Criminal Court with respect to Uganda's occupation of Ituri province in the Democratic Republic of Congo.[170]

Most controversy in this area centres around the cases where a foreign State fights against a non-state group in the territorial State but without the consent of the territorial State. In the view of this author, and contrary to the views described above, in such circumstances, there will be an international armed conflict between the foreign State and the territorial State. This will be the case because the use of force by the intervening foreign State on the territory of the territorial State, without the consent of the latter, is a use of force *against* the territorial State. This is so even if the use of force is not directed against the governmental structures

---

[167] See the discussion on foreign intervention on the side of the territorial State in section 7.2 above. See also Fleck, *Non-International Armed Conflicts,* 608: 'It is suggested that the non-international or international character of an armed conflict depends on the question whether or not a responsible territorial government has given its consent to military operations performed by the intervening State. Under the Westphalian system armed conflicts can be determined as international only in a case in which states . . . are involved as parties to the conflict.'

[168] See further discussion in ch. 12 below.

[169] See discussion in section 5 above on occupation.

[170] See *Armed Activities* case. For a similar view, see the decision of the ICC Pre-Trial Chamber in *Prosecutor v Lubanga*, para 220; also *Prosecutor v Katanga and Chui*, para 240.

of the territorial State, or the purpose of the use of force is not to coerce the territorial State in any particular way. That a use of force on the territory of another State (even if directed against non-state groups) without its consent is a use of force against the territorial State in breach of obligations to it can be seen from State practice and the jurisprudence of international tribunals. The International Court of Justice in the *Armed Activities* case held that:

> The Court considers that the obligations arising under the principles of non-use of force and non-intervention were violated by Uganda even if the objectives of Uganda were not to overthrow President Kabila, and were directed to securing towns and airports for reason of its perceived security needs, and in support of the parallel activity of those engaged in civil war.[171]

The Court further concluded that '[t]he unlawful military intervention by Uganda was of such a magnitude and duration that the Court considers it to be a grave violation of the prohibition on the use of force expressed in Article 2, paragraph 4, of the Charter'.[172] It should be recalled that article 2(4) prohibits uses of force *against* the territorial integrity or political independence of other States. Similarly, when Columbia attacked FARC forces in Ecuador in March 2008, the Organization of American States adopted a resolution stating the use of force had violated the territorial sovereignty of Ecuador. More generally, when States use force abroad, even against non-state groups, they routinely invoke article 51 of the UN Charter.[173] Article 51 is an exception to article 2(4) and invocation of that article is an acceptance that article 2(4) is engaged and that absent article 51, the use of force would be against the territorial integrity of another State.

Given that a use of force by one State on the territory of another, without the consent of the latter, is a use of force by the foreign State against the territorial State, a situation of armed conflict between the two automatically arises. An international armed conflict is no more than the use of armed force by one State against another. As Greenwood has stated, '[a]n international armed conflict exists if one State uses force against another State'.[174] To state otherwise is to assert that there can be an armed contention between States, possibly even an act of aggression by one State against another but that this is not covered by the rules which international law has designed to regulate such contentions between States. It matters not (and ought to matter not) whether the territorial State responds by using force against the foreign State. Common Article 2 to the Geneva Conventions makes it clear that the Conventions apply even if one of the parties does not acknowledge a state of war. It is also irrelevant to the existence of a state of international armed conflict whether the targeted entities are part of the governmental structure of the State or whether the purpose of the use of force is to affect the government of the State where force is being used. In the first place there is a distinction between a

---

[171] *Armed Activities* case, para 163.
[172] Ibid, para 165.
[173] See Israel's letters to the UN Security Council and Secretary-General on 12 July 2006 with respect to action against Hezbollah in Lebanon, S/2006/515, A/60/937 (12 July 2006).
[174] Greenwood, *Scope of Application*, 46, para 202.

State and a government. International armed conflicts are conflicts between States. A government is but one part of a State. A State is also made of people and territory in addition to a government in control of the territory.[175] Secondly, it would be difficult to discern what is meant by the governmental infrastructure of a State and no uniform answer can be given to that question. Whether airports, sea ports, electricity-generating plants, roads, bridges etc. are owned by the government of a State, or by private parties (as is the case in some countries) will depend on the economic approach adopted by that particular country. None of these things are intrinsically governmental. Thirdly, and most importantly, to attempt to distinguish between force directed at a non-state group and force which has as its overall purpose the intention to influence the government of the State is to condition the application of international humanitarian law on the mental state or motive of the attacker. It is to suggest that the very same acts of force directed by one State against the territory of another State would yield different legal results depending on the intention of the intervening State regarding whom it seeks to affect. The protections afforded to the civilian population and to the infrastructure of the territorial State ought not to depend on the motives of the foreign State. Additionally, this idea is problematic as the mental state or motive of the foreign State may not be easily discernible. What is important are the objective facts, which are: that force is being used by one State *against* another State (i.e. on its territory and without its consent).

The view that any use of force by a State on the territory of another without the consent of the latter brings into effect an international armed conflict between the two States has some support from scholars,[176] though it is probably not the majority view in the existing literature and, as noted above is not the view of the majority of the authors of this book. However, this view has the support of the international tribunals that have had occasion to consider the matter. First one may recall Judge Shahabuddeen's statement in the *Tadić* case that whether there was an international armed conflict depended on whether the Federal Republic of Yugoslavia was using force against Bosnia.[177] In his view, all that needed to be shown was the use of force by one State against another for an international armed conflict to come into being. Secondly, the International Court of Justice's opinion in the *Armed Activities* case supports the view taken here. The Court applied the law of international armed conflicts (the Geneva Conventions and Additional Protocol I) to the activities of Uganda in the Democratic Republic of the Congo and even to acts of Uganda outside the province of Ituri, which was held to have been under Ugandan occupation. The Court's decision was implicitly based on the view that there was an international armed conflict between Uganda and the Democratic Republic of the Congo, despite the fact that Uganda was in the territory of the

---

[175] Montevideo Convention on the Rights and Duties of States 1933, art. 1.
[176] See Fleck, *Non-International Armed Conflicts*, 607; Sassoli, *Transnational Armed Groups*, 5; J. Stewart, 'The UN Commission of Inquiry on Lebanon: A Legal Appraisal' (2007) 5 *Journal of International Criminal Justice* 1043.
[177] See *Tadić* Trial Judgment, Separate Opinion of Judge Shahabuddeen.

Democratic Republic of the Congo primarily to fight non-state groups.[178] In the *Targeted Killings* case, the Israeli Supreme Court also took the view that 'an armed conflict of international character [is] . . . one that crosses the borders of the state—whether or not the place in which the armed conflict occurs is subject to belligerent occupation'.[179]

That an international armed conflict exists where a State uses force against a non-state group on the territory of another State without the consent of the latter State was also confirmed by the UN Commission of Inquiry into the conflict in Lebanon in 2006.[180] The Commission was of the view 'that hostilities were in actual fact and in the main only between the IDF and Hezbollah. [However] The fact that the Lebanese Armed Forces did not take an active part in them neither denies the character of the conflict as a legally cognizable international armed conflict, nor does it negate that Israel, Lebanon and Hezbollah were parties to it'.[181]

One of the points emphasized by the Commission in reaching this finding was that:

> the State of Lebanon was the subject of direct hostilities conducted by Israel, consisting of such acts, as an aerial and maritime blockade that commenced on 13 July 2006, until their full lifting on 6 and 8 September 2006, respectively; a widespread and systematic campaign of direct and other attacks throughout its territory against its civilian population and civilian objects, as well as massive destruction of its public infrastructure, utilities, and other economic assets; armed attacks on its Armed Forces; hostile acts of interference with its internal affairs, territorial integrity and unity and acts constituting temporary occupation of Lebanese villages and towns by IDF.[182]

Indeed both Israel and Lebanon were of the view that the conflict was international despite the fact that Israeli action was primarily directed at Hezbollah and despite the fact that Lebanese armed forces did not respond in the conflict.[183]

The main judicial decision that appears to take a contrary view is the *Hamdan* decision of the US Supreme Court.[184] In that case the Court stated that Common Article 3 applies to persons detained by the US in connection with action taken against Al-Qaeda. The reasoning of the US Supreme Court in this part of the decision is rather confusing and it is not at all clear that it reaches the conclusion that there is a conflict with Al-Qaeda which is of a non-international character.

---

[178] See *Armed Activities* case.

[179] See *Targeted Killings* case, para 18.

[180] Human Rights Council, 'Report of the Commission of Inquiry on Lebanon pursuant to Human Rights Council resolution S-2/1*' A/HRC/3/2 (23 November 2006) paras 50–62.

[181] Ibid, para 55.

[182] Ibid, para 58.

[183] Ibid, paras 59 and 62.

[184] *Hamdan v Rumsfeld*. See also the decision of ICC Trial Chamber in *Lubanga, Trial Judgment*, which came to a different view: 'It is widely accepted that when a State enters into conflict with a nongovernmental armed group located in the territory of a neighbouring State and the armed group is acting under the control of its own State, "the fighting falls within the definition of an international armed conflict between the two States". However, if the armed group is not acting on behalf of a government, in the absence of two States opposing each other, there is no international armed conflict.' (para 541, footnote references omitted).

There are two ways of reading the *Hamdan* decision. One is that the Court applied Common Article 3 because it considered the conflict to be non-international. The other way to read it is that the Court was simply saying that Common Article 3 applied, at a minimum, to the conflict with Al-Qaeda. The US government had argued before the Court in that case that, firstly, it was engaged in a conflict with Al-Qaeda which was separate and distinct from the conflict in Afghanistan, and, secondly, that the conflict with Al-Qaeda was not an armed conflict to which the full Geneva Conventions applied. The Court responded by saying that: '*We need not decide the merits of this argument* because there is *at least* one provision of the Geneva Conventions that applies here even if the relevant conflict is not one between signatories' (emphasis added).[185]

Since the Supreme Court also quoted that part of the International Court of Justice's decision in the *Nicaragua* case, which held that Common Article 3 applies as a minimum even in international armed conflicts,[186] its decision is not decisive as to the classification of the conflict with Al-Qaeda, to the extent there was a separate conflict at all.[187]

Even if there is an international armed conflict between an intervening foreign State and a State on whose territory a non-state group is based, it might be argued that this has no bearing on the conflict between foreign State and the non-state group as that conflict would be non-international and there would be two conflicts running in parallel. The relationship between the foreign State and the non-state group would be governed by the law of non-international armed conflicts. However, the important point here is that the conflict with the non-state group will be so bound up with the international armed conflict between the two States that it will be impossible to separate the two conflicts. With respect to the conduct of hostilities and targeting in general, every act of targeting by the foreign State will not only be an attempt to target the non-state group (or members thereof) but will also at one and the same time be a use of armed force against the territorial State because it is a use of force on that State's territory without its consent. This means that every act of targeting or opening fire must comply with the law of international armed conflicts.

With regard to detention and the status of combatants, one anxiety that is expressed by some authors is that saying that there is an international armed conflict between a State and non-state group would imply that fighters of the non-state group have combatant immunity or are entitled to prisoner of war status.

---

[185] Ibid, sentence with fn 61 attached.
[186] Ibid, fn 63.
[187] It is worth noting that the position of the Obama administration is that the US is involved in an armed conflict with Al-Qaeda, but it does not state explicitly that this is a non-international conflict. However, reference is made to Common Article 3 which indicates that the US believes the conflict is a non-international conflict, see H. Koh, 'The Obama Administration and International Law' Remarks at the Annual Meeting of the American Society of International Law, Washington, DC (25 March 2010). See also, In Re: Guantanamo Bay Detainee Litigation, Respondents' Memorandum Regarding the Government's Detention Authority Relative to Detainees held at Guantanamo Bay (13 March 2009), available at: <www.justice.gov/opa/documents/memo-re-det-auth.pdf>, where there is similar ambiguity regarding the classification of the conflict (but where the US administration seeks to draw from the law of international armed conflicts).

However, this conclusion does not follow from the assertion that the foreign State is involved in an international armed conflict with the territorial State and that such hostilities are bound up with those against the non-state group. It is one thing to assert that the law of international armed conflict applies; it is another thing to see *how* that law applies. Applying the law of international armed conflict would not grant combatant immunity or indeed prisoner of war status to fighters from the non-state group, as they would not, in practically all cases, fulfil the criteria for these statuses. In the first place, the fighters being considered here would not, by definition, fight on behalf of the State or belong to it as we are only speaking of cases where the territorial State (or another State) is not involved in the hostilities directly or indirectly. If the fighters of the non-state group do belong to another State, the conflict would unquestionably be international. Secondly, they will usually not fulfil the other criteria for prisoner of war status.

However, questions remain as to whether members of that non-state group should be entitled to the benefits that the rest of the population are entitled to. In particular, if they are detained should they be accorded the protections to which civilians are entitled under the Fourth Geneva Convention? The answer to this question depends, first of all, on the applicability of the Fourth Geneva Convention to persons who take part in hostilities but who are not entitled to prisoner of war status.[188] Views on this are divided but the better view is that such persons, provided they fulfil the nationality criteria in article 4 of that Convention, are, in principle, entitled to such protections as are provided for in the Fourth Geneva Convention, subject to possible limitations imposed in accordance with article 5 of that Convention.[189] The next question would be whether the rules relating to detention apply given that those rules are restricted to protected persons in the territory of the belligerent and in situations of occupation. In the absence of a belligerent occupation, it may be asserted that battlefield unprivileged belligerents are not covered by those parts of the Fourth Geneva Convention relevant to detention.[190] Apart from these questions, in principle, there is no reason why persons in the territory where the conflict takes place should be deprived of protections that they ordinarily enjoy with regard to a foreign force. If a person were to be picked up by the foreign State and detained, it is impossible to see how the person's status as a civilian in the international armed conflict should be superseded by a claim that the person is a fighter in a non-international armed conflict. Such persons are protected persons under the Geneva Conventions and do

---

[188] For an extensive discussion, see Dörmann, *Unlawful Combatants*; R. Baxter, 'So-Called "Unprivileged Belligerency": Spies, Guerrillas and Saboteurs' (1951) 28 *British Yearbook of International Law* 325; D. Jinks, 'The Declining Significance of POW Status' (2004) 45 *Harvard Journal of International Law* 367; L. Vierucci, 'Prisoners of War or Protected Persons *qua* Unlawful Combatants? The Judicial Safeguards to which Guantanamo Bay Detainees are Entitled' (2003) 1 *Journal of International Criminal Justice* 284; J. Callen, 'Unlawful Combatants and the Geneva Conventions' (2004) 44 *Virginia Journal of International Law* 1025.

[189] For an extensive discussion, see Dörmann, *Unlawful Combatants*.

[190] Ibid.

not lose that status because they may have engaged in acts that are hostile to the foreign State.

So to summarize, the law that applies to transnational conflicts between a foreign State and a non-state group is the law of international armed conflicts where the foreign State intervenes without the consent of the territorial State. This application of the law of international armed conflict is consistent with the underlying reasons for the distinction between international and non-international armed conflicts. In the case of conflicts with non-state groups on the territory of another State, there is little reason to have the more limited regulation of non-international conflicts as the conflict is not an internal matter. The sovereignty and State autonomy reasons that are used to justify having more limited regulation of non-international armed conflicts do not apply where the State is acting outside its own territory. Deference to the sovereignty of the foreign State ought not to apply where that State acts outside its territory, as the sovereignty and autonomy of the territorial State are now also in issue. Importantly, the territorial State has interests at stake: interests in the protection of its territory and of its civilian population and infrastructure.

4

Conflict Classification and the Law Applicable to Detention and the Use of Force

*Jelena Pejic**

1. Introduction

The purpose of categorizing armed conflict and distinguishing this type of violence from other forms is to determine the applicable law and the rights and obligations of those responsible for, or affected by it. Classification is also necessary because it is generally held that international humanitarian law governing international and non-international armed conflict gives rise to significantly different levels of protection and because the scope of application of human rights law in armed conflict remains controversial. For the purpose of the case studies which follow, this chapter examines two of the main 'baskets' of rules making up international humanitarian law: the norms governing the deprivation of liberty of persons[1] and those regulating the use of force, with a view to identifying—in summary form—what the existing law is and where it may be lacking in the face of 'new' conflict classifications. In each section of this chapter, the interplay between international humanitarian law and human rights law is also discussed. Part 2 provides an overview of the principal sources of law applicable to armed conflict and to other situations of violence that do not meet that threshold. Part 3 focuses on the rules governing detention in armed conflict, with a particular emphasis on procedural safeguards in internment, as well as the legal and practical issues related to the transfer of detainees. Part 4 outlines the rules governing the use of force in armed conflict and outside of it, highlighting especially the issue of the interface between international humanitarian law and human rights law. Part 5 offers some concluding remarks.

* Legal Adviser, Legal Division, International Committee of the Red Cross (ICRC). The views expressed are the author's alone and do not necessarily represent the positions of the ICRC.

[1] The terms 'detention' and 'deprivation of liberty' are used interchangeably in this chapter.

2. Applicable law—an overview

An examination of the rules on detention and the use of force in armed conflict must start with a very brief reminder of the existing categories of armed conflict and the relevant legal sources.[2]

The existence of two categories of armed conflict under international humanitarian law—international and non-international—is generally not contested. International armed conflicts are those waged between States[3] or between a State and a national liberation movement[4] provided the requisite conditions have been fulfilled.[5] It is also generally accepted that an international armed conflict is triggered when a 'difference' between two States leads to the use of armed force by one against the other, regardless of the intensity of fighting or its duration.[6] The irrelevance of the intensity and duration of the hostilities has recently been called into question,[7] but it is submitted that there are, inter alia, good protection reasons not to link the existence of an international armed conflict to a specific level of hostilities.[8] International humanitarian law governing international armed conflict is comprised of a series of treaties, the most important of which are the 1949 Geneva Conventions for the protection of victims of war and the First Additional Protocol thereto of 1977.[9] It should also be recalled that international armed conflicts were for centuries governed primarily by rules of customary international humanitarian law, which remains an important source of applicable rules to this day (see further below).

A non-international armed conflict is one waged between a State and one or more organized non-state armed groups[10] or between such groups themselves.[11]

---

[2] The section which follows covers some of the ground dealt with in the preceding chapter and is provided in order to give the reader a summary of the law necessary to understand the subject matter of this chapter.

[3] Article 2 Common to the 1949 Geneva Conventions.

[4] Additional Protocol I, art. 1.

[5] Additional Protocol I, art. 96(3).

[6] J. Pictet (ed.), *Geneva Convention Relative to the Protection of Civilian Persons in Time of War: commentary* (1958) 23 (Pictet, *Commentary to the Fourth Geneva Convention*). For further discussion, see ch. 3 above.

[7] International Law Association, 'Final Report on the Meaning of Armed Conflict in International Law' (2010).

[8] Under existing law, if members of the armed forces of a State in dispute with another State are captured by the latter's armed forces, they are eligible for POW status regardless of whether there is fully fledged fighting between the two States. POW status and treatment are well-defined under international humanitarian law, including the fact that a POW may not be prosecuted for having taken a direct part in hostilities. It is not clear that captured soldiers would be as comprehensively protected under the domestic law of the detaining State, supplemented by human rights law. In addition, certain geopolitically important States are not party to the relevant global human rights treaty, the International Covenant on Civil and Political Rights (ICCPR).

[9] An additional source of treaty rules, relevant to some of the case studies in this volume, is the 1954 Hague Convention for the Protection of Cultural Property in the Event of Armed Conflict and its two Protocols.

[10] Article 3 Common to the 1949 Geneva Conventions; Additional Protocol II, art. 1(1).

[11] 1949 Geneva Conventions, Common Article 3.

International humanitarian law does not specify the criteria that have to be met for the threshold of non-international armed conflict to be reached, but they have been identified in practice, jurisprudence and the doctrine. As the issue of threshold for non-international armed conflict is dealt with in more detail in other chapters,[12] suffice it to say that a certain intensity of hostilities and the requisite organization of the non-state armed group are generally deemed indispensable for categorizing a situation of violence as a non-international armed conflict.[13] What should be noted, however, is that the typology of non-international armed conflicts has expanded over the past decade to comprise currently seven possible scenarios (the last two of which, admittedly, remain subject to controversy).[14] They are very briefly listed below:

- first, there are 'traditional' or 'classical' non-international armed conflicts in which government armed forces are fighting against one or more organized armed groups within the territory of a single State;

- second, an armed conflict that pits two or more organized armed groups between themselves may be considered a sub-set of 'traditional' non-international armed conflict when it takes place within the territory of a single State;

- third, certain non-international armed conflicts originating within the territory of a single State between government armed forces and one or more organized armed groups have also been known to 'spill over' into the territory of neighbouring States;

- fourth, the last decade, in particular, has seen the emergence of what may be called 'multinational non-international armed conflicts'. These are armed conflicts in which multinational armed forces are fighting alongside the armed forces of a 'host' State—in its territory—against one or more organized armed groups;

- fifth, a sub-set of multinational non-international armed conflict is one in which UN forces, or forces under the aegis of a regional organization are sent to help stabilize a 'host' government and become involved in hostilities against one or more organized armed groups in its territory;

- sixth, it may be argued that a non-international armed conflict ('cross-border') exists—alongside an international armed conflict—when the forces of a State are engaged in hostilities with a non-state party operating from the territory of a neighbouring State without the latter's control or support;

- a final, seventh type of non-international armed conflict waged across multiple territories ('transnational') is believed by some—almost exclusively in the United States—to currently exist between 'Al Qaeda and its affiliates' and the US.[15]

---

[12] See e.g. ch. 3, section 6.1 above.

[13] See *Prosecutor v Limaj*, IT-03-66-T, Judgment (Trial Chamber), 30 November 2005, para 90 and *Prosecutor v Ramush Haradinaj*, IT-04-84-T, Judgment (Trial Chamber), 3 April 2008, para 60.

[14] See J. Pejic, 'The Protective Scope of Common Article 3: More Than Meets The Eye' (2011) 93 (881) *International Review of the Red Cross* 1.

[15] 'Report of the United States of America Submitted to the U.N. High Commissioner for Human Rights In Conjunction with the Universal Periodic Review' (August 2010) paras 82 and 84, available at: <www.state.gov/documents/organization/146379.pdf>.

The main sources of treaty law governing non-international armed conflict are Common Article 3 to the 1949 Geneva Conventions, which is generally considered to also reflect customary law, and Additional Protocol II of 1977. Due to the paucity of treaty rules, it may be said that the significance of customary international humanitarian law is greater in non-international than in international armed conflict. In 2005 the International Committee of the Red Cross published the results of a ten-year Study of Customary International Humanitarian Law,[16] which considered that 148 out of 161 rules identified were applicable in both international and non-international armed conflict. The references to customary law in this chapter rely on the 2005 Study.[17]

It is well-established that, despite the views of a few important dissenters,[18] human rights law applies alongside international humanitarian law in armed conflicts[19] and that it also applies extraterritorially.[20] What is not settled is the interplay of the two branches of international law in situations of armed conflict and the extent of extraterritorial application of human rights law. It is submitted that international humanitarian law constitutes the *lex specialis*[21] in situations of international armed conflict as it was both developed for such conflicts and elaborates the rights and duties of States and persons affected with more specificity than any other body of international law. In international armed conflict, international humanitarian law is supplemented by human rights law. The domestic law of the States parties is also likely to be of importance, but primarily in relation to the adjudication of claims that may arise as a result of violations of international humanitarian law or human rights.

---

[16] J.M. Henckaerts and L. Doswald-Beck (eds), *Customary International Humanitarian Law*, Vol. I: Rules, Vol. II: Practice (2005) (Customary Law Study).

[17] Although the existence of a small number of such rules identified in the Customary Law Study is controversial, this article does not deal with those rules.

[18] See 'Second and Third Periodic Report of the United States of America to the U.N. Committee on Human Rights Concerning the International Covenant on Civil and Political Rights' Annex I, Territorial Scope of Application of the ICCPR (21 October 2005), available at: <www.state.gov/g/drl/rls/55504.htm>.

[19] *Legal Consequences of the Construction of a Wall in the Occupied Palestinian Territory* (Advisory Opinion) ICJ Rep 2004, 136, para 106 (*Wall* Advisory Opinion).

[20] Human Rights Committee, 'General Comment 31: Nature of the General Legal Obligation on States Parties to the Covenant' CCPR/C/21/Rev.1/Add.13 (2004) para 10 (General Comment 31).

[21] *Lex specialis* is a doctrine relating to the interpretation of laws, and can apply in both domestic and international law contexts. The doctrine states that a law governing a specific subject matter (*lex specialis*) overrides a general law that would otherwise be applicable (*lex specialis derogat legi generali*). According to some it is a rule of norm conflict avoidance, while according to others it is a rule of norm conflict resolution. It is submitted that it may be used for both purposes. For the opposite view, see M. Milanovic, 'Norm Conflicts, International Humanitarian Law and Human Rights Law' in O. Ben Naftali (ed.), *Human Rights and International Humanitarian Law*, Collected Courses of the Academy of European Law, Vol. XIX/1 (2010). Milanovic believes that the maxim is only useful as a tool of norm conflict avoidance, whereas resolution of a conflict of norms between international humanitarian law and human rights law must be sought in the political domain. The discussion is more than academic because human rights bodies may only interpret human rights norms in light of international humanitarian law (and thus resort to the *lex specialis* rule only as a tool of norm conflict avoidance), but cannot find a violation of international humanitarian law as such. The exception would be proceedings before the European Court of Human Rights in which art. 15(2) of the European Convention were invoked by a respondent State, but that has not happened.

The real conundrum occurs in non-international armed conflicts in which one of the parties is a State and the other is a non-state armed group (and even more so if the conflict involves only non-state armed groups). At least three issues arise.

First is the fact that the obligations of the State party under human rights treaties are not legally shared[22]—and in many cases could not be practically carried out— by the non-state party.[23] International humanitarian law thus remains the indispensable legal framework because it is the only body of international law aimed at the protection of persons that clearly binds both State and non-state parties in armed conflict. Given that the great majority of conflicts nowadays are non-international and that their typology is expanding, the abiding relevance of international humanitarian law in this context must be emphasized.

Second is determining the interplay of a State's international humanitarian law and human rights treaty obligations, which remains a difficult endeavour. It is not sufficient or helpful to state in general terms that human rights law continues to apply in armed conflict without elaborating on what this means in practice. Situations of armed conflict cannot be equated to times of peace, and some international humanitarian law and human rights rules produce conflicting results when applied to the same situation because they reflect the different reality for which each body of law was primarily developed. As a result, the relationship between the two bodies of law in a non-international armed conflict must be determined on a case-by-case basis (see below). As will be explained, this is particularly the case with rules governing procedural safeguards for security detention and those relevant to the use of force.

The third issue is the application of domestic law and its interplay with human rights law and international humanitarian law in a non-international armed conflict. There is no model of interplay that can be suggested as appropriate across the board, owing to the fact that domestic legal systems differ and that States' international law obligations also vary. However, it is once again the State party that is obliged to articulate the 'right' relationship between the national legal system and the State's international obligations, a concern that non-state armed groups generally do not share.

---

[22] For a different view, see A. Clapham, *Human Rights Obligations of Non-State Actors* (2006) 281–5. While it is the case, as Clapham notes, that a number of UN Security Council resolutions 'call on' the parties to a non-international armed conflict to respect human rights law (alongside international humanitarian law), the legal effect of such references is uncertain and subject to very different interpretations in the doctrine. Clapham himself acknowledges that non-state armed group human rights obligations apply 'to the extent appropriate to the context' (ibid, 284). Given that in most cases the human rights obligations allegedly binding non-state armed groups would be identical to those that clearly bind them under international humanitarian law, the value added of invoking human rights law remains unclear.
[23] It is submitted that the exception—to the exceedingly brief analysis that follows—would be highly sophisticated armed groups with stable control over a part of national territory that has enabled them to develop and perform government-like functions. In such cases the groups could be said to have de facto human rights *responsibilities*. The number of such contexts is currently very small. One such context was Sri Lanka until the defeat of the LTTE in 2009. See 'Report of the UN Secretary-General's Panel of Experts on Accountability in Sri Lanka' (25 April 2011), available at: <www.un.org/en/rights/srilanka.shtml>.

Outside armed conflict a peacetime legal regime based on domestic law and human rights law applies. In principle, a State's domestic law must be in accordance with its human rights obligations. Alongside treaties that a State may be a party to, customary law is also a source of human rights law. However, there is no international compendium of customary human rights norms, as a result of which the scope and content of customary rules remain open to significant differences in interpretation. Guidance on what may be said to constitute prevailing State practice followed out of a sense of legal obligation must thus be sought mainly in international jurisprudence and the decisions of other bodies with an interpretive function, as well as in the doctrine.

3. Detention in armed conflict

Deprivation of liberty is an inevitable and lawful incidence of armed conflict that is for the most part adequately dealt with in international humanitarian law (the exception, procedural safeguards for internment in non-international armed conflict, is discussed below). By way of reminder, international humanitarian law rules on deprivation of liberty protect persons who are already in the adversary's physical power, in contradistinction to those governing the use of force, i.e. the conduct of hostilities. The basic legal principle underpinning any form of detention in armed conflict is humane treatment. For the sake of clarity, international humanitarian law rules on detention (most of which overlap with human rights law) may be broadly divided into four groups:

1) Rules on the treatment of detainees in the narrow sense. These are norms that aim to protect the physical and mental integrity and well-being of persons deprived of liberty for whatever reason. They include the prohibition of murder, torture[24] and other forms of cruel, inhuman or degrading treatment ('ill-treatment'), mutilation, medical or scientific experiments, as well as other forms of violence to life and health. All of the acts are prohibited under both international humanitarian and human rights law. To the extent that the transfer of detainees may lead to violations of the right to life or of the prohibition of torture and other ill-treatment, this issue may also be categorized as belonging to treatment in the narrow sense and is dealt with below.

2) Rules on material conditions of detention. The purpose of these rules is to ensure that detaining authorities adequately provide for detainees' physical and psychological needs, which means food, accommodation, health,

---

[24] Under international humanitarian law torture is prohibited whether committed by a State or a non-state party to an armed conflict, whereas under human rights law torture is defined as severe physical or mental pain or suffering committed by State agents or by persons whose actions can be attributed to the State. However, the Statute of the International Criminal Court dropped the requirement of State involvement in torture in its definition of torture as a crime against humanity; see ICC Statute, art. 7(2)(e).

hygiene, contacts with the outside world, religious observance and others. Treaty-based and customary international humanitarian law provide a substantial catalogue of standards pertaining to conditions of detention, as do 'soft law' human rights instruments.[25] A common catalogue of norms could even be derived from both bodies of law.

3) Fair trial rights. Persons detained on suspicion of having committed a criminal offence are guaranteed fair trial rights in both armed conflict and other situations of violence. The list of fair trial rights is almost identical under international humanitarian and human rights law. Common Article 3 does not, admittedly, provide a list of judicial guarantees, but it is generally accepted that article 75(4) of Additional Protocol I—which was drafted based on the corresponding provisions of the International Covenant on Civil and Political Rights—may be taken to reflect customary law applicable in all types of armed conflict. International humanitarian law in fact reinforces human rights law as it allows no derogation from fair trial rights in situations of armed conflict. While criminal trials usually take place before domestic courts (with the exception of proceedings before international criminal courts), it is a given that national trials must conform to the relevant international fair trial standards. These may be deemed to be sufficiently clear and elaborate under both international humanitarian and human rights law.

4) Procedural safeguards in internment. For the purposes of this text, internment is defined as the non-criminal detention of a person based on the serious threat that his or her activity poses to the security of the detaining authority in an armed conflict. It is in the area of procedural safeguards in internment that differences emerge in law applicable to international and non-international armed conflicts, as well as between international humanitarian law and human rights law. The focus of this section of the chapter will therefore be on this group of rules, with a view to identifying possible gaps in the law, as well as the practical challenges.

3.1. Internment in armed conflict: international armed conflict

In international armed conflict, international humanitarian law permits the internment of prisoners of war (POWs) and, under certain conditions, of civilians.

---

[25] 'Standard Minimum Rules for the Treatment of Prisoners', Adopted by the First United Nations Congress on the Prevention of Crime and the Treatment of Offenders, held at Geneva in 1955, and approved by the Economic and Social Council by its resolution 663 C (XXIV) of 31 July 1957 and 2076 (LXII) of 13 May 1977, available at: <www2.ohchr.org/english/law/treatmentprisoners.htm>; 'Body of Principles for the Protection of All Persons under Any Form of Detention or Imprisonment', Adopted by General Assembly resolution 43/173 of 9 December 1988, available at: <www2.ohchr.org/english/law/bodyprinciples.htm>.

3.1.1 POW internment

POWs [26] are essentially combatants captured by the adverse party in an international armed conflict. As a term of art, 'combatant' denotes a legal status that, as such, exists only in this type of conflict. Under rules on the conduct of hostilities, a combatant is a member of the armed forces of a party to an international armed conflict who has 'the right to participate directly in hostilities'.[27] This means that he or she may use force against, i.e. target and kill or injure other persons taking a direct part in hostilities and destroy other enemy military objectives. Because such activity is obviously prejudicial to the security of the adverse party, the Third Geneva Convention provides that a detaining State 'may subject prisoners of war to internment'.[28] However, a POW may not be prosecuted by the detaining State for lawful acts of violence committed in the course of hostilities ('combatant privilege'), but only for violations of international humanitarian law, in particular war crimes, or other crimes under international law such as genocide or crimes against humanity.

In case of doubt about the entitlement to POW status of a captured belligerent, article 5 of the Third Convention provides that such person shall be protected by the Convention until his or her status has been determined by a competent tribunal.[29] This provision is often misunderstood as requiring judicial review. That is not the case, as article 5 tribunals are meant to operate in or near the zone of combat; they only determine status, not criminal or any other responsibility.[30]

It is generally uncontroversial that the Third Geneva Convention provides a sufficient legal basis for POW internment and that an additional domestic law basis is not required. The detaining State is not obliged to provide review, judicial or other, of the lawfulness of POW internment as long as active hostilities are ongoing, because enemy combatant status denotes that a person is *ipso facto* a security threat.[31] POW internment must end and POWs must be released at the cessation of active hostilities,[32] unless they are subject to criminal proceedings or are serving a criminal sentence.[33] They may also be released earlier on medical grounds[34] or on their own cognizance.[35] Unjustifiable delay in the repatriation of

---

[26] Geneva Convention III, art. 4.

[27] Additional Protocol I, art. 43(2).

[28] Geneva Convention III, art. 21.

[29] Geneva Convention III, art. 5.

[30] See commentary to art. 45(1) of Additional Protocol I on the nature of a 'competent tribunal' under art.5 of the Third Geneva Convention in Y. Sandoz, C. Swinarski and B. Zimmermann (eds), *Commentary on the Additional Protocols of June 8, 1977 to the Geneva Conventions of 12 August, 1949* (1987) para 1745.

[31] Judicial review under the domestic law of the detaining State could be sought to obtain the release of a POW who is detained despite the end of active hostilities. As mentioned further below, that is a grave breach of international humanitarian law.

[32] Geneva Convention III, art. 118.

[33] Geneva Convention III, art. 119.

[34] Geneva Convention III, art. 109(1) and 110.

[35] Geneva Convention III, art. 21.

prisoners of war at the close of active hostilities is a grave breach of Additional Protocol I.[36]

3.1.2 Internment of civilians

Under the Fourth Geneva Convention, internment—and assigned residence—are the most severe 'measures of control'[37] that may be taken by a State with respect to civilians whose activity is deemed to pose a serious threat to its security. It is uncontroversial that civilian direct participation in hostilities falls into that category. Despite the fact that only combatants are explicitly authorized under international humanitarian law to participate directly in hostilities,[38] the reality is that civilians often do so as well, in both international and non-international armed conflicts. (In such cases they are colloquially referred to as 'unprivileged belligerents' or wrongly referred to as 'unlawful combatants'.) Civilian direct participation in hostilities modifies the basic international humanitarian law rules under which civilians are entitled to protection against the dangers arising from military operations[39] and may not be made the object of attack.[40] It is expressly provided that civilians are protected from direct attack 'unless and for such time as they take a direct part in hostilities'.[41]

Apart from direct participation in hostilities other civilian behaviour may also meet the threshold of posing a serious security threat to the detaining power.[42] The Fourth Geneva Convention provides different wording in terms of permissible grounds for internment depending on whether an internee is detained in a State party's own territory ('if the security of the Detaining Power makes it absolutely necessary')[43] or is held in occupied territory ('imperative reasons of security').[44] It has been suggested that the difference in language only indicates that internment in occupied territory should in practice be even more exceptional than in the territory of a party to the conflict.[45]

The internment review process in a State party's territory would also appear to differ somewhat from that in occupied territory. In a State's own territory internment review is to be carried out by an 'appropriate court or administrative board',[46] while in occupied territory the Convention refers to a 'regular procedure' that is to

---

[36] Additional Protocol I, art. 85(4)(b).

[37] Geneva Convention IV, art. 27, 41 and 78.

[38] The only exception is the relatively rare occurrence of a *levée en masse*, provided for in art. 4(6) of the Third Geneva Convention.

[39] Additional Protocol I, art. 51(1). Given the consequences of civilian direct participation in hostilities it is clearly crucial to avoid broad interpretations. The ICRC's view is outlined further in the text.

[40] Additional Protocol I, art. 51(2).

[41] Additional Protocol I, art. 51(3) and Additional Protocol II, art. 13(3).

[42] Examples of activities that are not direct participation in hostilities but would constitute a serious security threat are the financing of combat operations, general recruitment for combat etc.

[43] Geneva Convention IV, art. 42(1).

[44] Geneva Convention IV, art. 78(1).

[45] Geneva Convention IV, Commentary, J. Pictet (ed.), ICRC, Geneva, 1958, 367.

[46] Fourth Geneva Convention, art. 43 (1).

be administered by a 'competent body'.[47] Despite these and other textual differences the rules are in essence the same. A person interned in international armed conflict has the right to submit a request for review of the decision on internment (to challenge it), the review must be expeditiously[48] conducted either by a court or an administrative board, and periodic review is thereafter to be automatic, on a six-monthly basis.[49] The Fourth Geneva Convention does not specify the right to legal assistance, but does not bar it either.

It is sometimes asked why international humanitarian law provides procedural safeguards for civilians interned in international armed conflict and not to POWs.[50] The simple answer is that, in reality, there is far less certainty as to the threat a captured enemy civilian actually poses than is the case with a combatant who is, after all, a member of the adversary's armed forces. In contemporary warfare civilians are, for example, often detained not in combat, but on the basis of intelligence information suggesting that they represent a security threat. The purpose of the review process is to enable a determination of whether such information is reliable and whether the person's activity meets the high legal standard that would justify internment.

Unlike combatants, who may not be prosecuted by a capturing State for direct participation in hostilities (combatant privilege), civilians who do so can be prosecuted for having taken up arms and for all acts of violence committed during such participation, as well as for war crimes or other crimes under international law that might have been committed. This rule is the same in international and non-international armed conflict. Contrary to certain assertions,[51] civilian direct participation is not a violation of international humanitarian law and is not a war crime per se under either treaty or customary law.[52]

Civilian internment must cease as soon as the reasons which necessitated it no longer exist.[53] It must in any event end 'as soon as possible after the close of hostilities'.[54] Unjustifiable delay in the repatriation of civilians is also a grave breach of Additional Protocol I.[55]

There is some debate among legal scholars whether, on its own, the Fourth Geneva Convention constitutes a sufficient legal basis for the internment of civilians in international armed conflict or whether it must be accompanied by domestic legislation. It is unclear why this question is posed only in relation to the Fourth Convention and not the Third for there is no indication that the treaties

---

[47] Fourth Geneva Convention, art. 78 (2).
[48] Fourth Geneva Convention, art. 41 and 78.
[49] Geneva Convention IV, Commentary, J. Pictet (ed.), ICRC, Geneva, 1958, 261, 368–9.
[50] See C. Garraway, ' "Combatants"—Substance or Semantics?' in M. Schmitt and J. Pejic (eds), *International Law and Armed Conflict: Exploring the Faultlines* (2007) 330.
[51] See e.g. Office of the Judge Advocate General, 'Law of Armed Conflict at the Operational and Tactical Levels' Joint Doctrine Manual, Canada, B-GJ-005-104/FP-021 (13 August 2001) 16–14, para 1609(3)(g), available at: <www.forces.gc.ca/jag/training-formation/index-eng.asp>.
[52] See e.g. the list of war crimes under art. 8 of the ICC Statute.
[53] Geneva Convention IV, art. 132; Additional Protocol I, art. 75(3).
[54] Geneva Convention IV, art. 46, 133(1).
[55] Additional Protocol I, art. 85(4)(b).

differ in the legal authority provided or in the level of elaboration of rights granted. It is believed that the Fourth Geneva Convention constitutes a sufficient legal basis for internment.

3.2. Internment in armed conflict: non-international armed conflict

International humanitarian law does not contain rules on procedural safeguards for persons interned in non-international armed conflict. This is presumably because the drafters of the Geneva Conventions, i.e. of Common Article 3, had in mind that domestic law would govern the due process aspect of deprivation of liberty, and because they chose not to take into account that internment might in practice be carried out by non-state armed groups. Additional Protocol II explicitly mentions internment,[56] thus confirming that it is a form of deprivation of liberty inherent to non-international armed conflict, but likewise does not list internment grounds or process rights.

In a traditional non-international armed conflict occurring in the territory of a single State between government armed forces and one or more 'insurgent' groups, domestic law, informed by the State's human rights obligations and international humanitarian law, constitutes the legal framework governing the deprivation of liberty by the State of non-state armed groups. Under some views, domestic law cannot allow non-criminal detention in armed conflict without derogation from the ICCPR even if the State provides judicial review as required under article 9(4) of the Covenant. On other views derogation would be necessary if the State suspended the right to habeas corpus and provided only administrative review of internment in a non-international armed conflict. According to still other positions, the right to habeas corpus can never be derogated from,[57] an approach, it is submitted, that is appropriate in peacetime, but does not always accommodate the reality of armed conflict, as will be discussed below. The obligations of States parties to the European Convention on Human Rights differ, as that instrument does not list security reasons as a permissible ground for the deprivation of liberty. It would thus appear that a derogation from article 5 of the Convention would be necessary even if internment with judicial review was provided. The interface between human rights law and the law governing armed conflict is unclear where the relevant human rights treaty, such as the African Convention on Human and Peoples' Rights, makes no provision for derogation.

Leaving aside what State obligations may be, the fact is that the other party in a non-international armed conflict is one or more organized non-state armed groups. Domestic law does not allow them to detain or intern members of a State's armed forces (or anyone else), and human rights law likewise does not provide a legal basis for detention by non-state armed groups. To claim otherwise is effectively to suggest that a non-state party would be legally bound to provide habeas corpus to individuals it captures and detains. It seems fairly obvious that this is neither

---

[56] Additional Protocol II, art. 5, 6.   [57] See e.g. General Comment 29, para 16.

a correct legal construction, nor a solution that could be implemented in practice.[58] Put differently, the increasingly widespread claim that human rights law must be resorted to when international humanitarian law is silent on a particular issue—such as procedural safeguards in internment—ignores the legal and other limits of the applicability of human rights law to non-state parties to non-international armed conflicts.

Identifying the legal framework governing internment is even more complicated in non-international armed conflicts involving States fighting outside their own territory. Only two examples out of the broader typology[59] will be recalled here.

The first are 'multinational non-international armed conflicts': armed conflicts in which multinational armed forces are fighting alongside the armed forces of a 'host' State—in its territory—against one or more organized armed groups. As the armed conflict does not oppose two or more States, i.e. as all the State actors are on the same side, the conflict must be classified as non-international, regardless of the international component, which can at times be significant. One example is the non-international armed conflict in Afghanistan following the termination of the international armed conflict which started in October 2001.[60]

A sub-set of multinational non-international armed conflict is one in which UN forces, or forces under the aegis of a regional organization such as the African Union, are sent to help stabilize a 'host' government involved in hostilities against one or more organized armed groups in its territory. There are in practice cases in which it may be argued that the international force has become a party to the conflict. This scenario raises a range of legal issues, among which is the legal regime governing multinational force conduct[61] and the applicability of the 1994 Convention on the Safety of UN Personnel.[62] It is nevertheless submitted that if and when UN or forces belonging to a regional organization become a party to a non-international armed conflict such forces are bound by international humanitarian law.

---

[58] The very few exceptions, as already mentioned, would be organized non-state armed groups that are akin to governments in terms of stable control of territory that enables them to exercise government-like functions. In such circumstances it may be argued that they are bound by customary human rights law, but the relevant customary law norm would simply be that 'arbitrary deprivation of liberty is prohibited'. While the obligation to provide habeas corpus might be a customary law norm binding governments, it is submitted that it would be a stretch to claim that it also binds non-state armed groups.

[59] See discussion in section 2 above.

[60] The international armed conflict in Afghanistan that started in October 2001 was considered by the ICRC to be a non-international armed conflict as of June 2002 when the Afghan government was established. Ever since then the US and NATO forces have been acting in support of the government against the Taliban and Al-Qaeda. Similarly, the international armed conflict that started in Iraq in March 2003 ended in June 2004, after which the foreign troops were acting in Iraq with the consent of the Interim Iraqi Government.

[61] The UN as an entity is not bound by human rights treaties.

[62] 1994 Convention on the Safety of United Nations and Associated Personnel. It does not envisage UN forces becoming a party to a non-international armed conflict and thus by implication grants them immunity from attack even when they do in fact take a direct part in hostilities in those circumstances.

In addition to the reasons for which it is believed that human rights law does not provide a legal basis for detention by non-state armed groups, uncertainty surrounding States' human rights obligations in the two multinational conflict scenarios outlined above arise as well. A few will be listed. First, as already mentioned, certain States reject the notion of application of human rights law in armed conflict as such.[63] Second, States who are members of a multinational force, whether acting under UN auspices or otherwise, might not be parties to the same human rights treaties, including the ICCPR, and may therefore have different legal obligations.[64]

Third, the extent of the extraterritorial reach of human rights law is a legal work in progress. The International Court of Justice and the Human Rights Committee have opined that States 'carry' their human rights obligations when they act abroad, but it is submitted that their broad pronouncements have not helped clarify the myriad legal, political and practical issues that arise and must be dealt with in situations of armed conflict on a case-by-case basis. Litigation before the European Court of Human Rights for States parties to that treaty has of course determined that they may not violate the prohibition of torture and other ill-treatment vis-à-vis persons they detain abroad, but that is already a norm of international humanitarian law. As regards procedural safeguards in detention, the European Court of Human Rights has opined that internment, i.e. non criminal detention in an (extraterritorial) armed conflict, is a breach of the European Convention unless there has been a derogation from article 5, or the UN Security Council in a binding resolution explicitly obliged States to undertake internment.[65] It is submitted that the Court's decision will have a chilling effect on the ability of Council of Europe States to take part in multinational operations abroad that involve deprivation of liberty.[66]

Fourth, a legal issue that no judicial or other body has opined on is whether States must derogate from their human rights obligation to protect personal liberty in order to detain persons abroad without providing habeas corpus

---

[63] 'United States Response to Specific Recommendations Identified by the Committee Against Torture' CAT/C/USA/CO (25 July 2006).

[64] This would not preclude the application of customary international human rights law.

[65] *Al-Jedda v The United Kingdom* (Judgment) App No. 27021/08 (7 July 2011). The case involved the internment of a dual Iraqi/UK national by UK forces in Iraq between 2004 and 2007, when the armed conflict had become non-international, which is why it is dealt with in this section of the chapter. However, the judgment does not address the issue of conflict classification and it is clear that the Court's reasoning would apply to civilian internment in international armed conflict as well. The Court focused on whether the UK had an 'obligation' to intern under the relevant UN Security Council resolutions, rather than dealing with whether the resolutions, and the international humanitarian law to which they referred, authorize internment, which is of course the case.

[66] The import of the Court's decision is, inter alia, that States parties to the European Convention may not intern civilians in armed conflict—even though non-criminal detention for imperative reasons of security may be necessary and is allowed under international humanitarian law—unless there is an explicit UN Security Council mandate or a derogation to art. 5 has been entered. The Court's decision could be read to imply that POW internment in international armed conflict would likewise be a breach of art. 5 of the European Convention unless those conditions are met. It is submitted that the decision has confused the interplay of international humanitarian law and human rights law in the area of detention and will make it legally, politically, and practically difficult for Council of Europe States to take part in military or stabilization operations abroad.

review.[67] If the application of human rights law is to be adapted to battlefield reality, in which providing judicial review in thousands or tens of thousands of cases may not be feasible, it would appear that a derogation should be made. What remains unresolved is which State involved in a non-international armed conflict should derogate—the one actually holding the detainees or the host State. In the first case it is unclear how detention abroad could be deemed to constitute a 'public emergency threatening the life' of the nation undertaking internment. (It is revealing that no State has ever derogated from its human rights obligations when acting extraterritorially.) In the second case, it is unclear why a host State should be expected to derogate if its domestic law does not allow internment and if its courts do not have the power to order the release of a person from multinational detention. These are not hypothetical, but very real queries, to which there is no response.[68]

Fifth, the legal effect of a bilateral treaty adopted between a detaining State and a host State or of a Chapter VII UN Security Council resolution authorizing internment by a multinational force may be debated. Can a bilateral treaty override the respective States' human rights obligations and provide a legal basis for internment without judicial review, particularly when there has been no derogation from their human rights obligations?[69] As regards Security Council authority, views are divided over whether a Chapter VII resolution authorizing a multinational force to 'use all necessary' means to fulfil its mandate may be read as permitting internment.[70] While there is good reason to believe that it may (if the mission can use force then it must logically be allowed to also intern), there are also compelling arguments against such a position (the clause is not specific enough to comply with the principle of legality).

The complex issues surrounding internment mentioned above raise the question of whether international humanitarian law may be interpreted to provide a legal basis to intern in non-international armed conflict for both sides to this type of armed conflict. Different positions have been enunciated thus far in exchanges among experts. According to views at one end of the range, international humanitarian law does not provide a legal basis to intern and human rights law, being the more specific body of rules in this case, constitutes the default legal regime that

[67] The *Al-Jedda* case mentioned above may be read to mean that the European Court of Human Rights will not allow non-criminal detention in armed conflict even if judicial review of the lawfulness of detention is provided.

[68] See 'Report of Expert Meeting on Procedural Safeguards for Security Detention in Non-International Armed Conflict' Chatham House and ICRC, London (22–23 September 2008), available at: <www.icrc.org/eng/assets/files/other/security-detention-chatham-icrc-report-091209.pdf>. The *Al-Jedda* case did not shed any light on these questions.

[69] The *Al-Jedda* case clearly states that bilateral agreements between States parties to the European Convention and other States cannot override Convention obligations (*Al-Jedda*, para 108). An additional question that may be posed is how a host State is to ensure that an intervening State complies with the host State's obligations under human rights law.

[70] As mentioned above, the European Court determined in the *Al-Jedda* case that internment must be clearly and explicitly authorized in a Chapter VII UN Security Council resolution in order to possibly displace the application of art. 5 of the European Convention (*Al-Jedda* paras 105,109–10).

must be applied.[71] For the reasons outlined above, it is believed that this is not legally correct as regards the authority to intern by non-state armed groups—and, more important—does not reflect the reality of warfare either for most such groups or the State(s) that may be involved. If human rights law can serve as the *lex specialis* to the *lex specialis* of international humanitarian law, then what is essentially being said is that armed conflict must be conducted according to rules primarily developed to be applied in time of peace.[72] This result is surely untenable as it ignores the critical differences between war and peace.

A second position acknowledges that armed conflict and peacetime are not the same, but suggests that, while human rights law remains the default regime, its application should be modified to take into account the reality of armed conflict. Thus, rather than requiring judicial review, other types of review could be applied to detention in non-international armed conflict on a case-by-case basis. Leaving aside other possible questions that could be posed, the most important is perhaps this: why should the rules governing detention under human rights law be diluted to accommodate a reality for which they were not originally crafted? And, what is to prevent the importation of new, diluted human rights standards into detention in peacetime? It is submitted that this could gravely undermine the *ratio legis* of human rights law, which is to prevent government abuse of rights that the State is obliged to observe—and is capable of observing—in peacetime.[73]

A third approach, endorsed here, is that both treaty and customary international humanitarian law contain an inherent power to intern and may in that sense be said to provide a legal basis for internment in non-international armed conflict. What international humanitarian law lacks are explicit rules on grounds for detention and the procedure that must be applied. This gap should be dealt with by development of the law, either in the form of non-treaty (soft law) standards or by adoption of a new international treaty on detention and internment in non-international armed conflict. The objective of the latter would be to elaborate a catalogue of procedural safeguards that would bind both State and non-state parties, but also allow for implementation in a manner that would reflect the different capabilities of the two sides in practice. While the feasibility of any such proposal remains to be seen, different actors have already attempted to address the problem of lack of procedural safeguards for internment in non-international armed conflict.

---

[71] See e.g. Human Rights First, 'Fixing Bagram: Strengthening Detention Reforms to Align with U.S. Strategic Priorities' (November 2009) 4, available at: <www.humanrightsfirst.org/wp-content/uploads/pdf/Fixing-Bagram-110409.pdf>. ('Detention is an essential element of armed conflict, but the grounds and procedures for detention must be consistent with international humanitarian law and the applicable standards of international human rights law. Common Article 3 and Additional Protocol II (AP II) do not provide procedural guidelines to govern reviews of detention in non-international armed conflicts. Thus it is necessary to refer to human rights law for guidance.')

[72] For an elaboration of this view see C. Droege, 'Elective Affinities? Human Rights and Humanitarian Law' (2008) 90 (871) *International Review of the Red Cross* 535–6.

[73] For a critique of the second position see N. Modirzadeh, 'The Dark Sides of Convergence: A Pro-Civilian Critique of the Extraterritorial Application of Human Rights Law in Armed Conflict' (2010) 86 U.S. Naval War College International Law Studies (Blue Book) Series 349–410.

3.2.1 Ways forward

The paucity of treaty rules on procedural safeguards in non-international armed conflict (as well as the fairly rudimentary nature of the process due to civilians in international armed conflict) led the ICRC to issue institutional guidelines in 2005 entitled 'Procedural Principles and Safeguards for Internment/Administrative Detention[74] in Armed Conflict and Other Situations of Violence'.[75] The rules formulated are based on law and policy and are meant to be implemented in a manner that takes into account the specific situation at hand. The guidelines are relied on by the ICRC in its operational dialogue with States, multinational forces and other actors. Only two issues dealt with in the document will be briefly mentioned here: grounds for internment and the internment review process.

As already mentioned, grounds for internment are not specified in international humanitarian law applicable in non-international armed conflict. For the guidelines, the ICRC relied on 'imperative reasons of security' as the minimum legal standard that should inform internment decisions in all situations of violence, including non-international armed conflict. This policy choice was adopted because it emphasizes the exceptional nature of internment and is already in wide use. It seems also to be appropriate in multinational non-international armed conflicts, in which foreign forces are detaining non-nationals in the territory of a host State, as the wording is based on the internment standard applicable in occupied territories under the Fourth Geneva Convention.[76] It is believed that the proposed standard strikes a workable balance between the need to protect personal liberty and the detaining authority's need to protect against activity seriously prejudicial to its security.

There should be no controversy that direct participation in hostilities is an activity that would meet the 'imperative reasons of security standard'. The key issue, of course, is what is direct participation in hostilities, a question that will be addressed further below. Conversely, internment may not be resorted to for the sole purpose of interrogation or intelligence gathering, unless the person in question is deemed to represent a serious security threat based on his or her own activity. Similarly, internment may not be resorted to in order to punish a person for past activity, or to act as a general deterrent to the future activity of another person.[77] As a general matter, internment should not be used in lieu of criminal prosecution when an effective judicial system is in fact available. In all cases it must be recognized that the imperative reasons of security standard is high, and careful

---

[74] The terms 'internment' and 'administrative detention' are used interchangeably.

[75] The institutional position is expressed in J. Pejic, 'Procedural Principles and Safeguards for Internment/Administrative Detention in Armed Conflict and Other Situations of Violence' (2005) 87 (858) *International Review of the Red Cross* 375. It was published as Annex 1 to the ICRC's Report on 'International Humanitarian Law and the Challenges of Contemporary Armed Conflicts' presented to the 30th International Conference of the Red Cross and Red Crescent held in Geneva in 2007.

[76] Geneva Convention IV, art. 78.

[77] See *A and B versus the State of Israel*, Supreme Court of Israel (sitting as the Court of Criminal Appeals) Judgment (30 June 2008).

evaluation of whether it has been met must take place in relation to each person detained.

As regards internment review, the ICRC's guidelines provide that a person must, inter alia, be informed promptly, in a language he or she understands, of the reasons for internment. An internee must likewise be informed that he or she has the right to challenge the lawfulness of his or her internment with the least possible delay before an independent and impartial body. In practice, mounting an effective challenge will presuppose the fulfilment of several procedural and practical steps, including: 1) providing internees with sufficient evidence supporting the allegations against them; 2) ensuring that procedures are in place to enable internees to seek and obtain additional evidence; and 3) making sure that internees understand the various stages of the internment review process and the process as a whole. Where internment review is administrative rather than judicial in nature, ensuring the requisite independence and impartiality of the review body will require particular attention. Internees should also benefit from expert legal assistance in the internment review process.

Automatic, periodical review of internment is a further procedural safeguard identified.[78] Periodical review obliges the detaining authority to ascertain whether the detainee continues to pose an imperative threat to security and to order release if that is not the case. The safeguards that apply to initial review are also to be applied at periodical review.

An overview of humanitarian problems observed in detention, particularly in non-international armed conflicts, was given by the ICRC to the 31st International Conference of the Red Cross and Red Crescent in November 2011, as well as the ICRC's views on how they may be addressed.[79] The resolution adopted at that conference provides that the ICRC should undertake further discussions and consultations with States with a view to presenting, at the 32nd International Conference, options as well as its recommendations on how to take the matter forward.[80]

In addition to ICRC initiatives, the Danish government has headed negotiations on a more narrowly defined, but related issue: the 'Handling of Detainees in International Military Operations'.[81] The aim is to provide States contributing forces to multinational missions—who are assumed to have different legal obligations—with a common platform for lawful participation in detention activities

---

[78] Periodical review is provided for in the Fourth Geneva Convention with respect to internees in the territory of a State party to an international armed conflict, as well as in occupied territory. See Geneva Convention IV, art. 43(1) and art. 78(2) respectively.

[79] See J. Kellenberger, 'Strengthening Legal Protection for Victims of Armed Conflicts—States' Consultations and Way Forward' Statement to the Permanent Missions in Geneva (12 May 2011), available at: <www.icrc.org/eng/resources/documents/statement/ihl-development-statement-2011-05-12.htm>.

[80] 31st International Conference of the Red Cross and Red Crescent 2011, Resolution 1: Strengthening Legal Protection for Victims of Armed Conflicts, available at: <www.icrc.org/eng/resources/documents/resolution/31-international-conference-resolution-1-2011.htm>.

[81] See T. Winkler, 'The Copenhagen Process on Detainees: A Necessity' (2009) 78(4) *Nordic Journal of International Law* 489–98.

regardless of the legal classification of the situation involved. The questions examined include the legal basis for detention, the relevant procedure, the length of permissible detention, review of detention, detainee transfer and others. The Copenhagen process continues as of this writing.

Not surprisingly, the UN Department of Peacekeeping Operations has also had to deal with issues related to detention by UN forces with increasing frequency over the past decade. In 2010, the Department issued Interim Standard Operating Procedures on Detention in United Nations Peace Operations which are binding on UN forces.[82] The document is useful in that it provides guidance on a range of practical issues but, for reasons that are not entirely clear, does not contemplate non-criminal detention by UN forces beyond 72 hours except in very rare circumstances.[83]

It should be noted that one legal and practical issue which the texts mentioned above do not deal with is the period of time after which the deprivation of liberty of a civilian in armed conflict may be said to constitute internment triggering the procedural safeguards that have been outlined above. In international humanitarian law applicable to international armed conflict it could be argued, based on article 136 of the Fourth Geneva Convention, that any detention longer than fourteen days constitutes internment. That is the outer time period after which a detaining State must notify a detainee to his or her State of origin and the ICRC. This is an issue that would deserve to be addressed in any future development of the law, particularly that governing non-international armed conflict.[84]

3.3. Transfer of detainees

The transfer among States of persons deprived of liberty in armed conflict has emerged as one of the key legal and practical challenges associated with detention over the past decade. The legal debate has centred on the meaning and scope of the principle of *non-refoulement* under international law, while the main practical difficulty has been its implementation in situations where multinational forces detain persons in the territory of a host State. What follows is a brief summary of what is believed to be the applicable law and how it should be interpreted in practice. Whether and when a common understanding on these same issues can be reached at the international level remains to be seen.

Non-refoulement is the principle of international law that prohibits a State from transferring a person to another State if there are substantial grounds to believe that he or she runs a real risk of being subjected to certain violations of his or her

---

[82] United Nations, Department of Peacekeeping Operations, Department of Field Support, 'Interim Standard Operating Procedures: Detention in United Nations Peace Operations' Ref. 2010.6 (25 January 2010).

[83] The Interim Procedures are being reviewed as of this writing.

[84] For an academic view urging States to engage in the elaboration of new law for armed conflicts with non-state armed groups see e.g. J.B. Bellinger III and V.M. Padmanabhan, 'Detention Operations in Contemporary Conflicts: Four Challenges for the Geneva Conventions and Other Existing Law' (2011) 105 *AJIL* 201–43.

fundamental rights. These include, in particular, torture or cruel, inhuman or degrading treatment or punishment; arbitrary deprivation of life (including as the result of a death sentence pronounced without fundamental guarantees of fair trial), and persecution on account of race, religion, nationality, membership of a particular social group or political opinion.[85] According to some views, an even broader list could be drawn up.[86]

The principle of *non-refoulement* is found, with variations in scope, in international humanitarian law, human rights law and refugee law and is also contained in a number of extradition treaties. Needless to say, the exact coverage of the principle and the violations that must be taken into account will depend on the specific norms applicable in a given context, i.e. on the relevant treaties and customary law.

The 1949 Geneva Conventions expressly provide for certain *non-refoulement* and wider pre-transfer obligations in international armed conflict. In respect of aliens, article 45(4) of the Fourth Geneva Convention stipulates that '[i]n no circumstances shall a protected person be transferred to a country where he or she may have reason to fear persecution for his or her political opinions or religious beliefs'.

A broader restriction on transfer is found in article 12(2) of the Third Geneva Convention, under which '[p]risoners of war may only be transferred by the Detaining Power to a Power which is a party to the Convention and after the Detaining Power has satisfied itself of the willingness and ability of such transferee Power to apply the Convention'. The Convention also provides that the transferring State must take corrective measures or request the return of POWs if it determines that the receiving State is failing to fulfil its obligations under the Convention.

Article 45(3) of the Fourth Convention foresees the same restrictions on transfers of civilians: 'Protected persons may be transferred by the Detaining Power only to a Power which is a party to the present Convention and after the Detaining Power has satisfied itself of the willingness and ability of such transferee Power to apply the present Convention.' The Fourth Convention also provides that the transferring State must take corrective measures or request the return of protected persons if it determines that the receiving State is failing to fulfil its obligations under the Convention.

There are no explicit international humanitarian law norms on *non-refoulement* in non-international armed conflict. However, a party to an armed conflict is bound by Common Article 3 in all circumstances. It may be argued that it would contravene the provisions of that article if a party transferred an individual

---

[85] Persecution as a ground for *non-refoulement* is provided for in international refugee law, but will not be further addressed in this chapter. See 1951 Convention Relating to the Status of Refugees, art. 33.

[86] See International Commission of Jurists, 'Declaration on Upholding Human Rights and the Rule of Law in Combating Terrorism ("Berlin Declaration")' (28 August 2004), available at: <www.unhcr.org/refworld/docid/41dec1f94.html>. Pursuant to Principle 10 on *non-refoulement*, 'states may not expel, return, transfer or extradite, a person suspected or convicted of acts of terrorism to a State where there is a real risk that the person would be subjected to a serious violation of human rights, including torture or cruel, inhuman or degrading treatment or punishment, enforced disappearance, extrajudicial execution, or a manifestly unfair trial; or be subject to the death penalty'.

under its control or authority to another party if there are substantial grounds to believe that the person would be tortured or otherwise ill-treated, or arbitrarily deprived of life. Put differently, similar to international humanitarian law in international armed conflict, which prohibits the circumvention of safeguards owed to protected persons by means of transfer to a non-compliant party, law applicable in non-international armed conflict should also not be circumvented by transferring internees to a party that will not respect its obligations under Common Article 3.[87]

In human rights law, *non-refoulement* is expressly provided for in article 3 of the Convention against Torture pursuant to which '[n]o State Party shall expel, return ("*refouler*") or extradite a person to another State where there are substantial grounds for believing that he would be in danger of being subjected to torture'. The Convention also states that '[f]or the purpose of determining whether there are such grounds, the competent authorities shall take into account all relevant considerations including, where applicable, the existence in the State concerned of a consistent pattern of gross, flagrant or mass violations of human rights'.

Non-refoulement can also be read as a fundamental component of the absolute prohibitions of arbitrary deprivation of life and of torture, cruel, inhuman or degrading treatment, provided for in articles 6 and 7 of the ICCPR.[88] This interpretation—shared by human rights bodies and many legal scholars—is based on the view that the rights in question are of such fundamental importance that a sending State cannot turn a blind eye to the risk that a person may be subjected to arbitrary deprivation of life or ill-treatment as a result of its decision on transfer. This does not mean that a poor human rights record in general will suffice to prevent a transfer, only that there must be a real risk that articles 6 and 7 of the ICCPR will be violated with respect to the individual concerned; in such a case, the transfer could be said to contribute indirectly to the prohibited treatment.[89]

The issue of whether the principle of *non-refoulement* applies only where a transferred person crosses an international border or may also apply to transfers between States within the same country remains unsettled. Some nations involved in transfers by their forces abroad have not accepted that they have a *non-refoulement* obligation in that context, while others who essentially share the same view suspended transfers in practice when they estimated that detainees would be at risk.

---

[87] See C. Droege, 'Transfers of Detainees: Legal Framework, *Non-Refoulement* and Contemporary Challenges' (2008) 90(871) *International Review of the Red Cross* 669.

[88] See Human Rights Committee, 'General Comment 20: Prohibition of torture and cruel treatment or punishment' HRI/GEN/1/Rev.1 (28 July 1994) 31, para 9; and 'General Comment 31', para 12. See the related case law of the European Court of Human Rights since *Soering v The United Kingdom* (Judgment) App No. 14038/88 (7 July 1989) para 91.

[89] The issue of the norms applicable to the transfer of persons between non-state armed groups may be posed in this context. While such groups are bound, at a minimum, by Common Article 3, and may thus be said to be subject to a *non-refoulement* obligation as interpreted above, it would be difficult to argue that they have corresponding obligations under human rights law if they are not deemed to be duty-bearers under that body of law.

This position has been criticized by human rights bodies[90] and national case law is inconclusive.[91]

The principle of no transfer to violations of the fundamental rights listed above should be—it is believed—upheld not only when a detainee is transferred across a State frontier, but also when he or she is being moved from the effective control or authority of one State to another within the same territory.[92] This should by no means be taken as lack of awareness of the very significant practical problems posed by the application of the principle of *non-refoulement* to transfers that do not entail the crossing of an international border. While there are no complete solutions at present, some good solutions do nevertheless exist. Among them are: 1) prolongation of detention by the State of custody, 2) transfer to third States, 3) transfer to select places of detention within the host State in which there is no risk of violations, 4) monitoring or 5) joint administration of places of detention in the host State for the purpose of enabling individual follow-up of transferees. It should be borne in mind that due to the narrow range of rights protected, observance of the principle of *non-refoulement* is not likely to impede the transfer of thousands of persons in practice; rather, it will stand in the way of the transfer of specific individuals who face a real risk.

The two most contentious issues related to the transfer of detainees are the procedural safeguards that should precede a transfer decision and the use, by a sending State, of 'diplomatic assurances' from a receiving State promising that a transferee's fundamental rights will be protected.

While neither treaty nor customary international humanitarian or human rights law provide for procedural safeguards that must be applied before transfer, such an obligation may be derived from the general international law principle that a person whose rights may be or have been violated has the right to an effective remedy.[93] In

---

[90] Committee against Torture, 'Conclusions and Recommendations: United Kingdom of Great Britain and Northern Ireland—Dependent Territories' CAT/C/CR/33/3 (10 December 2004) para. 5(e); Human Rights Committee, 'Concluding Observations: United States of America' CCPR/C/USA/CO/3/Rev.1 (18 December 2006) para 16.

[91] In a recent judgment, the Federal Court of Canada rejected the application of the Canadian Charter of Rights and Freedoms to persons detained in Canadian military custody in Afghanistan, while holding that international law did apply to such persons. It did not make any statements as to the applicability of specific international human rights treaties. Federal Court of Canada, *Amnesty International Canada and British Columbia Civil Liberties Association v Chief of the Defence Staff for the Canadian Forces, Minister of National Defence and Attorney-General 614 of Canada*, Federal Court of Canada, 2008 FC 336 (12 March 2008); the decision is on appeal. Similarly, the transfer of Iraqi detainees by UK forces to Iraqi authorities was litigated in the UK courts before eventually reaching the European Court of Human Rights, which disagreed with the national courts. See the judgment of the Court of Appeals in the case of *R (on the application of Al-Saadoon and Mufdhi) v the Secretary of State for Defence* [2009] EWCA Civ 7 (21 January 2009) and the European Court judgment in *Al-Saadoon and Mufdhi v the United Kingdom* (Judgment) App No. 61498/08 (2 March 2010).

[92] *Wall* Advisory Opinion, paras 108–11; *Case Concerning Armed Activities on the Territory of the Congo (Democratic Republic of the Congo v Uganda)* ICJ Rep 2005, 168, para 119 (*Congo v Uganda*); Committee against Torture, 'Conclusions and Recommendations: United States of America' CAT/C/USA/CO/2 (25 July 2006) para 15; *López Burgos v Uruguay*, HRC, Comm No. R.12/52, CCPR/C/13/D/52/1979 (29 July 1981) para 12.3; General Comment 31, para 10.

[93] In human rights law, this is articulated in art. 2(3) of the ICCPR. In the context of international armed conflict, owing also to ICRC efforts, a practice has developed allowing POWs to express fear of

the context of *non-refoulement*, this may be interpreted to mean that a process should be put in place enabling review of a transfer decision if and when the person involved alleges a real risk of abuse in the receiving State.[94] A number of procedural safeguards may be envisaged, such as: 1) timely information to the concerned person of the intended transfer; 2) the opportunity for the person concerned to express fears he or she may have about the transfer and to challenge the transfer before a body that is independent of the one that took the transfer decision; 3) the possibility for the person in question to make representations before the review body in order to explain the reasons he or she would be at risk in the receiving State; and 4) suspension of transfer during the review because of the irreversible harm that would be caused if the person was transferred. Where possible, the person should also be represented by counsel.

The process outlined above has in practice been followed by States in cases of expulsions, extraditions, deportations or other measures of removal of individuals from their territory. Typically, the remedy is before national courts. The phenomenon of transfers linked to multinational operations is, however, relatively new and takes place in obviously different circumstances. State practice has therefore, not surprisingly, been conflicting. Some States have granted detainees access to their courts (where their claims were rejected on the merits), while others have not taken that route. In this context, it should be borne in mind that a review of transfer need not be exclusively judicial in nature. As with procedural safeguards in internment, the key issue is whether the remedy is effective, i.e. whether the concerned person has a meaningful chance to obtain an independent and impartial decision against a transfer that would be contrary to the principle of *non-refoulement*.

3.3.1 Ways forward

It may be concluded that while the law and policy are a work in progress, it is clear that transfers between States occurring outside the transferring State's territory require practical responses at the international level as a matter of urgency. Workable solutions that would address the material limitations of States participating in multinational operations and their obligation to protect transferees from ill-treatment or arbitrary deprivation of life need to be devised.

In order to comply with their obligations under the principle of *non-refoulement*, sending States have increasingly resorted to transfer agreements under which the receiving State provides assurances that a transferred person will be treated in accordance with international standards ('diplomatic assurances'). While it is uncontroversial that such assurances do not, per se, relieve a sending State of its *non-refoulement* obligations, there are different views as to whether assurances may

repatriation to their State of origin and not to be repatriated if the circumstances point to a danger of violation of their fundamental rights upon return.

[94] See Sir E. Lauterpacht and D. Bethlehem, 'The Scope and Content of the Principle of *Non-Refoulement*', Opinion, in E. Feller, V. Turk and F. Nicholson (eds), *Refugee Protection in International Law: UNHCR's Global Consultations on International Protection* (2003) 87–177.

ever be resorted to. Some believe they cannot, while others focus on the conditions that must accompany them.

It is submitted that any diplomatic assurance received by a State constitutes only one among other relevant facts that are to be taken into account in assessing whether the fears of an individual in a given case are well founded. In determining the weight, if any, to be given to diplomatic assurances, a review body should be guided by the position adopted by various human rights organs, pursuant to which:

- in case of transfer to a State in which there is 'systematic practice of torture', assurances are unlikely to remove the risk and should not be resorted to;
- general assurances to the effect that the receiving State will abide by international standards, without specific assurances related to the particular individual in question, are not capable of removing the risk with regard to such person;
- diplomatic assurances may remove the risk only if accompanied by an independent and effective post-transfer monitoring mechanism.[95]

It must be emphasized that even though binding agreements incorporating a strong post-transfer monitoring mechanism can, in theory, eliminate the risk for the person concerned, experience has shown that assurances are not always complied with by the receiving State. It is difficult in practice to monitor compliance with an undertaking that persons deprived of liberty will not be ill-treated given that abuse frequently takes place behind closed doors and its occurrence is denied. Additionally, transferred persons may fear conveying allegations of ill-treatment to a monitoring body given that such information may put them at risk of reprisals when passed on to the detaining authorities. When assurances are violated it is also not always clear what, if any, remedy is available to the individual concerned. In sum, assurances should only be resorted to cautiously and with circumspection.

4. The use of force in armed conflict

Rules on the conduct of hostilities were historically developed for international armed conflict and are nowadays mainly provided for in Protocol I of 1977 additional to the Geneva Conventions, in Additional Protocol II (with far less elaboration) and in customary international humanitarian law. Common Article 3 is entirely devoted to the protection of persons in enemy hands and contains no rules on the conduct of hostilities. Practice, however, has unquestionably demonstrated that both State and non-state parties conduct hostilities in non-international armed conflicts meeting the Common Article 3 threshold. This was confirmed in the ICRC's 2005 Study on Customary International Humanitarian Law, which identified a number of conduct of hostilities rules applicable regardless of the

---

[95] See *Agiza v Sweden*, HRC, Comm No. 233/2003, CAT/C/34/D/233/2003 (2005) para 13.4.

classification of a conflict.[96] An exhaustive overview of the Study's rules on this issue cannot be undertaken, but a few relevant ones are mentioned further below. Before that, two preliminary remarks on rules governing conduct of hostilities are called for.

The first is that international humanitarian law rules governing the use of force are specific to the reality they govern and cannot be transposed to situations other than armed conflict. This is because the ultimate aim of military operations is to prevail over the enemy's armed forces. Parties to an armed conflict are thus permitted, or at least are not legally barred from, attacking each other's military objectives. Violence directed against those targets is not prohibited as a matter of law regardless of whether it is inflicted by a State or a non-state party. Acts of violence against civilians and civilian objects are, by contrast, unlawful because one of the main purposes of international humanitarian law is to spare civilians and civilian objects from the effects of hostilities. International humanitarian law thus regulates both *lawful* and *unlawful* acts of violence and is the only body of international law dealing with the protection of persons that takes such a two-pronged approach. There is no similar dichotomy in international human rights law[97] or in the international norms governing acts of terrorism, to name the two most obvious branches of international law that also seek to protect persons from violence.

The second feature not replicated in other bodies of international law is the principle of equality of rights and obligations of belligerents under international humanitarian law.[98] Pursuant to this body of norms, known as the *ius in bello*, each side to an armed conflict has to comply with the same rules. This is because the purpose of international humanitarian law is not to determine which party was 'right' in resorting to the use of armed force against the other (the purview of the *ius ad bellum*), but to ensure the equal protection of persons and objects affected by armed conflict regardless of the lawfulness of the first resort to force. Thus, any party to an armed conflict is equally prohibited from directly attacking civilians or civilian objects, but is not prohibited from attacking the adversary's military objectives.[99] In this sense international humanitarian law may be said to govern an essentially horizontal relationship between the parties to an armed conflict.

---

[96] There is also what has been called by Sivakumaran a 'threshold' approach that seeks to split up the law of non-international armed conflict, therefore including the application of norms regulating the conduct of hostilities, based on the intensity of the violence involved. According to this approach, 'a low-intensity internal armed conflict would be regulated through human rights law; a high-intensity internal armed conflict would be governed by international humanitarian law; the dividing threshold would be that of Additional Protocol II'. See S. Sivakumaran, 'Re-envisaging the International Law of Internal Armed Conflict' (2011) 22 *EJIL* 235–6.

[97] This is not to say that there cannot be lawful use of force by State agents under human rights law. Such use of force, however, is always undertaken in response to a previously unlawful act by an individual or group of persons. That is not the case with international humanitarian law, where direct participation in hostilities is either explicitly allowed or is not prohibited.

[98] M. Sassoli, 'La définition du terrorisme et le droit international humanitaire' (2007) *Revue québécoise de droit international (hors-série), Etudes en hommage à Katia Boustany* 31.

[99] The principle of equality of parties under international humanitarian law is not only legally important, but also serves to de facto enhance compliance with the norms by all sides involved.

Other bodies of international law, particularly human rights law, govern a primarily vertical relationship, between a State and individuals within its territory or jurisdiction.[100]

4.1. Rules on the conduct of hostilities in armed conflict

Just as humane treatment is the basic principle governing the treatment of persons in enemy hands, distinction is the fundamental principle in the conduct of hostilities. The ICRC Customary Law Study confirmed that parties to an armed conflict must at all times distinguish between civilians and combatants, and that attacks may only be directed against combatants.[101] It clarifies that civilians are persons who are not members of the armed forces and that the civilian population comprises all persons who are civilians.[102] The Study determines, as already noted, that civilians are protected against attack unless and for such time as they take a direct part in hostilities, an issue that will be examined further below.[103]

It is a norm of customary international humanitarian law that the parties to an armed conflict must at all times distinguish between civilian objects and military objectives and that attacks may only be directed against military objectives.[104] In so far as objects are concerned, military objectives are limited to those objects which by their nature, location, purpose or use make an effective contribution to military action and whose partial or total destruction, capture or neutralization, in the circumstances ruling at the time, offers a definite military advantage.[105] Civilian objects are all objects that are not military objectives. They are protected against attack, unless and for such time as they are military objectives. The Study confirms that indiscriminate attacks are prohibited and defines such attacks.[106]

Very importantly, the Study determines that the principle of proportionality must be observed in the conduct of hostilities in both international and non-international armed conflict[107] and that the parties must also adhere to rules governing precautions in attack or against the effects of attacks.[108] Given the very important and often misunderstood differences between the operation of these principles under international humanitarian law and human rights law—which reflect the differences between what is practically possible in war and in peacetime—a brief digression seems warranted.

The principle of proportionality in attack prohibits attacks against legitimate military objectives that may be expected to cause incidental death, injury to persons or damage to civilian objects, or a combination thereof, which would be excessive in relation to the concrete and direct military advantage anticipated. The crucial

---

[100] While it is true that States have a due diligence obligation and must do their best to prevent 'horizontal' violations of human rights by other actors, this principle does not go very far in protection terms when applied to situations in which the State has no control over the other actor, which is most often the case in hostilities in non-international armed conflict. See European Court of Human Rights, *Ergi v Turkey* (Judgment) App No. 23818/94 (28 July 1998).
[101] Customary Law Study, rule 1.   [102] Ibid, rule 5.   [103] Ibid, rule 6.
[104] Ibid, rule 7.   [105] Ibid, rule 8.   [106] Ibid, rule 12.
[107] Ibid, rule 14.   [108] Ibid, rules 15–24.

difference between the relevant international humanitarian law and human rights rules is that under the former, the principle of proportionality aims to limit incidental ('collateral') damage to protected persons and objects, while nevertheless recognizing that an operation may be carried out even if such damage is likely, provided that it is not excessive in relation to the concrete and direct military advantage anticipated. In contrast, the aim of the principle of proportionality under human rights law is to prevent harm from happening to anyone else except to the person against whom force is being used. Even such a person must be spared lethal force if there is another, non-lethal way of achieving the aim of a law-enforcement operation.[109]

The international humanitarian law principle of precautions in attack is multi-faceted in that it requires the application of a range of steps to ensure that civilians and civilian objects (but, legally, not persons taking a direct part in hostilities) are spared the effects of military operations.[110] It means, inter alia, that everything feasible must be done to make sure that the object of attack is indeed a military objective, i.e. to avoid erroneous targeting of civilians or civilian objects. It mandates that all feasible precautions in the choice of means and methods of warfare must be taken in order to avoid or at least minimize possible collateral damage, and that parties must refrain from an attack which may be expected to cause such damage. It also requires that an attack be suspended or cancelled if it becomes clear that an intended target is not a military objective, or if the attack may be expected to cause collateral damage. As is well known there are also precautions incumbent on the defending side. The corresponding human rights standards, outlined further below, are quite different.

The bottom line is that rules on the conduct of hostilities recognize that the use of lethal force against persons is inherent to waging war. This body of rules aims to avoid or limit death and other harm, particularly of civilians, but recognizes that the very nature of armed conflict is such that loss of life cannot be entirely prevented.

4.1.1 Meaning of the term 'direct participation in hostilities'

In addition to identifying rules believed to be uncontroversial in any type of armed conflict, the ICRC's Customary Law Study also revealed a number of areas where practice was ambiguous. It showed, for example, that it was not clear whether—for the purposes of the conduct of hostilities—persons fighting for organized non-state armed groups are to be considered members of armed forces or civilians. A related area of uncertainty identified, in both international and non-international armed

---

[109] See N. Lubell, 'Challenges in Applying Human Rights Law to Armed Conflict' (2005) 87 (860) *International Review of the Red Cross* 745. ('For example, under human rights law and the rules of law enforcement, when a State agent is using force against an individual, the proportionality principle measures that force in an assessment that includes the effect on the individual himself, leading to a need to use the smallest amount of force necessary and restricting the use of lethal force.')

[110] See J-F. Queguiner, 'Precautions Under the Law Governing the Conduct of Hostilities' (2006) 88 (864) *International Review of the Red Cross* 793.

conflict, was the absence of a precise definition of the term 'direct participation in hostilities'.

Given that civilians who directly participate in hostilities may be targeted—and killed—by the adversary, the consequences of the lack of a definition cannot be overstated. It was with a view to clarifying the law that in 2009 the ICRC published the Interpretive Guidance on the Notion of Direct Participation in Hostilities under International Humanitarian Law,[111] enunciating the organization's recommendations.[112] The Guidance was intended to provide military planners, commanders and others with legal standards elaborating the concept of direct participation in hostilities. The recommendations are thus necessarily broad/abstract in nature and need to be further 'translated' into operational tools in order to be applicable on the ground.

The first question addressed in the Interpretive Guidance is who is considered a civilian for the purposes of the principle of distinction because the answer determines the scope of persons protected against direct attack 'unless and for such time as they directly participate in hostilities'. The Guidance distinguishes between: 1) members of organized armed forces or groups, the latter defined as persons whose continuous function is to conduct hostilities on behalf of a party to an armed conflict; and 2) civilians, that is, persons who do not directly participate in hostilities, or who do so on a merely spontaneous, sporadic or unorganized basis. It concludes that, *for the purposes of the principle of distinction under international humanitarian law*, only the latter are deemed to be civilians.

This means that, in non-international armed conflict, persons who are not members of State armed forces or of organized armed groups are considered civilians and may not be targeted unless and for such time as they are engaged in a specific act of direct participation[113] (see below). Conversely, organized armed groups constitute the armed forces of a non-state party to a non-international armed conflict. The decisive criterion for individual membership in an organized armed group is whether a person performs a continuous function for the group involving his or her direct participation in hostilities ('continuous combat function'). As long as this is the case, he or she ceases to be a civilian for the purpose of the conduct of hostilities and loses protection against direct attack. This does not imply de jure entitlement to combatant privilege, which in any event does not exist

---

[111] See N. Melzer, *Interpretive Guidance on the Notion of Direct Participation in Hostilities under International Humanitarian Law* (2009) (Interpretive Guidance).

[112] For articles criticizing certain aspects of the Interpretive Guidance, and a response to the critiques, see 42 *New York University Journal of International Law and Politics* (Spring 2010), which is devoted to that topic.

[113] Pursuant to the Interpretive Guidance, in international armed conflict all persons who are neither members of the armed forces of a party to the conflict nor participants in a *levée en masse* are entitled to protection against direct attack unless and for such time as they take a direct part in hostilities. Members of irregular armed forces (e.g. militia, volunteer corps, etc.) who belong to a State party to a conflict are considered part of its armed forces. They are not deemed civilians for the purposes of the conduct of hostilities even if they fail to fulfil the criteria required by international humanitarian law for combatant privilege and POW status. Membership of irregular armed forces belonging to a party to the conflict is to be determined based on the same functional criteria that apply to organized armed groups in non-international armed conflict.

in non-international armed conflict. Rather, it distinguishes members of the organized fighting forces of a non-state party from civilians, i.e. persons who directly participate in hostilities on a merely spontaneous, sporadic or unorganized basis. Some critique has been directed at the notion of 'continuous combat function' because it is allegedly based on status rather than behaviour as the basis for targeting.[114] It is submitted that the critique is misplaced as the Guidance does not—and could not—introduce combatant status into non-international armed conflict. On the contrary, as the very term indicates, membership in an armed group is linked to the continuous combat *function* a person carries out.

The second question dealt with is what conduct amounts to direct participation in hostilities. Pursuant to the Guidance, a specific act must fulfil the following cumulative criteria: 1) it must be likely to adversely affect the military operations or military capacity of a party to an armed conflict or, alternatively, to inflict death, injury or destruction on persons or objects protected against direct attack (*threshold of harm*); 2) there must be a direct causal link between the act and the harm likely to result either from that act, or from a coordinated military operation of which that act constitutes an integral part (*direct causation*); and 3) the act must be specifically designed to directly cause the required threshold of harm in support of a party to the conflict and to the detriment of another (*belligerent nexus*).

Applied in conjunction, the three requirements are believed to permit a workable distinction between activities amounting to direct participation in hostilities and those which, although occurring in the context of an armed conflict, are not part of the conduct of hostilities and do not lead to loss of protection from direct attack. In addition, measures preparatory to the execution of a specific act of direct participation in hostilities, as well as the deployment to and the return from the location of its execution, are deemed to constitute an integral part of it.

The third issue addressed in the Guidance are the modalities that govern the loss of protection against direct attack. They include the time during which members of State armed forces or of organized armed groups, as well as individual civilians, may be subject to direct attack (mentioned above), and the rules and principles governing the use of force against them. As regards the latter, the Guidance determines that (...) 'the kind and degree of force which is permissible against persons not entitled to protection against direct attack must not exceed what is actually necessary to accomplish a legitimate military purpose in the prevailing circumstances'.[115] This recommendation, in particular, has been criticized as being contrary to international humanitarian law, which does not include any explicit restriction on the targeting and killing of persons who are legitimate military objectives.[116] It has also, wrongly, been interpreted as requiring a 'capture rather than kill' obligation in the conduct of hostilities.

---

[114] See 'Report of the Special Rapporteur on Extrajudicial, Summary or Arbitrary Executions, Philip Alston' A/HRC/14/24/Add.6 (28 May, 2010) para 65.

[115] Interpretive Guidance, recommendation IX.

[116] See W. Hays Parks, 'Part IX of the ICRC 'Direct Participation in Hostilities' Study: No Mandate, No Expertise, and Legally Incorrect' (2010) 42 *New York University Journal of International Law and Politics* 799.

In respect of the first critique, the ICRC's view, as explained in the Interpretive Guidance, is based on the interplay between the principles of military necessity and humanity that underlie the entire normative framework of international humanitarian law. Just as important, the recommendation is drawn from the interpretation given by relevant States to the interface of those principles as reflected in their military manuals.[117]

The second critique misreads the plain language of the recommendation and of the accompanying commentary. The latter specifically states that 'the absence of an unfettered "right to kill" does not necessarily imply a legal obligation to capture rather than kill regardless of the circumstances'.[118] The commentary also explains that: 'what kind and degree of force can be regarded as necessary in an attack against a particular military target involves a complex assessment based on a wide variety of operational and contextual circumstances. The aim cannot be to replace the judgment of the military commander by inflexible or unrealistic standards; rather, it is to avoid error, arbitrariness, and abuse by providing guiding principles for the choice of means and methods of warfare based on his or her assessment of the situation.'[119]

The Interpretive Guidance ends with a reminder that civilians who cease direct participation in hostilities and individuals who cease to be members of an organized armed group by disengaging from a continuous combat function regain full civilian protection against direct attack. However, in the absence of combatant privilege they are not exempted from prosecution under the domestic law of the detaining State for acts committed during direct participation or membership. They may also be held individually responsible for war crimes or other crimes under international law.

4.2. Use of force in occupied territory

Occupation is by definition a situation of international armed conflict to which the four Geneva Conventions apply pursuant to Common Article 2.[120] The fact that a territory is occupied does not, however, mean that an occupying power cannot be simultaneously faced with hostilities and with the obligation to restore and ensure public order and safety, i.e. to carry out its law-enforcement duties under international humanitarian law.[121] Thus, one of the most important challenges in

---

[117] See e.g. NATO, 'Glossary of Terms and Definitions' AAP-6V, 2-M-5; United States, Department of the Army, Field Manual 27-10 (1956) para 3; US Department of the Navy, The Commander's Handbook on the Law of Naval Operations, NWP 1–14M/MCWP 5–12-1/COMDTPUB P5800.7A (2007), 5-2, para 5.3.1; France, Ministry of Defence, Manuel de Droit des Conflits Armés (2001) 86 f.; Germany, Federal Ministry of Defence, Triservice Manual ZDv 15/2: Humanitarian Law in Armed Conflicts (August 1992) para 130; Switzerland, Swiss Army, Regulations 51.007/IV, Bases légales du comportement à l'engagement (2005) para 160. Historically, the modern concept of military necessity has been strongly influenced by the definition provided in art. 14 of the 'Lieber Code' (United States: Adjutant General's Office, General Orders No. 100, 24 April 1863).

[118] Interpretive Guidance, 78.

[119] Ibid, 80.

[120] Geneva Convention IV, Commentary, J. Pictet (ed.), ICRC, Geneva, 1958, 21.

[121] See Regulations annexed to Hague Convention IV of 1907, art. 43, and Geneva Convention IV, art. 64.

contemporary occupations is ascertaining when an occupying power may use force according to rules on the conduct of hostilities and when reliance on law-enforcement standards in occupation provided for by international humanitarian law and/or human rights law is called for. There are no clear answers and legal experts have different views on both the general interplay of conduct of hostilities and law-enforcement rules in occupation, as well as on their application in specific cases.[122]

While an analysis of the various legal approaches that may be adopted is outside the scope of this review, it must be noted that a significant number of authorities recognize that the conduct of hostilities and law-enforcement paradigm apply simultaneously in occupation. The prevailing view seems to be that law enforcement is the default regime in relation to the use of force in occupied territory, particularly in cases of stable and calm occupation. What is in dispute, however, is whether an occupying power's obligations to restore and maintain public order and safety are to be entirely informed by human rights standards on law enforcement (outlined below) or on the law-enforcement standards contained in the relevant international humanitarian law treaties, supplemented by human rights law.

Another issue is the elements or criteria on the basis of which it can be determined when an occupying power would be entitled to switch from the default paradigm to a conduct of hostilities framework in order to quell armed violence in occupied territory. It is generally believed that a distinction should be made between armed violence linked to the original armed conflict that led to the occupation and that emanating from organized armed groups not affiliated with the occupied State. In the first case, conduct of hostilities rules would be applicable by the occupying State against the armed forces of the occupied State, as well as affiliated militias or other resistance movements belonging to the latter, if active hostilities endured or had resumed within the context of the original international armed conflict.

In practice, hostilities and other acts of violence are most often directed against the occupying power not by the occupied State's armed forces, but by organized armed groups not formally 'belonging to' it within the meaning of international humanitarian law. This poses the question of when the conduct of hostilities paradigm is considered to have been triggered. It may be argued that the requisite threshold is that of non-international armed conflict (organization of the group and the requisite level of violence), and that a separate non-international armed conflict may thus exist in occupied territory in addition to hostilities within an international armed conflict.

As mentioned above, the legal and practical issues related to the use of force in occupied territory are many and constitute a work in progress. In 2008 and 2009 the ICRC organized three expert meetings devoted to examining different aspects of the legal framework governing occupation.[123]

---

[122] 'Report on the ICRC Project on Occupation and Other Forms of Administration of Foreign Territory, Third Meeting: Use of Force in Occupied Territory', Geneva, 29–30 October 2009, T. Ferraro (ed.), ICRC, 2011, forthcoming (on file with the author).

[123] A report summarizing the experts' discussions was not issued at the time of writing.

4.3. Use of force under human rights law

Among all the areas that are regulated by both international humanitarian law and human rights law the greatest differences, it is submitted, are found in the respective rules governing the use of force.

Human rights law was conceived to protect persons from abuse by the State and does not rely on the notion of the conduct of hostilities between parties to an armed conflict, but on law enforcement. The basic human rights norm is that everyone has the inherent right to life and that no one may be 'arbitrarily' deprived of life.[124] Rules on the use of force in law enforcement essentially provide guidance on how life is to be protected when it is necessary to prevent crime, to effect or assist in the lawful arrest of offenders or suspected offenders and to maintain public order and security. They are not treaty based, but contained in soft law, the interpretations of human rights bodies at the international level and in jurisprudence, which is not uniform across the regional human rights systems. Outlined below in summary form are some relevant principles drawn from the Basic Principles on the Use of Force and Firearms by Law Enforcement Officials,[125] a soft law instrument that arguably reflects customary law.

The basic principle enunciated in that instrument is that law-enforcement officials shall in carrying out their duty, as far as possible, apply non-violent means before resorting to the use of force and firearms. They may use force and firearms only if other means remain ineffective or without any promise of achieving the intended result. Whenever the lawful use of force and firearms is unavoidable, law-enforcement officials shall, inter alia: 1) exercise restraint in such use and act in proportion to the seriousness of the offence and the legitimate objective to be achieved; and 2) minimize damage and injury, and respect and preserve human life. Where injury or death is caused by the use of force and firearms by law-enforcement officials, they must report the incident promptly to their superiors.

Law-enforcement officials may not use firearms against persons except:

- 'in self-defence or defence of others against the imminent threat of death or serious injury,
- to prevent the perpetration of a particularly serious crime involving grave threat to life,
- to arrest a person presenting such a danger and resisting their authority, or
- to prevent his or her escape',

and may do so 'only when less extreme means are insufficient to achieve these objectives'.[126] In any event, intentional lethal use of firearms may only be made when strictly unavoidable in order to protect life.

---

[124] ICCPR, art. 6(1).
[125] Basic Principles on the Use of Force and Firearms by Law Enforcement Officials (1990) (Basic Principles on the Use of Force).
[126] Basic Principles on the Use of Force, principle 9.

In any case where the use of firearms might be necessary as described above, law-enforcement officials must identify themselves as such and give a clear warning of their intent to use firearms. They must leave sufficient time for the warning to be observed, unless to do so would unduly place the law-enforcement officials at risk or would create a risk of death or serious harm to other persons, or would be clearly inappropriate or pointless in the circumstances of the incident.

Governments and law-enforcement agencies must establish effective reporting and review procedures for all incidents in which law-enforcement officials use firearms in the performance of their duty, or where injury or death is caused by the use of force and firearms by law-enforcement officials. Persons affected by the use of force and firearms or their legal representatives must have access to an independent process, including a judicial process. In the event of the death of such persons, this provision applies to their dependants.

The bottom line, as regards the use of lethal force under law-enforcement principles governed by human rights law is that lethal force may be used only as a last resort, when other means are ineffective or without promise of achieving the intended result (but such means must always be available). Human rights jurisprudence has clarified that a 'strict' or 'absolute' necessity standard is attached to any use of lethal force, meaning that it may not exceed what is strictly or absolutely necessary to maintain, restore or otherwise impose law and order in the particular circumstances.[127] The use of lethal force is also subject to a proportionality requirement under which 'it would not be permissible to use lethal force if the harm expected to result may be regarded as disproportionate compared to the gravity of the threat or offence to be removed'.[128]

It may be concluded that the logic and criteria governing the use of lethal force under a human rights law-based law-enforcement paradigm differ significantly from the logic and rules on the conduct of hostilities under international humanitarian law due to the different circumstances for which the respective norms are intended. The key issue therefore is the interplay of these bodies of law in situations of armed conflict. Needless to say, the answer is much clearer in international than in non-international armed conflict and turns on the issue of *lex specialis*.

In its very first statement on the application of human rights in situations of armed conflict, the International Court of Justice in the 1996 *Advisory Opinion on the Legality of the Threat or Use of Nuclear Weapons*, observed that the protection of the ICCPR:

> does not cease in times of war, except by operation of Article 4 of the Covenant whereby certain provisions may be derogated from in time of national emergency. Respect for the right to life is not, however, such a provision. In principle, the right not arbitrarily to be deprived of one's life applies also in hostilities. The test of what is an arbitrary deprivation of life, however, then falls to be determined by the applicable *lex*

---

[127] N. Melzer, *Targeted Killing in International Law* (2008) 228. Melzer provides an outline of the 'qualitative', 'quantitative' and 'temporal' elements of the strict necessity standard based on human rights jurisprudence (idem) (Melzer, *Targeted Killing*).

[128] Melzer, *Targeted Killing* 232.

specialis, namely, the law applicable in armed conflict which is designed to regulate the conduct of hostilities. Thus whether a particular loss of life, through the use of a certain weapon in warfare, is to be considered an arbitrary deprivation of life contrary to Article 6 of the Covenant, can only be decided by reference to the law applicable in armed conflict and not be deduced from the terms of the Covenant itself.[129]

In its *Advisory Opinion on the Legal Consequences of the Construction of a Wall in the Occupied Palestinian Territory*[130] the Court made a broader statement about the interplay of human rights law and international humanitarian law, reiterating that the latter is the *lex specialis* to the general law of human rights. While the Court did not refer to international humanitarian law as *lex specialis* in the relevant part of its 2005 judgment in the *Case Concerning Armed Activities on the Territory of the Congo*,[131] it is not clear whether this omission is of great significance (as some legal experts believe). The facts as determined by the Court involved massive violations of both international humanitarian law and human rights, which is simply what the Court confirmed.

Whatever the case may be, it is submitted that international humanitarian law constitutes the *lex specialis* governing the assessment of the lawfulness of the use of force in an international armed conflict—when, of course, lethal force is resorted to against combatants and other persons directly participating in hostilities. This body of rules was specifically designed for such conflicts and regulates the use of force in sufficient detail. Attacks against legitimate military targets, including personnel, in combat operations can hardly be based on law-enforcement standards, namely the duty to attempt arrest before force is used. Some challenges inherent to situations of occupation have already been mentioned above. It should be noted that an attempt to carve out rules for 'targeted killings' in the specific context of occupation—merging conduct of hostilities and some law-enforcement standards—was made by the Israeli Supreme Court in its judgment in the *Targeted Killing* case.[132] Another fact pattern involving the killing of six Iraqi civilians, each in different circumstances, by UK forces during the occupation of Iraq was ruled on in 2011 by the European Court of Human Rights.[133] While the *Al-Skeini* case established important principles regarding the extraterritorial reach of the European Convention for States parties, it did not address the substantive interplay of international humanitarian law and human rights law regarding the use of force (which was at issue in four out of the six cases). This is because no applicant alleged a substantive breach of the right to life under article 2 of the Convention in the particular circumstances.[134]

---

[129] *Legality of the Threat or Use of Nuclear Weapons* (Advisory Opinion) ICJ Rep 1996, 226, para 25.

[130] *Wall* Advisory Opinion, para 106.

[131] *Congo v Uganda*, para 216.

[132] *The Public Committee against Torture in Israel v The Government of Israel*, High Court of Justice, HCJ 769/02 (13 December 2006).

[133] *Al-Skeini and others v The United Kingdom* (Judgment) App No. 55721/07 (7 July 2011) (*Al-Skeini*).

[134] The Court did determine that in five of the six cases the UK had not fulfilled its procedural duty to carry out an effective investigation into alleged violations of the right to life under art. 2 of the European Convention (*Al-Skeini*, paras 168–77).

The interplay of international humanitarian law rules and human rights standards on the use of force is less clear in non-international armed conflict for a range of reasons, only some of which can be briefly mentioned here.

- The first is the existence and operation of the *lex specialis* principle in non-international armed conflict. While a compelling case may be made for the application of rules on conduct of hostilities in international armed conflict (at least by those who believe that *lex specialis* is a useful concept, such as this author), the general lack of corresponding treaty rules in non-international armed conflict has led to views that there is no *lex specialis* and that human rights law fills the gap.[135] This position, however, overlooks the fact that the great majority of rules on the conduct of hostilities are customary in nature and are applicable regardless of conflict classification, as determined by the ICRC's Customary Law Study. Relevant international humanitarian law therefore exists and is being applied in practice.

- The issue of who may be targeted under international humanitarian law, i.e. how to interpret the rule that civilians are protected from direct attack unless and for such time as they take a direct part in hostilities, creates legal and practical uncertainty about how it should be applied in non-international armed conflict. It is hoped that the Interpretive Guidance on the Notion of Direct Participation in Hostilities might prove to be useful in providing the necessary legal clarity, but only time can tell. It is important to bear in mind that the Guidance deals with direct participation under an international humanitarian law lens only, without prejudice to other bodies of law, particularly human rights law, which may be concurrently applicable in a given situation.

- The jurisprudence of international human rights bodies and regional courts is not uniform in its approach to the relationship between international humanitarian law and human rights in general, including in respect of the scope of protection of the right to life in armed conflict. As already mentioned, the Human Rights Committee has made statements of a broad nature on the subject. In its General Comment No. 31, the Committee stated: 'As implied in general comment 29, the Covenant applies to situations of armed conflict to which the rules of international humanitarian law are applicable. While, in respect of certain Covenant rights, more specific rules of international humanitarian law may be specially relevant for purposes of the interpretation of Covenant rights, both spheres of law are complementary, not mutually exclusive.'[136] This may be read

---

[135] L. Doswald-Beck, 'The Right to Life in Armed Conflict: Does International Humanitarian Law Provide All the Answers?' (2006) 88(864) *International Review of the Red Cross* 903. ('Specific, clear and well-established rules of IHL can be considered to be *lex specialis*. However, where there is any kind of doubt, or where the rules are too general to provide all the answers, then human rights law will fill the gap, provided that this law is not incompatible with the overall fundamental aim and purpose of IHL. It is submitted that the human rights law relating to the right to life is suitable to supplement and interpret IHL rules relating to the use of force for non-international conflicts and occupation, as well as the law relating to civilians taking a "direct part in hostilities".')

[136] General Comment 31, para 11.

to mean that where a rule of international humanitarian law is *lex specialis* in non-international armed conflict, such as a rule on the conduct of hostilities, it does not derogate from the Covenant right, but rather must be consulted to determine whether that right has been violated.

- The Inter-American Commission's approach essentially follows the ICJ's views on the relationship between norms of the two bodies of law. The Commission has said that human rights law is not displaced by international humanitarian law during armed conflicts, but has acknowledged that in situations of armed conflict, international humanitarian law may serve as *lex specialis* in interpreting and applying international human rights instruments.[137]

- In contrast, the European Court of Human Rights has so far not enunciated an opinion on the relationship between these two bodies of law. It has consistently applied essentially law-enforcement rules to killings in non-international armed conflict, which suggests that it rejects international humanitarian law as the *lex specialis* in such situations (even though some of the principles invoked are clearly international humanitarian law-based). The Court's cases have mainly involved situations in which lethal force used in non-international armed conflict resulted in the deaths of persons not taking a direct part in hostilities, i.e. to situations in which the State party did not take sufficient precautions in attack.[138] Due to the facts, it could have reached the same conclusions on the (un)lawfulness of the planning and execution of the operations at issue whether it had applied international humanitarian law or human rights law. The real test of the Court's approach will be when it is confronted with a case that involves what would be deemed incidental but lawful civilian deaths under the laws of armed conflict, or the targeting of fighters in non-international armed conflict. The Court's finding could

---

[137] IACHR, 'Report on Terrorism and Human Rights' OEA/Ser.L/V/II.116 (22 October 2002) paras 57–62. (Para 61: 'In situations of armed conflict, both international human rights law and international humanitarian law apply. Nevertheless, the American Convention and other universal and regional human rights instruments were not designed specifically to regulate armed conflict situations and do not contain specific rules governing the use of force and the means and methods of warfare in that context. Accordingly, in situations of armed conflict, international humanitarian law may serve as *lex specialis* in interpreting and applying international human rights instruments. For example, both Article 4 of the American Convention and humanitarian law applicable to armed conflicts protect the right to life and, thus, prohibit summary executions in all circumstances. However, reference to Article 4 of the Convention alone may be insufficient to assess whether, in situations of armed conflicts, the right to life has been infringed. This is in part because the Convention is devoid of rules that either define or distinguish civilians from combatants and other military targets. Nor does the Convention specify the circumstances under which it is not illegal, in the context of an armed conflict, to attack a combatant or civilian or when civilian casualties as a consequence of military operations do not imply a violation of international law. Consequently, in such circumstances, one must necessarily look to and apply definitional standards and relevant rules of international humanitarian law as sources of authoritative guidance in the assessment of the respect of the inter-American Instruments in combat situations.')

[138] See e.g. *Isayeva, Yusupova and Bazayeva v Russia* (Judgment) App No. 57947/00 (24 February 2005); *Isayeva v Russia* (Judgment) App No. 57950/00 (24 February 2005); *Ergi v Turkey* (Judgment) App No. 23818/94 (28 July 1998).

potentially lead to incompatibility between the respective international humanitarian law and human rights rules. The fact that States parties to the ECHR have never invoked article 15 of that treaty—which allows no derogation from the right to life 'except in respect of deaths that result from lawful acts of war'—may well contribute to such a result.

- Last, but by no means least, is the issue of the legal framework applicable to the conduct of hostilities by non-state armed groups, whether against State armed forces or other such groups. What has been said above in relation to the application of human rights law to detention by organized armed groups is equally valid here and will not be repeated. What must, however, be noted is the almost complete lack of examination in the literature of the legal and practical effects of the possibly lopsided obligations of States and non-state armed groups in the use of lethal force. (The reason why this is absent in human rights case law is obvious). In consequence, many tough questions, including how the international humanitarian law principle of the equality of rights and obligations of the parties to a non-international armed conflict is to be maintained remain without a satisfactory answer.

What can be concluded from the above is that the use of lethal force by States in non-international armed conflict requires a case-by-case analysis of the interplay of the relevant international humanitarian law and human rights rules based on the specific facts. For States, the legal result reached will depend on the treaties they are party to, customary law and of course the relevant provisions of domestic law. Needless to say, political considerations will often have a considerable, if not decisive, effect on the legal reasoning adopted. It is also evident that in non-international armed conflict—as well as in international one—State armed forces must be trained to distinguish and switch between a war-fighting and a law-enforcement situation and be provided with clear rules of engagement on the use of force. As regards non-state armed groups, it is at least clear that they are bound by international humanitarian law.

5. Concluding remarks

The starting point of this chapter was that the existing categorization of conflict into international and non-international is sufficient to encompass existing and new types of armed conflict. There is no doubt that international armed conflict involves two or more States (or hostilities between a State and a movement of national liberation, an unlikely scenario nowadays). Rules of international humanitarian law governing detention and the use of force in international armed conflict are numerous and are for the most part, detailed enough to be considered the *lex specialis* applicable in international armed conflict. This does not imply that clarification of certain legal concepts or rules should not be undertaken but simply that, overall, the law contains no glaring gaps with respect to detention and the use of force that would make it inadequate for the reality it seeks to govern.

International humanitarian law applicable to non-international armed conflicts governs violence between State armed forces and organized non-state armed groups or between such groups themselves. Even though the typology of non-international armed conflicts is expanding, it is believed that these 'new' conflicts may be legally and practically folded into a non-international armed conflict classification. While it is evident that treaty-based rules governing detention and the use of force in non-international armed conflict are far less developed than the corresponding rules for international armed conflict, the identification of customary law rules has significantly facilitated the determination of what the existing law is. International humanitarian law rules on the use of force in both international and non-international armed conflict are thus fairly similar and seem to be broadly adequate to regulate hostilities in all types of non-international armed conflict, particularly since recommendations on interpreting the key notion of direct participation in hostilities have also been made. International humanitarian law norms governing certain aspects of detention are likewise generally known and accepted (treatment, conditions of detention, fair trial). What is lacking are clear rules on procedural safeguards for internment in non-international armed conflict that would both set out State and non-state armed group obligations and be realistically applicable in the varied circumstances in which deprivation of liberty takes place. It has been submitted that development of the law would be desirable.

The transfer of detainees between and within States involved in an armed conflict raises a multitude of legal challenges that are being identified as the practice evolves, particularly in non-international armed conflicts involving international forces operating in a host State. The basic rules are known, but their implementation on the ground remains a work in progress. Until broader international agreement can be reached, pragmatic solutions that respect both the rights of detainees and the capabilities of States must be sought.

The greatest legal and practical challenge identified in the chapter is the interplay of international humanitarian law and human rights law in armed conflict, especially in non-international armed conflicts. While a majority of the relevant rules of these branches of international law overlap and may be simultaneously applied, it has been submitted that significant differences nevertheless exist with respect to two issues: procedural safeguards for the internment of civilians and the use of force in armed conflict. The rules applicable under both regimes do not produce the same results and are not interchangeable because they were crafted for essentially different realities. As a result, an assessment of the lawfulness of the taking of life and internment in armed conflict is fraught with uncertainty and must be approached on a case-by-case basis.

The chapter also highlighted the fact that the ongoing legal debate on the interplay of international humanitarian law and human rights law and its effects on the conduct of States has for the most part ignored the non-state party to the non-international armed conflict equation. Given that this type of conflict is prevalent today and raises by far the most pressing humanitarian concerns, that omission can only be deemed glaring.

PART II

5

Northern Ireland 1968–1998

*Steven Haines**

1. Introduction

From the late 1960s, Northern Ireland, a part of the United Kingdom, experienced violent sectarian conflict between two rival communities, one largely Protestant and claiming loyalty to the British Crown, the other largely Roman Catholic and seeking a united republican Ireland. There had been outbreaks of violence before this, of course. Indeed, the history of sectarian motivated violence in the region has a history going back to the early seventeenth century, shortly after the Scottish king James VI assumed the crown of England as James I and both Scottish and English settlers were provided with land in the so-called Plantation of Ulster, displacing the indigenous Irish in the process. The sectarian dimension to the social division bound up with the majority Irish desire for independence developed into a running political sore. Although the division within Ireland affected the entire island, it became particularly focused on the north-eastern counties. In Ireland as a whole, the majority of the population was Catholic. In six of the nine counties of the north-eastern province of Ulster, however, a Protestant majority dominated. Eventually the division within Ireland produced both the Irish War of Independence (after which all but the Protestant-dominated six Ulster counties left the UK) and an Irish Civil War (which saw rival groups within the newly independent Irish Free State fighting over the acceptability of the very partition of the island that had brought it into being).

While those two early twentieth century wars would themselves be interesting case studies, they are simply a part of the historical background to this chapter, which is concerned with the most recent manifestation of sectarian and political violence in and about the six Ulster counties that remained in the UK following partition. They constitute what is now formally known as Northern Ireland, itself a constituent part of the UK.

* The author thanks Ben Brzezicki, Kristal Piñeros Medina, and Lena Borth for their research assistance in the preparation of this chapter.

The period covered by this chapter commenced with the outbreak of civil disturbances in Belfast and Londonderry in 1968, which led to the deployment of the British Army the following year. While a measure of violence continues, this chapter considers only the thirty years from 1968 to 1998 (often referred to as the 'Troubles'). The Good Friday Agreement of 1998 followed an initial 'ceasefire' declared by both the Provisional Irish Republican Army (PIRA) and Loyalist paramilitaries in 1994. The Agreement laid the foundations for the current set of political arrangements involving cross-sectarian devolved government based on an Assembly at Stormont (near Belfast) and a power-sharing executive. This was brokered by a process that involved the two communities in Northern Ireland (including the relevant non-state armed groups) and the governments in both London and Dublin. The arrangements represent a major achievement of Tony Blair's period as British Prime Minister but one that would not have been possible without cooperation from all quarters.[1]

While sectarian violence may remain a feature of life in Northern Ireland, it is much less intensive than it was. Periodic incidents of violence are dealt with by the Police Service of Northern Ireland (PSNI), which is itself a product of the peace process (replacing the Loyalist dominated and divisive Royal Ulster Constabulary (RUC) in 2001). The formal British military involvement in security operations lasted from 14 August 1969 to 31 July 2007 and the PSNI is no longer reliant on what is referred to in the UK's constitutional and administrative law (as well as its military doctrine) as 'military aid to the civil power' (MACP).[2]

The extent of military involvement and the numbers of casualties make it appropriate to consider whether or not the violence was such as to cross the threshold into armed conflict. Accordingly, this chapter analyses the security circumstances between 1968 and 1998 in order to establish whether or not an armed conflict occurred and, if so, how it should be categorized: as either non-international or international armed conflict. While this second issue may appear largely irrelevant, some consideration must be given to violent events beyond Northern Ireland, on the British mainland, in the Republic of Ireland, in Germany, the Netherlands, Belgium and Gibraltar.

The first section of this chapter gives a general description of the events that unfolded between 1968 and 1998 and starts with a brief description of the 'rival forces', both government and non-state actors, before moving on to provide a summary of the principal phases of the conflict. Following this essential background, it asks whether there was at any time an armed conflict in the Province and it discusses how this should be categorized if there was. It then addresses in turn the

---

[1] For an insider account of the Blair-led process see J. Powell, *Great Hatred, Little Room: Making Peace in Northern Ireland* (2008).

[2] UK Ministry of Defence, 'British Defence Doctrine' Joint Doctrine Publication 0-01 (2008) 3, A-1. Since 1998 the UK military doctrine dealing with Military Aid to Civil Authorities (MACA) tasking has undergone a substantial review prompted by the terrorist attacks on the US in 2001. The detailed categorization of military assistance has been altered as a result—see UK Ministry of Defence, 'Operations in the United Kingdom: The Defence Contribution to Resilience' Joint Doctrine Publication 02 (2007). Throughout the period that is the focus of this chapter domestic military counter-terrorist operations were a form of MACP, a sub-set of MACA, as previously defined.

application of force and detention. Finally, it deals with whether or not the existing rules of international humanitarian law are problematic and what consequences might have resulted from a difference in the way the conflict was categorized.

2. General summary of the conflict

Looking back on events stretching back over four decades, it is possible to analyse the period of hostilities and draw some conclusions about their course. One legal analyst (Colm Campbell) has divided the period into three: outbreak and militarization 1969–1976; criminalization 1977–1994; and transition 1995–2004.[3] The Army's own report on the Troubles describes: the early years 1969–1973; the later 1970s; the 1980s; and the 'long tail to the campaign' from 1990 onwards. Neither Campbell's nor the Army's chronological divisions proved entirely appropriate for the purposes of this chapter, however, and the events have been reviewed for their relevance to conflict threshold and categorization purposes. As a result, this chapter defines the periods as follows: civil disturbances 1968–1971; insurgency 1971–1974; terrorism 1975–1994; and conflict resolution 1994–1998.[4] Before discussing the events during those four periods, it will be useful briefly to describe the protagonists. In general terms there were three 'sides' to the conflict: the Security Forces; Republican groups; and Loyalist groups.

2.1. The rival forces

The principal protagonists during the armed hostilities were the Security Forces in Northern Ireland (SFNI) and the Provisional Irish Republican Army (PIRA);

---

[3] C. Campbell, '"Wars on Terror" and Vicarious Hegemons: the United Kingdom, International Law and the Northern Ireland Conflict' (2005) 54(2) *International and Comparative Law Quarterly* 326 (Campbell, *Wars on Terror*).

[4] Somewhat surprisingly, there is as yet no comprehensive account of the military campaign covering the 'Troubles' from start to finish (and relying on sources from all sides) that can be considered the standard reference. Fortunately, the account that follows can use information on facts and events that is generally available and which is not in dispute to an extent that has significance for this chapter. Statistics, in particular, are well-known and promulgated. A key and reliable source of such is the British Army's own final report of the military engagement; see UK Ministry of Defence, 'Operation Banner: An Analysis of Military Operations in Northern Ireland' Army Code 71842 (July 2006) (Operation Banner Report). Another source of facts and figures is P. Bew and G. Gillespie, *Northern Ireland: A Chronology of the Troubles 1968–1999* (1999) (Bew and Gillespie, *A Chronology*). Although full accounts are not available, there were several partial accounts published after the particularly intense periods of violence that occurred during the 1970s and the years immediately following. Examples from which the details for this historical section are drawn include R. Fisk, *The Point of No Return: The Strike Which Broke the British in Ulster* (1975) (Fisk, *The Point of No Return*); R. Evelegh, *Peacekeeping in a Democratic Society: The Lessons of Northern Ireland* (1978); D. Patrick, *Fetch Felix: The Fight Against the Ulster Bombers 1976–77* (1981); M. Dewar, *The British Army in Northern Ireland* (1985); D. Hamill, *Pig in the Middle: The Army in Northern Ireland 1969–1984* (1985). A more recent work is M. Mulholland, *The Longest War: Northern Ireland's Troubled History* (2002) (Mulholland, *The Longest War*). The standard work on the Irish Republican Army is T.P. Coogan, *The I.R.A.* (2000) (Coogan, *IRA*), but see also R. English, *Armed Struggle: The History of the IRA* (2003).

other non-state organized armed groups were also involved, both Republican and Loyalist.

2.1.1 The Security Forces in Northern Ireland (SFNI)

The Security Forces combined the RUC and the Armed Forces. The latter was principally, but not exclusively, the regular British Army.[5] A locally raised militia, known for much of the Troubles as the Ulster Defence Regiment (UDR), was formally a part of the Army but was exclusively deployed within Northern Ireland; it was formed early during the Troubles for purely internal security purposes. In 1992, the UDR merged with the Royal Irish Rangers to become the Royal Irish Regiment, with the former UDR battalions remaining restricted operationally to a security role within Northern Ireland and designated as a 'Home Service Force'.

While the bulk of the regular Armed Forces' units were barracked or deployed within secure bases, individual members of the RUC and UDR lived within their communities and were, as a consequence, extremely vulnerable to attack. This was especially true of reserve or part-time members of each, who also worked in their civilian jobs within the community. A milkman doing his rounds, a farmer working in the fields, a social worker visiting a family on a housing estate—all also reserve or part-time RUC or UDR—were easy 'soft' targets for the terrorists. Two hundred and four UDR/Royal Irish Regiment soldiers were killed during the Troubles, for example, 162 of whom (about 80 per cent) were off duty at the time they were killed.

In 1969, when armed hostilities broke out, there were only three battalions of regular infantry based in Northern Ireland. Three years later, in 1972 and at the height of the campaign, however, the Army deployed almost 30,000 troops. Approaching 300,000 regular members of the British armed forces served in Northern Ireland during the Troubles; over 600 were killed. In 1972 alone, well over a hundred British armed forces' personnel were killed in Northern Ireland. With the notable exception of the almost 300 killed in the Falklands War in 1982, in no year since 1972 have the numbers of British fatalities in conflict reached the level in that year; annual fatalities in neither Iraq nor Afghanistan have reached those levels. During the early 1970s it was not uncommon for 10,000 soldiers to be deployed on the streets of Belfast and Londonderry. Significantly, those figures do not include additional UDR soldiers, the regiment at its largest consisting of eleven battalions deployed across Northern Ireland (although not in West Belfast, Republican areas of Londonderry or the so-called 'bandit country' of South Armagh). Tens of thousands of local men and women donned UDR or Royal Irish Regiment uniform at some point during the 37-year campaign. If one adds to total numbers

---

[5] Although frequently included in statistics as a part of the Army, the Royal Marines are a part of the Royal Navy, which also ran coastal security and anti-gun running patrols around the coast and in Carlingford Lough on the southern border with the Republic, and provided most of the support helicopter cover. The RAF also provided helicopter support, with RAF Regiment units guarding Aldergrove Airport and providing battalion-size formations as an occasional input to the infantry battalion plot.

of regular Armed Forces and UDR personnel the figures for the RUC when hostilities were at their most intense in the 1970s, there were upwards of 50,000 SFNI personnel available in the Province to maintain internal security in a territory with a population of approximately one and a half million.[6]

2.1.2 Republican groups

At the start of the period under review, the IRA numbered no more than about 120 active members. Numbers increased during the first three years of the Troubles and in both 1972 and 1973 the total was well over 2000. The Army's Operation Banner Report estimates that about 10,000 people were involved in some way in the IRA between 1969 and 1972.[7] The IRA's poor showing in the days of rioting in August 1969 led to serious infighting within the organization and the emergence of two distinct IRA factions known as the 'Officials' and the 'Provisionals'.

The Officials (OIRA) were ideologically Marxist but with a leadership which did not generally favour violent action. Indeed, although the vast majority of OIRA members and supporters were Catholic Nationalists, a significant element of its leadership wished to appeal across the communities to achieve a degree of bi-sectarian working-class solidarity. Nevertheless, in the months following August 1969, they did resort to a limited violent campaign. This was relatively short-lived, however, and came to an effective end with the OIRA's declared ceasefire in 1972. That ceasefire was not uncontroversial within the OIRA and some of its membership caused a further split, forming the Irish National Liberation Army (INLA) in 1974.

In contrast to the Marxist inspired OIRA and INLA, PIRA was fundamentally an Irish nationalist group and, while arguably predominantly socialist in its political orientation, was by no means in tune with the OIRA's Marxist ideological position. Politically it was far closer to the mainstream Nationalist communities from which it drew its not inconsiderable support. PIRA asserted itself as the defender of those Nationalist communities and committed itself to waging a war on their behalf, if such proved necessary. What it was anxious to avoid was any criticism of the kind to which the pre-split IRA had been subjected following the August 1969 riots. It was PIRA that became the principal Nationalist or Republican paramilitary organiza-tion and which waged the most prominent violent campaign against the British authorities and Loyalist institutions through the period. It rapidly became a highly professional, extremely effective, well-led and well-organized irregular fighting force with a hierarchical military structure and clear, well-disciplined, lines of command. The SFNI experienced severe difficulty throughout the various phases of the Troubles containing PIRA's activities. It was linked to Sinn Fein, which was widely

---

[6] Clearly this does not imply that there were at times as many as 50,000 actually on foot patrol or similar within the Province. Within those numbers were those off duty, those taking meal breaks, preparing for deployment, etc., as well as those in largely support functions (e.g. Army personnel deployed to maintain vehicles and other equipment). Nevertheless, the numbers were substantial relative to the population of the region.

[7] Operation Banner Report, 3-2.

regarded as its 'political wing', something both PIRA and Sinn Fein preferred to deny.

Although the INLA also remained a serious paramilitary threat from 1974 onwards, neither it nor its own 'political wing', the Irish Republican Socialist Party (IRSP), could at any point be regarded as representative of a politically significant proportion of the Nationalist community. Through much of the course of the Troubles, the majority of the Nationalist community in fact supported the moderate—and certainly non-violent—Social Democratic Labour Party (SDLP). Others, while preferring non-violence, still supported Sinn Fein through the ballot box, especially in areas in which the party could deliver some tangible community benefit. Even though not all Sinn Fein voters were actively enthusiastic PIRA sympathizers, support for the 'paramilitary wing' within the Nationalist communities in the two cities of Belfast and Londonderry and in the predominantly rural border areas was more than sufficient to sustain it in the conduct of its persistent violent campaign through three decades.

Further 'IRA' splits occurred later during the period. The so-called Real IRA, for example, a group of PIRA members opposed to a negotiated settlement, was responsible for the Omagh bombing on 15 August 1998. That bomb killed twenty-nine innocent shoppers in the main street of the town. A further 220 were injured. It attracted horror and outrage, both within Northern Ireland and internationally and resulted in both the Real IRA and the INLA declaring ceasefires.[8] Indeed, while it is arguably distasteful to put it in such terms, the Omagh bombing had the positive consequence that it solidified support for a negotiated settlement.

2.1.3 Loyalist groups

Although there were a number of Loyalist paramilitary organizations ('a bewildering array' to quote the Army's Operation Banner Report[9]), the hostilities were not regarded as being between those groups and PIRA. While the Ulster Defence Association (UDA), formed out of a ragbag collection of local vigilante groups in the early months of the Troubles, had over 2000 members at its peak, neither it nor any of the other extremist Loyalist groups was as organized or effective as PIRA. Apart from surprising, albeit brief, outbreaks of violence against the SFNI, Loyalist paramilitaries' activities were mostly confined to terrorizing the Nationalist community (or, indeed, their own), running what were essentially criminal enterprises involved in extortion, the running of protection rackets and other forms of serious crime, much of it targeted on, and to the profound disadvantage of, the Loyalist community itself. Some of the members of such groups as the UDA, the Ulster Volunteer Force (UVF) and the Red Hand Commando (RHC) were extremely violent, ruthless and profoundly dangerous, but in terms of their ability to achieve—or even pursue—any serious politico-military objective, they were comprehensively ineffective. Essentially, they were no

---

[8] See Coogan, *IRA*, 704–06.   [9] Operation Banner Report, 3-3.

more than disparate collections of criminal thugs. Despite their contribution to the overall level of violence, they are not discussed in this chapter since they need not be considered as participants in the hostilities in Northern Ireland between PIRA and the UK authorities.

2.2. Civil disturbances 1968–1971

To say that Northern Ireland was, by the mid-1960s, divided along sectarian lines is to understate the situation. To use simple but largely accurate descriptions, Protestants were Loyalists, they were principally descended from Scots planter families, they were the best educated, they were economically better off and they tended to dominate the professional classes. In contrast, Republicans (also referred to as Nationalists) were Catholic, descended from indigenous Irish families, were less well-educated and were economically disadvantaged, with relatively few achieving senior professional positions within Northern Ireland. These communities, while they were spread generally across Northern Ireland, were largely ghettoized in the two major cities of Belfast and Londonderry, which were profoundly divided societally, and in rural areas, most notably South Armagh, the population of which was almost entirely Republican.

The coterminous nature of the societal cleavages exacerbated political divisions and resulted in a genuine feeling of deprivation within the Catholic Republican communities. Not only were they significantly opposed to partition, they were also incensed by a combination of economic deprivation and serious concerns to do with civil rights. Indeed, it was the civil rights issue that provided the catalyst leading to violent conflict in 1968, a year which, incidentally, saw riots and civil action across Europe often compared with the 1848 'year of revolutions'. It also coincided with mass demonstrations in the United States prompted by opposition to the Vietnam War. The year 1968 was a major year of protest internationally; deprived Catholic Republicans in Northern Ireland needed very little prompting to join in.

The civil rights protests that took place in 1967 and subsequently were largely inspired and organized by the Northern Ireland Civil Rights Association (NICRA). Its campaign was peaceful and based on similar principles to the Civil Rights Movement led by Martin Luther King in the US. A civil rights march was organized by NICRA in Londonderry in October 1968 and further marches took place in early 1969, all prompting violent Loyalist responses. Tensions between the rival communities had been rising steadily from 1967 onwards. What came to be seen as the eventual spark that ignited armed hostilities was the so-called 'battle of the Bogside' in August 1969 (the Bogside being a Nationalist and profoundly deprived area of Londonderry). This was not, however, prompted by a civil rights march but by the annual planned march of the Loyalist Apprentice Boys whose route took them past the Nationalist Bogside. Rioting between Loyalists and Nationalists broke out on 12 August. The RUC was deployed with reinforcements from across Northern Ireland but, given their predominantly Protestant membership, were seen by the Nationalists as siding with Loyalist rioters. After two days of intense rioting, the British and Northern Ireland governments agreed to the deployment of the British Army to restore order.

These events in Londonderry sparked off violent sectarian riots across Northern Ireland, in particular in Belfast, Newry and Strabane. In Belfast, a stray RUC bullet killed a nine-year-old Catholic child in a room in the Divis Flats. During the riots in Belfast, eight were killed and over 700 injured. A great many Nationalist families were also forced out of their homes. In these circumstances, the intervention by the British Army in August of 1969 was initially seen as very positive by Nationalist communities threatened by Loyalist rioters but with absolutely no confidence in the RUC to protect them. Soldiers were welcomed onto the streets and famously provided with mugs of tea by members of the Nationalist Catholic communities. At the same time, those communities were strongly critical of the IRA which was perceived as having done almost nothing to protect them from Loyalist attacks, prompting the assertion by many Nationalists that 'IRA' stood for 'I Ran Away'.

The situation that saw the British Army welcomed and the IRA castigated by the Nationalist communities was brief indeed, however. The Army had the extremely difficult task of remaining strictly neutral between the rival Nationalist and Loyalist communities: arguably impossible, given the ultimate aims of the two sides and the Army's clear association with 'British Rule'. In very short order, the Army found itself the focus of increasing hostility from the Nationalist communities it had originally been deployed to protect.

The two or three years from 1968 were marked by serious civil unrest, especially within the working class urban areas of Belfast and Londonderry. The marches and protests mounted by the two rival communities had the appearance of an uncontrolled and unsystematic descent into emotional sectarian violence. At the outset the IRA was too small and disorganized seriously to undermine internal security. Nevertheless, the IRA and its two rival factions, the OIRA and PIRA, eventually took advantage of the situation to expand membership and intensify activities. The circumstances were conducive to this. PIRA in particular re-established itself in this period as the principal 'defender' of Nationalist communities (after the pre-split IRA's embarrassing showing in 1969). In retrospect it is possible to identify this period as one of PIRA recruitment and development against a backdrop of increasing Nationalist community support for its aims and objectives. PIRA was greatly assisted in its development by the SFNI's actions in response to sectarian violence. During an operation in July 1970, for example, 3000 troops enforced a curfew in the Falls Road area, the Nationalist ghetto in West Belfast. Well over a thousand rounds of ammunition were fired as the Army fought with PIRA insurgents. Four people were killed. Later that year the first British soldier was killed. What had started as civil disturbances was becoming something more intensive.

2.3. Insurgency 1971–1974

By early 1971, PIRA had successfully established itself to the point at which its leadership felt able to launch an all out campaign against the British forces deployed in Northern Ireland. PIRA commenced its overt attacks on the Army and executed an insurgency campaign under cover of the violent sectarian riots that continued unabated.

Targeted attacks on the Security Forces increased through the early stages of that year. In response, the British and Stormont governments decided to introduce a policy of internment, something that had worked in previous periods of IRA activity, in particular in the late 1950s. On 9 August the Army mounted Operation Demetrius and detained 350 Nationalists on suspicion of IRA involvement. Unfortunately, because of an inadequate intelligence picture, many of these had little or nothing to do with the IRA (either PIRA or OIRA) when they were detained. Their internment, however, prompted significant numbers to join and become active in the organization of which they had been falsely accused of being members.

The following year, 1972, was undoubtedly the worst year for the SFNI. It started with the tragedy of Bloody Sunday in January. Fourteen people were killed in Londonderry when the Army became embroiled in a disastrous response to a civil rights march. In the course of that year over 100 British soldiers were killed by PIRA, with 500 others wounded in concerted attacks throughout Northern Ireland. PIRA also commenced a similarly concerted bombing campaign, principally against commercial targets. Well over 1000 bombs were exploded, with substantial 'collateral' civilian casualties. On 21 July a total of twenty-two bombs were detonated in Belfast city centre, killing seven civilians and two soldiers. This increase in PIRA's armed activity actually prompted the OIRA seriously to review its own involvement. The result was the OIRA decision to withdraw itself from the campaign of armed violence and to announce the ceasefire which then remained in force.

Despite the OIRA ceasefire, the substantial increase in PIRA activity prompted a violent response from Loyalist paramilitaries. The UVF and the UDA began conducting assassinations of Nationalists. Their targeting was crude, to say the least. It seemed that almost any Catholic was at risk, an approach which demonstrated very clearly the inadequacies of the Loyalist paramilitaries' ability to wage a focused campaign with precise objectives. There also took place a progressive process of what one might describe as 'ethnic cleansing', with both Catholics and Protestants driven from their homes in previously mixed residential areas in which they found themselves to be in a minority. The combination of public unrest and paramilitary activity continued—indeed, increased—to such an extent that the British Government concluded that the Northern Ireland administration had completely lost control of internal security. Direct Rule was imposed from London, intended as a temporary measure pending the creation of some form of government that would be acceptable to both sides of the sectarian divide.

In the five months from March to July 1972, there were over 6000 shooting incidents in Northern Ireland, almost 3000 in July alone. The PIRA was operating extremely effectively as an insurgent force. Nevertheless, the security situation across Northern Ireland was not uniformly serious. The violence was concentrated in particular areas of Belfast and Londonderry and in predominantly Nationalist rural areas. Security Forces' personnel were under serious threat in, for example, West Belfast and yet it was entirely possible for off-duty soldiers and police to enjoy a quiet night out in a pub just a few miles away, in towns like Bangor. This contributed to the impression that certain high-risk areas were under the effective control of PIRA. It was certainly true that the risks to the SFNI were extremely high in the areas of Nationalist concentration like West Belfast and the Bogside in Londonderry. It would be too easy, however, to conclude that these areas were effectively under the exclusive control of PIRA. The Army maintained a presence in them throughout the insurgency. If the authorities wished to assert their predominance, they merely moved in, a development that PIRA was never in a position effectively to prevent. At no point was it necessary for the Army to conduct sustained and high-intensity urban warfare in order to gain access to the high-risk areas. On the other hand, it would be going too far to claim that the Army was in complete control; it was not.[10] Faced with this conundrum, the authorities decided to mount a major operation to break the insurgency and establish control. To do this, however, it needed to reinforce the SFNI with units from the mainland UK and the British Army of the Rhine (BAOR).

In the early hours of 31 July 1972 the Army launched Operation Motorman in Belfast and Londonderry. With substantial reinforcements, including forces landed from Royal Navy amphibious shipping, a total of 28,000 troops moved into the high-risk areas. To quote the Army's Op Banner Report:

> The operation was launched at 0400 hours on Monday 31 July when an outer cordon was set up around the cities. The Bogside and Creggan estates in Londonderry and the Andersonstown and Ballymurphy estates in Belfast were sealed off and troops moved in to clear the barricades. All areas were secured by 0700 hours with no security force casualties and two terrorist fatalities in Londonderry.[11]

The operation lasted until 1 December, with large numbers of PIRA volunteers rounded up and interned. It effectively halted the PIRA insurgency and set the scene for further successes in the months that followed. In the second half of 1973, for example, 1798 members of PIRA were arrested, including one 'brigade commander' and eight 'battalion commanders'.

The final months of 1973 and through 1974 was a period during which a process aimed at achieving some measure of political settlement was pursued. The result was the Sunningdale Agreement. As part of that process, a significant number of internees (including many that had been rounded up during Motorman and its aftermath) were released. Unfortunately, the Loyalist community was opposed to the Agreement and in 1974 mounted the Ulster Workers' Council strike;[12] the Executive collapsed and the Nationalist community regarded this as further evidence of the Loyalists' intransigence; the insurgency began to re-emerge. PIRA

---

[10] For a flavour of the challenges the Army faced at street level, see General Sir R. Dannatt, *Leading from the Front: The Autobiography* (2010) 37–48.

[11] Operation Banner Report, 2–10.

[12] This was well reported in Fisk, *The Point of No Return*.

attempted what was in effect an offensive in the summer of 1974, but between June and August over 600 PIRA members were again arrested. With that level of attrition, the organization was forced to rethink its whole approach. Its decision was to implement an internal reorganization, by establishing a cellular structure, the intention being to ensure its own security. In 1975 PIRA announced a ceasefire, largely to go through the process of regrouping in this way.

Following that reorganization, PIRA ceased being effectively capable of mounting a traditional insurgency, however. The active service units intentionally operated independently. Insurgency would have required greater numbers of 'volunteers' to operate together in concerted attacks on the Security Forces. The need for organizational security effectively undermined its ability to operate as an insurgent force. The cellular structure was an advantage for an organization operating in very low-intensity situations in which covert action and operational confidentiality were important, but it is not clear whether PIRA willingly resorted to its new organizational structure or adopted it reluctantly as a necessary reaction to internment and the British counter-insurgency approach. Nor is it clear whether PIRA subsequently resorted to terrorism because it was the only way it could then mount a violent campaign against British rule, or whether PIRA deliberately set out to become an effective terrorist organization because its leadership believed that this would be the best way of achieving its long-term strategic goal of British withdrawal. If the latter is true, the reorganization was a great success, paving the way for PIRA to become an extremely successful terrorist group by the later 1970s capable of sustaining a campaign indefinitely and remaining a constant challenge for the British government. Whatever the truth of the matter, the consequence of PIRA's approach was that general insurgency stopped after 1974.

2.4. Terrorism 1975–1994

In late 1975 PIRA abandoned its ceasefire and commenced once again its attacks on the Security Forces. From October to December that year it killed seventeen members of the SFNI and wounded a further fifty-seven. Its attacks were fewer than had previously been the case during the full insurgency phase but they were selective and effectively carried through. Although many of the PIRA 'volunteers' were known to the SFNI, the ending of internment meant that they could only be detained if there was sufficient evidence to pursue a criminal prosecution. In most cases this was simply not available or was based on intelligence, the sources of which were too sensitive to be revealed in the process of criminal prosecution. Although there was a view that internment had been a successful element of the counter-insurgency strategy, especially when coupled with Op Motorman, and it was frustrating for members of the SFNI to be able to identify PIRA activists but not be able to detain them, in the longer term the benefit of departing from this approach was that it served to establish the rule of law in Northern Ireland and reduced the numbers of new recruits to the terrorists' cause. Internment had enhanced the ability of PIRA to recruit the numbers necessary for the insurgency.

Abandoning it meant that recruitment was never again to be stimulated by its negative impact on the Nationalist community; that effectively prevented the development of the sort of organization that could easily revert to insurgency in the future since there were simply not enough 'volunteers' to mount such a campaign.

From the mid-1970s onwards the principal British approach was to contain the terrorists and to keep their activities to a sufficiently low level that life in Northern Ireland could continue to a reasonable degree. While suggestions that there had been established a so-called 'acceptable level of violence' were understandably controversial, the fact was that in large swathes of the six counties normal life did carry on and the communities in general settled into an uneasy acceptance of the situation in which they found themselves. This was especially the case outside the ghettos of Belfast and Londonderry and away from the predominantly Nationalist populated border areas. Those areas certainly remained high risk for the SFNI, but they were far from being genuinely 'no-go areas'.[13]

From time to time major incidents seemed to reflect the level of violence during the insurgency. The annual 'marching season' was always a tense time in public order terms. From time to time PIRA demonstrated that it was more than capable of mounting major operations against the SFNI and other symbols of British 'occupation'.[14] But the major terrorist incidents, although far too frequent, were by no means a daily, weekly or even monthly occurrence, nor were they ubiquitous within Northern Ireland. PIRA did take the campaign to mainland Britain where the targets were softer and their activities were more difficult to monitor and predict. The problem also spread to the continent with servicemen and women serving with the British forces in Germany subject to attack. Importantly, however, the terrorist campaign was never of a nature that seriously undermined the government's determination not to 'give in to terrorism'. Neither side in the terrorism/counter-terrorism relationship seemed able fully to succeed in its aims.

Given the extent to which the rival communities were affected by the security situation, eventually there emerged the potential for some sort of political process. Other factors made such a development more likely. In the 1990s, tentative talks commenced between the government and PIRA which led to the latter's ceasefire in 1994. The PIRA leadership, realizing that terrorism alone would not carry the day, had adopted a dual approach, combining terrorist violence with legitimate political activity through the involvement of Sinn Fein in local government within

[13] The so-called 'no-go areas' became something of a myth that some assumed meant PIRA effectively held the ground and that the SFNI simply could not venture into them; this was never the case. See e.g. Campbell, *Wars on Terror*, 329.

[14] E.g. the 'Warrenpoint Bombing' on 27 August 1979 when 18 soldiers were killed in a brilliantly executed double bombing attack (on the same day that Lord Mountbatten was assassinated at his holiday home in the Republic). The author assumed responsibility for running all naval operations within the SFNI on that day. A mixed unit of Royal Marines and Royal Navy sailors operating in Warrenpoint Docks were the first response team on the scene of the bombing after the first bomb exploded and before the second was detonated.

Nationalist communities. By the mid-1990s Northern Ireland was also experiencing a developing economy which meant that the appalling deprivation within the working-class communities was giving way to relative affluence. That led to those communities seeking to enjoy better fortune and served to persuade PIRA and Sinn Fein leaderships to seek an alternative to all out hostility. From the time of the 1994 PIRA ceasefire, Northern Ireland was experiencing what might be referred to as the post-conflict peace-building phase, with negotiations between the parties, at first tentative and in secret but eventually conducted in a wave of publicity, especially during the negotiations that led to the Good Friday Agreement in 1998. Arguably the policy of never negotiating with terrorists (particularly associated with Prime Minister Margaret Thatcher, who had so nearly been the victim of a PIRA bomb at the Conservative Party's annual conference in Brighton in 1984) was an important and vital part of the process that drove PIRA into negotiations and to consider a ceasefire. Eventually, however, the government had to negotiate with those who were still engaged in terrorism in order to bring it to a conclusion.

2.5. Conflict resolution 1994–1998

In 1994 PIRA declared a ceasefire and coupled this with a decision to pursue its objectives by principally political means. Effective conflict resolution commenced with initial talks between the PIRA leadership and the Conservative government in London led by John Major. These were seen as less than successful by PIRA and, in 1996, it revoked its ceasefire, bombing Canary Wharf in London and injuring 200 in a bombing in Manchester. The last British soldier killed in Northern Ireland died in February 1997 but this was followed five months later by the final PIRA ceasefire in the wake of the change of government in London. Further talks then involved British Prime Minister Tony Blair, the Irish Taoiseach and the leaders of all the Northern Ireland political parties, including most notably Gerry Adams and Martin McGuiness of Sinn Fein and Ian Paisley of the Democratic Unionist Party, a consequence of which was the marginalization of the more moderate Northern Ireland political parties (essentially the SDLP and the Official Unionists). The talks also involved a number of international figures who became significantly influential in the peace process, including US President Bill Clinton and his envoy George Mitchell, former Finnish President Martti Artisaari and Canadian General John de Chastelain. The formal result was the Good Friday Agreement of 1998, with a power-sharing solution that saw both Republicans and Loyalists cooperating in a joint administration for Northern Ireland. While violence was not completely over, the security situation and general tenor of life in Northern Ireland had, been transformed by this political process.

3. Classification of the hostilities

3.1. Views of the parties and others on classification

3.1.1 The United Kingdom

The British government at no point formally acknowledged that the violence generated by PIRA or any other non-state armed group reached the Common Article 3 threshold, preferring to stress the criminal nature of the organizations' activities and the ability of domestic measures to deal with the problem. The violence was criminalized by the government, which refused to see the State as part of the conflict.[15] The UK Home Secretary and the Prime Minister of Northern Ireland asserted in 1971 that the authorities were 'at war with the IRA' or with the terrorists.[16] Both of these comments by senior political figures can be regarded as evidence of resort to political hyperbole; they certainly did not appear to be considered comment intended to affect the legal classification of the situation within the Province. Indeed, when the Irish government had previously attempted to raise the issue within the UN in 1969, the UK Permanent Representative to the UN commented to the effect that the situation within the Province was entirely a UK domestic matter and not for consideration within the UN. Quoting article 2(7) of the UN Charter, he added: 'Events in Northern Ireland are . . . an internal matter for the United Kingdom Government. It is within the competence of the Government of the United Kingdom to restore and maintain order. That we are doing.'

It has been suggested to the author that various legal advisers working within the British government (in particular military lawyers within the Army) considered that the threshold of a Common Article 3 non-international armed conflict had been reached in the 1970s, but that view was not, of course, reflected in any official pronouncement made by the British government, which always formally asserted that the PIRA's activities were simply breaches of the criminal law.[17]

One interesting angle to investigate in this context is British policy and action in relation to the international process of developing the law of armed conflict. In 1974 the Diplomatic Conference on the Reaffirmation and Development of International Humanitarian Law in Armed Conflicts began the negotiations that would lead eventually to the signing of the two 1977 Protocols Additional to the 1949 Geneva Conventions, Protocol II of which dealt with non-international armed conflicts. The start date of the conference coincided with the end of what

---

[15] See e.g. discussion in C. Campbell, 'The Frontiers of Legal Analysis: Reframing the Transition in Northern Ireland' (2003) 66(3) *Modern Law Review* 338.

[16] Campbell, *Wars on Terror*, 325, quoting Mulholland, *The Longest War*, 92; and Bew and Gillespie, *A Chronology*, 36.

[17] Unattributable information provided to the author. See also 'Armed Conflicts and Parties to Armed Conflicts under IHL: Confronting Legal Categories to Contemporary Realities' (Autumn 2010) 40 *Collegium* 115, where mention is also made of this.

we have identified as the insurgency phase of the hostilities in Northern Ireland.[18] While the UK signed the protocols in 1977, it did not ratify until 1998, by which time the hostilities were reaching a conclusion. Ratification only became 'increasingly likely' after 1994, the year of the PIRA ceasefire.

3.1.2 PIRA

Early in the period, PIRA continued the long-held claim, dating from the Irish Civil War, that it was fighting a war of national liberation. The IRA had always sought the liberation of the whole of the island of Ireland. The acceptance by many Republicans of the Anglo-Irish Treaty in the 1920s was never recognized by the IRA. Indeed, it continued the armed struggle and, although it was defeated in the subsequent Irish Civil War, its members persisted in regarding themselves as the legitimate liberation movement, refusing to recognize the government in Dublin and believing the IRA Army Council to be the legitimate government of the whole of the island of Ireland. Following Gerry Adams' election as Sinn Fein leader in 1983, the combined movement of Sinn Fein and PIRA moved increasingly towards a political process and in 1986 it recognized the Dail (Irish Parliament) as legitimate, thus effectively ending any basis for a claim that PIRA was engaged in an international armed conflict with the British authorities. The only State that ever gave any support to PIRA's claim to be engaged in an international armed conflict was Libya.

3.1.3 Others

The Republic of Ireland was the most affected State and its response was potentially important. The government requested a meeting of the UN Security Council in August 1969 as civil disturbances were intensifying. It also requested that a UN peace-keeping force be deployed to the Province. When the Irish Foreign Minister subsequently addressed the Security Council in pursuit of this approach he made the point that the Republic did not regard the British presence in Northern Ireland as legitimate.[19] The suggestion may have been that Republicans in Northern Ireland were engaged in a struggle for national liberation, although no reference was made in the Foreign Minister's statement to a situation of armed conflict; instead he referred to 'the virtual collapse of the civil machinery of law and order'. Although the Republic was supported by the Soviet Union in their effort to put the matter on the Council's agenda, the Council meeting was adjourned and the matter went no further; the UK had been successful behind the scenes. The Republic then

---

[18] Campbell has noted that the decision to 'criminalize' the situation in Northern Ireland from 1974 onwards coincided with the start of the Diplomatic Conference. (Campbell, *Wars on Terror*, 329.) Although the dates match, it is not considered likely that British policy towards security in Northern Ireland was driven by such concerns.

[19] See Security Council meeting, S/PV.1503 (20 August 1969). See also E. Schwelb, 'Northern Ireland and the United Nations' (1970) 19(3) *International and Comparative Law Quarterly* 483 and Campbell, *Wars on Terror*, 329–30.

attempted to take the matter to the General Assembly, where its inclusion on a provisional agenda was once again blocked in the General Committee by reference to article 2(7) of the UN Charter and the argument that the situation in Northern Ireland was a purely internal matter.[20] After these brief attempts within the UN to raise the issue, the Republic then seemed to back away from further attempts to intervene.[21] One reason for the Republic's decision to do this, suggested informally to the author, was that the government had begun to realize that it was not in its own security interests to pursue this line.[22] From the mid-1970s onwards, the two States cooperated in security policy and operationally (although there was never any effective cross-border deployment in either direction, occasional accidental or unauthorized crossings notwithstanding). The Thatcher-Haughey agreement on cross-border security coordination was one example of this cooperation and, as various peace processes developed, including that in the early 1970s, there was increasing communication between London and Dublin. The reality was that the Irish government was as concerned about PIRA activity as was the British, and it was almost certainly concerned about the likely consequences if the island of Ireland were to become politically united, which would have included Dublin coping with a Loyalist revolt in the northern six counties.

Libya provided support to PIRA by periodically supplying it with arms. It would appear, however, that no State chose to make any formal statement about the status of the conflict in Northern Ireland. In correspondence with the Republic, the United States expressed the view prior to the 1969 attempt to inscribe the matter on the Security Council agenda that there was 'no appropriate basis to intervene with regard to the domestic situation or civil disturbances of other sovereign countries'.[23] While the absence of comment from some other States could be merely a form of cautious 'diplomatic silence', the clear fact is that no general view was expressed that Britain was engaged in a non-international armed conflict with PIRA.

As far as the International Committee of the Red Cross is concerned, there is no record of it ever having publicly stated its position on the categorization of the conflict. That is not to say that it was not engaged; it certainly was. The ICRC's annual reports in the early 1970s make reference to Northern Ireland and, in particular, focus on visits to detention facilities in the Province at the invitation of

---

[20] See e.g. discussion in Daniel C. Williamson 'Taking the Troubles across the Atlantic: Ireland's UN Initiatives and Irish-US Diplomatic Relations in the Early Years of the Conflict in Northern Ireland, 1969–72' (2007) 18 *Irish Studies in International Affairs* 175.

[21] The Irish approach to the UN commenced with a letter of 17 August 1969 signed by the Irish Permanent Representative to the UN, C.C. Cremin, which was followed by a note from the Foreign Minister, Patrick Hillery, on 18 August (letter dated 17 August 1969 from the Permanent Representative of Ireland addressed to the President of the Security Council, S/9394 and letter dated 18 August 1969 from the Minister for External Affairs of Ireland addressed to the President of the Security Council, S/9396).

[22] Unattributable information provided to the author by a former Irish legal official.

[23] Quoted in Daniel C. Williamson 'Taking the Troubles across the Atlantic: Ireland's UN Initiatives and Irish-US Diplomatic Relations in the Early Years of the Conflict in Northern Ireland, 1969–72' (2007) 18 *Irish Studies in International Affairs* 179.

the British government. For example, between 5 and 7 October 1971 an ICRC delegate and a medical practitioner visited Crumlin Road Prison in Belfast, Long Kesh Internment Camp near Lisburn, and Armagh Prison, with a second series of visits that December, including to the prison ship *Maidstone* in the port of Belfast. During the second visit the delegates met 500 detainees and the ICRC *Annual Report 1971* states that they were able to meet and discuss with detainees 'freely and without witnesses'. Their reports were sent directly to the government of Northern Ireland.[24] The fact that these visits were allowed by the government did not imply any change of attitude to the classification of the hostilities.

Generally, therefore, there was very little evidence of significant opinion driving towards the classification of the situation in Northern Ireland as an armed conflict of either sort (international or non-international). The UK denied it had reached the threshold. Ireland toyed with the idea of making this an issue but then backed off from it. The ICRC probably considered it to be some form of armed conflict but never went on public record to that effect. PIRA did believe it was fighting a war of national liberation, until political considerations prompted its leadership to recognize the political institutions in Dublin as legitimate. And, of course, there is the odd case of Libya. So there is no serious analysis from the interested parties that decisively concludes one way or the other.

3.2. Analysis of the classification

The questions considered in this section include whether the level and character of the violence at any time reached the threshold of a non-international armed conflict. If it did, when did the hostilities reduce to the point at which the armed conflict ended? And was there ever a situation of international armed conflict?

For the whole of the period covered by this chapter, the question whether the hostilities should be classified as non-international armed conflict would have to be determined by reference to Common Article 3 of the Geneva Conventions, because Additional Protocol II did not apply until its ratification by the UK in 1998. Common Article 3 is deliberately vague in that it does not provide a precise definition of what constitutes a non-international armed conflict. The Pictet Commentary makes the point that the Diplomatic Conference formulating the Geneva Conventions 'wisely' abandoned the attempt to provide a precise definition with strict criteria.[25] As Pejic has more recently noted 'no definition would be capable of capturing the factual situations that reality throws up'.[26] Nevertheless, as she comments in the current volume, 'a certain intensity of hostilities and the requisite organization of the non-state armed group are generally deemed indispensable for categorizing a situation of violence as a non-international armed

---

[24] International Committee of the Red Cross, 'Annual Report 1971' (1972) 38–9.

[25] J. Pictet et al, *Geneva Convention for the amelioration of the condition of the wounded and sick in armed forces in the field: a commentary* (1952) 49.

[26] J. Pejic, 'Status of Armed Conflicts' in E. Wilmshurst and S. Breau, *Perspectives on the ICRC Study on Customary International Humanitarian Law* (2007) 85.

conflict'.[27] For the International Criminal Tribunal for the Former Yugoslavia, non-international armed conflict constitutes 'protracted armed violence between governmental authorities and organized armed groups within a State': this is virtually identical to the Statute of the International Criminal Court's 'protracted armed conflict between governmental authorities and organized armed groups or between such groups'.[28] There are two key questions in relation to Northern Ireland, therefore:

- Did the violence that occurred at any time represent more than merely internal disturbances or tensions that needed to be dealt with purely within the scope of domestic law enforcement? and
- Did the organization of PIRA satisfy the criteria for non-international armed conflict?

As has been illustrated above, the initial phase characterized by civil disturbances (during which the IRA was ill prepared, small in numbers and badly organized) was followed by a period of concerted insurgency with a reinforced PIRA organized within a clear military hierarchy overtly taking on the SFNI. That was followed by a lengthy terrorist phase before an effective period of conflict resolution and peace-building began in the mid- to late-1990s.

Leaving the period of civil disturbances from 1968 to 1971 aside, the scale of the subsequent PIRA insurgency, especially during 1972, coupled with what the SFNI needed to do to halt it, took the hostilities significantly above the level that could be described uncontroversially as merely civil disturbances. Relevant factors include the intensity of PIRA's activities, the numbers they deployed and the harm, in terms of fatalities and injuries, they inflicted on the SFNI. Added to this is the scale of the SFNI reinforcement during Operation Motorman, when almost 30,000 troops were deployed in Belfast and Londonderry, in order to impose a tactical defeat on PIRA. There remains some doubt however as to precisely when the level of insurgent and counter-insurgent activity reached the threshold of armed conflict. Different analysts may well arrive at different answers in that respect. The bulk of them, however, would be unlikely to deny that by 1972 there was at least prima facie evidence that a non-international armed conflict was in train. While the British authorities may well have denied this for policy reasons, PIRA believed itself to be fighting an armed conflict, it was organized to do so with sufficient volunteers operating to inflict serious casualties on the SFNI and, in the main, it must be admitted that most PIRA targeting was against SFNI personnel.

For much of the twenty years from 1974 onwards, there was what may be described as a permanent background level of violence interspersed with sporadic incidents of extreme violence. Those incidents could be of high intensity in and of themselves. The Warrenpoint bombing on 27 August 1979 was an obvious case in

---

[27] See ch. 4, section 2 above.
[28] See *Prosecutor v Tadić*, IT-94-1-AR72, Decision on Defence Motion for Interlocutory Appeal on Jurisdiction (Appeals Chamber), 2 October 1995, para 70; and ICC Statute, art. 8(2)(f).

point, but it occurred against a background level of violence that certainly did not result in daily fatalities. In that year there were on average less than two bombings and three shootings per day resulting in about one SFNI and one civilian death per week. This was in contrast to 1972, during which there were on average five bombings and thirty shooting per day, resulting in an average of one killing every day (the majority being civilians).[29]

While it is probably true to say that the threshold of a Common Article 3 non-international armed conflict was reached in the early-1970s, it is very much less clear at what point the armed conflict terminated. As the years went by, the security situation in Northern Ireland improved, the economy picked up, political discourse began to materialize and the conditions developed in which a political break-through became possible. The background violence reduced but periodically violence erupted and many were killed and injured as a result. A degree of judgment is necessary in attempting to identify precisely when the violence dropped to a level consistent with mere 'civil disturbances'. The point might be the end of the insurgency in 1974, or alternatively 1994 and the PIRA ceasefire that year, notwithstanding PIRA's subsequent brief return to violence in 1997. Importantly, terrorist atrocities can and frequently do occur outwith the state of armed conflict. While many may disagree, the conclusion here is that the non-international armed conflict did not extend into the post-1974 phase. One reason for the choice of this date is that the reorganization of PIRA delivered a clear effect in terms of the group's apparent inability to mount its side of a non-international armed conflict.

From the point at which the IRA factionalized and PIRA began to build up to insurgency, the latter was invariably well-organized. It had an effective command structure, it was internally well-disciplined (indeed, ruthlessly so) and it was capable of conducting operations, not only throughout Northern Ireland but also elsewhere in Britain and Europe. It seems to have met the organizational criteria for non-international armed conflict up to the point at which it declared its final ceasefire following the Canary Wharf and Manchester bombings in 1997. Its forced reorga-nization in 1974 and 1975, a reaction to the SFNI's counter-insurgency operations, does seem to have had the effect of preventing it continuing fully fledged insurgen-cy operations, however. Its new structure was a deliberately fashioned, systemati-cally implemented and a disciplined response to the challenging operational environment in which PIRA found itself. It is submitted that it would be unrea-sonable to deny that PIRA post-1974/75 met the organizational criterion for non-international armed conflict. Nevertheless, while it arguably met those criteria throughout the period from about 1971 to 1998, its particular internal organiza-tional choice after 1974 was a major factor in the reduction of the level of violence below the threshold for non-international armed conflict. In this particular case, there was a very close relationship between the nature of the organization and the intensity of insurgent activity it was able to deliver.

---

[29] Figures taken from Dewar, *The British Army in Northern Ireland* (1985) 232.

A final consideration is whether any phase of the hostilities could be classified as an international armed conflict (notwithstanding PIRA's belief that it was engaged in a liberation struggle). During the entire period, hostilities were largely contained within Northern Ireland, although they did spill over into both the wider UK and into other States, most notably the Irish Republic and parts of western Europe. The UK ambassadors in both Dublin and The Hague were assassinated (in 1976 and 1979 respectively), as was Lord Mountbatten at his holiday home at Mullaghmore in the Irish Republic (in August 1979). In 1980 PIRA admitted targeting British armed forces' personnel based in West Germany. This had also involved PIRA operations in the Netherlands and Belgium. British counter-terrorist operations were also mounted beyond the UK, most notably in the British Overseas Territory of Gibraltar in 1988, in response to a suspected terrorist plot to mount an attack on British forces there.[30]

These trans-boundary aspects notwithstanding, at no time was the UK in a state of armed conflict with another State in relation to British rule in Northern Ireland. While relations with the Republic of Ireland were not invariably excellent, and security cooperation was not always what it might have been, at no time did relations become so bad that the two States came close to direct hostilities with each other. The fact that Republican terrorist groups, PIRA in particular, were operating in Northern Ireland from 'bases' in the Republic raised understandable issues. The government in Dublin was not, however, providing support to PIRA and actively opposed its cross-border activities. A March 1980 agreement between Prime Minister Thatcher and Charles Haughey, the Irish Taoiseach, improved operational links between the Security Forces on both sides of the border but it was not an indication of an absence of prior cooperation.[31]

The extension of PIRA's operations to the UK mainland, to West Germany and elsewhere on the continent were, at most, evidence of a non-international armed conflict conducted on a foreign State's territory. Support to PIRA provided by Libya, in the form of arms supplies, did nothing to improve Anglo-Libyan relations but the situation never gave rise to any recognition of an international armed conflict between those two States. The obvious and largely uncontroversial conclusion must be that the violence in Northern Ireland and elsewhere was never an international armed conflict.

---

[30] The name given to this operation was 'Operation Flavius'. This resulted in a case being taken to the European Court of Human Rights; the circumstances are comprehensively described in *McCann and Others v United Kingdom* (Judgment) App No. 18984/91 (27 September 1995) (*McCann v the United Kingdom*).

[31] The Royal Navy conducted operations on the border in Carlingford Lough and in the area around Warrenpoint. Royal Navy and Royal Marine units engaged there were equipped with radios for direct communications with Security Forces in the Republic; but this was not to facilitate cross-border operations by Security Forces on either side of the border. (The author was responsible for overseeing all naval operations within the Province between 1979 and 1981.)

4. The application of force

While the rules for the application of force (rules on opening fire) promulgated by the parties are an important factor to be taken into account when analysing the characteristics of any armed conflict, in the case of Northern Ireland one clear difficulty is the absence of any reliable source material establishing the existence of any such rules promulgated and applied by PIRA. Although it argued until 1986 that it was engaged in a national liberation struggle that enabled it to regard itself as fighting an international armed conflict, PIRA seems throughout the period to have been disregarding important rules of international humanitarian law, especially the principle of distinction. In the absence of any evidence of PIRA rules on opening fire but certain evidence of serious non-compliance with international humanitarian law, the assumption is that there were no PIRA rules. In contrast, there is clear evidence of rules applied by the Security Forces.

Throughout the period of hostilities, the British rules for opening fire were predicated on the notion of the minimum use of force consistent with what is often referred to today as the 'law-enforcement paradigm'. To quote from the Northern Ireland 'Yellow Card' issued to all armed forces' personnel: 'Firearms must only be used as a last resort'; a requirement that was in the opening paragraph of the card and printed in capitals to make it stand out. A challenge needed to be issued before opening fire, unless to do so would 'increase the risk of death or grave injury' or unless the act of opening fire was in direct response to fire already opened against the Security Forces (or those whose security was their responsibility). Opening fire against a person was only authorized if he or she was 'committing or about to commit an act likely to endanger life, and there is no other way to prevent the danger' or if that person had just killed or injured someone, had refused to surrender when challenged and 'there is no other way to make an arrest'. Aimed shots only were allowed. This meant single deliberately aimed shots, even if the weapon used was physically capable of rapid automatic fire. No more rounds than necessary were to be fired.[32]

The rules represent a policy directive within the legally permitted application of force, a feature of all legitimate rules of engagement. They were clearly breached on occasion but those members of the Security Forces who did fail to comply could be, and some were, subject to criminal prosecution.[33] It would be impossible seriously to claim that all actual breaches were subject to full investigation and the subsequent prosecution of those responsible. Breaches either may not have been

---

[32] The quotes are from UK Ministry of Defence, 'Instructions for Opening Fire in Northern Ireland' Army Code No. 70771, issued to the author during his service in Northern Ireland and retained in his possession.

[33] The highest profile example was the conviction in 1993 of Lance Corporal Lee Clegg for the 1990 murder of an occupant of a car that failed to stop at an Army-manned vehicle checkpoint in West Belfast. Clegg was sentenced to life imprisonment but had his conviction quashed in 1998 following new forensic evidence being made available. He was finally acquitted during a re-trial in 1999. See *R v Clegg* [1995] 1 AC 482.

revealed during post-contact debriefing or, arguably, prima facie unlawful applications of force may not have led to prosecution for want of adequate evidence or because they were not unreasonable in the precise circumstances. Notwithstanding these considerations, the British government's policy was to restrict opening fire to law-enforcement standards.

4.1. The 'shoot to kill' controversy

Nevertheless, there have been suggestions of a 'shoot to kill' policy. The allegations were that, in certain circumstances, some members of the Security Forces (including members of the SAS, other military personnel and members of the RUC) employed force deliberately to kill rather than attempt to arrest those they were targeting. Three incidents in November and December 1982, resulting in six deaths all involving the RUC, were followed by additional notable incidents in Strabane (23 February 1985), Loughgall (8 May 1987) and Gibraltar (Operation Flavius on 8 March 1988).

In May 1984 an enquiry into the 1982 RUC operations was opened under the direction of Greater Manchester Police's Deputy Chief Constable John Stalker. This was rendered extremely controversial when, in June 1986, Stalker was suspended over allegations that he had associated with known criminals. Stalker was eventually cleared of those allegations but the leadership of the enquiry was assumed by Colin Sampson of the West Yorkshire Police. Sampson's conclusions were never made public. In his memoirs, Stalker stated that he failed to find clear evidence of a 'shoot to kill' policy but that he believed there to have been a 'clear understanding' that RUC officers were expected to comply with it.[34] A total of fourteen PIRA and INLA members were killed in the later three incidents from 1985 to 1988 and the European Court of Human Rights considered several cases between 1982 and 1995 including the case arising from the 1988 Operation Flavius in Gibraltar.[35]

If a 'shoot to kill' policy had been adopted, it would have been contrary to the general rules contained in the Yellow Card as it would have involved a breach of the principle of minimum use of force and would have been contrary to human rights norms. Notwithstanding the judgments of the European Court of Human Rights, there are two comments that ought to be made in relation to the claim that a 'shoot to kill' policy was applied. The first is that in law-enforcement conditions it may well be necessary at times to apply force in a manner that will inevitably lead to death. When targeting a bomber preparing to activate a radio-controlled improvised explosive device, for example, a shot to the head resulting in instant death may be necessary to ensure non-activation. Such targeting would require, in most cases, the application of force by specialist and highly trained members of either the police or military. In such circumstances 'shoot to kill' would not breach human rights norms representing, as it would, the minimum use of force in the circumstances.

---

[34] J Stalker, *Stalker: Ireland, 'Shoot to Kill' and the 'Affair'* (1987).
[35] See *McCann v the United Kingdom*.

The second possible origin of allegations of a 'shoot to kill' policy is related to the manner in which any law-enforcement official or member of the armed forces targets a person, if that level of force is appropriate. All soldiers are trained to fire at the main part of the human torso as the most effective means of ensuring that a round hits its target and has the desired 'stopping' effect.[36] By way of illustration, a 7.62mm round fired from the standard weapon carried by the Army in Northern Ireland (the Self Loading Rifle, for much of the period) would, as a minimum, generate serious life-threatening trauma on passing through the body, especially if the round seriously damaged the main organs. While death was not the intention, it could well be the result. While there was claimed to be no official 'shoot to kill' policy, there was inevitably a significant risk that the application of such force would result in the death or very serious injury of the person targeted.

Notwithstanding these two points, the controversy generated by the incidents noted was understandable. The British government has always denied the official existence of such a policy, although it has not been possible to discount altogether the application of such an approach. The high level denial of an official policy is perhaps more significant than the unauthorized application of such an approach, or its illegal authorization at the tactical level. The incidents recorded can be regarded as profoundly regrettable breaches of opening fire rules designed for a situation officially regarded as falling below the threshold for non-international armed conflict. The same conclusions as to the impermissibility of the force alleged to have been used would have applied even if the UK had classified the hostilities as an armed conflict.

5. Detention

Two forms of detention, differing significantly from the forms of criminal detention and imprisonment standard in UK law, were employed in the early 1970s.[37] Internment without trial was introduced in 1971 but abandoned by the end of 1975. 'Special category' imprisonment was introduced in 1972 and abolished in 1976. Both were determined by the prevailing internal security situation.

5.1. Internment

Human rights law allows for derogations from human rights obligations 'in times of war or other emergencies threatening the life of the nation'.[38] Certain rights are non-derogable, including, for example, the right not to be tortured in any circumstances, including during interrogation while detained. The right not to be

---

[36] The author, who served with the Security Forces between 1977 and 1982, was himself trained to use a weapon in this manner.

[37] The information on detention below is based on the account included in the judgment of the European Court of Human Rights in *Ireland v The United Kingdom* (Judgment) App No. 5310/71 (18 January 1978) (*Ireland v the United Kingdom*).

[38] European Convention on Human Rights, art. 15.

arbitrarily detained is, however, not itself specifically listed as a non-derogable right so, on first sight, it might appear that internment would be permitted following derogation. Internment was phased out in Northern Ireland between July and December 1975, prior to which it was perhaps not unreasonable for the British government to assume that its derogation allowed for internment. On 22 August 1984 the UK withdrew its notice of derogation under the European Convention. Since internment was phased out in 1975 and since the UK withdrew its deroga-tion in 1984, the development of human rights law has challenged the assumption that underpinned the British use of internment. Notable in this respect is a ruling in the European Court of Human Rights from 1993[39] and General Comment 29 of the Human Rights Committee.[40]

The conclusion reached from this account is that internment in Northern Ireland was not effected under the terms of international humanitarian law but (rightly or wrongly) through the process of derogation from the obligations contained within the European Convention on Human Rights. It would be inappropriate to backdate the effect of such determinations as those contained in either General Comment 29 or the jurisprudence of the European Court of Human Rights and to argue that internment as used in Northern Ireland was tantamount to some form of POW detention under international humanitarian law. For that reason, while the introduction of internment represents an interesting aspect of the manner in which the British and Northern Ireland authorities dealt with PIRA insurgency and terrorism, it does not in any way affect the way we might choose to interpret the category of conflict being experienced at the time—that is to say it does not point us to a conclusion that the conflict was an armed conflict.

5.2. Special category status

This is of some interest, not least because it indicates an official recognition of some measure of difference between what might be described as 'common criminals' on the one hand and 'members of armed groups' on the other. Special category prisoners were detained in separate compounds, were not obliged to wear prison uniform, were not expected to work while detained and were accorded privileges, including extra visits and food parcels. These departures from routine conditions of criminal imprisonment were similar in many respects (although certainly not identical) to the privileges granted to prisoners of war, although the British and Northern Ireland governments were adamant in denying any such linkage. In November 1975, the Secretary of State for Northern Ireland announced the phasing out of 'special category status' which had been introduced in 1972; phasing out began on 1 March 1976, after which date no convicted member of a non-state armed group was granted such status.

---

[39] *Brannigan and McBride v the United Kingdom* (Judgment) App No. 14553/89 (26 May 1993).
[40] HRC, 'General Comment 29: States of Emergency (art. 4)' CCPR/C/21/Rev.1/Add.11 (31 August 2001).

The reaction to this change was the commencement of the so-called 'dirty protest' by convicted terrorists, especially in HM Prison Maze. Prisoners at first refused to wash and smeared excrement over the walls and floors of their cells and, more seriously, embarked on the hunger strikes of 1980 and 1981. The infamous death of the first hunger striker, Bobby Sands, who had been elected as a Westminster MP during his action, was followed by further deaths that indicated the strong determination of both the prisoners themselves and the British government under Margaret Thatcher. Once it became obvious that the government was not to be moved, the hunger strikes were called off. Given that 'special category status' was somewhat less harsh than the restrictions imposed on other criminally convicted prisoners, the only possible relevance is to do with the appearance of a form of quasi-POW status. In non-international armed conflict there is no right to be accorded POW status and the introduction of 'special category status' certainly risked Republican supporters regarding detention arrangements as an effective if reluctant acceptance by the British authorities of the existence of an international armed conflict predicated on PIRA's claim to be a national-liberation movement. The reactions (both amongst the prisoners themselves and among their supporters in the Republican communities in Northern Ireland who engaged in violent demonstrations, especially in the wake of hunger strikers' deaths) should be seen in this context. It is easy to suggest that 'special category status' was a mistake, although those who initiated it had done so for not entirely cynical reasons.

6. Other issues

6.1. Weapons issues

One clear issue of note in relation to Security Force operations in Northern Ireland was the methods used for riot control. The use of so-called 'plastic bullets' and CS-Gas generated controversy. The firing of plastic bullets into groups of demonstrators in an attempt to disperse them did lead to injury and occasional fatalities. Arguably, however, they were a largely non-lethal minimum use of force in the circumstances used and complied with the law-enforcement paradigm.

In the case of CS-gas, its use in armed conflict is legally more controversial than its use in law enforcement because of the ban on the use of chemical weapons as a method of warfare. Arguably, even during armed conflict, such agents when used for riot control are strictly not 'weapons or methods of warfare' and there is a view that resort to them would not breach the chemical weapons ban which was in any case not then in force. The classification of the hostilities did not therefore affect the legitimacy of the use of CS-gas.[41]

---

[41] The 1925 Geneva Gas Protocol had prohibited 'the use in war of asphyxiating, poisonous or other gases'. In 1970, the UK stated that CS-gas was outside the scope of the Protocol. The view that riot control agents are not weapons, means or methods of warfare was expressed by the US at the time of its ratification of the Protocol in 1975. The 1993 Chemical Weapons Convention obviously post-dated the bulk of the period concerned (MoD, *Manual of the Law of Armed Conflict* (2004) 11).

6.2. Interrogation

The manner of interrogation used by the Security Forces in the early months of the Troubles was a notable—arguably infamous—feature of the conflict in Northern Ireland. Of particular note were two instances of 'interrogation in depth' conducted between the 11 and 17 August 1971 and between 11 and 18 October 1971. The interrogations were conducted by the RUC following training of their interrogators by British Army personnel in April 1971. The techniques were essentially those previously employed by British Security Forces in a variety of colonial internal security situations during the 1950s and 1960s. They are summarized as 'the five techniques' as follows: hooding; subjection to continuous and monotonous noise; deprivation of sleep; deprivation of food and water (other than one round of bread and one pint of water every six hours); and wall standing.

The 'five techniques' were initially adjudged to be torture by the European Commission on Human Rights. In the later judgment of the European Court of Human Rights the Court distinguished between torture and inhuman or degrading treatment, judging the five techniques in the circumstances in question to have constituted the latter rather than the former.[42] The British government had itself initiated an investigation and ordered a report by a Committee of Privy Counsellors headed by Lord Parker of Waddington. This had been delivered in March 1972[43] and contained a powerful dissenting (or minority) report by Lord Gardiner condemning the use of the techniques.[44] Although the European Court of Human Rights did not reach its judgment until 1977, the British government had already ordered the abandonment of the 'five techniques' once they had become controversial.[45] As with internment, although the issue of interrogation in the early months of the period under review is an interesting and profoundly important one in the general sense, it does not influence the way in which we might choose to categorize the conflict in Northern Ireland.

[42] *Ireland v the United Kingdom.*
[43] 'Report of the Committee of Privy Counsellors appointed to consider authorised procedures for the interrogation of persons suspected of terrorism' (the Parker Report) (March 1972).
[44] Ibid, Minority Report.
[45] The 'five techniques' were the cause of controversy once again in the context of Iraq, in relation to the circumstances surrounding the death in 2003 of Baha Mousa, an Iraqi civilian, while he was in the custody of a British battlegroup. The Baha Mousa Public Inquiry conducted a thorough review of the history of the 'five techniques', including their controversial application in Northern Ireland up to 1971, their withdrawal from use in 1972 and the subsequent consideration of them by the European Court of Human Rights in *Ireland v the United Kingdom* (1978). Despite their re-emergence in Iraq in 2003, there was no suggestion in the Baha Mousa Public Inquiry Report that the 'five techniques' had been used in Northern Ireland after 1971. See in particular Baha Mousa Public Inquiry Report (8 September 2011) Part IV, 411–60.

7. Conclusions

The Northern Ireland case study is an interesting one because it deals with a situation that was not treated as an armed conflict; the identification of a crossing of the threshold (in both directions) is not straightforward and the result is far from obvious, especially when it comes to determining when the intensity of violence dropped below the threshold at some point from 1974 onwards. The conclusion is that the Common Article 3 threshold was reached, but not for the entirety of the period under review (1968 to 1998). The early months of the sectarian violence (from 1969 to some point in 1971) did not constitute an armed conflict because of the nature of that violence and the inadequate organization of the relevant non-state armed group (IRA/PIRA). From mid-1971 onwards, however, during the PIRA insurgency, there was a non-international armed conflict that reached the Common Article 3 threshold. The level of violence may be regarded as having reduced to a level below the threshold as the insurgency failed and as PIRA resorted to techniques more commonly associated with a campaign of terrorism. From 1974 onwards, PIRA certainly met the organizational criterion; the key issue is whether or not the criterion of level or intensity of violence was met. Opinions will undoubtedly differ on this but the conclusion of this author is that while it may undoubtedly be argued that it was up to the time of the PIRA ceasefire in 1994 or, perhaps, up to the time of the Good Friday Agreement in 1998, it was not in fact. A non-international armed conflict occurred between some point in 1971 and ended at some point towards the end of 1974.

This review of the Northern Ireland hostilities has not revealed problems relating to international humanitarian law, largely because the UK did not treat this as an armed conflict but as a situation of law enforcement. In applying its domestic law, the government adopted additional legal provisions not applicable elsewhere in the country. The human rights obligations of the UK applied to these as to the whole conduct of its management of the violence. In relation to both the application of force and detention, the UK as a matter of law and official policy remained generally within what would have been legally permissible in a non-international armed conflict, notwithstanding the issue of interrogation techniques that breached human rights standards. If the UK had acknowledged an armed conflict to be in train at any point during the Troubles, it would have been able to justify different approaches to the application of force and detention. Successive governments were reluctant to give such acknowledgement, however. The British position was that all members of organized armed groups were invariably to be treated as criminals and to face the full effects of the criminal law through prosecution in the courts. Notwithstanding the relatively brief application of both Internment and Special Category Status, members of non-state armed groups were to be imprisoned with no special privileges accorded them on account of their motivation. This policy could have been followed, of course, even if the UK had acknowledged the existence of a non-international armed conflict (in which prisoner of war status does not exist), but it would arguably have risked increasing controversy as to prisoners' status and treatment in detention. In the view of this writer, it is difficult to see what political advantage would have accrued to the government by adopting the line that a non-international armed conflict was in train.

From PIRA's point of view, while for political reasons it claimed to be fighting a war of liberation (certainly before the mid-1980s), it is far from clear that it appreciated the potential consequences to them of a determination that they were engaged in armed conflict. Quite apart from the more liberal opening fire arrangements that would have been legally available to the Security Forces, compliance with the principle of distinction would have been required of them; this seemed to be of no concern to those carrying on various manifestations of the bombing campaign throughout the Troubles.

Chronology

1967	Northern Ireland Civil Rights Association (NICRA) founded.
1968	Civil Rights demonstrations and marches commence.
14 August 1969	British Army deployed following rioting in Londonderry and Belfast.
October 1969	Protestant rioting in Belfast.
December 1969	Irish Republican Army (IRA) splits into Provisional and Official factions.
1970	Ulster Defence Regiment (UDR) formed.
31 October 1970	Provisional IRA kills first British soldier.
9 August 1971	Internment (without trial) introduced; Army mounts Operation Demetrius.
30 January 1972	'Bloody Sunday' in Londonderry (Army kills 13 demonstrators).
2 February 1972	British Embassy in Dublin burned down.
24 March 1972	London imposes Direct Rule on Northern Ireland.
29 May 1972	Official IRA ceasefire.
20 June 1972	Special Category Status detention introduced.
26 June 1972	Brief Provisional IRA ceasefire during talks with government in London.
21 July 1972	Bloody Friday in Belfast (9 killed, 130 injured by 19 PIRA bombs).
31 July 1972	Operation Motorman mounted by Army.
6–9 December 1973	Sunningdale Conference.
14–29 May 1974	Ulster Workers' Council Strike against Power Sharing.
21 November 1974	Birmingham Pub Bombing (19 killed, 182 injured).
9 February–7 April 1975	Second Provisional IRA ceasefire.
1 May 1975	Constitutional Convention elections.
24 July–5 December 1975	Internment phased out.
1 March 1976	Special Category Status abolished.
9 March 1976	Constitutional Convention dissolved.
21 July 1976	British ambassador to Dublin assassinated.
11 March 1977	26 UVF terrorists sentenced to a total of 700 years in prison.
27 June 1977	OIRA/PIRA feud in Belfast (4 killed, 18 injured).
17 February 1978	PIRA firebomb the La Mon Restaurant (12 killed, 23 injured).

13 March 1978	Republic prisoners commence 'Dirty Protest' at Maze Prison.
22 March 1979	British ambassador to The Hague assassinated.
30 March 1979	Airey Neave MP assassinated by Irish National Liberation Army (INLA) outside House of Commons.
27 August 1979	Warrenpoint bombing, assassination of Lord Mountbatten in Republic of Ireland.
March 1980	PIRA admits responsibility for attacks on British Army in West Germany.
27 October 1980	First Hunger Strike commences at Maze Prison.
1 March 1981	Second Hunger Strike commences at Maze Prison.
5 May 1981	Death of Hunger Striker Bobby Sands, rioting in Londonderry and Belfast. Nine hunger strikers die between 12 May and 20 August.
4 September 1981	INLA withdraws from Hunger Strike.
3 October 1981	PIRA calls off Hunger Strike.
October–November 1981	PIRA bombing campaign in London.
14 November 1981	Rev Robert Bradford MP assassinated by PIRA.
20 July 1982	Bomb in Regents Park, London.
6 December 1982	INLA bombing of Droppin' Well Inn, Ballykelly.
1983	Gerry Adams elected Sinn Fein leader and began the process of seeking a settlement by way of both political and military action.
12 October 1984	Grand Hotel, Brighton bombing, 5 killed, 34 injured in an attempt to 'blow up the Cabinet' of Margaret Thatcher.
15 November 1985	Anglo-Irish Agreement.
1988	SAS mount operation in Gibraltar to prevent bombing; 3 killed.
1993	Series of Loyalist bombings and shootings.
October 1993	Shankill Road bombings.
31 August 1994	PIRA ceasefire.
October 1994	Loyalist ceasefires.
9 February 1996	PIRA revoked ceasefire; bombing of Canary Wharf, London.
15 June 1996	Manchester bombing; 200 injured but none killed.
12 February 1997	Last British soldier killed in the conflict.
July 1997	PIRA reinstated ceasefire.
1998	Real IRA bombing of Omagh. INLA ceasefire and the signing of the Good Friday (or Belfast) Agreement.

6

The Democratic Republic of the Congo 1993–2010

Louise Arimatsu

1. Introduction

On 30 June 2010, the Democratic Republic of the Congo celebrated its fiftieth anniversary of independence from Belgian rule. But if independence had promised to be an opportunity for disavowing violence as a way of life that had been the Congo's history under one of the most brutal manifestations of European colonialism, the following five decades were to disappoint.[1] To describe the Congo as a site of perpetual violence marked by recurring full-scale armed conflict and lost opportunities is to risk repeating—with no excuse[2]—the trajectory paved by Conrad with the phrase 'heart of darkness', and thus to consolidate identities and histories that serve to perpetuate dominant images and structural prejudices.[3] Nevertheless it is difficult to speak of the Congo without reference to its violent history, not least because the carnage and gratuitous sexual violence which has become synonymous with the country continues unrelentingly to dominate the lives of its people to this day.

As if the Congolese people needed to be reminded of their past, a month after celebrating their anniversary a draft UN report documenting the most serious violations of human rights and international humanitarian law committed in the DRC in the decade starting 1993 (the Mapping Report) was leaked to the press.[4] Given its temporal scope, judgment was directed inwards at the Congo and its immediate neighbours, powerfully illustrating how decisions as to the appropriate time frame for critical scrutiny are loaded with value judgments and that all historical accounts are necessarily founded on arbitrary decisions that generate partial narratives.[5]

This study nevertheless also begins in the early 1990s. The chapter subdivides Congo's history of violence into four key periods: 1) the period prior to the First

---

[1] See generally, J. Van Lierde (ed.), *Lumumba Speaks: The Speeches and Writings of Patrice Lumumba 1958–1961* (1963), specifically J.-P. Sartre, 'Introduction', 41.

[2] As Said has observed, 'Conrad could probably never have used Marlow to present anything other than an imperialist world-view, given what was available for either Conrad or Marlow to see of the non-European at the time'. E. Said, 'Two Visions in Heart of Darkness' in E. Said (ed.), *Culture and Imperialism* (1993) 22, 23.

[3] See K. Dunn for a fuller discussion on how it is widely accepted that national identity is not an ontological category but merely a form of cultural production. K. Dunn, *Imagining the Congo: the International Relations of Identity* (2003). Although Conrad did not originate the image of the Congo, his powerful descriptions continue to resonate and thus partially constitute identities to this day.

[4] UN High Commissioner for Human Rights, 'Report of the Mapping Exercise documenting the most serious violations of human rights and international humanitarian law committed within the territory of the Democratic Republic of the Congo between March 1993 and June 2003' (August 2010) (Mapping Report).

[5] This was clearly at issue with the 'Report of the Secretary-General's Investigative Team charged with investigating serious violations of human rights and international humanitarian law in the Democratic Republic of the Congo' S/1998/581 (29 June 1998) (1998 Report of the SGIT on the DRC). Responding to the strong objections raised by then President Laurent-Desire Kabila, the temporal scope of the report was eventually backdated to begin on 1 March 1993 rather than from the original start date of September 1996, enabling Kabila to deflect some measure of responsibility. Letter dated 29 June 1998 from the Secretary-General addressed to the President of the Security Council, S/1998/581 (29 June 1998).

Congo War extending from the spring of 1993 until summer 1996; 2) the period starting with the outbreak of the First Congo War in July 1996 until the summer of 1998; 3) the period spanning the Second Congo War until the establishment of the transitional government in July 2003; and finally 4) the period since the end of the Second Congo War during which time large-scale fighting has continued to dominate life in the eastern provinces. Each section begins with a cursory overview of the history of the conflicts and identifies the main protagonists. This is followed by a critical examination of the legal framework within which both external observers and those involved in the hostilities claimed was applicable.[6] Whether the categorization of the specific armed conflict under consideration altered the behaviour of the parties in respect of the rules on opening fire and those relating to capture and detention are examined to ascertain what legal and practical problems were—and still are—encountered with the bifurcation of the law.

2. The legacy of Colonialism and the Cold War: March 1993–summer 1996

2.1. History

Tension had been mounting between the various tribal groupings in the eastern province of North Kivu for some years prior to the outbreak of the large-scale violence in March 1993. Disputes over land use and ownership rights had polarized local communities with members of the Hunde, Nande and Nyanga—who considered themselves to be the 'indigenous' tribes—contesting the ownership rights of the Banyarwanda or 'immigrant' communities, many of whom had relocated as refugees from Rwanda after Zaire's independence in 1960.[7] On 20 March 1993, following an inflammatory speech by the governor of North Kivu questioning the right of the Banyarwanda to Zairian nationality and calling on the Zairian security forces to assist the Hunde and Nyanga to 'exterminate' the group, armed militias linked to both tribes attacked the Banyarwanda at Ntoto market, west of Masisi, killing up to 500 civilians.[8] Over the ensuing months, the Nyanga and Hunde militias, sometimes referred to as the Mai-mai or Bangilima,[9] launched further attacks against the Banyarwanda (comprised of both Hutus and Tutsis). As the

---

[6] Over the last five decades, almost every conceivable 'type' of conflict has been waged on the DRC's territory; for a useful typology of non-international armed conflicts, see ch. 4 above, section 2.

[7] For an in-depth account of the Congo wars, see generally, F. Reyntjens, *The Great African War* (2009) (Reyntjens, *The Great African War*). For a concise account of the background to the conflict, see 'Report of the Special Rapporteur on the situation of human rights in Zaire', E/CN.4/1995/67 (23 December 1994) (1994 SR Report on Zaire).

[8] Amnesty International, 'Zaire: Violence Against Democracy' (16 September 1993) (AI, *Zaire*).

[9] The Bangilima is an armed group comprised of members of the Nande ethnic group and mercenaries from Haut-Zaire and FAZ deserters who claimed to be defending the interests of the Zairian people to halt the territorial ambitions of the Banyarwanda. For a general overview on the Mai-mai armed group (mayi-mayi), see Appendix to the report produced by MONUC, 'First assessment of the armed groups operating in the Democratic Republic of the Congo' S/2002/341 (5 April 2002).

violence spread, Hutu-armed units, supported by the Zairian armed forces (*Forces Armées Zaïroises* (FAZ)), began targeting Hunde civilians in retaliation.[10] By the time calm was finally restored towards the end of the year, thousands had reportedly been killed and up to a quarter of a million people displaced.[11]

By February 1994, with the intervention of President Mobutu and the deployment of troops of the *Division Spéciale Présidentielle* (DSP), some semblance of order and stability had returned to the province. However, this was to be short-lived. In the aftermath of the genocide in neighbouring Rwanda, and with the Rwandan Patriotic Front (RPF) gaining ground, North Kivu was flooded with over 700,000 refugees, primarily of Hutu ethnicity, fleeing Rwanda.[12] Among the refugees who crossed the border into Zaire during late spring and early summer were members of the armed forces of the previous regime—the *Forces Armées Rwandaises* (FAR)—and the Interahamwe who had played a pivotal role in the Rwandan genocide. By year end, growing concern over the massive influx of refugees in the Kivus prompted Zairian opposition parties to unite to condemn the damaging effects that the presence of the refugees was having on the local ecology and the socio-economic and security conditions of the indigenous communities.[13] Mobutu, on the other hand, appeared to regard the refugees as an expedient means by which his political future could be consolidated: the unchecked cross-border raids by the ex-FAR and Interahamwe from Zaire's territory had the potential to ignite a full-scale armed conflict with his new adversaries in Rwanda and divert attention from his abysmal human rights record which was increasingly coming under domestic and international scrutiny and criticism.

The precise nature of the relationship between Kinshasa and the foreign insurgents based in eastern Zaire during this period remains oblique. Nonetheless, the ability of the ex-FAR and other armed groups to launch attacks repeatedly into Rwanda between July 1994 and mid-1996 indicates that the Zairian authorities were, at best, indifferent to the rearming and retraining of these armed groups on Zairian territory.[14] Despite the imposition of an international arms embargo,[15] the persistent reports of arms being channelled for the ex-FAR through Goma[16]

---

[10] Mapping Report, 58–9.

[11] According to some reports, by August over 20,000 had been killed and a quarter of a million displaced. G. Prunier, 'The Catholic Church and the Kivu Conflict' (2001) 31 *Journal of Religion in Africa* 139–62 (Prunier, *The Catholic Church*). Others have put the death toll at closer to 6000 with a quarter of a million displaced. 'Ethnic Conflict in North-Kivu', available at: <www.grandslacs.net>. Amnesty International estimated that 3000 were killed (AI, *Zaire*); MSF estimated that roughly 6000–15,000 had been killed and 250,000 displaced. According to a report by the Special Rapporteur 3000 were killed and 225,000 displaced (1994 SR Report on Zaire).

[12] By 1995 it was estimated that 1.4 million Rwandese refugees were living in the camps in Zaire. 'Second Report of the Secretary-General on Security in the Rwandese Refugee Camps' S/1995/65 (25 January 1995).

[13] Prunier, *The Catholic Church*, 139–62. For a graphic account see 1994 SR Report on Zaire.

[14] Regular cross-border 'skirmishes' on the Zaire/Rwanda border characterized this period although from time to time there were more serious incidents.

[15] SC res. 918 (1994).

[16] Human Rights Watch, 'Rearming with Impunity' (May 1995); 'Rwandan exiles received arms' *The Times* (28 March 1995).

(despite the avid denials by Zaire) eventually led to the adoption of Security Council resolution 997 in June 1995 calling for military observers to be stationed in Zaire to monitor and restrict the sale and supply of arms destined for use within Rwanda.[17] In September 1995 an International Commission of Inquiry (ICOI) was established[18] to investigate, in addition to the sale of arms to the ex-FAR, allegations that such forces were receiving military training in neighbouring States.[19] Although seriously hampered by a general lack of cooperation, the Commission found that in particular 'Zaire, or elements within Zaire, appear to continue to play a central role as a conduit for arms supplies to and military training of Rwandan and Burundian insurgents on its soil'.[20]

By autumn 1995, North Kivu was once again embroiled in full-scale conflict as Hunde and Nyanga militias, confronted by the sudden increase in the Hutu population and fearing a loss of power, launched offensives against Hutu communities.[21] The catalyst for this renewed fighting was the announcement by the Zairian government in August 1995 that all Rwandan refugees were to be expelled, prompting the mass movement of the Hutu refugees from the UNHCR camps to other destinations in North Kivu where they inevitably met with local resistance.[22] As the violence escalated, massacres by Hutu militias against the Hunde and Tutsi and by Hunde militia against the Tutsi and Hutu gradually led to the creation of ethnically homogenous areas.[23] In March, the conflict had spread to other localities in North Kivu where the Bangilima continued to target the Banyarwanda. By April, the Banyarwanda were under attack in South Kivu[24] the Kasai people under attack by the Shaba[25] and ethnic violence among a host of different communities had spread to the provinces of Bas-Zaire and Haut-Zaire.

Over the following year, there was a significant realignment of alliances that eventually resulted in a fundamental split between the Hutu and Tutsi Banyarwanda. In addition, there was a gradual transformation of the *Mutuelle des Agriculteurs et Eleveurs du Virunga* (MAGRIVI) from what was originally a political organization campaigning on the cultural/political rights of the Hutu community, into a radicalized militia which became increasingly aligned with the Interahamwe.[26]

---

[17] See 'Third report of the Secretary-General on Security in the Rwandese Refugee Camps' S/1995/304 (14 April 1995) and 'Report of the Secretary-General on the Implementation of Paragraph 6 of Security Council Resolution 997 (1995)' S/1995/552 (9 June 1995).

[18] SC res. 1013 (1995).

[19] E.G. Berman, 'The International Commission of Inquiry (Rwanda): Lessons and Observations From the Field' (2001) 45 *American Behavioral Scientist* 616–26.

[20] Letter dated 1 November 1996 from the Secretary-General Addressed to the President of the Security Council, S/1997/1010 (24 December 1997), para 108(e).

[21] 1994 SR Report on Zaire, para 92.

[22] 'Zaire expels 2,000 refugees despite UN appeal' *Financial Times* (22 August 1995).

[23] By spring 1996, most of the Tutsi population had fled from Masisi while records suggest that over 200,000 Tutsis had left eastern Zaire for Rwanda fearing the increasing attacks by the Hutu Banyarwanda and the ex-FAR/Interahamwe coupled with the resumption of hostilities between the Hutu Banyarwanda and the Mai-mai.

[24] 'Report of the Special Rapporteur on the situation of human rights in Zaire' E/CN.4/1996/66 (29 January 1996), sub-section B (1996 SR Report on Zaire).

[25] 1994 SR Report on Zaire, sub-section C.

[26] 1996 SR Report on Zaire, sub-section C1.

During the two year period of inter-ethnic armed conflict lasting until summer 1996, the FAZ mounted two successive operations to restore order, each of which ended in failure. Although accused of siding with the Interahamwe and Hutu militias, the motivation of many of the members of the FAZ was more 'the result of economic calculations than of political or ethnic bias [as] they essentially fought for those who paid for their services'.[27] Unpaid and lacking in discipline, the armed forces were often directly complicit in the atrocities perpetrated against the civilian population and the refugees. The total death toll during this armed conflict has been estimated to range from 6000 to 40,000; the number of displaced, 400,000.[28]

2.2. Classification of the conflict

2.2.1 Classification of the conflict by the parties and by others

There is little evidence to suggest that the parties to the violence in March 1993 concerned themselves with the classification of the conflict. Although by year end the UN Department of Humanitarian Affairs described the situation as an armed conflict that was being fought on ethnic lines,[29] the international community, by and large, did not express a view on the matter. Of those States that appeared to take some interest in Zaire,[30] the rising incidents of violence were treated as the tragic consequence of a political clash that was unfolding between President Mobutu and his political opponent, Prime Minister Etienne Tshisekedi. Extra-judicial executions, 'disappearances', torture and the arbitrary and unlawful detention of opposition leaders, supporters and journalists by Mobutu's security forces were well documented and clearly on the increase. But the gravity of the ethnic violence that was unfolding in North Kivu and the legal implications that this implied were under-played by most observers.[31] By contrast, the human rights community was warning, as early as September 1993, that 'the current situation in Zaire is amounting to a civil war in many respects. Adhering to Common Article 3 of the Geneva Conventions is a first step which should be followed by the adoption of safeguards contained in international human rights standards.'[32]

---

[27] Reyntjens, *The Great African War*, 18. See also discussion in ch. 3 and 15.

[28] 1996 SR Report on Zaire, IV.

[29] Department of Humanitarian Affairs, 'Consolidated United Nations Inter-Agency Appeal for Emergency Humanitarian Assistance—Zaire' DHA/93/133 (December 1993).

[30] Belgium, France and the United States—referred to as the troika—were the key external 'players' during this period.

[31] In his statement before the Subcommittee on Africa, George Moose, Assistant Secretary for African Affairs at the State Department described what was unfolding as 'a pernicious pattern of government-provoked or tolerated violence against minority ethnic groups'. In his statement, John Hicks, Acting Assistant Administrator for Africa at the Agency for International Development, described the violence as 'civil strife in and around Kinshasa'. 'Zaire, a country in crisis: hearing before the Subcommittee on Africa of the Committee on Foreign Affairs' House of Representatives, 103rd Congress, 1st session (October 1993).

[32] AI, *Zaire*.

As in 1993, the mass violence that engulfed North Kivu and the surrounding areas from late 1994 onwards was largely ignored by the international community, which chose to focus on the refugee crisis as a distinct and separate problem from the ethnic conflicts that were being fuelled by the Zairian authorities.[33] Although the US State Department voiced its concern about the 'increasing incidents of inter-ethnic violence in the north Kivu region' and condemned 'the exploitation of ethnic tensions for political or material gain',[34] there seemed little appetite to discuss, in public, the nature of the conflicts.[35]

2.2.2 Author's classification

That the violence which erupted in March 1993 in North Kivu satisfied the threshold of a non-international armed conflict and was therefore governed by Common Article 3 is now widely accepted.[36] But it is worth taking a further look as to why this should be so. As the 2010 Mapping Report observes, 'the legal classification of the acts of violence that took place [in this period] ... depends on the nature and degree of organisation of the militias involved and the intensity of the violence'.[37] In other words, the two key criteria that must be satisfied before a situation of violence is objectively determined to be a non-international armed

---

[33] Human Rights Watch, 'Forced to Flee: Violence Against the Tutsis in Zaire' (1 July 1996); Fédération Internationale des Ligues des Droits de l'homme, July 1996, Vol. 8, No. 2(A).

[34] Press briefing by Nicholas Burns, State Department spokesperson (21 May 1996).

[35] On 17 July 1994, as armed members of the FAR and Interahamwe retreated across the border into Zaire, Goma airport was shelled, probably by members of the advancing Rwandan Patriotic Front. '50 Refugees Killed in Stampede; 60 Killed by Mortars' *Associated Press* (18 July 1994); 'Conditions in Goma-Zaire 16–20 July 1994' (21 July 1994), available at: <www.rwandadocumentsproject.net/gsdl/ collect/usdocs/index/assoc/HASH019f/abb0420f.dir/2370.pdf>. The shelling of the airport led to the death of 'more than a hundred Zairian citizens' prompting a formal complaint by Zaire to the President of the Security Council, see Letter dated 19 July 1994 from the Chargé d'Affaires A.I. of the Permanent Mission of Zaire to the United Nations Addressed to the President of the Security Council, S/1994/861 (22 July 1994). The wording of the letter is instructive in that the Zairian government describes the attack as amounting to the 'non-compliance by the Rwandese belligerent with the spirit and letter of the relevant Council resolutions relating to the immediate implemen- tation of the cease-fire in Rwanda'. Had the RPF, at that time in question, been regarded as the armed forces of Rwanda, the shelling would more likely have been described as an armed attack that would allow for the lawful use of force in self-defence by Zaire. By early 1995 Kagame—who was then head of the RPF—was looking for opportunities to enter into an armed conflict with Zaire, see Reyntjens, *The Great African War*, 47.

[36] A 1998 report commissioned by the UN Secretary-General into the violence found that the fighting was 'sufficiently serious to trigger the application of Common Article 3 of the Geneva Conventions' although no conclusions as to the specific identity of protagonists or violations perpe- trated were reached. Nonetheless the report concluded that the deliberate massacre of unarmed civilians by armed groups during the period amounted to a serious violation of international human- itarian law. 1998 Report of the SGIT on the DRC, paras 77 and 91.

[37] Mapping Report, para 476. In holding that 'an armed conflict exists whenever there is a resort to armed force between States or protracted armed violence between governmental authorities and organized armed groups or between such groups within a State' the *Tadić* case in the ICTY established the test that is now commonly applied to determine the existence of an armed conflict, see *Prosecutor v Tadić*, IT-94-1- AR72, Decision on the Defence Motion for Interlocutory Appeal on Jurisdiction (Appeals Chamber), 2 October 1995, para 70 (*Tadić*). See also *Prosecutor v Akayesu*, ICTR-96-4-T, Judgment (Trial Chamber), 2 September 1998, para 620 and further discussion in ch. 3 and 4 above.

conflict to which Common Article 3 applies are the intensity of the violence and the organization of the parties to the conflict. These criteria distinguish an armed conflict from such forms of violence as 'banditry, unorganized and short-lived insurrections, or terrorist activities, which are not subject to international humanitarian law'.[38] Although the duration of the violence serves as an indicator of intensity,[39] it is the loss of human life and the scale of injuries inflicted, the level of the destruction caused to the social infrastructure, and the disruption to normal life as exemplified by the displacement of populations that, together, evidence the intensity of the violence. The scale of the violence perpetrated in eastern Zaire in both 1993 and 1994 onwards was such that the threshold of intensity was satisfied.[40]

The second element, that of organization, requires that parties involved in the hostilities (be they militias or other armed actors) possess the capacity to sustain military operations based on some form of command structure.[41] The logic of introducing this element is to distinguish between armed conflict and general situations of violence that States insist are better regulated by domestic law rather than by international law. The evidence collated by various UN fact-finding bodies and human rights organizations based in and outside Zaire, as well as media accounts of the conflict, indicate that those involved in the violence in both 1993 and 1994 were organized into identifiable militia groups principally linked by tribal or ethnic affiliations. Moreover, the fact that armed groups such as the Mai-mai and Bangilima were clearly able to mount coordinated attacks to which the MAGRIVI/Hutu militia were able to respond with equally well-coordinated counter-attacks, evidenced a degree of command structure needed to satisfy the conditions of Common Article 3.[42]

The question posed in the Mapping Report of whether the arrival in July 1994 of the refugees and foreign forces changed the legal nature of the conflict, given the presence of other armed groups on Zairian territory, is worth further consideration. The authors of the Report reject this possibility on the grounds that a non-international armed conflict cannot become an international armed conflict unless: 1) a third-party State intervenes militarily in the conflict, or if 2) some of the parties to the conflict are acting in the name of that third-party State.[43] This statement of the law skirts the question of what form and degree of *indirect* involvement on the part of another State is required to transform a non-international into an

---

[38] See discussion in ch. 3, section 6 above.

[39] The *Tadić* Trial Chamber's reference to 'protracted armed violence' raised the question of whether the *duration* of the violence was a separate element of the test for the existence of an armed conflict. The matter was considered by the Trial Chamber in *Haradinaj* which concluded that the phrase as interpreted and applied by subsequent Trial Chambers referred to the intensity of the armed violence rather than to its duration. *Prosecutor v Ramush Haradinaj et al*, IT-04-84-T, Judgment (Trial Chamber), 3 April 2008, paras 37–49.

[40] Mapping Report, para 476.

[41] Evidence of 'organization' may also include the existence of a headquarters, of disciplinary rules and mechanisms and of territorial control. Furthermore, the ability to gain access to weapons and other military equipment, the ability to recruit members and to provide training and to speak with one voice, have all been cited as factors that support the existence of the necessary level of organization. See further ch. 3 above.

[42] See Mapping Report, para 476.

[43] Ibid, para 477.

international armed conflict, a matter on which opinion remains divided. The *Tadić* Appeal Chamber's answer, despite stretching the boundaries of judicial creativity to its limits, has provided the precedent subsequently relied upon by other tribunals. Thus, the now widely-accepted criterion that transforms what is ostensibly a non-international armed conflict, or an armed conflict between a State and an organized armed group, into an international armed conflict is that another State has 'overall control' over the armed group. Such control exists 'when a State (or, in the context of an armed conflict, the Party to the conflict) *has a role in organising, coordinating or planning the military actions* of the military group, in addition to financing, training and equipping or providing operational support to that group'.[44] Attempts to reconcile this test with those identified by the ICJ as providing the appropriate attribution tests for the acts of non-state actors within the context of state responsibility is not only futile, because impossible, but unnecessary.[45] As the ICJ has observed, 'logic does not require the same test to be adopted in resolving the two issues which are very different in nature: the degree and nature of a State's involvement in an armed conflict on another State's territory which is required for the conflict to be characterized as international, can very well, and without logical inconsistency, differ from the degree and nature of involvement required to give rise to that State's responsibility for a specific act committed in the course of a conflict'.[46]

Although the Report concludes that 'it cannot be argued that the ex-FAR were at this stage the army of a third-party State nor that they were acting in its name or as its agent', the possibility that Zaire may have had overall control over at least some of the armed groups that were launching attacks against Rwanda during the two-year period from mid-1994 until mid-1996, is given little consideration. Had evidence emerged to show that Zaire did in fact have the requisite control over those elements of the ex-FAR or Interahamwe which were engaged in hostilities against Rwanda, the conflict would clearly have been internationalized with the possibility that there were several conflicts—international and non-international—taking place concurrently.

2.3. The use of force

Although Zaire was bound by the main human rights and international humanitarian law conventions well before the conflicts of the 1990s, it was not party to Additional Protocol II until 2002.[47] Nevertheless, there are a number of fundamental rules of international humanitarian law of a customary nature that govern

---

[44] *Tadić*, para 137.

[45] On the tests for attribution in the context of State responsibility, see *Case Concerning Application of the Convention on the Prevention and Punishment of the Crime of Genocide (Bosnia and Herzegovina v Serbia and Montenegro)* ICJ Rep 2007, 43, paras 385–401 (*Genocide Convention* case).

[46] *Genocide Convention* case, para 405; see also discussion in ch. 3 above. The question of what test applies in assessing whether an organized armed group 'belongs to' a party to a conflict in the context of occupation is discussed below at section 5.

[47] Burundi had ratified both Additional Protocols I and II in 1993, Rwanda in 1984 and Uganda in 1991. In December 2002 the DRC deposited its instrument of accession to Additional Protocol II and a declaration accepting the competence of the International Fact-Finding Commission provided for by art. 90 of Additional Protocol I.

the conduct of the parties engaged in hostilities irrespective of the type of armed conflict being waged.[48] Accordingly, all parties to the armed violence were bound by the principle of distinction[49] which requires 'the contending parties to refrain from directly attacking the civilian population and individual civilians and to distinguish in their targeting between civilians and combatants and other lawful military objectives'.[50] The evidence collated from this period reveals that many of the armed militia were unconcerned with distinguishing between those who were taking a direct part in the fighting and the civilian population and, indeed, civilians were often deliberately targeted on the basis of ethnic or group identity.[51] Nor is there any indication that even in attacks against legitimate military objectives did the parties take into consideration the principle of proportionality, which prohibits such attacks if the harm caused to civilians and civilian objects would be excessive in relation to the concrete and direct military advantage anticipated.[52] But the armed groups were not alone in failing to observe these fundamental principles. For example, during December 1993 the Special Rapporteur on Extrajudicial, Summary or Arbitrary Executions[53] transmitted numerous appeals to the Zairian government concerning allegations involving the 'indiscriminate' use of force by the DSP which had resulted in the deaths of civilians.[54]

2.4. Detention

In the absence of a fully developed body of rules governing detention in non-international armed conflict, the basis and conditions of detention in respect of armed non-state actors continues to be governed by domestic law informed by human rights obligations.[55] However, the lack of clearly defined rules is in some respects of peripheral concern where Zaire was concerned since, even in peacetime, the Zairian authorities were systematically failing to meet minimum human rights standards as enumerated in the Standard Minimum Rules for the Treatment of

---

[48] Common Article 3 is concerned with the protection of persons in enemy hands and consequently contains no rules on the conduct of hostilities. See discussion in ch. 4, section 4 above.

[49] In its codified form, the principle is provided in Additional Protocol II, art. 13(2).

[50] *Abella v Argentina*, Inter-American Commission on Human Rights, Case No. 11.137, Report No. 55/97 (18 November 1997). See also J.M. Henckaerts and L. Doswald Beck, *Customary International Humanitarian Law* (2005), rules 1 and 7 (ICRC Customary Law Study).

[51] Although the Investigative Team found that Common Article 3 governed the violence during the period July 1994 to October 1996, it is worth noting that the offences perpetrated by the ex-FAR and Interahamwe against the local population in North Kivu were described as 'crimes, including homicide' rather than as war crimes; see 1998 Report of the SGIT on the DRC. Although 'intentionally directing attacks against the civilian population as such or against individual civilians not taking direct part in hostilities' is now recognized as constituting a war crime (ICC Statute, art. 8(2)(e)(i)), whether at the time in question individual criminal responsibility attached to the prohibition is doubtful.

[52] See ch. 4, section 4.1 above.

[53] The Special Rapporteur was authorized to consider deaths due to the use of force by law-enforcement officials as well as violations of the right to life during armed conflicts and was therefore mandated to take into consideration the Geneva Conventions and the Additional Protocols when assessing a particular situation.

[54] 1994 SR Report on Zaire.

[55] See further discussion in ch. 4 above.

Prisoners.[56] In its submission to the Secretary-General in February 1994, the International Federation of Human Rights observed,

> the number of disappeared persons in Zaire is extremely hard to determine because there are no registration books in detention centres. The lack of this type of document is a flagrant contravention of rule 7 of the Standard Minimum Rules for the Treatment of Prisoners. Conditions of detention in Zaire are utterly alarming in general: torture and ill-treatment appear to be common practice; detainees are usually deprived of food and medical care. Arbitrary detention is a widely practised method of intimidation.[57]

2.5. Co-applicability of international humanitarian law and international human rights law

As far as human rights organizations and the UN bodies were concerned, these two bodies of law were treated as applying concurrently throughout the period of the armed conflicts despite the nebulous relationship between them. As noted above, the language used by the Special Rapporteur on Extrajudicial, Summary or Arbitrary Executions would suggest that the normative framework within which the use of force by the State authorities was being judged was the law of war; in other words, as the *lex specialis*, the standard being applied was that found in international humanitarian law. Yet human rights organizations were at the same time describing the killings resulting from the armed confrontations not only at the hands of the armed forces but also those between the various ethnic groups as 'arbitrary executions', pointing to the continued relevance of human rights law.[58] Although the interplay between international humanitarian law and international human rights law remains indeterminate, what is clear is that those incidents that were scrutinized and roundly condemned by external observers involved the deliberate or indiscriminate killing of civilians and thus were patently unlawful under both legal regimes.

3. The First Congo War: from a global site of conflict to a regional one (July 1996–July 1998)[59]

3.1. History

In October 1996 large-scale violence broke out in South Kivu when the Banyamulenge,[60] who had endured years of state-sponsored discrimination and persecution, became the subject of a provocative and belligerent declaration by the deputy

---

[56] Adopted by the First United Nations Congress on the Prevention of Crime and the Treatment of Offenders, held at Geneva in 1955 and approved by the Economic and Social Council by its resolution 663C (XXIV) of 31 July 1957 and 2076 (LXII) of 13 May 1977.

[57] Written statement dated 4 February 1994 by the International Federation of Human Rights addressed to the Secretary-General and circulated in accordance with ESC resolution 1296, E/CN.4/1994/NGO/13 (4 February 1994) (IFHR Statement). See also AI, *Zaire*.

[58] IFHR Statement, para 3.

[59] Since its first encounter with the West, the territory of the DRC has been the site of confrontation between the 'great powers' not least during the Cold War.

[60] The Banyamulenge are Banyarwanda who arrived and settled in South Kivu from South West Rwanda before 1885. For further details see Reyntjens, *The Great African War*, 22.

governor of the province.[61] Although the full extent of the involvement of the Rwandan Patriotic Army (RPA) in the Banyamulenge rebellion may not have been widely known at the time, there was nevertheless considerable evidence pointing to its active engagement in the conflict. Nonetheless, Rwanda's vehement denials when confronted by Zaire's accusations of intervening in its internal affairs, enabled the *Alliance des Forces Démocratiques pour la Libération du Congo-Zaïre* (AFDL),[62] a Congolese rebel movement led by Laurent-Desire Kabila, to take public 'credit' for having orchestrated the uprising and to mount a full scale civil war that would topple Mobutu seven months later.[63]

Foreign incursions into Zaire can be traced to as early as 4–5 June 1996 when Ugandan soldiers (Uganda People's Defence Force (UPDF)) launched an attack on the village of Bunagana killing up to thirty-six civilians of Hutu ethnicity. Zaire's attempt to bring the matter to the attention of the Security Council was largely ignored given the shifting global priorities among its former allies who, in the post-Cold War climate, were keen to distance themselves from Mobutu's authoritarian and corrupt regime.[64] During this same period, incursions by Rwanda were also recorded with compelling evidence to suggest that by July, Rwandan soldiers were already deployed in South Kivu despite statements by public officials refuting such allegations.[65] The direct interventions by Rwanda, Uganda and more latterly Angola, as well as the indirect intervention of Burundi, in what was ostensibly a civil war in Zaire, were subsequently justified by the respective parties as necessary for reasons of national security. It was widely recognized that Zaire's territory had for some years been used as the base from which various rebel movements were able to launch attacks at each of Zaire's neighbours: the ex-FAR and Interahamwe into Rwanda; the Allied Democratic Forces (ADF) into Uganda; the *Conseil National Pour la Défense de la Démocratie-Forces pour la Défense de la Démocratie* (NCDD-FDD) into Burundi; and the *União Nacional para a Independência Total de Angola* (UNITA) into Angola.[66]

---

[61] On 7 October the deputy governor of South Kivu claimed that the Banyamulenge community were destabilizing the region and had to leave within a week or 'be hunted down as rebels'; A. Goldman, 'Nowhere to Go but Home' *BBC Focus on Africa*, January–March 1997, 14.

[62] The AFDL 'united' four anti-Mobutu opposition groups: the People's Revolutionary Party (PRP) headed by Laurent Kabila; the National Resistance Council for Democracy (CNRD) a Lumumbist guerrilla group; the Democratic Alliance of Peoples (ADP) a Congolese Tutsi group; and the Revolutionary Movement for the Liberation of Zaire (MRLZ).

[63] See e.g. H. Solomon, 'Some Reflections on the Crisis in Zaire' Institute for Security Studies, Occasional Paper 15 (February 1997). See also M. McNulty, 'The collapse of Zaire: implosion, revolution or external sabotage?' (1999) 37 *Journal of Modern African Studies* 53–82, at 75 (McNulty, *The collapse of Zaire*).

[64] For request from Zaire dated 10 June 1996, asking for an urgent meeting of the Security Council to consider the matter, see Letter dated 8 June 1996 from the representative of Zaire, concerning an alleged military attack by Uganda against Zaire, S/1996/413 (8 June 1996).

[65] Reyntjens, *The Great African War*, 48–9.

[66] According to McNulty, 'the imperative for the states of the undeclared alliance which backed the AFDL...was regional security. The AFDL victory was intended to remove a major source of instability for those countries, while allowing the Kigali government to inflict swift and violent punishment on the perpetrators of the 1994 genocide garrisoned in eastern Zaire. This aspect of the

The scale and intensity of the violence that unfolded in eastern Zaire from October onwards was unprecedented.[67] The targets of the military operations by the AFDL, RPA and UPDF were the UNHCR refugee camps in the Kivus which were being used as safe havens by the armed insurgents. With little regard for the welfare of the refugees, the camps were systematically shelled and the fleeing Rwandan Hutu refugees deliberately targeted by the AFDL and RPA.[68] On 22 October, Zaire publicly accused both Rwanda and Burundi of having launched an armed attack in North Kivu and Katanga[69] and by November all three major towns on the border with Rwanda—Uvira, Bukavu and Goma—had fallen to the AFDL rebels and RPA troops. Over the first weeks of the conflict an estimated 9000 people were killed, most of whom were civilians and anywhere between 250,000 to 500,000 people were displaced.[70] Given the scale of the humanitarian catastrophe that was unfolding in Zaire, on 15 November the Security Council convened to consider the deployment of a multinational force to deliver humanitarian aid and facilitate the voluntary repatriation of the refugees to Rwanda.[71] Despite complaints by Zaire of Rwandan 'aggression', with the exception of Botswana the participants in the debate limited their comments to the 'safe' topic of the plight of the refugees.[72] Botswana's interjection—that the abuse of the refugee camps by armed insurgents 'can only lead to increased tension along the Rwanda-Zaire border and transform what began as an internal conflict into an inter-State conflict with far-reaching regional ramifications'—exposed the reluctance on the part of the international community to recognize the reality of what was already taking place in Zaire.[73]

That the Rwandan army (the RPA) had played a pivotal role in the military campaign of a Congolese rebel movement (the AFDL) was confirmed by Rwandan president Paul Kagame, then Defence Minister, in the now infamous interview with *The Washington Post* of 9 July 1997.[74] According to Kagame, Rwanda's three

campaign was driven by the need for Rwanda (and similarly for Uganda and Burundi) to secure their western borders against attack from within Zaire . . . '; McNulty, *The collapse of Zaire*, 56.

[67] See reports issued by Amnesty International (e.g. 'Deadly Alliances in Congolese Forests' (December 1997)) and Human Rights Watch cited in the Mapping Report as well as the Mapping Report itself documenting the mass atrocities perpetrated during the period.

[68] 'Report of the joint mission charged with investigating allegations of massacres and other human rights violations occurring in eastern Zaire (now DRC) since September 1996' A/51/942 (2 July 1997) paras 42–7 (Report of the Joint Mission). See also Medicins sans Frontières, 'Forced Flight: A Brutal Strategy of Elimination in Eastern Zaire' (27 May 1997).

[69] In response to Prime Minister Kengo Wa Dondo's public statement accusing Rwanda of involvement in the conflict, Rwanda's spokesperson Major Rutayisire replied: 'We are not involved in operations in North Kivu.' See *Financial Times* (22 October 1996).

[70] On the refugee crisis in eastern Zaire, see *Financial Times* (22 October 1996) and *Independent* (28 October 1996).

[71] The measure would be mandated under SC res. 1078 (1996).

[72] S/PV.3713, Security Council meeting (15 November 1996) (S/PV.3713). Resolution 1080 was adopted allowing for the deployment of a multinational force under Chapter VII; nevertheless, a successful campaign by Rwanda and the AFDL to discourage the deployment of the force led to the abandoning of the plan.

[73] S/PV.3713.

[74] J. Pomfret, 'Rwandans Led Revolt in Congo' *The Washington Post* (9 July 1997).

strategic objectives—to 'dismantle the [refugee] camps'; 'to destroy the structure' of the ex-FAR and Interahamwe; and to overthrow Mobutu—involved planning the rebellion, supplying arms, munitions and training facilities for the rebel forces and ensuring that key operations were directed by mid-level commanders of the RPA.[75] Evidence suggests that Uganda had also recruited, trained and commanded 15,000 fighters to support the AFDL rebellion[76] and that the Ugandan armed forces were actively involved in the hostilities in December 1996.[77] Burundi's role in the conflict has been described as 'complicit' rather than active although there is some evidence to indicate that Burundi's armed forces (*Forces Armées Burundaises* (FAB)) did directly participate in the hostilities on at least one occasion.[78] The Angolan armed forces (*Forças Armadas Angolanas* (FAA)) intervened directly in April 1997 although Angola had already intervened indirectly in February by facilitating the deployment of the '*Tigres*' or Katangese *Gendarmes*[79] who were instrumental in the capture of Kisangani. By March 1997, the AFDL rebels had taken control of much of eastern Zaire but with the intervention of the *Gendarmes* and Angolan soldiers, the rebels were able to advance swiftly to Kinshasa. On 16 May, Mobutu fled the capital and on the same day Laurent Kabila proclaimed himself to be President.

During the seven-month conflict, widespread atrocities had been perpetrated by all sides; but the greatest responsibility for the wanton killing of the Hutu refugees lay with the AFDL and the Rwandan armed forces.[80] The feeble attempt on the part of the AFDL to justify the mass killings on the grounds that 'a war was going on'[81] was dismissed by the Special Rapporteur, whose recommendation to establish a commission to report on 'the gross violations of the right to life committed in

[75] In his *Washington Post* interview, Kagame confirmed that the RPA had engaged with pro-Mobutu UNITA rebels outside Kinshasa before finally entering the capital with the AFDL.

[76] Reyntjens, *The Great African War*, 58–9. See also 'Zairean rebel forces capture key town' *Financial Times* (3 December 1996), suggesting that the fall of Kisangani was led by Ugandan forces rather than the AFDL.

[77] Reyntjens, *The Great African War*, 59–61 and fn 55.

[78] Ibid, 61.

[79] Given that the *Gendarmes* were incorporated into the FAA, it could be maintained that Angola's intervention under the 'overall control' test came with the deployment of the *Gendarmes* in late February/early March 1997. Refuting allegations that Angola had sent men and weapons to support Kabila, Angola's Ambassador justified the build-up of Angolan forces in Cabinda province as necessary to 'defend national sovereignty and the civilian population against the military activity of separatist groups operating in the enclave'; see *Independent* (18 March 1997). See also 'Angola is accused of invading Zaire' *The Times* (26 April 1997) and 'Angolan factions are drawn into Zairean civil war' *The Times* (3 May 1997).

[80] There is also considerable evidence to show that, as they retreated, members of the FAZ were involved in the commission of mass atrocities directed at the civilian population. For a hard-hitting account of the atrocities perpetrated in the conflict, see Amnesty International, 'Deadly alliances in the Congolese forests' AFR 62/33/97 (3 December 1997).

[81] See comments by Kabila's Chef de Cabinet, Moise Nyarugabo in the 'Report by the Special Rapporteur on the situation of human rights in the area occupied by rebels in eastern Zaire' E/CN.4/1997/6/Add.2. (2 April 1997) para 39 (1997 SR Report on Zaire).

eastern Zaire against refugees and the local population' was to result in a series of damning reports.[82]

3.2. Classification of the conflict

3.2.1 Classification of the conflict by the parties and by others

The difficulties encountered in classifying the armed conflict(s) that raged in Zaire between 1996 and 1998 is evidenced by the changing analyses that have been expounded over the years by the parties to the conflict as well as by external observers. Zaire's repeated attempts to convince the international community that by the latter half of 1996 it was engaged in an international armed conflict with Rwanda and Uganda went unheeded as those States directly involved in the fighting oscillated between denying and implicitly conceding involvement in the fighting. Amidst claim and counter-claim, it was often the political rhetoric that triumphed over the law—and even of fact—simply because it was politically expedient for the vast majority of States not to challenge the narratives of denial. However, what was accepted without question was that in October 1996 the violence had crossed the threshold of 'merely [comprising] internal disturbances or tensions'. This was so in light of the 'serious incidents reported' and the fact that the rebel forces had 'controlled certain parts of Zairian territory'. The law of armed conflict therefore applied.[83]

The Banyamulenge rebellion was initially depicted by those in the region as internal in nature—as 'a spontaneous revolutionary uprising by the oppressed peoples of Zaire to sweep away dictatorship'. On a superficial level the dominant narrative, which treated the rebellion as one that was waged between AFDL rebels supported by the Banyamulenge to rid Zaire of Mobutu, appeared convincing.[84] Although closer inspection suggested otherwise, even those outside the region— with the exception of France—were generally reluctant to describe the conflict other than as internal.[85] The consequence of the deliberate strategy to mask the involvement of foreign actors through covert operations and the use of ambiguous

---

[82] As the Special Rapporteur noted, ' . . . many of the alleged incidents could not be justified even in time of war, since war too is subject to regulations and there are limits to what is permissible in combat'; see 1997 SR Report on Zaire.

[83] In its 1997 report the Joint Mission of the UN Commission for Human Rights which had been charged with investigating the allegations of human rights violations in eastern Zaire since September 1996 stated, 'there is absolutely no doubt that the incidents in question occurred in the context of an armed conflict'; Report of the Joint Mission, para 83.

[84] That the rebellion was essentially one that was comparable with the 1993 conflict in North Kivu and thus non-international in character was not an uncommon narrative; see UN Department on Humanitarian Affairs, 'IRIN briefing on the conflict in South Kivu' (7 October 1996). See also, McNulty, *The collapse of Zaire*, 54 and material cited in fn 2.

[85] 'After a visit to Zaire . . . by the Dutch cooperation minister Jan Pronk, a Dutch official accused Paris of denying reality in its efforts to persuade the international community to let it halt the rebel advances. "The French want to discuss a situation that doesn't exist" he said. "They refuse to allow any talk of the Zairean conflict as internal. Paris only wants it discussed in terms of a foreign invasion. That way it can justify foreign intervention to prop up what it sees as a pro-French government."' *The Guardian* (11 March 1997). In January 1997, when the Belgians had publicly referred to Rwanda's

rhetoric left some observers with little choice but to characterize the conflict as 'neither solely regional nor solely national'.[86] And despite the fact that by early autumn there were many who were aware that the inter-ethnic conflict had 'become international',[87] it was some considerable time later that the international dimension of the conflict was formally recognized by the international community.

In spite of the overwhelming evidence of foreign intervention, even *after* Kabila's 'victory', the 'civil war' narrative prevailed.[88] Struggling to accommodate the political rhetoric within the boundaries of the law, the Joint Mission of the UN Commission for Human Rights framed its analysis of the conflict within a rigid textual reading of Common Article 3 to the Geneva Conventions. That the provision speaks of 'armed conflict not of an international character occurring in the territory of one of the High Contracting Parties' enabled the Mission to reason that:

> it is also clear that the conflict involves third countries and has repercussions for other States (return of refugees, new refugee flows, etc.). Nevertheless, the conflict is taking place within the territory of one State. Although the Zairian Government denounced foreign intervention, the entire international community has treated the conflict as a non-international conflict.[89]

Whether precluded from reaching any other conclusion, or simply abdicating responsibility, the Mission reasoned, 'based on the foregoing, the joint mission is of the view that the provisions of article 3 common to the four Geneva Conventions must be applied to the conflict in eastern Zaire'.[90] A year later, when the UN Secretary-General's Investigative Team (SGIT) reconsidered the classification of the conflict, the lack of evidence as to the degree and nature of foreign involvement in the conflict led them to fall back on the default position: that, at a minimum, Common Article 3 applied. The reasoning of the SGIT is worth recalling in full, although whether the absence of compelling evidence alone explains the conclusion is open to question since President Kagame's interview detailing Rwanda's role in the conflict had been in the public domain for nearly a year:

> The conflict can be considered internal, or non-international, in that the forces aligned against the established government of then Zaire were under the leadership of the AFDL which at the time was an insurgent movement whose main objective was to overthrow the existing government. Nevertheless, the parties concerned recognise that elements of the armed forces of at least one neighbouring country, Rwanda, participated actively in the conflict, largely in the pursuit of their own goals, in particular, that of eliminating a threat to the national security of Rwanda based on the presence of large hostile armed groups in the border areas. It is certain that the conflict *had both national and international*

---

involvement in the conflict, there had been an angry rebuttal by both Rwanda and the AFDL; Reyntjens, *The Great African War*, 55–6.

86 1997 SR Report on Zaire, para 120.
87 Comments by former President of Tanzania, Julius Nyerere cited ibid.
88 See e.g. Peter Rosenblum 'Kabila's Congo' 97 (619) *Current History*, May 1998.
89 Report of the Joint Mission, para 81.
90 Ibid, para 84.

dimensions. There was, in effect, a convergence of two conflicts both of which were essentially internal—one between the AFDL and the government of Zaire, the other pitting the Government of Rwanda against remnants of the former armed forces of Rwanda and the allied armed political militia, the Interahamwe, taking place largely in the territory of a neighbouring State. The two conflicts were closely intertwined, with the forces of the AFDL and Rwandan army, in particular, often acting as a single force. There is also some evidence of the participation of elements of the armed forces of other countries on the side of the insurgents, as well as that of mercenaries on the side of the then Government of Zaire, but many key questions about the nature and extent of foreign participation remain unanswered at this time. In short the Team was not able to obtain sufficient evidence on the role of the foreign armed forces to determine whether the international aspect of the conflict was so predominant as to consider the conflict an international one, for the purposes of international humanitarian law. Consequently, the standards applied for purposes of this report are those of Common Article 3 of the Geneva Conventions, which are applicable to all armed conflicts, internal as well as international.[91]

3.2.2 Author's classification

The finding by the Joint Mission of the UN Commission for Human Rights that the conflict was non-international in scope *because* fought *within* the territory of a single State merits comment. It is now widely accepted that to adopt a narrow textual reading of Common Article 3 is unwarranted since the classification of a conflict is contingent not on the geographical location of the hostilities but on the parties to the conflict. As long as the armed conflict is one fought between government forces and an organized armed group (or between such groups), it is non-international irrespective of location. The critical question was whether the extent of Rwanda's involvement in support of the AFDL was such that the conflict was international rather than non-international in character. Although the SGIT was unable even to marshal sufficient evidence to corroborate allegations that neighbouring States were directly implicated in the fighting and therefore concluded that the conflict was non-international in nature, twelve years later, the authors of the Mapping Report reached a different determination. According to the report,

> [w]ith all the information available today, the importance of the role of third-party States in the first war, which led to the overthrow of the Mobutu regime, cannot be dismissed. Although, in 1998, the Investigative Team...believed it was not in a position to classify the type of armed conflict that took place in the Congo during this period...this is no longer the case. The involvement of Rwanda and Uganda in the conflict, from the outset, in setting up and organising the AFDL, operational planning and logistical support, such as providing weapons and training to some of the combatants, is now recognised by the highest authorities in the countries concerned.[92]

---

[91] 1998 Report of the SGIT on the DRC.
[92] Mapping Report, para 478. The authors of the report refer not only to the *Washington Post* interview with Kagame, but also a subsequent interview by General Kabarebe of the RPA who in 2003 had described himself as having led the military operations of the AFDL. In addition to interviews

But is the Mapping Report's conclusion convincing? Were there not in fact several concurrent conflicts being fought on Zaire's territory during this period as inferred by the SGIT, notwithstanding its inability to establish that at least one was international in scope? That the armed encounters between members of the various foreign armed forces on the territory of Zaire and the armed forces of Zaire (including for example the FAZ and/or DSP) were international armed conflicts and therefore governed by international humanitarian law in its entirety is beyond dispute. Insofar as the hostilities between the AFDL and the armed forces of Zaire were concerned, the rules applicable in international armed conflict should have also applied based, as the Mapping Report concludes, on the extent and degree of control that foreign States had over the AFDL.[93] The intimate connection between the AFDL and Rwanda during this period indicates that the overall control test was satisfied and that all hostilities between the AFDL and the armed forces of Zaire constituted an international armed conflict. The rebuttable presumption that necessarily applies is that the AFDL fighters were entitled to combat immunity and, on detention, to POW status. Yet State practice fails to support this conclusion.

As noted above, rules applicable in non-international armed conflict continued to govern the hostilities between the armed forces of the foreign States deployed on Zaire's territory and the respective foreign rebel groups that were operating from Zaire's territory. The hostilities between the organized armed groups would also have been subject to the same rules including, for example, the clashes between the AFDL and the ex-FAR and Interahamwe or the West Nile Bank Front (WNBF) or UNITA. But as is all too apparent in conflicts involving multiple State and non-state actors each of which are engaged in as many separate hostilities, the bifurcated nature of the law as now constituted is potentially hugely problematic if the rules that apply in non-international and international armed conflict diverge. Nevertheless, that none of the parties in these conflicts was able to consistently satisfy even the minimum standards encapsulated in Common Article 3 renders these problems superfluous.[94]

A second question that arises concerns non-international conflicts that are being fought extraterritorially without the consent of the territorial State. State practice, albeit sparse, indicates that if the territorial State is neither willing to disarm the non-state actor nor to consent to the intervention of the armed forces of the State under attack, international law permits the latter to resort to force in self-defence to the extent that the preconditions of self-defence are satisfied.[95] In such cases, the vast majority of legal experts are of the view that the rules of non-international

conducted on the ground, evidence of the active involvement of elements of the UPDF in certain provinces is cited in support of the international character of the conflict.

[93] In June 1996, the RPA was training Banyamulenge rebels in northwest Burundi.

[94] See e.g. 1998 Report of the SGIT on the DRC, para 93: 'the AFDL was responsible for violations of IHL including the detention of malnourished children being treated in a hospital, killing of wounded patients in another hospital, the beating and killing of nurses in those hospitals, denial of access by relief organisations to camps for displaced persons containing large numbers of ill and wounded person and the failure to collect and care for the sick and injured violated CA3.'

[95] N. Lubell, *Extraterritorial Use of Force Against Non-State Actors* (2010), chs 1–3.

armed conflict apply.[96] The inherent difficulty with this position for the State resorting to self-defence is that while the State may be acting lawfully, the armed forces operating extraterritorially may nonetheless be subject to domestic criminal prosecutions in the territorial State for having resorted to force without lawful authority on foreign soil since neither combatant status or privilege exists in non-international armed conflict.[97] But until such time as there is a hostile encounter between the armed forces of the respective States, the non-international armed conflict paradigm will prevail.

3.3. The use of force in armed conflict

As noted above, the principle of distinction is a fundamental principle that applies irrespective of the type of conflict. Consequently, disagreements over the classification of the conflicts during this period did not alter the fact that each of the warring parties was obliged not to attack civilians and civilian objects. The deliberate targeting of refugees fleeing from the camps by the AFDL and the RPA not only amounted to war crimes but crimes against humanity.[98] Insofar as the shelling of the camps was concerned, the principle of proportionality applied irrespective of classification. The ex-FAR and Interahamwe may have been legitimate military targets but those shelling the camps were under a legal obligation to consider whether the expected deaths and injury to civilians or damage to civilian objects would be excessive in relation to the concrete and direct military advantage anticipated. International humanitarian law also prohibits indiscriminate attacks; in other words attacks which employ a method or means of combat which cannot be directed at a specific military objective or the effects of which cannot be limited as required by law. The widespread shelling of the refugee camps was not only disproportionate but amounted to an indiscriminate attack. Thousands of refugees were pursued across the entire expanse of Congo's territory by the AFDL/RPA amd finally slaughtered; this indicates not simply a breach of the obligation to take precautions against the effects of attacks, but almost certainly that civilians were the direct targets of attacks.

3.4. Detention

Since different rules on internment apply in international and non-international armed conflict, the fact that there were multiple parallel conflicts being fought on

---

[96] For an alternative view, see discussion in ch. 3, section 9 above.

[97] This may explain why States that deploy their armed forces extraterritorially in response to attacks by non-state actors without the consent of the territorial State are willing, as a matter of policy, to apply international armed conflict rules. There may therefore be an emerging trend to categorize such conflicts as international since several specific benefits accrue. The international armed conflict framework would enable the deployed forces to lawfully resort to force in their engagement with the non-state actor and retain their right to combat immunity and POW status on capture.

[98] The crimes committed may also amount to genocide to the extent that it was the Hutu ethnic groups who were specifically targeted by the AFDL and RPA; for further details see Mapping Report, paras 509–18.

Zaire's territory during this period makes analysis complex. This challenge is compounded by the absence of official information on Zaire's detention policy and access to accurate and comprehensive data on who was being interned, on what grounds their detention was justified, and under what conditions they were being held. Nevertheless, there is considerable evidence, collated by human rights organizations, to show that during the period spanning the conflicts, 'arbitrary' arrests by the FAZ were frequent with large numbers of civilians being detained in military detention centres and prisons, particularly in eastern Zaire.[99]

As the conflict escalated, the Zairian authorities began detaining ever-increasing numbers of civilians, primarily of Tutsi ethnic origin, as well as journalists and human rights activists.[100] International humanitarian law offers no express guidance on the legal basis of internment in non-international conflict nor what conditions should apply to such internment since domestic law, conditioned by the human rights obligations of the State, has traditionally constituted the legal framework governing the deprivation of liberty.[101] There is some evidence to suggest that the Zairian authorities relied on a broad interpretation of 'reasons of security' to justify its detention practice.[102] But even if a large majority of detainees did in fact present a real security risk, there were clearly many who were interned merely by virtue of their ethnic affiliation, thereby constituting a serious infringement of human rights norms. Moreover, the apparent *en bloc* internment of certain sectors of the community was a disproportionate measure that amounted to collective punishment.[103] As far as the conditions of detention were concerned, appalling living conditions coupled with widespread mistreatment, often amounting to torture, were regularly documented; with no procedural guarantees for periodic review, detainees were left in a perpetual state of uncertainty as to whether their captivity would last for days or years.

If the government's record was deplorable, the AFDL and its allies together with other armed groups in the conflict were guilty of far worse. The policy pursued by the AFDL of taking no prisoners meant that, more often than not, members of the armed forces and civilians alike, who found themselves under the control

---

[99] See e.g. Amnesty International, 'Lawlessness and insecurity in North and South Kivu' (November 1996) 17.

[100] Most were held in detention centres run by the civil guard and/or in prisons across the country; Amnesty International, 'Rape, killings and other human rights violations by the security forces' (19 February 1997) 7.

[101] See further discussion in ch. 4, section 3.2 above.

[102] In July 1997, the *Collectif des Associations des droits de l'homme* (CADDHOM) produced a report ('Rapport d'activités janvier à juin 1997') denouncing the 'mass arbitrary arrests in South Kivu' while in a further report covering the period from July–December 1997 ('Rapport des activités janvier-mai 1997') CADDHOM makes reference to the 'startling number of arbitrary and illegal arrests in South-Kivu'. A number of other organizations, such as *Groupe justice et libération*, also document the widespread incidents of 'unlawful' arrests ('activity report for January–May 1997'). During 1996, the ICRC visited 603 people detained in connection with the violence and who were described as presenting a 'security threat'; ICRC, 'Annual Report' (1996) 64.

[103] See rule 103 of the ICRC Customary Law Study.

of the rebels, were generally executed.[104] Moreover, following the fall of Kinshasa, requests by the ICRC to visit any new detainees were rejected by the AFDL.[105]

The rules on internment in international armed conflict, particularly those pertaining to the treatment of POWs, are well-developed.[106] That these rules have the potential to 'create' a problem is exemplified by the decision of the Zairian authorities in October 1996 to parade before the media ten Rwandan detainees, described as 'prisoners-of-war', who had allegedly been captured while engaged in a military operation at Bukavu airport. Zaire's objective was to prove to the international community the depth of Rwanda's involvement in the conflict in eastern Zaire and to challenge the dominant narrative that the violence in the territory was non-international in scope. Nonetheless, to demonstrate that it was engaged in an international armed conflict, Zaire arguably violated article 13 of the Third Geneva Convention which provides that POWs 'must at all times be humanely treated [and]...must at all times be protected, particularly against acts of violence or intimidation and against insults and public curiosity'. This provision has been read to include the filming of POWs such that they would be individually recognizable thereby potentially causing humiliation.[107]

Whether the States parties accorded POW status to all captured members of the opposing forces is unknown. What is also unclear is whether those interned were held under conditions that complied with the obligations set out in the Third Geneva Convention and whether they were repatriated at the end of the hostilities. What is notable is that there is no evidence to indicate that captured members of the AFDL meeting the conditions of combatant status were accorded POW status by the Zairian authorities.

3.5. The concurrent applicability of international human rights law

During this period of armed conflict the international community assumed the co-applicability of international humanitarian law and international human rights.[108] However, what remained unaddressed was the legal basis upon which

---

[104] See generally, paras 42–47 of the Report of the Joint Mission and specifically para 48 which states: 'even in the case of genuine combatants, it should be recalled that neither the Banyamulenge and the Alliance rebels nor the Interahamwe militias and former FAR members take prisoners. This fact was acknowledged by the person known as the Alliance representative in Europe, a Mr E. Angulu...'. Informative testimony gathered by Amnesty International about the arrests, arbitrary detentions and torture practised by the ADFL on a widespread and systematic basis can be found in its reports'. See Amnesty International, 'DRC: Deadly Alliances in Congolese Forests' (3 December 1997) 34–47.

[105] ICRC, 'Annual Report' (1997) 60.

[106] See further discussion in ch. 4, section 3.1 above.

[107] The following January the Zairian authorities once more, in breach of the Third Geneva Convention, paraded on national television two 'prisoners-of-war'—a Ugandan corporal and a Rwandan lieutenant—to demonstrate the involvement of Uganda in the armed conflict; Reyntjens, *The Great African War*, 59, citing Agence France Press Kinshasa (31 January 1997).

[108] Letter dated 29 June 1998 from the Secretary-General addressed to the President of the Security Council, S/1998/581 (29 June 1998) reads: 'All the parties to the violence that racked Zaire, and especially its eastern provinces, during the period under consideration have committed serious violations of human rights or international humanitarian law'. Likewise, the 1998 SR Report on Zaire, para 89 states: 'there continue to be very serious violations of many human rights, including the right to life,

human rights law applied to the conduct of the foreign armed forces fighting in the Congo as well as the precise interplay between the specific rules that comprised each normative regime.

4. The Second Congo War: Africa's World War (2 August 1998–July 2003)

4.1. History

Although by mid-1997, relative peace and order had been restored in the rest of the country, the east remained volatile. In the Kivus, grave human rights abuses continued to be a regular occurrence with frequent reports of the RPA and other unidentified 'armed groups of Tutsi ethnicity' being involved in mass killings of civilians, ostensibly in retaliation for the continued raids into Rwanda by the ex-FAR and Interahamwe. Disgruntled by the new regime's inability to address effectively the activities of the insurgents, Rwanda, Uganda and Burundi secured a number of security arrangements with the now re-named DRC. As early as September 1997 the DRC's armed forces, the *Forces Armées Congolaises* (FAC), and the RPA had agreed to carry out joint operations against the various rebel groups in the Masisi region. During this period the FAC, comprised primarily of members of the Banyamulenge and Banyarwanda, continued to be commanded by officers of the RPA. Thus, despite Rwanda's announcement in the same month that it had withdrawn its troops from Congolese territory, the reality was quite different; otherwise referred to as 'soldiers without borders' the RPA remained on Congolese territory engaging, in some cases, in joint operations with the FAC but often acting unilaterally.[109] At Kabila's invitation, UPDF soldiers were also deployed on Congolese soil to combat the various rebel groups that were seeking to overthrow President Museveni; as with the RPA, UPDF troops were involved in both unilateral and joint operations with the FAC.[110]

As the months went by, Kabila found himself under growing pressure from both within and outside the DRC. The SGIT was beginning to ask difficult questions about the mass atrocities perpetrated during the First Congo War while, internally,

---

to physical and psychological integrity, liberty of person, freedom of association, due process and freedom of expression and opinion.'

[109] Rwanda's presidential spokesperson, Claude Dusaidi was also reported to have admitted, 'all [RPA troops] have been called back, except if some of them are still there in virtue of an accord with Laurent-Desire Kabila, [that is] something I am not informed about'. *Le Monde* (27 September 1997), cited by Reyntjens, *The Great African War*, 145 fn 4; see also accompanying text.

[110] *Case Concerning Armed Activities on the Territory of the Congo (Democratic Republic of the Congo v Uganda)* ICJ Rep 2005, 168, paras 36 and 46 *(Congo v Uganda)*. See also the Protocol on Security along the Common Border entered into between the DRC and Uganda on 27 April 1998.

there was mounting dissatisfaction with the continued presence of foreign forces operating on Congolese soil.[111] Anti-Tutsi sentiment among the local populations in the eastern provinces was further fuelled by the illicit transfer of land, natural resources and local industries to interests in both Rwanda and Uganda. In a bid to distance himself from his former allies and to diffuse the ethnic tension in the east, Kabila authorized the deployment of troops from other provinces to 'dilute' the make-up of the FAC in the Kivus. The strategy backfired, igniting violent confrontations between those non-Tutsi elements of the FAC and the RPA. The deepening fragmentation of the FAC along ethnic lines prompted Kabila to act once more and, in March 1998, a further contingent of FAC soldiers from Katanga were deployed to the region to contain the growing influence of the 'Tutsi elements' who were refusing to obey the orders of non-Tutsi officers. The latter meanwhile had been showing greater reluctance to fight the Mai-mai, ex-FAR and Interahamwe rebels and in some cases were tacitly aiding the insurgents.

Throughout the spring, relations between Kabila and Kagame[112] and Museveni deteriorated rapidly. In mid-July the UPDF unilaterally installed an operational base 15 kilometres inside Congolese territory and, amidst rumours of an impending coup organized by the Chief of Staff of the FAC, Colonel Kabarebe (a Rwandan national), on 26 July Kabila publicly ordered the withdrawal of 'all foreign forces' from the DRC.[113] On 2 August the RPA and Banyamulenge troops took control of Goma, Uvira and Bukavu, igniting the Second Congo War. Three days later, three civilian airlines transporting 600 to 800 Rwandan soldiers were rerouted to Bas-Congo, west of Kinshasa while, in the east, history appeared to be repeating itself with the speedy advancement of the Ugandan, Rwandan and Burundian troops in support of the Banyamulenge forces.[114]

As in 1996, ten days into the conflict a Congolese rebel movement united against the incumbent regime—the *Rassemblement Congolais pour la Démocratie* (RCD)— announced that it was responsible for initiating the war despite the weight of evidence indicating otherwise. But unlike 1996, following a request for assistance by Kabila, the Southern African Development Community (SADC) member States of Angola, Zimbabwe and Namibia intervened with military force. On 20 August, Zimbabwean troops arrived in Kinshasa and two days later, several Angolan battalions, supported by the air force, heavy artillery and armoured vehicles defeated the rebels in Bas-Congo forcing them, together with the RPA and UDPA to retreat.[115] By the end of September, Chad, Libya and Sudan had entered the conflict directly and indirectly in support of Kabila.

---

[111] *Association Zaïroise de Défense de Droits de l'Homme* (AZADHO) communiqué released on 4 December 1997 demanded the Congolese government 'lift all ambiguity surrounding the nationality of the soldiers operating in the [Kivu] province and . . . make sure that soldiers of the Rwandan army are prohibited from operating there, under whatever pretext'. Cited by F. Ryntjens, 'Briefing: the Second Congo War: More than a Remake' (1999) 98 *African Affairs* 245.

[112] Although Paul Kagame was Rwanda's Vice President, he clearly had full control and authority over all defence and foreign policy decision-making.

[113] *Congo v Uganda*, para 30.

[114] All three States justified their use of force on the grounds of self-defence.

[115] Reyntjens, *The Great African War*, 197.

That same month, a new rebel group led by Jean-Pierre Bemba—the *Mouvement national pour la libération du Congo* (MLC)—was created with the backing of Uganda which was closely 'involved in the recruitment, education, training, equipment and supplying of the MLC and its military wing, the [*Armée de libération du Congo*] ALC'.[116] According to the DRC, the UPDF also provided tactical support including artillery cover for ALC troops during military operations.[117] Within a matter of months, a substantial part of Congolese territory in several north-eastern provinces had fallen under UPDF control; shortly thereafter, administrative responsibility over a large part of Orientale province was, according to Uganda, delegated to the MLC.[118]

As the violence escalated it spread to other provinces, most notably Orientale Province, North Katanga and Equateur, bringing in ever greater number of parties to the conflict. On one level, the conflict pitted Kabila (with some elements of the FAC) and the armed forces of Zimbabwe (Zimbabwe Defence Forces (ZDF)), Angola (FAA), Namibia (Namibia Defence Force (NDF)), Chad (*Armée nationale tchadienne* (ANT)) and Sudan, against the military wing of the RCD, the *Armée nationale congolaise* (ANC), the MLC/ALC, RPA, UPDF and FAB.[119] Over time, and as alliances shifted, the Mai-mai entered the conflict in support of Kabila, as did the Burundian rebel group, the FDD and the ex-FAR and Interahamwe.[120] Despite denials by the DRC, there was strong evidence to indicate that the FAC were 'arming, training and supplying these armed groups'.[121]

In March 1999, growing disagreement between Rwanda and Uganda on the direction of the war led to the RCD dividing into a pro-Rwandan wing (RCD-Goma) and pro-Ugandan wing (RCD-ML). In June 1999, the Ugandan autho-

---

[116] *Congo v Uganda*, para 32.
[117] Ibid.
[118] Ibid, para 31.
[119] Mapping report, para 308.
[120] The Mai-mai were originally opposed to Kabila and fought against the AFDL during the First Congo War. But because their principal 'enemy' was the RPA, during the Second Congo War they fought against RCD-Goma and with the FAC.
[121] 'Report of the Secretary-General on the UN Mission in the DRC' S/2000/30 (17 January 2000); see also, Letter dated 18 November 1998 from the Secretary-General Addressed to the President of the Security Council, S/1998/1096 (18 November 1998). Of the estimated Rwandan Hutu armed forces on Congolese soil (15,000), approximately half were integrated into the Congolese Armed Forces (FAC); International Crisis Group, 'Africa Briefing, Disarmament in the Congo: Investing in Conflict Prevention' (12 June 2001). For Kabila, this was necessary because he had inherited a dysfunctional, disillusioned and undisciplined armed force (FAZ) from Mobutu. As a consequence he pursued a strategy of arming, supplying, training and organizing not only the ex-FAR/Interahamwe but also the FDD (*Conseil National Pour la Défense de la Démocratie-Forces pour la Défense de la Démocratie*) and ADF (Ugandan Allied Democratic Forces), together, these armed groups became Kabila's front line infantry. The FDD comprised the second largest armed group on Congolese soil and they too, were partially integrated in the FAC and moved between the DRC, Burundi and Tanzania. Both the Rwandan and Burundian Hutus fought alongside each other and with the Mai-mai. The briefing paper observed that 'despite the multitude of groups and warlords and despite different national agendas, the ex-FAR/Interahamwe, the FDD and the Mai Mai groups are operating increasingly as an integrated army, largely as a result of Congolese and Zimbabwean support and training. They have shown great sophistication and greater co-ordination in the last few months, and the ethnic Hutu-Tutsi agenda seems increasingly to influence the ideology of the Mai Mai, who see themselves as resisting Tutsi occupation in the DRC'. Ibid.

rities created a new province in the vicinity of its border with the DRC from a part of Orientale Province which was renamed Kibali-Ituri. Although the former deputy governor of Orientale was appointed as de jure administrator, Colonel Muzoora of the UPDF exercised de facto the duties of the governor and the UPDF was in effective control of the territory until its withdrawal on 2 June 2003.[122]

During the early months of the conflict, a number of attempts were made on the part of the UN and Organization of African Unity (OAU) to negotiate a ceasefire between the parties. The Lusaka ceasefire agreement, which was eventually adopted in July 1999, called for the disarmament of all armed groups and the withdrawal of all foreign troops from the Congo; regrettably it did little to alter the situation on the ground.[123] As the conflict continued civilians, and especially women and girls, became the object of unprecedented levels of sexual violence. The sheer scale of the massacres, rapes and pillaging perpetrated during the Second Congo War renders any attempt to document the violations of international humanitarian law and international human rights law hugely challenging, if not impossible.

The international community nonetheless remained optimistic that the Lusaka Agreement would form the basis of a sustainable ceasefire and had accordingly agreed to the deployment of a UN 'peace-keeping' force—the *Mission de l'Organisation des Nations-Unies au Congo* (MONUC)—to monitor its implementation.[124] In August 1999, the Council authorized the deployment of up to ninety military liaison personnel to facilitate the implementation of the ceasefire and in November all personnel deployed to the DRC under previous resolutions were brought together to constitute MONUC.[125] The following February the Council adopted resolution 1291 and, under its Chapter VII powers, authorized MONUC to monitor the cessation of hostilities and extended to it the right to use force in self-defence and to protect civilians under imminent threat of physical violence.[126] By the spring the conflict had reached a military stalemate with the country partitioned into three main blocs: the government and its allies had consolidated their hold over the south and west; Uganda, together with the MLC and RCD-ML controlled the north; and Rwanda together with RCD-Goma had secured the east.

In early May, a dramatic shift in one of the alliances unfolded when serious fighting erupted between the UPDF and the RPA over the control of Kisangani. The use of heavy artillery by the parties resulted in hundreds of civilian deaths, thousands being injured, severe property damage and the displacement of tens of

---

[122] 'Sixth Report of the Secretary General on UN Mission in the DRC' S/2001/128 (12 February 2001).

[123] By the terms of the agreement the signatory States comprising the DRC, Namibia, Rwanda, Uganda, Zimbabwe and Angola agreed to the cessation of hostilities within 24 hours of the signing. The representatives of the RDC and MLC declined to sign. The agreement also required belligerents to cease the movement of military forces and all acts of violence against the civilian population.

[124] 'Report of the Secretary-General on the UN Preliminary Deployment in the DRC' S/1999/790 (15 July 1999).

[125] SC res. 1279 (1999).

[126] SC res. 1291 (2000).

thousands.[127] In response to a plea by the Secretary-General[128] the Security Council, acting under Chapter VII, adopted resolution 1304 condemning unreservedly the fighting between UPDF and RPA in Kisangani that was held to be 'in violation of the sovereignty and territorial integrity' of the DRC and 'demanded the forces and those allied to them to desist from further fighting'. The resolution further demanded the immediate withdrawal of Ugandan and Rwandan forces from the DRC and that 'all other foreign military presence and activity, direct and indirect, in the DRC be brought to an end'.[129] Under mounting international pressure, on 22 June Uganda began withdrawing its forces as a 'unilateral gesture in support of the Kampala disengagement plan' and undertook to withdraw the remaining troops in accordance with the Lusaka Agreement. In early August, Rwanda followed suit with an announcement that its troops would likewise be withdrawn. Despite these public statements both parties continued to maintain their troop presence in the DRC until autumn 2002.

On 16 January 2001 President Kabila was assassinated, creating a window of opportunity for breaking the impasse. Ten days later his son, Joseph Kabila, was sworn in as the new President and, in his first address to the nation, called for 'an immediate and unconditional withdrawal of aggressor States', the revival of the Lusaka peace accord, and the organization of an 'Inter-Congolese Dialogue' (ICD). The Dialogue eventually led to the 2002 Sun City Agreement between the government, the MLC and RCD and paved the way for multipartite government and democratic elections.

On 30 July 2002, Rwanda and the DRC signed the Pretoria Accord. In exchange for the full withdrawal of the RPA, Kabila agreed to deal robustly with the ex-FAR and Interahamwe which had, in the interim years, regrouped to form the Democratic Forces for the Liberation of Rwanda (FDLR). By early October MONUC was able to confirm the departure of RPA troops from Congolese territory while the DRC government 'took the first tangible measures to comply with the terms of the agreement by interning a great many FDLR members before repatriating them to Rwanda'.[130] Meanwhile on 6 September, the Luanda Agreement between Uganda and DRC was signed paving the way for the withdrawal of the UPDF forces from Congo's territory. In mid-December, the *Global and All-Inclusive Agreement* was signed by the Government, MLC, RCD, RCD-ML, RCD-N and Mai-mai enabling the establishment of a transition government by the following summer. Despite the *All Party Agreement*, fighting continued in the east involving the Mai-mai, dissident factions of the RCD-Goma and the FDLR.

[127] See inter-agency assessment mission to Kisangani established pursuant to Security Council resolution 1304 (2000) which documents over 760 civilian deaths, 1700 wounded and over 4000 houses damaged or destroyed.
[128] 'Third report of the Secretary-General on the UN Mission in the DRC' S/2000/566 (12 June 2000), para 81.
[129] SC res. 1304 (2000).
[130] ICRC, 'Annual Report' (2002).

The Second Congo War is said to have claimed over 4 million lives and displaced a further 4 million people.[131]

4.2. Classification of the conflict

4.2.1 Classification of the conflict by the parties and by others

There is no doubt that as far as Kabila was concerned, by August 1998 the Congo was engaged, first and foremost, in an international armed conflict with Rwanda and Uganda.[132] This view was clearly shared by those SADC States which intervened militarily to assist Kabila in ridding Congo's territory of 'foreign' soldiers. Justifying his country's decision to send troops on the basis that 'we are convinced that the rebel force is supported from Uganda and Rwanda', Zimbabwe's Defence Minister added, 'it became very clear that our sister country has been invaded'.[133] Likewise Angola's Deputy Foreign Minister, Jorge Chikoti, defended his country's military involvement in the war to assist Kabila as a response to what was 'an unprovoked invasion' of Congo by Uganda and Rwanda that 'violates a principle of sovereignty and territorial integrity'.[134] By early September, even President Nelson Mandela, who was originally equivocal about intervening in the Congo, announced his support for the military intervention; in the face of 'aggression', he reasoned, Kabila, as President of the DRC, was entitled 'to call for assistance from his allies in Zimbabwe, Angola and Namibia'.

Kinshasa's view of its conflict with the RCD and MLC rebels presents a complex picture. Although it was common knowledge that the RCD and MLC rebels were supported by both Rwanda and Uganda, there is little evidence to indicate that the government viewed either of the armed groups to be under the overall control of, or belonging to any other State party to the *degree* that merited the operation of international armed conflict rules in its hostilities with the rebels. Moreover, on an operational level Kabila and his allies appeared to treat the conflicts with the RCD and MLC as non-international in character. Yet equally, Kabila's intransigent refusal to negotiate directly with the rebels because they were mere 'proxies' of Rwanda and Uganda would suggest that the overall control test was met and consequently the conflicts with the rebels were regarded as merely one aspect of the broader international armed conflict.[135]

---

[131] Internal displacement monitoring centre, cited in 'DRC: Nearly four million displaced or otherwise vulnerable' *IRIN News* (16 February 1999).

[132] In his address at the 12th Non-Aligned Movement Summit in South Africa on 2 September 1998, President Kabila called for the immediate withdrawal of Ugandan and Rwandan troops from Congo. See 'Kabila makes surprise summit entrance' *BBC News* (2 September 1998). See also, 'White Paper on Massive Violations of Human Rights and of the basic rules of International Humanitarian Law by the aggressor countries (Uganda, Rwanda and Burundi in the eastern part of the Democratic Republic of the Congo' annexed to letter dated 24 February 1999 from the permanent representative of the DRC to the President of the Security Council, S/1999/205 (25 February 1999).

[133] IRIN, Press Release (19 August 1998).

[134] 'Angola admits involvement in Congo' *BBC News* (31 August 1998).

[135] During the preliminary stages of the Lusaka ceasefire agreement, Kabila had refused to meet with the rebels arguing that 'the DRC had been invaded by Rwanda and Uganda, and that the rebel movements were mere proxies'; Reyntjens, *The Great African War*, 248.

The repetitive denials on the part of both Rwanda and Uganda as to the deployment of their respective troops in the Congo[136] did not deter the international community from recognizing that by the end of August 1998, an *international* armed conflict was being waged on Congolese territory. This is evidenced by the adoption of a statement made by the President of the Security Council on behalf of its members, urging all States to refrain from any interference in each other's internal affairs and calling for an immediate ceasefire and withdrawal of all foreign forces from Congolese territory. Notably, the Council urged all parties 'to respect and protect human rights and respect humanitarian law, in particular the Geneva Conventions of 1949 and the Additional Protocols of 1977, as applicable to them'.[137] But the view that some of the fighting in the Congo was international in character was not one that was unanimously accepted, as exemplified by the opinion of the Special Rapporteur who, in his September 1998 report observed:

> Towards the end of August, and at Kabila's request, the armed forces of Zimbabwe and Angola intervened in support of his regime; thus, with Rwanda and Uganda openly backing the rebels, there were at least five countries involved. Notwithstanding the foregoing, in the Special Rapporteur's view, the conflict remains an internal armed conflict, subject to article 3 of all four 1949 Geneva Conventions.[138]

Although the Special Rapporteur was to retract his opinion a year later, the initial confusion as to the classification of the conflict is perhaps best explained by taking account of the legal regime that existed just prior to August 1998. It is common ground that where foreign armed forces engage in an armed conflict against non-state actors with the full consent of the territorial State the hostilities are subject to non-international armed conflict rules. Thus, to the extent that both Rwandan and Ugandan armed forces were deployed in the DRC at Kabila's invitation, any and all armed confrontations between those forces and the rebels, in spite of the extraterritorial nature of the operations, were governed by Common Article 3 and the relevant customary international law rules.[139]

---

[136] E.g. following the decision on the part of some SADC members to intervene in the DRC, Uganda's presidential spokesperson Hope Kivangere condemned the decision on the ground that it risked 'escalating the conflict which in our opinion is a purely internal matter'; IRIN, Press Release (19 August 1998). Moreover, it was not until November 1998, that then Vice-President Kagame admitted for the first time that Rwandan soldiers were assisting the rebel forces in the Congo; BBC online network 'Rwanda admits having troops in Congo' 6 November 1998.

[137] UN Security Council, 'Presidential Statement on the situation concerning the DRC' S/PRST/1998/26 (31 August 1998).

[138] 1998 SR Report on Zaire, paras 26–7. Even in his report of 8 February 1999, the Special Rapporteur continued to maintain that the conflict was non-international in character. 'Towards the end of August, at Kabila's request, the armed forces of Zimbabwe, Angola, Chad and Sudan intervened in support of his regime, so that, with the open participation of Rwanda and Uganda on the rebel side, at least some seven countries ended up involved in the conflict. Notwithstanding this internationalization of the conflict, in the Special Rapporteur's view, it remains an internal armed conflict, subject to article 3 common to the four 1949 Geneva Conventions.' 'Report of the Special Rapporteur on the situation of human rights in the Democratic Republic of the Congo' E/CN.4/1999/31 (8 February 1999), paras 40–41 (1999 SR Report on the DRC).

[139] In its pleadings before the ICJ the DRC confirmed that both armed forces were on Congolese territory by invitation. The Court therefore observed, '[i]t seems certain that from mid-1997 and

What then was the effect of Kabila's unambiguous withdrawal of consent at the Victoria Summit on 8 August 1998? It is self-evident that the continued presence of RPA and UPDF troops on Congo's territory violated the principle of non-intervention but this fact alone would not have altered the legal regime that governed the armed encounters between those forces and the insurgents on Congo's territory. Nor would the entry of Zimbabwe, Angola and Namibia in support of Kabila have necessarily altered the applicable legal regime unless and until such time as armed hostilities broke out among the armed forces of the respective States. As Common Article 2 to the Geneva Conventions makes abundantly clear, '... the present Convention shall apply to all cases of declared war or of any other armed conflict which may arise between two or more of the High Contracting Parties, even if the state of war is not recognized by one of them'.

Thus, rules applicable in non-international armed conflict would have governed the fighting between SADC members and the Congolese rebel groups, the RCD and MLC, unless it could be shown that one or both armed groups were in fact under the overall control of Rwanda and/or Uganda. Even so, it is difficult to explain why the Special Rapporteur chose to disregard the weight of evidence implicating the direct involvement of the RPA and UPDF in the hostilities in the autumn of 1998.[140]

Revisiting his original opinion on the classification of the conflict/s and citing evidence of state practice as the basis for his re-evaluation, in September 1999, the Special Rapporteur concluded:

> Various facts make it necessary to reconsider this viewpoint. Foreign armies, including those who responded to the appeal by President Kabila to intervene in accordance with Article 51 of the Charter of the United Nations and those described by the Security Council as 'uninvited' countries, have exchanged prisoners in accordance with the provisions of the Third Geneva Convention of 1949; prisoners have been visited and exchanged in territories of the 'uninvited' countries; there have been clashes typical of

during the first part of 1998 Uganda was being allowed to engage in military action against anti-Ugandan rebels in the eastern part of Congolese territory.... [I]t is clear from the materials put before the Count that in the period preceding August 1998 the DRC did not object to Uganda's military presence and activities in its eastern border area. The written pleadings of the DRC make reference to authorized Ugandan operations from September 1997 onwards.' *Congo v Uganda*, para 45.

[140] It would seem that the Special Rapporteur was possibly persuaded by reports that Kinshasa was 'simply dealing with an insurrection staged by France'. 1998 SR Report on Zaire, para 19. Moreover, not only were States denying any involvement in the conflict, but some were actively seeking to destroy any trace of evidence pointing to their involvement. This is exemplified by the news item reporting the death of 89 Burundian soldiers in clashes with the FAC who were 'clandestinely' transported back to Burundi because Burundi continued to deny any military involvement in the conflict. 'DRC: Burundian soldiers reportedly killed near Moba' *IRIN News* (10 December 1998). For a persuasive alternative view on the 'start date' of the armed conflict between the DRC and Uganda, see separate opinion of Judge Kooijmans who suggests that it was only when Uganda acted upon the invitation of Rwanda and sent a battalion to occupy the airport of Kisangani—located at a considerable distance from the border area—on 1 September 1998 that it grossly overstepped the limits set by customary international law for the lawful exercise of the right of self-defence. Accordingly the measures taken by Uganda prior to this incident were for the purpose of repelling the persistent attacks of the Ugandan rebel movements in the DRC and thus would have been governed by non-international armed conflict rules; *Congo v Uganda*, paras 33–4.

any war between foreign national forces in Congolese territory; and 'uninvited' States have signed the Lusaka Ceasefire Agreement, which specifically refers to prisoners of war and the mixed nature of the conflict. The Special Rapporteur therefore believes that there is in fact a combination of internal conflicts (RCD against the Kinshasa Government and MLC against Kinshasa) and international conflicts, such as the conflict between Rwanda and Uganda in Congolese territory, clashes between the Rwandan and Ugandan armies and FAC. In the international conflicts, respect for the four Geneva Conventions is required, while, in the internal conflicts, the provisions of the article 3 common to the four Conventions are applicable.[141]

That there were international and non-international conflicts being fought simultaneously on Congo's territory was a view shared by a vast majority of external observers. What is less clear is whether the conflicts between Kinshasa and the two main rebel groups were regarded as separate non-international conflicts or whether they were considered to be part of the wider international armed conflict.[142]

With no immediate end to the conflict in sight, from March 1999 Kinshasa began to describe the eastern provinces and in particular the Kivus as being 'occupied' by the armed forces of Uganda and Rwanda.[143] In contrast to Rwanda, which insisted on defining its presence in the DRC exclusively in the language of self-defence,[144] Uganda oscillated between conceding some measure of responsibility as an occupying power[145] and rejecting such status on the grounds that with the limited number of troops it had deployed on the ground, it could not possibly control, let alone administer, the territory despite of the weight of evidence that indicated otherwise.[146] The international community remained silent on the issue until early 2001 following Kabila's assassination. The renewed fighting between the

[141] 'Report of the Special Rapporteur on the situation of human rights in the DRC' A/54/361 (17 September 1999) para 20.

[142] See e.g. US Department of State '1998 DRC Country Report on Human Rights Practices' (26 February 1999) which states: 'In the ensuing civil war [between the Government and the RCD], elements of the armed forces of Burundi, Rwanda, and Uganda operated inside the country in support of the rebels; elements of the armed forces of Angola, Chad, Namibia, and Zimbabwe operated inside the country in support of the Government; and the nongovernmental armed groups [Interahamwe, ex-FAR, Mai-mai, ADF] operated inside the country on the side of the Government, often as guerrillas inside RCD-occupied territory.'

[143] S/PV.3987, Security Council meeting (19 March 1999). See also statement by President Kabila at a special sitting of the Security Council on 24 January 2000 describing Rwanda, Uganda and Burundi as 'occupiers'. S/PV.4092, Security Council meeting (24 January 2000). During this debate, Canada's representative noted, 'the territorial integrity of the Democratic Republic of the Congo is contested by foreign military forces occupying vast swathes of its eastern provinces'.

[144] 'Report of the Special Rapporteur on situation of human rights in the DRC' A/56/327 (31 August 2001) para 20. For an interview with President Kagame on the topic, see e.g. 'Rwanda's Kagame Defends Congo Occupation' *CNN News* (6 September 2000).

[145] The Secretary-General's Sixth Report on MONUC states: 'MONUC dispatched a military and humanitarian team to Kampala and Bunia on 24 January [2001]. In Kampala the Ugandan Army Commander accepted that UPDF was responsible for the security of the civilian population in the Bunia area and undertook to make every effort to contain the violence.' 'Sixth Report of the Secretary General on UN Mission in the DRC' S/2001/128 (12 February 2001) para 27. By contrast, in its Rejoinder dated 6 December 2002, Uganda continued to reject the thesis that it was an occupier; *Congo v Uganda*.

[146] The Security Council became far more willing to condemn both Rwanda and Uganda after June 2000 following the third clash between the two States which had resulted in the killing and wounding

Hema and the Lendu in Bunia (the capital of Ituri district), prompted the European Union presidency to issue a statement on 1 February reminding Uganda of its obligations as the occupying power:

> the situation has been exacerbated by the continued military presence of the Ugandan army in this part of the DRC which hampers the efforts to re-establish peace there. The region is at present under the de facto control of the Ugandan army . . . the European Union calls on Ugandan authorities, responsible for upholding the respect for human rights in areas under their control, to do their utmost to put an end to these massacres . . . [147]

On 12 February, the Sixth Report of the Secretary-General on MONUC was released indicating that the UPDF was in effective control of Bunia;[148] shortly thereafter Security Council resolution 1341 was adopted expressly reminding all parties of their obligations under the Fourth Geneva Convention and stressing—for the first time—that 'occupying forces should be held responsible for human rights violations in the territory under their control'.[149] Two months later, the Secretary-General's Panel of Experts on the Illegal Exploitation of Natural Resources released its first report cataloguing the extensive looting and exploitation of the Congo's natural resources by the 'occupying forces', Uganda, Rwanda and Burundi.[150] In 2005, the ICJ found Uganda to have violated its obligations as an occupying power to prevent acts of looting, plundering and exploitation of Congo's natural resources.

4.2.2 Author's classification

Although the Second Congo War has been described as 'legally complex',[151] what makes unravelling this particular conflict (or rather tangled web of conflicts) more challenging than most are the difficulties encountered in ascertaining the necessary facts upon which an informed assessment can be undertaken. Not only were there an extraordinary number of States and non-state armed groups engaged in the fighting but there were multiple international and non-international conflicts being fought concurrently on the Congo's vast territory.[152] While some conflicts were

---

of hundreds of civilians in Kisangani; 'DRC: IRIN Special Report on the Ituri clashes' (3 March 2000), available at: <www.irinnews.org/Report.aspx?ReportID=12700>.

[147] European Union, 'Declaration of the Presidency on behalf of the European Union on the Hema-Lendu conflict' 5693/01 (1 February 2001).

[148] 'Sixth Report of the Secretary General on UN Mission in the DRC' S/2001/128 (12 February 2001).

[149] SC res. 1341 (2001) para 14.

[150] Letter dated 12 April 2001 from the Secretary-General to the President of the Security Council, S/2001/357 (12 April 2001). See also statement made by the US representative during the Security Council debate on the DRC on 3 May 2001, referring to the 'occupying powers'; S/PV.4317, Security Council meeting (3 May 2001). For a useful account, see Human Rights Watch, 'Uganda in Eastern DRC: Fueling Political and Ethnic Strife' (March 2001).

[151] Per Argentine representative to the Security Council who continued, 'in our view, it is neither exclusively internal nor exclusively international'; S/PV.3987, Security Council Meeting (19 March 1999).

[152] As well as the international armed conflicts and those conflicts that were possibly transformed from non-international into international ones by the indirect involvement of another State on the side of the non-state actor, there were also countless non-international armed conflicts waged between armed groups including those between the Mai-mai and the RCD-Goma in eastern Congo and

unmistakably international or non-international in character, classifying others remains more problematic. And this is because there simply is no reliable information regarding the precise nature of the relationship between some State parties to the conflict and some armed groups. Moreover, if at the start of the conflict these relationships were murky—thus making any assessment of control difficult at best—as the armed groups splintered, reconstituted and realigned themselves with the different belligerent States over the course of the conflict, gauging the element of control becomes even more testing.

Did the Special Rapporteur's 1999 revised evaluation of the legal framework more accurately reflect reality? As State practice demonstrates, there was no dispute among the States parties to the conflict that the armed confrontations between their respective military forces were subject to international armed conflict rules. In addition to statements made during the initial months of the conflict, that international armed conflict rules applied is evidenced not only by the granting of POW status to captured combatants of the opposing forces but by the terms of the Lusaka Peace Accord which expressly provided for the repatriation of combatants detained during the conflict.[153]

Whether the hostilities involving either the RCD or MLC should have been qualified as international armed conflict is far from certain. Although the threshold

---

between the Hema and Lendu militias in Ituri. In each of these cases, the evidence collated by, for example, MONUC and human rights NGOs based in the territory indicate that the two preconditions of Common Article 3—intensity of the violence and organizational attributes of the groups—were satisfied. See e.g. the decision of the Pre-trial Chamber in *Prosecutor v Germain Katanga and Mathieu Ngudjolo Chui* which found that there was 'sufficient evidence to establish substantial grounds to believe that between August 2002 and May 2003, an armed conflict took place in the territory of Ituri between a number of local organised armed groups including, *inter alia*, the *Union des Patriotes Congolais* ("the UPC")/*Forces Armées pour la Libération du Congo* ("the FPLC"), the *Front Nationaliste et Intégrationniste* ("the FNI"), the *Force de Résistance Patriotique en Ituri* ("the FRPI") and the *Parti pour l'Unité et la Sauvegarde de l'Intégrité du Congo* "the PUSIC"). These armed groups: (i) had a certain degree of organisation, insofar as such groups acted under a responsible command and had an operative internal disciplinary system; and (ii) had the capacity to plan and carry out sustained and concerted military operations, insofar as they held control of parts of the territory of the Ituri District.' See *Prosecutor v Germain Katanga and Mathieu Ngudjolo Chui*, ICC-01/04-01/07-717, Decision on the Confirmation of Charges (Pre-Trial Chamber I), 30 September 2008, para 239 (*Katanga and Chui*). The Mapping report also concludes at para 239: 'both the participation of foreign armed forces on Congolese territory and the direct support in terms of equipment, weaponry and combatants provided to several rebel groups through the period of the "second war" confirm that an international armed conflict was taking place in the DRC at the same time as internal conflicts between different groups of Congolese militiamen.'

153 Chapter 3 of the Lusaka Agreement states:

'3.1 Upon the cease-fire taking effect, all Parties shall provide the ICRC/Red Crescent with relevant information concerning their prisoners of war or persons detained because of the war. They shall subsequently accord every assistance to the ICRC/Red Crescent representatives to enable them to visit the prisoners and detainees and verify any details and ascertain their condition and status.

3.2. On the coming into force of the Agreement, the Parties shall release persons detained because of the war or taken hostage within three days of the signing of the Cease-fire Agreement and the ICRC/Red Crescent shall give them all the necessary assistance including relocation to any provinces within the DRC or any other country where their security will be guaranteed.'

of control is lower than that required to incur State responsibility,[154] the overall control test should not be mistaken as being easy to satisfy. As was emphasized by the ICTY Appeal Chamber, 'extensive and compelling' evidence is required to show that a State is 'genuinely in control of the units or groups'.[155] This, the Appeal Chamber reasoned, is particularly so where 'the general situation is one of turmoil, civil strife and weakened State authority'.[156] In *Lubanga* the Pre-Trial Chamber of the ICC was unable to find that an international armed conflict existed in the period from June 2002 to December 2003 under the *Tadić* test, presumably because insufficient evidence had been put before it of Uganda's 'role in organising, co-ordinating or planning the military actions of the military [non-state] group, in addition to financing, training and equipping the group or providing operational support to it'.[157]

In contrast, the *Katanga and Chui* Pre-Trial Chamber found that in addition to there being evidence to establish the direct involvement of the UPDF in Ituri during 2002–2003,

> [t]here is also sufficient evidence to establish substantial grounds to believe that Uganda was one of the main suppliers of weapons and ammunitions to these armed groups [the FNI/FRPI] and that the respective recipients' ability to successfully attack other groups was aided by this Ugandan military assistance. As a result, the Chamber finds that there is sufficient evidence to establish substantial grounds to believe that the conflict that took place in Ituri District between, at least, August 2002 and May 2003 was of an international character.[158]

Of all the conflicts in the DRC, it is those that were waged in Ituri during Uganda's occupation that are the most challenging to assess. There is no doubt that Uganda was the occupying power in Ituri from June 1999 until the withdrawal of the UPDF in 2003. As the ICJ noted, the presence of the UPDF in a particular location alone was insufficient to satisfy article 42 of the 1907 Hague Regulations which provides that 'territory is considered occupied when it is actually placed under the authority of the hostile army'. It was the factual substitution of Congolese authority with that of the UPDF (through, for example, the creation of a new province, the appointment of a de jure administrator and the exercise of de facto administrative powers) that functioned to impose the duties of an occupying State on Uganda.[159]

---

[154] In applying the effective control test to determine whether Uganda could be held responsible for the acts for the acts of the MLC, the ICJ concluded that the link was too tenuous. While there was ample evidence to show that Uganda had provided the MLC with both training and military support there was insufficient evidence to satisfy the element of effective control; *Congo v Uganda*, para 160. Whether the same conclusions might be drawn with respect to Rwanda and RCD-Goma is dependent on the evidence.

[155] *Tadić*, paras 138–9.

[156] *Tadić*, para 139.

[157] *Prosecutor v Thomas Lubanga Dyilo*, ICC-01/04-01/06, Decision on the Confirmation of Charges (Pre-Trial Chamber I), 29 January 2007, para 211. The Chamber distinguished between two periods: July 2002 to June 2003, and June 2003 to December 2003; in the first it determined that the conflict was of an international character.

[158] *Katanga and Chui*, para 240.

[159] See *Legal Consequences of the Construction of a Wall in the Occupied Palestinian Territory* (Advisory Opinion) ICJ Rep 2004, 136 for customary status of the Regulations.

As the occupying power, Uganda was required, inter alia, to take all feasible measures to restore, and ensure, as far as possible, public order and safety in the occupied area, while respecting, unless absolutely prevented, the laws in force in the DRC.[160] Moreover, the UPDF continued to be governed by international armed conflict rules in its hostile engagements with other State parties.

What is more complex is the legal framework that should have governed the hostilities between Uganda and the organized armed groups within the occupied territory. The answer to this question demands careful analysis and is best considered by examining the specific facts on the ground. Even prior to Uganda's occupation, there existed in Ituri protracted armed conflicts between various armed groups including the Hema, the Lendu and Ngiti militia. These conflicts were further aggravated by the involvement of the main national rebel groups—the MLC, RCD-ML and RCD-Goma—with each supporting the different local militia in an attempt to expand their own power bases in the Province.[161] Non-international armed conflict rules would have applied to hostilities between the various armed groups but only if the two preconditions—intensity and organization—were satisfied. Over the years, these conflicts were fuelled by the involvement of Uganda, Rwanda and the DRC, each of which supported one or other group at different times. With the intervention of State parties—directly and indirectly—the conflicts clearly had the potential to become international in character. But did Uganda's occupation of Ituri alter the classification of the conflict or did non-international armed conflict rules continue to prevail in the hostilities between Uganda and these groups? It is difficult to see how the occupation per se would have transformed the classification of the conflicts. The reclassification from non-international to international armed conflict could only have occurred had a relationship of overall control evolved between those organized armed groups operating in the occupied territory and another State party to the conflict. Only if it could be shown that an armed group belonged to or was acting on behalf of a State to the degree that satisfied the overall control test, would the hostilities between the UPDF and the group be governed by international armed conflict rules.

---

[160] Hague Regulations 1907, art. 43.

[161] During its occupation, Uganda was actively involved in the conflicts between the Hema and Lendu and provided weapons, training and support to each group as well as to the national rebels groups, the RCD-ML and MLC, among others. In 2002, internal disagreement within the RCD-ML resulted in violent conflict between the APC (the military wing of the RCD-ML) and the Union of Congolese Patriots (UPC) commanded by Lubanga, a leading Hema. During this period the Lendu militia were closely aligned with the RCD-ML. In June, the Ugandan authorities (which had helped to launch the RCD-ML) intervened to arrest Lubanga; nevertheless two months later, in August 2002 the UPDF took part in a joint operation with the UPC to oust the APC from Bunia. As the UPC gained power, Kinshasa began to strengthen the APC, Lendu and Ngiti militia providing weapons and training. These groups all shared a common objective: to expel the occupier. Having taken control of Bunia, the UPC began to pursue closer links with RCD-Goma and Rwanda and by January 2003, an alliance was established whereby RCD-Goma would provide military and political support to the UPC; there is also compelling evidence to indicate that Rwanda provided weapons, training and advice. In the face of this threat, Uganda supported the creation of anti-UPC coalition bringing together the Front National Integration (a Lendu political party) and the Patriotic Force Resistance in Ituri (a Ngiti political party). During 2002–03, amidst the ever-shifting alliances, over 5000 civilians were slaughtered across Ituri and tens of thousands displaced.

Based on this analysis, the decisions of the ICC Pre-Trial Chamber in the two cases of *Lubanga* and *Katanga and Chui* are problematic. In *Lubanga*, the Pre-Trial Chamber decided that 'as a result of the presence of the Republic of Uganda as an occupying Power', the conflict was of an international character from July 2002 to 2nd June 2003, the date of the effective withdrawal of the Ugandan army.[162] But however deep Uganda's involvement in the armed conflicts between the UPC and the FNI/FRPI, that alone cannot alter the normative regime from that of a non-international to an international armed conflict. Uganda clearly remained bound by the latter rules as it was engaged in an ongoing international conflict with Kinshasa; nevertheless, its hostilities with the UPC were governed by non-international armed conflict rules. Only if the requisite link between the UPC and Kinshasa (or for that matter any other State party) was demonstrated could an international armed conflict exist. The Chamber expressly notes that there was insufficient evidence to establish substantial grounds to believe that Rwanda and/or the central government of the DRC directly intervened in the armed conflict in the territory of Ituri district between August 2002 and May 2003.[163] It therefore follows that only if adequate evidence is tendered to demonstrate the overall control of the UPC by a State party, namely Rwanda or the DRC, can the charges pertaining to war crimes in an international armed conflict be upheld.[164] This raises the question of whether a distinction, in respect of the necessary evidential threshold of control, should be made between those armed groups who assert that they are fighting on behalf of the territorial State in situations of occupation and those that are under the overall control of a foreign State, including the occupying State. Thus, to take the example of the link between Kinshasa and the APC, Lendu and Ngiti militia in late 2002, might not the fact that they shared the common objective—to rid the Province of the occupier—amount to adequate evidence to demonstrate that those armed groups fulfilled the criteria of 'belonging to a Party' in an international armed conflict?[165]

---

[162] *Prosecutor v Thomas Lubanga Dyilo*, Decision on the Confirmation of Charges, Pre-Trial Chamber I (ICC- 01/04-01/06-803) 29 January 2007, para 220.

[163] *Katanga and Chui*, para 241.

[164] On 14 March 2012, Trial Chamber I released its judgment in the case of the *Prosecutor v Thomas Lubanga Dyilo* (ICC-01/04-01/06. Its analysis and findings in respect of classification correspond with the analysis in this text; see in particular paras 523–67.

[165] Some support for this can be found in the Pictet commentary to art. 4 of the Third Geneva Convention which states: 'International law has advanced considerably concerning the manner in which this relationship shall be established. The drafters of earlier instruments were unanimous in including the requirement of express authorization by the sovereign, usually in writing, and this was still the case at the time of the Franco-German war of 1870–1871. Since the Hague Conferences, however, this condition is no longer considered essential. It is essential that there should be a "de facto" relationship between the resistance organization and the party to international law which is in a state of war, but the existence of this relationship is sufficient. It may find expression merely by tacit agreement, if the operations are such as to indicate clearly for which side the resistance organization is fighting (24).' The *Tadić* Appeal Chamber also appeared to infer that a distinction might be warranted between the territorial State and foreign States when it stated: 'If . . . the controlling State is not the territorial State where the armed clashes occur or where at any rate the armed units perform their acts, more extensive and compelling evidence is required to show that the State is genuinely in control of the units or groups . . .' *Tadić*, para 38.

One unusual feature of the Second Congo War is seen in the armed conflicts that were fought between belligerent States on Congolese soil and which did not directly involve the DRC, as with the hostilities between Rwanda and Uganda over the control of Kisangani and the conflict between Uganda and Sudan over accusations that the latter was providing assistance to anti-Uganda insurgents including the FUNA, UNRF II, the National Army for the Liberation of Uganda (NALU) and the LRA.[166] These extraterritorial wars would have been international armed conflicts captured by Common Article 2. Since international humanitarian law is essentially comprised of rules that regulate the relationship between the belligerents, the geographical location of the conflict is increasingly being treated as immaterial.[167] Of course that is not to infer that the law is oblivious to the harm wreaked on the local population and/or property damage inflicted since in addition to regulating the relationship between the belligerents, the very purpose of international humanitarian law is to protect those who are not involved in the conflict.

4.3. Use of force

As far as the conduct of hostilities was concerned, the classification of the conflicts did not appear to have had any practical effect on the behaviour of any of the parties. The systematic violation of fundamental treaty and customary rules was a common feature of the conflicts irrespective of normative framework.[168] The principle of proportionality did little to curtail the use of force, while few observed the principle of distinction.[169] More often than not, civilians were deliberately targeted, often by virtue of their perceived ethnic affiliation. Government forces and their Angolan and Zimbabwean allies were guilty of indiscriminately shelling cities and towns killing hundreds of civilians and there was little attempt to distinguish between military objectives and civilian objects.[170] In the summer of 1998, the ANC/RPA/UPDF coalition took control of the Inga hydroelectric power station in the Bas-Congo, stopping the turbines on the dam for three weeks thereby depriving the province of power and water supplies. This action arguably violated the principle of distinction and rendered useless property that was essential to the survival of the population such as medical centres and the hospitals which resulted in increased number of deaths particularly among children.[171] The aerial bombardment of towns in Orientale province by FAC in January 1999 came under heavy criticism for violating the principle of distinction although in February FAC took

---

[166] *Congo v Uganda*, para 121.

[167] I have argued elsewhere that the law of war as it originally evolved was not bound by territorial conceptions. In other words, territorialized legal reasoning is a relatively modern phenomenon; L. Arimatsu, 'Territory, boundaries and the law of armed conflict' (2009) 12 *Yearbook of International Humanitarian Law* 157–92.

[168] See 1998 SR Report on Zaire, citing violations of IHL attributable to each of the parties to the conflict.

[169] See e.g. 1999 SR Report on the DRC at para 128 which states: 'The main victims of the war on both sides are civilians, including children and even nursing babies.' See also Mapping Report, paras 311–91.

[170] 1999 SR Report on the DRC, para 49 and Mapping Report, para 333. See rule 7 of the ICRC Customary Law Study.

[171] For details, see Mapping Report, para 334. Rule 54 of the ICRC Customary Law Study states, 'attacking, destroying, removing or rendering useless objects indispensable to the survival of the civilian population are prohibited'.

active measures to warn the civilian population of imminent aerial bombardment in compliance with their obligation to take precautions in attack.[172] The use of heavy weaponry by the RPA and UPDF in densely populated areas in August 1999 also came under heavy criticism for having violated the principles of distinction and proportionality and for failing to take precautions in attack. But in early May the following year when fighting broke out between the parties, Uganda took measures to warn the local population of imminent bombardment and to facilitate evacuation thereby resulting in far fewer civilian casualties. Nevertheless, the clash between the two forces in June 2000 which involved indiscriminate attacks with heavy weapons led to heavy civilian casualties in spite of the UPDF's efforts to arrange for the evacuation of the combat zones prior to the outbreak of hostilities.[173]

Insofar as the hostilities between the foreign armed forces and the various rebel groups were concerned, in practice there was little respect for any rules although non-international armed conflict rules continued to govern. The same rules would also have governed the armed confrontations between SADC members and those rebel groups that were using the DRC as a base from which to launch attacks into the territories of the respective States as, for example, in the case of Angola and UNITA. But the regrettable reality was that none of the parties appeared to comply with even the most basic international humanitarian law rules particularly in respect of civilian protection.

4.4. Detention

With the outbreak of the conflict, many Tutsis, Banyamulenge and those suspected of being rebel sympathizers were detained by the State authorities. By November 1998 detainee numbers had reached nearly 2000 many of whom were women and children. Most were imprisoned in overcrowded prisons and detention centres in appalling conditions while others were held in unauthorized prisons renowned for torture.[174] From July 1999 onwards, some of those detained were allowed to leave the country under the terms of an agreement between Kinshasa, UNHCR, the ICRC and several host countries.[175]

Despite having no lawful authority to do so, the rebels established many clandestine 'prisons' in the private homes of high-ranking RCD members, in specially adapted containers and in decommissioned aircraft that were described as 'torture centres' or 'extermination centres'.[176] Throughout the conflict, in the areas under government control, journalists, lawyers, religious leaders, human rights workers, politicians and trade union leaders were detained, generally on the charge of 'collusion with the rebels'.[177] The period of detention varied from days to

---

[172] Mapping Report, para 359. See rule 15 of the ICRC Customary Law Study.
[173] Mapping Report, para 362.
[174] 1999 SR Report on the DRC, para 50.
[175] Mapping Report, para 311.
[176] 1999 SR Report on the DRC, para 109.
[177] 'Report of the Special Rapporteur on situation of human rights in the DRC' E/CN.4/2001/40 (1 February 2001).

years. In rebel-held areas, the forcible repatriation of Rwandan and Burundian refugees was not uncommon, in violation of the principle of *non-refoulement*.[178]

However, amidst the irrational and all too often frenzied violence, a handful of rules were upheld particularly in respect of those detained in the course of the conflict by the armed forces of the respective belligerents. Records indicate that as early as September 1998, both the DRC and Rwanda had informed the ICRC of the mutually agreed conditions of access to detained prisoners of war as well as other captured persons. In June 1999, the Chadian Foreign Minister, Mahamay Saleh Annadif, publicly confirmed that Chad was holding 119 'prisoners of war' including twenty-seven Ugandans and about ten Rwandans who had been visited by the ICRC. Under the supervision of the ICRC, agreement was reached with Uganda and Rwanda for a return of Chadian POWs held by those countries in exchange for the repatriation of the POWs held by Chad. The remaining prisoners, according to the Foreign Minister, comprised Congolese rebels, who were to be 'handed over to the DRC authorities'.[179]

Under the auspices of the Political Committee, which was established by the 1999 Lusaka ceasefire agreement, the exchange of POWs and release of detainees in cooperation with the ICRC was facilitated throughout June 2000. Thus, in addition to direct negotiations between States,[180] on 16 June the Committee announced that all the parties had complied with the requirements of the ICRC and Red Crescent and that the release and exchange of prisoners had commenced when a total of 181 POWs were exchanged mainly involving Rwandan, Zimbabwean, Namibian and DRC forces who had been detained by the various belligerents.[181] Moreover, it was confirmed that the POWs had all been registered and regularly visited by the ICRC during the period of their captivity. Also in June the ICRC had transported thirty-five Zimbabwean and eleven Namibian POWs from Rwanda to the DRC and returned eighty-eight Rwandan POWs from the DCR; thirty-five Zimbabweans were taken from the DRC to Zimbabwe while forty-three Rwandan POWs were returned from Zimbabwe.[182]

In addition to the issue of POW repatriation, the Lusaka agreement, to which both the rebel movements became signatories,[183] expressly dealt with the far more contentious topic of the release of all those 'persons detained because of the war'.[184]

---

[178] Ibid. See further discussion in ch. 4 section 3.3 above.

[179] 'DRC: Chad to hand over prisoners of war' *IRIN News* (11 June 1999).

[180] E.g. during a meeting on 3 June 2000 between Kabila and Kagame the release of POWs had been discussed; 'Third report of the Secretary-General on the UN Mission in the DRC' S/2000/566 (12 June 2000).

[181] S/PV.4159, Security Council meeting (16 June 2000); see also 'Fourth report of the Secretary-General on the UN Mission in the DRC' S/2000/888 (21 September 2000) documenting the exchange of POWs at para 34: 'the authorities of the DRC released 88 Rwandan prisoners; Zimbabwe released 43 Rwandan prisoners; and Rwanda released 11 Namibian and 35 Zimbabwean prisoners.'

[182] In its annual report for 2000, the ICRC record having been involved in the repatriation of POWs and civilians, including 97 Rwandan POWs from the Congo to Rwanda, 9 Congolese POWs from Chad to Kinshasa and 156 Rwandan civilian internees from the Congo to Rwanda.

[183] The MLC was signed on 11 August while, due to internal disagreements, the RCD did not sign until 31 August 1999. The agreements had already been signed by the States involved in the conflict—Angola, DRC, Namibia, Rwanda, Uganda and Zimbabwe—on 10 July 1999.

[184] Lusaka Agreement, ch. 3.

Under the agreement, the signatories agreed not only to 'accord every assistance to the ICRC/Red Crescent representatives to enable them to visit the prisoners and detainees and verify any details and ascertain their condition and status' but, on the coming into force of the Agreement, to 'release persons detained because of the war or taken hostage within three days of the signing of the Cease-fire Agreement and the ICRC/Red Crescent shall give them all the necessary assistance including relocation to any provinces within the DRC or any other country where their security will be guaranteed'.[185] What is unclear is who was included in the term 'hostage', which remained undefined.[186] However, a striking distinction (at least on paper) is made between those who had taken an active part in the hostilities within the context of the Congolese 'civil war', in other words, the MLC and RCD rebels, who were treated as coequals under the Agreement, and other armed groups on Congo's territory. This differentiation is perhaps best exemplified by the agreement reached between the signatories in respect of the formation of a new Congolese National army whose soldiers would comprise 'the Congolese Armed Forces (FAC) and the armed forces of the RCD and MLC'. By contrast, there was consensus that other armed groups (including the ex-FAR, ADF, LRA, the Uganda National Rescue Front (UNRF II), Interahamwe, the Former Uganda National Army (FUNA), FDD, WNBF, UNITA) would be disarmed under the auspices of the Joint Military Commission working in collaboration with MONUC/OAU which would have the authority to track down and disarm such groups.

4.5. International human rights law

As on all previous occasions involving armed conflict on Congolese soil, the UN bodies treated human rights law as applying concurrently with international humanitarian law. The targeting of the civilian population and the failure to distinguish were repeatedly condemned as both gross human rights violations and violations of the laws of war.[187] Moreover, in his regular reports to the Security Council the Secretary-General continued to draw attention to the failure of both the government and the rebels to uphold human rights norms in the territories under their control.[188] While on one level, UN reports might be explained as

---

[185] Lusaka Agreement, section 3.2. Notably, commenting on access to both government and rebel held detainees, the ICRC noted that during 2000 'the customary rules were respected, in particular the right speak privately to detainees. The ICRC visited some 2,000 people deprived of their freedom on both sides of the front line'. The following year no new POWs were registered with the ICRC; however, the number of people arrested for reasons of 'State security' or 'in connection with the conflict' especially in eastern DRC remained high with a total of 796 new detainees being registered in 2001; ICRC, 'Annual Report' (2001).

[186] As highlighted by the Special Rapporteur, how this would work in practice remained uncertain since 'those whom the RCD regarded as "hostages" were considered by the Kinshasa Government to be "protected persons"; the word "hostages" is not defined in annex A of the Ceasefire Agreement'; 'Report of the Special Rapporteur on the situation of human rights in the DRC' E/CN.4/2000/42 (18 January 2000).

[187] Ibid, paras 119–20.

[188] E.g. the Secretary-General's second report on MONUC, dated 18 April 2000, refers to the human rights situation in the DRC 'whether in Government or rebel-held territory' as 'grave'. The

rhetorical gestures in part, it is unsatisfactory that the ICJ found Uganda in breach of its obligations to secure respect for the applicable rules of international human rights law, without clarifying the basis upon which such obligations accrue.[189] It remains unclear whether the Court's finding was based on the extraterritorial applicability of the treaties in question or whether those obligations arose out of the requirement for the occupying power to respect the laws in force in the DRC.

5. Transition or repetition? (2003–2011)

5.1. History

The establishment of a transitional government of national unity in 2003 did little to quell the armed conflicts in the eastern provinces; independent reports estimated that at the end of 2007, as many as 45,000 people continued to die every month as a result of the fighting.[190] Although Kabila had stopped arming the FDLR in 2002, his failure to act decisively to disarm the insurgents was to lead, once again, to large-scale armed conflict in North Kivu from the latter half of 2008 until early 2009. In the intervening years, the Congolese armed forces—renamed the *Forces Armées de la République Démocratique du Congo* (FARDC)[191]—had conducted a number of modest operations against the FDLR in South Kivu with limited results. But MONUC's efforts to disarm the rebels fared no better.[192] Ethnic tensions in local communities continued to simmer primarily, though not exclusively, as a result of the perceived status of the province as a de facto annex of Rwanda. But it was the poorly managed reorganization of the FARDC and the replacement of an ex-ANC commander and other senior members of the military hierarchy in South Kivu that triggered RCD-Goma to take direct action in June 2004. Led by Laurent Nkunda, the rebels seized Bukavu which resulted in the killing of several hundred civilians. Although under international pressure Nkunda was forced to retreat, his temporary demise seriously undermined Rwanda's influence in the province. The

report continues, 'the ongoing conflict has only served to exacerbate the already dire situation. Reports continue to be received of massacres, executions, arbitrary arrests, illegal detentions, torture, inhuman and degrading treatment of suspects and detainees, as well as the imposition of restrictions on freedom of expression, association and movement'; 'Second Report of the Secretary-General on UN Mission in the DRC' S/2000/330 (18 April 2000) para 55.

[189] *Congo v Uganda*, para 178.

[190] Burnet Institute and International Rescue Committee, 'Mortality in the Democratic Republic of Congo' (February 2008).

[191] The Global All-inclusive Agreement provided for the establishment of a unified Congolese defence force, the creation of a superior defence council chaired by the president and charged with guiding and providing advice on the restructuring and integration of the army, as well as for the disarmament of armed groups.

[192] Reyntjens, *The Great African War*, 210–11. In July 2003, the Security Council had authorized an increase in MONUC's military strength to 10,800 personnel; nonetheless, its mandate remained primarily reactive in that it was authorized to 'take the necessary measures in the areas of deployment of its armed units, and as it deems it within its capabilities...to protect civilians and humanitarian workers under imminent threat of physical violence'; SC res. 1493 (2003).

incident also proved damaging for MONUC which had failed to intervene despite having the mandate to resort to force to protect the civilian population.[193]

In response to the criticisms, MONUC began to adopt a more 'robust' posture and in 2005 a programme to forcibly disarm the rebel groups was implemented together with 'cordon-and-search' operations against 'illegal armed groups'.[194] By August 2005, it was apparent that MONUC's role in the DRC had altered significantly, with the Secretary-General reporting on 'MONUC-led robust military operations' in Ituri Province and large-scale military operations being conducted in South Kivu. In particular, Operation Falcon Sweep and Operation Iron Fist—joint military operations with FARDC—involved a large number of troops and an increase in 'the intensity of MONUC military operations' resulting in the destruction of six FDLR camps.[195]

Meanwhile, Nkunda had withdrawn to North Kivu where he formed the *Congrès national pour la défense du peuple* (CNDP) ostensibly to champion the rights of Congolese Tutsi community.[196] As relations between Kigali and Kinshasa once again deteriorated, Nkunda's CNDP increasingly found themselves to be the beneficiaries of Rwanda's patronage.[197] Throughout 2007 the CNDP began to extend their control over an ever-widening territory stretching up to the Congolese border with Uganda. In the core support areas of Masisi and Rutshuru, Nkunda introduced new administrative practices and changes to the police and security sector, as well as to the land distribution and tax systems.[198]

By summer 2008, tension was escalating as the CNDP and FARDC prepared for war and the RPA began reinforcing its troops along the border. In October clashes between the CNDP and FARDC resulted in the death of hundreds of civilians and the displacement of 250,000. As the FARDC retreated, villages were pillaged and wide-scale sexual violence was perpetrated by all sides.[199] At the end of October, with his fighters based just outside Goma, Nkunda declared a unilateral ceasefire. Severely weakened, Kabila approached both the EU and SADC for assistance but as the international community played for time, it was the intervention of the Secretary-General's Special Envoy for the Great Lakes Region, Olusegn Obasanjo, together with the Secretariat of the International Conference on the

---

[193] SC res. 1291 (2000).

[194] MONUC was encouraged to adopt a far more pro-active approach in its engagement with armed non-state actors and, in particular, with the FDLR; SC res. 1592 (2005).

[195] 'Eighteenth Report of the Secretary-General on the UN Mission in the DRC' S/2005/506 (2 August 2005).

[196] International Crisis Group, 'Congo: Bringing Peace to North Kivu' (31 October 2007).

[197] In an interview with a Belgian newspaper on 6 September 2008, Kagame was reported to have commended Nkunda for resorting to violence against the FARDC; cited in International Crisis Group, 'Congo: Five Priorities for a Peacebuilding Strategy' (May 2009) (ICG, *Five Priorities*).

[198] The CNDP 'continued to consolidate its hold in areas under its occupation, including by establishing a parallel police force and civil administration, including a de facto customs service at Bunagana, near the border with Uganda'; 'Fourth Special Report of the Secretary-General on the UN Mission in the DRC' S/2008/728 (21 November 2008).

[199] A census of UNICEF and related medical centres reported treatment of 18,500 persons for sexual violence in the first 10 months of 2008, 30 per cent of whom were children. In June 2008, 2200 rape cases were registered in North Kivu alone; ICG, *Five Priorities*, 4.

Great Lakes Region (ICGLR), which paved the way for a dialogue between Kabila and Kagame.

In January 2009, in an unexpected turn of events, the RPA was deployed to North Kivu in a joint operation with FARDC. Two days into the joint operation, Nkunda was detained by the RPA and, under the new leadership of General Bosco Ntaganda, an understanding was reached for the integration of the CNDP forces into the FARDC. Thirty-five days after the start of Operation 'Umoja Wetu', the joint operation came to an end with the withdrawal of RPA troops. Responsibility for security in the provinces was left in the hands of the FARDC with MONUC in support.

Within weeks, the FARDC launched a major anti-FDLR military operation— Kimia II—in the Kivus with MONUC providing logistical support. MONUC had been mandated to 'use all necessary means' in disarming the FDLR, ex-FAR/ Interahamwe, the LRA and the dissident militia of Laurent Nkunda, and its priority was to ensure that the rapprochement between the DRC and Rwanda was maintained by supporting the military campaigns against the FDLR.[200] Moreover, MONUC's participation in the operations, it was claimed, would assist in ensuring respect for international humanitarian law and international human rights thereby serving to better protect the civilian population. Lasting for ten months, the operation proved hugely contentious. Although its numbers were depleted, the FDLR remained active in the Kivus and continued to threaten the local population while the deployment of over 60,000 FARDC troops in the provinces resulted in greater insecurity for the local population. Subjected to retribution campaigns by the FDLR and serious human rights violations by the FARDC, women and girls, in particular, suffered the consequences of a highly militarized environment in which rape became endemic.[201] The mass atrocities committed by the FARDC placed MONUC in a difficult position as its mandate required it to ensure the protection of civilians under imminent threat of physical violence 'emanating from any of the parties engaged in the conflict' which clearly extended to the armed forces.[202]

During 2009, amidst concerns that MONUC could be held responsible for the violation of international humanitarian law and international human rights law committed by FARDC troops, revised terms of collaboration were entered into between the UN and the government of the DRC.[203] The new regime placed greater

---

[200] SC res. 1794 (2007).

[201] International Crisis Group, 'Congo: No Stability in Kivu despite Rapprochement with Rwanda' Africa Report No. 165 (16 November 2010).

[202] SC res. 1856 (2008); this obligation was re-affirmed in SC res. 1925 (2010) para 12 when MONUC was renamed the United Nations Organization Stabilization Mission in the DRC, or MONUSCO.

[203] It would appear that as far as the UN Legal Office was concerned, resolution 1856 required MONUC's involvement in any and all joint operations with the FARDC to be conditioned on respect for international humanitarian law, international human rights law and refugee law. In other words, military and operational support was governed by the policy of 'conditionality'; see 'MONUC—draft policy on conditionality of support to the FARDC' Note to Mr Le Roy (12 October 2009), available at: <www.innercitypress.com/doss8boot121609.html>.

emphasis on civilian protection, with continued MONUC support conditioned on respect for international law.[204] Although MONUC's involvement in the third joint military operation 'Amani Leo' (from January 2010) was governed by the new regime, during 2010 the UN's Office for the Coordination of Humanitarian Affairs reported rising levels of violence against civilians, not least by the FARDC.[205]

In addition to the Kivus, high levels of violence were also documented in Orientale and Katanga provinces. With the withdrawal of Ugandan and Rwandan armed forces from Orientale Province in 2002, fighting between the various armed groups in Ituri intensified in late 2002 and early 2003. As the violence escalated among the different armed groups including the Hema-dominated Union of Congolese Patriots (UPC), the Lendu-dominated Front for National Integration (FNI), the southern Hema-dominated Party for Unity and Safeguarding of the Integrity of Congo (PUSIC) and the People's Armed Forces of Congo (FAPC), hundreds of civilians were slaughtered in the town of Bunia and tens of thousands displaced.[206] However, by 2010, the FARDC with the support of MONUSCO (the successor to MONUC) had made considerable progress in securing some semblance of peace in the district; meanwhile MONUSCO has also continued to provide support to joint FARDC-UPDF operations against the LRA.[207]

During the early transition period, in addition to the FARDC forces, the ANC and the Mai-mai continued to operate in Katanga. Following a minor rebellion in October 2004 by a handful of Mai-mai militia, FARDC troops, under the command of Colonel Ilunga Ademar, entered Kilwa and, meeting no resistance, took control of the village within two hours of arriving. The soldiers then proceeded to loot many of the homes, systematically rape the women and girls, torture the villagers who were accused of collaborating with the 'rebels' and execute more than 100 people.[208] A year later, after considerable international pressure, Colonel Ademar and seven soldiers were prosecuted for war crimes and other crimes committed in Kilwa. The military prosecutor invoked article 8 of the ICC Statute and articles 173 and 174 of the Code of Military Justice together with supplementary charges including arbitrary detention, torture and murder. In June 2007 the Military Court acquitted the defendants in respect of all the charges concluding that the villagers had been killed during 'fierce' fighting between the rebels and the FARDC.[209]

---

[204] In practice, this has meant that MONUSCO has refused logistical support to a number of FARDC requests due to the presence of 'problematic' commanders.

[205] International Crisis Group, 'After MONUC, should MONUSCO continue to support Congolese military campaigns?' (19 July 2010).

[206] Some sources estimate that at least 5000 civilians were killed in Ituri between July 2002 and March 2003.

[207] 'Report of the Secretary-General on MONUSCO' S/2010/512 (8 October 2010). In early 2011, the security situation further deteriorated with an escalation in violence by the LRA although aid agencies continue to report on frequent human rights abuses by the FARDC; 'Security deteriorates in Uele districts' *IRIN News* (11 March 2011).

[208] 'Sixteenth report of the Secretary-General on the UN Mission in the DRC' S/2004/1034 (31 December 2004).

[209] RAID/Global Witness, 'Kilwa Massacre: Timeline of Key Events 1998–2010', available at: <http://raid-uk.org/docs/KilwaClassAction/Kilwa_timeline_EN_8Nov10.pdf>.

5.2. Classification of the conflict

5.2.1 *Classification of the conflict by the parties and by others*

The armed conflicts that have continued to ignite on Congolese territory following the establishment of the transitional government and the withdrawal of the 'uninvited' foreign armed forces have been treated by Kinshasa and other external observers as non-international in character in that they have all entailed violent clashes between the FARDC and various rebel groups or fighting among such groups.[210] Although the DRC's ratification in 2002 of Additional Protocol II introduced the possibility that some armed conflicts would be governed not only by Common Article 3 but by that Protocol, there is no evidence of the parties to any of the conflicts seeking to declare the Protocol to be applicable to the fighting. The international community has also avoided any express reference to the Protocol, choosing merely to remind the parties to 'comply fully with their obligations under international law, including international humanitarian law, human rights law and refugee law'.[211] In contrast, international human rights organizations took the view, from as early as 2007, that the armed conflicts between the FARDC and the CNDP and FDLR were governed by Additional Protocol II.[212]

5.2.2 *Author's classification*

Additional Protocol II applies to non-international armed conflicts 'which take place in the territory of a High Contracting Party between its armed forces and dissident armed forces or other organized armed groups which, under responsible command, exercise such control over a part of its territory as to enable them to carry out sustained and concerted military operations and to implement this Protocol'.[213] The criteria that must be satisfied before the Protocol becomes operational are clearly higher than the Common Article 3 threshold of application.[214] Nevertheless, since both the CNDP and FDLR operated under a responsible command and each exercised control over a part of the territory such as to enable them to carry out sustained and concerted military operations and to implement its terms,

---

[210] See ICRC's 2008 Annual Report at 99 which assumes the existence of a non-international armed conflict in the Kivus. Also see the conclusions of the Mapping Report in respect of the armed conflict in Katanga Province following the 2002 Pretoria Agreement which led to the withdrawal of Rwanda troops. The intensity of the violence together with the level of organization of the groups involved in the hostilities was such that an internal armed conflict continued to be waged; Mapping Report, para 486.

[211] UN Security Council, 'Presidential Statement on the situation concerning the DRC' S/PRST/2008/38 (21 October 2008); see also S/PV.6024, Security Council meeting (26 November 2008) and S/PV.6055, Security Council meeting (22 December 2008).

[212] See Human Rights Watch, 'Renewed Crisis in North Kivu' (October 2007); Amnesty International, 'Written Submission to the Human Rights Council' A/HRC/S-8/NGO/1 (27 November 2008).

[213] Additional Protocol II, art.1.

[214] See *Prosecutor v Sesay, Kallon & Gbao* (RUF case), SCSL-04-15-7, Judgment (Trial Chamber), 2 March 2009, paras 96–99 (RUF case).

Additional Protocol II applied to the conflicts.[215] Although the Protocol advances the basic set of rules provided in Common Article 3 by strengthening the protections due to civilians and developing the rules pertaining to the conduct of hostilities, the evolution of customary international humanitarian law rules for non-international conflict has rendered the treaty rules almost redundant.[216]

The violence and insecurity endured by the people of Congo throughout the 1990s clearly did not end with the withdrawal of foreign soldiers, the deployment of UN peacekeepers, or the establishment of a transitional government of unity. Non-international armed conflicts, caused, fuelled and perpetuated by the struggle for control over resources, have continued to blight lives. The intensity of the fighting in many cases leaves little doubt that the armed encounters should have been governed by non-international armed conflict rules; however, where the conditions of an armed conflict were simply not met, domestic law informed by human rights law remained the appropriate normative framework. Whether the atrocities allegedly committed by FARDC troops at Kilwa were perpetrated in the context of an armed conflict is questionable; but as serious human rights violations, the appropriate criminal charges lay in realms of domestic law.[217]

The most politically sensitive and legally complex issue that has arisen in recent years concerns the role of MONUC and MONUSCO[218] in the DRC's armed conflicts. Against the backdrop of the organization's evolving role from observer status to active participant in some of the hostilities in the DRC,[219] opinion has divided as to what normative regime most appropriately governs UN forces in such circumstances. The authority of MONUC (and MONUSCO) derives primarily from Chapter VII Security Council resolutions on the basis that the situation in the DRC 'constitutes a threat to international peace and security in the region'.

In 2000, resolution 1291 was adopted, authorizing the first deployment of military personnel with the mandate to use force, primarily in self-defence but also to defend civilians under imminent threat of physical violence.[220] During the

---

[215] As with Common Article 3, the criteria are applied objectively irrespective of the subjective conclusions of the parties; *Prosecutor v Akayesu*, ICTR-96-4-T, Judgment (Trial Chamber), 2 September 1998, paras 622–7.

[216] According to the ICRC Customary Law Study, 148 out of 161 rules identified were applicable in both international and non-international armed conflict; see also RUF case, paras 60–5.

[217] See the statement issued by the UNHCR immediately following the verdict: 'I am concerned at the court's conclusions that the events in Kilwa were the accidental results of fighting, despite the presence at the trial of substantial eye-witness testimony and material evidence pointing to the commission of serious and deliberate human rights violations.' 'High Commissioner for Human Rights Concerned at Kilwa Military Trial in the Democratic Republic of the Congo' UN Press Release (4 July 2007).

[218] On 1 July 2010, MONUC was replaced by the United Nations Organization Stabilization Mission in the Democratic Republic of the Congo (MONUSCO) in accordance with Security Council resolution 1925 of 28 May 2010 to reflect the new phase reached in the country.

[219] The Security Council originally authorized the deployment of up to 90 UN military personnel who were given the responsibility for liaising with the parties to the Ceasefire Agreement, assisting the Joint Military Command [JMC] and for briefing the Secretary-General on the situation on the ground; SC res. 1258 (1999) para 8.

[220] The resolution allowed for an increase in military personnel numbers of up to 5537. MONUC was authorized to take 'the necessary action, in the areas of deployment of its infantry battalions and as

first half of the decade, MONUC's ability to intervene to protect the civilian population was severely curtailed by the lack of manpower.[221] To enable it to carry out its functions, successive resolutions have steadily allowed for the increase in military personnel that, as of June 2011, stands at 19,815.[222]

MONUC's mandate has likewise evolved and expanded in response to the changing situation on the ground.[223] By 2004, growing calls for it to adopt a more proactive approach in protecting civilians culminated in the Council authorizing MONUC to use 'all necessary means' (albeit 'within its capacity') to carry out its protection mandate[224] and in 2005 it was authorized to employ more robust tactics in dealing with organized armed groups.[225] MONUC's increasing involvement in the armed conflicts inevitably led to questions being asked as to whether it was at any given moment a 'party' to the conflict so that international humanitarian law applied and whether its participation risked 'internationalizing' the armed conflicts.[226]

Although there was originally some doubt as to whether international humanitarian law applied to UN forces, it is now widely accepted that it does, although what remains hazy are under what circumstances the rules apply, the scope of the relevant rules and the holders of the obligations.[227] There is consensus that insofar

it deems it within its capabilities, to protect United Nations and co-located JMC personnel, facilities, installations and equipment, ensure the security and freedom of movement of its personnel, and protect civilians under imminent threat of physical violence'; SC res. 1291 (2000) para 8.

[221] For background, see 'Third Special Report of the Secretary-General on the UN Mission in the DRC' S/2004/650 (16 August 2004).

[222] SC res. 1445 (2002) para 10; SC res. 1493 (2003) para 3; SC res. 1565 (2004) para 3; SC res. 1621 (2005) para 1; SC res. 1635 (2005) para 2; SC res. 1736 (2006); SC res. 1843 (2008) para 1; SC res. 1856 (2008) para 1; and SC res. 1906 (2009) para 1.

[223] E.g. by 2003, MONUC was authorized to 'take the necessary measures in the areas of deployment of its armed units, and as it deems it within its capabilities' to protect not only those interests listed in resolution 1291 but also humanitarian workers under imminent threat of physical violence and to contribute to the improvement of the security conditions in which humanitarian assistance is provided; SC res. 1493 (2003). In 2004, in response to the armed conflicts in eastern provinces MONUC was given the additional task of inspecting the cargo of aircraft and transport vehicles using the port, airports, airfields, military bases and border crossings in the Kivus and Ituri to prevent the illicit supply of arms; SC res. 1533 (2004).

[224] Resolution 1565 extended MONUC's mandate (see in particular paras 4, 5 and 7) and in doing so, the Security Council authorized it to 'all necessary means' to carry out some of the tasks listed in paras 4 and 5. See also SC res. 1906 (2009).

[225] In resolution 1592, the Security Council emphasized that in accordance with the mandate extended under resolution 1565, MONUC was authorized to use 'cordon and search' tactics in respect of armed non-state actors to prevent attacks on civilians and to disrupt the military capability of such groups; SC res. 1592 (2005) para 7.

[226] An analogous argument was raised by the Defence in the RUF case and rejected by the Court; RUF case, para 973.

[227] As the UN Secretariat had argued for very many years, the UN as an international organization was not in a position to become a party to the 1949 Geneva Conventions, not least because it was unable to implement many of its provisions. Even its critics have conceded that 'conceptually, the UN cannot be considered a "Party" to a conflict nor a "Power" as understood by the Conventions'. Nevertheless, as Sassoli observes, 'in practice, . . . peacekeeping and peace-enforcement operations can involve, with or against the will of the UN, hostilities with the same characteristics and humanitarian problems to be solved by IHL as traditional armed conflicts'. M. Sassoli 'International humanitarian law and peace operations, scope of application *ratione materiae*' in G.L. Beruto (ed.), *International*

as UN command and control operations are concerned, it is the UN that is responsible for the conduct of the forces.[228] To reinforce its commitment to international humanitarian law, the UN has taken the position that where its forces are actively involved in situations of armed hostilities, and those forces are engaged therein as 'combatants', the rules encapsulated in the *Secretary-General's Bulletin on the Observance by United Nations Forces of International Humanitarian Law* provide the relevant normative framework.[229] As emphasized by the UN, two cumulative conditions are required for international humanitarian law to apply to a UN operation: the existence of an armed conflict in the area of its deployment and the active engagement of the force in the conflict as 'combatants' to the extent that they are taking a direct part in the hostilities.[230] Putting to one side the difficulties faced in determining whether or not MONUC was a party to the conflicts, there is no question that the conflicts remained non-international in character since all the military operations were conducted either with the support of the DRC or in close collaboration with the FARDC.

5.3. The use of force

As far as the use of force by (and against) UN peacekeepers is concerned, the critical question is not the classification of the conflict but whether the peacekeepers are at

---

Humanitarian Law, Human Rights and Peace Operations, Conference Proceedings, 31st Round Table on Current Problems of International Humanitarian Law, San Remo (4–6 September 2008).

[228] See further discussion in ch. 3 above, section 8. See also letter of 3 February 2004 from the United Nations Legal Counsel to the Director of the Codification Division in 'Responsibility of international organizations: Comments and observations received from international organizations' A/CN.4/545 (25 June 2004) 17, which states: 'As a subsidiary organ of the United Nations, an act of a peacekeeping force is, in principle, imputable to the Organization, and if committed in violation of an international obligation entails the international responsibility of the Organization and its liability in compensation.' The authority of the Security Council flows to the UN Secretary-General who appoints the Task Force Commander who reports directly to, and takes orders from the Secretary-General. Nonetheless, this does not preclude the parallel responsibility of troop-contributing States for the activities of their soldiers or police that form part of the UN peace-keeping operation. See generally, P. Klein, 'The Attribution of Acts to International Organizations' in J. Crawford, A. Pellet and S. Olleson (eds), *The Law of International Responsibility* (2010) 306–14.

[229] Critics have voiced concerns that the rules listed in the Bulletin are inadequate given the brevity of the document compared with the plethora of rules in convention and customary law that apply in international armed conflict. Some concern has also been raised as to how the Bulletin is to be interpreted in the context of the 1994 Convention on the Safety of United Nations (UN) and Associated Personnel. The most compelling argument for the direct applicability of convention and customary law rules to UN forces is that the *ius in bello* applies to all in times of armed conflict and is not contingent on the legal status of those using force or whether they have been authorized to do so by the Security Council. See generally 'International Humanitarian Law, Human Rights and Peace Operations' Conference Proceedings, 31st Round Table on Current Problems of International Humanitarian Law, San Remo (4–6 September 2008), in particular, D. Shraga, 'The applicability of international humanitarian law to peace operations, from rejection to acceptance' and M. Sassoli 'International humanitarian law and peace operations, scope of application *ratione materiae*'.

[230] Some experts have observed that the use of the term 'combatant' is misleading since 'combatant' status applies only in international armed conflict. Although this has led to the criticism that the Secretary-General's Bulletin can only apply in such conflicts, practice indicates that the rules contained in the Bulletin have been treated as binding in non-international armed conflict.

any particular moment, a party to the conflict. As with most peace-keeping missions, it was assumed that MONUC's personnel, given its original mandate, were civilians and therefore entitled to civilian protection under international humanitarian law and the specific protections encapsulated in the 1994 Convention on the Safety of United Nations (UN) and Associated Personnel.[231] MONUC personnel clearly had the right to resort to force in self-defence in the discharge of their mandate although the resort to lethal force was understood as a last resort measure conditioned on the principles of necessity and proportionality interpreted according to human rights standards.[232] By the end of the 1990s, in recognition of the special role played by peacekeepers in armed conflict situations, the international community deemed the targeting of those who were engaged in peace-keeping activities to amount to a war crime in both international and non-international armed conflict.[233]

Over the years, as MONUC's mandate evolved, it became increasingly apparent that some of its personnel were no longer exclusively engaged in peace-keeping activities but rather were beginning to take a direct part in the hostilities to an extent to warrant the loss of civilian status.[234] What criteria might be taken into account to assess whether or not peacekeepers have crossed the threshold that deprives them of civilian protection, is a difficult question.[235] Although the ICRC's Interpretive Guidance on the notion of direct participation in hostilities proves a

---

[231] UN peacekeepers are protected persons by virtue of the fact that they are civilians and thus, as the SCSL makes clear, 'the prohibition against attacks on peacekeeping personnel does not represent a new crime. Instead, as personnel and objects involved in a peacekeeping mission are only protected to the extent that "they are entitled to the protection given to civilian or civilian objects under the international law of armed conflict", this offence can be seen as a particularisation of the general and fundamental prohibition in international humanitarian law against attacks on civilians and civilian objects'; RUF case, para 215. See also ICRC Customary Law Study, rule 33.

[232] 'Peacekeepers are only authorised to use force in self-defence. It is now settled law that the concept of self-defence for these missions has evolved to include the "right to resist attempts by forceful means to prevent the peacekeeping operation from discharging its duties under the mandate of the Security Council"'; 'United Nations Peacekeeping Operations, Principles and Guidelines' (18 January 2008) 34–5 (UNPO, *Principles and Guidelines*). See also RUF case, para 228: 'The Chamber acknowledges that the operative United Nations doctrine on this issue is that peacekeeping operations should only use force as a measure of last resort, when other means have failed'; and at para 233: '. . . the use of force by peacekeepers in self-defence in the discharge of their mandate, provided that it is limited to such use, would not alter or diminish the protection afforded to peacekeepers.' See also discussion in ch. 4 above.

[233] ICC Statute, art. 8(2)(b)(iii) and art. 8(2)(e)(iii).

[234] See RUF case in which the SCSL held, 'it is also the Chamber's view that by force of logic, personnel of peacekeeping missions are entitled to protection as long as they are not taking a direct part in the hostilities—and thus have become combatants—at the time of the alleged offence. Where peacekeepers become combatants, they can be legitimate targets for the extent of their participation in accordance with international humanitarian law. As with all civilians, their protection would not cease if the personnel use armed force only in exercising their right to individual self-defence'; RUF case, para 233.

[235] As the SCSL suggests, it is the 'totality of the circumstances' that must be considered when determining whether or not at the material time UN personnel are entitled to civilian protection including the relevant Security Council resolutions for the operation, the specific operational mandates, the role and practices actually adopted by the peace-keeping mission during the particular conflict, their rules of engagement and operational orders, the nature of the arms and equipment used by the peace-keeping force, the interaction between the peace-keeping force and the parties involved in

useful tool,[236] by contrast to other civilians who take a direct part in the hostilities, UN forces do so on the basis of lawful authority derived primarily from Security Council resolutions complemented and supplemented by status of forces agreements with host States.

Based on the criteria identified in the Interpretive Guidance, the evidence indicates that MONUC was a 'party' to at least one or more of the pre-existing non-international conflicts in Ituri and Kivu in 2005 when it began to conduct far more proactive military operations both on a unilateral and joint basis with the FARDC. At least until the latter half of 2006, MONUC forces were engaged in combat operations and thus governed by the rules set out in the Secretary-General's Bulletin. Although some of the rules elaborated in the Bulletin have been criticized for not being customary in status, the Bulletin nevertheless provides the relevant binding legal framework for UN forces when they are engaged as a party in combat operations.[237] The ten-section Bulletin comprises rules pertaining to the principle of distinction; the means and methods of warfare; the treatment of civilians and person *hors de combat*; the treatment of detainees; and the protection of the wounded, the sick and medical and relief personnel.[238] The Bulletin does not distinguish between the types of conflict and therefore sections 5 and 6, which include rules on distinction, precautions in attack, proportionality, the prohibition on reprisals and the rules pertaining to the means and methods of warfare, apply equally to non-international and international armed conflict.

By 2007, MONUC's involvement in the military operations against the rebel groups had diminished and it was principally consigned to logistical support and operational training. For example, in the hostilities between the CNDP and FARDC in North Kivu, MONUC's role was limited to providing logistical and medical assistance.[239] As such, it was no longer a party to the conflict and consequently its forces were entitled to civilian protection.[240] As the violence intensified in early 2008, MONUC's part in the armed conflicts appeared to take on a different dimension. It provided intelligence, logistical support, operational advice, transportation of ammunition and rations, and the evacuation of FARDC casualties from conflict

---

the conflict, any use of force between the peace-keeping forces and the parties in the conflict, the nature and frequency of such force; RUF case, paras 234 and 1906–25.

[236] N. Melzer, 'Interpretive Guidance on the Notion of Direct Participation in Hostilities under International Humanitarian Law' (2009).

[237] The provisions that have been criticized for going beyond customary law include sections 6.3, 6.7 and 6.8. These include the prohibitions on using methods of warfare intended to cause widespread, long-term and severe damage to the natural environment, rendering useless objects indispensable to the survival of the civilian population, and causing the release of dangerous forces with consequent severe losses among the civilian population.

[238] 'Secretary-General's Bulletin: Observance by United Nations forces of international humanitarian law' ST/SGB/1999/13 (6 August 1999).

[239] 'Twenty-third Report of the Secretary-General on the UN Mission in the DRC' S/2007/156 (20 March 2007) and 'Twenty-fourth Report of the Secretary-General on the UN Mission in the DRC' S/2007/671 (14 November 2007).

[240] As the SCSL has made clear, the personnel of a peace-keeping mission are entitled to the protection afforded to civilians only insofar as the peacekeepers are not taking a direct part in hostilities; RUF case, para 1906.

zones.[241] Given the level of its involvement, the nature of the support, and the function it was performing, there are strong arguments for concluding that in 2008 MONUC was once more a party to the conflict.

In recognition of MONUC's transformed role on the ground, in December 2008, the Security Council adopted resolution 1856 urging it to implement its mandate through 'robust rules of engagement' and further authorized it to engage in joint military operations with the FARDC.[242] MONUC's concept of operations and the rules of engagement were subsequently revised to take account of 'provisions regarding fire support, air-to-ground engagements, preventing collateral damage and levels of authorization for the use of specific weapons systems'. These revisions were needed, according to the Secretary-General, 'to remove restrictive clauses on the terms of the use of force during the conduct of military operations, as outlined in the concept of operations'.[243] There is no doubt that from January 2010 onwards MONUSCO's forces have been actively engaged in Operation Amani Leo as 'combatants' within the meaning of the Secretary-General's Bulletin.

To accept that the status of peacekeepers in armed conflict is potentially a fluid one is to recognize the need to respond to the realities on the ground. But such a position is not without its problems. The consequence of adaptability is uncertainty, since the lawfulness of the use of force is inextricably tied to and contingent on the specific role of the peacekeeper at any given moment in time.[244] In taking on a combat function, those MONUC forces engaged in hostilities with the various rebel groups clearly benefited from a form of 'combat immunity' that derived from the terms of their mandate as outlined in successive Security Council resolutions.[245] But it also necessarily followed that during such times MONUC forces were lawful targets.[246] The unresolved question is what effect, if any, this has on *other* peace-keeping contingents deployed on the host State's territory not least because targeting peacekeepers who are entitled to civilian protection amounts to a war crime.

---

[241] 'Twenty-fifth Report of the Secretary-General on the UN Mission in the DRC' S/2008/218 (2 April 2008).

[242] SC res. 1856 (2008).

[243] 'Twenty-seventh Report of the Secretary-General on the UN Mission in the DRC' S/2009/160 (27 March 2009), paras 90–91.

[244] C. Garraway, 'To Kill or Not to Kill? Dilemmas on the Use of Force' (2009) 14 *Journal of Conflict & Security Law* 499 at 510.

[245] The concept of combat immunity is generally regarded as applicable only in international armed conflict since the authority to resort to force in non-international armed conflict rests exclusively with the State or by way of Chapter VII Security Council resolutions.

[246] Because the 1994 Convention on the Safety of United Nations and Associated Personnel criminalizes attacks against UN personnel, questions arose as to the relationship between the Convention and international humanitarian law when peacekeepers were engaged as combatants. Although art. 2 provides that the Convention 'will not apply to an UN operation authorized by the Security Council as an enforcement action under Chapter VII (of the UN Charter) in which any of the personnel are engaged as combatants against organised armed forces and to which the law of international armed conflict applies', the ICC Statute expressly clarified the relationship between the two regimes by defining war crimes to include attack against peacekeepers 'as long as they are entitled to the protection given to civilians or civilian objects under the international law of armed conflict'.

5.4. Detention

Additional Protocol II explicitly mentions internment,[247] thus confirming that it is a form of deprivation of liberty inherent to non-international armed conflict. Nonetheless, the Protocol is silent as to the grounds of internment and due process rights.[248]

MONUSCO's detention policy, as with all other UN operations, is governed by the 2010 Interim Standard Operating Procedures on Detention issued by the UN Department of Peacekeeping Operations. The policy document expressly requires that the rules must be applied in a manner consistent with international human rights law, international humanitarian law and refugee law and moreover, that the *lex specialis* of international humanitarian law pertaining to detention is not affected by the Procedures. Under the Procedures, any person detained by UN personnel shall be released or handed over to the relevant detaining authorities of the territorial State as soon as possible and within forty-eight hours of capture.[249] Handover is precluded where there are substantial grounds for believing that there is a real risk that the detained person will be tortured or ill-treated, persecuted, subjected to the death penalty or arbitrarily deprived of life; in any of those circumstances, the only available option, albeit somewhat counter-intuitive, is release.[250] In providing practical guidance, the document thus exposes the fundamental problem that lies at the root of most UN operations in non-international armed conflict and post-conflict situations: that there is often an unbridgeable gulf between the aspirations of the law and the reality on the ground.

5.5. International human rights law

Although there is no dispute that international human rights law governs UN operations, Security Council resolutions authorizing the deployment of such missions—whether civilian or military—rarely make express reference to the applicability of the legal regime to UN personnel.[251] Resolution 1865 (2008), in authorizing joint military operations with the FARDC, nonetheless explicitly provides that such operations are to be conducted 'in accordance with international humanitarian, human rights and refugee law'.[252]

---

[247] Additional Protocol II, art. 5 and 6.

[248] See further discussion in ch. 4, section 3.2 above.

[249] In exceptional circumstances, a detainee may be kept in UN custody for longer; paras 73–5.

[250] The principle of *non-refoulement*—found in various guises in international humanitarian law, human rights law and refugee law—prohibits States (and therefore UN missions) from transferring a person, irrespective of status, to another State if there are substantial grounds to believe that he or she runs a real risk of being subjected to certain violations. See further discussion in ch. 4, section 3.3 above.

[251] 'International human rights law is an integral part of the normative framework for United Nations peacekeeping operations. . . . United Nations peacekeeping operations should be conducted in full respect of human rights and should seek to advance human rights through the implementation of their mandates'; UNPO, *Principles and Guidelines*, 14.

[252] SC res. 1856, paras 3(g) and 14.

6. Conclusion: Framing the DRC within the law

6.1. Difficulties of classification

The primary difficulty of classification is not that the law is indeterminate but that the facts pertaining to the situation under consideration are unclear or disputed. As this case study demonstrates, collating the necessary evidence to determine accurately the appropriate legal framework is often, if not always, impeded by conflicting narratives and the volatile chaos that is the very nature of armed conflict. In the case of the Congo, these challenges are amplified by its geography and history. Congo's vast territory coupled with its porous borders and its history of perpetual cross-border migrant flows and associated violence makes reliable evidence-gathering an almost impenetrable task and even allegations of the active deployment of foreign troops on its territory have been difficult to confirm. These impediments have been further compounded by State interests and a deep moral ambiguity that both intervention and non-intervention has engendered among the international community. As a consequence, the political rhetoric has often prevailed over factual evidence. This is so both in respect of the existence of an armed conflict and of the parties to the conflict.

Whether a situation of violence has crossed the Common Article 3 threshold to warrant the application of international humanitarian law rather than remaining subject to domestic law is an evidential question requiring that the violence has reached a certain level of intensity and that those implicated in initiating and perpetuating it are doing so in an organized manner through some command structure. The jurisprudence of tribunals has assisted in identifying what factors might be taken into account when considering both elements but it is the latter criterion that has proved more problematic since the organizational command structure and the practice of non-state armed groups are frequently not easy to discern. A related question pertaining to organized armed groups is whether motivation is a relevant factor. Particularly in the period following the Second Congo War, much of the violence has involved the control over natural resources for financial gain. Opinion has divided on whether such conduct is more appropriately regulated through the law-enforcement paradigm rather than the law of armed conflict. International humanitarian law's indifference as to the actor's motive is founded on good reason.

Over the last five decades, the Congo's territory has been the site of every conceivable 'type' of armed conflict.[253] As its history vividly illustrates, spill-over conflicts have fuelled international conflicts and all too often neighbouring States have incited further internal violence to advance their own interests. What is revealing is that despite the progressive development of the law applicable to non-international armed conflict, which has extinguished the divide between the two types of conflicts except on a very few issues, States have continued to insist on

---

[253] See the typology in ch. 4, section 2 above.

the distinction. Of course this is only to be expected since classification is itself the inexorable offshoot of sovereign authority that insists on the absolute monopoly of violence within its territorial boundaries. This reasoning has resulted in a difference of opinion among legal scholars as to what normative regime applies to conflicts involving a State and an organized armed group fought on the territory of another State without the consent of the territorial State. In other words, were the armed conflicts between the UPDF and LRA or between the RPA and Interahamwe waged on Congolese soil without the consent of Kinshasa subject to international or non-international armed conflict rules? The view taken on this issue necessarily determines the answer to whether an occupying power is bound by international armed conflict rules in all its violent encounters with organized armed groups within occupied territory.[254] While the vast majority of experts are agreed that the classification of a conflict is determined by the parties to the conflict and therefore non-international armed conflict rules apply, the minority view cannot be dismissed lightly.[255]

In addition to the co-existence of multiple international and non-international armed conflicts, it would appear that the DRC has been the site of a number of non-international armed conflicts that have been transformed into international ones with the indirect involvement of another State in support of the organized armed group against the government. The overall control test, that now functions to determine when that threshold of indirect involvement has been met, was the outcome of judicial creativity on the part of the *Tadić* Appeals Chamber which found itself in a legal straitjacket. The utility of the test within international criminal law's system is not disputed although the evidential threshold that must be met before a conflict is found to be unambiguously international appears to be high.[256] Moreover, what remains unsettled is whether the test for finding that an organized armed group 'belongs' to a Party to the conflict is an identical test to that which determines 'overall control'. The Appeals Chamber may have extrapolated the latter from the former but the concept of 'belonging' to a Party as found in treaty law is clearly preconditioned on the existence of an international armed conflict.

Two difficulties that have not been addressed fully by the international community concern peace-keeping operations and classification. First, when UN forces undertake military operations against the armed forces of the territorial State or the armed forces of a foreign State on the territory of the host State, it would follow that the armed conflict would become international in character. The question then arises as to whether the UN forces would be governed by international humanitarian law in its entirety or be subject only to the rules provided in the Secretary-General's Bulletin. If it is the former, how then would some of the rules

---

[254] A general rule however should not be read as precluding the possibility of the exception.

[255] See further discussion in ch. 3, section 5.1 above.

[256] ICOI could not adduce sufficient evidence linking the training and supplying of weapons to the ex-FAR/Interahamwe to the Zairian State despite evidence implicating members of the Zairian government in such activities for personal profit.

encapsulated in the Geneva Conventions be implemented in practice, not least in respect of detention? A second difficulty concerns the geographical reach of a conflict. If, as is the case with MONUSCO, UN forces become a party to the conflict in one geographical area and as a consequence lose their civilian immunity, does the same apply to all peacekeepers deployed within the territorial boundaries of the State? Such a result is not only counter-intuitive but, clearly, hugely problematic for troop-contributing States.

6.2. Use of force and detention

As far as the conduct of hostilities is concerned, the classification of the different conflicts appeared to matter little to the parties engaged in the armed violence. This appears to be so for two distinct reasons. First, the developments in customary international law suggest there is little difference between the rules that govern the conduct of hostilities in international and non-international armed conflict. Thus, for those parties that did comply with the rules, the classification of the conflict was immaterial. This is best illustrated by the example of MONUC which in its *military operations* has, by and large, complied with the laws pertaining to the conduct of hostilities as provided in the Secretary-General's Bulletin.[257] Second, the classification of the conflict was simply not a consideration for those who did not comply with any of the rules.

However, by contrast with the rules on opening fire, classification obviously mattered to the States parties in respect of internment. There is ample evidence to show that during the Second Congo War each of the States parties distinguished between lawful combatants and other armed groups by according the former POW status when detained. Whether those interned as POWs were in fact accorded their full rights under the Third Geneva Convention is not known. The rudimentary infrastructure and procedural mechanisms existing at the time in the DRC would suggest that many of the provisions would have been difficult to implement in practice. Whether other States were able to comply fully with their Convention obligations is also not known. The extent to which the classification of the conflict mattered to the States involved in the Second Congo War is further evidenced by the express reference to the repatriation of POWs in the Lusaka Peace Accords.

The absence of international law rules regulating detention in non-international armed conflict resulted in grave consequences for all those who were detained in the course of the armed conflicts in the Congo. This lacuna enabled all parties to claim wide powers of detention and to define the terms of detention. During the conflicts, the State authorities, under both Mobuto and Kabila, claimed sweeping powers of detention on the grounds of 'reasons of security' with little concern for integrating procedural guarantees or for complying with minimum standards on the conditions of detention. The right to detain was also asserted by rebel groups during the Second Congo War which was clearly at odds with both domestic law

---

[257] MONUC's reputation is not entirely unblemished as some of its peacekeepers have come under severe criticism for sexual exploitation.

and human rights law since neither envisages the right of non-state actors to detain.[258]

The absence of an express prohibition on *refoulement* in non-international armed conflict resulted in many Rwandan and Burundian refugees being forcibly returned to their respective States. During both the Congo Wars, it was not uncommon for refugees—including children—to be 'repatriated' to unknown fates.[259] Although Common Article 3 can be read to incorporate the principle of *non-refoulement*, the absence of express rules all too often functioned to facilitate the forcible return of refugees.[260]

6.3. Looking to the future

The Congo's wars have been characterized by the failure on the part of the vast majority of armed actors to comply with the most basic principle of international humanitarian law: that attacks may not be directed against civilians.[261] The history of Congo's violence reveals time and again how the principle of distinction—the cornerstone of law of armed conflict—played little, if any, part in the armed encounters between government forces and rebel groups and in the fighting among such groups. Rather, civilians have been deliberately targeted by all the parties. In an attempt to account for why the principle has had no purchase, the ICRC observed in the aftermath of the First Congo War: 'As the conflict was marked by sharply drawn ethnic divisions and the proliferation and fragmentation of armed groups, a humanitarian message based on the respect of people not or no longer taking part in the fighting generally had little if any chance of being heard.'[262]

The failure on the part of successive governments since independence to nurture a disciplined armed force linked primarily by national loyalty resulted in internal fragmentation and divisions based on ethnic affiliation. This has inevitably meant that in times of conflict, the Congo's armed forces have often proved, at best, unreliable and, at worst, complicit in the mass atrocities perpetrated against the civilian population on ethnic lines. Over the last decade, the international community has invested heavily in the reform of the DRC's security sector through the deployment of MONUC and MONUSCO. The value of such initiatives cannot be over-stated since they have the potential to alter behaviour by embedding a culture based on the rule of law, not least, international humanitarian law. But how else might a country begin to tackle the problem of armed violence between parties that view the principle of distinction as an intrinsically counter-productive means by which to achieve their objectives? The measures that Kabila's administration adopts in light of the findings of the Mapping Report will be subject to close

---

[258] See further discussion in ch. 4, section 3.2 above.
[259] Mapping Report, para 256.
[260] See further discussion in ch. 4, section 3.3 above.
[261] See ICRC Customary Law Study, rule 1.
[262] ICRC, 'Annual Report' (1997) 62.

scrutiny,[263] for not until criminal sanctions are enforced against those who specifically target civilians is it likely that conduct will alter. What is clear is that the DRC faces multiple challenges on an unprecedented scale that it cannot hope to address without some measure of external assistance.

At the State celebrations marking the fiftieth anniversary of its independence, President Kabila described the moment as representing a 'new departure' for the DRC. It is yet to be seen whether Kabila will retrace the path paved by his two predecessors, or deliver on his promise and in so doing disavow Fanon's prediction that 'the apotheosis of independence is transformed into the curse of independence'.[264]

Chronology

March 1993	Large-scale violence breaks out between the Hunde, Nande and Nyanga tribes and the 'immigrant' communities comprising the Banyarwanda in Masisi.
April–July 1994	Civil war in Rwanda; RPF seizes power; 2 million Hutu refugees flee—in particular to Zaire (DRC).
Autumn 1995	Large-scale violence in North Kivu (Hutu v Hunde and Tutsi; Hunde v Tutsi and Hutu), Rwandan Hutu attack targets within Rwanda from Zaire refugee camps.
June–July 1996	Banyamulenge in South Kivu are persecuted.
September 1996	Banyamulenge conflict supported by Rwanda.
October 1996	AFDL formed with Laurent-Desire Kabila as spokesperson (US pro-AFDL; France pro-Mobuto). Refugee camps attacked in North and South Kivu. Uganda invades Zaire.
18–31 October 1996	Uvira, Bukavu and Goma fall.
4 November 1996	Nairobi I regional summit on Zaire.
November–December 1996	Mass return of Rwandan refugees; others flee westward. Humanitarian intervention to protect refugees aborted.
16 December	Nairobi II regional summit.
25 December	Bunia falls.
February 1997	Angola enters on the side of the anti-Mobuto coalition.
18 February 1997	Security Council resolution 1079 (5-point peace plan).
March 1997	Kisangani falls. Massive slaughter by RPA of Rwandan refugees in Zaire.
19 March 1997	Nairobi III regional summit.
April 1997	Fall of Lubumbashi and Kikwit.
May 1997	Fall of Kinshasa. Kabila sworn in as President.

---

[263] Following the release of the Mapping Report and speaking on behalf of President Kabila, Ambassador Ileka Atoki's commented, 'like all Congolese people, I want to see justice for these crimes and I want to help rebuild our country on the basis of the rule of law'. See 'Justice for the victims in Congo' *The Huffington Post* (1 October 2010).

[264] F. Fanon 'Concerning Violence' in F. Fanon (ed.), *The Wretched of the Earth* (1963) 76–7.

February 1998	Mutiny by Banyamulenge soldiers in Bukavu.
26 July 1998	Kabila orders foreign militaries to leave the DRC.
2 August 1998	Goma, Bukavu and Uvira fall.
5 August 1998	RPA attack Kitona; Angola intervenes to defend Kabila.
12 August 1998	RCD formed.
19 August 1998	SADC authorizes deployment of Angolan, Zimbabwean and Namibian forces to support Kabila.
August–October 1998	Kisangani and Kindu fall.
October–November 1998	Uganda and Rwanda admit to having armed forces in DRC; MLC formed.
May–June 1999	Hostilities between RPA and UPDF in Kisangani.
May 1999	RCD splits into RCD-ML and RCD-Goma.
June 1999	Ugandan General Kazini 'creates' province of Kibali-Ituri and appoints governor.
10 July 1999	Lusaka Accord.
July 1999	Mass atrocities in Ituri.
August 1999	Hostilities between Rwanda and Uganda in Kisangani.
October 1999	MONUC deployed.
28 August 2000	Arusha Accord on Burundi.
16 January 2001	Kabila assassinated.
26 January 2001	Joseph Kabila assumes office.
25 February 2002	Inter-Congolese Dialogue in Sun City.
April 2002	Transitional government between Kabila and Bemba.
30 July 2002	Pretoria Accord between Rwanda and DRC.
6 September 2002	Luanda Accord between Uganda and DRC.
September 2002	Rwanda withdraws forces.
6 May 2003	UPDF withdraws from Ituri.
May 2004	Nkunda captures Bukavu.
26 October 2004	US tripartite-agreement (Uganda, Rwanda, DRC) to deal with 'negative forces'.
July–October 2006	Elections—Kabila sworn in as president.
October 2006	Offensive in eastern DRC by CNDP headed by Laurent Nkunda with support from Rwanda (to protect the Banyamulenge).
August 2007	Fighting in Kivu between Congolese army (FARDC) and CNDP; CNDP v Mai-mai; FDLR v Congolese army.
December 2008	Mass atrocities by LRA in northern Congo; announcement of joint operation by DRC and Rwanda v CNDP and FDLR in the Kivus.
February 2009	Rwandan forces withdrawn.
March 2009	Operation Kimia II (MONUC and Congolese army v FDLR).
December 2009	Kimia II suspended.
January 2010	MONUC-supported operation Amani Leo launched.

7

Colombia

*Felicity Szesnat and Annie R. Bird**

1. Introduction

Colombia continues to experience the longest running and constantly evolving armed conflict in the world today. There has been a great deal of fluctuation both in the intensity of the fighting, and the range and organization of the actors involved over nearly half a century of hostilities. Analysing all of the issues raised by so many years of conflict in-depth is impossible within the constraints of this chapter. Therefore, the authors look briefly at its origins and evolution, but concentrate on the period from 1994 to the present day, this being the period of the greatest intensity in fighting, with the greatest number of actors involved, and raising the most controversial issues in relation to the classification of conflicts. These issues include: whether criminal violence can ever be classified as being an armed conflict to which international humanitarian law is applicable; whether recognition of belligerency is still a viable concept in international law today; under what circumstances the acts of paramilitary groups may be attributed to the State in which they operate; and finally, in what circumstances hostilities carried out by one State in the territory of another State qualify as an international or a non-international armed conflict.

In discussing issues relevant to characterizing the conflict, this chapter focuses on a few selected groups only, namely, those viewed as being representative of the range of issues confronting anyone attempting to classify the Colombian conflict: the *Fuerzas Armadas Revolucionarias de Colombia* (FARC) and *Ejército de Liberación National* (ELN), as they constitute the two main non-state armed groups fighting against the Colombian authorities; the *Autodefensas Unidas de Colombia* (AUC), as it formed the umbrella body for paramilitary groups active from 1994 to 2003, when the demobilization process began; the Black Eagles and *Organización Nueva Generación,* as they represent best the two ends of the spectrum of 'new illegal' armed groups which have arisen from the ashes of the AUC post-demobilization;[1]

* We are grateful to Dr Clara Sandoval-Villalba for comments on earlier drafts. Responsibility for the content of this chapter, however, lies solely with the authors.

[1] The term 'new illegal armed groups' is used in Colombia to denote groups arising post-demobilization of the AUC; however, in this chapter, the term 'non-state armed groups' will be used to describe all groups which engage in hostilities, and which are not State organs.

and finally, a purely criminal enterprise, *Los Rastrojos*, will be considered, since this group has been involved in active hostilities against both FARC and the ELN, as well as the Colombian armed forces. The roles of Ecuador, Venezuela and the United States (US) in the conflict will also be examined, particularly in the context of Operation Phoenix, carried out in March 2008 by Colombia mostly within Ecuadorian territory.[2]

2. Brief outline of the Colombian hostilities

Colombia has experienced many conflicts during its history; estimates are that it faced 'more than 50 armed conflicts' during the nineteenth century alone.[3] This current phase of hostilities, which is said to date from 1964, has its roots in the assassination on 9 April 1948 of Jorge Eliécer Gaitán, the Liberal Party's presidential candidate, which sparked off riots in the capital, Bogotá.

The riots gave rise to '*La Violencia*', a ten-year period of civil conflict in the Colombian countryside between supporters of the Colombian Liberal Party and the Colombian Conservative Party, which resulted in between 200,000 to 300,000 deaths, even though these groups were not well organized.[4] *La Violencia* ended in 1957 with an agreement between the Liberals and the Conservatives to establish the *Frente Nacional*, which saw the two parties taking turns to govern the country.[5] Nevertheless, the conflict continued in rural areas, where peasant armies joined with leftist guerrillas to gain or retain possession of land.[6] These groups were able to wage hostilities, but were unable to form a central command, and did not control much territory. Still, they were sufficiently bothersome to the Colombian State that, in 1955, various 'military expeditions' were mounted against them.[7] In 1957, these groups ceased armed activity against the State.[8]

This period also witnessed the start of an extensive collaborative effort between the US and Colombia to develop the latter's internal security apparatus.[9] This led

---

[2] This is not the only occasion on which Colombia has been accused of violating another State's sovereignty, but it is the best-known incident, hence its selection for analysis.

[3] United Nations Office on Drugs and Crime, *Crime and Instability: Case Studies on Transnational Threats* (2010) 9 (UNODC, *Case Studies*).

[4] J.F.G. Forero, 'Colombia in Armed Conflict? 1946–1985' Papel Político, Universidad Javeriana (2005) 50 (Forero, *Colombia in Armed Conflict*).

[5] Inter-American Commission on Human Rights, 'Report on the Demobilization Process in Colombia' (2004), para 34.

[6] Congressional Research Service, 'Colombia: Conditions and US Policy Options' (12 February 2001) 8 (CRS, *Colombia and US*).

[7] Forero, *Colombia in Armed Conflict*, 55–7.

[8] Ibid, 60.

[9] D.M. Rempe, 'The Past as Prologue? A History of US Counterinsurgency Policy in Colombia, 1958–66' (March 2002) 4 (Rempe, *A History of US Counterinsurgency*). The Colombian armed forces and the police force (civilian in nature) are both defined as 'public forces'. They fall under the Ministry of Defence for fiscal reasons, and because they both engage in 'counter-insurgency' operations. The Commander of the Armed Forces commands the army, navy and air-force, whilst the National Police has its own director, a general, who coordinates the activities of the police in collaboration with the

to vastly expanded internal security activities in Colombia under the US Military Assistance Program. In addition, a distinction began to emerge between armed groups which were involved in purely criminal activities, and those armed groups which used criminal means to fund their political aims.[10]

2.1. The 1960s

The 1960s saw the emergence of several new non-state armed groups in remote areas of the country, in particular, ELN and FARC, although FARC had been operating previously under the name *Bloque Sur*.[11]

FARC remains the largest and oldest insurgent group in the Americas. It claims to be a revolutionary, agrarian, anti-imperialist Marxist-Leninist organization of Bolivarian inspiration that represents the rural poor in a struggle against Colombia's wealthier classes. At its inception, FARC had fewer than 400 fighters;[12] this had almost doubled by the end of the 1960s.[13] FARC's first armed encounter with Colombian forces occurred in 1966 in Quindio.[14]

ELN was formed in 1963 by 'Catholic radicals and left-wing intellectuals',[15] and ideologically was influenced by the Cuban Revolution.[16] ELN started out with around 40 fighters, and grew to having 100 fighters at the end of the decade;[17] it carried out its first military action in January 1966.[18] However, both FARC and ELN were small groups which were rather disorganized, capable only of sporadic violence.

Nevertheless, the threat posed by these groups led to the government's adoption of Decree 3398 in 1965, which provided the basis for civilian participation in military activity in Colombia. Article 33 of the Decree allowed the Ministry of Defence to arm and control *Comunidades Campesinas para la Vigilancia* (Peasant Vigilante Communities).[19] In 1968, Law 48 was adopted, which transformed Decree 3398 into permanent legislation, authorizing the State to create civilian patrols and the Ministry of Defence to provide them with weapons usually reserved for the military, to be used for search, control and destroy operations. The military's vision for self-defence groups was as follows: to repel guerrilla activities; recruit loyal officers for the reserve; and train them in combat techniques, defence tactics

Armed Forces Commander. Therefore, wherever the term 'public forces' appears in this chapter, it should be read as including both armed forces and police forces.

[10] Rempe, *A History of US Counterinsurgency*, 31.
[11] UNODC, *Case Studies*, 9, 74.
[12] The term 'fighters' will be used to describe those employing violence on behalf of non-state armed groups, rather than other terms such as guerrilla, terrorist, insurgent etc., which have other, specific legal implications, or which have become pejorative in their use.
[13] Forero, *Colombia in Armed Conflict*, 75.
[14] Ibid, 63–4.
[15] S. Hansom, 'FARC, ELN: Colombia's Left-Wing Guerillas' (2009) 1, available at: <www.cfr.org/publication/9272/> (Hansom, *Left-Wing Guerillas*).
[16] Forero, *Colombia in Armed Conflict*, 63.
[17] Ibid, 75.   [18] Ibid, 63–4.
[19] *Decreto Legislativo* 3398 de 1965.

and psychological indoctrination. The military also stated that, ' . . . the network of self-defence represents a powerful instrument for the defence of the nation against domestic or international offensive actions. Its organization must be at all times under military control'.[20]

In spite of the military's vision for these 'self-defence groups', they were not particularly violent around this time.[21]

2.2. The 1970s

In the 1970s, FARC was active in nine different areas, and grew to having 3000 members. It had a hierarchical command and control structure, and adopted a political programme.[22] Originally, FARC fighters were easily identifiable: they wore uniforms and carried their assault rifles openly, and their units moved around the countryside in large formations.[23] For the first fifteen years or so of its existence, FARC banned farmers living within its territory from growing coca. However, FARC later permitted and even encouraged farmers to grow coca, taxing farmers and using these taxes to fund its political and military activities.[24]

ELN, in contrast, nearly sank without trace. In September 1973, two brothers of the ELN commander-in-chief, Fabio Vasquez, were killed by the Colombian army, along with nineteen other fighters. About a year later, Vasquez 'abandoned' the ELN, delivering a 'near-fatal blow' to ELN in the process.[25]

2.3. The 1980s

In 1982, FARC changed its military structure and adopted a more aggressive military programme.[26] In 1984, the Colombian government held its first peace talks with the organization, leading to a tentative ceasefire. In 1985, a 'legitimate' political party, the *Unión Patriótica* (UP), was launched, supported by FARC amongst others. In 1986, the UP gained representation in Congress in the general elections.

---

[20] See M. Escobar, 'Seize the State, Seize the Way: State Capture as a Form of Warlords Politics in Colombia' PhD thesis (2011) ch. 1, p. 3 (Escobar, *Seize the State*); M. McClintock, *Instruments of Statecraft: U.S. Guerrilla Warfare, Counterinsurgency, and Counterterrorism: 1940–1990* (1992) 223–4; República de Colombia, Comando General de las Fuerzas Militares, 'Reglamento de Cooperación Civil Militar' (1986) 33, 40–4, 68, 72; Comando General de las Fuerzas Armadas, 'Reglamento de Combate de Contraguerrillas' EJC 3–10 Reservado (1969).

[21] For a more detailed description of this period, see Human Rights Watch, 'The "Drug War" in Colombia: The Neglected Tragedy of Political Violence (An Americas Watch Report)' (1989) 11–18 (HRC, *The Drug War*); Human Rights Watch, 'The Killings in Colombia (Los asesinatos en Colombia)' (April 1989) 50–5.

[22] International Crisis Group, 'The History and Current State of FARC' (March 2009), available at: <www.crisisgroup.be/flash/farc_mar09/farc.html> (ICG, *FARC*).

[23] T. Pfanner, N. Melzer and K. Gibson, 'Interview with Sergio Jaramillo Caro' (2008) 90 (872) *International Review of the Red Cross* 824 (Pfanner et al, *Interview*). At the time of the interview, Sergio Jaramillo Caro was the Colombian Vice-Minister of Defence.

[24] ICG, *FARC*.

[25] International Crisis Group, 'Colombia: Prospects for Peace with the ELN' (4 October 2002) 11.

[26] It also renamed itself FARC-EP (FARC-*Ejercito del Pueblo*).

In response to the UP's political success, death squads linked to paramilitary groups began a violent campaign against the party, killing an estimated 3000 of its members, and assassinating its leader and presidential candidate in 1987. As a direct result of this assassination, FARC withdrew from the 'legal' political sphere, and focused on building up its military strength.

During the 1980s, FARC carried out an increasing number of kidnappings— mainly of high-profile people—with the aim of exerting political pressure on the Colombian government. Later in the decade, FARC's kidnappings were mostly carried out for financial reasons, as a source of funding. In addition, by 1982, FARC had entered into formal agreements with drug barons regarding drug production, levying taxes on the drugs industry and using this money to finance its political and military operations. By the end of the 1980s, FARC was also involved in most phases of coca production and trafficking, and had taken control of these phases. This was mostly because FARC had had a disagreement with the Medellin cartel, ending its links with this cartel.

During this period, the strength of non-state armed groups was such that the Colombian government made a number of efforts to negotiate with them, flourishing as they did in its remote, undeveloped rural areas. In 1984, President Betancur negotiated a ceasefire with FARC and released many imprisoned fighters, but ELN rejected the government's ceasefire proposal. Initially, paramilitary groups had begun to emerge in the 1980s to provide private security for important economic and political sectors in Colombia (including local drug barons, ranchers, business people and politicians), who used them to protect their interests from non-state armed groups; these non-state armed groups were at that time funding themselves partly through kidnapping and extorting money from those sectors.[27]

Although Law 48 provided for civilians to be armed by the State, and some of these civilians were also involved in paramilitary activity, it would be incorrect to view the Colombian government as solely responsible for the rise of the paramilitaries. Admittedly, the emergence of paramilitaries was part of the State's counter-insurgency strategy, but the involvement of paramilitaries themselves in drug trafficking progressively located them outside the orbit of State control.[28] Nevertheless, some government officials invoked Law 48 as justification for their support of these groups. However, in 1989, most of Law 48 was revoked, making self-defence groups illegal.[29]

2.4. Early 1990s to 2002

FARC ended its truce with the government in 1990 after some 2000 to 3000 of its members who had demobilized were murdered, mostly by paramilitary groups.[30]

---

[27] A. Carrillo-Suarez, '*Hors de logique*: Contemporary Issues in International Humanitarian Law as Applied to Internal Armed Conflict' (1999) 15(1) *American University International Law Review* 7 (Carrillo-Suarez, *Contemporary Issues*).

[28] Escobar, *Seize the State*, 1.

[29] Decrees 813, 814, 815 and 1194 were used to revoke most of Law 48. For a more detailed description of this period, see HRC, *The Drug War*.

[30] US State Department, 'Background Note: Colombia' available at: <www.state.gov/r/pa/ei/bgn/35754.htm>.

FARC carried out its first large-scale military attack in 1996, against the *Las Delicias* military base, and succeeded in killing 54 soldiers, and capturing 60. Over the next two years, FARC carried out more large-scale attacks, many against military targets, reaching the peak of its military powers in the late 1990s.[31] During this time, FARC and ELN had expanded their operations to such an extent that they influenced or controlled local government in over half the country's 1000 municipalities.[32]

Fighters in non-state armed groups were well-equipped, often even better than Colombian soldiers, and were paid salaries and pensions.[33] In 2001, the Colombian Defense Ministry stated that FARC had 16,492 members. With between 3000 and 6000 fighters, ELN had not changed much in size since 1998.

FARC's previous practice of wearing uniforms and operating in large formations changed in the 1990s: FARC fighters are said to have begun wearing civilian clothing, and no longer carried their weapons openly. They began moving around in small groups, their commanders having banned fighters from moving around in 'company-size formations'.[34] Most analysts argue that during this time, FARC and ELN fighters were highly disciplined soldiers, although some believed that their discipline was attributable to fear of punishment, rather than loyalty to their organization.[35] Later indications were that traditional discipline had broken down.

The degree to which FARC fighters enjoyed popular support among the inhabitants of areas in which they operated is debatable. In areas they controlled, or where their influence was strong, FARC provided many of the public services usually performed by government, or negotiated with elected officials to undertake certain projects.[36] Moreover, FARC created a clandestine political party, the Bolivarian Movement for a New Colombia, 'which actively co-govern[ed] in areas of guerrilla influence'.[37] An alternative view held that the inhabitants had no alternative but to submit to FARC's rule.

In 1998, when President Pastrana took office, he initiated peace talks with FARC. To facilitate this process, he approved FARC's demand for the establishment of a demilitarized zone, consisting of 42,000 square kilometres (the size of Switzerland); FARC enjoyed 'free rein' in this area, which was their safe haven.[38] This zone was supposed to be a neutral territory in which talks could be held; however, it was also a strategic territory for FARC.[39] No full and lasting peace agreement was reached during this period.

2.4.1 Paramilitary groups

Due to the increase in violent attacks carried out by fighters from non-state armed groups, the rural rich and politicians increasingly relied on private security groups

---

[31] ICG, *FARC*.   [32] CRS, *Colombia and US*, 1.
[33] Ibid, 9.   [34] Pfanner et al, *Interview*, 824.
[35] CRS, *Colombia and US*, 9.   [36] Ibid, 9.
[37] A. Alape, 'The Possibilities for Peace' NACLA Report on the Americas (March/April 1998) 36.
[38] 'Bomb Kills Peasant, 2 FARC Rebels in Colombia' *Latin American Herald Tribune* (2009).
[39] Conciliation Resources, 'Negotiations with the FARC' (2004), available at: <www.c-r.org/our-work/accord/colombia/negotiations-farc.php>.

for protection. This idea was supported by Governor Uribe in Antioquia, who promoted the establishment of civilian rural defence groups in 1994, called '*Convivir*'. Over 400 *Convivir* groups were created, until the Constitutional Court declared them unlawful in 1997.[40] By that time, *Convivir* groups had been accused of committing human rights abuses; some were also believed to have served as fronts for, or were otherwise linked to, paramilitary groups.[41]

Along with *Convivir*, as well as other 'self-defence' groups around the country, a number of paramilitary groups began forming, such as the *Autodefensas Campesinas de Córdoba y Urabá* (ACCU). ACCU was formed in 1994, since it was felt that the government was not doing enough to defeat non-state armed groups. The founding of ACCU was based on the principle of establishing civilian rural defence groups. During the early 1990s, ACCU continued to recruit new members, and to expand its control of territory.[42]

These various scattered paramilitary groups consolidated in 1997 with the creation of an umbrella body—the *Autodefensas Unidas de Colombia* (AUC). In addition, at least some *Convivir* groups supported its creation. AUC's foundational document stated that the group was 'a politico-military movement. Based upon the right of legitimate defence AUC had an anti-subversive character and claimed for transformations within the State but did not seek to threaten its integrity'.[43] AUC comprised nearly 4000 fighters, organized into different types of units, such as military units, vigilante units, death squads, logistic and intelligence units.[44] AUC was organized on a regional basis, each region having a 'general staff' (*estados mayores regionales*). Regional leaders also served on the national general staff (*estado mayor conjunto*), which coordinated the regional groups' strategy.[45] Each paramilitary fighter received a salary, food, a uniform and weapons and ammunition; these costs were met by ranchers, business people and drug barons.[46] From 1998 to 2001, AUC's strategy mainly comprised a terror campaign—in collusion with the public forces—against the alleged 'social bases' of FARC and ELN; the focus was thus on civilians, and not on attempting to defeat non-state armed groups.

---

[40] In November 1997, the Colombian Constitutional Court held that *Convivir* members would neither be permitted to gather intelligence information, nor employ military grade weapons. Legal supervision of *Convivir* increased, and in early 1998, dozens of *Convivir* groups had their licences revoked because they did not turn in their weapons when requested to, and withheld information about their personnel.

[41] See Congressional Research Service, 'Colombia: The Uribe Administration and Congressional Concerns' (14 June 2002) 3. According to the US State Department's Country Reports on Human Rights Practices for 1997, 'The [Colombian] Ombudsman's 1997 report to Congress, however, reiterated his office's opposition to the *Convivir* program ... [because] it involved citizens in the armed conflict, stripped them of their protected status, and converted them into legitimate targets of attack'. US State Department, 'Country Reports: Colombia' (1997) 462.

[42] International Crisis Group, 'Colombia's New Armed Groups' Latin American Reports 20 (2007) 3 (ICG, *New Armed Groups*).

[43] Cited in Escobar, *Seize the State*, ch. 3, p. 9.

[44] ICG, *New Armed Groups*, 3.

[45] Carrillo-Suarez, *Contemporary Issues*, 7.

[46] Ibid, 8.

It has been argued that AUC facilitated the paramilitaries' transition from private drug barons' armies to political actors, and represented finding a 'public objective' to cover their 'private goal', in order to justify their increasing territorial expansion.[47] AUC had access to a variety of financial resources, mainly through the cocaine and heroin markets, assisted by complex regional and/or local alliances with elites and organized crime. So, although AUC allied itself with the Colombian government against other non-state armed groups, it was simultaneously at loggerheads with the State in the fight against drugs.[48]

2.5. 2002 to the present day

2.5.1 FARC and ELN

In 2002, after FARC hijacked a commercial airliner, President Pastrana ended peace talks, giving FARC forty-eight hours to leave the demilitarized zone. After this, FARC increasingly began attacking civilians and civilian targets. On the day that Uribe was inaugurated as the President of Colombia, FARC launched an attack on the presidential palace, killing twenty civilians. As a result, President Uribe began a vigorous campaign to defeat FARC, and other non-state armed groups in Colombia.[49] In 2003, military operations *Libertad* I and II, carried out under the auspices of *Plan Colombia*, led to FARC being driven out of the *Cundimamarca* Department.[50] In 2004, President Uribe received generous US support for *Plan Patriota*, which created mobile military units to launch an offensive against FARC in its southern Colombian strongholds.[51]

In 2008, FARC suffered a number of setbacks,[52] but, under the new leadership of Alfonso Cano, it launched 'Plan Rebirth', which included taking the offensive back into Colombian cities. The Plan saw an increase in bomb attacks in Bogotá, and called for a 'war of attrition', through targeting the military by using anti-personnel mines and snipers, and attacking infrastructure to undermine an economy already

[47] F. Cubides, 'Los paramilitares como agentes organizados de violencia. Su dimensión territorial' in F. Cubides, C. Olaya and C.M. Ortiz (eds), *Violencia y desarrollo municipal* (1995); F. Cubides, 'De lo privado y de lo público en la violencia colombiana: los paramilitares' in J. Arocha, F. Cubides and M. Jimeno (eds), *Las violencias: inclusión creciente* (1998); and F. Cubides 'Narcotráfico y paramilitarismo: ¿Matrimonio indisoluble?', in A. Rangel (ed.), *El poder paramilitar*, (2005); F. Cubides, *Burocracias armadas. El problema de la organización en el entramado de las violencias colombianas* (2005).

[48] F. Gutiérrez and M. Barón, 'Estado, control territorial paramilitar y orden político en Colombia. Notas para una economía política del paramilitarismo' in F. Gutiérrez, M.E. Wills and G. Sánchez (eds), *Nuestra guerra sin nombre. Transformaciones del conflicto en Colombia* (2006) 272.

[49] 'Profiles: Colombia's Armed Groups' *BBC News* (5 November 2011) (BBC, *Colombia's Armed Groups*).

[50] ICG, *FARC*.

[51] A. Isacson, 'The End of the 'Plan Colombia' Era' *Just the Facts Blog* (26 October 2010).

[52] E.g. FARC commander Manual Marulanda died of a heart-attack in March, and Raul Reyes, the FARC second-in-command, was killed during Operation Phoenix; 15 high-profile hostages (including Ingrid Betancourt, a former Colombian presidential candidate) were rescued from FARC by the Colombian military.

hard hit by the global economic crisis.[53] However, FARC has been unable to regain its former territory.[54]

Although in the last few years some of FARC's commanders have been killed, the organization retains the capability to conduct large operations, especially through its 48th Front. Despite setbacks, FARC continues with its campaign against the Colombian authorities, even though it is claimed that FARC has become somewhat demoralized since 2008. It is currently estimated that FARC has 6000–12,000 fighters, forming 110 operational units,[55] and still controls around 15 to 20 per cent of Colombian territory,[56] although this is mostly in mountainous and jungle areas, rather than urban centres.[57]

As for ELN, its current command structure consists of a 15-member high-command, divided into the Central Command and its National Directorate.[58] Questions have been raised about whether the ELN command structure is fully in control of all its fronts.[59] It is estimated that ELN has around 2200 to 3000 members, a significant reduction of its military capability, which was at its peak in the late 1990s.[60] Currently, ELN is said to have several units which are trained in special operations, as well as the manufacture of explosives.[61] ELN also organizes and operates networks of 'unarmed militia'.[62] It has engaged in bombing campaigns and extortion against both multinational and domestic oil companies, attacking oil pipelines on numerous occasions.[63] However, the Colombian government claims that military actions carried out by ELN dropped from 195 per year in 2002, to 19 per year in 2007.[64] ELN is said to be seeking to participate formally in political life in Colombia, but this has not yet happened.[65] ELN and the Colombian government have been holding peace talks since May 2004, but these have so far not resulted in any ceasefire.[66]

2.5.2 *Paramilitary groups*

By 2002, it was estimated that there were approximately 12,000 fighters in AUC,[67] which was operating in the majority of Colombia's provinces.[68] AUC had become

---

[53] J. McDermott, 'FARC Rallies its Battered Troops' *BBC News* (2 March 2009).

[54] ICG, *FARC*.

[55] BBC, *Colombia's Armed Groups*; Hansom, *Left-Wing Guerillas*, 2.

[56] G. Coffey, 'Colombia's War in the Andes' International Institute for Strategic Studies Report (2008) (Coffey, *Colombia's War*).

[57] ICG, *FARC*.

[58] International Crisis Group, 'Colombia: Moving Forward With the E.L.N.?' Latin America Briefing (2007) 4 (ICG, *ELN*).

[59] Ibid, 4.   [60] Hansom, *Left-Wing Guerillas*, 2.   [61] Ibid.

[62] ICG, *ELN*, 4.   [63] Hansom, *Left-Wing Guerillas*, 3.

[64] ICG, *ELN*, 2.   [65] Hansom, *Left-Wing Guerillas*, 1.

[66] Ibid, 4.

[67] ICG, *New Armed Groups*, 4.

[68] Presidencia de la República Oficina Alto Comisionado para la Paz, 'Proceso de Paz con las Autodefensas' *Informe Ejecutivo* 8.

increasingly involved in drugs trafficking, eventually deriving 70 per cent of its income from drugs.[69]

In December 2003, AUC entered into a peace agreement with the government that led to the collective demobilization of over 32,000 AUC members. In addition, more than 20,000 members of FARC, AUC, ELN, and other illegal armed groups individually surrendered their arms. By April 2006, the High Commissioner for Peace announced that the demobilization process was complete;[70] however, it was not completely effective. Some paramilitaries did not demobilize; others demobilized, only to re-emerge some time later to take up arms once more, claiming that the Colombian government had broken its promises to them.[71] Other demobilized paramilitaries later became involved with drug-trafficking organizations.[72]

In 2005, links were discovered between the Colombian Intelligence and Security Service (DAS) and the paramilitaries. In May 2006, ten elite counter-narcotics police officers were killed by an army unit; this raised fears that the drug cartels and paramilitaries had infiltrated key State institutions. The 'para-politics' scandal, which erupted in 2006,[73] led to the Supreme Court issuing arrest warrants for several members of Congress for collaborating with paramilitaries. By April 2008, nearly 100 government officials had either been sentenced, or were being investigated, for colluding with paramilitaries, including: at least fifteen members of Congress, President Uribe's cousin and former President of Congress Mario Uribe Escobar, the army chief General Mario Montoya, former head of DAS Jorge Noguera, and former president of the Superior Council of the Judicature José Alfredo Escobar Araújo.[74]

Post-demobilization investigations and trials also found 'department governors, former and current legislators, and other senior government and military figures guilty of collusion with paramilitary groups'.[75]

---

[69] ICG, *New Armed Groups*, 3.

[70] International Crisis Group, 'Colombia Conflict History' (updated June 2011) (ICG, *Colombia History*).

[71] On 3 February 2010, Carlos Franco, director of the Presidential Program for Human Rights and Humanitarian Law, declared in an interview that he was of the opinion that paramilitarism in Colombia was extinguished (declaration available at: <http://web.presidencia.gov.co/sp/2010/feb-rero/03/11032010.html>). However, Philip Alston's report, published 31 March 2010, states: 'Senior members of the Fiscalía also admitted that the JPU [Justice and Peace Unit] lacks the capacity and resources to conduct the strategic and complex investigations and prosecutions necessary to prevent the structure of paramilitary groups from surviving and being replicated'. Human Rights Council, *Report of the Special Rapporteur on Extrajudicial, Summary or Arbitrary Executions, Mission To Colombia*, 20, para 55.

[72] ICG, *New Armed Groups*, Executive Summary.

[73] See e.g. C.W. Cook, 'Colombia: Issues for Congress' (9 November 2007) 4–5. E.g. AUC leader Salvatore Mancuso publicly claimed that approximately 35 per cent of congressional members supported his organization.

[74] ICG, *New Armed Groups*, 5. 'Colombia's 'Parapolitics' Scandal Casts Shadow Over President' *The Guardian* (23 April 2008). US Office on Colombia, 'Understanding Colombia Series: Para-Politics Scandal', available at: <www.usofficeoncolombia.org/understanding_colombia/pdf/para_politics.pdf>.

[75] ICG, *Colombia History*.

2.5.3 The emergence of new armed groups

The so-called 'new illegal armed groups' (referred to hereinafter as 'new armed groups', to distinguish them from other groupings involved in the conflict) emerged after AUC had been demobilized.[76] New armed groups sometimes established business relations with elements of both FARC and ELN.[77] It is estimated that there are several thousand fighters involved in approximately eighty new armed groups,[78] which have a presence in around 100 municipalities.[79]

Many of these armed groups retain, or have 'inherited', a military-type structure, and exert military control over their territory, e.g. the *Organización Nueva Generación* (ONG). ONG is an example of 'paramilitary continuity', with members wearing uniforms and armbands, and undertaking some counter-insurgency operations.[80] The Black Eagles (BE) appear to be on the opposite end of the continuum to ONG, and are said to be 'dedicated solely to guarding the drug business'.[81] Three of the original leaders of BE were ex-AUC members.[82] However, BE is thought to be unstructured, with 'no clear chain of command'.[83]

There have been reports of both the BE and ONG engaging (separately) in fighting with FARC and ELN.[84] However, there have also been reports of these groups collaborating with both FARC and ELN on drugs trafficking.[85] ONG and BE reportedly have issued threats against community leaders, left-wing activists, trades union activists and human rights defenders, just as AUC did in the past. Whether this is an indication that these groups will take on the counter-insurgency positions of AUC or not is yet to be seen.[86]

Many groups are engaged primarily in drug trafficking. There is disagreement over whether one such group, *Los Rastrojos*, is a drug cartel, or a successor to the now defunct AUC,[87] although evidence indicates the former. However, *Los Rastrojos* has political interests, and stands accused of financing candidates in congressional elections in 2010.[88] It operates an 'armed wing', and consists of approximately 1500 members. It controls territory mostly in the south-east of Colombia, but is said by Colombian authorities to be expanding into the more central Antioquia department.[89] There is also evidence that *Los Rastrojos* and ELN have fought each other on several occasions.

In order to deal with new armed groups, the police have established a special search unit—a 'highly mobile task force'—although it focuses mostly on BE.[90] However, there have also been many reports that members and/or units of the

---

[76] ICG, *New Armed Groups*, 6.   [77] ICG, *Colombia History*.
[78] ICG, *New Armed Groups*, Executive Summary.
[79] As compared to AUC, which operated in 711 municipalities prior to demobilization.
[80] ICG, *New Armed Groups*, 12.   [81] Ibid, 9.   [82] Ibid.
[83] Ibid, 6.   [84] Ibid, 26.   [85] Ibid, 12.   [86] Ibid, 26.
[87] See further section 4.4 in this chapter on criminal violence as armed conflict.
[88] 'Los Rastrojos Gang Infiltrates Colombian Elections' *Colombia Reports* (13 April 2010).
[89] Ibid.
[90] ICG, *New Armed Groups*, 20.

Colombian public forces have either been 'tolerating the new armed groups and criminal gangs or even actively working with them'.[91]

2.6. Effects of the armed conflict

Huge numbers of Colombians, both civilians and fighters, have been killed since the violence began in 1963. One exhaustive study claims that nearly four million people were the direct victims of armed violence from 1964 to 2004 alone. If one were also to include those injured and direct family members of victims, the proportion of the population affected would be upwards of 40 to 50 per cent.[92] Many Colombians have been displaced by the conflict: there are approximately three million internally displaced persons in Colombia, and there are estimated to be around 82,300 Colombian refugees in Ecuador.[93]

3. Classification of the Colombian conflict by the relevant actors

3.1. Colombia

Various organs of the Colombian State have classified the hostilities differently, at different times. This is probably due in part to the fluctuation in the intensity of the hostilities, and in part due to changes in the political leadership of the country.

Initially, the Colombian executive classified the hostilities as a Common Article 3 armed conflict. After ratifying Additional Protocol II in 1995, President Samper unilaterally declared that both Common Article 3 and Additional Protocol II bound public servants—including the army and the police.[94] However, he stated that his decision was made as 'a matter of constitutional law and public policy', rather than classifying the conflict on an objective basis, using traditional international humanitarian law thresholds.[95]

In the wake of the events of 11 September 2001, President Pastrana called FARC 'terrorists', and said that they were waging a 'war against civilians' and a 'war against civilian society'. However, he did concede that there was an ongoing armed conflict in Colombia, but did not clarify whether he viewed it as coming within Common Article 3 or also within Additional Protocol II.

President Uribe's democratic security policy re-framed the conflict in terms of terrorism. Uribe said that he viewed the conflict as neither an armed conflict, nor a 'civil war', referring instead to what he termed the 'terrorist threat'. However, in

---

[91] Ibid, 21.
[92] El Instituto de Estudios para el Desarrollo y la Paz (INDEPAZ), 'Las Cifras del Conflicto' Comunicaciones (22 March 2007).
[93] Coffey, *Colombia's War*; UNHCR, '2008 Global Trends: Refugees, Asylum-seekers, Returnees, Internally Displaced and Stateless Persons' (16 June 2009) 7, 19.
[94] Carrillo-Suarez, *Contemporary Issues*, 18.
[95] Ibid.

September 2005, he stated that if ELN were to declare a ceasefire, he would no longer refer to 'terrorist threats', but would accept that an armed conflict existed.[96]

In its *Directiva Permanente* No. 10 of 2007, the Ministry of Defence declared that the provisions contained in both Common Article 3 and Additional Protocol II were applicable to the situation in Colombia. Whether this may be interpreted to imply that the Colombian authorities accepted the armed conflict as having an Additional Protocol II character, or whether this declaration merely confirmed the authorities' position that it chose to apply the Protocol as a matter of policy is unclear.[97]

As for the new armed groups which formed after the adoption of the Justice and Peace Law, the Colombian government has categorized them as *bandas criminales* (criminal gangs), and has said that it will deal with them using a law-enforcement paradigm.[98] Furthermore, it has said that these new groups 'will not receive any kind of recognition, but rather will be pursued as common criminals'.[99]

In May 2011, after a meeting including the Commanders of the Armed Forces, President Santos said, '[t]he armed forces are operating under the umbrella of International Humanitarian Law, which presumes the existence of an internal armed conflict'.[100] Once more, no indication was given as to whether the Colombian government viewed the armed conflict as coming within Additional Protocol II or only falling within Common Article 3.

The Colombian Supreme Court, in the *Gian Carlo Guttierez Suarez* case, ruled that the conflict had crossed the threshold necessary to classify it as an armed conflict.[101] It recognized that the armed conflict had been underway for the past forty years,[102] ruling that both Common Article 3 and Additional Protocol II were applicable.[103]

3.2. FARC

FARC has argued that their territorial control and military power mean that they should be recognized as belligerents in the classical sense of the term; FARC therefore refuses to recognize the applicability of Additional Protocol II rules,

---

[96] Fundación Ideas para la Paz, 'Siguiendo el conflicto: hechos y análisis de la semana' (9 September 2005). The Colombian Commission of Jurists is of the opinion that, in spite of the government's denial, the hostilities fall within Additional Protocol II. *Tiempos de sequía, Situación de derechos humanos y derecho humanitario en Colombia 2002–2009*, Comisión Colombiana de Juristas, 57.

[97] Ministerio de Defensa Nacional, Directiva Permanente No. 10 (2007) (*Directiva Permanente*). See statement of the Vice-Minister for Defence: Pfanner et al, *Interview*, 825: 'It may turn out that we are in agreement on a legal characterization that encourages the application of international humanitarian law. (...) rather than actually saying "this is an armed conflict", what matters is to be able to say "this is the kind of force I need to use because these criteria have been met". (...) it is immaterial whether you call that "a conflict"; the truth is that in practice your military operations are enablers for law enforcement'.

[98] ICG, *New Armed Groups*, Executive Summary.

[99] Ibid, 25.

[100] 'Santos Upholds Redefinition of Colombia's "Armed Conflict"' *Colombia Reports* (10 May 2011).

[101] *Gian Carlo Gutierrez Suarez*, Supreme Court of Colombia, Radicado No. 32.022 (21 September 2009) 59 (*Gutierrez Suarez* case).

[102] Ibid, 91.   [103] Ibid, 189.

other than those contained in their own 'humanitarian law statute',[104] stating that recognition of belligerency requires that the rules governing international armed conflicts be applied, and not those governing armed conflicts of a non-international character.[105]

3.3. ELN

ELN has frequently said that it is bound by international humanitarian law, and has incorporated these norms into several of its internal codes of conduct. In the late 1990s, ELN specifically stated that it had the 'capacity to apply Protocol II for the purposes of regulating the internal conflict'.[106] It may be assumed, therefore, that ELN views the conflict as an armed conflict, having reached the threshold of Additional Protocol II—at least, in the 1990s.

3.4. AUC

AUC has, in the past, referred to the conflict as an 'internal armed conflict'. However, it is not clear from these references whether AUC saw the non-international armed conflict as reaching the threshold of Additional Protocol II or only that of Common Article 3.[107]

3.5. Other States

3.5.1 Ecuador

The Colombian authorities have taken contradictory positions regarding Ecuador in relation to Colombia's conflict with FARC. On the one hand, Colombia has claimed to have evidence allegedly proving that there are links between FARC and Ecuador;[108] on the other hand, Colombia and Ecuador have undertaken joint operations against FARC in the past, and Ecuador has also taken action against FARC independently, handing over captured FARC detainees to Colombia. Ecuador's approach to dealing with FARC on its own territory takes the form of conflict prevention, using social and economic means, and through a police presence

---

[104] It appears that FARC does not have one single document outlining the international humanitarian law rules it believes it should adhere to; rather, there are several documents with different rules such as *Reglamento Interno* (Internal Regulations), *Estatuto* (Statute), *Reglamento de Regimen Disciplinario* (Rules of Discipline), *Normas Internas del Comando* (Internal Norms of the Command) and *Normas de Comportamiento con las Masas* (Norms for the Behaviour with the Masses), which at point 11 says, '[o]fficers and combatants should study and practice the norms of international humanitarian law in accordance to the conditions of our revolutionary war'.

[105] Carrillo-Suarez, *Contemporary Issues*, 25.

[106] Ibid, 26.

[107] Ibid, 29–30.

[108] The computers seized from the FARC camp in the Ecuadorian border region with Colombia on 1 March 2008 were examined by Interpol, which found them not to have been tampered with in the aftermath of Operation Phoenix. See 'INTERPOL releases Forensic Report requested by Colombia on seized FARC computers and hardware' Interpol Press Release (15 May 2008).

towards building a 'law-abiding society'.[109] Ecuador has thus adopted a law-enforcement paradigm in dealing with FARC; in other words, Ecuador does not appear to believe it is involved in an armed conflict with FARC.

Ecuador has said that it does not recognize either ELN or FARC as 'belligerents', or 'terrorists'; rather, it views FARC and ELN as irregular groups.[110] In response to Colombia's statements about FARC activity on Ecuadorian territory, Ecuador said that it had dismantled 117 FARC camps on its territory in the past four years, and had arrested eleven fighters in the past year;[111] in addition, Ecuadorian President Correa declared a 'zero tolerance' policy towards FARC.[112] 'Limited military cooperation' between Ecuador and Colombia apparently began after the Organization of American States (OAS) negotiated an agreement between the two countries in 2009, although it is not clear precisely what this military cooperation entails.[113]

In a statement made by the Ecuadorian Minister of Foreign Affairs, it was said that Ecuador 'rejects the presence of Colombian irregular groups in the country', and 'reiterates its firm decision not to allow the territory of the nation to be used by others to carry out military operations or to be used as a base of operations, as part of the Colombian conflict'.[114] This could be interpreted to mean that Ecuador views the conflict as being a non-international armed conflict solely between Colombia and FARC (as well as possibly other non-state armed groups).

In spite of the above, there have been allegations of cooperation between Ecuador and FARC. For example, a Commission established by President Correa to investigate Operation Phoenix, as well as whether FARC was being supported by Ecuador, reported its findings in December 2009. The Commission found that Gustavo Larrea, who had been the Ecuadorian Interior and Security Minister, had 'direct links' to FARC, as did Jose Ignacio Chauvin (Larrea's deputy); and that a retired general, Rene Vargas Pazzos, rented a farm to a FARC commander. However, the Commission did not find that any current officials in Correa's administration, or Correa himself, had links to FARC.[115]

3.5.2 *Venezuela*

Computers seized by Colombia from a FARC camp were alleged to contain information regarding 'close ties' between Venezuela and FARC. One e-mail reportedly detailed how FARC planned to buy 'surface-to-air missiles, sniper rifles and radios' in Venezuela in 2008, in a deal brokered by General Henry Rangle

[109] US Senate Committee on Foreign Relations, 'Playing with Fire: Colombia, Ecuador and Venezuela' (28 April 2008) 8.

[110] 'Ecuador no reconocerá beligerancia a Farc' *El Tiempo* (23 January 2008).

[111] F. Robles, 'Correa: Colombia's Strike Ruined Hostage Release' *Miami Herald* (6 March 2008) (Robles, *Colombia's Strike*).

[112] K.A. McBride, 'Colombian-Ecuadorian Relations: One Year After' *Americas Quarterly Web Exclusive* (26 March 2009), available at: www.as-coa.org/article.php?id=1557.

[113] Ibid.

[114] Ministry of Foreign Affairs, 'Ecuadorian Government Protests Assassination of Raul Reyes in Ecuador' Communiqué of the government of Ecuador (1 March 2008).

[115] 'Ecuador Officials Linked to Colombia Rebels' *Time Magazine* (15 December 2009).

Silva, the Director of Venezuela's Police Intelligence Agency, and Ramon Rodri-guez Chacin, a former Venezuelan Interior Minister. Interestingly, another e-mail was supposed to contain an offer from FARC to train Venezuelan officers in 'guerrilla warfare'.[116] The Colombian authorities have also claimed that FARC has in the past received financial help from President Chavez, to the amount of US$300 million.[117] In addition, Colombia has accused Venezuela of providing FARC with three 'Swedish-made anti-tank weapons'.[118] Venezuela has denied all these allegations.

The Venezuelan National Assembly voted in January 2008 to support President Chavez in his call to Colombia to recognize the 'belligerent status' of both FARC and ELN. President Chavez has said of FARC, '[t]hey are armies, real armies … that occupy a space in Colombia'.[119] Although it is therefore clear that Venezuela believes that the conflict in Colombia should be fought according to the rules of international armed conflict, in practice, the Venezuelan position has little impact on the classification of the armed conflict. In addition, although Venezuela has recognized belligerency in the case of FARC, it does not appear to have observed the requirement that recognition brings into effect the principle of neutrality. FARC is known to have camps and bases in Venezuelan territory, but there is no evidence that Venezuela has taken any action against FARC in this regard, unlike Ecuador. President Chavez is reported to have said in the past that Venezuela 'shared a border not with Colombia, but with territory controlled by the FARC'.[120]

3.5.3 The US

Since 1989, when the Cold War ended and drug trafficking was declared to be a threat to the national security of the US, Colombia became the number one recipient of US military aid in the Americas, mostly due to growing concerns about the rapid rise to power of FARC, and, to a lesser extent, AUC paramili-taries.[121] In July 2000, the US Congress approved US$1.3 billion in supplemental funding for the region-wide 'Plan Colombia', most of which was earmarked for Colombia. Almost half of this funding was dedicated to a programme to set up and train two new Colombian Army Counter-Narcotics battalions.[122] In addition, Colombian military personnel received (and continue to receive) training in the US, or from US instructors in Colombia.[123] In the early 2000s, the US had 1400

---

[116] 'Venezuela Still Aids Colombia Rebels, New Material Shows' *The New York Times* (2 August 2009).

[117] Coffey, *Colombia's War*; 'FARC Rebels Arrested in Ecuador' *BBC News* (7 March 2008). It is not clear whether these documents have ever been proven to be authentic or not.

[118] Hansom, *Left-Wing Guerillas*, 3.

[119] 'Chavez: Take FARC Off Terror List' *CNN World* (11 January 2008).

[120] 'Venezuela Tolerates FARC Rebels in Border Region' *Los Angeles Times* (21 January 2009).

[121] Congressional Research Service, 'Colombia: Summary and Tables on U.S. Assistance, FY1989–FY2003' (3 May 2002).

[122] Ibid.

[123] US State Department, 'Background Note: Colombia' available at: <www.state.gov/r/pa/ei/bgn/35754.htm>.

military personnel and contractors operating in Colombia;[124] this limit was set by the US Congress. However, the US is not authorized to use military force in Colombia, and all of its activities there require authorization by the Colombian government.[125]

The US is 'the most influential foreign actor in Colombia'.[126] It has frequently referred to the conflict in Colombia as an 'internal armed conflict', such as in the 2010 US State Department Country Report: 'The 46-year internal armed conflict continued between the government and terrorist organizations, particularly the Revolutionary Armed Forces of Colombia (FARC) and the National Liberation Army (ELN)'.[127] This would seem to indicate that the US believes that the conflict in Colombia has been, at minimum, a non-international armed conflict within Common Article 3 since 1964.

3.6. Other institutions

The Inter-American Commission on Human Rights (IACHR) refers, in all its documents, to the 'internal armed conflict' in Colombia; however, this is by virtue of the fact that Colombia itself has 'openly acknowledged the factual reality of its involvement in such a conflict and the applicability of Article 3 common to the . . . Geneva Conventions [and] . . . the 1977 Protocol Additional to the Geneva Conventions'.[128] The IACHR therefore has not considered it necessary itself to deal with the issue of whether objectively, the violence in Colombia constitutes a non-international armed conflict within Common Article 3 or one which also reaches the threshold of Additional Protocol II.

The UN Human Rights Committee (UNHRC) consistently refers to the Colombian conflict as an internal armed conflict: ' . . . it is a complex internal armed conflict, which is exacerbated by organized violence . . . '.[129] However, the UNHRC has not stated whether it considers the Additional Protocol II threshold to have been reached.

The International Committee of the Red Cross (ICRC) classifies the conflict in Colombia as an ' . . . internal armed conflict to which common Article 3 and Additional Protocol II apply . . . '. The ICRC has long been involved in the Colombian conflict, and was first granted authorization to visit people detained in connection with it in 1969.[130]

---

[124] CorpWatch, 'Colombia: Private Firms Take on U.S. Military Role in Drug War' (22 May 2001). There appear to have been at least four private security companies operating in Colombia under US authority.

[125] 'US Set to Boost Military Role in Colombia' *MSNBC News* (15 July 2009). However, see section 7 below on Operation Phoenix, in respect of the role played by the US.

[126] Human Rights Watch, 'Colombia: Events of 2009'.

[127] US Department of State, 'Country Reports: Colombia' (2010).

[128] Inter-American Commission on Human Rights, 'Third Report on the Human Rights Situation in Colombia' (1999) 4.

[129] 'Report of the United Nations High Commissioner for Human Rights on the Situation of Human Rights in Colombia' (2010) 4 (UNHCHR, *Colombia 2010*).

[130] ICRC, 'Colombia: The ICRC Continues to Support Those Affected by Conflict' (2005).

4. Authors' classification of the Colombian conflict

Before attempting to classify the conflict, or its different phases, several issues with a direct impact on classification are identified and discussed.[131] These include: the role of the US, Venezuela and Ecuador in the conflict (relevant to whether or not the activities of these States internationalize the conflict); whether or not FARC qualifies for recognition of belligerency; the role of paramilitary groups pre- and post-demobilization, and their relationship with the Colombian State (relevant to whether their actions may be attributed to the Colombian State); and finally, whether a group involved in purely criminal violence against either other non-state armed groups or the Colombian State may ever be said to be a party to an armed conflict. The authors' classification of the conflict follows the discussion of these issues.

4.1. Has the Colombian armed conflict been 'internationalized' through the intervention of foreign States?

The foreign States most active in the Colombian conflict are the US, Ecuador, and Venezuela. With regard to the US, which has provided significant funding to the Colombian military since the 1970s, all US activities require authorization by the Colombian government. The US is therefore involved in the armed conflict, not as a party to it, but solely in support of, and at the invitation of, the Colombian authorities. It cannot be argued that US involvement has 'internationalized' the conflict.

With regard to Ecuador, insufficient evidence exists to support claims that Ecuador has supported FARC. Colombian Police Director Oscar Naranjo alleged that 'Correa [Ecuadorian President] has been supporting FARC politically and militarily, and had endangered the security of Colombia'.[132] An Ecuadorian Commission of Enquiry also found that the former Ecuadorian Interior and Security Minister, amongst others, had direct links to FARC.[133] In spite of this, no evidence has been found to suggest that any Ecuadorian politicians or officials were acting according to official Ecuadorian government policy in developing and maintaining these links, nor is it clear precisely what these links entailed.

Colombia also claimed to have found evidence in the FARC encampment after Operation Phoenix which showed that FARC had contributed to President Correa's election campaign.[134] If FARC had been proven to have contributed to

---

[131] It should be noted that Colombia acceded to the Geneva Conventions on 8 November 1961, and to Additional Protocol II on 14 August 1995 (Additional Protocol II came into force on 14 February 1996). Colombia has also acceded to the International Covenant on Civil and Political Rights, and the American Convention on Human Rights.

[132] m&c Americas News, 'Colombia Calls Ecuador Border Violation Self-Defence (Roundup)' (3 March 2008), available at: <www.monstersandcritics.com/news/americas/news/article_1393839 .php/Colombia_calls_Ecuador_border_violation_self_defence_Roundup>.

[133] See section 2 above, outlining the conflict from 1963 to the present.

[134] For further discussion on Operation Phoenix, see section 7 below.

Correa's campaign, then this must surely undermine any argument that Ecuador was in either effective or overall control of FARC. Furthermore, Ecuador has taken some action against FARC in the past, such as destroying some of its camps, and arresting a number of its fighters.

As for Venezuela, there is evidence that it has, at a minimum, either been unable or unwilling to act against FARC in the past. It has been established that FARC has fighters based in camps in Venezuela, but that Venezuela, unlike Ecuador, has not attempted to destroy these camps, nor arrest any of the fighters. Amongst other things, Colombia has accused Venezuela of supporting FARC financially (to the amount of around US$300 million), and supplying FARC with weapons.

None of these allegations, even if proven true, are sufficient to indicate that either Ecuador or Venezuela exercise either effective or overall control over any of the non-state armed groups active in Colombia.[135] Therefore, it cannot be said that the armed conflict has been internationalized owing to the involvement of any third States.

4.2. Recognition of belligerency? The case of FARC

The authors concur with the position of both Akande and Scobbie on the recognition of belligerency,[136] namely that it is still an active concept, and that it may be either explicitly or implicitly conferred on a non-state armed group. FARC has argued that the extent of its territorial control and military power means that it should be granted recognition as a belligerent party in the classical sense of the term.[137] Accordingly, FARC has bound itself to applying international armed conflict rules during hostilities, as laid down in its 'humanitarian law statutes'.[138] Colombia has always dismissed FARC's claim to recognition of belligerency,[139] whilst at the same time making various statements—during the 1990s in particular— which may well be capable of being interpreted as amounting to tacit recognition of belligerency.[140] It conceded that FARC has conducted widespread fighting

---

[135] In line with the criteria laid down in the *Nicaragua* and *Tadić* cases; see also ch. 3, section 7 above.

[136] As stated in ch. 3, section 5.3 and ch. 9, section 4.4 of this volume.

[137] However, were FARC found to be in the effective or overall control of a third State, e.g. Venezuela, then recognition of belligerency would not be legally possible. ELN also asked to be recognized as a belligerent party in a document published 22 January 2008, available on its website at: <www.eln-voces.com/index.php?option=com_content&view=article&id=130:editinsu096&ca-tid=18:comunicados&Itemid=74>.

[138] Carrillo-Suarez, *Contemporary Issues*, 25.

[139] See e.g. 'Las Farc no tendrián estatus beligerante' *El Colombiano* (6 May 2011).

[140] H. Lauterpacht, *Recognition in International Law* (1947) 176 (Lauterpacht, *Recognition*). Lauterpacht identifies the following criteria for the recognition of belligerency:

> [F]irst, there must exist within the State an armed conflict of a general (as distinguished from a purely local) character; secondly, the insurgents must occupy and administer a substantial portion of national territory; thirdly, they must conduct the hostilities in accordance with the rules of war and through organized armed forces acting under a responsible authority; fourthly, there must exist circumstances which make it necessary for outside States to define their attitude by means of recognition of belligerency.

Note that there remains disagreement amongst both scholars and courts as to the correct criteria for the recognition of belligerency.

across Colombia; that it controlled and administered substantial Colombian territory;[141] that it has organized armed forces;[142] and that it has its own 'humanitarian law statutes', which reflect international humanitarian law rules applicable in international armed conflicts.[143] However, if it is accepted that a State has the political discretion to recognize belligerency or not, then it must be concluded that Colombia has never recognized FARC as belligerents, given its explicit denials in this regard.

Lauterpacht held that the 'most affected' States must feel it 'necessary...to define their attitude by means of recognition of belligerency...'.[144] Some, if not most, affected States in this conflict must surely be those neighbouring Colombia: Ecuador and Venezuela.[145] The Venezuelan government has said in the past that it views FARC as amounting to 'belligerent or irregular forces',[146] and, in January 2008, the Venezuelan National Assembly voted to support President Chavez in his call on Colombia to recognize the 'belligerent status' of both FARC and ELN.[147] Chavez said, '[t]hey are armies, real armies... that occupy a space in Colombia'.[148]

Recognition of belligerency by third States supposedly brings into play the principle of neutrality. Although appearing to have recognized belligerency explicitly in the case of FARC, Venezuela does not appear to have adopted the principle of neutrality as regards either FARC or Colombia,[149] particularly in view of the fact that it appears to allow FARC to maintain camps on its territory. Ecuador has stated that it is 'neutral' in relation to this conflict, although it is not clear precisely what is meant by this, as Ecuador has given Colombia permission in the past to undertake hostilities against FARC on Ecuadorian territory, and has itself taken action against

---

[141] As evidenced by Colombia's creation of a demilitarized zone consisting of 42,000 square kilometres, as demanded by FARC as a precursor to establishing peace talks. The vast majority of this territory was already under the control of FARC, so it was arguably merely an official recognition of an existing fact.

[142] There is disagreement as to what constitutes 'responsible' command: whether it is merely an identifiable military hierarchy which is capable of giving orders which are carried out, or whether 'responsible' means, in addition, that any orders given comply with international humanitarian law, and any breaches of that law are investigated and punished.

[143] Colombia has accused FARC of breaching international humanitarian law on numerous occasions, and therefore not adhering to the requirement that a non-state armed group must conduct hostilities in accordance with the law. However, committing violations of international humanitarian law does not, as such, exclude a non-state armed group from being recognized as belligerents.

[144] Lauterpacht, *Recognition*, 176.

[145] Both Ecuador and Venezuela's territory has been used by FARC to establish bases for their fighters, and hostilities have taken place in their territory.

[146] J.J. Brittain and R.J. Sacouman, 'Uribe's Colombia is Destabilising a New Latin America' *CounterPunch* (2008), available at: <www.ecuador-rising.blogspot.com/2008_03_01_archive.html>.

[147] K. Janicke, 'Venezuela Legislature Supports Belligerent Status for Colombian Rebels' *Venezuelanalysis.com* (2008).

[148] 'Chavez: Take FARC Off Terror List' *CNN World* (11 January 2008).

[149] Hansom, *Left-Wing Guerillas*, 3–4; for further information on the relationship between Venezuela/Ecuador and FARC, see section 3.5 above. The principle of neutrality is argued to apply only to international armed conflicts, and non-international armed conflicts in which recognition of belligerency has been accorded; however, there are other authors who argue that this concept is defunct, or that the principle should be extended to non-international armed conflicts by analogy, where those conflicts spill over into the territory of third States.

FARC fighters on its territory. Given this seemingly contradictory behaviour, it is impossible to come to any conclusion as to whether Ecuador's neutrality statement could be read as implying recognition of belligerency.

In conclusion, the effect of recognition of belligerency by Colombia in the case of FARC would be that the armed conflict between them would be subject to the rules applicable to international armed conflicts. Although recognition of belligerency has the same effect as classifying hostilities as an international armed conflict, that is, it determines that the rules of international humanitarian law applicable to international armed conflicts must be implemented, it does not itself alter the classification of the armed conflict.[150] The conflict between Colombia and FARC would, therefore, remain a non-international armed conflict, as recognition of belligerency does not bestow statehood, and only recognized States may be parties to international armed conflicts. Hostilities between FARC and any other non-state armed group would continue to be governed by Common Article 3, where that other group itself qualified as a party to the armed conflict in accordance with the requirements of that provision.[151]

4.3. The relationship between paramilitary groups and the Colombian government, as it affects the classification of the armed conflict

Originally, there were several Colombian laws which authorized the arming of civilians by the State, leading to the formation of paramilitary groups as part of the State's counter-insurgency strategy. Later, evidence emerged, particularly during the 'para-politics' scandal, of strong links between paramilitary groups, government officials and the military.[152] This raises the question of the test which should be employed to determine the relationship between paramilitaries and the Colombian State for the purposes of the classification of the armed conflict.

This section focuses solely on the situation in which the State with whom the paramilitary group is alleged to have links is also the State on whose territory hostilities are occurring. The authors argue that the test for determining the relationship between a paramilitary group and a State for the purposes of classification of an armed conflict differs from those involved in attributing the acts of paramilitaries to a State for the purposes of State responsibility for those acts. As a result, the authors argue that the situation in Colombia differs markedly from the situations confronted by the International Court of Justice (ICJ) in *Nicaragua*,[153]

---

[150] However, although recognition of belligerency has no legal role to play in the classification of conflicts for the purposes of international humanitarian law, it does amount to a classification of sorts under public international law.

[151] These requirements are: that a group is organized to a certain extent, and conducts hostilities which are prolonged, or of a certain level of intensity.

[152] See discussion at section 2.5.2 above.

[153] *Military and Paramilitary Activities in and against Nicaragua (Nicaragua v United States of America)* ICJ Rep 1986, 14.

and the International Criminal Tribunal for the Former Yugoslavia (ICTY) in *Tadić*,[154] and that, therefore, neither the effective nor overall control tests are appropriate in this context.

The authors submit that the correct test for determining attribution where the group in question operates on the territory of the State concerned is the agency test, as outlined in the *La Rochela Massacre Case* by the Inter-American Court of Human Rights. The Court held that:

> The Court notes that in the instant case the State allowed the involvement and cooperation of private individuals in the performance of certain duties (such as the military patrol of public order areas, the employment of arms designed for the exclusive use of the armed forces or the performance of military intelligence activities), which, in general, are within the exclusive competence of the State and where the State has a special duty to act as a guarantor. Therefore, the State is directly responsible, either as a result of its acts or omissions, for all the activities undertaken by these private individuals in the performance of the foregoing duties, particularly if it is taken into consideration that private individuals are not subject to the strict control exercised over public officials regarding the performance of their duties.[155]

Although the Court laid down this test in considering the responsibility of Colombia for human rights law violations committed by paramilitary groups, rather than for purposes of the classification of hostilities in order to determine the applicable legal framework, nevertheless the authors moot this form of the agency test as the correct test to be employed in these circumstances. Unlike the relationship between the US and the Contras in Nicaragua, where the US was the foreign State, Colombia arguably has more control over what happens on its own territory, both in terms of establishing a paramilitary group, and subsequently for ensuring that that group abides by the requisite legal framework. The agency test is therefore much more appropriate than those of complete dependence and control (as required by article 4 of the International Law Commission's Articles on State Responsibility), effective control (as required by the ICJ) or overall control (as required by the ICTY).[156]

According to the evidence presented in earlier sections of this chapter of strong links between the paramilitary groups and the Colombian government, the authors argue that paramilitary action should be attributed to the Colombian State for classification purposes, at least until demobilization began in 2002. As to the effect on classification of this attribution, any hostilities involving paramilitaries would be classified the same as if the Colombian State were involved alongside or instead of these paramilitaries.

---

[154] *Prosecutor v Tadić*, IT-94-1-AR72, Decision on Defence Motion for Interlocutory Appeal on Jurisdiction (Appeals Chamber), 2 October 1995.

[155] *Case of the Rochela Massacre v Colombia*, Inter-American Court of Human Rights, Case No. 11.995, Report No. 42/02 (11 May 2007) 32–3, para 102.

[156] See discussion in ch. 3, section 7.1 regarding the different circumstances in which a foreign State operates through a non-state armed group against another State.

4.4. Can criminal violence ever qualify as an armed conflict?

When FARC was founded in 1966, its aim was to overthrow the Colombian government through armed struggle, replacing it with a government based on Marxist principles.[157] However, FARC has financed its political aims largely through criminal acts, such as kidnapping-for-ransom, extortion, various forms of smuggling and, increasingly, involvement in all phases of the international drugs trade (as producers, manufacturers and exporters).[158] As a result, it is estimated that FARC earns between US$500 and US$600 million annually from illegal drugs alone.[159] Of its 110 operation units, around sixty-five units are reported to be involved in the drugs trade in one way or another.[160] As a result, some analysts argue that FARC has ceased to have any political vision or aims, and that it has become a criminal organization or 'business' instead,[161] whilst others hold that FARC retains an ideological dimension which distinguishes it from other actors.

On the other side of the spectrum are groups such as *Los Rastrojos*, which is said to be involved in purely criminal activities (mostly drugs trafficking), and which appears to have no political agenda or ideological leanings. *Los Rastrojos* has in the past engaged in hostilities with Colombian public forces, and, separately, with FARC and ELN for control of drug-trafficking routes.

The question which thus arises is whether groups which are purely criminal in nature can ever be said to be parties to an armed conflict.[162] In other words, must a non-state armed group have a political motive in order for it to qualify as a party to a non-international armed conflict? Alternatively, should involvement in criminal enterprise exclude a non-state armed group from qualifying as a party to an armed conflict?

Before considering the legal dimensions of this issue, the practical difficulties of determining whether particular hostilities are purely political, purely criminal or a mix of the two should be noted.[163] Both FARC and ELN are involved in the drugs trade, but both also fight against the Colombian State for political reasons; furthermore, they have, on occasion, also fought each other. How is the determination as to whether fighting is taking place for criminal or political reasons to be made? If non-state armed groups were to claim a political agenda or aims, would this suffice? Or would States demand the right to determine whether an armed group it opposes has a political motive or not?

Non-state armed groups frequently turn to crime to fund their political struggles, as there are very few legal avenues open to them to raise money. Regardless of the fact that many non-state armed groups nevertheless hold to their political aims, States have a propensity for labelling them ordinary criminals. As Pictet rightly

---

[157] BBC, *Colombia's Armed Groups.*   [158] Ibid.
[159] Hansom, *Left-Wing Guerillas,* 2.   [160] Ibid.
[161] BBC, *Colombia's Armed Groups.*
[162] See also discussion of this issue in ch. 2, section 3.2 and ch. 3, section 6.1.
[163] Rempe, *A History of US Counterinsurgency,* 304–27.

stated, '[i]n a civil war the lawful Government, or that which so styles itself, tends to regard its adversaries as common criminals'.[164]

There was discussion of this issue at the Diplomatic Conference of 1949. Some States were unhappy with the initial draft of Common Article 3, saying that '. . . it would cover in advance all forms of insurrection, rebellion, anarchy, and the break-up of States, and even plain brigandage'. Others said that they were reluctant to give the status of belligerents to '. . . its enemies, who might be no more than a handful of rebels or common brigands . . . There was also a risk of ordinary criminals being encouraged to give themselves a semblance of organization as a pretext for claiming the benefit of the Convention . . .'. No States dissented from this position; it may therefore be assumed that there was unanimity amongst States in this regard. However, these concerns were expressed mostly in opposition to the notion that ordinary criminals could ever acquire the status of belligerents; history has shown that no such status has ever been bestowed on ordinary criminals. In spite of States' concerns, the final text of Common Article 3 does not per se exclude criminal groups from qualifying as parties to armed conflicts.

Increasing numbers of States, particularly in Latin America, have utilized their militaries against criminal armed groups.[165] Criminal groups and non-state armed groups alike are frequently similarly well-organized, control territory and are able to engage in protracted fighting, utilizing sophisticated weaponry; the ensuing hostilities often do not appear to differ in substance. Civilians are often equally at risk from hostilities involving non-state armed groups as they are from hostilities involving criminal armed groups, and may well benefit from the application of international humanitarian law in these circumstances.

If non-state armed groups engage in criminal activities, and if they are nonetheless recognized as a party to an armed conflict, there is no reason why members of these groups cannot be held to account for any alleged crimes they may have committed during that conflict, within the domestic system of the affected State. The law provides more than adequately for this outcome. Therefore, the authors argue that, at a minimum, Common Article 3 should be applicable where criminal groups engage in hostilities that otherwise meet all the criteria to qualify as a non-international armed conflict.

4.5. Classification of hostilities involving groups active in the Colombian armed conflict

Having considered the issues outlined above, and having regard to the criteria for the two forms of non-international armed conflict,[166] the authors have drawn the following conclusions:

---

[164] J. Pictet (ed.), *The Geneva Conventions of 12 August 1949: Commentary* (1958) 27.
[165] E.g. Mexico, Brazil and Honduras.
[166] See ch. 3, section 6.

- *Colombian State v FARC*: this constituted an armed conflict within Common Article 3 until the mid-1990s; thereafter, it reached the threshold of Additional Protocol II, and so remains at the time of writing.
- *Colombian State v ELN*: this was a Common Article 3 conflict until the mid-1990s, and an Additional Protocol II conflict thereafter until late 1990s. At the time of writing, it is deemed to come within Common Article 3, as ELN is still carrying out attacks, although fewer than in the past with fewer fighters at its disposal.
- *Colombian State v AUC*: although there are limited instances of the AUC and the Colombian State in conflict with each other, any hostilities between the two constituting an armed conflict would qualify under Common Article 3.
- *Colombian State v new armed groups which arose after the 2003 demobilization process*: there is currently no evidence that new paramilitary groups are acting as agents of the Colombian State, even though evidence suggests that certain elements of the State cooperate and collude with some of these groups. However, the Colombian State mostly and officially actively works against these new armed groups. Therefore, should any hostilities occur which amount to an armed conflict between the Colombian State and these groups would qualify as a Common Article 3 conflict (unless these groups could be shown to meet the criteria of Additional Protocol II).
- *FARC v ELN*: by virtue of the fact that both groups are non-state actors, any conflict between these two groups may only ever amount to a Common Article 3 conflict.
- *FARC or ELN v AUC*: hostilities post-2003, in which AUC was considered to be a non-state actor—e.g. between AUC and FARC/ELN in relation to dominating the drugs trade—could only ever amount to a Common Article 3 conflict. In respect of hostilities pre-2003, where AUC was deemed to be an agent of the Colombian authorities, the conflict between either FARC or ELN and AUC could have come within either Common Article 3 or Additional Protocol II, depending on whether, at the particular time in question, Additional Protocol II criteria were met. On this basis, it is arguable that from the mid-1990s to 2003, hostilities between these groups would be classified as coming within Additional Protocol II.
- *FARC or ELN v new armed groups arising post-2003 demobilization process*: classification of any hostilities between these groups would depend on whether the threshold of Common Article 3 had been reached; any conflict between FARC or ELN and these new groups may, at most, qualify under Common Article 3.
- *Colombian armed forces/FARC/ELN v drug cartels* (e.g. *Los Rastrojos*): any hostilities between either the Colombian State, FARC or ELN and a drug cartel would need to reach the threshold of Common Article 3 in order to be

classified as, at most, a Common Article 3 non-international armed conflict.[167]

5. Rules on opening fire

This section, and the next, will focus solely on the rules governing the use of force and detention currently in effect in Colombia, as there is insufficient space in this chapter to deal with all the various regimes which have governed these two areas in Colombia over the past five decades. The Colombian Ministry of Defence issued a *'Directiva Permanente'* in June 2007, containing the rules of engagement to be followed by the armed forces to ensure compliance with international humanitarian and human rights law.[168] The Directive confirmed the applicability of Common Article 3 and Additional Protocol II to the conflict, and that, therefore, the principles of legality, distinction, necessity and proportionality must govern all military actions.

It further stated that: 1) troops must distinguish between civilians and those directly participating in hostilities and protect civilians in all circumstances; 2) military objectives must be properly identified, and can be attacked; 3) the means and methods employed must be proportional to the military advantage to be gained, and that attacking civilians does not provide any military advantage; 4) killing fighters who are directly participating in hostilities is legitimate where the use of force is proportional; 5) killing persons outside active hostilities or when the use of force is not absolutely necessary will be considered as violating the right to life; and 6) troops are not exempt from respecting international humanitarian or human rights law where armed groups are themselves in violation of those rules.

The Directive formed the basis for the recent *Manuel de Derecho Operacional* (Manual of Law Governing Operations), issued to soldiers in the form of an administrative order, rather than an act of parliament.[169] The Manual itself distinguishes between two different situations, and prescribes different sets of rules for each: operations during hostilities (red card ops),[170] and operations to maintain security (blue card ops).[171] Blue card rules reflect international human rights law rules to be implemented by soldiers when conducting law-enforcement

---

[167] Even if FARC were to be recognized as belligerents, the conflict between FARC and a drug cartel could only qualify as a Common Article 3 non-international armed conflict, as it would remain a conflict between two non-state armed groups.

[168] Colombian Ministry of National Defence, 'Comprehensive Human Rights and IHL Policy' (2007), available at: <http://mindefensa.gov.co/irj/go/km/docs/Mindefensa/Documentos/descargas/Documentos_Home/Politica_DDHH_MDN.pdf>.

[169] Comando General Fuerzas Militares, 'Manuel de Derecho Operacional' (2009) (Manuel de Derecho Operacional).

[170] 'Operaciones en escenarios de hostilidades—tarjeta roja' and 'Operaciones para el mantenimiento de la seguridad—tarjeta azul'. C. von der Groeben, 'The Conflict in Colombia and the Relationship Between Humanitarian Law and Human Rights Law in Practice: Analysis of the New Operational Law of the Colombian Armed Forces' (2011) 16(1) *Journal of Conflict and Security Law* 141 (Von der Groeben, *New Operational Law*).

[171] Von der Groeben's translation of the blue card rules is as follows (150): '1. Resort to the use of force shall remain the last option. 2. Identify yourself as a member of the Military Forces. 3. Give a

operations, whilst Red card rules governing hostilities, on the other hand, have been argued to be an admixture of international humanitarian law and human rights law rules.[172] Red card rules state:

> ... force against a military objective or licit target may be used whenever:
>
> 1. The use of force falls within an operational order; and it is identified as military objective or licit target, at the moment of using weaponry.
> 2. If the circumstances permit, demobilization and capture are favored over deaths in combat.
> 3. Force shall be used in a directed way and not indiscriminately, reducing as far as possible harm against goods and protected people.
> 4. The use of force is always permissible in self-defense or if another person's life is in danger.[173]

International humanitarian law permits the use of force, but it does not require it; therefore rule 2 ('...demobilisation and capture are favored over deaths...'), it is argued, does not denote the insertion of a human rights rule into a mostly humanitarian law paradigm. Rather, rule 2 reflects a policy decision, which is probably due to the influence of international human rights law. In 2008, the then Vice Minister of Defence said, '...we regard IHL as *lex specialis* to human rights law in those situations where, mainly because of the level and organization of the violence, you have to conduct offensive military operations. However, we have also said that we fully recognize that human rights obligations remain in force.'[174]

Rule 1 incorporates the principle of distinction, whilst rule 3 requires that hostilities should not be indiscriminate, and appears to incorporate the principle of humanity. Rule 3 also requires, '...reducing as far as possible harm against goods and protected people'; however, it is not at all clear that the reduction of harm is the same as the proportionality principle, which prohibits, according to article 51(5)(b) of Additional Protocol I, 'an attack which may be expected to cause incidental loss of civilian life, injury to civilians, damage to civilian objects, or a combination thereof, which would be excessive in relation to the concrete and direct military advantage anticipated'. The 'reduction of harm' is surely not the same as ensuring damage is not excessive; if this is another attempt to integrate human rights law into international humanitarian law then it may potentially lead to breaches of the latter.

Given that international humanitarian law permits the use of force during armed conflict, rule 4 appears to be superfluous, unless, again, this represents the Colombian authorities' attempt to reflect human rights law principles. However, rule 4 is consistent with the armed conflict paradigm, in that it appears that, rather than encouraging troops to use the full force of international humanitarian law

---

clear warning of your intention to use firearms. 4. Use force proportionally to the threat which is to be averted. 5. The use of force is always permissible in self-defense or if another person's life is in danger'.

[172] Von der Groeben, *New Operational Law*, 151.
[173] Ibid.   [174] Pfanner et al, *Interview*, 828.

irrespective of the situation they are confronted with, the Red card rules encourage troops to consider means other than lethal force.

In order to determine whether Red or Blue card rules are to be applied, the Colombian authorities have set up two distinct, but inter-linked mechanisms: an Advisory Board (*'Grupo Asesor'*), and, separately, new posts within the armed forces entitled Legal Operations Advisers (*'Asesor Juridico Operacional'*). The Board consists of the heads of the intelligence agencies, the national police and the armed forces; meeting only once or twice a year, its primary task is to classify the situation—as it currently stands—in relation to each non-state armed group. Pursuant to this classification, the Board decides whether Red or Blue card rules are to be adopted when engaging with each non-state armed group. This procedure has the advantage that decisions about classification, within the public forces, should be consistent. However, in meeting so infrequently (it is claimed that meetings have 'hardly taken place at all thus far'),[175] the Board runs the risk of being out of touch with current developments, which may potentially lead to the wrong rules being applied.

The Legal Operations Advisers are a new addition to the armed forces, and are responsible for advising military commanders as to the rules to be implemented during a specific operation. However, they are limited by the classification set down by the Board: if the Board has classified a situation as being one to which Blue card rules apply, the Adviser cannot recommend Red card rules to the commander. In other words, an Adviser cannot classify, or change the classification, of a conflict.

It is impossible to tell from the Red card rules how the conflict has been classified, other than that it is a non-international armed conflict; that is, whether Common Article 3 or Additional Protocol II is applicable. In relation to the Blue card rules, which constitute a law-enforcement paradigm, these may be utilized during an armed conflict, but are more likely to be implemented in non-armed conflict situations.

Despite issuing the Directive in 2007, and the Manual in 2009, there have been many allegations of violations of these rules by the Colombian public forces, including the deliberate targeting of civilians, and extra-judicial executions.[176] As for FARC and ELN, as mentioned previously, both groups have said that they are bound by international humanitarian law; however, both groups have been accused of violations, including taking 'direct action against the civilian population, using prohibited weapons and anti-personnel mines, and attacking civilian premises and property'.[177]

6. Rules on detention

As mentioned in the previous section, rule 2 on the Red card states that, 'if the circumstances permit, demobilization and capture are favored over deaths in

---

[175] Von der Groeben, *New Operational Law*, 156–7.
[176] E.g. Amnesty International, 'Report on Colombia' (2009).
[177] UNHCHR, *Colombia 2010*.

combat'. As to what is done with fighters post-capture, in January 2008 a new system in relation to rules on detention took effect.[178] In theory, within thirty-six hours of being detained, detainees must be brought before a judge in order to determine if that detention is valid. If it is deemed to be valid, formal charges must be brought against the detainee within thirty days, and the criminal trial itself must begin within ninety days of the first date of detention. In the majority of felony cases, suspects must be released if formal charges are not filed within 180 days of the initial date of detention. Where a detention is alleged to be arbitrary, habeas corpus is available to address this issue.[179]

Members of the Colombian armed forces are not authorized to execute warrants of arrest; they are generally accompanied by members of the Prosecutor General's Corps of Technical Investigators (CTI), who are empowered to issue and execute such warrants. However, members of the armed forces are permitted to detain members of non-state armed groups who are captured during active hostilities, as warrants of arrest are not required where suspects are detained during the alleged commission of offences, or flee from the scene of an alleged offence.[180]

The Directive issued by the Ministry of Defence (referred to above) also contains rules on detaining those captured during hostilities. It states that there must be strict adherence to the rules on capture and detention, and that article 12 of Law 589 of 2000 (dealing with forced disappearances) must be respected. Furthermore, it states that those captured must be turned over to the competent authorities, along with information including the date and time of the alleged transgression, and the reason for the apprehension or detention.

The rules for detention, as outlined above, are clearly based within a framework of international human rights law, and not international humanitarian law. International humanitarian law neither specifies the lawful grounds for detaining persons, nor what procedures should be followed in reviewing detention.

The Colombian government has stated that it does not hold any 'political prisoners'; however, nearly 4000 detainees were held by the Colombian authorities during 2009, accused of 'rebellion' or 'aiding and abetting insurgence'. The ICRC is permitted by the authorities to visit these detainees.[181] In fact, Directive No. 10 of 2007 includes a paragraph granting the ICRC immediate access to detainees.

In August 1996, FARC captured sixty Colombian members of the armed forces after an assault on the *Las Delicias* outpost; after this, FARC issued a statement saying that it was treating these detainees humanely, in accordance with the '... provisions established in Protocol II ...'. These detainees were released, seemingly in good health, by FARC ten months later.[182] However, numerous allegations have been made in recent years that FARC no longer appears to respect

---

[178] For a detailed description of this legal framework and how it works in practice, see Human Rights Council, *Report of the Working Group on Arbitrary Detention, Mission to Colombia*, 16 February 2009.

[179] US Department of State, 'Country Reports: Colombia' (2010).

[180] Ibid.

[181] US Department of State, 'Country Reports: Colombia' (2010).

[182] Carrillo-Suarez, *Contemporary Issues*, 43.

international humanitarian law rules on detention. For example, allegations were made in 2009 against FARC's prison director, Heli Mejia Mendoza, that Colombian soldiers were treated inhumanely, such as being constantly chained up.[183] There are numerous allegations of mistreatment, torture and extra-judicial killings of people said to have been detained by the Colombian authorities, as well as other breaches of the current rules of detention, for example, not charging persons within thirty days of first being detained.

7. Operation Phoenix

This chapter turns next to Operation Phoenix, a military strike carried out on 1 March 2008 by Colombian forces against FARC fighters based in Ecuadorian territory. In particular, the operation raises questions about how to classify military operations which are carried out in the context of a non-international armed conflict, but which take place across State borders.

The Colombian authorities have given two conflicting versions of how Operation Phoenix was both planned and conducted. In the first version, the Colombian government stated that its ground troops were in pursuit of FARC fighters, who crossed the Ecuadorian border and fired on its armed forces from within Ecuadorian territory. Colombia said it then called for an air strike on these fighters, which was carried out from within Colombian airspace. Once fighting had stopped, Colombian forces were flown into Ecuador to 'secure the area and neutralize the enemy', in accordance with the 'hot pursuit' doctrine.[184] This version has subsequently been challenged by Ecuador, and discredited, not least by the general who conducted the operation himself.[185]

In the second version, the Colombian authorities claimed that they had received information that Reyes (the FARC second-in-command) was going to be staying in a FARC camp based in Colombian territory, and planned an attack on this basis. However, they then received further intelligence stating that Reyes had just moved to a FARC camp in Ecuadorian territory, close to the Colombian border,[186] but took the decision to attack the FARC camp regardless of where it was situated,[187] believing it to be a 'legitimate target'.[188] At around midnight on 1 March 2008,

---

[183] 'FARC Jailer is Colombia's to Try' *The China Post* (21 June 2009).

[184] L.E. Nagle, 'Colombia's Incursion into Ecuadorian Territory: Justified Hot Pursuit or Pugnacious Error?' SSRN Paper (2008) 1 (Nagle, *Hot Pursuit*); S. Brodzinsky, 'Colombia's Cross-Border Strike on FARC Irks Neighbours' *Christian Science Monitor* (3 March 2008).

[185] General Padilla, 'Fenix Narrada por el General Freddy Padilla' *El Tiempo* (1 March 2009). In addition, President Correa stated that there was 'no sign of pursuit' at or around the scene of the fighting; see 'Ecuador Recalls Ambassador to Colombia for Consultations After Death of "Reyes" in the Country' *El Tiempo* (2 March 2008).

[186] Nagle, *Hot Pursuit*, 1.

[187] OAS Commission, 'Report of the OAS Commission that Visited Ecuador and Colombia' Twenty-Fifth Meeting of Consultation of Ministers of Foreign Affairs (2008) 6 (OAS Commission Report).

[188] 'Colombia se levantó de la mesa en la audiencia que evalúa demanda de Ecuador por la operación Fénix' *El Tiempo* (19 March 2010).

Colombia's air force carried out air strikes, launching their assault from Colombian territory,[189] and dropping ten bombs on the camp in Ecuador.[190]

Both Colombian versions of Operation Phoenix concur that after the initial air strike, Colombian ground forces, consisting of both military and police, arrived at the camp in Ecuador, and on arrival, were fired on by surviving FARC fighters.[191] The Colombian forces returned fire, and, when they had control of the camp, removed two bodies, those of Reyes and an Ecuadorian citizen, Franklin Guillermo Aisalla Molina, taking them back to Colombia, leaving all other bodies and three wounded people behind.[192] Colombian armed forces also said that they removed computers from the camp.

7.1. Classification of Operation Phoenix by the participants and others

7.1.1 Colombia

Colombia has acknowledged that it entered Ecuadorian territory without permission from the Ecuadorian authorities.[193] Prior to launching Operation Phoenix, Colombia asserts that it had repeatedly warned Ecuador that non-state armed groups were based in Ecuadorian territory, and had asked Ecuador to act against these groups. Colombia claimed that it had documented numerous cases in which FARC fighters fired on Colombian forces from across the border in Ecuador.[194]

The then Colombian Defence Minister, Juan Manuel Santos, said that Operation Phoenix amounted to 'legitimate acts of war, legitimate acts in defence of democracy'.[195] Colombia's Foreign Minister Fernando Araujo Perdomo justified Colombia's attack, saying, '[t]he terrorists, among them Raul Reyes, have had the habit of murdering in Colombia and invading the territory of neighboring countries to find refuge'. Therefore, the Minister continued, 'Colombia did not violate the sovereignty, but instead acted under the principle of legitimate defense'. Furthermore, the Colombian authorities stated that such a strike was justified under international law because FARC is a terrorist group, and the Colombian military was engaged in a 'hot pursuit' operation.[196]

Colombia claimed to have found evidence in the FARC encampment in Ecuador that both Venezuela and Ecuador had been supporting FARC militarily and financially, and that this evidence supported Colombia's argument that Operation Phoenix was 'an act of self-defence'.[197]

---

[189] Nagle, *Hot Pursuit*, 1.
[190] OAS Commission Report, 6; it is still unclear exactly what transpired during the attack on the FARC camp in Equadorian territory.
[191] OAS Commission Report, 6.
[192] Nagle, *Hot Pursuit*, 1; 'Colombia Confirms One Ecuadorian Among Dead in Cross-Border Raid' *Deutsche Presse-Agentur* (24 March 2008) (DPA, *Colombia's Cross-Border Raid*).
[193] OAS Commission Report, 7.
[194] Robles, *Colombia's Strike*.
[195] DPA, *Colombia's Cross-Border Raid*.
[196] Nagle, *Hot Pursuit*, 2.
[197] DPA, *Colombia's Cross-Border Raid*.

7.1.2 Ecuador

The Ecuadorian President, Rafael Correa, was not informed about Operation Phoenix before it took place; rather, Colombian President Uribe called him the following Saturday morning to tell him of the operation.[198] Uribe explained that this was because the attack took place in 'hot pursuit' of FARC fighters.[199] Correa responded to the discovery that, in addition to carrying out hostilities on Ecuadorian soil, Colombian forces had also spent several hours in Ecuador documenting the attack, by saying that it was 'not an incursion—it was an invasion' by Colombia.[200] He also termed the operation an act of 'aggression'.[201] Two days after the strike, Ecuador severed diplomatic ties with Colombia. In addition, the Ecuadorian government issued a call for an international arrest warrant to be issued for Defence Minister Santos, for ordering the air strike.[202] The petition lodged by Ecuador against Colombia in the Inter-American Court of Human Rights confirms Ecuador's lack of consent to Colombia carrying out hostilities on its territory.[203]

The Ecuadorian authorities disputed the Colombian account of the operation, saying that the 'smart bombs' which were fired would require special planes and experienced pilots to handle them, arguing that Colombia did not have such resources.[204] Ecuadorian military sources claimed that the planes used in the attacks were flown by Americans, possibly employees of the private security company DynCorp.[205] President Correa later said that the FARC fighters were 'bombed and massacred...surely with the assistance of foreign powers'; alleging these 'foreign powers' to be US forces.[206] It is not clear from these statements whether Ecuador was claiming to have been attacked jointly by the US and Colombia; in other words, whether it considered Operation Phoenix to have been an international armed conflict. It should be noted, however, that a US Senate report dealing with the operation makes no reference to any US involvement in it.[207] In April 2008, President Correa warned the Colombian government and FARC to stay out of his country, saying future incursions would be considered an 'act of war'.[208]

---

[198] Nagle, *Hot Pursuit*, 2.   [199] Ibid.   [200] Robles, *Colombia's Strike.*

[201] DPA, *Colombia's Cross-Border Raid.*

[202] 'Ecuador, Colombia Set Patch-Up Talks on Security, Bilateral Ties' *United Press International* (14 October 2009).

[203] *Ecuador v Colombia*, Inter-State Petition on Admissibility in the Matter of Franklin Guillermo Aisalla Molina, Inter-American Court of Human Rights, Report No. 112/10, Inter-Petition IP-02 (2010) para 17 (*Ecuador v Colombia*).

[204] K. Lucas, 'Ecuador: Manta Air Base Tied to Colombian Raid on FARC Camp' *IPS* (21 March 2008).

[205] Coffey, *Colombia's War.*

[206] Nagle, *Hot Pursuit*, 2.

[207] US Senate Committee on Foreign Relations, 'Playing with Fire: Colombia, Ecuador and Venezuela' (28 April 2008) (US Senate, *Playing With Fire*).

[208] Ibid, 4.

7.1.3 *Responses by other States to Operation Phoenix*

President Chavez of Venezuela called Operation Phoenix a 'war crime'; as to the allegation that Venezuela had been supporting FARC, he denied this.[209] Brazil condemned the Colombian strike, calling it a 'territorial violation'. Brazil's Foreign Minister called on Colombia to apologize to Ecuador, and to explain any 'mitigating circumstance', such as 'if the raid was mounted in self-defense or was a "hot pursuit" action'.[210]

The President of Chile, Michelle Bachelet, termed the operation an 'aggressive breaching of the border'.[211] Nicaragua broke off diplomatic relations with Colombia, because of what President Daniel Ortega referred to as 'political terrorism' on the part of Colombia.[212] Peruvian President, Alan Garcia, called the Operation a 'violation of Ecuadorian sovereignty', and condemned it.[213]

The US termed Operation Phoenix a 'violation of territorial integrity', but also said that the 'methods used by the FARC, and other like groups, violate both Colombia's sovereignty and the sovereignty of other countries where they operate, regardless of how these groups are classified, whether terrorist, irregular or belligerent'.[214]

The OAS debated the issue, and unanimously agreed on a resolution regarding Operation Phoenix; the OAS Permanent Council stated that Colombia had violated the 'principles of international law' by crossing into Ecuadorian territory.[215] The OAS subsequently established a commission to investigate the operation,[216] which visited both Colombia and Ecuador in March 2008. It concluded that the Colombian military had entered Ecuadorian territory without the consent of the Ecuadorian government, which constituted 'a violation of the sovereignty and territorial integrity of Ecuador and the principles of international law'.[217]

None of the responses reproduced above reflect on the classification of Operation Phoenix for international humanitarian law purposes (save for President Chavez's comment about the operation being a 'war crime', although he did not say what kind of an armed conflict he believed was involved). This is yet again indicative of the difficulties inherent in interpreting States' responses to such incidents, especially for the purposes of trying to establish State practice in relation to the classification of conflicts.

---

[209] 'Chávez financió y dio refugio a las FARC' *El Pais* (11 May 2011).
[210] 'Brazil Condemns Colombia's Ecuador Raid' *Reuters* (3 March 2008).
[211] DPA, *Colombia's Cross-Border Strike*.
[212] 'Nicaragua cuts ties with Colombia' *BBC News* (8 March 2008).
[213] 'Ecuador's Correa on LatAm Tour' *Prensa Latina* (3 November 2009).
[214] US Senate, *Playing With Fire*, 9.
[215] *Ecuador v Colombia*.
[216] The Commission was established on the basis of the Permanent Council's resolution CP/Res. 930 (1632/08). It was headed by the Secretary-General, and consisted of four ambassadors designated by him.
[217] OAS Commission Report, 10.

7.2. Authors' classification of Operation Phoenix

Various possibilities for the classification of Operation Phoenix are discussed before the authors arrive at a conclusion at the end of this section. Several aspects of the conduct of the operation remain in dispute and classification may be affected should new information come to light.

Colombia initially stated that hostilities with FARC commenced in Colombian territory, before spilling into Ecuadorian territory, arguing that this amounted to a 'hot pursuit'. However, the hot pursuit doctrine is a maritime law concept,[218] and there is no basis in treaty law outside the law of the sea for drawing an analogy on land.[219] Even if an analogy could be drawn which extended to actions on land, it would fail since a hot pursuit must end where the territory of a third State begins. The classification of Operation Phoenix as a continuation of a non-international armed conflict through hot pursuit is therefore dismissed.[220]

Operation Phoenix could be classified as an extraterritorial non-international armed conflict, since all the parties to the hostilities were also parties to the original non-international armed conflict in Colombia; the same goes for the targets of the attack. The only difference between the original non-international armed conflict and the hostilities conducted under the auspices of Operation Phoenix was that the latter took place in a third State, rather than on Colombian soil.[221] It has been argued elsewhere in this book that any non-international armed conflict which crosses a State's border and continues into a second State (territorial State) without its consent, must be an international armed conflict by virtue of that lack of consent.[222] Although Operation Phoenix was carried out by Colombian forces on Ecuadorian soil without Ecuadorian consent, the authors oppose this argument. An international armed conflict clearly requires that there be an armed conflict between two States: in this case, Ecuadorian forces were not involved in any way in hostilities against Colombia.

In relation to the issue of consent, if the territorial State consented to the attack, that attack would constitute the continuation of a non-international armed conflict. If consent was sought before hostilities commenced, but was refused by the territorial State, the conflict may arguably be classifiable as an international armed

---

[218] N. Poulantzas, *The Right of Hot Pursuit in International Law* (2002).

[219] Were it to be agreed that the hot pursuit doctrine exists in these circumstances, this may well preclude classification of Operation Phoenix as an international armed conflict.

[220] In addition, Colombia has since repudiated its own statements regarding Operation Phoenix being carried out according to the 'doctrine' of hot pursuit. However, this is not to say that there may not be State practice developing which accepts the notion of a doctrine of hot pursuit on land in customary law (or regional custom); however, examining this idea is outside the scope of this chapter.

[221] There is some disagreement as to whether extraterritorial non-international armed conflicts which are classified as reaching the Additional Protocol II threshold in the State in which the primary conflict is being waged, are subject to the Protocol when waged in another State, or whether only Common Article 3 is applicable. Article 1(1) of the Protocol ostensibly limits the Protocol's application to 'the territory of a High Contracting Party' to the Convention. This issue cannot be dealt with here due to space limitations.

[222] See ch. 3, section 9 above.

conflict. If no such consent was sought prior to Operation Phoenix, the authors argue that it would depend on the reaction of the territorial State to the ensuing hostilities as to whether the conflict would amount to an international or a non-international armed conflict.

In the case of Operation Phoenix, Colombia did not seek prior permission for carrying out the attack, and, when engaging in the operation, Colombia did not target Ecuadorian facilities or citizens. The authors argue that this does not constitute the use of force by Colombia against Ecuador, and therefore the operation cannot be characterized as an international armed conflict. There is no evidence that Colombia had *animus belligerendi* towards Ecuador; however, if Colombia were shown to have *animus* against Ecuador, Operation Phoenix could arguably be classified as an international armed conflict.[223]

When Ecuador learnt of Operation Phoenix, it did not respond by attacking Colombia, nor did it describe the operation as an international armed conflict or a war, although it did accuse Colombia of committing an act of aggression. This, however, is not the same as considering the operation an international armed conflict. A further possibility for arguing that Operation Phoenix constituted an international armed conflict is to be found in allegations by Colombia that Ecuador had been supporting FARC. However, in the view of the authors, the level of support alleged to have been provided (if proven) would neither reach the threshold of effective control (*Nicaragua*), nor of overall control (*Tadić*), and therefore this possibility does not arise.

The authors therefore conclude that Operation Phoenix should be classified as a non-international armed conflict: an extraterritorial continuation of the non-international armed conflict involving Colombia and FARC.

7.3. Rules on opening fire in Operation Phoenix

There is no information in the public domain regarding any specific rules of engagement which may have been issued to the Colombian public forces for Operation Phoenix. It is assumed, therefore, that the Colombian government's *Directiva Permanente*, issued in June 2007, governed the operation, or at least, that any rules of engagement which may have been used would not conflict with the Directive.[224] The Directive, as discussed earlier, confirmed that all the provisions of Common Article 3 and Additional Protocol II were applicable to the armed conflict between Colombia and FARC; Colombia has not claimed at any time that Operation Phoenix was anything other than a non-international armed conflict.

One of the difficulties in assessing whether the provisions contained in Common Article 3 and Additional Protocol II were adhered to during Operation Phoenix, is that the facts of the operation are in dispute. Colombian forces alleged that they were fired on by FARC fighters,[225] and that, as a result, they returned

---

[223] See e.g. comparable discussion in ch. 13, section 4.1 below.
[224] For a discussion of this Directive, see section 5 above.
[225] OAS Commission Report, 6.

fire. On anyone's reading of the definition of direct participation in hostilities, this use of force would be uncontroversial. However, allegations were made that FARC members were asleep in their camp at the time of the attack;[226] and that some FARC fighters were executed by Colombian forces.[227] The Directive orders troops to distinguish between civilians and those taking a direct part in hostilities; however, it is unclear what definition of direct participation Colombia adhered to at that time.[228] In relation to the allegations of execution-style killings, this is prohibited no matter what the classification of an armed conflict is.

Furthermore, the Directive states that the means and methods employed must be proportional to the military advantage to be gained from them. This raises the question as to whether dropping ten bombs over a two-hectare radius around the camp would be a proportionate use of force.[229] It appears that there were about fifty people in this area at the time of the bombings, including civilians, twenty-six of whom were killed, and at least three injured.[230]

It is therefore concluded that any issues raised by the use of force in Operation Phoenix were neither due to problems with the classification of the operation, nor the international humanitarian law rules applicable as a result of classification, but rather the interpretation and implementation of these rules.

7.4. Rules on detention in Operation Phoenix

Again, the facts on the ground are in dispute, making it difficult to render any accurate assessment of detention rules. Colombia's Directive of 2007 does not specifically include any rules on detention, however, the Directive does state that those killed outside active hostilities or when the use of force is not absolutely necessary, will be considered as having had their right to life violated; this is a rule of international human rights, not of international humanitarian law. Nevertheless, under the international humanitarian law paradigm, it could be interpreted as saying that there is an obligation to detain where the use of force is not essential.

In the case of Operation Phoenix, it was alleged that those targeted in the camp were asleep at the time. If this was the case, the Colombian forces may have been obliged to detain, rather than kill, the FARC fighters.[231] Furthermore,

---

[226] This allegation was made by one of the surviving FARC fighters, and was supported by Ecuadorian investigators, who said that the fighters were in their pyjamas, and had appeared to have been attacked in their sleep.

[227] See *Ecuador v Colombia*, in which Ecuador alleges that one of its citizens was 'extrajudicially executed by members of the Colombian security forces'. *Ecuador v Colombia*, para 1.

[228] For further discussion on the concept of direct participation in hostilities, see ch. 4, section 4 above. Aspects of the definition are still in dispute.

[229] OAS Commission Report, 6.

[230] *Ecuador v Colombia*, paras 111–12.

[231] Unless the notion of targeting people on the basis of their status as fighters, rather than their behaviour, is accepted.

the Colombian authorities took two bodies back to Colombia with them, but left three wounded fighters behind. It is unclear why these fighters were not detained by Colombia, although it was possible that they were not Colombian citizens. It is not clear whether those wounded in the attack were either detained or arrested by Ecuadorian forces after they arrived at the scene of the attack.

In respect of the detention of FARC fighters by Ecuador, there is not much information available as to how fighters arrested by Ecuador are treated after arrest, except for the case of Ricardo Palmera, in 2004.[232] He was arrested by the Ecuadorian authorities in Quito at the request of the US and Colombia, and was deported to Colombia under an extradition agreement, to face charges of murder, kidnapping and rebellion. However, the Colombian authorities extradited him to the US at the end of 2004 to stand trial there, without being tried for any crimes allegedly committed in Colombia.

8. Conclusions

This chapter addressed a number of difficulties in the course of classifying the conflict. Assessing the appropriate classification of any hostility is frequently hindered by a lack of information in the public domain, which is fundamental to making a proper determination, and is further hindered by disputes between the actors concerned as to the accuracy of such information. In the case of Colombia, these factors constituted particular obstacles in attempting to establish the precise nature of the relationship between paramilitaries (both pre- and post-demobilization) and the Colombian government; the status and impact of the relationship between foreign States and non-state armed groups, for example the alleged relationship between Venezuela or Ecuador and FARC; and the sequence of events during Operation Phoenix.

Further, the longer an armed conflict continues, the more fluctuations are likely to occur, both in the intensity of the hostilities, and in the organizational structure of groups involved. Keeping track of all these changes makes it difficult to assess when a situation reaches, or falls below, the requisite thresholds for Common Article 3 or Additional Protocol II.

As well as facing these practical problems, there were theoretical difficulties in classifying the hostilities involving Colombia. These included determining what constitutes the correct test for actions of paramilitaries to be attributed to the State for classification purposes, and the correct test for establishing attribution to foreign States for acts committed by non-state armed groups. For the latter, there is still disagreement as to whether the effective or overall control test should be employed, or whether there is yet another, more appropriate test. Other difficulties lay in determining whether, under international humanitarian law, criminal groups may ever qualify as parties to an armed conflict, and whether

---

[232] Aka Simon Trinidad, who played a major role in FARC's financial operations.

recognition of belligerency is still an active concept, and if so, whether the criteria for recognition, and the obligations flowing therefrom remain unchanged. This chapter also had to consider whether an attack by one State against a non-state armed group present (temporarily or permanently) in the territory of another State constituted a continuation of a non-international armed conflict, or a separate (parallel) international armed conflict.

The decision by the Colombian government to apply Additional Protocol II as a matter of policy has meant that some of the problems that could have arisen in relation to classification and its consequences were rendered moot. There was no need to distinguish between the two thresholds for non-international armed conflict because the violence, at least since the 2007 *Directiva Permanente* and the Military Manual,[233] was regarded as either constituting the maintenance of the security situation, or 'hostilities'. However, had Operation Phoenix been classified as an international armed conflict there would have been a difference in the law applicable both to the use of force on the ground and to detention.

Both the *Directiva Permanente* and the Military Manual contain admixtures of international humanitarian and human rights law, which may well be confusing in practice, especially in relation to rules on opening fire. Since international humanitarian law does not specify on which lawful grounds persons may be detained, or what procedures should be followed in reviewing detention, the Colombian authorities turned to human rights law to provide a framework for detention.

In an armed conflict such as this, where there are multiple actors (State public forces, paramilitaries, non-state armed groups—some of which meet Common Article 3 criteria, and some of which meet the criteria of Additional Protocol II—and criminal armed groups), the most practical legal solution would be to apply customary international humanitarian law rules across the board (the issue of criminal groups qualifying as parties to the armed conflict notwithstanding). International human rights law is available to 'fill in the gaps'. Of course, not all of the rules delineated by the ICRC as being customary international humanitarian law have been accepted as such by all States. And, notwithstanding the lack of distinction in the ICRC Study between the rules applicable under Common Article 3 and Additional Protocol II, these remain the two distinct legal thresholds in respect of the treaty law governing non-international armed conflicts.

---

[233] See sections 5 and 6 of this chapter.

Chronology

9 April 1948	Jorge Eliecer Gaitan, Liberal Party Presidential candidate, was assassinated.
1948–1957	*La Violencia* (ten-year period of civil conflict between supporters of the Colombian Liberal Party and the Colombian Conservative Party) commenced.
1963	ELN was established.
1964	FARC was established.
1965	Decree 3398, which provided for civilian participation in military activity, was adopted.
1968	Law 48, which transformed Decree 3398 into permanent legislation, was passed.
1982	FARC held its 7th Guerilla Conference, renamed itself FARC-EP, and adopted a more aggressive military programme.
1984	A ceasefire was negotiated between Colombia and FARC/M-19; ELN refused to participate in it.
1985	*Union Patriotica* was launched, supported by FARC amongst others.
1986	UP gained representation in Congress.
1987	UP leader was assassinated.
1990	FARC ended ceasefire with State.
1994	*Convivir* was established by national law.
	ACCU was established by Carlos Castaño.
1996	First large-scale attack was carried out by FARC against *Las Delicias* military base.
1997	Paramilitary groups created umbrella organization—the AUC.
1998	Peace talks initiated with FARC; demilitarized zone the size of Switzerland established to facilitate talks.
2000	Plan Colombia was launched by US, which gave more than US$860 million to Colombia to fight the 'war on drugs'.
2003	Paramilitary demobilization began.
2005	Justice and Peace Law was established.
2006	Para-politics scandal broke.
2008	Operation Phoenix was carried out; top paramilitary leaders were extradited to the US; 'new illegal armed groups' emerged.
2009	FARC and ELN announced ceasefire between them.
2010	Venezuela cut diplomatic ties with Colombia, after Colombia accused Venezuela of providing sanctuary to FARC fighters; senior FARC commander was killed by Colombian forces.
2011	FARC released several hostages as a peace gesture to the Colombian government.

8

Afghanistan 2001–2010

*Françoise J. Hampson**

1. Introduction

Whilst the focus of this chapter is on the situation in Afghanistan since September 2001, it is necessary to consider briefly the period surrounding the Soviet intervention in 1979, in order to understand the background to the various possible permutations in the relationships between different groups. The Soviet Union sent armed forces into Afghanistan in December 1979 in order to 'assist' the then government. There was an increasing level of conflict between the government and various organized armed groups, organized along tribal or clan lines, operating in a loose coalition. Over time, the armed groups received significant assistance, notably in the form of weaponry, from Western States. Following the departure of the Soviet forces from Afghanistan by February 1989, many were surprised at the length of time for which the government held on to power. Eventually, in 1992 it fell to the forces of the loose coalition, known as the Mujahedeen. There were increasing disagreements between the groups forming the coalition, resulting in fighting between them, which had a particularly serious impact on Kabul. The government headed by Ahmad Shah Massoud, the most effective of the military commanders against the Soviet forces, was recognized as the government of Afghanistan by several, notably Western, States.

In an environment of fighting, disorder and chaos, some elements of the population, at least in the south-east of the country, welcomed the arrival of an unusual force, the Taliban, which gained increasing control over territory from their stronghold in Kandahar. In areas which they seized, they provided a measure of stability, order and dispute resolution. It was only as they consolidated their control that the Taliban engaged in severe levels of repression, with a particularly serious impact on women. The Taliban took over Kabul in 1996 and started to run the country. The Taliban were recognized as the government of Afghanistan by Pakistan, Saudi Arabia and the UAE but by no other States. It is alleged that President Musharraf of Pakistan encouraged Pakistanis to go to Afghanistan to fight

* I am grateful for research assistance with this chapter from Theresa DiPerna and to Felicity Szesnat for editing assistance.

alongside the Taliban. Their ranks were allegedly also swelled by around 3000 members of the Pakistani armed forces. The proportion of the territory subject to Taliban control increased but they did not have control over all Afghanistan. In particular, Massoud, leading the Northern Alliance, held out against the Taliban from his base in the Panjshir valley. Two individuals posing as journalists arranged to meet Massoud and, on 9 September 2001, blew up both themselves and him. It is not clear if the timing of the killing was linked to the operations in the United States two days later or if it was a coincidence.

Those involved in the 9/11 attacks against the United States (US) were neither Afghans nor, for that matter, Iraqis. The United Nations (UN) Security Council, in resolution 1368 (2001) of 12 September 2001, recalled the inherent right of self-defence in a preambular paragraph, even though the suspected perpetrators were non-state actors.[1] NATO, for the first time in its history, invoked article 5 of the treaty, enabling all NATO members to come to the assistance of the US.[2] Statements from Osama bin Laden strongly implied that Al-Qaeda was responsible for the 9/11 attacks.[3] The Security Council, in resolution 1373 (2001) of 28 September 2001, reaffirmed that States are required to give no support, whether active or passive, to terrorists and are required to take steps to deny them safe havens in their territory. The US asked the Taliban, whom the US did not recognize as the government of Afghanistan, to hand over for trial the leaders of Al-Qaeda. After a period of time, the Taliban refused to accede to the request.[4] As a result, the US and its Coalition partners had to fight the apparent de facto government of Afghanistan in order to be able to reach Al-Qaeda, their real goal.[5]

Afghanistan was at all relevant times a party to the four Geneva Conventions of 1949. It became a party to Additional Protocols I and II only on 10 November 2009. It acceded to the International Covenant on Civil and Political Rights (ICCPR) on 24 January 1983. At no point between September 2001 and the

---

[1] '...*Determined* to combat by all means threats to international peace and security caused by terrorist acts, *Recognizing* the inherent right of individual or collective self-defence in accordance with the Charter, 1. *Unequivocally condemns* in the strongest terms the horrifying terrorist attacks which took place on 11 September 2001 in New York, Washington, D.C. and Pennsylvania and *regards* such acts, like any act of international terrorism, as a threat to international peace and security.'

[2] NATO, Press Release (2001)124 (12 September 2001), available at: <www.nato.int/docu/pr/2001/p01-124e.htm>; E. Buckley, 'Invocation of Article 5: five years on' (2006) *NATO Review*.

[3] Initially, responsibility was established by national security agencies, relying on intercepted communications; C. Blackhurst and P. Lashmar, 'Piece by Piece, The Jigsaw of Terror Revealed' *The Independent* (30 September 2001); J. Tagliabue and R. Bonner, 'A NATION CHALLENGED: GERMAN INTELLIGENCE; German Data Led U.S. to Search For More Suicide Hijacker Teams' *The New York Times* (29 September 2001); Office of the Prime Minister, 10 Downing Street, 'Responsibility for the Terrorist Atrocities in the United States, 11 September 2001' (November 2001), full text reproduced at: <http://news.bbc.co.uk/1/hi/uk_politics/1579043.stm>. On 29 October 2004, Osama bin Laden accepted responsibility in a video broadcast by Al-Jazeera.

[4] In his book, *My Life with the Taliban* (2010), Abdul Salam Zaeef states that the Taliban offered to hand over Osama bin Laden for trial if the US established a prima facie case but that the US provided no evidence of his connection with the events of 9/11.

[5] Arguably in contrast to the Israeli operation against Hezbollah in Lebanon; see ch. 12. The contributions of different States to Operation Enduring Freedom in the first phase of the conflict are set out at D. Gerleman et al, 'Operation Enduring Freedom: Foreign Pledges of Military & Intelligence Support' CRS Report for Congress (17 October 2001).

time of writing has Afghanistan sought to derogate under the Covenant. It should, perhaps, be noted that it signed the Convention on the Elimination of Discrimination against Women (CEDAW) on 14 August 1980 but only ratified it on 5 March 2003. It acceded to the Statute of the International Criminal Court on 10 February 2003.

2. October 2011 to the installation of Hamid Karzai

The reason for the start of this period is obvious: the planning and conduct of an armed conflict against the Taliban and Al-Qaeda following the attacks in the US on 9/11. Operation Enduring Freedom (OEF) began on 7 October 2001 when the US-led Coalition launched air attacks into Afghanistan, notifying the UN Security Council that this was done in self-defence and in order to avert further attacks.[6] It is more difficult to ascertain the ending of the period, in particular at what point there was in being a body competent to request external assistance on behalf of Afghanistan and when such assistance was sought. At a meeting in Bonn in late November 2001, provisional arrangements were agreed with regard to the post-Taliban administration of Afghanistan. The agreement was signed on 5 December 2001. The internationally recognized administration of President Rabbani gave way to an Interim Afghan Authority (IAA), headed by Chairman Hamid Karzai, on 22 December 2001, as agreed at the Bonn meeting. On 25 January 2002, the composition of a Special Independent Commission was agreed for the convening of an Emergency Loya Jirga. That was held from 11 to 19 June 2002 and endorsed the appointment of Hamid Karzai as President, pending elections. The four groups present at the meeting in Bonn requested the early deployment of a security force.[7] The International Security Assistance Force (ISAF) was accordingly established by Security Council resolution 1386 (2001) of 20 December 2001. The resolution referred to a letter from the permanent representative of Afghanistan to the United Nations which contained, as an annex, a letter from the acting Minister of Foreign Affairs of the IAA; that letter gave the consent of the government of Afghanistan to the deployment of a multinational security force.[8] ISAF was given a Chapter VII mandate for six months which was subsequently renewed for further periods.

---

[6] Letter from Permanent Representative of the USA to the UN addressed to the President of the Security Council, S/2001/946 (7 October 2001). The UK letter stated that the action was 'directed against Usama Bin Laden's Al-Qaeda terrorist organization and the Taliban regime that is supporting it'; letter dated 7 October 2001 from the Chargé d'affaires a.i. of the Permanent Mission of the United Kingdom of Great Britain and Northern Ireland to the United Nations addressed to the President of the Security Council, S/2001/947 (7 October 2001).

[7] At Annex 1, para 3 of the Bonn Agreement the signatories requested the Security Council to consider authorizing the early deployment of a UN mandated force.

[8] Letter dated 19 December 2001 from the Permanent Representative of Afghanistan to the United Nations addressed to the President of the Security Council, S/2001/1223 (19 December 2001). In a previous letter of 14 December, consent had been given to the deployment of a multinational force on the basis of Chapter VI of the UN Charter. The letter of 19 December referred to the deployment of a force on the basis of either Chapter VI or Chapter VII of the Charter. The letter said that the government had agreed to the deployment of a force and not that it had requested it.

The choice of date for the ending of the first phase of the post 9/11 conflict depends on the point at which the conflict ceased to be against the government of Afghanistan and became instead one fought with the consent of a new government. In other words, consent is the key factor. For the consent to be effective, it is necessary that the entity giving consent should have the authority to do so in international law. It is not clear whether that authority comes from recognition or whether it requires some form of domestic representative endorsement, in this case the endorsement of Hamid Karzai as President by the Loya Jirga. It is also possible that the Security Council by Chapter VII resolution can assert or imply a consent that is not in fact present. It will be assumed that, from its first deployment, ISAF was present in Afghanistan with the effective consent of the national authorities.

2.1. Views of the parties on classification of the hostilities

There were at least two ongoing sets of hostilities, the first between the Northern Alliance and the Taliban/Al-Qaeda, and the second involving the Coalition and Taliban/Al-Qaeda. In relation to the second there is some difficulty in identifying the parties.

2.1.1 *Who were the parties?*

a. Taliban/Al-Qaeda
The Taliban were arguably the de facto government of a High Contracting Party to the Geneva Conventions of 1949. It is not relevant for the characterization of the conflict that the US did not recognize the government. What matters is that it recognized the State and that the State was a High Contracting Party. However, it was possibly not the case that the US did not recognize any authority as the government of Afghanistan; it appears that the recognition of the Massoud government was never withdrawn. The increasing lack of formality with regard to recognition of governments makes it difficult to determine the facts. If the Massoud government was still recognized, the Americans may have regarded the Northern Alliance, or at least part of it, as the armed forces of Afghanistan. This could have a significant bearing on the classification of the conflict if recognition plays a role where there are two authorities vying for power and one of them has been recognized.[9] Alternatively, given the priority which the Geneva Conventions attach to facts, it may be the case that the forces of the State are those forces in fact exercising authority over the majority of the territory, irrespective of any question of recognition.[10]

---

[9] This is the only case studied in which recognition of a party to conflict might have an impact on classification. It would result in a conflict between the US and her allies and the recognized Afghan authorities on one hand and the Taliban and Al-Qaeda on the other. That would appear to represent an armed conflict not of an international character.

[10] The only reference to recognition in the treaty provisions dealing with the applicability of the Geneva Conventions of 1949 is to non-recognition of the state of war between two States, rather than

One source of factual confusion concerns whether any elements of Al-Qaeda were integrated into the Taliban forces, as opposed to fighting alongside them or for the same general cause. There would appear to be three possibilities: elements of Al-Qaeda were fully integrated; Al-Qaeda forces fought alongside the Taliban but as a separate militia fighting the same cause; or Al-Qaeda only fought as a separate force, albeit one making common cause with the Taliban. Only the first two options would imply that the defenders constituted one force and that there was therefore only one conflict involving the US and its Coalition partners.[11] The third option, whether alone or in combination with the other two options, would imply that there were two separate armed conflicts, one between the US and its Coalition partners against the Taliban, possibly with Al-Qaeda elements integrated into the Taliban armed forces, and the other between the US and its Coalition partners against Al-Qaeda, fighting independently of the Taliban. The issue of the presence of Pakistani nationals fighting with or alongside the Taliban does not appear to be relevant to the question of classification.[12] It is not known whether any members of the Pakistani armed forces were present in Afghanistan during the conflict with the US-led Coalition or whether they had left the territory as soon as it became clear that an armed conflict was imminent.

A further element of uncertainty affecting the classification of the conflict is the relationship between the Taliban and Al-Qaeda. If Al Qaeda were acting under the effective or overall control of the Taliban, then, even if fighting as separate units, the totality of fighters might constitute one force.[13] But it might not be inappropriate to consider also the possibility that the Taliban was acting under the effective or overall control of the Al-Qaeda. Whilst there may have been less difference in military capabilities than is usually the case in such situations, there appears however to be no evidence that this was the case. A third possibility was that the policies of the two entities were so integrated that they could be regarded as effectively one party to the conflict.

It is not clear what views the participating States took concerning the identity of the persons against whom they were fighting. It appears that both US military and CIA personnel on the ground in Afghanistan made no practical distinction when referring to the Taliban, Al-Qaeda and other enemy fighters.[14] Taliban fighters also

to non-recognition of a party as the authority representing the State; Common Article 2 to the Geneva Conventions of 1949.

[11] On the responsibility of a State for the acts of an organized armed group fighting under either its overall or effective control, see ch. 3, section 7.1 above.

[12] There is evidence that a significant number of Pakistanis and other foreigners were evacuated prior to the fall of Kunduz, possibly with the complicity of the US; A. Raschid, *Descent into Chaos* (2008).

[13] This chapter does not take a view on the question whether either the 'effective' or 'overall' control, or some other test, is the correct one for the purpose of classification of a conflict, since there is no need to do so in the circumstances of this case. For further discussion, see ch. 3, section 7.1 above.

[14] The original military plan for the campaign in Afghanistan proposed that the US would 'destroy the al-Qaeda network inside Afghanistan along with the illegitimate Taliban regime which was harboring and protecting the terrorists'. See GlobalSecurity.org, 'Operation Enduring Freedom —Afghanistan, Planning and Implementation', available at: <www.globalsecurity.org/military/ops/enduring-freedom -plan.htm>. With regard to the later phase of the conflict, see also M. Cole, 'Watching Afghanistan fall'

did not appear to make distinctions between enemy combatants nor between enemy combatants and civilians.[15]

b. The Coalition

The US was fighting alongside Coalition partners. As to the other States within the Coalition, the UK regarded itself as a key contributor to OEF, albeit that the operation between October and December 2001 may have been 'effectively conducted under US leadership'.[16] Another partner in effect was the Northern Alliance, a collection of Afghan-organized armed groups. It has been suggested by some commentators[17] and in some reports[18] that the Northern Alliance was 'closely supervised', 'controlled' by or 'taking orders' from the US; however, while the US conceded having had a 'relationship'[19] with various opposition groups on the

Salon.com (27 February 2007), available at: <http://rempost.blogspot.com/2007/02/watching-afghanistan-fall.html>. This site provided real-time accounts and quotations from US forces and local CIA officials on the ground in northern Afghanistan repeatedly referring to all enemy fighters synonymously, regardless of their actual affiliations with either the Taliban, Al-Qaeda or other fighting groups, as either 'the enemy', 'insurgents' or as 'Al-Qaeda'. The repeated and synonymous usage of these single classifications of fighters who, in reality, had varying affiliations, had become so commonplace amongst US personnel on the ground that local Afghans adopted this same approach and used 'al-Qaida to refer to any anti-U.S. insurgent', a name that reportedly '…came to them by way of the Americans'.

[15] See e.g. 'Informer Killings Show Growing Taleban Control' Institute for War and Peace Reporting (9 March 2007) (quoting unnamed Taliban Commander in the Sangin district: 'We are beheading and hanging those who have given information about our operations to ISAF and the government.') Allegedly anyone who cooperated with the central government or with foreign troops counted as a traitor and an infidel.

[16] UK House of Commons, Foreign Affairs Committee, 'Eighth Report, Global Security: Afghanistan and Pakistan' (Session 2008–09) para 214 (FAC, *Global Security: Afghanistan and Pakistan*).

[17] See e.g. Y. Arai-Takahashi, 'Disentangling Legal Quagmires: The Legal Characterisation of the Armed Conflicts in Afghanistan Since 6/7 October 2001 and the Question of Prisoner of War Status' (2002) 5 *Yearbook of International Humanitarian Law* 67–8.

[18] See e.g. L. Harding et al, 'Fatal Errors that Led to Massacre' *The Guardian* (1 December 2001), stating that US Special Forces reportedly instructed Northern Alliance soldiers to pour diesel fuel into the basement of the Qala-i-Janghi fortress and ignite it in an effort to flush out rebelling, Taliban prisoners. 'US and Northern Alliance Retake Afghan Fortress from Rebelling Prisoners' History Commons.org (27 November 2001); see also C. Soloway, 'Tale of an American Talib' *MSNBC News* (1 December 2001); but see C. Gall, 'A Nation Challenged: Rebellion; Alliance Declares Revolt is Crushed' *The New York Times* (27 November 2001), reporting that: 'Some 16 American and British Special Operations forces were on the scene again today, taking positions just inside the fort's main entrance, although they did not appear to be joining the action to put down the rebellion themselves.'

[19] Then US Defense Secretary Donald H. Rumsfeld, in a Pentagon press briefing with Gen. Pete Pace, Vice Chairman of the Joint Chiefs of Staff (30 November 2001), full transcript printed in 'Rumsfeld Briefs Press on War Effort' *The Washington Post* (30 November 2001), answering a question as to whether opposition groups in Afghanistan, such as the Northern Alliance, would make the decision as to whether prisoners, such as Mullah Omar and Osama bin Laden, would be handed over to US custody, stated that: 'We have a relationship with all of these elements on the ground. We have provided them food, we've provided them ammunition, we've provided air support, [and] we've provided winter clothing. We've worked with them closely, we have troops embedded in their forces and have been assisting with overhead targeting and resupply of ammunition. It's a relationship.' When pressed further about whether US military personnel would be conducting interrogations and whether US military personnel had the authority to take custody of those they wished to question from those forces who were holding them, Secretary Rumsfeld replied: 'You can be certain that in the event we find someone we want that we will have the authority to receive them from those that actually currently have custody of them.'

ground in Afghanistan throughout the conflict, US government officials described assertions that they had control over the Northern Alliance or any other opposition groups in Afghanistan as 'overstatements'.[20] For example, US officials publicly stated in November 2001 that although they acknowledged that US Special Forces and Central Intelligence Agency (CIA) officers had been taking part in the interrogations of some prisoners, control over those prisoners remained in the hands of the various rebel factions holding them.[21] No evidence has been found that either the Northern Alliance or other Afghan opposition groups thought that they were under either the effective or overall control of the US.[22] Although it is possible that a perception existed amongst Coalition allies that the US was exercising some operational command and control over the Northern Alliance and other resistance groups, there is at least some evidence that the Northern Alliance had its own operational and tactical goals which the US claimed to have been militarily and politically incapable of stopping even when those operational and tactical goals clashed with US goals.[23]

A more difficult question concerns the nature of the Northern Alliance. Was it one force or a loose coalition of separate forces? If it was the latter (though this is perhaps unlikely), those separate forces may have had different relations with the

---

[20] Then United States Navy, Rear Admiral John D. Stufflebeem, Deputy Director for Operations, Readiness and Capabilities, Joint Staff, Department of Defence News Briefing, with PA Victoria Clarke, US Department of Defense Office of the Assistant Secretary of Defense (Public Affairs), News Transcript (29 November 2001), responding to a question during a Pentagon press briefing regarding the difficulty of having northern Afghan ethnic groups entering the Pashtun area and the complications that that creates for the peace process, for the US government, then Rear Adm. John D. Stufflebeem replied: 'We are not controlling any opposition group. We are working with opposition groups. We are not dictating what their objectives are or may not be. We certainly have made suggestions. We certainly have responded to requests and questions that they have asked us. We have provided tactical information when asked. We have volunteered what would be American expectations or coalition expectations of detainees that they might have, in terms of treatment.' Following Rear Adm. Stufflebeem's response to this question, then ASD PA Victoria Clarke, added: 'I'm not aware of advice being offered. I would just underscore what the admiral has said, which the secretary has said repeatedly, to say that we can control or dictate what the opposition groups might do is just—it's just an overstatement. We can't.'

[21] W. Pincus and S. Mufson, 'Prisoners' Fate, Treatment Not In U.S. Hands, Officials Say' *The Washington Post* (30 November 2001), quoting a 'Senior Pentagon Official': 'We don't have possession of the prisoners'. Asserting that he did not know how many were being held, or in what conditions and locations, he said, 'That's like asking me what conditions prisoners in France are being held in . . .' nor, he said, had the United States to his knowledge said anything to Northern Alliance leaders about how prisoners should be treated.

[22] See e.g. K. Gannon, '10 years on, a first-person view of Afghan collapse' *Jamaica Observer* (29 October 2011), asking Abdul Rasool Sayyaf, a powerful Afghan warlord where his men would go subsequent to the US having strongly urged its allies, (the Northern Alliance), to make sure their heavily armed ethnic militias did not storm Kabul when the Taliban left, he merely laughed at the naiveté of the Americans replying, 'No one can keep us out'. See also R. Cryer, 'The Fine Art of Friendship: *Jus in bello* in Afghanistan' (2002) 7 *Journal of Conflict and Security Law* 45–7.

[23] M. Tanner, 'Northern Alliance Rout Taleban' Institute for War and Peace Reporting, RCA Issue 82 (21 February 2005), quoting then US Defense Secretary Donald Rumsfeld in response to the Northern Alliance's rapid force advancements after their having captured Herat in western Afghanistan and whether the US could prevent them from capturing the capital city of Kabul: 'We don't have enough forces on the ground to stand in their way.'

US. No evidence has been found of the view of the Coalition, the Taliban or the Northern Alliance itself.

2.1.2 Classification of the conflict by the parties

The evidence with regard to the classification of the conflict(s) by the parties and what rules they thought were applicable is not only patchy; in addition, it is often only available after the event, without making it clear to what period in the evolution of events it is referring. Further, the evidence may indicate a result or conclusion without establishing whether that is the party's view of what was legally required or simply what they decided to do. Two issues need to be kept distinct: the first is whether the armed conflict was an international or a non-international armed conflict; the second is what law was applicable.

The US seemed to have accepted that it was involved in an international armed conflict with Afghanistan but maintained its view that its opponents were not entitled to combatant privileges.[24] Initially, they denied the applicability of the

---

[24] This was at least the case following the Presidential Memorandum of 7 February 2002 (see below); prior to that date different US agencies took different views: see e.g. C. Garraway, 'Afghanistan and the Nature of Conflict' in M. Schmitt (ed.), *The War in Afghanistan: A Legal Analysis* (2009). For the text of the Presidential Memorandum on Humane Treatment of Taliban and al Qaeda Detainees (7 February 2002) (Presidential Memorandum of 7 February 2002), see ibid, 157–9; the Memorandum stated inter alia 'Our recent extensive discussions regarding the status of al Qaeda and Taliban detainees confirm that the application of Geneva Convention Relative to the Treatment of Prisoners of War of 12 August 1949, (Geneva) to the conflict with al Qaeda and the Taliban involves complex legal questions. By its terms, Geneva applies to conflicts involving "High Contracting Parties," which can only be states. Moreover, it assumes the existence of "regular" armed forces fighting on behalf of states. However, the war against terrorism ushers in a new paradigm, one in which groups with broad, international reach commit horrific acts against innocent civilians, sometimes with the direct support of states. Our nation recognizes that this new paradigm—ushered in not by us, but by terrorists—requires new thinking in the law of war, but thinking that should nevertheless be consistent with the principles of Geneva.

    1. Pursuant to my authority as commander in chief and chief executive of the United States, and relying on the opinion of the Department of Justice dated 22 January 2002, and on the legal opinion rendered by the attorney general in his letter of 1 February 2002, I hereby determine as follows:

        a. I accept the legal conclusion of the Department of Justice and determine that none of the provisions of Geneva apply to our conflict with al Qaeda in Afghanistan or elsewhere throughout the world because, among other reasons, al Qaeda is not a High Contracting Party to Geneva.

        b. I accept the legal conclusion of the attorney general and the Department of Justice that I have the authority under the Constitution to suspend Geneva as between the United States and Afghanistan, but I decline to exercise that authority at this time. Accordingly, I determine that the provisions of Geneva will apply to our present conflict with the Taliban. I reserve the right to exercise the authority in this or future conflicts.

        c. I also accept the legal conclusion of the Department of Justice and determine that common Article 3 of Geneva does not apply to either al Qaeda or Taliban detainees, because, among other reasons, the relevant conflicts are international in scope and common Article 3 applies only to "armed conflict not of an international character."

        d. Based on the facts supplied by the Department of Defense and the recommendation of the Department of Justice, I determine that the Taliban detainees are unlawful combatants and, therefore, do not qualify as prisoners of war under Article 4 of Geneva. I note that, because Geneva does not apply to our conflict with al Qaeda, al Qaeda detainees also do not qualify as prisoners of war.'

Geneva Conventions to the conflict but then changed their view.[25] In the February Presidential Memorandum the implication was that there was one conflict with the Taliban and another with Al-Qaeda, both of which were international in character but as to the second of which the Geneva Conventions did not apply. There is no indication that any other members of the Coalition at the relevant time regarded themselves as fighting two separate conflicts: an international one with the State of Afghanistan represented by the Taliban and a non-international one with Al-Qaeda. They appear to have accepted from the start that they were parties to an international armed conflict.[26]

This memorandum was issued before the decision of the US Supreme Court in *Hamdan v Rumsfeld*, 548 U.S. 557 (2006). It should be remembered that the US is not a party to Additional Protocol I. Whilst parties to Additional Protocol I tend to use the term combatant as meaning persons who come within art. 43 of the Protocol and are therefore entitled to combatant privileges, the US tends to use the term to describe those who fight. It appears to prefer the term lawful belligerent for those referred to by others as combatants. This can make it difficult accurately to construe the statements of US spokesmen. In remarks to Harvard Law Students, John B. Bellinger, Legal Adviser to the US Secretary of State, made it clear that the US was involved in an armed conflict but he did not characterize it as an international or a non-international armed conflict. 'The U.N. Security Council reaffirmed that right, saying that under Article 51 of the U.N. Charter, we were entitled to take action in self-defence. That is what our coalition forces were doing in Afghanistan. They were not there as policemen . . . . . Many Europeans, for their part, have agreed that from 2001 to 2002 at minimum there was, in fact, a war. There was a legal state of armed conflict in Afghanistan, where we were fighting the Taliban and Al Qaeda.'; J.B. Bellinger, 'Remarks on the Military Commissions Act' (2007) 448 *Harvard International Law Journal Online* 1.

   [25] Para 1(b) and (c) of the Presidential Memorandum of 7 February 2002 accepted that the Geneva Conventions applied to the conflict between the US and the Taliban, which was international in character (and see J. Bellinger, former Legal Adviser to the US State Department, to this effect in 'Legal Issues in the War on Terrorism—A Reply to Silja N.U.Voneky' (2007) *German Law Journal* 871. Before this, memorandum views of US Departments were divided: Department of Justice, John Yoo and Robert Delahunty Memorandum to William J. Hayner II, General Counsel, Department of Defense, 'Re Application of Treaties and Laws to al Qaeda and Taliban Detainees' (9 January 2002), reprinted in K. Greenberg and J. Dratel (eds), *Torture Papers: The Road to Abu Ghraib* (2005), stated that the conflict with Taliban and Al-Qaeda was neither international (because Afghanistan is a failed State and so cannot be considered a High Contracting Party within the meaning of Common Article 2) nor non-international (because it is not internal); Department of State, Memorandum from William H. Taft IV, Legal Adviser, Department of State, to John Yoo, Deputy Assistant Attorney General, Office of the Legal Counsel, United States Department of Justice, 'Your Draft Memorandum of January, 9' (11 January 2002) 11: 'The situation as between the United States and the Taliban is one of an armed conflict arising between two or more High Contracting Parties under Article 2.'

   [26] While the UK was not explicit about the nature of the armed conflict, the implication was that it was engaged in an international armed conflict with Afghanistan. In response to a question in the UK House of Commons on 30 October 2001 about whether the UK was 'at war' the Foreign and Commonwealth Office (FCO) Minister replied: 'The military coalition is engaged in an armed conflict in self-defence against those who perpetrated the terrorist attack of 11 September and those who harbour and sustain them.' See UKMIL, (2001) *British Yearbook of International Law* 697. In response to a question asked in the UK House of Lords on 30 January 2002 about the grant of POW status to members of Her Majesty's armed forces, in view of restrictions of the rights of Taliban and Al-Qaeda militants, the Minister replied: 'Members of the UK Armed Forces engaged in international armed conflict who are captured by an enemy would be prisoners of war under the terms of the 3rd Geneva Convention 1949 and we would expect them to be treated accordingly. The question of whether or not a person is entitled to prisoner of war status depends on the application of the criteria in Article 4 of that convention to the particular facts and circumstances in the individual case.' See UKMIL, (2002) *British Yearbook of International Law* 920. As regards Canada, see Canada: National Defence and the Canadian Forces, Board of Inquiry, 'In-Theatre Handling of Detainees' (2009): 'When Canadian

It is not easy however to ascertain the date on which the Coalition took the view that the international armed conflict had come to an end and that a non-international armed conflict was in progress. The view of the ICRC was that the Coalition was engaged in an international armed conflict from October 2001 until the convening of the Loya Jirga in Kabul in June 2002 and the subsequent establishment of an Afghan transitional government on 19 June 2002.[27] No evidence has been found of the classification of the conflict by the Taliban, Al-Qaeda or the Northern Alliance. Nor has evidence been found of the views as to the classification of the conflict between the Taliban and Northern Alliance by either of the parties or of the members of the Coalition.

2.2. Author's view of the classification of the conflicts

The conflict between the Taliban, possibly with integrated elements of Al-Qaeda, against the US and its Coalition partners was an international armed conflict within the definition provided by Common Article 2 of the Geneva Conventions. The conflict between elements of Al-Qaeda fighting independently of the Taliban and the US and its Coalition partners, insofar as there was any such independent fighting, would appear to have been a non-international armed conflict, since the State participants were all found on one side of the conflict.[28] It may however be

---

forces take part in armed conflict outside Canada, both national and international law guides their conduct. The Canadian legal framework is based on traditional state-to-state armed conflict and those rules are applicable to Canadian forces in Afghanistan even though Canada maintains that the conflict there involves opponents not normally recognized as lawful combatants under the laws of armed conflict.' See also A. Cole, 'Legal Issues in Forming the Coalition' in M. Schmitt (ed.), *The War in Afghanistan: A Legal Analysis* (2009): 'Early coalition contributions to the invasion of Afghanistan also reflected the generally held view that this was an international armed conflict. The deployment of forces and the details of their rules of engagement (ROE) were based on the premise that this was a conflict between the "coalition of the willing" on the one hand and Taliban forces, al Qaeda and the Afghan army on the other.' (Cole, *Forming the Coalition*.)

[27] 'Following the convening of the Loya Jirga in Kabul in June 2002 and the subsequent establishment of an Afghan transitional government on 19 June 2002, which not only received unanimous recognition by the entire community of States but could also claim broad-based recognition within Afghanistan through the Loya Jirga process, the ICRC has changed its initial qualification as follows: "The ICRC no longer views the ongoing military operations in Afghanistan directed against suspected Taliban or other armed groups as an international armed conflict."' Letter to the UK House of Commons by Philip Spoerri, Legal Adviser, International Committee of the Red Cross (28 November 2002), available at: <www.publications.parliament.uk/pa/cm200203/cmselect/cmintdev/84/84ap09.htm>. See also ICRC, 'International humanitarian law and terrorism: questions and answers' (1 January 2011). This was also the view of many commentators after the event: see e.g. S. Ojeda, 'US Detention of Taliban Fighters: Some Legal Considerations' in M. Schmitt (ed.), *The War in Afghanistan: A Legal Analysis* (2009) 358; R. Geiss and M. Siegrist, 'Has the Armed Conflict in Afghanistan Affected the Rules on the Conduct of Hostilities?' (2011) 93 *International Review of the Red Cross* 13, (Geiss and Siegrist, *Armed Conflict in Afghanistan*).

[28] Commentators' views diverge as to the existence or not of a separate conflict with Al-Qaeda at this point; for the view that the Coalition was involved in two armed conflicts, one against the Taliban and one against Al-Qaeda, see e.g. C. de Cock, 'Counter-Insurgency Operations in Afghanistan. What about the "Jus ad Bellum" and the "Jus in Bello": Is the Law Still Accurate?' 13 *Yearbook of International Humanitarian Law* (2010) 97, (de Cock, *Counter-Insurgency Operations in Afghanistan*). For the view that they were involved in a single armed conflict, see e.g. Geiss and Siegrist, *Armed Conflict in Afghanistan* at 13, 14.

doubted whether it is feasible in this context to distinguish between operations of and against Al-Qaeda and the Taliban. Even if it is possible to make the legal distinction, for all practical purposes this was a single international armed conflict.

The conflict between the Northern Alliance and the Taliban was a non-international armed conflict, but was it within Common Article 3 or the customary law equivalent of Additional Protocol II? If the Northern Alliance was one force, that force would need to be able to mount sustained and concerted military operations for any customary law equivalent of Additional Protocol II to be applicable. If it was a collection of separate organized armed groups, there is the possibility that that requirement was met by some groups and not by others. In that case, those groups satisfying the requirement might, if they could establish that they had a responsible command and, possibly, that they had the requisite control of territory, be involved in the customary law equivalent to an Additional Protocol II non-international armed conflict with the Taliban, whereas the other groups not able to mount such operations would only have been involved in a Common Article 3 non-international armed conflict. It is not clear whether it is necessary to prove control of territory in order for Additional Protocol II, or its customary law equivalent, to be applicable or whether it is sufficient to establish concerted and sustained military operations.[29]

3. The installation of Hamid Karzai to the present

Following either the adoption of Security Council resolution 1386 (2001) or the installation of Hamid Karzai as President, there was no longer an armed conflict between the Coalition and the armed forces of Afghanistan.[30] The Taliban forces became a non-state organized armed group. The US believed that two conflicts were being conducted in the territory. First, there was the continuation of the previous conflict, OEF, waged against the remnants of Al-Qaeda and elements of the Taliban, principally in the border area between Afghanistan and Pakistan and eventually in Pakistan itself.[31] Initially, US forces were only involved in that conflict, together with limited numbers of forces from some of the States who had participated in the Coalition.

Secondly, and at the same time, ISAF, mandated under Security Council resolution 1386 and subsequent resolutions, was involved in dealing with attacks against targets in other parts of Afghanistan, including central government and the governorates. While ISAF was confined initially to a very restricted geographical area, principally around Kabul, the geographical scope of its mandate

---

[29] See ch. 3, section 6.2.

[30] See above, section 2.1.2, for the view that the international armed conflict did not come to an end until a later date, perhaps June 2002.

[31] This chapter does not consider cross-border operations in Pakistan, whether in continuation of an engagement which started in Afghanistan or as free-standing operations linked to the conflict in Afghanistan. The characterization of such operations is considered in other chapters, e.g. ch. 3, section 9; ch. 12, section 3.2; ch. 13, section 4; ch. 14, section 3.

was broadened until it covered all the territory.[32] ISAF was composed of forces some of which had taken part in the prior international armed conflict, but many of which had not. In much of Afghanistan, national contingents (not forces of mixed nationality) were in charge of particular geographical areas. There was an acute need for every type of nation-building and institution-building. Whilst significant sums had been pledged at the Bonn Conference and subsequently, progress on the ground was very slow, but initially, ISAF encountered limited opposition.

From late 2002, the attention of two of the key players was primarily elsewhere, in Iraq. From 2003 until 2007/08, the US in particular seems to have taken its 'eye off the ball'. During this period, the Taliban had the opportunity to regroup and to become an organized fighting force again. Initially, they staged attacks against the ISAF forces, notably in and around Helmand province. This resulted in the Taliban taking significant casualties. The Taliban then diversified their attacks and also engaged in 'hit and run' strikes, particularly by improvised explosive device (IEDs). This resulted in an increase in ISAF casualties. As attention returned to Afghanistan, US forces became increasingly involved in ISAF, as well as continuing OEF operations.

Increasing concern was expressed at the scale of civilian casualties. This was the result both of ISAF and OEF operations, notably air strikes, and also of Taliban operations. The concern was expressed by Hamid Karzai and Afghans themselves, as well as by commentators in the West.[33] The Taliban appear to have felt some pressure about the issue because they announced steps that would be taken to minimize civilian casualties.[34] It is not clear whether this was done out of any sense of legal obligation, on account of religious obligations, or to preserve their support base. US military commanders recognized the need to reduce civilian casualties in order to win the battle of hearts and minds and adopting a counter-insurgency doctrine (COIN), imposed rules of engagement more restrictive than required by the law.[35] It is not clear how effective these policies were in reducing insecurity and Taliban attacks throughout Afghanistan.

---

[32] See e.g. SC res. 1386 (2001); SC res. 1510 (2003). See also NATO, 'ISAF: History', available at: <www.isaf.nato.int/history.html>.

[33] See e.g. Human Rights Watch, 'Troops in Contact' Report (2008): in 2007 over 1,600 civilians were killed in the conflict. 950 died as a result of Taliban and Al-Qaeda actions, whereas 434 of the casualties were attributable to US and NATO actions; and UN Secretary-General's report of September 2008: 'The insurgency's dependence on asymmetric tactics has also led to a sharp rise in the number of civilian casualties. Civilians are also being killed as a result of military operations carried out by Afghan and international security forces, in particular in situations in which insurgents conceal themselves in populated areas.' See 'Report of the Secretary-General on the Situation in Afghanistan and Its Implications for International Peace and Security' A/63/372-S/2008/617 (23 September 2008).

[34] 'Taliban Issues Code of Conduct' *Al-Jazeera News* (28 July 2010); a later version is to be found at annex to M. Munir, 'The Layha for the Mujahideen: An Analysis of the Code of Conduct for the Taliban fighters under Islamic Law' (2011) 93 *International Review of the Red Cross* 103 (Munir, *The Layha for the Mujahideen*).

[35] The COIN doctrine was set out in the US Army Field Manual 3–24 (FM 3–24). See further below at section 4.

The ISAF mandate has been renewed at periodic intervals.[36] The later resolutions refer to both ISAF and OEF and to a framework of counter-terrorist operations. The ISAF mandates have required the parties to respect international humanitarian and human rights law, without defining the relevant obligations. The mandates have been adopted under Chapter VII of the UN Charter and permit the forces to use 'all necessary means' in the attainment of the mandated goals.[37]

With two apparently separate military operations in Afghanistan, OEF and ISAF, the question arises whether these are two separate forms of armed conflict and who are the parties to them. As regards the Coalition partners, the US and the UK's conduct of operations in Afghanistan was closely coordinated;[38] however, there were some concerns expressed by the British that while the UK may '... have had people embedded in the analytical stage of the discussion of US policy towards Afghanistan ... the Americans insisted on taking the embedded British officers out [of the discussion] when they moved on to the strateg[ic] stage ...' and referred to such circumstances as the UK having '... access without influence'.[39] From the UK's perspective, the nature of the relationship between US forces and the UK was that of a 'key contributor' to ISAF, until NATO formally took overall command in 2003 with a rotating command.[40]

The UK also viewed itself, but to a lesser extent, as a key contributor to OEF. It was not until 2003 that NATO 'rapidly came back into the picture, not least because the US came to recognize the need for long-term assistance in managing societies that had been freed from oppressive regimes by US uses of force'.[41] Reportedly, although both ISAF and OEF came under US oversight in a bid to improve coordination, as Professor Roberts testified before the UK's House of Commons Foreign Affairs Committee, 'the arrangements for coordinating the work of these three distinct forces [ISAF, OEF and Afghan National Security Forces] continue to pose problems' because while ISAF 'coordinates the efforts of the provincial reconstruction teams, it does not directly "command" them, and instead command lines are "stove-piped" to national embassies and capitals'.[42] Whereas the US, UK and Canada have tended to see Afghanistan as a counter-insurgency operation, allies such as Germany and some others regard it as more of a stabilization mission, resulting in divisions and tensions both within ISAF, and between ISAF and OEF.[43]

---

[36] Resolution 2011 (2011) was adopted on 12 October 2011.

[37] See e.g. SC res. 1413 (2002); SC res. 1510 (2003); SC res. 1623 (2005); SC res. 1746 (2007); SC res. 2011 (2011).

[38] 'Case Study: Afghanistan' in House of Commons, Foreign Affairs Committee, 'Global Security: UK-US Relations' (28 March 2010) 24.

[39] Lord Wallace of Saltaire, Evidence given before the UK Foreign Affairs Committee (11 November 2009), ibid at EV 10; and see Q 25.

[40] Ibid.

[41] FAC, *Global Security: Afghanistan and Pakistan*, para 14.

[42] 'A Strategic Conflict Assessment of Afghanistan' *Post-War Reconstruction & Development Unit* (November 2008) 39, ibid at para 16.

[43] FAC, *Global Security: Afghanistan and Pakistan*.

3.1. Views of the parties as to classification of the conflicts

3.1.1 *Operation Enduring Freedom (OEF)*

The views of the US with regard to the classification of OEF in 2002 and subsequently are unclear, but at the time of writing it appears to regard it as a non-international armed conflict. The UK also drew a distinction between ISAF and OEF, in both of which it participated, describing the role of OEF as to prevent the threat of attack 'from Al Qaida and Taliban remnants' and the role of ISAF in accordance with its Security Council mandate.[44]

3.1.2 *ISAF*

The views of some of the different contributing States have varied over the years. For a significant period of time, the German contingent in the north of Afghanistan denied that it was involved in an armed conflict at all.[45] Others of the contributing States classified it as a non-international armed conflict.[46] UNAMA, the United Nations Assistance Mission in Afghanistan, regards it as a non-international armed conflict,[47] as does the ICRC, as noted above, and the Afghanistan Independent Human Rights Commission.[48]

---

[44] Speech by Secretary of State for Defence to UK House of Commons (20 June 2002); see also speech on 20 March 2002.

[45] This seems to have been largely motivated by domestic political concerns. The question was thrown into sharp relief by the Kunduz incident; European Center for Constitutional and Human Rights, 'German Air Strike near Kunduz: A Year After' (30 August 2010). However, the German Federal Prosecutor's decision to close the case against German soldiers responsible for the NATO air strike near Kunduz characterized the conflict as a non-international armed conflict. See C. von der Groeben, 'German Federal Prosecutor Terminates Investigation Against German Soldiers with Respect to NATO Air Strike in Afghanistan' *EJIL Talk* (29 April 2010).

[46] As regards the UK for example, in a decision of the Asylum and Immigration Tribunal, *GS (Existence of Internal Armed Conflict) Afghanistan v Secretary of State for the Home Department*, CG [2009] UKAIT 00010 (23 February 2009) it was noted: 'The Secretary of State concedes that as at 7 January 2009 for the purpose of International Humanitarian Law (IHL) there is an internal armed conflict in Afghanistan extending to the whole of the territory of Afghanistan.'

[47] See UNAMA, 'Afghanistan: Annual Report on Protection of Civilians in Armed Conflict 2010' (March 2011): 'UNAMA takes the position that the armed conflict in Afghanistan is a non-international armed conflict between the Government of Afghanistan supported by international military forces (also referred to in this report and within Afghanistan as "Pro-Government Forces") and various non-state armed groups (also referred to in this report and within Afghanistan as "Anti-Government Elements").

The non-state armed groups encompass organized armed groups of diverse backgrounds, motivations and command structures, including those characterized as the Taliban, the Haqqani network, Hezb-e-Islami and others. All parties to the armed conflict—Afghan armed forces, international military forces and non-state armed groups—have clear obligations under international law to protect civilians.' See also UNAMA, 'Afghanistan: Midyear Report 2011, Protection of Civilians in Armed Conflict' (July 2011) (UNAMA Midyear Report 2011).

[48] 'The ongoing conflict in Afghanistan is defined as a non-international armed conflict because it is between state parties (the Afghan government, NATO member states and their partners) and non-state groups.' 2008 Report 'representing the Afghan perspective on the operations of Pro-Government Forces': see AIHRC, 'From Hope to Fear: An Afghan Perspective on Operations of Pro-Government Forces in Afghanistan' (23 December 2008) 7.

3.2. Author's view of the classification of the conflicts

There are three conflicts in the territory of Afghanistan: that involving OEF, that involving ISAF, and that between the Taliban and the State of Afghanistan. As regards the first, the Taliban no longer represent the armed forces of Afghanistan and insofar as the US may have viewed OEF after 2002 as being involved in an international armed conflict, it is not clear on what that possible view was based: without a State on the other side, or armed forces within the overall or effective control of a State, there cannot be an international armed conflict.[49] The OEF hostilities therefore comprise a non-international armed conflict. It is not clear however whether the opposing party is Al-Qaeda or a mixture of remnants of the Taliban and Al-Qaeda. In the case of the latter, it is not clear whether they are fighting as one force and who is under the control of whom. The US is not a party to Additional Protocol II and therefore only the provisions of Common Article 3 and customary international humanitarian law can apply.

For both OEF and the hostilities in which ISAF are involved, a number of questions arise regarding the nature and extent of the non-international armed conflicts. First, where the level of the intensity of the conflict is only at a level at which Common Article 3 (or its customary law equivalent) applies, does the whole range of rules of international humanitarian law regarding the conduct of hostilities apply?[50] Secondly, if, as this writer submits, certain of the provisions equivalent to those in Additional Protocol II would apply if the threshold for armed conflict set out in that Protocol is also to be found in customary international law, the questions arise whether the criterion of control in Additional Protocol II or any customary law equivalent require that the territory be controlled within the State which is a party to the conflict; and whether it requires control against opposition or whether it is possible to rely on unopposed control. Sustained and concerted military operations do not appear to be mounted against the US and its Coalition partners *within* part of Pakistan but it is arguably the area *from which* sustained and concerted attacks are carried out in Afghanistan. Is that sufficient to trigger the applicability of Additional Protocol II or its customary law equivalent?

The size of the territory thus affected has progressively increased. In some places and at some times, the ISAF forces have come under sustained and concerted attack. It is not clear whether the opposing forces controlled territory in the conventional sense.[51] If there are limited US ground forces in the area, there is limited opportunity for the opposing forces to demonstrate their ability to conduct concerted and sustained military operations. They may be able to demonstrate control of territory, but not the requisite type of operations. Another possibility is

[49] For discussion of whether an international armed conflict can arise by virtue of US operations into Pakistan, see section 4.1 of ch. 13 (Al-Qaeda) below.
[50] For discussion of this question, see section 4 below. See ch. 4 above for the contrary view that the rules in international and non-international armed conflict are largely the same, without any distinction in customary international law between levels of non-international armed conflict.
[51] See discussion in A. Bellal, G. Giacca and S. Casey-Maslen, 'International Law and Armed Non-state Actors in Afghanistan' (2011) 93 *International Review of the Red Cross* 56–8.

that no one is in control of territory. Each party to the conflict is able to do enough to prevent the other side from claiming control, but without being able to do enough to assert it themselves. Is it sufficient if those forces have the ability to move freely within the territory in question, or is something more expected in the way of control, such as the exercise of governmental functions?

Different contingents have had to cope with varying levels of violence at different times and places. This raises the question of the geographical scope of international humanitarian law. Is it possible to have, in different parts of one country, disturbances not reaching the threshold of a non-international armed conflict, a Common Article 3 non-international armed conflict, and the customary equivalent to an Additional Protocol II conflict—or does the classification reflecting the highest level of disruption apply wherever there is fighting? It is submitted that it is indeed possible to have different classifications of armed conflict in different parts of a territory, although this will of course require armed forces to be ready to adapt swiftly to changing conditions. Similar to the geographical application of the law is the temporal application. Does the criterion of protracted nature (which is interpreted as requiring a certain intensity)[52] continue to apply once the situation is characterized as an armed conflict or can the classification vary from day to day or at least week to week?

It should be remembered that Afghanistan ratified the Additional Protocols on 10 November 2009. If a conflict between a host State and non-state forces is characterized as coming within Additional Protocol II, does this affect the characterization of fighting between a UN mandated force assisting the State and those non-state forces? Does that depend on the facts on the ground and on whether the assisting State in question has ratified Additional Protocol II? If the UN-mandated force is assisting the State, is it bound by whatever characterization affects the conflict in which that State is involved, even if some contingents have not ratified the treaty in question? Is a State, by virtue of its assumption of an international obligation, required to ensure that all relevant activities within its territory, whether conducted by itself or another State, conform to its undertakings? Such an argument could apply not only to obligations under international humanitarian law, but also under human rights law.[53]

Further, the question of the hostilities between the State of Afghanistan and the Taliban must be considered. Where one or more States are assisting the territorial State in a struggle against insurgents, is there one conflict between the territorial State and the insurgents, with the assisting States bound by the characterization of the primary conflict, or does each State have a separate belligerent relationship with the fighters?[54] In that case, even if Additional Protocol II is applicable between the

---

[52] See ch. 3, section 6.1 above.

[53] See ch. 4 above. This also raises a question as to the scope of State responsibility in international law.

[54] In earlier situations, such as the Soviet invasion of Afghanistan, it was assumed that the assisting/intervening State had an independent relationship with the insurgents; H.-P. Gasser, 'Internationalised Non-international Armed Conflicts: Case Studies of Afghanistan, Kampuchea and Lebanon' (1983) 33 *American University Law Review* 145.

territorial State and the insurgents (as it is, in at least some places, in this case), it would not be applicable between the latter and assisting States. Whether or not genuine difficulties in characterizing the conflict matter, depends on the difference the alternative characterizations make to the rules applicable. It should be remembered that the area of difficulty is that between Common Article 3 and Additional Protocol II.

These are not questions based on confused factual situations, but rather arise from uncertainty as to the legal criteria for applicability of Additional Protocol II. In practice, however, no State appears to have raised these issues. Most States acted as though there was a Common Article 3 non-international armed conflict. Some, at least at certain times, have acted as though Common Article 3 has not been applicable, but this appears to be for political rather than legal reasons.

4. Rules on opening fire

In the first phase of the conflicts, there is no evidence that the Coalition distinguished between whether they were fighting the Taliban (international armed conflict) or Al-Qaeda (non-international armed conflict). Since Afghanistan was not, at the time, a party to Additional Protocol I, members of the Coalition who were parties were not obliged to apply its provisions in relation to that conflict, but such evidence as does exist suggests that they applied the targeting principles as policy or customary law. It is not clear whether those States which thought that members of the Taliban were not entitled to combatant privilege only targeted those taking a direct part in hostilities, or whether the view on combatant privilege only affected rights upon detention.[55] In practical terms, in that phase of the conflict, the principal targets were training bases, equipment and command and control infrastructure, including communications. In addition, close air support was provided to the Northern Alliance at the scene of fighting. There were therefore many self-evidently legitimate targets. Whilst collateral casualties had to be taken into account, there is no evidence that the difficult question of who can be targeted and in what circumstances, which has arisen subsequently, was of much difficulty in the early phase.[56]

As regards the second phase of the conflict, the rules of international humanitarian law applicable to ISAF and OEF operations should have been the same, on the basis of the classification of both of them as non-international armed conflicts. It appeared that the NATO forces on the one hand and the US forces on the other, both

---

[55] The Presidential Memorandum of 7 February 2002 refers to Geneva Convention III but makes no reference to rules on targeting.

[56] That is not to say that there were no problems arising from the application of force in this initial phase; e.g. an ICRC building was targeted by mistake. 'US Jets Hit Red Cross in Kabul' *Associated Press* (26 October 2001).

used 'hostile intent' as a criterion for employing airpower in defensive operations . . .
However, NATO defined the term as 'manifest and overwhelming' force, whereas the
US standard was 'the threat of imminent use of force.' In other words, the NATO
standard placed greater emphasis on the necessity criterion of self-defense and was
more restrictive temporally. Employing the same term differently created confusion
regarding the availability of air support in TIC situations, especially when US and
NATO forces were supporting each other. It also created an impression that the US
forces were quick to pull the trigger.[57]

A further point of difference is that ISAF forces have a Chapter VII mandate which
enables them to use all necessary means in achievement of the mandate;[58] that does
not however appear to have made a difference regarding the rules adopted for
opening fire.

As indicated above, in ISAF operations claims of disproportionate civilian
casualties have been a major influence on the framing of rules applicable to the
conduct of hostilities. The US Counter-Insurgency Doctrine attaches considerable
significance to these issues.[59] The range of restrictions imposed by General
McChrystal on when ISAF forces could open fire[60] was alleged to have given rise
to higher ISAF casualties.[61] General Petraeus introduced a measure of additional
flexibility for ISAF forces, whilst still focusing on the need to avoid civilian and
collateral casualties. The rules are clearly more restrictive than the law is thought to
allow. Nevertheless a report of the UK House of Commons Foreign Affairs

---

[57] M. Schmitt, 'Targeting and International Humanitarian Law in Afghanistan' in M. Schmitt
(ed.), *The War in Afghanistan: A Legal Analysis* (2009) (Schmitt, *Targeting in Afghanistan*).

[58] As opposed to a Chapter VI mandate in which force is only authorized in defence of the
contingent, mission property or the mandate. This leaves aside the question whether a Chapter VII
mandate *could* permit rules on conduct of hostilities which offer significantly less protection than those
in international humanitarian law.

[59] The COIN manual states for example 'An operation that kills five insurgents is counterproduc-
tive if collateral damage leads to the recruitment of fifty more insurgents' at 309. Schmitt, *Targeting in
Afghanistan*, 307.

[60] The US ROE are classified, but one commentator, on the basis of accounts from individual
soldiers, suggested that the rules required: 'No night or surprise searches; villagers are to be warned
prior to searches; Afghan National Army or Afghan National Police must accompany U.S. units on
searches; U.S. soldiers may not fire at insurgents unless they are preparing to fire first; U.S. forces
cannot engage insurgents if civilians are present; only women can search women; troops can fire on
insurgents if they catch them placing an improvised explosive device but not if insurgents walk away
from where the explosives are.'; F.M. Maloof, 'It's not just the enemy killing U.S. soldiers' *WorldNet-
Daily* (13 December 2009). The rules were criticized for being defensive rather than offensive ROE, 'as
evidenced by recent charges of murder against two U.S. Army snipers because they had targeted a
Taliban commander who reportedly wasn't holding a weapon', ibid. A further problem concerned the
need for varying authorizations for different kinds of operations. For an affirmation of the sufficiency
of the rules, however, see N. Springer, 'Many Paths up the Mountain: Population-Centric COIN
in Afghanistan' *Small Wars Journal* (2010).

[61] In the first phase of the conflict, there were few Coalition casualties because most of the ground
fighting was done by the forces of the Northern Alliance. That changed with the deployment of
considerable numbers of ground forces to both OEF and ISAF. In the first phase of ISAF operations, in
some places there was only sporadic fighting. In other places, there were major clashes with the Taliban,
resulting in significant Taliban casualties. There is a tension between the desire to avoid Coalition
casualties and the need to avoid civilian casualties.

Committee in 2009 stated that 'the use of air power and acts of considerable cultural insensitivity on the part of some Coalition Forces over an extended period have done much to shape negative perceptions among ordinary Afghans about the military and the international effort in Afghanistan'.[62]

Differing views of international law and the domestic law and policies of the national contingents of ISAF also had a major influence on their targeting. As one commentator put it:

> Different nations took different views of whom they were engaged with in an armed conflict, so coalition targeting arrangements had to ensure that the nation that owned the assets likely to be allocated to the particular target was satisfied that the individuals they were likely to kill were within its own national understanding of who was a combatant. It is fair to say that the United States took a wider view of whom might legitimately be targeted than some of its European allies. The US approach reflected the widespread political and public support at home, while the European position reflected their more cautious national positions.[63]

While, for understandable reasons, the ROE of contributing forces were not made public, the rules on opening fire would have been specific to the task or mission within the overall framework of the ROE. There has been discussion in the media about changes in national ROE to enable contingents to work well together, adopting similar interpretations of self-defence; the Danish are reported to have said that changes were made because 'we couldn't all have different Rules of Engagement'.[64] Since German forces in the north of Afghanistan claimed for a time not to be involved in an armed conflict at all, the only basis on which they could open fire would appear to have been the Afghan rules on the use of force by security personnel. That is presumably based on a law and order paradigm. It is not clear whether there was any authority under domestic German law for the extra-territorial use of force by German soldiers outside the context of armed conflict.[65] The Kunduz incident highlighted the problems for the German contingent,[66] arising not from difficulties with the rules themselves, but rather from the failure properly to classify the situation as an armed conflict.

Generally speaking, however, it was not the issue of classification of the conflict but the policies of the contributing States which had the main influence on the targeting rules. The means by which the targeting restrictions were introduced included:

> coalition and national rules of engagement (ROE), no-strike lists (for reasons such as IHL or host-nation sensitivities), restricted target lists (in which attack requires special

---

[62] FAC, *Global Security: Afghanistan and Pakistan*, para 2.

[63] Cole, *Forming the Coalition*, 146.

[64] Danish Battalion Commander Frank Lissner, 'Rules of battle change for Danish forces in Afghanistan' *Military World* (9 July 2009), available at: <www.military-world.net/Afghanistan/1907.html>.

[65] C. von der Groeben, 'Criminal Responsibility of German Soldiers in Afghanistan: The Case of Colonel Klein' (2010) 11(5) *German Law Journal* 469–92.

[66] Ibid.

preapproval, e.g., due to negative cultural implications), individual target folder restrictions (such as a requirement to use a particular munition or strike a particular 'desired point of impact'), Joint Air Operations Plans, execute orders, fragmentary orders, fire support coordination measures and soldier cards. The net result was a dense and often confusing normative environment, one in which IHL played a minor role relative to policy and operational considerations.[67]

As regards the Taliban, evidence for their views on the conduct of hostilities is slim, whether during the phase of international armed conflict with the Coalition forces,[68] or during the non-international armed conflicts in which they were involved. At least three editions of a code of conduct for Taliban fighters have been published since 2009, but there is little collected evidence on the extent to which the provisions are followed.[69] A commentator has observed that the code 'may be said to show respect for some fundamental humanitarian rules. However, many rules contained in it have no basis either in Islamic law or in international humanitarian law and may even contradict both of them'.[70] For instance, the Taliban include civilians, such as government workers, members of the Afghan Cabinet and Parliament, contractors, drivers and translators, on its list of targets to kill or capture, in violation of international humanitarian law.[71]

Whatever may have happened in practice, the classification of a conflict as coming within either Common Article 3 or within Additional Protocol II or their customary equivalents could potentially have significant implications for the rules on opening fire.[72] The extent to which the rules applicable vary as between Common Article 3 situations and those within Additional Protocol II is unclear. Over the past fifteen years, a significant number of customary rules applicable in

---

[67] Schmitt, *Targeting in Afghanistan*, 314. Indeed De Cock discusses whether in the light of COIN operations the rules of international humanitarian law have become obsolete or less relevant, where destruction and capture of enemy forces as the main centre of gravity has shifted to winning the hearts and minds of the local population; C. de Cock, *Counter-Insurgency Operations in Afghanistan*, 97.

[68] The evidence of Afghan State practice of an earlier period in relation to the rules on means and methods of fighting and the protection of the victims of war cited in the ICRC Customary Law Study (2005) is very limited. It is certainly the case that the fighting in Afghanistan from 1979 to 2001 was marked by an apparent disregard of the relevant and applicable rules of the law of armed conflict. During the Soviet operations, the conflict was a non-international armed conflict and only Common Article 3 was applicable but the fighting was marked by serious and well-attested violations of even that rudimentary framework. The subsequent fighting was again characterized as a non-international armed conflict. At that time, it was unclear whether there were rules of a 'Hague law' type applicable in non-international armed conflicts. Nevertheless, it appears legitimate to call into question whether *any* Afghan fighting forces had any culture of respect for certain rules whilst fighting. This is perhaps surprising, given that Islam has rules on who cannot be targeted during armed conflict. It may be that local cultural values prevailed over religious precepts. It is possible that there was an assumption that the two sets of values were the same, but that they reflected what in fact were cultural values.

[69] The UNAMA report of 2011 concluded that 'although Taliban rhetoric on preventing civilian casualties has improved, UNAMA has not documented improved compliance with international humanitarian law...The Taliban continue to directly target civilians and use indiscriminate weapons...'; UNAMA Midyear Report 2011, 12.

[70] Munir, The Layha for the Mujahideen, 102.

[71] UNAMA Midyear Report 2011, Preface and 13.

[72] For the law applicable in non-international armed conflict see ch. 3, sections 3 and 6 and ch. 4, section 4.

non-international armed conflicts are alleged to have emerged. They include a prohibition against attacking civilians unless and for such time as they take a direct part in hostilities and, possibly, a prohibition against causing excessive or indiscriminate civilian harm. Whilst the case law of the ICTY, the ICRC Study on Customary Humanitarian Law and the Statute of the International Criminal Court all refer to the existence of these 'Hague law' type rules in non-international armed conflicts, they do not distinguish between non-international armed conflicts under Additional Protocol II and under Common Article 3. Insofar as these rules imply an armed conflict paradigm and not a law and order paradigm in relation to the circumstances for opening fire, it is not clear whether they should be regarded as customary law in a Common Article 3 situation. It might be possible to argue that they are applicable where there are sustained and concerted military operations and where the only reason that the conflict is not within Additional Protocol II is that the territorial State is not a party to the conflict. It is more problematic where the level of violence does not attain that threshold.

An area of potential legal difficulty concerns the meaning of 'direct participation in hostilities'. There is first uncertainty as to the temporal and functional scope of the concept. That has been clarified, with relatively little controversy, by the Interpretive Guidance of the ICRC.[73] Linked to that is the much more controversial question whether there exist groups who forfeit the protection to which civilians are entitled much more generally than when they are taking a direct part in hostilities.[74] The issue of targeting members of organized armed groups exercising continuous combat functions is most likely to arise in the case of air strikes, whether by aircraft or drones, and intelligence-led ground operations. Since by definition the person is not at the time taking a direct part in hostilities, it puts a premium on the accuracy of the intelligence about the individual.[75] The third problem is in knowing whether the concept of direct participation in hostilities exists in customary law and, if so, whether it is confined to Additional Protocol II situations, as is the case with treaty law, or whether it also applies in situations coming within Common Article 3.[76]

There have been difficulties in the Afghanistan situation in establishing the circumstances in which it is appropriate to open fire or to target a person or thing. The situation has clearly illustrated the difficulties in distinguishing between a peaceful civilian and an armed opposition fighter.[77] But these do not appear to have been a result of problems in classifying the conflicts or of doubt about the legal rules applicable in the light of that characterization. The principal problems seem

---

[73] N. Melzer, 'Interpretive Guidance on the Notion of Direct Participation in Hostilities under International Humanitarian Law' (2009).

[74] See discussion in F. Hampson, 'Direct Participation in Hostilities and the Interoperability of the Law of Armed Conflict and Human Rights Law' in R. Pedrozo and D. Wollschlaeger (eds), *International Law and the Changing Character of War* (2011) 187.

[75] If he were taking a direct part in hostilities, he could be targeted on that basis.

[76] For discussion of the difficulties of applying the concept in Afghanistan and the use of the 'likely and identifiable threat' standard of targeting, see Schmitt, *Targeting in Afghanistan*, 317.

[77] See e.g. discussion in Geiss and Siegrist, *Armed Conflict in Afghanistan*, 22–4.

rather to be the result of uncertainty as to the facts and a concern that, for military and political reasons, greater precautions in attack needed to be adopted than were required by the law itself. Even the possible exception, the uncertainty surrounding the temporal and functional scope of 'direct participation in hostilities', seems to be mixed up, in practice, with the military and political constraints.

It should be remembered that not everything that occurs during the course of an armed conflict is regulated by international humanitarian law. The normal incidents of the maintenance of law and order exist alongside military operations.[78] Such incidents include dealing with 'ordinary' crimes, in other words crimes not related to the conflict, the policing of demonstrations and, in some circumstances, activities at roadblocks. Such activities are regulated by the rules applicable to law-enforcement, including human rights law.[79] It is not always easy to distinguish which is applicable in a given situation, but it makes a significant difference to the rules applicable to opening fire. Generally speaking, under law-enforcement rules, it is only lawful to open fire as a last resort and on account of the threat posed by the behaviour at the time of the person targeted. In other words, a person cannot be targeted simply on account of allegedly belonging to an organized armed group.

5. Rules on detention

5.1. First phase of the conflicts: October 2001–June 2002

Initially, few detainees were taken by foreign forces. This was largely owing to the fact that the hostilities at the outset largely consisted of air operations. People were detained by the Taliban and the Northern Alliance. As increasing numbers of foreign ground forces were deployed, the issue of detention assumed greater prominence.

Of those detained by foreign forces, by far the majority were detained by the US, even if they were sometimes captured by its allies.[80] At the outset, the determination by the Bush administration as to the non-applicability of the Geneva Conventions to Taliban and Al-Qaeda detainees as 'unlawful combatants' meant that they were without the protection of either Geneva Convention III applicable to POWs, or of Common Article 3.[81] Where the fighting was subject to the rules of

---

[78] Geiss and Siegrist, *Armed Conflict in Afghanistan*, 11 and 40.

[79] For a brief discussion of the relevance of human rights law, see section 6. The controversial question of the scope of the extraterritorial applicability of human rights law is addressed in ch. 4, section 2.

[80] M. Waxman, 'United States Detention Operations in Afghanistan and the Law of Armed Conflict' (2009) 39 *Israel Yearbook on Human Rights* 2.

[81] A position only modified by *Hamdan v Rumsfeld*, 548 U.S. 557, 629–31 (2006). See G. England, US Deputy Secretary of Defense, 'Application of Common Article 3 of the Geneva Conventions to the Treatment of Detainees in the Department of Defense' Memorandum to the Secretaries of the Military Departments et al (7 July 2006), available at: <www.defenselink.mil/home/dodupdate/For-the-record/documents/20060711.html>.

international armed conflict, the applicable law should have been clear. Captured combatants were to be detained as POWs. Persons captured whilst fighting were to be presumed to be combatants until their status was determined.[82] If the detaining power considered a person prima facie entitled to that status was not in fact so entitled, there is provision for status determination on an individualized basis.[83] Civilians could only be detained with a view to criminal proceedings, or subject to internment on security grounds. In the view of some States, any person who is not a combatant is a civilian.[84] This is not the view of the US. Where a detainee is determined to be a civilian who has taken a direct part in hostilities, he or she can be detained as a civilian but can also be prosecuted, if so provided under applicable domestic law, for having taken part in the fighting.[85] The blanket denial by the US of prisoner of war (POW) status to members of the Taliban, on the basis that the Geneva Conventions did not apply as a matter of law, was not consistent with the Conventions. The US position was subsequently modified as a result of legal action,[86] resulting in the creation of machinery to enable status determination at least of those in Guantánamo Bay.[87] The modification occurred during the second phase. In the first phase, the principal concern of monitoring groups such as Human Rights Watch was the law applicable to the detainees.[88]

The Northern Alliance, which was engaged in a non-international armed conflict with the government, had no authority in domestic or international law to detain anybody.[89] Common Article 3 of the Geneva Conventions prohibits ill-treatment of detainees. There were widespread allegations not only of summary execution, but also of the killing of detainees.[90] There is no evidence as to whether,

---

[82] Geneva Convention III, art. 5. See also discussion of the US practice in G. Solis, 'Law of War Issues in Ground Hostilities in Afghanistan' in M. Schmitt (ed.), *The War in Afghanistan: A Legal Analysis* (2009) 222. For the view that 'President George W. Bush was legally correct in concluding that neither al-Qaeda nor the Taliban met the prerequisites for prisoner of war status, but for the wrong reasons' see W.H. Parks, 'Combatants' in M. Schmitt (ed.), *The War in Afghanistan: A Legal Analysis* (2009) 284.

[83] Geneva Convention III, art. 5(2); Additional Protocol I, art. 45(1).

[84] UK Ministry of Defence, *The Manual of the Law of Armed Conflict* (2004) xx. Combatant is being used in the sense of Additional Protocol I, art. 43, that is, a person who is entitled to fight.

[85] See generally, R. Goldman and B. Tittemore, 'Unprivileged Combatants and the Hostilities in Afghanistan: Their Status and Rights Under International Humanitarian and Human Rights Law' ASIL Task Force on Terrorism (December 2002); F. Hampson, 'Detention, the "War on Terror" and International Law' in H. Hensel (ed.), *The Law of Armed Conflict: Constraints on the Contemporary Use of Military Force* (2007); M. Waxman, 'The Law of Armed Conflict and Detention Operations in Afghanistan' in M. Schmitt (ed.), *The War in Afghanistan: A Legal Analysis* (2009) 344 (Waxman, *Detention Operations in Afghanistan*).

[86] *Hamdan v Rumsfeld.*

[87] *Boumediene v Bush*, 128 S. Ct. 2229 (2008). See e.g. Waxman, *Detention Operations in Afghanistan*, 350.

[88] T. Malinowski, 'What to do with our "detainees"?' Human Rights Watch (28 January 2002).

[89] The question of detention in situations covered by Additional Protocol II will be considered in the next sub-section.

[90] Human Rights Watch World Report 2003, Afghanistan, available at: <www.hrw.org/legacy/wr2k3/asia1.html>. Notorious allegations include the Dasht-i-Leili massacre in December 2001 in which it is alleged that forces under the control of General Dostum caused the suffocation of a large number of detainees in metal containers; 'Starved, hurt and buried alive in Afghanistan' *The Independent* (2 May 2002), and the manner in which a prison riot was dealt with in Mazar-i-Sharif in November 2001; Human Rights Watch World Report 2002, Afghanistan, available at: <www.hrw.org/legacy/wr2k2/asia1.html>.

in 2001–2002, the Taliban, Al-Qaeda or the Northern Alliance accepted that legal rules were applicable to the treatment of detained opponents.

5.2. Second phase of the conflicts: June 2002–present

During this phase, all three conflicts were subject to the rules of non-international armed conflict. In the case of the Afghan government's conflict with the Taliban, only Common Article 3 of the Geneva Conventions was applicable until the State ratified Additional Protocol II on 10 November 2009. The Afghan government was also bound by the human rights treaties which the State had ratified, including the International Covenant on Civil and Political Rights (ICCPR). OEF and ISAF were subject to Common Article 3 and customary humanitarian law applicable in non-international armed conflicts. Members of ISAF or the Coalition who had ratified the ICCPR and/or the Convention against Torture (CAT) and/or the European Convention on Human Rights (ECHR) were bound by the provisions on detention and ill-treatment.[91]

Common Article 3 prohibits the ill-treatment of detainees, but does not address the grounds or incidents of detention. In particular, unlike the position in international armed conflicts, it does not identify permitted grounds of detention or the modalities of the review of the lawfulness of detention. It is likely that this is because, at the time of drafting, it was assumed that non-international armed conflicts would be within the territory of the State in question, which would be able to rely on domestic law provisions, possibly modified by emergency legislation.

The precise extent of the applicability of human rights law to detention in situations of conflict is unclear. It appears to prohibit arbitrary detention, but does not define 'arbitrary'. The problem is exacerbated under the ECHR, which exhaustively lists the only permitted grounds of detention. In a situation of domestic emergency, it is necessary for the State to derogate if it wishes to introduce internment or administrative detention. No State has ever derogated with regard to a situation outside national borders.

In short, classification makes a significant difference to the rules of international humanitarian law. The rules applicable to international armed conflicts address both grounds and incidents of detention. Those applicable to non-international armed conflicts are silent with regard to both.[92] Classification made no difference to the applicability of human rights law but, in practice, the different views of the members of ISAF with regard to the extraterritorial applicability of human rights law caused significant problems of interoperability in the area of detention. Whilst the US was of the view that detention was not subject to international legal regulation and was free of domestic judicial scrutiny, its European partners were

---

[91] The extraterritorial applicability of CAT is accepted by all parties. The US disputes the extraterritorial applicability of the ICCPR. Parties to the ECHR accept that it applies to extra-territorial detention, but the extent of its applicability is unclear.

[92] Under Additional Protocol II, there are due process guarantees in the case of criminal proceedings. The Protocol does not address the incidents of detention in the case of administrative or security detention.

concerned about detaining anyone, not knowing how intrusive the European Court of Human Rights might be. In other words, different members of the Coalition appeared not only to interpret their international obligations differently, but also to have radically different approaches to international law itself. The European members of the Coalition sought to avoid the *risk* of being in violation of their obligations. The US gives the impression of only appearing to be concerned about indisputable breaches of international law.

The US appears to have been of the view that there were no rules of international law establishing grounds of detention or review of detention. Given its view as to the non-extraterritorial applicability of human rights law, this is hardly surprising, but it seems to imply that the US believes that there is no customary international humanitarian law addressing these issues. The situation regarding ill-treatment in detention ought to be different since the US recognizes that the CAT, to which it is a party, applies extraterritorially. It was concerned that domestic law, particularly constitutional law, might be invoked, which was why a detention centre (in Guantánamo Bay) was opened outside US territory. The results were predictable.

The US was not only detaining thousands in Afghanistan, but was transferring to Afghanistan persons detained elsewhere in the 'global war on terror'.[93] The detentions were allegedly arbitrary and there was no judicial or quasi-judicial system of review. Initially, most detainees were held in a facility near Kandahar before being transferred to Guantánamo Bay. Subsequently, the principal detention facility was at Bagram airbase. By the second half of 2002, there were allegations of severe ill-treatment in the principal US detention facility at Bagram airbase. It is alleged that two prisoners died of injuries inflicted during detention in December 2002.[94]

It took some time before human rights groups were able to obtain information. Most of the reports are subsequent to 2004, but they often relate to the situation from mid-2002 onwards. In a major report in 2004, Human Rights Watch claimed that detentions were arbitrary, there was no mechanism for reviewing the lawfulness or necessity of detention, and ill-treatment, including torture, was widespread.[95] In an open letter to the Secretary for Defense in December 2004,

---

[93] See ch. 13 below.

[94] A US Army investigation established the circumstances in which they died, following an initial finding of death through natural causes. Five soldiers pleaded guilty to assault and other crimes and a sixth was found guilty at trial. The longest sentence any of them received was five months in a military prison; 'Times Topics: Bagram Detention Center (Afghanistan)' *The New York Times* (16 November 2009). See also Human Rights Watch, 'United States: Reports of Torture of Al-Qaeda Suspects' (26 December 2002); and Human Rights Watch, 'U.S.: New Detainee Deaths Uncovered in Afghanistan' (14 December 2004). Human Rights Watch, quoting military officials, states that eight persons have died in detention in Afghanistan since 2001.

[95] Human Rights Watch, 'Enduring Freedom' (9 March 2004); 'U.S. forces also routinely arrest civilians taking no direct part in hostilities, sometimes in contexts in which the arrests seem arbitrary or based on poor or faulty intelligence. As shown in this section, U.S. forces sometimes take into custody all men of military age found within the vicinity of an operation. Other times, it seems persons are targeted for arrest because U.S. officials have determined they are a security risk or are useful for intelligence purposes-for instance, clerics or local tribal leaders who might be politically involved with the Taliban, or civilians spotted near the site of a recent attack. Human Rights Watch has interviewed many Afghans who were arrested for simply being at the wrong place at the wrong time.' See also, Human Rights Watch, 'Afghanistan: Abuses by U.S. Forces' (9 March 2004).

Human Rights Watch noted fewer allegations of ill-treatment from Bagram, but an increase from other detention facilities in Gardez, Khost, Urgon, Ghazni and Jalalabad.[96]

By 2005, there were allegations of secret places of detention run by the CIA.[97] It is not clear whether such places were created to avoid legal scrutiny, since there was at that stage no scrutiny of places of detention run by the military. The US has sought to distinguish between the two when responding to the questions of the Committee against Torture and the Human Rights Committee (HRC) under the ICCPR.[98] The legal basis for such a distinction is not clear, since CIA agents and private contractors acting under the control of CIA agents engage the responsibility of the US under international law. Detainees in the secret places of detention did not get the benefit of visits from the ICRC. The practice may constitute an 'enforced disappearance' in relation to the detainees and their next-of-kin. Detainees were transferred not only to other places under US control, such as Guantánamo Bay and secret detention facilities in European States, but also to the authorities of other States, many of which had widespread and systematic practice of torturing detainees.

As legal writs were filed relating to the detainees in Guantanamo Bay, Congress introduced legislation to try to restrict possible challenges. In 2005, the Detainee Treatment Act sought to impede access to federal courts for torture or habeas corpus claims. The 2006 Military Commissions Act included ex post facto immunity for violations of the 1996 War Crimes Act. A near blanket denial of the relevance of international law and a compliant Congress resulted in a huge responsibility falling on the shoulders of domestic courts.[99]

Statements made by President Obama when he was a candidate during the presidential election campaign led to the belief that his election would make a significant difference to the whole question of detention linked to the 'global war on terror'. Whilst some of the practices were modified, there was no change to the essential structure.[100] A case had been filed with a US district court seeking habeas corpus relief for six foreigners detained outside Afghanistan and transferred

[96] Human Rights Watch, 'An Open Letter to US Secretary of Defense Donald Rumsfeld' (14 December 2004).

[97] Human Rights Watch, 'U.S. Operated Secret 'Dark Prison' in Kabul' (20 September 2005); Amnesty International, Cageprisoners, the Center for Constitutional Rights (CCR), the Center for Human Rights and Global Justice at New York University School of Law, Human Rights Watch, and Reprieve, 'Off the Record: US Responsibility for Enforced Disappearances in the "War on Terror"' (8 June 2007); see also, Human Rights Watch, 'US: Failure to Provide Justice for Afghan Victims' (17 February 2007); the conviction of one CIA contractor was the exception that proves the rule.

[98] See Conclusions and Recommendations of the Committee against Torture, CAT/C/USA/CO/2 (25 July 2006) and Concluding Observations of the Human Rights Committee, CCPR/C/USA/CO/3/Rev.1 (18 December 2006).

[99] For a discussion of the US case law briefly referred to below, see A. Deeks 'Litigating How We Fight' in R. Pedrozo and D. Wollschlaeger (eds), *International Law and the Changing Character of War* (2011) 428. The article also discussed cases in other States, in particular in the UK.

[100] On the second day of his Presidency, he announced the closure of CIA black sites and said that the agency would henceforth be subject to the interrogation rules in the revised *Army Field Manual* (2006).

there.[101] The Bush administration sought to distinguish the apparently similar *Boumediene* case, which it had lost in the Supreme Court, by arguing that Afghanistan was an active theatre of war. On 8 September 2008, the Justice Department filed a response to al-Bakri's habeas corpus motion which stated:

> Federal courts should not thrust themselves into the extraordinary role of reviewing the military's conduct of active hostilities overseas, second-guessing the military's determination as to which captured alien as part of such hostilities should be detained, and in practical effect, superintending the Executive's conduct in waging a war . . . . [Al-Bakri] places much emphasis on his allegations that he is a Yemeni citizen who was captured in Bangkok, Thailand, while on a trip there in December 2002, and that the [CIA] detained him for some months before transferring him to US military custody in Bagram, Afghanistan . . . . [His] allegation that he was not captured on a battlefield in Afghanistan is immaterial.[102]

Judge John D. Bates asked the incoming Obama administration whether it wished to modify its pleadings. The government in February 2009 said that it maintained its previously articulated position; relying on the Military Commissions Act, it maintained that *Boumediene* does not apply to 'enemy aliens in the active war zone'.[103]

On 2 April 2009, Judge Bates issued his opinion in which he stated that the petitioners in *Maqaleh* 'are virtually identical to the detainees in *Boumediene*'. He applied the multi-factored analysis that the Supreme Court had devised in *Boumediene*: first, the citizenship and status of the detainee and the adequacy of the process through which that status determination was made; second, the nature of the sites where apprehension and then detention took place; and third, the practical obstacles inherent in resolving the prisoner's entitlement to the writ. On these grounds, Bates dismissed the habeas corpus petition of Wazir because he was an Afghan national, despite the fact that he had been rendered from Dubai for reasons the government never explained. In relation to the other three, the two Yemenis and the Tunisian, Bates decided that federal courts did have jurisdiction to consider their habeas corpus petitions because they were foreign citizens of other countries, because the Unlawful Enemy Combatant Review Board process at Bagram was even more deficient than the Combatant Status Review Tribunals that the Supreme Court had rejected in *Boumediene*, and because US control over the facility is 'practically absolute', like Guantánamo. On appeal by the government, a three-judge panel of the DC Circuit unanimously overruled Bates' decision

---

[101] The case was originally filed on behalf of Fadi al-Maqaleh, a Yemeni who was 20 when he was arrested sometime in 2003. To that was added a petition on behalf of Haji Wazir, an Afghan currency trader who was arrested in 2002 in Dubai, where he had a shop. They were combined in *Maqaleh v Gates*. A month after the decision in the Supreme Court in *Boumediene*, the two applicants sought to have the decision applied to them. At that point, two additional petitions were added: Amin al-Bakri, a Yemeni gem trader who was arrested in Thailand in 2002, and Redha al-Najar, a Tunisian who was arrested at his home in Karachi, Pakistan, in 2002.

[102] L. Hajjar, 'Bagram, Obama's Gitmo' 41 *Middle East Report* (Fall 2011). This argument would presumably also be applicable to detention in international armed conflicts.

[103] Ibid.

on the grounds that Bagram is not like Guantánamo: it is in an active theatre of war, there is no similar long-term occupancy or indication that the US wants to maintain permanent control, and the Afghan government, unlike Cuba, is an ally in the war.[104] The *Maqaleh* petitioners amended their petition, citing changes in government policy and interpretations of applicable law (notably the Obama administration's acknowledgement that its detention authority under the Authorization for the Use of Military Force[105] is subject to international law, which prohibits arbitrary and indefinite detention), and the announcement of 8 June 2010 by the administration that it intends to maintain 'indefinite' control over a portion of the new detention facility in Parwan that had opened on the airbase the previous December. The US has also asserted its right to continue to detain indefinitely non-Afghan prisoners who were or could in the future be transferred there from other countries.

Against this back-drop of resisting all judicial scrutiny, some changes have been made to the operation of the system in practice. As part of the review and reform of detainee operations in Afghanistan, on 29 August 2009, General Douglas Stone, who had been asked to conduct an investigation, reportedly told senior military officials that at least two-thirds of Bagram detainees pose no threat to the US or Afghanistan, and recommended their release. In September 2009, the Obama administration replaced Bagram's existing review procedures with a new Detainee Review Board process that, for all intents and purposes, is identical to the Combatant Status Review Tribunals (CSRT) the Supreme Court had determined to be deficient for Guantánamo.[106]

---

[104] *Maqaleh v Gates*, 605 F.3d 84 (21 May 2010); see also Human Rights Watch, 'US: Court Ruling Revokes Protection for Bagram Detainees' (21 May 2010).

[105] Authorization for Use of Military Force (18 September 2001) Public Law 107–40 [S. J. RES. 23], 107th Congress.

[106] Human Rights Watch, 'The Bagram Detainee Review Boards: Better, But Still Falling Short' (1 June 2010):'The DRBs established by the Obama administration—operating since September under interim guidelines—are designed not only to review the basis for detention but also to serve as a relationship-building exercise between the US military and the local population. In March, the US military invited several international non-governmental organizations, including Human Rights Watch, to observe the new DRBs for the first time.... The DRBs are intended to determine whether each detainee has been properly detained by US forces. If the military panel determines that he may appropriately be detained, there remains an additional consideration: will he pose a future threat to US or coalition forces if released? If the answer is no, the man is supposed to be set free. There is also a third option: detainees may be turned over to the custody of the Afghan government for criminal prosecution. Since September 2009, more than 80 detainees have been recommended for release, and the US government reports that the current release rate is around 50 per cent. While this high release rate might be based on the new consideration of whether detainees pose a future threat, it also suggests that some of these men should never have been detained in the first place.... the DRBs remain flawed. As with the CSRT, detainees don't have access to legal counsel. Instead, they have a military officer called a Personal Representative appointed to assist them. But they don't truly represent them—there is no lawyer-client confidentiality and no reason for the detainees to trust the US military officers. As it is, conscientious Personal Representatives are overworked—there are 800 detainees and only 8 Personal Representatives. Although detainees can meet with family members in person or by video conference, they are unable to meet with a lawyer. And secret evidence—unavailable to the detainee—continues to be used in almost every case.'

In a speech on 21 May 2009, President Obama set out his strategic vision on detention, one day after Congress voted to deny him the funds to close Guantá-namo Bay.[107] He made clear a preference for the bringing of criminal prosecutions whenever possible. He wanted to work with Congress to craft legislation that would set out an 'appropriate legal regime' for holding terrorism suspects without trial; the framework would include clear procedures, fair standards and a thorough process for periodic review, which would make it an improvement on the arbitrary system of detention used during the Bush administration. In November 2009, the media began reporting ICRC concerns about continuing torture in Afghanistan. In April 2010, the BBC reported testimonies of nine prisoners who said they had been subjected to beatings, sexual humiliation, sleep deprivation, isolation and other stress and duress tactics at a facility on the Bagram airbase called 'Tor jail', which translates in Pashtu as the 'black jail', separate from the new prison.[108] On 11 May, the ICRC confirmed the existence of a secret prison to which it had no access. Tor jail is run not by the CIA, but by the US Defense Intelligence Agency and the Joint Special Operations Command (JSOC), which has authorization to use interroga-tion methods detailed in Appendix M to the *Army Field Manual*.[109] After initially denying the existence of such a facility, Defense Department officials subsequently claimed that it is an 'interrogation facility', not a 'detention site', and therefore the ICRC does not have a right to see those held there nor do the regular interrogation rules apply. Allegations of abuse also have emerged about JSOC units at undis-closed forward operating bases across the country.

In the case of other members of the Coalition, the problem of detentions in Afghanistan presents a different face. From the outset, they have been reluctant to detain and to be obliged to run detention facilities. It is difficult to determine to what extent they would have reacted differently had they been taking part in an international armed conflict, but the reaction of the UK, which was involved in the conflict in Iraq, may be instructive. When seeking to justify the detention of a British/Iraqi dual-national in Iraq on 10 October 2004, the UK relied on the authority it claimed was included in a Security Council resolution.[110] It did not seek to rely on any justification available under the customary law of armed conflict applicable in non-international armed conflict.[111] No attempt was made to argue that the test applicable to the detention of civilians in an international armed

---

[107] For transcript of the speech at the national Archives Museum, see <www.whitehouse.gov/the_press_office/Remarks-by-the-President-On-National-Security-5-21-09/>.

[108] The Open Society Foundation published an investigative report into these allegations, Open Society Institute, 'Confinement Conditions at a US Screening Facility on Bagram Air Base' (14 October 2010). Eighteen of the 20 released detainees who were interviewed by the Foundation had been detained at Tor jail, half of them in the period since President Obama took office.

[109] Appendix M is designed to induce debility, disorientation and dread in captured persons, and contains tactics otherwise removed from US interrogators' handbooks. It permits captives to be held in isolation at detention sites for an initial 30 days, a period that can be extended up to 90 days.

[110] *Al-Jedda v the United Kingdom* (Judgment) App No. 27021/08 (7 July 2011). The govern-ment's preliminary argument was that the applicant was not within the jurisdiction of the British government.

[111] The Coalition Provisional Authority handed over authority to the Iraqi Interim Government on 28 June 2004, after which the British and American forces were present in Iraq with alleged consent.

conflict—internment necessary for imperative reasons of security—was the appropriate test in a non-international armed conflict, even though that was the factual reason for the applicant's detention. This either implies uncertainty as to grounds of detention under customary law in non-international armed conflicts or uncertainty as to the willingness of the European Court of Human Rights to take account of the law of armed conflict. It is striking that the argument does not appear to have been made.

Members of the Coalition have good reason to believe that the ECHR applies extraterritorially to some extent to some issues.[112] Their concern regarding the implications of the Convention was not based on the existing case law under the Convention but based on fear as to what it might be. At the same time, on the ground there was a need to detain individuals thought to represent a serious security threat to their forces and/or the civilian population. The result was that they were willing to detain people for up to, but no more than, ninety-six hours. By then, the individual had to have been transferred to another Coalition partner, in practice the US or the Afghan authorities, or be released.[113] This approach was not limited to the European members of the Coalition.[114] In an attempt to achieve a common platform, the Danish government embarked on the Copenhagen Process on the handling of detainees in military operations.[115] It seeks to identify both the legal framework and the legal rules applicable, and to share best practice.

ISAF contributors other than the US clearly believe that there are international law rules applicable to detention in non-international armed conflicts but they are not sure of the content of those rules. Outside the Copenhagen Process, there appears to have been no attempt to try to shape an articulation of those rules, such as identifying plausible grounds of detention and the review mechanism. They accept legal accountability and try to avoid being found in violation, notably of the ECHR. The problems concern the scope, in such situations, of article 5 of the Convention and not article 3, which prohibits torture, inhuman and degrading treatment. The non-US members of ISAF all appear to accept the definitions of ill-treatment found in the practice of CAT and the case law of the ECHR.[116]

The other key player with regard to detention is the Afghan government. No issues arise with regard to the disputed scope of extraterritorial applicability of human rights law. It is clearly applicable, alongside Afghan domestic law and

---

On that basis, by October 2004, the non-international armed conflict rules were the relevant international humanitarian law rules applicable.

[112] They conceded the applicability of the ECHR to extraterritorial detention in *Bankovic and others v Belgium and others* (Decision) App No. 52207/99 (12 December 2001) para 37. The Court has subsequently applied the Convention to extraterritorial detention, as in the case of *Ocalan v Turkey* (Judgment) App No. 46221/99 (12 May 2005).

[113] The 96 hours criterion appears to address the requirement that a person be brought promptly before a judicial officer to authorize detention. It does not address the question of the lawfulness of the ground of detention.

[114] See section 5.3 on transfers below.

[115] See ch. 4, section 3.2 above.

[116] This is unlike the US, a party to CAT, which has sought to justify practices which clearly conflict with that case law e.g. 'waterboarding'.

relevant rules of international humanitarian law. There is an argument that Afghanistan is required to ensure that any States which operate in Afghanistan with the consent of the government respect Afghanistan's international obligations.[117] That would apply to the full range of Afghanistan's human rights obligations and not simply those applicable extraterritorially. Any violation would be that of Afghanistan, rather than of the assisting State.

As of 2001, there was a framework of domestic law in Afghanistan, but it is not clear whether the law itself was in conformity with Afghanistan's international obligations. An even greater problem was the lack of respect for the law in practice, whether that concerned the prohibition of arbitrary detention or ill-treatment. In 2003, responsibility for detainees was placed in the hands of the Ministry of Justice, rather than the police. Insufficient attention was paid by the international community to the respect for the rule of law in practice. In an attempt to secure some measure of accountability, the Afghan Independent National Human Rights Commission was given the responsibility of monitoring conditions of detention, including ill-treatment. The Afghan government adopted a strategy for addressing these issues in 2004, but little appears to have been done to put it into practice. Since then, the situation has gone backwards. There have been consistent and widespread allegations of ill-treatment at the hands of the Afghan National Security Directorate.[118] In January 2012, a decree was promulgated which would transfer responsibility for detainees to the Interior Ministry, reversing the 2003 reform.[119] In view of the track record of the Afghan police, particularly the local police,[120] and the failure of the Interior Ministry to secure effective accountability, human rights groups have expressed concern that the decree could herald an increase in the prevalence of ill-treatment.

The problem for the Afghan authorities has nothing to do with the classification of the conflict or the consequences of classification. The Afghan government does not appear to dispute the scope and content of its obligations under international humanitarian law and human rights law. The problem is rather the failure to implement in practice its national and international legal obligations and to provide effective redress to the population whose rights have been violated.

Non-state actors, such as the Taliban, are bound by non-international armed conflict rules, but not directly bound by human rights law. That said, the State's

[117] This is a question of the scope of State responsibility, both generally and specifically with regard to human rights law.
[118] E.g. Human Rights Watch, 'Afghan Torture is no Secret' (4 May 2010); Human Rights Watch has been raising its concerns with the Afghan government and third States since 2002. See also, Human Rights Watch, World Report 2010, Afghanistan, available at <www.hrw.org/world-report-2010/afghanistan>; Afghan Independent Human Rights Commission, 'Causes of Torture in Law Enforcement Institutions' (April 2009); United Nations Assistance Mission in Afghanistan, UN Office of the High Commissioner for Human Rights, 'Treatment of Conflict Related Detainees in Afghan Custody' (October 2011).
[119] Human Rights Watch, 'Afghanistan: Decree Increases Detainees' Risk of Torture' (10 January 2012).
[120] Human Rights Watch, 'Afghanistan: Rein in Abusive Militias and Afghan Local Police' (12 September 2011); Human Rights Watch, '"Just Don't Call It a Militia": Impunity, Militias and the "Afghan Local Police"' (September 2011).

human rights obligations include the obligation to protect individuals from violations at the hands of third parties. The Taliban codes of conduct include rules about the treatment of detainees.

5.3. Transfer

In international armed conflicts, a State may not transfer a person to a State not party to the Conventions. In addition, in the case of the transfer of prisoners of war, there is a residual responsibility on the part of the State effecting the transfer. If the receiving State does not respect its obligations under the Convention, the transferring power may need to seek the POW's return.[121] In non-international armed conflicts, the forced displacement of the civilian population is prohibited, except where the security of the population or imperative military necessity so requires. It is not clear whether customary law applicable in non-international armed conflicts prohibits the transfer of individuals, where the receiving authority does not acknowledge or respect in practice its international humanitarian law obligations to such transferees. It is also not clear whether a State is prohibited from transferring a detainee to another territory but still subject to the State's control.[122] Human rights law prohibits the transfer of a person to a State where he is likely to be subjected to torture, cruel, inhuman or degrading treatment. This is prohibited both by virtue of the interpretation of the provisions on ill-treatment by human rights bodies and, for parties to CAT, by virtue of express provision in the treaty.[123]

The restrictions on transfer have been a major source of difficulty for all States, particularly the non-US members of ISAF. In a non-international armed conflict outside national territory, the way round most of the detention problems would be an immediate transfer to national authorities. As shown above, ill-treatment is practised in many Afghan centres of detention, notably those run by the National Directorate of Security (NDS). Pressure has been put on members of ISAF by both national and international NGOs and, in some cases, by domestic litigation, not to transfer detainees to the Afghan authorities.[124] States have sought to get round the

---

[121] Geneva Convention III, art. 12; see also Geneva Convention IV, art. 45.

[122] Under art. 45 of Geneva Convention IV, a State cannot transfer an individual from occupied territory to its own territory.

[123] CAT, art. 3; the prohibition of transfer under the Convention only applies where the risk is of torture (i.e. not cruel, inhuman or degrading treatment).

[124] Amnesty International, 'Afghanistan: Stop Transfer of Detainees' (7 February 2008); Human Rights Watch, 'Canada/Afghanistan: Investigate Canadian Responsibility for Detainee Abuse' (27 November 2009): 'Senior Canadian diplomat Richard Colvin, who was based in Afghanistan in 2006–07, told a House of Commons committee last week that persons taken prisoner by Canadian forces in Afghanistan and transferred to Afghan custody during that time period were likely tortured. Colvin testified that he made repeated warnings about detainee abuse. He said that his warnings were at first ignored by senior Canadian government officials, but he was then later instructed to "be quiet and do what we were told."'; Human Rights Watch, 'Afghan Torture is no Secret' (4 May 2010): 'Canada has accepted so-called diplomatic assurances from the Afghan government that detainees will not be tortured, and believes it can monitor the conditions of the persons it transfers to Afghan custody. Such assurances are generally ineffective, and monitoring only allows an opportunity to find out about

problem by securing diplomatic assurances and by putting in place arrangements to monitor the fate of transferred detainees. Following reports as to continuing torture in many places of detention, many States have chosen to suspend transfers, even where such follow-up arrangements were in place.[125] It is not known whether there were any cases of transfers by the non-US members of ISAF to third States other than the US.

A separate problem arises in relation to transfer to US authorities.[126] It is not clear whether, at certain times, it could have been argued that there was a real risk of ill-treatment in US detention facilities. Even if the original detention was not arbitrary, there was a real risk that rights relating to the incidents of detention, such as periodic review, would not be respected.

The US effected two types of transfers: first, it transferred detainees to Guantánamo Bay, particularly in the early years of the conflict. Human rights law appears only to address continuing State responsibility for detention and treatment, rather than the transfer itself. Only international humanitarian law appears to address geographical transfers. The transfer of detainees to secret US detention facilities in third States would seem to involve the same questions as transfer to Guantánamo Bay, with the additional question of the complicity of the State which allowed the US to have a secret detention facility in its territory.[127] Second, the US transferred detainees to the authorities of third States whose record suggested a very real risk of torture for the detainees.[128]

All the discussion of transfers has been in the context of human rights law. That would not have been the case had the transfers occurred in the context of an international armed conflict. The problem again is not the content of the rules applicable in non-international armed conflict, but either the lack of rules or uncertainty as to the content of customary non-international armed conflict rules.

---

torture after it happens.'; Human Rights Watch, 'Transfers to Afghan Custody Violate Canada's International Legal Obligations' (5 May 2010), which refers to 'credible allegations' that detainees handed over by Canadian troops to the NDS in 2007 were mistreated by Afghan government officials. Similar concerns have been raised with Australia, with regard to both transfers to the US and to the Afghan authorities, see Amnesty International, 'Australia's new Afghan prisoner policy could violate international law' (14 December 2010). As far as litigation is concerned, see *Amnesty International Canada v Canada (Minister of National Defence)* 2007 FC 1147, 2007 Carswell FC, 3688 at 19. In the UK, the High Court ruled that detainees could not be transferred to the National Security Directorate in Kabul, but that transfers could continue to NDS facilities in Kandahar and Lashkar Gah, provided existing safeguards were 'strengthened by observance of specified conditions'; *Maya Evans v MOD* [2010] EWHC 1445 (Admin) (25 June 2010).

[125] A few days before the release of UNAMA Report on Treatment of Conflict Related Detainees in Afghan Custody (October 2011), NATO stopped the transfer of detainees to several Afghan detention facilities, including both NDS and police facilities.

[126] Amnesty International refers to transfers both to the US and Afghan authorities; Amnesty International, 'Afghanistan: Stop Transfer of Detainees' (7 February 2008).

[127] Council of Europe, Parliamentary Assembly, Committee on Legal Affairs and Human Rights, 'Alleged secret detentions in Council of Europe member states' AS/JUR (2006) 03 rev. It should be remembered that unacknowledged detention accompanied by transfer raises the question of enforced disappearances, but that is attributable to the lack of acknowledgement of the detention, and not to the transfer.

[128] E.g. Egypt, Syria, Tunisia, and Morocco.

6. International human rights law

As noted in chapter 4 above, the relationship between human rights law and international humanitarian law in situations of armed conflict remains unsettled.[129] Human rights law has been referred to in this chapter principally in the context of detention, but it is relevant to all phases of the conflict and possibly to other issues. In particular, it may be applicable to the decision to open fire. This is likely to be the case where, in the circumstances, the decision has to be analysed in terms of a law-enforcement paradigm, but it may apply more widely.[130]

The area in which human rights law was of most practical importance was in the field of detention. Members of ISAF bound by the ICCPR or the American Convention on Human Rights (ACHR) had to take account of their provisions.[131] Both those treaties proscribe arbitrary detention.[132] There may be some flexibility in the determination of what is arbitrary in situations of armed conflict. A much more difficult situation arises for States parties to the ECHR. Article 5 of the ECHR lists exhaustively the only permitted grounds of detention. They do not include administrative detention or internment. In order to be able to justify detention on those grounds, it is necessary for a European State to derogate. There is as yet no case law on whether a State can derogate with regard to an emergency in another State. No State has, as yet, attempted to do so.[133] Had Afghanistan derogated under the ICCPR, there might have been an argument as to whether a European member of ISAF could rely on that derogation. That might be

---

[129] See discussion in ch. 4, section 2.

[130] See eg *Al Skeini and others v the United Kingdom* (Judgment) App No. 55721/07 (7 July 2011), which concerned deaths in Iraq. The Court examined only whether the applicants were within the jurisdiction of the UK and whether there was an obligation to conduct an investigation into the deaths, rather than the decision to open fire itself. See generally, F. Hampson, 'Is Human Rights Law of Any Relevance to Military Operations in Afghanistan?' in M. Schmitt (ed.), *The War in Afghanistan: A Legal Analysis* (2009) 486 (Hampson, *Military Operations in Afghanistan*).

[131] CAT applies outside national territory by virtue of its express terms. The conduct is prohibited in both international and non-international armed conflicts. Respect for the Convention should therefore have caused no problem, at least in relation to the conduct of Coalition forces. The US had difficulties with the Committee against Torture owing to its view as to the treatment to which the prohibitions applied.

[132] ICCPR, art. 9; American Convention on Human Rights, art. 7. HRC, 'General Comment 31 on the Nature of the General Legal Obligation Imposed on States Parties to the Covenant', CCPR/C/21/Rev.1/Add.13 (26 May 2004), to which no State has objected, states at para 10: 'This means that a State party must respect and ensure the rights laid down in the Covenant to anyone within the power or effective control of that State Party, even if not situated within the territory of the State Party.... This principle also applies to those within the power or effective control of the forces of a State Party acting outside its territory, regardless of the circumstances in which such power or effective control was obtained, such as forces constituting a national contingent of a State Party assigned to an international peace-keeping or peace-enforcement operation.' The case law of the Inter-American Court and Commission of Human Rights, acting under the Convention (rather than the Organization of American States Charter and the American Declaration) does not yet establish to what extent the Convention has extraterritorial effect.

[133] It is possible that, as a result of the recent decision in *Al-Jedda v the United Kingdom*, States will in future seek to do so.

relevant to the HRC, but it is not obvious how the European Court of Human Rights could take it into account.

Questions might also be raised about the implications of the Security Council mandate for the human rights obligations of ISAF contributing States,[134] the implications of Afghanistan's own human rights obligations for ISAF States,[135] and the issue of civil or criminal liability for ISAF troops who did not prevent fundamental human rights abuses committed by other forces with which they were allied. None of the difficulties mentioned here are the result of problems in classifying the hostilities. They result from the lack of relevant rules in non-international armed conflicts, uncertainty as to the scope of the human rights requirements in situations of extraterritorial emergency and the continuing need to find the right accommodation between the two bodies of rules—international humanitarian law and international human rights law.

7. Conclusions

The conflicts in Afghanistan have presented a large number of problems of international humanitarian law and human rights law, some of which have been touched on in this chapter. The question is whether those problems result from difficulties of classification of the relevant conflicts.

7.1. Classification

It is clear that, in 2001, there was an international armed conflict between the Taliban (the government of Afghanistan) fighting alongside Al-Qaeda and the Coalition. There should have been no legal problem with this classification, but the US initially denied the applicability of the Geneva Conventions thereby avoiding the purpose of classification, which is to signpost the relevant law. Although there have subsequently been analyses of that phase which separates it into two armed conflicts—one between the Coalition and the Taliban (international) and one between the Coalition and Al-Qaeda (non-international)—there is no evidence that the parties either made the twofold classification or used two sets of rules.

There is some controversy about the time at which the international armed conflict ended, but, in the submission of this writer, it was after the overthrow of the Taliban as the government. At that point there were two operations, OEF and ISAF. There is a question as to whether there was one conflict or two. Was the fighting in eastern Afghanistan (OEF) a continuation of the previous conflict, or part of the conflict in relation to which ISAF was assisting the new government of

---

[134] Contrast the treatment of the issue in *Behrami and Behrami v France* and *Saramati v France, Germany and Norway* (Decision) App No. 71412/01 and 78166/01 (2 May 2007) and the judgment of the European Court of Human Rights in *Al-Jedda v the United Kingdom*.

[135] See discussion of issue in Hampson, *Military Operations in Afghanistan*.

Afghanistan? Whether it was one conflict or two, any conflict was a non-international armed conflict, since no State armed forces were involved on the other side. There was no problem with regard to the minimum threshold of applicability for Common Article 3; the only reason it was at one time a problem for Germany related to domestic political reasons.

As discussed above in sections 2.3 and 3.2 there may be questions as to whether the non-international armed conflict crossed the threshold of applicability of Additional Protocol II, either at all or in relation to different areas of Afghanistan; but these issues do not appear to have had any importance in practice. The significance of the possible applicability of Additional Protocol II is not great since it arises only after Afghanistan's ratification of Additional Protocol II (in November 2009) and, because of the wording of the Protocol—which is artificially not applicable to non-international armed conflicts in the territory of another State not a party to the conflict—probably does not affect any of the members of ISAF, whether or not parties to the Protocol. Classification under customary law as regards the type or types of non-international armed conflict is a real problem in theory, not least owing to the lack of evidence regarding State practice and the difficulty in establishing *opinio iuris;* but again this does not appear to have had any significance in practice.

7.2. Consequences

As regards the first phase there should have been no real problems with the rules applicable; the chief difficulty arose because of the US blanket denial of status to the Taliban and its wish, apparently, to be free to deal with the detainees without any restriction imposed by international law. In the second phase, the non-international armed conflict in which ISAF was involved included stability operations requiring a wide range of tasks. Leaving aside the gaps in the law relating to detention issues, the question arises whether the law applicable to non-international conflict is adequate to deal with the breadth of the activities necessary in stability and counter-insurgency operations including policing functions, where, as in Afghanistan, the 'foreign' troops are present for a long period and in circumstances sometimes similar to occupation. This question relates to the substantive law rather than classification, but needs to be addressed in considering whether the different legal categories of armed conflict are adequate to encompass all forms of contemporary military operation.[136]

In general the legal rules as to opening fire did not raise issues of difficulty; for military and political reasons greater restrictions were applied than required under the law. There were problems of interoperability, with national constraints and with determining what rules were applicable given uncertain facts (particularly with regard to assessments as to whether civilians were directly participating in

---

[136] See e.g. discussion in K. Watkin, 'Stability Operations: A Guiding Framework for "Small Wars" and Other Conflicts of the 21st Century?' in M. Schmitt (ed.), *The War in Afghanistan: A Legal Analysis* (2009) 421.

hostilities), but those are not problems with the law itself. In theory, problems might also have arisen because of the uncertainty as to whether rules of customary international humanitarian law applicable in non-international armed conflict, especially those concerning means and methods of warfare, apply in all such conflicts or only those which cross the threshold of Additional Protocol II. No such problem appears to have arisen in practice. Issues of detention however presented major difficulties, not on account of classification itself or on account of the choice of the rules applicable, but owing to the *lack* of clear rules, especially with regard to grounds of detention and procedural safeguards, for example as to review of detention. The difficulties were exacerbated by uncertainty as to the extraterritorial applicability of human rights law.

7.3. In sum

The legal problems encountered in the course of the hostilities against and within Afghanistan did not result from difficulties in classifying the conflicts. The phase of non-international armed conflict does, however, exemplify a situation where formal classification does not always help with the problems on the ground, particularly in relation to operations the conduct of which varies not according to the legal classification of the conflict, but according to the nature of the task and the constraints of policy.[137] It was the gap in international humanitarian law relating to non-international armed conflict, controversies with regard to the scope of applicability of international human rights law, and multiple participants with different views of the law and policy which caused most of the problems in practice.

Chronology

1979	Soviet Army invades Afghanistan and props up communist government.
1980	Babrak Karmal installed as ruler, backed by Soviet troops.
1986	Babrak Karmal replaced by Najibullah as head of Soviet-backed regime.
1988	Soviet Union signs an agreement, following negotiations between the United States, the USSR, Pakistan and Afghanistan, pledging to withdraw its troops from Afghanistan.
1989	Last Soviet troops leave, but civil war continues.
1992	Najibullah's government toppled.
1996	Taliban seizes control of Kabul.

---

[137] See e.g. discussion by Schmitt of the move from law to legitimacy: 'the conduct of hostilities in Afghanistan illustrated a shift from law toward legitimacy. As governments, non-governmental organizations, academics and others raise expectations, there is decreasing emphasis on strict legal analysis.' Schmitt, *Targeting in Afghanistan*, 329.

8 December 1998	Security Council resolution 1214 (1998) demands that all Afghan factions cooperate in bringing indicted terrorists to justice.
15 October 1999	Security Council resolution 1267 (1999) notes that Osama bin Laden is indicted in the US, demands that he be surrendered to be brought to justice and applies broad sanctions.
9 September 2001	Ahmad Shah Massoud, leader of the Northern Alliance, is assassinated.
October 2001	US-led bombing of Afghanistan begins following the September 11 attacks on the US. Northern Alliance forces enter Kabul.
November 2001	The UN invites major Afghan factions (but not the Taliban) to a conference in Bonn. On December 5, the Bonn Agreement is signed, endorsed by UN Security Council resolution 1383. The agreement installs Hamid Karzai as head of the Interim Administration of Afghanistan.
20 December 2001	Security Council resolution 1386 (2001) authorizes the establishment of ISAF. On 22 December, President Rabbani hands power to the new Interim Afghan Administration, established in Bonn and headed by Hamid Karzai.
January 2002	Deployment of first contingent of ISAF.
June 2002	Hamid Karzai is elected by Loya Jirga to head the country's transitional government.
January 2004	Loya Jirga adopts new constitution.
October–November 2004	Hamid Karzai wins presidential elections.
September 2005	Afghans vote in parliamentary elections.
October 2006	ISAF assumes responsibility for security across the whole of Afghanistan.
February 2009	ISAF States pledge to increase military and other commitments in Afghanistan after US announces dispatch of 17,000 extra troops.
August 2009	Presidential and provincial election; in October Karzai is declared winner of the presidential election.
December 2009	US President Barack Obama decides to boost US troop numbers in Afghanistan by 30,000, bringing total to 100,000.

9

Gaza

Iain Scobbie[*]

1. Introduction

Although Israel became the belligerent occupant of Gaza in 1967 following the Six-Day War, the period under analysis in this chapter starts with the outbreak of the second *intifada* in September 2000 and ends in May 2011. Classifying the Gaza conflict is complex. Was there a conflict—or conflicts—throughout the whole of this period? Was it international or non-international, and if the former, how is it possible to have an international conflict when one party is not a State? While it is clear that one of the parties to the conflict was Israel, what entity, or entities, comprised the other? Was the conflict with the Palestinian people as a whole, or only those in Gaza, or with the various armed groups operating within Gaza (such as Islamic Jihad), or with the Harakat al-Muqāwama al-Islāmiyya (the Islamic Resistance Movement, that is, Hamas), or only with Hamas' military wing, the Izzidin al-Qassam Brigade? Or was it with some combination of these actors? Does Israel still occupy Gaza or was the occupation terminated by Israel's disengagement, by Hamas' accession to power in Gaza, or by subsequent events such as Egypt's re-opening of the Rafah crossing in late May 2011 which allows the passage of people in and out of Gaza?

2. Description of the situation

2.1. Background

Some simplification of the complexity of the situation is inevitable, but the principal facts relevant to the classification of the hostilities which have occurred during this period are as follows.

Negotiations in July 2000 at Camp David between Israel and the Palestine Liberation Organization ended in deadlock. As a result, the second *intifada*

[*] I am grateful to my colleagues Sarah Hibbin and Alon Margalit, and to Professor David Kretzmer, for their comments on earlier drafts of this chapter. Responsibility for the content of this chapter, however, lies solely with me.

started on 28 September 2000. Since then, the Israel Defense Forces (IDF) have undertaken numerous military operations in Gaza.[1] In April 2004, the Israel Cabinet announced its original Disengagement Plan, which had the stated objective of ending the occupation. In September 2005, Israel effected its disengagement by evacuating Israeli settlers from Gaza, withdrawing its troops from the territory and formally terminating its military rule. It did, however, retain a substantial degree of control over matters such as Gaza airspace, land borders, offshore areas and utility supplies. Before Israel's disengagement from Gaza in 2005, Gaza was subject to belligerent occupation by Israel: this was expressly affirmed by Israel's Supreme Court, sitting as the High Court of Justice, in *Ajuri v IDF Commander*.[2]

In the January 2006 election to the Palestinian Legislative Council, the legislature of the Palestinian National Authority, Hamas obtained an overall majority. The election was assessed internationally to be 'well administered under the difficult circumstances of ongoing conflict and occupation'.[3] On 25 June 2006, Hamas armed forces captured Israel Defense Forces Corporal Gilad Shalit. This resulted in Israel launching Operation Summer Rains on 28 June 2006 in an attempt to suppress rocket fire from Gaza and secure the release of Corporal Shalit.[4]

In March 2007, a Hamas-led national unity government was formed for the Palestinian National Authority by Hamas and Fatah, the nationalist political party founded in the late 1950s, which is the largest group in the Palestine Liberation Organization and which dominated Palestinian politics from the Six-Day War until the 2006 election. This arrangement quickly broke down and in June 2007, following its success in an armed struggle with Fatah in Gaza,[5] Hamas assumed overall control of Gaza. As a consequence, Palestinian Authority President Abbas, himself a member of Fatah, dismissed the Hamas-led government. Since then, the West Bank has been under Fatah control, and Gaza under Hamas.[6] Hamas Prime Minister Haniya has denied that this has led to a separate Gaza State being created, asserting, 'The Gaza Strip is an indivisible part of the homeland and its residents are

---

[1] See e.g. 'Israeli military operations against Gaza, 2000–2008' (2009) 38(3) *Journal of Palestine Studies* 122.

[2] See *Ajuri v IDF Commander*, HCJ 7015/02 (3 September 2002), opinion of President Barak, para 22.

[3] National Democratic Institute for International Affairs/Carter Center, 'Final report on the Palestinian Legislative Council Elections 25 January 2006' (2006) 23, available at: www.accessdemocracy.org/files/2068_ps_elect_012506.pdf.

[4] On 18 October 2011 Gilad Shalit was released following an agreement between Israel and Hamas which included the release by Israel of 1027 Palestinian prisoners.

[5] For an overview of the dynamics of this dispute, see N.J. Brown, 'The Hamas-Fatah conflict: shallow but wide' (2010) 34(2) *Fletcher Forum of Word Affairs* 35.

[6] See e.g. House of Commons Foreign Affairs Committee, 'Global Security: Israel and the occupied Palestinian territories, Fifth report of session 2008–2009' (2009) 14, para 8 (House of Commons, *Global Security*): 'From June 2007, therefore, the two Occupied Palestinian Territories were under the effective control of two separate political authorities, with fundamentally different stances towards Israel and the peace process.'

an integral part of the Palestinian people'.[7] This view was echoed by President Abbas during Security Council debates on Operation Cast Lead.[8]

Rocket fire from Gaza into southern Israel increased in the months following Hamas' assumption of control in Gaza. For its part, after the Hamas takeover, Israel, which controls the Israel-Gaza crossings, declared Gaza to be hostile territory[9] and imposed a terrestrial blockade on the territory. It kept the crossings largely closed and severely restricted the range of goods that could be transported through them. Sporadic Israeli incursions into Gaza in pursuit of terrorist targets, and other forms of clashes between Israeli forces and Palestinians in and around the territory, continued.

In June 2008, Egypt brokered a six-month ceasefire between Hamas and Israel. This led to a reduction in rocket fire from Gaza, but not a complete halt. The progressive breakdown of the ceasefire, and Hamas' ultimate decision not to extend the truce, paved the way for the launching of Operation Cast Lead by Israel in December 2008 to January 2009. Israel and Hamas each claimed that the other was responsible for the collapse of the ceasefire. Israel blamed Hamas for failing to halt rocket fire, and Hamas blamed Israel for failing to implement apparent commitments in the ceasefire agreement to provide greater access through Gaza's border crossings.[10] According to the Israel Security Agency (Shin Bet), there were 1276 rocket launchings from Gaza in 2007 and 1785 in 2008 (before the start of Operation Cast Lead). This rocket fire killed two Israelis in 2007 and four in 2008. According to the UN Office for the Coordination of Humanitarian Affairs in the Occupied Palestinian Territory, 301 Palestinians were killed in Gaza in 2007 and 389 in the first ten months of 2008 as a direct result of the conflict with Israel.[11]

In June 2010, following international pressure, particularly after the interception of the Mavi Marmara flotilla by Israel on 31 May 2010,[12] Israel relaxed its restrictions on the movement of goods into Gaza.[13] The Mavi Marmara flotilla

---

[7] 'Hamas takes full control of Gaza' *BBC News* (15 June 2007).

[8] S/PV.6061, Security Council meeting (6 January 2009) 5, remarks by Abbas (Palestine) (SC 6061st meeting).

[9] See Israeli Ministry of Foreign Affairs, 'Behind the headlines: Israel designates Gaza a "hostile territory"' (24 September 2007), available at: <www.mfa.gov.il/MFA/About+the+Ministry/ Behind +the+Headlines/Gaza+designated+a+%E2%80%9CHostile+Territory%E2%80%9D+24-Sep-2007.htm> (MFA, *Gaza Designated as Hostile Territory*).

[10] See e.g. SC 6061st meeting, remarks by Shalev (Israel) 6–7, and Al-Faisal (Saudi Arabia) 23; House of Commons, *Global Security*, 15, para 10.

[11] House of Commons, *Global Security*, 14–15, para 9.

[12] On this incident, see R. Buchan, 'The international law of naval blockade and Israel's interception of the *Mavi Marmara*' (2011) 58 *Netherlands International Law Review* 209; D. Guilfoyle, 'The Mavi Marmara incident and blockade in armed conflict' (2010) 81 *British Yearbook of International Law* 171 (Guilfoyle, *The Mavi Marmara incident*); J. Kraska, 'Rule selection in the case of Israel's naval blockade of Gaza: law of naval warfare or law of the sea?' (2011) 13 *Yearbook of International Humanitarian Law* 367 (Kraska, *Israel's Naval Blockade*); and A. Sanger, 'The contemporary law of blockade and the Gaza freedom flotilla' (2011) 13 *Yearbook of International Humanitarian Law* 397 (Sanger, *Contemporary Law of Blockade*).

[13] Israeli Security Cabinet, 'Decision on easing the blockade against the Gaza Strip' (20 June 2010), reproduced in (2010) 40 *Journal of Palestine Studies* 196.

was an attempt organized by non-governmental organizations to deliver humanitarian aid in breach of the maritime blockade imposed on Gaza at the start of Operation Cast Lead.

In April 2011, it was reported that a reconciliation agreement had been signed in Cairo between Fatah and Hamas which might lead to a new national unity government that would control both the West Bank and Gaza.[14] While the April 2011 conciliation agreement could have a profound impact on how the situation in Gaza should be classified, its degree of implementation and implications are far from clear at the time of writing. Accordingly, it must be largely disregarded in this analysis.

During the period under consideration, a number of official reports have examined various incidents or episodes of the hostilities which have given rise to particular international concern. For example, the Goldstone Report[15] was issued as a result of Operation Cast Lead. The interception of the Mavi Marmara flotilla has been examined in five official reports: one commissioned by the UN Human Rights Council (the Hudson-Phillips Report), one by the Israeli government (the Turkel Commission Report), two by the Turkish government (the interim and final reports of the Turkish National Commission of Inquiry) and one by the UN Secretary-General (the Palmer Report).[16] Although both Operation Cast Lead and the Mavi Marmara interception raise significant legal issues in themselves, they were only episodes in the broader context of hostilities involving Gaza and Israel. This analysis does not focus on these incidents or the reports on them. Having said that, one aspect of Operation Cast Lead does take on a particular importance, namely Israel's declaration of its blockade of Gaza's coast. The views expressed by States in UN fora during debates on Cast Lead are also of some interest.

2.2. Restrictions relating to Gaza

The Revised Disengagement Plan provides that 'Israel will guard and monitor the external land perimeter of the Gaza Strip, will continue to maintain exclusive authority in Gaza air space, and will continue to exercise security activity in the

---

[14] See 'Hamas and Fatah agree to form a caretaker government' *The Guardian* (27 April 2011). An unofficial translation of the agreement is available at: <http://middleeast.about.com/od/palestinepalestinians/qt/Fatah-Hamas-Reconciliation-Agreement.htm>.

[15] Human Rights Council, 'Human rights in Palestine and other occupied Arab territories: report of the United Nations Fact Finding Mission on the Gaza conflict' A/HRC/12/48 (15 September 2009) (The Goldstone report).

[16] Human Rights Council, 'Report of the international fact-finding mission to investigate violations of international law, including international humanitarian and human rights law, resulting from the Israeli attacks on the flotilla of ships carrying humanitarian assistance' A/HRC/15/21 (27 September 2010) (The Hudson-Phillips Report); 'The Public Commission to examine the maritime incident of 31 May 2010' (January 2010) (The Turkel Commission Report); Turkish National Commission of Inquiry, 'Interim report on the Israeli attack on the humanitarian aid convoy to Gaza' (September 2010) and 'Report on the Israeli attack on the humanitarian aid convoy to Gaza' (February 2011); and 'Report of the Secretary-General's Panel of Inquiry on the 31 May 2010 Flotilla Incident' (September 2011) (The Palmer Report).

sea off the coast of the Gaza Strip'.[17] Israel's border controls include the mainte-nance of restricted land areas within Gaza: a 300 metre 'no-go' area in which access is totally prohibited at risk of death, and high-risk areas which extend 1000–1500 metres from the border where firing on people, as well as land-levelling and property destruction by the IDF are 'common and wide-spread'.[18]

Israel physically controls all crossing points into Gaza, with the exception of the Rafah crossing between Egypt and Gaza. After disengagement, in November 2005, Israel and the Palestinian Authority concluded an agreement to regulate passage through the Rafah crossing, which was made subject to an annexed statement of principles, and placed under the supervision of the European Union Border Assistance Mission (EU BAM), with remote monitoring by Israeli security person-nel.[19] Following the capture of Corporal Shalit in June 2006, Israel dictated the opening and closing of the Rafah crossing by virtue of its control of the tripartite liaison office, which had to be operational for the crossing to open. In mid-2007, it was reported that the crossing had been closed approximately 80 per cent of the time that the parties had agreed it should be open.[20]

After Hamas assumed control of Gaza, Israel announced that it would freeze the operation of the agreement on the Rafah crossing, as the Palestinian Authority personnel that had operated the crossing were unable to reach it. Israel further objected that it was unable to monitor the persons passing through. The crossing last opened with EU BAM monitoring on 9 June 2007. Although Egypt could open the crossing on its side, it generally refrained from doing so, and in 2010 the Rafah crossing was 'closed for public use for a total of 324 days, except for some cases with prior coordination'.[21] In May 2011, as a result of the Fatah-Hamas reconciliation agreement and the fall of President Mubarak, Egypt eased restrictions which had been placed on the passage of Gaza residents through the Rafah crossing,

---

[17] Prime Minister's Office, 'Cabinet resolution regarding the Disengagement Plan' (6 June 2004), section 3(1) (Revised Disengagement Plan).

[18] The Office for the Co-ordination of Humanitarian Affairs calculates that these areas amount to 17 per cent of the total land mass of Gaza, and 35 per cent of its arable land, see OCHA, 'Between the fence and a hard place: the humanitarian impact of Israeli-imposed restrictions on access to land and sea in the Gaza Strip' (August 2010) 8–10, available at: <www.ochaopt.org/documents/ocha_opt_special_focus_2010_08_19_english.pdf>; see also, Palestinian Centre for Human Rights, 'Fact sheet: the buffer zone in the Gaza Strip' (October 2010), available at: <www.pchrgaza.org/facts/factsheet-bufferzone-aug.pdf>.

[19] The legal instruments dealing with the Rafah crossing, including the 15 November 2005 Israel-PA Agreement on Movement and Access and annexed Agreed Principles for Rafah Crossing, and 23 November 2005 Agreed Arrangement on the European Union Border Assistance Mission at the Rafah Crossing Point on the Gaza-Egyptian Border (concluded at the invitation of Israel and the Palestinian Authority) may be found at: www.eubam-rafah.eu/node/2303. See also, B'Tselem, 'Gaza Strip, Rafah Crossing', available at: <www.btselem.org/gaza_strip/rafah_crossing>.

[20] See Euro-Mediterranean Human Rights Network, 'Third Annual Review on Human Rights in EU-Israel Relations 2005–2006' (June 2007) 9 and 32; Gisha, 'Rafah crossing: who holds the keys' (March 2009) 119–21 (Gisha, *Rafah Crossing*); World Bank, 'Potential alternatives for Palestinian trade: developing the Rafah trade corridor' (21 March 2007) 4.

[21] UN General Assembly, 'Report of the Commissioner-General of the United Nations Relief and Works Agency for Palestine refugees in the Near East, 1 January–31 December 2010' A/66/13 (2011) 7, para 32; for an analysis of Egyptian policy regarding the crossing, see Gisha, *Rafah Crossing*, 125–32.

but not those placed on the passage of goods. The position at the time of writing is not, however, entirely clear.

2.3. The aims of Hamas

Although Hamas has the long-term aim of establishing an Islamic State on the entire territory of Mandate Palestine, that is Israel, the West Bank and Gaza, it also recognizes the interim objective of establishing a Palestinian State in the West Bank and Gaza. Its actions have tended to strike a balance between the pursuit of these two aims, although its long-term aim remains central to Hamas' ideology.[22] The latter was identified and emphasized in its 1988 Charter, article 11 of which affirms the integrity and nature of the territory of Mandate Palestine: 'the land of Palestine is an Islamic land entrusted to the Muslim generations until Judgement Day. No one may renounce all or even part of it ... This is its status in Islamic law.'[23] This aim is reflected in an antipathy to peaceful solutions aimed at solving the Palestine conflict, because no part of Palestine may be given up: 'There is no solution to the Palestinian problem except through struggle.'[24] Moreover, 'the ongoing conflict between the Arabs and the Muslims and the Zionists in Palestine is a fateful civilizational struggle incapable of being brought to an end without eliminating its cause, namely, the Zionist settlement of Palestine': this can only be done through 'a comprehensive holy struggle in which armed struggle is a basic instrument'.[25] Nevertheless, in an interview with the *New York Times* in May 2009, the Hamas Politburo Chief Khalid Mishal stated:

> The most important thing is what Hamas is doing and the policies it is adopting today ... Hamas has accepted the national reconciliation document. It has accepted a Palestinian state on the 1967 borders including East Jerusalem, dismantling settlements, and the right of return based on a long-term truce. Hamas has represented a clear political program through a unity government. This is Hamas's program regardless of the historic documents. Therefore, it is not logical for the international community to get stuck on sentences written 20 years ago.[26]

---

[22] See K. Hroub, *Hamas: political thought and practice* (2000) 60–1 and 69–86 (Hroub, *Hamas*), and also his *Hamas: a beginner's guide* (2006) 37–41 (Hroub, *A Beginner's Guide*); B. Milton-Edwards and S. Farrell, *Hamas: the Islamic Resistance Movement* (2010) 14–17 (Milton-Edwards and Farrell, *Resistance Movement*); A. Tamimi, *Hamas: a history from within* (2007) 147–69 (Tamimi, *A History from Within*).

[23] 'Hamas Charter' (18 August 1988), translated in Hroub, *Hamas*, 273 (Hamas Charter); see also, 'Hamas, Introductory memorandum, Third: The political identity of Hamas' in Hroub, *Hamas*, 295.

[24] Hamas Charter; for Hamas' attitude to the Peace Process, see J. Gunning, *Hamas in politics: democracy, religion, violence* (2007) 195–240; Milton-Edwards and Farrell, *Resistance Movement*, 68–84; and M. Rabbani, 'A Hamas perspective on the movement's evolving role: and interview with Khalid Mishal, part II' (2008) 37 *Journal of Palestine Studies* 61–2 (Rabbani, *A Hamas Perspective*).

[25] 'Hamas, Introductory memorandum, Fourth: The view of Hamas on the nature of the struggle and the way to conduct it' translated in Hroub, *Hamas*, 295–6.

[26] 'Hamas Politburo Chief Khalid Mishal: remarks on Hamas Charter, President Obama, comparisons with Hizballah, and other matters, New York Times, 5 May 2009, excerpts' (2009) 38 *Journal of Palestine Studies* 215–16 (Mishal New York Times Interview); see also, J. Solomon and J. Barnes-Dacey, 'Hamas Chief Outlines Terms for Talks on Arab-Israeli Peace' *The Wall Street Journal* (31 July 2009).

Commentators underline that Hamas leaders and spokesmen have rarely referred to the Charter since its inception, and their 'language has become virtually indistinguishable from that of any freedom fighter in Latin America, South Africa, or East Asia'.[27] Since the mid-1990s Hamas has increasingly focused on the interim aim of ending Israeli occupation.[28]

Hamas' military wing, the Izzidin al-Qassam Brigade,[29] was formed in 1992 and military action increasingly became a method to pursue its political aims. In May 2010, however, it was reported that Mishal, the Hamas leader, had stated that Hamas would end its conflict with Israel if Israel withdrew to its 1967 borders.[30] In May 2011, Mahmoud Zahar, the Hamas foreign minister, stated that Hamas would be willing to accept a Palestinian State within the 1967 borders although it would not recognize Israel as this would be contrary to its aim to liberate all of Palestine.[31] In the Jordanian newspaper *al-Sabeel* in July 2010, Mishal explained that there was 'a difference between saying there is an enemy called Israel on the one hand and acknowledging its legitimacy on the other; the former is not really recognition. In short, we refuse to recognize the legitimacy of Israel because we refuse to recognize the legitimacy of occupation and theft of land'.[32]

Hamas' stated aims may be thought to contain a degree of ambiguity as although there is some acceptance of a two-State solution based on the 1967 borders, it has not renounced its claim to all of the territory of Mandate Palestine. This is consonant with its disjunction of interim and long-term aims, and rooted in its ideological position that 'the land of Palestine is an Islamic land entrusted to the Muslim generations until Judgement Day'.

3. The views of States and others on the classification of the conflict

Although Gaza was not a State, or part of a State, during the period under consideration,[33] the consequence of its occupation by Israel as a result of the Six Day War is that, in September 2000, the conflict was an international armed

---

[27] Tamimi, *A History from Within*, 147–56; also Hroub, *A Beginner's Guide*, 33–5; and Hamas Political Bureau, 'This is what we struggle for' in Tamimi, *A History from Within*, 268: 'Hamas is a national liberation movement whose military effort is directed solely and exclusively at the foreign occupiers'.

[28] Hroub, *Hamas*, 44; S. Roy, 'Religious nationalism and the Palestinian-Israeli conflict: examining Hamas and the possibility of reform' (2004) 5 *Chicago Journal of International Law* 253.

[29] For an overview of the Qassam Brigade and its activities, see Milton-Edwards and Farrell, *Resistance Movement*, 110–33.

[30] 'Hamas renews offer to end fight if Israel withdraws' *Reuters* (30 May 2010); see also, Mishal New York Times Interview, 216; and Rabbani, *A Hamas Perspective*, 80. Hroub argues that the creation of a Palestinian State in the West Bank and Gaza has been accepted as an 'interim solution' by Hamas since its creation, see Hroub, *Hamas*, 73–84.

[31] 'Hamas accepts 1967 borders, but will never recognize Israel, top official says' *Haaretz* (11 May 2011); 'Hamas leader: State on 1967 borders, but no Israel recognition' *JTA News* (11 May 2011).

[32] 'Hamas Leader Khalid Mishal: remarks on Hamas's policies, al-Sabeel, Amman, July 2010' (2010) 40 *Journal of Palestine Studies* 187 (Mishal al-Sabeel Interview).

[33] Any implications of the Palestinian attempt to seek membership of, or recognition as a State from, the UN during the 2011 session of the General Assembly, are irrelevant to the instant analysis.

conflict, subject to the provisions of the Fourth Geneva Convention.[34] The question must be addressed whether this classification changed either by virtue of Israel's disengagement from Gaza in September 2005, or by Hamas' accession of power over Gaza in June 2007.

3.1. Before disengagement (2000–2005)

3.1.1 *Israel's views*

In its First Statement to the *Sharm el-Sheikh Fact-finding Committee* (the Mitchell Commission), the Government of Israel stated that since the start of the second *intifada*:

> Israel is engaged in an armed conflict short of war. This is not a civilian disturbance or a demonstration or a riot. It is characterised by live-fire attacks on a significant scale, both quantitatively and geographically—around 2,700 such attacks over the entire area of the West Bank and the Gaza Strip. The attacks are carried out by a well-armed and organised militia, under the command of the Palestinian political establishment, operating from areas outside Israeli control.[35]

The notion of an 'armed conflict short of war' was devised by the IDF Military Advocate General's Corps to categorize the violence experienced during the second *intifada*. It was presumably intended not to correspond to either an international or a non-international armed conflict, and thus is a purported novel classification which introduces ambiguity regarding the applicable law. In 2003, Menachem Finkelstein, then IDF Military Advocate General, explained that this notion was adopted because: 'the scale and intensity of the events justifies the classification as an armed conflict. On the other hand, war is classically defined as being a conflict between the military organizations of two or more states, a condition not met in our scenario.'[36]

As 'war' is a term which has been consciously dropped from the lexicon of international law, to be replaced by the factual test of whether an armed conflict exists, it is odd to see this discredited term function as the basis for the attempted introduction of a new legal category which, moreover, has not been consistently employed by the Israeli government.[37] It also ignores the test set out in the *Tadić* jurisdiction decision in 1995 that 'an armed conflict exists whenever there is a resort

---

[34] The reasoning of the International Court of Justice in the *Wall* Advisory Opinion regarding the de jure application of the Fourth Geneva Convention to the West Bank is applicable, *mutatis mutandis*, to Gaza, as both Israel and Egypt were parties to the Fourth Geneva Convention at the time when Gaza was occupied; see *Legal Consequences of the Construction of a Wall in the Occupied Palestinian Territory* (Advisory Opinion) ICJ Rep 2004, 136, 173–7, paras 90–101 (*Wall* Advisory Opinion).

[35] Sharm el-Sheikh Fact-finding Committee, 'First Statement of the Government of Israel' (28 December 2000) para 282.

[36] M. Finkelstein, 'Legal perspective in the fight against terror—the Israeli experience' (2003) 1 *IDF Law Review* 343–4: note omitted (Finkelstein, *Israeli Experience*).

[37] See the arguments presented by the Israeli government on the nature of the conflict in *Public Committee against Torture in Israel et al v Government of Israel et al*, High Court of Justice, Israel, HCJ 796/02 (13 December 2006) (*Targeted Killing* case)—discussed below.

to armed force between States or protracted armed violence between governmental authorities and organized armed groups or between such groups within a State'.[38]

One may also question if this attempt to reconceptualize the nature of the conflict was necessary. The Palestinian territories, including Gaza, were undoubtedly under Israeli occupation at this time, as the Israeli High Court had expressly affirmed.[39] Israel would consequently have been justified in treating the situation as an international armed conflict. The *intifada* did not give rise to the issue of whether the conflict should be reclassified, but rather called for the formulation of appropriate rules of engagement by the IDF. Further, the party opposing Israel in this 'armed conflict short of war' was claimed to be 'neither the Palestinian people nor the Palestinian Authority . . . [but] only those organizations and individuals involved in terror activities'.[40] This has been a constant Israeli refrain. Thus during the prosecution of Operation Cast Lead, it claimed: 'The targets of this operation are the terrorists and their infrastructure alone. We are not at war with the Palestinian people, but with Hamas and other terrorist groups in Gaza . . . The people of Gaza do not deserve to suffer because of the killers and murderers of the terrorist organizations.'[41]

Although this identifies diverse groups as forming the adverse party to Israel in the Gaza conflict, the inclusion of groups other than Hamas is, perhaps, of a secondary nature. Indeed, Israel places emphasis on the conflict with Hamas, and appears to ascribe to Hamas responsibility for all attacks which emanate from Gaza, either directly or indirectly through a failure to prevent attacks by others. For example, when the Israeli Security Cabinet declared that Hamas was 'hostile territory' in September 2007, it stated: 'The responsibility for this determination lies squarely with Hamas, which controls the Gaza Strip and supports and encourages the ongoing terrorist activity emanating from that area.'[42]

This gives reason to focus the question of classification on the Israel-Hamas conflict to the exclusion of other groups hostile to Israel.

In any event, although the Israeli government has appeared to vacillate regarding the precise classification of the conflict since the start of the second intifada in September 2000—whether it has been international, non-international, or some new variant of conflict which is perhaps akin to a 'war on terror'—it was nonetheless clear that it had been engaged in an armed conflict in its own and in the occupied Palestinian territories.

---

[38] *Prosecutor v Tadić*, IT-94-1-AR72, Decision on the Defence Motion for Interlocutory Appeal on Jurisdiction (Appeals Chamber) 2 October 1995, para 70 (*Tadić* Jurisdiction).

[39] See e.g. *Ajuri v IDF Commander*, HCJ 7015/02 (3 September 2002), opinion of President Barak, para 22.

[40] Finkelstein, *Israeli Experience*, 344.

[41] S/PV.6060, Security Council meeting (31 December 2008), remarks by Shalev (Israel) 6 (SC 6060th meeting); see also, identical letters dated 27 December 2008 from the Permanent Representative of Israel (Shalev) to the Secretary-General and President of the Security Council, S/2008/816 (27 December 2008); and identical letters dated 6 January 2009 from the Permanent Representative of Israel (Shalev) to the Secretary-General and President of the Security Council, S/2009/6 (6 January 2009).

[42] MFA, *Gaza Designated as Hostile Territory.*

At times, this rather ambiguous position has been endorsed by Israel's Supreme Court, sitting as the High Court of Justice: for instance in January 2008 in *Jaber al Bassouini Ahmed et al v Prime Minister and Minister of Defense*, the Court referred only to an 'armed conflict' without clarifying whether it was an international or a non-international armed conflict.[43] Gisha, one of the non-governmental organizations (NGOs) which presented the petition in the *al Bassouini* case, observed that this was a 'dramatic departure' from the Court's earlier jurisprudence which had applied the law of occupation to Gaza and the West Bank. In ruling on the issue presented, whether the reduction of the fuel and electricity supply to Gaza planned by the military would cause a humanitarian crisis, Gisha reported that the Court curtailed argument on the question of the applicable law, and pressed the petitioners to address the factual question only.[44]

On the other hand, in a subsequent case arising from events alleged to have occurred during Operation Cast Lead, the Court ruled:

> The normative framework that applies to the armed conflict between the State of Israel and Hamas is complex. It centers around international legal rules regarding armed conflicts of an international nature (international armed conflict). Although classification of the armed conflict between the State of Israel and Hamas as an international conflict gives rise to a number of difficulties, we have treated this conflict as an international armed conflict in a series of judgments.

Further the Court accepted that, during Operation Cast Lead, the law of belligerent occupation might also apply to Gaza as 'the application of the laws of occupation under international humanitarian law is conditional upon the potential to exercise governmental authority in a territory following the entry of military forces, and not necessarily upon practical exercise of such authority by them'. It did not, however, reach a definitive ruling on this point, as the Israeli government had agreed that 'the humanitarian laws relevant to the petition apply'.[45] These included provisions of the Fourth Geneva Convention.

3.1.2 Hamas' views

No statement which clearly formulates Hamas' position on how the conflict should be classified under international law has been found. It sees itself as a national liberation movement 'that struggles for the liberation of the Palestinian occupied territories and for the recognition of Palestinian legitimate rights'.[46] In a 1996

[43] *Jaber al Bassouini Ahmed et al v Prime Minister and Minister of Defense*, HCJ 9132/07 (30 January 2008), opinion of President Beinisch, para 12 (*Al Bassouini* case).
[44] Gisha, 'Briefing: Israeli High Court decision authorizing fuel and electricity cuts to Gaza (HCJ 9132/07, issued 30 January 2008)' (31 January 2008).
[45] *Physicians for Human Rights and others v Prime Minister and others, and joined case*, HCJ 201/09, 248/09 (19 January 2009), opinion of Chief Justice Beinisch, para 14, translated in *Oxford Reports on International Law in Domestic Courts* (*ILDC*) 1213 (IL 2009) (*Physicians for Human Rights* case).
[46] Hamas Political Bureau, 'This is what we struggle for' in Tamimi, *A History from Within*, 265; see also, Hamas Political Bureau, 'The Islamic Resistance Movement (Hamas)' in Tamimi, *A History from Within*, 279–80.

memorandum presented to a conference at Sharm al-Sheikh, Hamas claimed that 'international law and conventions give to every individual and group, especially those falling under military occupation by a foreign power, the right to self-defence with every available means'.[47]

3.2. Israel's disengagement from Gaza (2005 onwards)

3.2.1 *Israel's views*

The jurisprudence of Israel's High Court, for example in the *Ajuri* case, as well as the arrangements made for Israel's disengagement make it clear that, before the implementation of the Revised Disengagement Plan in August 2005, Israel considered that Gaza was territory occupied by Israel. Indeed, in cases brought by Israeli settlers in Gaza immediately before disengagement which sought review of the government's plan, the Israeli government argued and the High Court affirmed that it was occupied territory.[48]

When Prime Minister Sharon announced the initial 16 April 2004 Disengagement Plan, article 2 provided that the completion of withdrawal entailed that there would be 'no permanent Israeli civilian or military presence' in the evacuated areas, and therefore there would 'be no basis for the claim that the Gaza Strip is occupied territory'.[49] This express reference to Gaza as 'occupied territory' was deleted in the 6 June 2004 Revised Disengagement Plan which was approved by the Cabinet. Its primary implication was set out in Principle Six (Political and Security Implications), which provided that the 'completion of the plan will serve to dispel the claims regarding Israel's responsibility for the Palestinians within the Gaza Strip'.[50]

Israel has claimed that its evacuation of Gaza had the consequence that as there was no longer any permanent presence of Israeli security forces within Gaza:[51] 'From this point on, the full responsibility for events occurring in the Gaza Strip and for thwarting terror attacks against Israeli targets will be in the hands of the Palestinian Authority and its apparatuses.'[52]

Consequently, the IDF Chief of Southern Command, Major-General Dan Harel, promulgated a decree proclaiming the end of military rule in Gaza and annulling the 6 June 1967 proclamation which had originally instituted military rule.[53]

---

[47] Hamas, 'An important memorandum from the Islamic Resistance Movement (Hamas) to the Kings, Presidents, and Ministers meeting at Sharm al-Sheikh' (13 March 1996), translated in Hroub, *Hamas*, 307.

[48] See *Matar and others v The Commander of the Israeli Defence Force in Gaza*, *ILDC* 73 (IL 2005) para 7; and also *Nango and others v Israel and others*, HCJ 05/7918, *ILDC* 156 (IL 2005) para H1.

[49] Prime Minister's Office, 'Disengagement Plan' (16 April 2004).

[50] Revised Disengagement Plan.

[51] Ibid, section 2(A), art. 3.1.

[52] IDF, Declaration regarding end of military rule in Gaza Strip (12 September 2005), available at: <www.mfa.gov.il/MFA/Government/Communiques/2005/Exit+of+IDF+Forces+from+the+Gaza+Strip+completed+12-Sep-2005.htm> (IDF, Declaration of 12 September 2005).

[53] Ibid.

The view that Israel had relinquished control over and responsibility for Gaza and its population was endorsed by Israel's High Court in January 2008 in the *al Bassiouni* case, in which the petitioners challenged Israel's restrictions on the supply of electricity and gas to Gaza. In this decision, the Court relied on the government of Israel's assertion that it was no longer in effective control of Gaza, and thus no longer occupied the territory. The Court ruled:

> since September 2005 Israel no longer has effective control over what happens in the Gaza Strip. Military rule that applied in the past in this territory came to an end by a decision of the government, and Israeli soldiers are no longer stationed in the territory on a permanent basis, nor are they in charge of what happens there. In these circumstances, the State of Israel does not have a general duty to ensure the welfare of the residents of the Gaza Strip or to maintain public order in the Gaza Strip according to the laws of belligerent occupation in international law. Neither does Israel have any effective capability, in its present position, of enforcing order and managing civilian life in the Gaza Strip. In the prevailing circumstances, the main obligations of the State of Israel relating to the residents of the Gaza Strip derive from the state of armed conflict that exists between it and the Hamas organization that controls the Gaza Strip; these obligations also derive from the degree of control exercised by the State of Israel over the border crossings between it and the Gaza Strip, as well as from the relationship that was created between Israel and the territory of the Gaza Strip after the years of Israeli military rule in the territory, as a result of which the Gaza Strip is currently almost completely dependent upon the supply of electricity from Israel.[54]

This view was endorsed in the Turkel Commission Report on the interception of the Mavi Marmara flotilla.[55]

Nevertheless, although Israel's High Court affirmed that disengagement had terminated the occupation of Gaza, this appears to have had no impact on its view that the continuing conflict should be classified as an international armed conflict. Post-disengagement, in the *Targeted Killing* case, Israel's Supreme Court made its definitive ruling on the nature of the conflict between Israel and hostile Palestinian elements. In the leading opinion, President Emeritus Barak emphasized, in his summary of the respondents' arguments, that:

> 10. . . . Respondents' [ie, the Government of Israel *et al*] stance is that the question whether the laws of belligerent occupation apply to all of the territory in the area is not relevant to the issue at hand, as the question whether the targeted killings policy is legal will be decided according to the laws of war, which apply both to occupied territory and to territory which is not occupied, as long as armed conflict is taking place on it.

> 11. Respondents' position is that . . . there is no longer any doubt that an armed conflict can exist between a state and groups and organizations which are not states . . . Regarding

[54] *Al Bassiouni* case, para 12; affirmed *Anbar et al v GOC Southern Command et al* and *Adalah et al v Minister of Defence et al*, HCJ 5268/08 and HCJ 5399/08 (9 December 2009) para 6. For commentary, see Y. Dinstein, *The international law of belligerent occupation* (2009) 278–9 (Dinstein, *Belligerent Occupation*); and Y. Shany, 'The law applicable to non-occupied Gaza', paper delivered at the *Complementing IHL: exploring the need for additional norms to govern contemporary conflict situations* conference (Jerusalem, 1–3 June 2008).

[55] The Turkel Commission Report, 50–3, paras 45–7.

the classification of the conflict, respondents originally argued that it is an international armed conflict, to which the usual laws of war apply. In their summary response (of January 26 2004), respondents claim that the question of the classification of the conflict between Israel and the Palestinians is a complicated question, with characteristics that point in different directions. In any case, there is no need to decide that question in order to decide the petition. That is because according to all of the classifications, the laws of armed conflict will apply to the acts of the State. These laws allow striking at persons who are party to the armed conflict and take an active part in it, whether it is an international or non-international armed conflict, and even if it belongs to a new category of armed conflict which has been developing over the last decade in international law—a category of armed conflicts between states and terrorist organizations . . . [56]

The premise of President Emeritus Barak's opinion was that 'between Israel and the various terrorist organizations active in Judea, Samaria, and the Gaza Strip . . . a continuous situation of armed conflict has existed since the first intifada'.[57] He ruled that although the normative system regulating this armed conflict was complex, the situation amounted to an international armed conflict: 'the fact that the terrorist organizations and their members do not act in the name of a state does not turn the struggle against them into a purely internal state conflict'.[58] President Emeritus Barak thus emphatically rejected the respondents' revised plea that it was difficult to classify the nature of the conflict ruling, 'for years the starting point of the Supreme Court—and also of the State's counsel before the Supreme Court—is that the armed conflict is of an international character. In this judgment we continue to rule on the basis of that view'.[59]

This ruling was expressly reaffirmed by Chief Justice Beinisch in the case brought by Physicians for Human Rights during Operation Cast Lead.[60]

Before the Turkel Committee, the Israeli Military Advocate-General gave evidence on the difficulty of classifying the conflict between Israel and Hamas, and testified that 'after Operation Cast Lead, Israel adopted the position that it is bound by the laws of war that apply to both international armed conflict and non-international armed conflict'.[61] The Report concluded that 'there is a consensus that the conflict between the State of Israel and the Hamas is an international armed conflict, although the reasons that have led various parties to this conclusion vary'.[62]

3.2.2 Hamas' views

It is difficult to discern Hamas' view on whether disengagement terminated the occupation, or had any implications for the classification of the conflict from the standpoint of international law. On the one hand, Mishal has stated that 'resistance . . . has succeeded in driving the occupiers out of southern Lebanon and Gaza',[63] but virtually in the same breath talked about 'our legitimate right to resist

---

[56] *Targeted Killing* case, paras 10–11.   [57] Ibid, para 16.   [58] Ibid, para 21.
[59] Ibid, para 21.   [60] *Physicians for Human Rights* case, para 14.
[61] The Turkel Commission Report, 46–7, para 40.
[62] Ibid, 47, para 41; see also, 49–50, para 44.
[63] Mishal al-Sabeel Interview, 189.

occupation and aggression'.[64] In 2009, however, he stated 'Israel is practicing the occupation. Israel is controlling every aspect of Palestinian life. Israel is imposing the siege'.[65] Nevertheless, as these statements were all made during newspaper interviews, one should perhaps not place much reliance upon them.

3.2.3 Views of other States

During Operation Cast Lead, it appears that a majority of States considered Gaza still to be occupied, despite Israel's disengagement and Hamas' seizure of power in Gaza in June 2007. In the relevant Security Council debates, a number of States expressed this opinion, and a statement to that effect was made on behalf of the 118 member States of the Non-Aligned Movement.[66] This represents the view of the majority of States (including the United Kingdom),[67] and is shared by the UN Secretary-General,[68] the Human Rights Council,[69] and the Chairman of the Committee on the Exercise of the Inalienable Rights of the Palestinian People.[70] This was also the view of the International Fact-Finding Mission established following the operation.[71] It is perhaps significant that this position was not disputed during these Security Council meetings, or during the parallel debates in the General Assembly.[72] Further, before both bodies a majority of States called upon Israel to apply the Fourth Geneva Convention in its dealings with Gaza:[73]

---

[64] Ibid, 188–90.

[65] Mishal New York Times Interview, 216; see also, Rabbani, *A Hamas Perspective*, 68: 'our conviction that the Palestinian situation is not normal because we are not a state but under occupation', and ibid, 80: 'our real political objective is not a cease-fire but rather ending the occupation' (quoting Mishal).

[66] SC 6060th meeting, remarks by representatives of Palestine (4, 5), Libya (7, 8), South Africa (9), Costa Rica (16), Egypt (18, 19); SC 6061st meeting, remarks by representatives of Palestine (5), Libya (12, 13), League of Arab States (24–6), Egypt (28), Jordan (29–30), Lebanon (31), Morocco (32), Qatar (33); S/PV.6061(Resumption 1), Security Council meeting (7 January 2009), remarks by representatives of Malaysia (3), Cuba, on behalf of member States of the Non-Aligned Movement (4), Pakistan (9–10), Iran (12), Nicaragua (14), Ecuador (16), Bolivia (17) (SC 6061st meeting, Resumption 1); and S/PV.6063, Security Council meeting (8 January 2009), remarks by representative of Palestine (10).

[67] See Foreign and Commonwealth Office, 'Annual Report on Human Rights 2008' Cm 7557 (March 2009) 149: 'Although there is no permanent physical Israeli presence in Gaza, given the significant control Israel has over Gaza's borders, airspace and territorial waters, Israel retains obligations as an occupying power under the Fourth Geneva Convention.'

[68] SC 6060th meeting, remarks by UN Secretary-General (4).

[69] HRC res. S-9/1, A/HRC/RES/S-9-1 (12 January 2009).

[70] SC 6061st meeting, Resumption 1, remarks by Badji (Chairman of the Committee on the Exercise of the Inalienable Rights of the Palestinian People) 11.

[71] The Goldstone Report, 85, paras 276–7. This assessment was expressly re-affirmed in The Hudson-Phillips Report, 15, paras 62–4.

[72] See General Assembly Plenary, Tenth Emergency Special Session, 32nd and 33rd meetings, GA/10807 (15 January 2009) (Dept of Public Information summary), and General Assembly Plenary, Tenth Emergency Special Session, 34th and 35th meetings, GA/10809/Rev.1* (16 January 2009) (Dept of Public Information summary).

[73] SC 6060th meeting, remarks by representatives of Burkina Faso (15), Costa Rica (16), Egypt (18), League of Arab States (19); SC 6061st meeting, remarks by representatives of Vietnam (15), Mexico (20), Jordan (28); and SC 6061st meeting, Resumption 1, remarks by representatives of Cuba, on behalf of the member States of the Non-Aligned Movement (4), Pakistan (10), and Nicaragua (13).

again, no State contested this claim. Both the Goldstone Report and Hudson-Phillips Report also affirmed that, as occupant of Gaza, Israel was bound by the provisions of the Fourth Geneva Convention.[74]

3.3. Hamas' accession to power in Gaza (2007)

Assuming, for the moment, that the occupation of Gaza was not terminated by Israeli disengagement, did the disintegration of the Fatah-Hamas unity government in 2007 and Hamas' assumption of power within Gaza make a change in this respect?

In a meeting between the US Ambassador to Israel and the Israeli Military Intelligence Director Yadlin on 13 June 2007, as the conflict between Hamas and Fatah was nearing its close:

> The [US] Ambassador commented that if Fatah decided it has lost Gaza, there would be calls for Abbas to set up a separate regime in the West Bank. While not necessarily reflecting a consensus GOI [Government of Israel] view, Yadlin commented that such a development would please Israel since it would enable the IDF to treat Gaza as a hostile country rather than having to deal with Hamas as a non-State actor.[75]

In due course the Israeli Security Cabinet did exactly that, with its designation of Gaza as 'hostile territory' on 19 September 2007, although it described this as 'a factual (rather than legal) description of the region controlled by Hamas'.[76] Further, on 8 December 2008, shortly before the launch of Operation Cast Lead on 27 December, Yadlin met with Representative Wexler, who was part of a US congressional delegation. Yadlin stated that the Palestinians had established two entities, one in the West Bank which was supported by Israel, and the other constituting a terrorist entity in Gaza.[77] This division between Gaza and the other occupied Palestinian territories was maintained by Israel before the Security Council during debates on Operation Cast Lead, when its representative, Shalev, stated that '[a]s long as Hamas rules Gaza, rejecting the Quartet principles and seeking Israel's destruction, Gaza can never be part of a Palestinian State'.[78]

In the General Assembly, Tenth Emergency Special Session, 32nd and 33rd meetings, GA/10807 (15 January 2009), the application of the Fourth Convention was demanded by Brockmann (GA President), Cuba, on behalf of the Non-Aligned Movement, and Algeria, and in the 34th and 35th meetings (GA/10809/Rev.1*) by Venezuela, Kuwait, Burkina Faso and Afghanistan.

[74] The Goldstone Report, 85, para 276; The Hudson-Phillips Report, 15, paras 62–3.
[75] 'Military Intelligence Director Yadlin comments on Gaza, Syria and Lebanon' cable from the US Embassy in Tel Aviv, 07TELAVIV1733 (13 June 2007) para 6, available at: <http://wikileaks.ch/cable/2007/06/07TELAVIV1733.html>.
[76] MFA, *Gaza Designated as Hostile Territory*. For commentary, see C. James, 'Mere words: the "enemy entity" designation of the Gaza Strip' (2009) 32 *Hastings International and Comparative Law Review* 643.
[77] 'CODEL Wexler's meeting with Military Intelligence Chief Yadlin' cable from the US Embassy in Tel Aviv, 08TELAVIV2745 (8 December 2008), available at: <http://files.vpro.nl/wikileaks/date/2008-12_0.html>.
[78] SC 6061st meeting, remarks by Israel (8).

To some extent, the two entity view has been reflected by others. For example, the 2009 House of Commons Foreign Affairs Committee report, *Global security: Israel and the occupied Palestinian territories*, concluded that 'the Israeli-Palestinian conflict must now be understood as essentially a three-way situation, comprising Israel, the West Bank and the Palestinian Authority, and Gaza and Hamas'.[79] On the other hand, this view was disputed during Security Council debates on Operation Cast Lead; for example, the representative of Qatar stated that Palestinian national differences should not be used 'as an excuse to divide the Palestinian people and Palestinian land'.[80] This view of the unity of the Palestine territories was reflected in Security Council resolution 1860 (2009) which called for a cessation of the hostilities. The second preambular paragraph of this resolution stressed 'that the Gaza Strip constitutes an integral part of the territory occupied by Israel in 1967 and will be a part of the Palestinian State'.[81]

4. Author's analysis of the classification of the conflict (September 2000–March 2011)

At least until its disengagement from Gaza in September 2005, Israel was clearly the belligerent occupant of Gaza, and the law of international armed conflict therefore applied. While Gaza is not of course a State, the fact of belligerent occupation leads to this result. The legal implications of Israel's disengagement are, however, contested. Israel claims that because it no longer maintains a permanent military presence in Gaza, it is no longer the belligerent occupant of Gaza and has, as expressly intended by the Disengagement Plan, no remaining responsibilities for its population. This is disputed by other international actors. Even after the accession to power of Hamas, Israel's claim that it no longer occupies Gaza has not been accepted by UN bodies, most States, nor the majority of academic commentators, because of its exclusive control of its border with Gaza and crossing points, including the effective control it exerted over the Rafah crossing until at least May 2011, its control of Gaza's maritime zones and airspace, which constitute what Aronson terms the 'security envelope' around Gaza,[82] as well as its ability to intervene forcibly at will in Gaza.[83]

---

[79] House of Commons, *Global Security*, 58, para 127.

[80] SC 6061st meeting, 34; see also, ibid, remarks by Palestine (5) and Egypt (28).

[81] The unity of the territories was also recognized by the Human Rights Council which, in the final stages of Operation Cast Lead, adopted resolution S-9/1 on 12 January 2009. This referred to the 'ongoing Israeli military operation in the Occupied Palestinian Territory, particularly in the occupied Gaza Strip', and to Israel as the occupying power.

[82] G. Aronson, 'Issues arising from the implementation of Israel's disengagement from the Gaza Strip' (2005) 34 *Journal of Palestine Studies* 51–3.

[83] For a range of views, see e.g. E. Benvenisti, 'The law on the unilateral termination of occupation' in T. Giegerich and U. Heinz U (eds), *A wiser century? Judicial dispute settlement, disarmament and the laws of war 100 years after the Second Hague Peace Conference* (2009); A. Bockel, 'Le retrait israelien de Gaza et ses consequences sur le droit international' (2005) 51 *Annuaire français de droit international* 16; S. Darcy and J. Reynolds, '"Otherwise occupied": the status of the Gaza Strip from the perspective

This controversy must be addressed. If, as Israel contends, disengagement terminated occupation, then presumably the conflict should be classified as a non-international armed conflict because, during the period under consideration, Gaza (and a fortiori Hamas) was not a State. If, on the other hand, disengagement failed legally to terminate the occupation, then the conflict between Israel and Gaza should continue to be classified as an international armed conflict, subject to the provisions of the Fourth Geneva Convention, rather than adopting the studied ambiguity of 'armed conflict short of war' preferred by the IDF.

4.1. Withdrawal of troops leading to termination of occupation?

There are possible objections to classification of the situation as one of occupation. It has been argued[84] that, by virtue of the physical withdrawal of its ground troops, Israel relinquished effective control of Gaza and thus terminated the occupation. Article 42 of the Hague Regulations provides that '[t]erritory is considered occupied when it is actually placed under the authority of the hostile army. The occupation extends only to the territory where such authority has been established and can be exercised'.

The issue, however, is not the creation of an occupation, which as a practical matter would appear to require the use of ground forces to create and maintain control, but whether an existing occupation was terminated by disengagement. This might well involve different considerations, as the conditions required to end an occupation are not as clearly delineated in the governing instruments as those which determine whether and when an occupation has been established. As von Glahn comments, 'most books on international law make little mention of the intricate and numerous problems arising at the end of ... military occupation'.[85]

Traditionally, the test for the termination of an occupation was seen as a simple question of fact. 'Occupation comes to an end when an occupant withdraws from a territory, or is driven out of it':[86]

---

of international humanitarian law' (2010) 15 *Journal of Conflict and Security Law* 211 (2010); Dinstein, *Belligerent Occupation*, 276–80; H.-P. Gasser, 'Notes on the law of belligerent occupation' (2006) 45 *Military Law and Law of War Review* 233–4; M. Mari, 'The Israeli disengagement from the Gaza Strip: an end of the occupation?' (2005) 8 *Yearbook of International Humanitarian Law* 356; E. Samson, 'Is Gaza occupied? Redefining the legal status of Gaza' (2010) 83 *Mideast Security and Policy Studies*; I. Scobbie, 'An intimate disengagement: Israel's withdrawal from Gaza, the law of occupation and of self-determination' (2004) 11 *Yearbook of Islamic and Middle Eastern Law* 3, reprinted in V. Kattan (ed.), *The Palestine question in international law* (2008) 637; and Y. Shany, 'Binary law meets complex reality: the occupation of Gaza debate' (2008) 41 *Israel Law Review* 68.

[84] See e.g. Y. Shany, 'Faraway, so close: the legal status of Gaza after Israel's disengagement' (2006) 8 *Yearbook of International Humanitarian Law* 369.

[85] G. von Glahn, *The occupation of enemy territory: a commentary on the law and practice of belligerent occupation* (1957) 257 (Von Glahn, *The occupation of enemy territory*); see also, A. Roberts, 'The end of occupation: Iraq 2005' (2005) 54 *International and Comparative Law Quarterly* 27 (Roberts, *Iraq 2005*).

[86] L. Oppenheim, *International law: a treatise, Vol. II* (7th edn, 1952) 436 (Oppenheim, *International Law*); see also, W. Heintschel von Heinegg, 'Factors in war to peace transitions' (2003) 27 *Harvard Journal of Law and Public Policy* 845: 'The end of an occupation is a question of fact. It will be brought about by any loss of authority over the territory in question.'

the moment the invader voluntarily evacuates [occupied] territory, or is driven away by a *levée en masse*, or by troops of the other belligerent, or of his ally, the former condition of things *ipso facto* revives. The territory and individuals affected are at once, so far as International Law is concerned, considered again to be under the sway of their legitimate sovereign.[87]

The assumption embedded in this test is that occupation terminates when authority passes back into the hands of the displaced sovereign. This must be a genuine transfer and not simply a pretence which masks a retention of authority by the occupant. To employ Roberts' phrase, 'it is the reality not the label that counts',[88] since 'the withdrawal of occupying forces is not the sole criterion of the ending of an occupation; and the occupant has not necessarily withdrawn at the end of all occupations'.[89]

As Oppenheim observes, the requirement in article 42 that occupation extends only to the territory where the adversary's authority 'has been established and can be exercised' is 'not at all precise', but that when an occupant is able to assert authority over territory 'it matters not with what means, and in what ways, his authority is exercised'.[90] The test is one of effective control, and von Glahn considers that an occupation might be maintained through the control of the adversary's airspace: 'Since international law does not contain a rule prescribing the military arm through which an effective belligerent occupation is to be exercised, it might be theoretically possible to maintain necessary control through the occupant's air force alone'.[91]

Once an occupation is established, is there any reason why effective control could not be maintained through aerial warfare? Indeed, the importance of air power was stressed by Major General Amos Yadlin in 2004 after he became head of Israeli military intelligence. An Israeli air force officer, he stated: 'Our vision of air control zeroes in on the notion of control. We're looking at how you control a city or a territory from the air when it's no longer legitimate to hold or occupy that territory on the ground.'[92]

To regard Israel's withdrawal of ground troops from Gaza as determinative is to ignore the implications which might flow from Israel's continued control of Gaza's airspace which in itself could give reason to argue that this disengagement was insufficient to terminate the occupation.

4.2. Inability to carry out obligations of occupier?

It has been argued, and affirmed by Israel's High Court in the *Al Bassiouni* case,[93] that, by the act of disengagement, Israel divested itself of the responsibility to

---

[87] Oppenheim, *International Law*, 618.
[88] Roberts, *Iraq 2005*, 47.   [89] Ibid, 28.
[90] Oppenheim, *International Law*, 435.
[91] Von Glahn, *The Occupation of Enemy Territory*, 28–9.
[92] Quoted in D. Li, 'The Gaza Strip as laboratory: notes in the wake of disengagement' (2006) 35 *Journal of Palestine Studies* 48.
[93] *Al Bassiouni* case, para 12.

ensure 'public order and civil life' in Gaza—the primordial obligation of an occupant under article 43 of the Hague Regulations[94]—and thus unilaterally terminated the occupation. But although an occupant has the legal duty to establish an administration in territory it occupies, today this 'is the rare exception rather than the rule'.[95] Thus, in the *Armed Activities* case, Judge Kooijmans noted in his separate opinion: 'Occupants feel more and more inclined to make use of arrangements where authority is said to be exercised by transitional governments or rebel movements or where the occupant simply refrains from establishing an administrative system.'[96] Just because an occupant fails to fulfil its duties as occupant does not deprive it of that status, as Israel's High Court has itself recognized:

> application of Chapter 3 of the Hague Regulations and application of the parallel provisions of the Fourth [Geneva] Convention are not conditional upon the set-up of a special organizational system taking the form of military government. The obligations and powers of a military force which stem from its effective seizure of territory exist and come into being due to the very fact of military seizure of the territory, ie, even if the military force only effects control via its ordinary combat units.[97]

4.3. Israel's continuing control

Before disengagement, as a consequence of the 1995 Israel-PLO Interim Agreement on the West Bank and Gaza Strip, Israel devolved responsibility for the maintenance of 'public order and civil life' to a transitional government, namely, the Palestinian Authority. The authors of the Fourth Geneva Convention had envisaged that a transfer of competence to local authorities could occur during a prolonged occupation, without terminating that occupation.[98] The Interim Agreement envisaged the creation of the Palestinian Interim Self-Government Authority (styled 'the Council' in the Agreement), but provided that pending its establishment, its powers were to be exercised by the Palestinian Authority.[99] Article I(1)

---

[94] Following Schwenk, it is submitted that 'public order and civil life' is a more accurate translation of the key phrase 'l'ordre et la vie publics' in the authoritative French text of art. 43 than the more commonly used phrase 'public order and safety'. See E. Schwenk, 'Legislative power of the military occupant under Article 43, Hague Regulations' (1944) 54 *Yale Law Journal* 393 fn 1 and 398. This mistranslation has also been noted by Israel's High Court, see *Christian Society for the Holy Places v Minister of Defence and others*, 52 *International Law Reports* 512, opinion of Deputy President Sussman at 513–14.

[95] See E. Benvenisti, *The International Law of Occupation* (1993) 4–5: also UK Ministry of Defence, *The Manual of the Law of Armed Conflict* (2005) 276, para 11(3)(1) (UK *Manual*); *Prosecutor v Tadić*, IT-94-1-T, Judgment (Trial Chamber), 7 May 1997, 204–5, para 584; and *Prosecutor v Blaškić*, IT-95-14-T, Judgment (Trial Chamber), 3 March 2000, 51, para 149.

[96] *Case Concerning Armed Activities on the Territory of the Congo (Democratic Republic of the Congo v Uganda)* ICJ Rep 2005, 168, separate opinion of Judge Kooijmans, 306 at 317, para 41.

[97] *Tzemel v Minister of Defence*, HCJ 102/82, (1982) 37(3) PD 365 at 373, quoted with approval in *Physicians for Human Rights* case, para 14.

[98] See J. Pictet (ed.), *Commentary to Geneva Convention IV Relative to the Protection of Civilian Persons in Time of War* (1958) 62–3 (commentary to art. 6), and 272–6 (commentary to art. 47).

[99] 1995 Interim Agreement, art. I(2) provides:

> Pending the inauguration of the Council, the powers and responsibilities transferred to the Council shall be exercised by the Palestinian Authority established in accordance with the

provided that powers and responsibilities which were not transferred by the Agreement to the Palestinian Authority would continue to be exercised by Israel, while the latter expressly retained 'the responsibility for protecting the Egyptian and Jordanian borders, and for defense against external threats from the sea and from the air'.[100]

Given Israel's continuing control over its border with Gaza, as well as over Gaza's airspace and maritime zones, it is submitted that disengagement did not radically alter the overall structure of control created by the Interim Agreement, which itself had not terminated the occupation. The re-opening of the Rafah crossing has not affected the preponderance of Israel's control over Gaza to any significant extent, as it allows only the passage of restricted classes of people, and not the passage of goods. If the fundamental elements of control which are associated with occupation were not terminated by disengagement, this entails a failure to achieve the aim which was ostensibly intended. Although Hamas replaced the Palestinian Authority as the effective government in Gaza in June 2007, this should be seen as only a functional substitution which did not alter the realities of continued Israeli overall control.

Further, in the *List* case, the US Military Tribunal at Nuremberg, when considering the effect of resistance to occupation, ruled:

> While it is true that the partisans were able to control sections of these countries [Greece, Yugoslavia and Norway] at various times, it is established that the Germans could at any time they desired assume physical control of any part of the country. The control of the resistance forces was temporary only and did not deprive the German Armed Forces of its status of an occupant.[101]

The view that effective occupation could lie in the *capacity* to assert control was also affirmed by the ICTY in *Prosecutor v Naletilić and Martinović* where it ruled that one of the guidelines to determine whether an occupation was established was whether 'the occupying power has a sufficient force present, or the capacity to send troops within a reasonable time to make the authority of the occupying power felt'.[102] Israeli land forces have re-entered Gaza on numerous occasions since disengagement, and it has therefore, in the terms of the *List* formula, demonstrated that, albeit with effort, it 'could at any time [it] desired assume physical control of any part of the country'.[103]

Gaza-Jericho Agreement, which shall also have all the rights, liabilities and obligations to be assumed by the Council in this regard. Accordingly, the term 'Council' throughout this Agreement shall, pending the inauguration of the Council, be construed as meaning the Palestinian Authority.

[100] 1995 Interim Agreement, art. XII(1); see further Annex I, Protocol Concerning Redeployment and Security Arrangements, art. XIII (Security of the Airspace) para 4, which provides in part '[a]ll aviation activity or use of the airspace by any aerial vehicle in the West Bank and the Gaza Strip shall require prior approval of Israel...' and art. XIV (Security along the Coastline of the Sea of Gaza).

[101] *Trial of Wilhelm List and others* (the *Hostages* trial) (1949) VIII *Law Reports of Trials of War Criminals* 55–6, quotation at 56.

[102] *Prosecutor v Naletilić and Martinović*, IT-98-34-T, Judgment (Trial Chamber), 31 March 2003.

[103] For a survey of Israel's operations within Gaza from disengagement to Operation Cast Lead, see 'Israeli military operations against Gaza, 2000–2008' (2009) 38 *Journal of Palestine Studies* 133–8.

Moreover, unless occupation continued, it would be counter-intuitive that States should demand that Israel itself provide humanitarian aid in Gaza, especially at the height of an active conflict, and a loosening of the terrestrial 'blockade' it had imposed.[104] Although some argue that an occupant owes post-occupation human-itarian obligations where territory has become dependent upon it as the result of occupation,[105] in the circumstances, Dinstein's view appears to be better. He commented, 'the notion that a Belligerent Party in wartime is in duty bound to supply electricity and fuel to its enemy is plainly absurd. The sole reason for the existence of an obligation to ensure such supplies for the benefit of the civilian population—even at a minimal level—is that the occupation is not over'.[106]

The issue of whether Gaza was still occupied following the disengagement remains controversial but it is submitted that Israel did not relinquish control of Gaza in August 2005, but simply withdrew, or redeployed, the most visible aspect of its control—the stationing of troops within Gaza. Israel remains in occupation.

The key to this conundrum might lie in Israel's position, expressed since the formulation of its 'armed conflict short of war' doctrine, and made before the Security Council,[107] that the conflict in Gaza obtains between Israel and the armed organizations ranged against it, and not with the Palestinian population as a whole. The existence of parallel conflicts cannot be ruled out conceptually:[108] for example, in an international armed conflict between States, one could simultaneously be engaged in a conflict with local forces which are not aligned to the opposing State party and thus be engaged in both an international and a non-international armed conflict.

In the case of Gaza, it may be argued that, on the one hand, the occupation, and thus an international armed conflict, persists as the over-arching legal structure between Israel and Gaza, and in particular in relation to the obligations Israel owes to the Gazan population *qua* occupier. On the other hand, a separate and distinct

---

[104] See e.g. Letter from the Permanent Representative of France to the President of the Security Council on behalf of the EU, S/2008/841 (31 December 2008); Letter from the Permanent Representative of Qatar to the Secretary-General, S/2009/12 (7 January 2009); Letters from the Permanent Representative of Cuba to the Secretary-General on behalf of the Non-Aligned Movement, A/63/673-S/2009/13 (7 January 2009), S/2009/15 (8 January 2009), and S/2009/33 (14 January 2009); SC 6060th meeting, remarks by Libya (8), France (9–10), Indonesia (11), United Kingdom (12), Italy (13), China (15), Burkina Faso (16), and Belgium (17); SC 6061st meeting, remarks by Austria (14), Vietnam (15), Japan (19), Mexico (20), China (21), Russia (22) and League of Arab States (26); and SC 6061st meeting, Resumption 1, remarks by Malaysia (3), Cuba, on behalf of the Non-Aligned Movement (4), Czech Republic, on behalf of the EU and other States (7), Indonesia (9), Nicaragua (14), Australia (16) and Ecuador (16).

[105] See e.g. S. Bashi and T. Feldman, *Scale of Control: Israel's Continued Responsibility in the Gaza Strip* (2011) 47–57; and B. Rubin, 'Disengagement From The Gaza Strip And Post-Occupation Duties' (2010) 42 *Israel Law Review* 528.

[106] Dinstein, *Belligerent occupation*, 279.

[107] E.g. Shalev (representative of Israel) SC 6060th meeting: 'We are not at war with the Palestinian people, but with Hamas and other terrorist groups in Gaza.'

[108] This is at the very least implicit in the ICTY ruling in *Tadić* Jurisdiction, para 73, that there could exist 'situations that the parties themselves considered at different times and places as either internal or international armed conflicts, or as a mixed internal-international conflict'. See also, chs 6 and 10 of this volume.

conflict exists between Israel and Hamas as an armed group, despite the fact that the latter is the effective government of Gaza.[109] If such a bifurcation of this conflict is possible, and it is legally coherent to argue that one relationship exists with a population and another with its government as Israel claims, then Hamas' ascent to power would appear to be irrelevant to the classification of the conflict between Israel and Gaza per se.

4.4 A separate conflict with Hamas?

Since the outbreak of the second *intifada* in September 2005, the international consensus (shared by Israel's High Court) is that hostilities between Israel and Hamas should be classified as an international armed conflict. While statements made in international fora indicate that this classification flows from the continuing occupation, Israel rejects this rationale. Indeed, as the Turkel Commission noted, although this classification is generally accepted, diverse reasons are given in its support.[110] As Hamas is a non-state actor,[111] the presumptive classification of the conflict should be as a non-international armed conflict. 'Even if one assumes that at no time since 1967 did any parts of the West Bank and Gaza cease being territory to which the international law of belligerent occupation applied, this does not necessarily mean that any armed conflict which arises between armed groups in these areas and Israel itself is of an international nature.'[112]

An important consideration in classifying the conflict is Israel's declaration of a blockade directed against Hamas on 3 January 2009[113] during the course of Operation Cast Lead, a blockade which has continued in force. This, it is

---

[109] Compare Guilfoyle, *The Mavi Marmara Incident*, 187.

[110] The Turkel Commission Report, 47, para 41. The final report of the Turkish National Commission of Inquiry rejected the view that the conflict should be classified as an international armed conflict, on the ground that Israel had not recognized it as such (see 60–3), while the Palmer Committee Report concluded that 'the conflict should be treated as an international one for the purposes of the law of blockade' (41, para 73; see also, 83–5, paras 20–4). It is difficult to estimate the weight that should be placed on the Palmer Report as it was 'dependent upon the investigations conducted by Israel and Turkey' (9, para 11); it expressly stated that 'the legal issues at large in this matter have not been authoritatively determined by the two States involved and neither can they be by the' Palmer Committee itself (10, para 14); and opined that '[t]oo much legal analysis threatens to produce political paralysis' (10, para 15).

[111] As Israel is not a party to Additional Protocol I, Hamas' self-designation as a national liberation movement, and thus the effect of art. 1(4) which internationalizes conflicts in which 'peoples are fighting against . . . alien occupation . . . in exercise of their right of self-determination' is irrelevant to this analysis.

[112] D. Kretzmer, 'Targeted Killing of Suspected Terrorists: Extra-Judicial Executions or Legitimate Means of Defence?' (2005) 16 *European Journal of International Law* 209 (Kretzmer, *Targeted Killing*).

[113] The declaration of the blockade, No. 1/2009 *Blockade of Gaza Strip*, provides:

All mariners are advised that as of 03 January 2009, 1700 UTC, Gaza maritime area is closed to all maritime traffic and is under blockade imposed by Israeli Navy until further notice.

Maritime Gaza area is enclosed by the following coordinates: 31 35.71 N, 34 29.46 E; 31 46.80 N, 34 10.01 E; 31 19.39 N, 34 13.11 E; 31 33.73 N, 33 56.68 E.

A diagram of the area subject to blockade is reproduced in C. Migdalovitz, 'Israel's Blockade of Gaza, the Mavi Marmara Incident, and Its Aftermath' (Congressional Research Service, 2010) 16, and as Annex D to Part One of The Turkel Commission Report.

submitted, is conclusive in determining the status of the conflict. In rejecting a petition which sought to obtain a declaration that Israel lacked jurisdiction to intercept the Mavi Marmara flotilla on 31 May 2010, President Beinisch of the Israeli High Court stated:

> In light of Hamas' control of the Gaza Strip, Israel has taken various steps meant to prevent direct access to the Gaza Strip, including the imposition of a naval blockade on the Strip, which, according to the State's declaration, is meant to block the infiltration of weapons and ammunition into Hamas ranks which have carried out shooting and terrorist attacks in Israeli territory for years with the goal of harming civilians.[114]

Imposing the blockade constituted a recognition of the belligerency of Hamas which, if nothing else, serves to internationalize the conflict.

The declaration of a blockade is a belligerent act which, traditionally, can only be imposed during an international armed conflict:[115] 'Blockade is a belligerent right, and can only be exercised against a state with which the blockading power is at war. A power may prohibit foreign trade with its own ports; but such prohibition does not carry with it the same rights of interference with foreign vessels as are conferred by a regularly constituted blockade.'[116]

Until Common Article 3 of the Geneva Conventions was adopted in 1949, international law was on the whole not concerned with the conduct of civil conflict unless the belligerent State, or neutral States which thought that their interests were directly affected by the conflict, recognized the belligerency of the insurgent forces.[117] This effectively 'internationalized' the conflict, by making its conduct subject to the laws of war.

---

[114] A. Glickman, 'High Court rejects flotilla suits: Soldiers defended their lives' *YNet News* (6 March 2010).

[115] See e.g. W. Heintschel von Heinegg, 'Blockade' in R. Wolfrum (ed.), *Max Planck Encyclopedia of Public International Law* (2008) para 25; Kraska, *Israel's Naval Blockade*, 386–91; M. Krauss, 'Internal conflicts and foreign States: in search of the state of law' (1978) 5 *Yale Studies in World Public Order* 186–7 (fn 47) (Krauss, *Internal Conflicts*); J.B. Moore, *A digest of international law* (1906), Vol. 7, 780–3, 785–6 and 808 (Moore, *A Digest*); S.C. Neff, *The rights and duties of neutrals: a general history* (2000) 22; R.R. Oglesby, *Internal war and the search for normative order* (1971) 40 and 42–3 (Oglesby, *Internal War*); V.A. O'Rourke, 'Recognition of belligerency and the Spanish war' (1937) 31 *AJIL* 402 (O'Rourke, *Recognition of belligerency*); Sanger, *Contemporary Law of Blockade*, 421; M.M. Whiteman, *Digest of international law* (1968), Vol. 10, 868–72 (Whiteman, *Digest*); and G.G. Wilson, 'Insurgency and international maritime law' (1906) 1 *AJIL* 56.

[116] 17 January 1876 letter from the Earl of Derby to Lord Odo Russell, reproduced in Moore, *A Digest*, Vol. 1, 808.

[117] On recognition of belligerency, see Moore, *A Digest*, Vol. 1, 164–205; G. Hackworth, *Digest of International Law* (1940) Vol. 1, 318–27 (Hackworth, *Digest*); Whiteman, *Digest*, Vol. 2, 486–523; *Spanish Civil War Pension Entitlement* case, Federal Republic of Germany, Federal Social Court (14 December 1978), 80 *International Law Reports* 666; *Tatem v Gamboa*, England, Kings Bench (30 May 1938), 9 *International Law Reports* 81; J. Crawford, *The creation of States in international law* (2nd edn, 2006) 380–2 and 418–21; A. Cullen, 'Key developments affecting the scope of internal armed conflict in international humanitarian law' (2005) 183 *Military Law Review* 74–8; Krauss, *Internal Conflicts*, 185–94; R. Higgins, 'International law and civil conflict' in E. Luard (ed.), *The international regulation of civil wars* (1972) 170–1; H. Lauterpacht *Recognition in international law* (1947) Part III (Lauterpacht, *Recognition*); Y.M. Lootsteen, 'The concept of belligerency in international law' (2000) 166 *Military Law Review* 109; L. Moir, *The law of internal armed conflict* (2002) 4–18 (Moir, *Internal Armed Conflict*); A.D. McNair, 'The law relating to the civil war in Spain' (1937)

During the nineteenth century, blockades and the right to stop and search neutral vessels on the high seas were acknowledged to be lawful methods of warfare during civil wars if, and only if, the belligerency of the insurgent non-state forces had been recognized, whether expressly or implicitly. States adhered to this view that the legal validity of a blockade was dependent on their recognition of the belligerency of the insurgent forces during the most significant internal conflict of the early twentieth century, the Spanish Civil War (1936–1939). Recognition of belligerency was not accorded by third States during this conflict, with the result that:

> When one says that belligerent rights are not admitted or conceded, that applies to both sides. There is no more right in a government that is fighting a civil war to interfere as a belligerent with ships on the high seas because they are a government, than there is such a right on the part of the insurgents. Both sides are exactly in the same position.[118]

Recognition of belligerency by third States thus conferred, inter alia, the right of blockade on the parties to a civil war. Conversely, the imposition of a blockade by the belligerent State upon ports and coastline in the hands of the insurgents amounted to an implicit recognition by it that the insurgents were belligerents,[119] and thus entitled to exercise belligerent rights: 'there is no escape from the conclusion that, by claiming to exercise belligerent rights as against the insurgents, the lawful government not only acquires those rights as against outside States but also automatically confers belligerent rights upon the insurgents in relation to itself and others.'[120]

Further, even if a blockade imposed by a belligerent State fails to meet the legal requirements of a valid blockade, and is thus a legal nullity, the recognition of belligerency arising from its declaration subsists.[121]

The Turkel Commission was of the opinion that, in contemporary international law, recognition of belligerency 'has become less important and today is almost irrelevant'.[122] It is true that the UK *Manual of the Law of Armed Conflict* observes that '[t]he doctrine has declined to the point where recognition of belligerency is almost unknown today',[123] and some commentators claim that the doctrine has fallen into desuetude.[124] Technically, the claim of desuetude is wrong, as that

---

53 *Law Quarterly Review* 474–84; Oglesby, *Internal War*, ch. 3; Oppenheim, *International Law* 249–53; O'Rourke *Recognition of belligerency*; and H.A. Wilson, *International law and the use of force by national liberation movements* (1988) 22–9.

[118] Sir John Simon, in relation to the British government's refusal to recognize the Spanish government's attempt to establish a blockade in August 1936, quoted in Whiteman, *Digest*, Vol. 2, 511.

[119] See e.g. Moore, *A Digest*, Vol. 1, 166, 182 and 190; Hackworth, *Digest*, Vol. 1, 320; and Whiteman, *Digest*, Vol. 2, 502–3.

[120] Moore, *A Digest*, Vol. 1, 201.

[121] Lauterpacht, *Recognition*, 197–8.

[122] The Turkel Commission Report, 46, para 39.

[123] UK *Manual*, 384, para 15.1.2.

[124] See e.g. L. Doswald-Beck, 'The legal validity of military intervention by invitation of the government' (1985) 56 *British Yearbook of International Law* 189; Guilfoyle, *The Mavi Marmara incident*, 191–2; Oglesby, *Internal War*, ch. 7; A. Paulus and M. Vashakmadze, 'Asymmetrical war and

doctrine applies only to treaties and, moreover, it does not lie in simple non-use. Obsolescence per se is not a recognized ground for treaty termination. Desuetude requires evidence of the parties' intention and consent to abandon the treaty.[125] A similar consideration applies to the extinction of a doctrine rooted in customary international law. States must be seen to adopt a position which contradicts their previous practice in order to extinguish the rule through the emergence of contrary custom. Practice affirming the continued existence of the doctrine of recognition of belligerency may be found at least from the late 1950s and early 1960s, and no evidence of contrary practice has been found.[126] The doctrine might be in decline but it is not yet dead.

While Gaza, as an integral part of the occupied Palestinian territories, is not a State, a clear analogy may be drawn with the declaration of a blockade during a civil war. If the government of a State proclaims a blockade in relation to territory occupied by insurgent forces, this amounts to a recognition of the belligerent status of those forces, and thus the conflict is classified as an international armed conflict.[127] Indeed, this was the conclusion to which the Turkel Commission itself leaned—'there is a consensus that the conflict between the State of Israel and Hamas is an international armed conflict'[128]—although it also opined that even if it were a non-international armed conflict the armed conflict rules regarding blockade would still apply given the 'decline' of the doctrine of recognition of belligerency and the convergence of rules applicable in both types of conflict.[129] As Sanger notes, this latter claim is unsupported by legal argument,[130] and for the reasons

the notion of armed conflict—a tentative conceptualization' (2009) 873 *International Review of the Red Cross* 99; Moir, *Internal Armed Conflict*, 18–21; and Sanger, *Contemporary Law of Blockade*, 421–5. See also, A. Cullen, *The concept of non-international armed conflict in international humanitarian law* (2010) 22–3.

[125] On desuetude, see e.g. G. Le Floch, 'La désuétude en droit international public' (2007) 111 *Revue Général de Droit International Public* 609; M.J. Glennon, 'How international rules die' (2004) 93 *Georgetown Law Journal* 939; R. Kolb, 'La désuétude en droit international public' (2007) 111 *Revue Général de Droit International Public* 577; and A. Vamvoukos, *Termination of treaties in international law: the doctrines of rebus sic stantibus and desuetude* (1985) Part II.

[126] See e.g. 1957 Protocol to the Convention on Duties and Rights of States in the Event of Civil Strife, art. 2; 'Memorandum by the Attorney-General on legal implications of the Korean conflict' National Archives, CAB/129/42, Records of the Cabinet Office (50) CP 207 (14 September 1950); E. Lauterpacht, 'The contemporary practice of the United Kingdom in the field of international law—survey and comment' (1956) 5 *International and Comparative Law Quarterly* 405 (31 January 1956 UK statement that it did not recognize a state of belligerency between Chinese nationalists and communists); 'Memorandum by the Director of the Office of Far Eastern Affairs' (1945) VII Foreign Relations of the United States 262 (7 March 1945); 'Department of State memorandum: legal aspects of the Indonesian government's right to block certain ports held by insurgents' (1 March 1958) XVII/XVIII FRUS (1958–1960); and 'Memorandum from the President's Special Assistant (Schlesinger) to President Kennedy' (17 April 1961) XXII FRUS 260 (1961–1963). Lauterpacht reaffirmed the vitality of the doctrine in the 7th edition of Oppenheim's *International law, Vol. II*; see Oppenheim, *International Law*, 209–12, paras 59–59a, 370–1, para 126.

[127] See the Harvard Draft Convention on the Rights and Duties of Neutral States in Naval and Aerial War (1939) 33 *AJIL* Supplement 209; Lauterpacht, *Recognition*, 194, see 193–9 generally; and *Tatem v Gamboa*, England, Kings Bench (30 May 1938), 9 *International Law Reports* 81.

[128] The Turkel Commission Report, 47, para 41.

[129] Ibid, 48–9, para 42.

[130] Sanger, *Contemporary Law of Blockade*, 434.

given above, it is inaccurate: the declaration of a blockade against a non-state actor entails that the conflict should be classified as international.

While some might think this controversial, it is submitted that the accumulation of considerations indicates that the conflict between Israel and Gaza (or between Israel and Hamas) from 2000 onwards should be classified as an international armed conflict.

5. Rules on application of force

Despite the lengthy period under consideration, the rules or practices on the application of force employed by both Israel and Hamas appear to have remained relatively stable throughout. While the initial Israeli description of the situation arising from the second *intifada* as an 'armed conflict short of war' is ambiguous, and does not designate either an international or a non-international armed conflict, it could be argued that the convergence of the law of armed conflict applicable in both reduces the practical impact of this distinction. Indeed, an official Israeli report on Operation Cast Lead states:

> [t]he Gaza Strip is neither a State nor a territory occupied or controlled by Israel. In these *sui generis* circumstances Israel as a matter of policy applies to its military operations in Gaza the rules of armed conflict governing both international and non-international armed conflicts. At the end of the day, classification of the armed conflict between Hamas and Israel as international or non-international in the current context is largely of theoretical concern, as many similar norms and principles govern both types of conflicts.[131]

The report further claimed that the rules of engagement issued for the operation emphasized four guiding principles—military necessity, distinction, proportionality and humanity—the formulation of which are clearly based on the law applicable during an international armed conflict contained in Additional Protocol I.[132] In the conflict with Hamas, it is claimed that Israeli forces must adhere to the provisions of the Fourth Geneva Convention, the Hague Regulations and those provisions of Additional Protocol I that reflect customary international law.[133] For instance, in discussing legitimate targets, the report makes close reference to article 52 of Additional Protocol I on the grounds that it expresses custom.[134] In contrast, the rules of engagement formulated for the interception of the Mavi Marmara flotilla assumed that those on board were 'civilians not taking a direct part in hostilities. The planned use of force was based on the same principles as those applicable in a law enforcement context, with the ROE primarily permitting the use of force in self-defense'.[135]

---

[131] Government of Israel, 'The operation in Gaza: factual and legal aspects' (July 2009) 11, para 30.
[132] Ibid, 82, para 222; see generally, 82–5, paras 222–9.
[133] Ibid, 11, para 31.
[134] Ibid, 38–40, paras 101–7.
[135] The Turkel Commission Report, 264, para 235.

One aspect of Israel's armed activities in the occupied Palestinian territory, including Gaza, has been its policy of the targeted killing of members of non-State armed groups hostile to Israel.[136] The legality of these operations was examined by Israel's Supreme Court in the *Targeted Killing* case where President Emeritus Barak concluded that this depended on the circumstances of each individual operation. He ruled:

> The approach of customary international law applying to armed conflicts of an international nature is that civilians are protected from attacks by the army. However, that protection does not exist regarding those civilians 'for such time as they take a direct part in hostilities' (§51(3) of *The First Protocol*). Harming such civilians, even if the result is death, is permitted, on the condition that there is no other less harmful means, and on the condition that innocent civilians nearby are not harmed. Harm to the latter must be proportionate. That proportionality is determined according to a values based test, intended to balance between the military advantage and the civilian damage. As we have seen, we cannot determine that a preventative strike is always legal, just as we cannot determine that it is always illegal. All depends upon the question whether the standards of customary international law regarding international armed conflict allow that preventative strike or not.[137]

Academic commentaries on this judgment, while not uncritical, are mainly sympathetic,[138] but nonetheless policies of targeted killing have proved to remain controversial. For example, in 2010, Philip Alston, the former UN Special Rapporteur on Extrajudicial, Summary or Arbitrary Executions, cautioned that the 'failure of States to comply with their human rights law and IHL obligations to provide transparency and accountability for targeted killings is a matter of deep concern. To date, no State has disclosed the full legal basis for targeted killings . . . Nor has any State disclosed the procedural and other safeguards in place to ensure that killings are lawful and justified, and the accountability mechanisms that ensure wrongful killings are investigated, prosecuted and punished. The refusal by States who conduct targeted killings to provide transparency about their policies violates the international legal framework that limits the unlawful use of lethal force against individuals'.[139]

---

[136] For a concise overview of Israel's targeted killing policy, see N. Melzer, *Targeted Killing in International Law* (2008) 27–36 (Melzer, *Targeted Killing*).

[137] *Targeted Killing* case, para 60.

[138] See e.g. the articles in the symposium on the case in 5 *Journal of International Criminal Justice* (2007), namely, A. Cassese, 'On Some Merits of the Israeli Judgment on Targeted Killings' 339; O. Ben-Naftali, 'A Judgment in the Shadow of International Criminal Law' 322; A. Cohen and Y. Shany, 'A Development of Modest Proportions: the application of the principle of proportionality in the *Targeted killings* case' 310; W.J. Fenrick, 'The *Targeted Killings* Judgment and the Scope of Direct Participation in Hostilities' 332; and R.S. Schondorf, 'The Targeted Killings Judgment: A Preliminary Assessment' 301.

[139] P. Alston, 'Report of the UN Special Rapporteur on Extrajudicial, Summary or Arbitrary Executions, Addendum: Study on Targeted Killings' A/HRC/14/24/Add.6 (28 May 2010) 26, para 87. For a range of views on the legality of targeted killings, see e.g. G. Blum and P. Heymann, 'Law and policy of targeted killing' (2010) 1 *Harvard National Security Journal* 145; Kretzmer, *Targeted Killing*; Melzer, *Targeted Killing*, and his 'Targeted Killings in an Operational Law Perspective' in T.D. Gill and D. Fleck (eds), *The Handbook of the International Law of Military Operations* (2010) 277; and

As for Hamas, features which appear to be embedded in its conduct of the conflict include its use of indiscriminate weapons systems, and its willingness to take reprisals against civilians. Hamas claims that its fighters 'adhere scrupulously to Islamic rules and standards that confirm all the contents of the Universal Declaration on Human Rights and the Fourth Geneva Convention'.[140] These instruments do not cover the means and methods of warfare, and the rockets fired from Gaza into southern Israel, which are often homemade, are inherently indiscriminate.[141] Hamas has justified attacks on Israeli civilians as retaliation for Israeli attacks on Palestinian civilians—for example, in 1994, it justified a series of suicide bombings as retaliation for the massacre in the al-Ibrahimi mosque in Hebron perpetrated by a settler, Baruch Goldstein.[142] Hamas has also used the asymmetry of the forces available to it and Israel to justify its attacks on civilians. These may be in pursuit of Hamas' policy 'to transform Israel from a land that attracts world Jews to a land that repels them by making its residents insecure'[143] in order to realize its long-term aim of creating an Islamic State in all of Mandate Palestine.

Hamas, nevertheless, has at times denied allegations that it has carried out indiscriminate attacks, reiterating that only military objects may be targeted and that Palestinian armed groups are committed to that principle. However, it has also claimed that these armed groups are not part of an organized army with technologically advanced weaponry and thus accidental deaths can, and will, occur.[144] Hamas has also rejected any findings that it committed war crimes during fighting between itself and Israel in 2009.[145]

The conduct of both sides during Operation Cast Lead was excoriated by the Goldstone Report which concluded, inter alia, that 'the instructions given to the Israeli forces moving into Gaza provided for a low threshold for the use of lethal weapons against the civilian population';[146] that Israeli forces engaged in indiscriminate and deliberate attacks against civilians;[147] and that official Israeli statements made in relation to Operation Cast Lead 'leave little doubt that disproportionate destruction and violence against civilians were part of a deliberate policy'.[148] In relation to Hamas and other Palestinian armed groups, Goldstone concluded that:

T. Ruys, 'License to Kill? State-Sponsored Assassination under International Law' (2005) 44 *Military Law and Law of War Review* 13.

[140] Hamas, 'An important memorandum from the Islamic Resistance Movement (Hamas) to the Kings, Presidents, and Ministers meeting at Sharm al-Sheikh' (13 March 1996), translated in Hroub, *Hamas*, 310.

[141] For details, see 'Palestinian weapons deployed against Israel during Operation Cast Lead' (2009) 38 *Journal of Palestine Studies* 193–7.

[142] See Hroub, *Hamas*, 242–51; and Tamimi, *A History from Within*, 159–61.

[143] Hroub, *Hamas*, 247.

[144] B'Tselem, 'Hamas report to U.N. shamefully evades responsibility' (24 February 2010), available at: <www.btselem.org/English/Israeli_Civilians/20100224_Hamas_Report.asp>.

[145] 'Hamas gives U.N. response to Gaza war crimes report' *Reuters* (3 February 2010).

[146] The Goldstone Report, 16, para 44.

[147] Ibid, chs X and XI.

[148] Ibid, 335, para 1211; see generally 324–35, paras 1174–212.

Given the apparent inability of the Palestinian armed groups to aim rockets and mortars at specific target and, the fact that the attacks have caused very little damage to Israeli military assets, it is plausible that one of the primary purposes of these continued attacks is to spread terror—prohibited under international humanitarian law—among the civilian population of southern Israel.[149]

6. Rules on capture and detention

During most of the period under consideration, detention of Gazan residents by Israel has, under Israeli law, been governed by the Internment of Unlawful Combatants Law which was first enacted in 2002 and amended in 2008. The Israeli government did not employ the extended powers of internment granted by the 2008 amendments during Operation Cast Lead.[150] This act was promulgated in response to the *Bargaining Chips* case, delivered by the Israel Supreme Court, sitting as an expanded panel of nine justices, on 12 April 2000.[151] The petitioners in this case had been brought to Israel by its security forces in 1986–1987 and prosecuted for being members of organizations hostile to Israel. After they completed their sentences (in 1991 and 1992), they were held in administrative detention pursuant to orders issued by the Israeli Minister of Defence under section 2 of the 1979 Emergency Powers Act (Detentions). In the leading opinion, Chief Justice Barak stated:

> There is no dispute between the parties that the Petitioners themselves pose no threat to the national security. They served their sentence and would normally be deported from Israel. There is no dispute that the ground for continuing detention of the Petitioners is the advancement of repatriating captive and missing [Israeli] servicemen... [T]he Petitioners are being held in administrative detention as bargaining chips in the difficult negotiations that Israel has been conducting in order to repatriate..[the] POWs and MIAs.[152]

Chief Justice Barak, speaking for the majority of the Court, rejected the legality of this detention, ruling: 'The State detains, using the executive branch, a person who has committed no offense and who presents no danger; his only sin being a bargaining chip. The violation of human liberty and dignity is so profound so as to be intolerable in a country which supports liberty and dignity, even if premised on considerations of national security.'[153]

---

[149] The Goldstone Report, 473, para 1722.

[150] B'Tselem/Hamoked, 'Without trial: administrative detention of Palestinians by Israel and the Internment of Unlawful Combatants Law' (2009) 53 (B'Tselem, *Without trial*). Dinstein employs a slightly different translation of the title of this legislation, namely the Detention of Unlawful Combatants Law; see Y. Dinstein, *The conduct of hostilities under the law of international armed conflict* (2004) 31.

[151] *Anonymous (Lebanese citizens) v Minister of Defence*, Final Decision, FCrA 7048/97 (12 April 2000), *ILDC* 12 (IL 2000) (*Bargaining Chips* case).

[152] *Bargaining chips* case, opinion of Chief Justice Barak, *ILDC* 12 (IL 2000) 4, para 2.

[153] Ibid, 10, para 19.

He found that the detention of individuals as hostages, 'a term encompassing the holding of persons as bargaining chips', was prohibited under international law, citing as authority article 1 of the 1979 International Convention against the Taking of Hostages and article 34 of the Fourth Geneva Convention.[154]

Before the promulgation of the 2002 Act, detention was governed by the 1988 Administrative Detentions (Temporary Provision) (Territory of Gaza Strip) Order. This Order was cancelled upon Israel's disengagement from Gaza in September 2005.[155] As Gaza was clearly under Israeli occupation until then, the Administrative Detentions Order can be seen as an exercise of the occupant's power to intern which is expressly recognized in articles 41–43, 68 and 78 of the Fourth Geneva Convention, the modalities of which are regulated by Section IV of the Convention.

In relation to two detainees from Gaza, who had been detained in January 2002 and January 2003, the constitutionality of the Internment of Unlawful Combatants Law was challenged in proceedings which culminated in the *A and B v Israel (Appeal Decision)* judgment, delivered by the Israeli Supreme Court on 11 June 2008.[156] The Court ruled that the law was constitutional and consistent with the requirements of the law of armed conflict. The appellants were detained under the Act on the basis that they 'were major activists in the Hezbollah organization who would very likely return to terror activities if they were released . . . and their release was likely to harm state security'.[157] In her opinion, President Beinisch noted that section 1 of the Act expressly stated that its purpose was to regulate the internment of unlawful combatants in a way that was consistent with Israel's obligations under international humanitarian law. She commented: 'The premise in this context is that an international armed conflict prevails between the State of Israel and the terrorist organizations that operate outside Israel (see HCJ 769/02 *Public Committee against Torture in Israel v Government of Israel* (the *Targeted Killings* case) . . . at paragraphs 18, 21; see also A. Cassese, *International Law* (second edition, 2005), at page 420).'

She continued that in interpreting the Act in a manner consistent with international humanitarian law, it should be borne in mind that international legal

[154] Ibid, 11, para 20.
[155] For a brief (and critical) account of the parallel administrative detention order operative in the West Bank, see B'Tselem, *Without trial*, 14–22.
[156] *A and B v Israel*, Appeal Decision (11 June 2008) CrimA 6659/06, 1757/07, 8228/07, 3261/08, *ILDC* 1069 (IL 2008) (*A and B v Israel*). The leading opinion was delivered by President Beinisch, in which the other two Justices concurred. For a brief background summary of this case, see B'Tselem, *Without trial*, 56, which also presents sample case studies at 59–63. It is perhaps worth noting in passing that the appellants in this case had been detained under the 1988 Administrative Detentions (Temporary Provision) (Territory of Gaza Strip) Order until its revocation on 12 September 2005, and then the Internment of Unlawful Combatants Law was substituted as the basis of their detention, with the court competent to undertake judicial review of the detention orders being the Tel Aviv-Jaffa District Court (see *ILDC* 1069 (IL 2008), opinion of President Beinisch, 6–7, paras 1–2). This indicates that, at some point, the detainees were transferred from Gaza to Israel, which was presumably in breach of art. 49(1) of the Fourth Geneva Convention. The question of unlawful transfer was apparently not raised in the case.
[157] *A and B v Israel*, 7, para 3.

norms have not been adapted to 'changing realities and the phenomenon of terrorism that is changing the form and characteristics of armed conflicts and those who participate in them'. Accordingly, the Supreme Court would 'interpret the existing laws in a manner that is consistent with new realities and the principles of international humanitarian law'.[158]

On the premise that international humanitarian law is not 'as a rule' intended to regulate the relationship between the State and its citizens, President Beinisch deduced that the Knesset intended the Internment of Unlawful Combatants Law 'to apply only to *foreign* parties who belong to a terror organisation that operates against the security of the state'. Its definition of 'unlawful combatant' thus included:

> residents of a foreign country that maintains a state of hostilities against the State of Israel, who belong to a terrorist organisation that operates against the security of the state and who satisfy the other conditions of the statutory definition of 'unlawful combatant'. This definition may also include inhabitants of the Gaza Strip which is no longer held under belligerent occupation.[159]

In subsequently justifying the consistency of the appellants' detention under the Internment of Unlawful Combatants law with international humanitarian law, President Beinisch relied on the provisions of the Fourth Geneva Convention and, in particular, the power of a party to a conflict to adopt 'control and security' measures under article 27. These included the powers of detention under articles 41–43. She ruled:

> the detention provisions set out in the Fourth Geneva Convention were intended to apply and realise the basic rule provided in the last part of article 27 of the convention . . . [T]his article provides that the parties to a dispute may adopt security measures against protected civilians in so far as this is required as a result of the war. The principle underlying all the detention provisions provided in the Fourth Geneva Convention is that it is possible to detai[n] 'civilians' for security reasons in accordance with the extent of the threat they represent. According to the aforesaid convention, there is a power of detention for security reasons, whether we are concerned with the inhabitants of an occupied territory or we are concerned with foreigners who were found in the territory of one of the states involved in the dispute. In the appellants' case, although the Israeli military rule in the Gaza Strip has ended, the hostilities between the Hezbollah organisation and the State of Israel have not ended, and therefore the detention of the appellants in the territory of the State of Israel for security reasons is not inconsistent with the detention provisions in the Fourth Geneva Convention.[160]

This ruling is obviously predicated on the view that the 'unlawful combatants' covered by the Act were civilians;[161] indeed, President Beinisch proceeded expressly to deny that the appellants were entitled to prisoner of war status,[162] although under the terms of the Act, like prisoners of war, they could be detained until the

---

[158] *A and B v Israel*, 10–11, para 9.   [159] Ibid, 11–12, para 11.
[160] See ibid, 13–15, paras 15–17: quotation at 14–15, para 17.
[161] Ibid 12, para 12.   [162] Ibid, 21–2, para 33.

time that hostilities against Israel by their parent organization came to an end.[163] However, as the declaration of the blockade amounted to Israel's recognition of Hamas as a belligerent and thus, formally, as a party to an international armed conflict, should this not entail that, in principle, its fighting members ought to be assimilated to members of regular armed forces who possess combatant status, combatant immunity and entitlement to prisoner of war status on capture rather than detention as 'unlawful combatants'?[164]

During Operation Cast Lead Hamas did not capture any IDF personnel, and so the questions of identifying the relevant standards of treatment and whether these were observed by Hamas did not arise. On the other hand, it seems more apt to consider Corporal Shalit, captured by Hamas on 25 June 2006, as a hostage being held as a 'bargaining' chip for the release of Palestinians detained by Israel (which accords with the circumstances of his eventual release) rather than as a prisoner of war, although the Goldstone Report classified him as a prisoner of war.[165]

B'Tselem, an Israeli NGO, claims that Israel detained five Gazan residents between 2005 and 2008, and thirty-four residents of Gaza during or subsequent to Operation Cast Lead, stating that most had been released by 30 September 2009.[166] This stands in stark contrast to the findings of the Goldstone Report which alleges that hundreds of Gazans were detained by the IDF during Cast Lead,[167] with approximately a hundred being taken to Israeli prisons.[168] On the evidence before it, the Goldstone Mission found that there was 'a pattern of

---

[163] Ibid, 22, para 34, 29–31, para 46, and 33–4, para 52.

[164] This is an open question. Does Israel's recognition of Hamas as a party to an international armed conflict entail that members of Hamas' armed wing, the Izzidin al-Qassam Brigade, constitute 'members of the armed forces of a party to the conflict' to employ the terms of art. 4(A)(1) of the Third Geneva Convention? In other words, should they be seen as regular forces, as opposed to members of an irregular force otherwise falling under art. 4(A)(2), were Hamas to be a party to the Third Geneva Convention? While Dinstein argues that 'regular forces are not absolved from meeting the cumulative conditions binding irregular forces' (Dinstein, *Conduct of Hostilities*, 36), this is disputed by other commentators; see e.g. A. Rogers, 'Combatant status' in E. Wilmshurst and S. Breau, *Perspectives on the ICRC Study on customary international humanitarian law* (2007) 114–15. Further, rule 4 of the ICRC Study provides that '[t]he armed forces of a party to the conflict consist of all organised armed forces, groups and units which are under a command responsible to that party for the conduct of its subordinates'. The commentary notes that 'the four conditions contained in the Hague Regulations and the Third Geneva Convention have been reduced to two conditions' (J.M. Henckaerts and L. Doswald-Beck, *Customary international humanitarian law, Vol. I: Rules* (2005) 14–16 (ICRC Customary Law Study)), with the requirement of visibility being relevant to entitlement to prisoner of war status. This is governed by rule 106, which requires combatants to distinguish themselves from the civilian population when they are engaged in an attack or in a military operation preparatory to an attack (see ibid, 384–6). This does not entail that combatants wear uniforms in all hostile action, although armies generally do so as a matter of practice. In fact, international humanitarian law does not define what constitutes a uniform. The obligation is one of distinction, not uniform, and as Parks observes, on the occasions that partisans wore uniforms during WWII, '"Uniform" varied, often being more like modern "gang" colors than a traditional military uniform'. See W.H. Parks, 'Special forces' wear of non-standard uniform' (2003) 4 *Chicago Journal of International Law* 539, see *passim*, and also T. Pfanner, 'Military uniforms and the law of war' (2004) 86 *International Review of the Red Cross* 93.

[165] The Goldstone Report, 373, para 1337.

[166] B'Tselem, *Without trial*, 54.

[167] Detentions are dealt with in ch. XV of the Goldstone Report, 300–24, paras 1103–73.

[168] Ibid, 301, para 1105.

behaviour on the part of the Israeli soldiers'[169] which amounted to the imposition of a collective penalty in violation of article 50 of the Hague Regulations and article 33 of the Fourth Geneva Convention. Further, some aspects of the treatment meted out to detainees constituted outrages on human dignity and 'required a considerable degree of planning and control . . . sufficiently severe to constitute inhuman treatment within the meaning of the Fourth Geneva Convention and thus a grave breach of the said Convention that would constitute a war crime'.[170] Similar allegations of the ill-treatment of detainees, including torture, have been made by the Israeli NGOs PCATI and Adalah.[171]

7. Other significant problems of international humanitarian and human rights law

Apart from the criticisms made of both Israel and Hamas regarding the means and methods of warfare they have employed, the Gaza conflict exhibits additional significant aspects of non-compliance with the law of armed conflict and human rights law.

Although Israel claims that its obligations under international human rights instruments do not apply outside its own territory, this was rejected by the International Court of Justice in the *Wall* Advisory Opinion.[172] Further, the position espoused by the Israeli government is belied by the jurisprudence of Israel's High Court which has repeatedly ruled that the human rights of the population of the occupied territories cannot be disregarded by the occupying forces.[173] Conversely, as Hamas does not control any Israeli territory, it can owe human rights obligations only to the local population. While there is room for criticism of its human rights record within Gaza,[174] at best this can be seen as only ancillary to the conflict with Israel, apart from its treatment of Gilad Shalit. Since it appears that he was being held as a hostage, as opposed to a prisoner of war, the views expressed by President Barak in the *Bargaining Chips* case are equally applicable to him.

---

[169] Ibid, 314, para 1162.

[170] Ibid, 323, paras 1169–70.

[171] See Public Committee against Torture in Israel/Adalah, 'Exposed: the treatment of Palestinian detainees during Operation Cast Lead' (June 2010), available at: <www.stoptorture.org.il/files/Exposed4-Treatment%20of%20Detainees%20Cast%20Lead_June%202010.pdf>.

[172] See *Wall* Advisory Opinion, 177–81, paras 102–13. As Judge Buergenthal concurred in this conclusion (see his declaration, ibid, 240, para 2), this was a unanimous ruling by the Court.

[173] See e.g. the opinions of President Barak in the *Targeted Killing* case (2005) para 18; in *Ajuri* case, paras 14–16; and in *Mara'abe et al v Prime Minister of Israel et al*, HCJ 7957/04 (15 September 2005) paras 24–8: in this last case, although President Barak declined to rule expressly on the formal applicability of the International Covenant on Civil and Political Rights in the occupied territories, he stated, '[w]hen this question arose in the past in the Supreme Court, it was left open, and the Court was willing, without deciding the matter, to rely upon the international conventions . . . We shall adopt a similar approach'.

[174] See e.g. The Goldstone Report, 373–81, paras 1339–66.

The humanitarian situation in Gaza raises issues of both human rights law and international humanitarian law. In July 2011, it was reported that 38 per cent of Gazans live in poverty; 54 per cent are food insecure, and over 75 per cent are aid dependent; and 31 per cent of the workforce is unemployed.[175] Many of these humanitarian problems in Gaza stem from the restrictions Israel has placed on the movement of people and goods in and out of the territory. This policy was initially implemented by the Israeli Security Cabinet decision to designate Gaza as a 'hostile territory' which expressly stated that it provided:

> a basis for sanctions on the Hamas regime. Israel cannot be expected to provide for those that attack its citizens, for example by providing fuel to vehicles being used to transport Kassam missiles, or supplying power to Hamas military installations. When has a state under constant attack supplied a hostile population with the provisions necessary to carry out these attacks?
>
> At the heart of this decision is the principle that although Israel remains committed to averting any humanitarian crises, it does not feel required to provide any supplies which go beyond that. It would be hypocritical to expect Israel to provide anything beyond the basic human needs of a population when a large number of its members, including the authorities, are engaged in systematic hostile activities.[176]

The terrestrial restrictions and maritime blockade of Gaza raise two principal issues: the question of the duty to provide humanitarian relief, and the related matter of the legality of the maritime blockade.

On the assumption that the occupation of Gaza continues, Israel as occupant has the duty under article 55 of the Fourth Geneva Convention to ensure food and medical supplies for the population to the fullest extent of the means available to it and, 'it should, in particular, bring in the necessary foodstuffs, medical stores and other articles if the resources of the occupied territory are inadequate'. Further, under article 59, if 'the whole or part of the population of an occupied territory is inadequately supplied', Israel is under a duty to agree to and facilitate relief schemes by all the means at its disposal, permit the free passage of relief consignments and guarantee their protection. The restrictions on terrestrial passage were imposed in September 2007, and although eased in June 2010,[177] still remain. In the *Al Bassiouni* case, the Israeli government argued that, as it no longer occupied Gaza, 'the State of Israel does not have a general duty to ensure the welfare of the residents of the Gaza Strip'.[178] But even if Israel is no longer the occupant, arguably it breached its duties under customary international law which requires parties to a

---

[175] Office for the Co-ordination of Humanitarian Affairs, 'Humanitarian situation in the Gaza Strip July 2011' (1 July 2011), available at: <http://unispal.un.org/UNISPAL.NSF/0/D6BCF7AEEEB FBBBE852578C600622956>.

[176] MFA, *Gaza designated as Hostile Territory*.

[177] Israeli Security Cabinet, 'Decision on easing the blockade against the Gaza Strip' (20 June 2010), reproduced in (2010) 40 *Journal of Palestine Studies* 196: for an assessment of the situation after this measure was adopted, see Office for the Co-ordination of Humanitarian Affairs, 'Easing the blockade: assessing the humanitarian impact on the population of the Gaza Strip' (March 2011), available at: <www.ochaopt.org/documents/ocha_opt_special_easing_the_blockade_2011_03_engl-ish.pdf>.

[178] *Al Bassiouni* case, para 12.

conflict to 'allow and facilitate rapid and unimpeded passage of humanitarian relief for civilians in need'.[179] Further, some, including the ICRC, argue that the effect of the restrictions is the imposition of a collective punishment on the population of Gaza which, in itself, breaches the law of armed conflict.[180]

Given the restrictions on access to Gaza, it has also been argued that the maritime blockade imposed on Gaza is unlawful on the ground that it causes damage to the civilian population which is, or may expected to be, excessive in relation to the concrete and direct military advantage anticipated from the blockade.[181] While this allegation was rejected by the Turkel Commission, the Hudson-Philips Report concluded it was well-founded.[182]

8. Conclusions

This chapter has concentrated on the structural issues of classification of the conflict in Gaza rather than specific operations and incidents. The attempt to classify this conflict was complicated both by the unique nature of Gaza[183] and by Israel's manipulation, and probably conscious manipulation, of legal categories. 'Disengagement' arguably did not terminate occupation as it retained existing structures of control, but was portrayed as such simply because of the absence of boots on the ground. Given the high-tech means of surveillance and attack employed by Israel, this was an attempt to deny responsibility for the territory while reaping the benefits of effective, albeit remote, control. Similarly, invention of the 'armed conflict short of war' category was unnecessary and confusing. A further problem arose from the divergent views expressed at times by the Israeli government and the High Court. As for Hamas, its views on the nature of the conflict are all but impossible to discern as it appears not to speak the language of international law.

Weighing the factors that the conflict in Gaza presents, on balance it appears that Israel continues to occupy the territory, with the consequence that the conflict

---

[179] See ICRC Customary Law Study, rule 55, 193–200; see also, Guilfoyle, *The Mavi Marmara incident*, 197–202; The Palmer Committee Report, 42–4, paras 77–80, and app. I, 'The applicable international legal principles' 87–9, paras 33–6; and Sanger, *Contemporary Law of Blockade*, 414–20 and 435–8.

[180] ICRC, 'Gaza closure: not another year!' News release 10/103 (14 June 2010). The Hudson-Phillips Report also concluded that the blockade amounted to collective punishment, see 12, para 54, as did the Final Report of the Turkish National Commission of Inquiry, see 78–81. Guilfoyle, *The Mavi Marmara incident*, 203–4 takes a more nuanced approach. See also, the Palmer Committee Report, app. I, 89–90, paras 37–39.

[181] See L. Doswald-Beck (ed.), *San Remo manual on international law applicable to armed conflicts at sea* (1995) 179, rule 102.

[182] See the Turkel Commission Report, 64–102, paras 61–97; and the Hudson-Phillips Report, 12, para 53: its assessment of the humanitarian situation in Gaza is at 9–11, paras 37–44. The Palmer Committee Report found that the blockade was lawful, see 44, para 89, while academic commentary favours the view that it was unlawful, see e.g. Guilfoyle, *The Mavi Marmara incident*, 203–4 and Sanger, *Contemporary Law of Blockade*, 443–4.

[183] As the Palmer Report stated: 'The specific circumstances of Gaza are unique and are not replicated anywhere in the world.' (41, para 73).

should be classified as an international armed conflict. If a distinct conflict exists between Israel and Hamas, then although presumptively this should be seen as a non-international armed conflict as Hamas is a non-state actor, Israel's imposition of the maritime blockade may be seen as a recognition of belligerency which internationalized the conflict.

On the whole, however, it might be doubted whether classification has a practical impact on how this continuing conflict should be conducted, given the convergence of customary law rules regulating international and non-international conflict. This is apparent in Israeli statements regarding the prosecution of Operation Cast Lead; it is easy to agree with the Israeli view that 'classification of the armed conflict between Hamas and Israel as international or non-international in the current context is largely of theoretical concern, as many similar norms and principles govern both types of conflicts'.[184] The principal issue where a difference is apparent is in relation to the treatment of detainees. If Israel is engaged in an international armed conflict with Hamas, should not captured Hamas fighters in principle be accorded prisoner of war status rather than be detained as 'unlawful combatants'? As the Palmer Committee observed, 'under the law of armed conflict a State can hardly rely on some of its provisions but not pay heed to others'.[185]

Much more serious, however, are the consequences of Israel's denial that it continues to occupy Gaza in relation to the implementation of the occupant's duties to provide, and facilitate the provision of, humanitarian relief. The unspecified minimum humanitarian standards invented by Israel to assuage the problems caused by its integration of the Gazan economy and infrastructure into its own and the resultant dependency, adverted to in the *al Bassouini* case, appear to fall below the humanitarian obligations incumbent on an occupant. But even if Israel is no longer the occupant, it still has the obligation, under customary international law, to 'allow and facilitate rapid and unimpeded passage of humanitarian relief for civilians in need'.[186]

Chronology

28 September 2000	Start of the Second *Intifada*.
6 February 2001	Likud leader Ariel Sharon elected Prime Minister in Israel replacing the Labor Party's Ehud Barak and promising 'peace and security'.
February 2003	Israel initiates a series of incursions in Gaza and Nablus.
4 June 2003	Aqaba Summit: Ariel Sharon and Palestinian Prime Minister, Mahmoud Abbas, agree to stop violence and end occupation according to the Road Map. Hamas and Islamic Jihad vow to continue violence.

---

[184] Government of Israel, 'The operation in Gaza: factual and legal aspects' (July 2009) 11, para 30.
[185] The Palmer Committee Report, 41, para 73.
[186] ICRC Customary Law Study, rule 55.

21 August 2003	Israel assassinates Hamas leader Ismail Abu Shanab in Gaza. Others killed in widespread operations in the West Bank.
19 November 2003	UN Security Council adopts resolution 1515 in support of the Roadmap for Peace.
25–26 October 2004	Knesset approves the Cabinet's Revised Disengagement Plan for the withdrawal of Israel settlers and ground forces from Gaza.
8 February 2005	Ariel Sharon, Mahmoud Abbas, President Mubarak of Egypt and King Abdullah of Jordan meet in Sharm El Sheikh. Abbas and Sharon announce an end to the violence. Israel will withdraw from Palestinian cities. The Second *Intifada* is deemed to be over.
August 2005	Israeli evacuation of Gaza settlements and four West Bank settlements begins on 15 August and is completed on 24 August.
25 June 2006	Hamas armed forces capture IDF Corporal Gilad Shalit.
27 June 2006	Israel begins operation Summer Rains and deploys ground forces in Gaza.
June 2006	Israeli targeted killings in Gaza and West Bank continue, while Hamas fires about 90 Qassam rockets into Sderot and other Western Negev communities.
26 November 2006	Israelis and Palestinians announce a truce to apply to Gaza. Israel holds to the truce, but rocket fire from Gaza continues.
15 June 2007	Hamas and Fatah forces clash in Gaza, with the result that Fatah is driven out of Gaza, and Hamas assumes control of the territory.
19 June 2008	Israel-Hamas truce in Gaza.
27 December 2008	Israel launches Operation Cast Lead. Hamas broadens rocket strikes to include Israeli towns and cities.
31 May 2010	Comoros-flagged but Turkish-owned ship MV Mavi Mamara, part of a flotilla of humanitarian aid, is boarded by Israeli commandos after attempting to run the Gaza blockade.
June–July 2010	Israel announces that it is easing the Gaza blockade.
April 2011	Reports of a reconciliation agreement between Fatah and Hamas.
May 2011	Egypt eases restrictions at the Rafah crossing.
18 October 2011	Gilad Shalit released as the result of an agreement between Israel and Hamas which includes the release of 1027 Palestinians held in Israeli prisons.

10

South Ossetia (2008)

*Philip Leach**

1. Introduction

This chapter analyses the 2008 South Ossetian armed conflict, involving the States of Georgia and Russia, and the armed forces of the de facto authorities of South Ossetia. It was a conflict which made media headlines for a few short days in August 2008, but it was rooted in the break-up of the Soviet Union and followed years of simmering tensions and sporadic hostilities in the region. It had a profound effect on the lives of those living in the region—effects which continue to this day (notably for the thousands of Internally Displaced Persons), and which will persist for many years.

In addition to the armed forces of the two States—Georgia and Russia—the conflict was characterized by the involvement of militia under the authority of, or aligned with, the political leadership of South Ossetia, a 'break-away' region in the north of Georgia, bordering Russia, whose status was, and remains, unrecognized by the international community. Classifying the conflict is not unproblematic. Was it an international armed conflict or a non-international armed conflict, or both? Is it rather to be characterized as an 'internationalized' non-international armed conflict or a 'mixed conflict'?[1] Accordingly, as regards the law of armed conflict, this chapter raises wider questions about the relationship between conflicts. It is no longer the case, as it once may have been, that scholars can legitimately focus on single conflicts. Increasingly, it is necessary to consider the implications of a more complex series of contemporaneous armed conflicts, and, for example, to ask at what point is a non-international armed conflict subsumed into an international armed conflict, and what is the relevance of the various tests laid down by the International Criminal Tribunal for Former Yugoslavia (ICTY) and the

* I am greatly indebted to Alexander Halban, Vaho Vakhtangidze (former European Human Rights Advocacy Centre interns), and Joanna Evans (Senior Lawyer, European Human Rights Advocacy Centre) for their invaluable research assistance, and in particular for their drafting of the description of the conflict. Thanks to Giorgi Chkheidze (Georgian Young Lawyers Association) for his advice on Georgian domestic law, and to the other contributors to this volume for their comments on earlier drafts, with special thanks to Charles Garraway and Françoise Hampson.

[1] S. Vité, 'Typology of armed conflicts in international humanitarian law: legal concepts and actual situations' (2009) 91(873) *International Review of the Red Cross* 85.

International Court of Justice (ICJ). This chapter also discusses the increasingly complex relationship between Hague law, Geneva law and human rights law, and the growing tensions between these various systems of law.

2. The hostilities

2.1. Historical context

During the Soviet era, South Ossetia had the status of an autonomous region (*oblast*) within the Georgian Soviet Socialist Republic (the Georgian SSR).[2] When the Georgian SSR declared its independence from the USSR in April 1991, South Ossetia remained part of the territory of Georgia. In September 1990, South Ossetia unilaterally declared its independence from the Georgian SSR.[3] However, in December 1990, the President of Georgia, Zviad Gamsakhurdia, summarily abolished the autonomous status of South Ossetia.[4]

Armed conflict followed in January 1991[5] and continued throughout the year, causing thousands of casualties and creating tens of thousands of refugees on both sides of the Georgian-Russian border.[6] By the end of 1991, the South Ossetians had expelled the majority of Georgian troops from the region and most of the territory of South Ossetia became subject to the de facto control of the secessionist government.[7]

On 21 December 1991, South Ossetia voted for independence from Georgia; a step which was followed by the 1992 referendum for independence and the adoption of the act of independence of 1992.[8] 98 per cent of South Ossetia's

---

[2] First created by the Central Executive Committee of Georgia and the Council of People's Commissars of Georgia, Decree No. 2 'On the Arrangement of the South Ossetian Autonomous Oblast' (20 April 1922), available at: <www.rrc.ge/law/decre_1922_04_20_e.htm?lawid=129&lng_3=en>. This was confirmed in each successive Georgian constitution: Constitution of the Soviet Socialist Republic of Georgia (1923) art.1, available at: <www.rrc.ge/law/konstG_1922_03_02_e.htm?lawid=127&lng_3=en>, Constitution of the Soviet Socialist Republic of Georgia (1927), art. 9, para 3, available at: <www.rrc.ge/law/Gkon_1926_07_05_e.htm?lawid=1109&lng_3=en>, Constitution (Basic Law) of the Soviet Socialist Republic of Georgia (1937), art. 19, available at: <www.rrc.ge/law/Gkon_1937_02_13_e.htm?lawid=1385&lng_3=en>, and Constitution (Basic Law) of the Soviet Socialist Republic of Georgia (1978), art. 71, available at: <www.rrc.ge/law/Gkon_1978_04_15_e.htm?lawid=1387&lng_3=en>. See further, A. Nußberger, 'The War between Russia and Georgia—Consequences and Unresolved Questions' (2009) 1(2) *Göttingen Journal of International Law* 341–64.
[3] Declaration of State Sovereignty of the Soviet Democratic Republic of South Ossetia (20 September 1990), available at: <www.rrc.ge/law/dekl_1990_09_20_e.htm?lawid=1194&lng_3=en>.
[4] International Crisis Group (ICG), 'Georgia: Avoiding War in South Ossetia', No. 159 (2004) 3, available at: <www.crisisgroup.org/~/media/Files/europe/159_georgia_avoiding_war_in_south_ossetia.pdf> (ICG, *Avoiding War*). See also, Global Security, 'South Ossetia—Background', available at: <www.globalsecurity.org/military/world/war/south-ossetia-3.htm>.
[5] ICG, *Avoiding War*, 3.
[6] Ibid, 5–6.
[7] See ICG, 'Georgia's South Ossetia Conflict: Make Haste Slowly', No. 183 (2007) 28, Appendix C, available at: <www.crisisgroup.org/media/Files/europe/183_georgia_s_south_ossetia_conflict_make_-haste_slowly.pdf (ICG, *Georgia's South Ossetia Conflict*).
[8] Declaration of Independence of the Republic of South Ossetia (29 May 1992), available at: <www.rrc.ge/law/dekl_1992_05_29_e.htm?lawid=363&lng_3=en>.

residents voted in favour of independence,[9] although the Georgian population of South Ossetia (28.97 per cent of the total population[10]) did not participate in the referendum. The referendum was not recognized by the international community.[11]

In late 1992, a Russian brokered ceasefire agreement was signed[12] and a Joint Peacekeeping Force was established, composed of Georgian, Ossetian and Russian armed forces.[13]

Georgia had ceased to exercise de facto control over the majority of South Ossetia.[14] The territories controlled by the autonomous government included the districts of Tskhinvali, Java, Znauri and parts of Akhalgori.[15] About 23,000 ethnic Georgians fled from South Ossetia and resettled in other parts of Georgia.[16] However, approximately one-third of the territory of South Ossetia remained under Georgian control including a part of Akhalgori, in the south-east of South Ossetia, and several ethnic Georgian villages around Tskhinvali, in central South Ossetia.[17]

In 1993, South Ossetia drafted its own constitution and in 1996 elected its first president.[18] In 2001, Eduard Kokoity became the de facto president of South Ossetia.[19] He stated that he would continue to strive for the reunification of South Ossetia with Russia.[20] A new referendum and presidential elections were held in November 2006 in South Ossetia and 99 per cent of the population voted in favour of independence, although, again, the ethnic-Georgian population of

---

[9] Human Rights Without Frontiers International (HRWF), 'Georgia—South Ossetia—Russia: the historical context of the August 2008 war' (2009) 5, available at: <www.hrwf.org/images/reports/2009/2009%20georgia%20south%20ossetia%20russia.pdf> (HRWF, *The Historical Context*).

[10] Independent International Fact-Finding Mission on the Conflict in Georgia (IIFFMCG), 'Report' Vol. II (2009) 65, available at: <www.ceiig.ch/pdf/IIFFMCG_Volume_II.pdf> (IIFFMCG, *Report II*).

[11] HRWF, *The Historical Context*, 5; see also, inter alia, the analysis in IIFFMCG, Report, Vol. I, 17, para 11.

[12] Agreement on Principles of Settlement of the Georgian-Ossetian Conflict (24 June 1992), available at: <www.rrc.ge/law/xels_1992_06_24_e.htm?lawid=368&lng_3=en>; HRWF, *The Historical Context*, 6. See also, L. Olson, 'The South Ossetia Case', Conciliation Resources, *Accord* (1999), available at: <www.c-r.org/our-work/accord/georgia-abkhazia/south-ossetia.php>. The terms of the ceasefire covered the termination of hostilities, the withdrawal of armed forces and the creation of a Joint Control Commission (JCC) comprising representatives of the parties to the conflict, whose role was to exercise control over the implementation of the ceasefire, the withdrawal of armed forces, the disbanding of self-defence forces and the maintenance of security in the region. The JCC was also to deal with economic rehabilitation, refugees and displaced people.

[13] Parliamentary Assembly of the Council of Europe (PACE), 'Situation in Georgia and the consequences for the stability of the Caucasus region' Report, Doc. 9564 (24 September 2002) paras 24–33, available at: <http://assembly.coe.int/Mainf.asp?link=/Documents/WorkingDocs/Doc02/EDOC9564.htm>.

[14] ICG, *Georgia's South Ossetia Conflict*, app. C.

[15] Ibid.

[16] Human Rights Watch (HRW), 'The Ingush-Ossetian Conflict in the Prigorodnyi Region' (1996), available at: <www.hrw.org/legacy/reports/1996/Russia.htm>.

[17] ICG, *Georgia's South Ossetia Conflict*, app. C

[18] HRWF, *The Historical Context*, 5.

[19] Ibid, 5–6.

[20] PACE, Doc. 9564, paras 26, 27. See also 'Eduard Kokoity: the aim of South Ossetia is unification with North Ossetia' *Yuzhnaya Osetiya* (10 June 2006) available at: <http://ugo-osetia.ru/6.50.html> [Russian].

South Ossetia did not vote and the referendum was not recognized by Tbilisi.[21] Eduard Kokoity was re-elected as president.[22] However, in spite of these internal declarations, during this period, South Ossetia was unsuccessful in gaining any international recognition as an independent State or in establishing international relations.[23]

2.2. Events of August 2008

2.2.1 *The armed conflict*

On the evening of 7 August 2008, Georgian troops commenced an artillery attack upon the capital of South Ossetia, Tskhinvali.[24] According to Georgia, the target of the attacks were the 'enemy forces' on the territory of South Ossetia.[25] At this stage, this meant the de facto South Ossetian armed forces. Although now acknowledged as the beginning of the armed conflict which was to follow in Georgia, the assault has been described as 'only the culminating point' of a long period of increasing tensions between Russia and Georgia and repeated outbreaks of violence in and around South Ossetia.[26] On 8 August 2008, Georgian ground troops entered Tskhinvali and fighting between Georgian and South Ossetian troops commenced.[27]

Also on 8 August 2008, Russia commenced a counter-attack, deploying ground forces towards Tskhinvali and conducting an aerial bombardment of Georgian troops in Tskhinvali and the vicinity.[28] Russian aircraft also began attacks upon several targets in undisputed Georgian territory.[29] The Russian operation would progess to include large-scale military actions in central and western Georgia and Abkhazia as well as the occupation of a significant part of the undisputed territory of Georgia.[30]

President Medvedev declared that the Russian Federation was exercising its right to self-defence under article 51 of the UN Charter and had responded to a Georgian attack on its peacekeepers in Tskhinvali, whose presence in the region was based upon the 1992 Sochi ceasefire agreement.[31]

---

[21] HRWF, *The Historical Context*, 6.   [22] Ibid.   [23] Ibid.

[24] PACE, resolution 1633 (2008), 'The consequences of the war between Georgia and Russia' (2 October 2008) para 5, available at: <http://assembly.coe.int/Mainf.asp?link=/Documents/AdoptedText/ta08/ERES1633.htm>.

[25] IIFFMCG, *Report II*, 209.

[26] IIFFMCG, *Report I*, 11, para 3; HRW, 'Up In Flames: Humanitarian Law Violations and Civilian Victims in the Conflict over South Ossetia' (2009) 23, available at: <www.hrw.org/sites/default/files/reports/georgia0109web.pdf> (HRW, *Up In Flames*).

[27] Ibid.

[28] Ibid.

[29] Ibid, 24.

[30] PACE, res. 1633 (2008) para 6. This chapter, however, focuses only on the conflict in and around South Ossetia.

[31] T. Hammarberg, Council of Europe Commissioner for Human Rights, 'Human Rights in Areas Affected by the South Ossetia Conflict. Special Mission to Georgia and Russian Federation' CommDH(2008)22 (2008) para 13, available at: <https://wcd.coe.int/ViewDoc.jsp?id=1338365&Site=CommDH&BackColorInternet=FEC65B&BackColorIntranet=FEC65B&BackColorLogged=FFC679 (*CommDH(2008)22*)>.

The Georgian authorities stated that they too were acting in self-defence following attacks by South Ossetian militia on Georgian villages and peacekeepers and the movement of Russian tanks through the Roki tunnel into South Ossetia on 7 August.[32] On 9 August 2008, President Saakashvili of Georgia declared a state of war in the whole territory of Georgia for fifteen days.[33] The fact of this declaration was communicated by the Georgian authorities to the Secretary General of the Council of Europe in a *note verbale* the following day, which also stated that no derogation of any rights under the European Convention on Human Rights had been made.[34]

It was reported that Georgian troops began a withdrawal from South Ossetia into undisputed Georgian territory on 10 August 2008.[35] Russian troops however continued operations both in South Ossetia and undisputed Georgian territory after 10 August 2008.[36]

2.2.2 The ceasefire agreement

On 12 August 2008, President Sarkozy, the then President of the Council of the European Union, proposed a peace initiative in the form of a six-point reconciliation plan.[37] However, despite an official announcement that Russian forces had ended all combat operations that day,[38] there is evidence to suggest that Russian troops continued to advance into Georgian territory up until 15 August 2008.[39] A separate military operation by Russian troops was also conducted in Abkhazia, resulting in the occupation of several cities in the region.

Nevertheless, the European Union ceasefire plan was signed by both Georgia and Russia on 15 and 16 August 2008 respectively.[40] The terms of the ceasefire included the withdrawal of Georgian troops to 'their usual bases' and Russian forces to 'the lines they held before the hostilities broke out', prior to 6 August.[41]

---

[32] HRW, *Up In Flames*, 23; IIFFMCG, *Report I*, 20, para 16.

[33] *CommDH(2008)22*, para 12.

[34] Ibid. Pursuant to art. 15(1) of the Convention, a State may take measures derogating from particular provisions of the Convention 'in time of war or other public emergency threatening the life of the nation'. The European Convention on Human Rights came into force in relation to Georgia on 20 May 1999 (and Protocol No. 4 to the Convention from 13 April 2000 and Protocol No. 1 to the Convention from 7 June 2002). The Convention came into effect in respect of Russia on 5 May 1998 (as did Protocols No. 1 and 4). See also, *Georgia v Russia* (Decision) App No. 38263/08 (13 December 2011) paras 1 and 73 (*Georgia v Russia* Admissibility Decision).

[35] HRW, *Up In Flames*, 24.

[36] Ibid, 25.

[37] President of Russian Federation, 'Press Statement following Negotiations with French President Nicolas Sarkozy' (12 August 2008), available at: <http://archive.kremlin.ru/eng/text/speeches/2008/08/12/2100_type82912type82914type82915_205208.shtml>.

[38] HRW, *Up In Flames*, 25; Ministry of Defence of the Russian Federation, 'The Russian Army will not conduct active military activities from 15.00 Tuesday' (13 August 2008), available at: <www.mil.ru/info/1069/details/index.shtml?id=49435> [Russian].

[39] HRW, *Up In Flames*, 25.

[40] Ibid. See also, I. Traynor, 'Georgia and Russia declare ceasefire' *The Guardian* (16 August 2008).

[41] Embassy of France in Washington, 'Georgia: the 6 Points Plan' (14 August 2008), available at: <http://ambafrance-us.org/spip.php?article1101 [English]; www.ambafrance-us.org/IMG/pdf/accord6points.pdf> [French]. The agreement included the following terms: the non-use of force; the

On 26 August 2008, the Russian Federation recognized South Ossetia and Abkhazia as independent sovereign States[42] in a move which has not been supported elsewhere in the international community (other than subsequently by Nicaragua[43] and latterly Venezuela in September 2009[44]).

2.3. The aftermath of the conflict

2.3.1 *The buffer zone*

From 15 August 2008 onwards, Russian troops began to withdraw from undisputed Georgian territory, leaving Gori city on 22 August 2008 but creating a 20-kilometre wide 'buffer zone' north of the city under the control of Russian forces. Many of the reports on the conflict refer to the territory north of the city of Gori 'between Tskhinvali and the check point in Karaleti' as the 'buffer zone'[45]—meaning the area adjoining South Ossetia and extending as far as the checkpoint in the village of Karaleti (approximately 7 km northwest of the city of Gori),[46] within undisputed Georgian territory. The 'buffer zone' was established by Russian military forces,[47] purportedly with the aim of keeping peace and order.[48] Entry and exit of civilians into the zone was regulated by use of military checkpoints. Georgian police were denied access.[49]

That Russian armed forces occupied and executed de facto control over this region has been acknowledged by a number of international bodies and non-governmental organizations (NGOs), including the United Nations High Commissioner for Refugees (UNHCR),[50] the Council of Europe Commissioner for Human Rights,[51] the Parliamentary Assembly of the Council of Europe (PACE)[52]

---

definitive cessation of hostilities; free access for humanitarian aid; the withdrawal of the Georgian military forces to their usual bases; the withdrawal of Russian military forces to the lines they held before hostilities broke out; the implementation of additional security measures by the Russian peacekeeping forces; and the opening of international discussions on the modalities of security and stability in Abkhazia and South Ossetia.

[42] HRW, *Up In Flames*, 26; President of the Russian Federation, Decree of 26 August 2008 No. 1261 'On the Recognition of South Ossetia', available at: <http://graph.document.kremlin.ru/doc.asp?ID=047560>. See also *Georgia v Russia* Admissibility Decision, para 20.

[43] President of the Republic of Nicaragua, Decree No. 46-2008, available at: <www.cancilleria.gob.ni/publicaciones/r_osetia_s.pdf> [Spanish]. 'Nicaragua recognises independence of South Ossetia and Abkhazia' *The New York Times* (4 September 2008).

[44] 'Putin praises Venezuela for recognition of Abkhazia, South Ossetia' *RiaNovosti* (10 September 2009), available at: <http://en.rian.ru/russia/20090910/156089350.html>.

[45] *CommDH(2008)22*, paras 2, 25.

[46] OCHA, Gori area, map (11 December 2008), available at: <http://reliefweb.int/node/11863>.

[47] *CommDH(2008)22*, para 25.

[48] President of the Russian Federation, 'Press Conference following Talks with President of France Nicolas Sarkozy' (8 September 2008) available at: <http://eng.kremlin.ru/text/speeches/2008/09/08/2208_type82912type82914type82915_206283.shtml>.

[49] HRW, *Up In Flames*, 26.

[50] UNHCR, 'UNHCR teams enter Georgia "buffer zone"' (16 September 2008), available at <www.unhcr.org/news/NEWS/48cfa9b01d.html>.

[51] *CommDH(2008)22*, para 89.

[52] See e.g. PACE, res. 1633 (2008) para 6.

and international NGOs.[53] Furthermore, numerous sources (including international bodies, such as the UNCHR,[54] the Council of Europe Commissioner for Human Rights[55] and PACE[56]) reported widespread looting, deliberate burning and torching of houses, physical assaults and other violations of the rights of civilians committed by the South Ossetian irregular militias and gangs in the 'buffer zone'. In a number of these reports the Russian Federation was criticized for its failure to prevent mass human rights violations and maintain order in the 'buffer zone', which, until October 2008,[57] was under the de facto control of the Russian Federation.[58]

The humanitarian situation in the 'buffer zone' was addressed by the Council of Europe Commissioner for Human Rights during this period in his 'Six principles for urgent protection of human rights and humanitarian security': 'The problem of the "policing vacuum" in the so-called "buffer zone" between Tskhinvali and Karaleti must be resolved urgently.'[59] In early September 2008, the Commissioner for Human Rights reported that following the initial assaults on Tskhinvali and assaults on Georgian villages in South Ossetia, 'lawlessness spread in the "buffer zone" controlled by Russia between Tskhinvali and Karaleti and forced many to leave even from there'.[60] The Commissioner further commented that the return of displaced persons was 'delayed for the majority of them as safety has not been guaranteed'[61] and that 'large areas must be demined from cluster bombs, mines and unexploded ordinance devices which now threaten ordinary people'.[62]

He concluded inter alia, that 'the policing vacuum in the "buffer zone" has to be addressed' . . . , 'systematic demining must be undertaken as a matter of highest priority'. . . . , 'the remaining problem about international access in the area must be resolved' and 'efforts must also be planned for a systematic, impartial collection of evidence about violations committed in connection with the hostilities'.[63]

On 8 September 2008, Russia agreed to withdraw all of its armed forces deployed outside the boundaries of South Ossetia and Abkhazia by 1 October 2008[64] whilst announcing that it intended to keep a total of 7600 troops within Abkhazia and South Ossetia[65] and seemingly in violation of the August 2008

---

[53] See e.g. HRW, *Up In Flames*, 33–5.
[54] See e.g. UNCHR, 'Reports of lawlessness creating new forcible displacement in Georgia' (26 August 2008), available at: www.unhcr.org/news/NEWS/48b424f94.html.
[55] *CommDH(2008)22*, paras 2, 3, 87, 88, 89.
[56] PACE, res. 1633 (2008) paras 13, 23.1.
[57] President of the Russian Federation, 'Press Conference' (8 September 2008).
[58] See e.g. *CommDH(2008)22*, para 87.
[59] Ibid, para 5(4).
[60] Ibid, para 2.
[61] Ibid, para 3.
[62] Ibid.
[63] Ibid, 21 (conclusions).
[64] President of the Russian Federation, 'Press Conference' (8 September 2008).
[65] HRW, *Up In Flames*, 26. See also 'Russia plans 7,600 force in Georgia rebel regions' *Reuters* (9 September 2008).

ceasefire agreements.[66] On 9 September 2008, Russia formally established diplomatic relations with South Ossetia.[67]

In January 2009, PACE condemned 'the Russian non-mandated military presence and building of new military bases within the separatist regions of South Ossetia and Abkhazia, as well as in Akhalgori, Perevi and Upper Abkhazia and in villages controlled by the central government of Georgia before the breakout of the conflict',[68] and deplored 'the continued refusal of Russia and the de facto authorities to allow access to Organisation for Security and Co-operation in Europe (OSCE) monitors to South Ossetia and to European monitors to both South Ossetia and Abkhazia'.[69]

In February 2009, an OSCE military monitoring patrol was detained by South Ossetian forces outside the administrative boundaries of South Ossetia and warning shots were fired at OSCE monitors by South Ossetian forces.[70] In March 2009, a Georgian police officer was killed and another four injured in an explosion caused by what appeared to be a trip-wired mine. A second exploded upon the arrival of a rescue team and injured a further two Georgian police officers.[71] Also in March 2009 it was reported that the Russian Ministry of Finance had approved a financial aid package for South Ossetia of 2.8 billion rubles ($97 million).[72]

In April 2009, a PACE report noted, inter alia:

> We are seriously concerned about the increased militarization of the break-away regions by Russia. This not only violates the ceasefire agreement and is in contradiction to the demands in Assembly Resolutions 1633(2008) and 1647(2009) but also increases the tensions in this already very volatile region undermining its stability.
>
> Russia continues to maintain military troops in Perevi, which is outside the administrative boundaries of South Ossetia...
>
> ... international monitors continue to report tensions and provocations along the administrative borders.[73]

---

[66] HRW, *Up In Flames*, 26.

[67] President of the Russian Federation, Order of 15 September 2008 No. 538-RP 'On the Signing of the Treaty on Friendship, Cooperation and Mutual Assistance between the Russian Federation and the Republic of South Ossetia', available at: <http://graph.document.kremlin.ru/doc.asp?ID=047792> [Russian]; President of the Russian Federation, 'Statements following the signing of the Treaties on Friendship, Cooperation and Mutual Assistance with the Republics of Abkhazia and South Ossetia' (17 September 2008), available at: <http://archive.kremlin.ru/eng/speeches/2008/09/17/1948_type82912type82914type82915_206565.shtml>; President of the Russian Federation, 'Beginning of Meeting with President of South Ossetia Eduard Kokoity' (13 July 2009) available at: <http://archive.kremlin.ru/eng/speeches/2009/07/13/1125_type82914_219559.shtml>.

[68] PACE, res. 1647 (2009), 'The implementation of Resolution 1633 (2008) on the consequences of the war between Georgia and Russia' (28 January 2009) para 5.4.

[69] Ibid, para 5.1.

[70] PACE, 'Follow-up given by Georgia and Russia to Resolution 1647 (2009)', Doc. 11876 (28 April 2009) para 12.

[71] Ibid.

[72] Ministry of Finance of the Russian Federation, 'On the signing of an accord between the Ministry of Finance of the Russian Federation and the Ministries of Finance of Abkhazia and the Republic of South Ossetia of 17 March 2009' (16 March 2009), available at: <www1.minfin.ru/ru/press/press_releases/printable.php?id4=7175> [Russian].

[73] Ibid, paras 9–10.

PACE further reported that the General Prosecutor's Office of Georgia had opened an investigation into deliberate violations of international humanitarian law in the course and the aftermath of the war. 'However, according to Georgian authorities, this investigation is hindered by the lack of access of the competent Georgian authorities to the former conflict zone inside the break-away region of South Ossetia.'[74]

PACE also noted that the Investigative Committee of the General Prosecutor's Office of Russia had finalized an investigation into genocide committed by Georgian troops against Russian citizens, as well as into crimes against the Russian military. The Deputy Head of the Investigative Committee confirmed that 'the committee did not plan to open an investigation into alleged violations of human rights and international humanitarian law during the war by Russian citizens or Russian military forces'.[75] PACE noted finally in this regard, that neither investigation 'have to date resulted in any persons being charged'.[76] PACE also reported that the Russian authorities and the de facto authorities continued to refuse access to OSCE monitors to South Ossetia as well as EU monitors to both South Ossetia and Abkhazia, 'in violation of the Sarkozy-Medvedev agreement and Assembly demands'.[77]

On 30 April 2009, an agreement regarding cooperation on the protection of State borders was signed by the President of Russia who stated that 'the powers for the protection of the borders of these republics, which these agreements have delegated to Russia, will be implemented in strict accordance with the national legislation of Abkhazia and South Ossetia. This is a crucial point and validation of the national sovereignty of the two republics'.[78]

Also in April 2009, Human Rights Watch published a report which concluded that many unexploded cluster munitions remained within Georgian and South Ossetian territory and recommended that both the Russian and Georgian authorities 'urgently . . . provide assistance for clearance in Georgia, including, if necessary in South Ossetia' as well as conducting 'independent, impartial and rigorous investigations into their use of cluster munitions and make public the findings'.[79]

In May 2009, UNHCR estimated that approximately 30,000 people (mainly ethnic Georgians) remained displaced as a result of the conflict[80] and in August 2009, Amnesty International reported that 'several hundreds of displaced people are, however, still unable to return to many areas adjacent to South Ossetia owing to their fears about security in the area'.[81]

---

[74] Ibid, para 24.   [75] Ibid, para 25.   [76] Ibid, para 26.   [77] Ibid, para 20.

[78] See President of the Russian Federation, 'Speech at Ceremony for Signing Bilateral Documents between the Russian Federation, the Republic of Abkhazia and the Republic of South Ossetia' (30 April 2008), available at: <http://archive.kremlin.ru/eng/speeches/2009/04/30/2000_type82912-type82914_215748.shtm>.

[79] HRW, 'A Dying Practice: Use of Cluster Munitions by Russia and Georgia in August 2008' (2009) 6, available at: <www.hrw.org/sites/default/files/reports/georgia0409web_0.pdf>.

[80] Amnesty International (AI), 'Civilians in the aftermath of war: The Russian-Georgian conflict one year on' (August 2009) 7.

[81] Ibid, 11.

In August 2009, Amnesty International noted that the European Union Monitoring Mission (EUMM) was the only internationally-mandated monitoring mission on the ground but was still unable to enter those areas controlled by Russian and/or de facto South Ossetian and Abkhazian authorities.[82] Furthermore, one year on from the conflict in August 2009, Amnesty International noted that 'to date, no one had been brought to justice by the Georgian or Russian authorities for the serious violations of international law which took place during the conflict and its immediate aftermath'.[83]

3. Views of the parties and others on conflict classification

3.1. Russia

Russia consistently viewed the conflict as an act of Georgian aggression against South Ossetia, which was disproportionate and in breach of the UN Charter and the agreements resolving the previous Georgian-Ossetian conflict. Russia maintained that its forces were legitimately present in South Ossetia as peacekeepers.[84]

Russia presented its intervention in South Ossetia as an act of self-defence under the UN Charter, to protect its peacekeepers, who were attacked by Georgian forces. It also argued that it intervened to protect other Russian citizens (that is, the majority of the South Ossetian population, which had been granted Russian passports en masse).[85]

Russia initially sought to present its role exclusively as a peace-keeping/defensive action, maintaining that the conflict was only between Georgian and Ossetian forces. This would suggest that it initially viewed the conflict as non-international. However, in its responses to the Independent International Fact-Finding Mission on the Conflict in Georgia (IIFFMCG) ('the *Tagliavini* Report'), Russia acknowledged that in view of the presence of its forces in Georgia the conflict could be characterized as an international armed conflict. It claimed that at the same time there was a separate non-international conflict between Georgia and Ossetia. It denied any military or political control over the South Ossetian forces. Russia responded to the *Tagliavini* Report, inter alia, as follows:

> Russia was a party in the military conflict with Georgia between 7 August (when Georgia attacked the Russian peacekeepers) and 12 August. We presume that the armed conflict between Russia and Georgia was over as of 12 August. We also believe

[82] Amnesty International (AI), 'Civilians in the aftermath of war: The Russian-Georgian conflict one year on' (August 2009), 7.
    [83] Ibid.
    [84] S/PV.5951, UN Security Council meeting (8 August 2008); S/PV.5952, UN Security Council meeting (8 August 2008); S/PV.5953, UN Security Council meeting (10 August 2008).
    [85] Letter dated 11 August 2008 from the Permanent Representative of the Russian Federation to the United Nations addressed to the President of the Security Council, S/2008/545 (11 August 2008); IFFMCG, Report, Vol. III, Russia: On Georgia's aggression against South Ossetia in August 2008; Russian President, 'Statement on the Situation in South Ossetia' (8 August 2008); Russian Ministry of Foreign Affairs, Spokesman (13 August 2008); Russian President, 'Statement' (26 August 2008). See also *Georgia v Russia* Admissibility Decision, paras 44–6.

that we should refer to two armed conflicts—a domestic one (an armed conflict that was not international in nature) in the territory of Georgia in which Russia was not a party, and an international armed conflict that occurred on the aforementioned dates in which Russia was a party.[86]

When asked by the IIFFMCG whether Russia's actions were governed by international humanitarian law, Russia replied: 'Yes, because an armed conflict existed between the Russian Federation and Georgia. By extension, both parties were bound by humanitarian law provisions governing such situations and conflicts. Furthermore, Georgia was bound by obligations arising from the law governing domestic (non-international) conflicts.'[87]

3.2. Georgia

Georgia presented its initial strike on Tskhinvali in the context of escalating attacks by South Ossetian troops on Georgian forces and civilians in the region.[88] It consistently argued that the South Ossetian forces were acting under the control and direction of Russia.[89]

Georgia dismissed Russia's claim to be undertaking a peace-keeping mission and presented Russia's intervention as an act of aggression, referring to Russian occupation of South Ossetia and undisputed parts of Georgia (the 'buffer zone'). Georgia therefore claimed that it was acting in self-defence against the Russian invasion, invoking article 51 of the UN Charter and customary international law.[90] Georgia argued that Russia violated international humanitarian law (and the Fourth Geneva Convention in particular).[91]

Georgia did not distinguish between the conflicts against Russian and South Ossetian armed forces. Instead, it characterized the whole armed conflict as international, arguing that Russia exercised effective control over the South Ossetian armed forces, making them agents of Russia and not a separate, non-state armed group. In its written submissions to the European Court of Human Rights (in the course of its inter-state case against Russia), Georgia argued that:

The conflict in the present case is properly characterised as international in nature. This is because the conflict involved two State parties: (1) the Russian Federation and

[86] IIFFMCG, *Report III*, Russia: Responses to Additional Legal Questions from IIFFMCG.
[87] Ibid.
[88] IIFFMCG, *Report III*, Georgia: The Aggression by the Russian Federation against Georgia.
[89] S/PV.5951, UN Security Council meeting (8 August 2008). See also *Georgia v Russia* Admissibility Decision, para 25.
[90] Letters dated 9 August 2008 from the Permanent Representative of Georgia to the United Nations addressed to the Secretary-General and the President of the Security Council, S/2008/544 (9 August 2008); S/PV.5952, UN Security Council meeting (8 August 2008); S/PV.5953, UN Security Council meeting (10 August 2008); S/PV.5961, UN Security Council meeting (19 August 2008); S/PV.5969, UN Security Council meeting (28 August 2008); OSCE, Special Permanent Council Meeting, 'Statement of the Georgian Delegation' (14 August 2008); IIFFMCG, *Report III*, Georgia: Use of Force Issues Arising out of the Russian Federation Invasion of Georgia, August, 2008.
[91] IIFFMCG, *Report III*, Georgia: Responses to legal questions from IIFFMCG.

(2) the Republic of Georgia (as the separatist forces are properly regarded as *de facto* organs[92] of the Russian Federation).

Objective evidence establishes that prior to the actual invasion by Russian forces on 7 August 2008: (a) there was resort to armed force by the Ossetian and Abkhaz separatists against the Republic of Georgia; and (b) the separatists were *de facto* organs of the Russian Federation. As a result, there was an international armed conflict in existence on or before 7 August 2008.

Likewise, in relation to the period from 7 to 12 August 2008, objective evidence shows that there was resort to armed force by the separatists, the Russian Federation and the Republic of Georgia. Therefore, it is beyond doubt that there was an international armed conflict in existence from 7 to 12 August 2008.

Furthermore, after the ceasefire on 12 August 2008, the situation is properly understood as one of occupation, which is also governed within IHL by the provisions pertaining to international armed conflicts. This is because objective evidence illustrates comprehensively that significant portions of Georgia remain occupied by forces of the Russian Federation and/or separatist forces acting as *de facto* organs of the Russian Federation.[93]

3.3. South Ossetia

South Ossetia consistently referred to Georgian aggression, which it alleged was disproportionate to any threat from its armed forces or those of Russia. It did not specify how it classified the conflict. However, as it referred to acts of military aggression by Georgia against 'the Republic of South Ossetia', and since it claims to be an independent State, it might be presumed that it regarded the conflict between Georgia and South Ossetia as an international armed conflict.[94]

3.4. Other parties

United Nations statements did not specify how it classified the conflict and did not initially directly refer to the Russian forces, but made reference to the 'Georgian-Ossetian conflict'.[95] The Council of Europe also did not specifically classify the conflict, but did refer to the war and/or armed conflict 'between Georgia and Russia',[96] implying an international armed conflict. It did not specify how it classified the fighting between Georgian and South Ossetian forces.

---

[92] As to the questions relevant to the '*de facto* organs' test in relation to state responsibility see also, art. 8 of the Draft articles on Responsibility of States for Internationally Wrongful Acts, with commentaries, 2001. See also the discussion in ch. 3, section 7.1 above.

[93] *Georgia v Russian Federation*, ECtHR, App No. 38263/08, Application by Georgia.

[94] South Ossetian President, Decree on the Introduction of a State of Emergency (17 August 2008); IIFFMCG, *Report III*, South Ossetia: View of the Conflict.

[95] See e.g. S/PV.5953, UN Security Council meeting (10 August 2008). The generality of Security Council resolutions as to the nature of, and parties to, conflicts is commented on by Jelena Pejic in J. Pejic, 'Status of Armed Conflicts' in E. Wilmshurst and S. Breau (eds), *Perspectives on the ICRC Study on Customary International Humanitarian Law* (2007) 78 (Pejic, *Status of Armed Conflicts*).

[96] PACE, 'The consequences of the war between Georgia and Russia', Doc. 11724 (1 October 2008), Monitoring Committee, co-rapporteurs: Mr Luc Van den Brande and Mr Mátyás Eörsi; PACE, 'The consequences of the war between Georgia and Russia', Doc. 11732 rev (1 October

Like the Council of Europe, the EU also placed particular emphasis on the Russian invasion of Georgia, but did not specifically classify the conflict.[97] The OSCE originally referred to 'the Georgian-Ossetian conflict' (implying a non-international armed conflict), but after the conflict had ended, tended to refer to 'the Georgian-Russian conflict' (implying an international armed conflict).[98]

The US and UK emphasized, in particular, Russian involvement and responsibility. The US condemned Russia's aggression and infringement of Georgia's territorial integrity. It saw Russia's role as going beyond any peace-keeping mission, making Russia a clear party to the conflict; implying an international armed conflict.[99] The UK's position as presented at the UN sought to demonstrate how Russia had become a party to the fighting, which was characterized as an international armed conflict between it and Georgia. Sir John Sawers, then the UK's Permanent Representative to the UN, said at the UN Security Council:

> I think the facts make it clear that this is a conflict between Georgia and Russia. Russian spokesmen try to present the problem as a conflict between Georgia, South Ossetia and Abkhazia, with Russia's role one of peacekeeper. That claim was always doubtful. The last two weeks have demonstrated beyond any doubt that Russia is a party to the conflict. Indeed, Russia's letter last week, saying that they were acting under Article 51 of the United Nations Charter, confirmed that they are a party to the conflict, and Russian actions since 7 August have gone way beyond those of a peacekeeper or mediator. So let us not pretend that this is anything other than a conflict between Russia and Georgia, a conflict which Russia has clearly won militarily. Russian forces in Georgia are now, in effect, an army of occupation, and they will remain so until they withdraw to the positions held prior to 7 August and force levels return to those that prevailed then.[100]

Human Rights Watch referred to two armed conflicts—an international conflict between Georgia and Russia, and a non-international conflict between Georgia and South Ossetia. However, it did not consider in detail Georgia's argument that Russia's effective control of the Ossetian forces made the entire conflict international.[101]

2008), Legal Affairs and Human Rights Committee, rapporteur: Mr Christos Pourgourides. See also, 'The occupation by Russia of a part of Georgia is unacceptable, according to PACE co-rapporteurs' Press Release (22 August 2008); 'Russia and Georgia must abide by Council of Europe principles, said PACE monitoring co-rapporteur' Press Release (23 August 2008).

[97] Conclusions of the Presidency of the Extraordinary European Council at Brussels, 1 September 2008.

[98] See e.g. 'OSCE Chairman calls for a halt to all military action, re-establishment of contact in the Georgian-Ossetian conflict' Press Release (8 August 2008); 'OSCE Chairman welcomes Russian President's decision to end military operation in Georgia' Press Release (12 August 2008); 'OSCE Permanent Council holds special meeting, Georgian Foreign Minister addresses delegations' Press Release (28 August 2008).

[99] See e.g. S/PV.5961, UN Security Council meeting (19 August 2008); OSCE, 726th Permanent Council Meeting (14 August 2008), Statement of the United States Mission.

[100] S/PV.5961, UN Security Council meeting (19 August 2008) 9–10.

[101] HRW, *Up In Flames.*

3.5. The International Independent Fact-Finding Mission on the Conflict in Georgia (IIFFMCG)(the Tagliavini Report)[102]

The Tagliavini Report found that neither the Georgian attack on South Ossetia nor the Russian invasion of Georgia were justified under international law, and both lacked proportionality and necessity. It gave extensive consideration to the question of whether the conflict was one single, international conflict—because of Russia's effective control of South Ossetia (as argued by Georgia)—or concurrent international and non-international conflicts (as argued by Russia).[103] It suggested that there was fairly strong evidence of Russian control over Ossetian forces, but it did not come to a firm conclusion. The Tagliavini Report also suggested that customary international humanitarian law was largely the same in all types of armed conflict, making the distinction less important.

4. Author's analysis of classification

4.1. International armed conflict

Russia and Georgia are parties to the Geneva Conventions 1949 and the two Additional Protocols of 1977. Russia is also a party to the Hague Convention and Regulations IV of 1907. Many of these rules have also become part of customary international law and would apply to all armed conflicts, irrespective of classification.[104]

There is no question that the hostilities between Russia and Georgia amounted to an international armed conflict, as defined by Common Article 2(1) of the Geneva Conventions: 'cases of declared war or of any other armed conflict which may arise between two or more of the High Contracting Parties, even if the state of war is not recognized by one of them.' Indeed, this categorization has been acknowledged by both Russia and Georgia and has widely been recognized by other States and international organizations (see above). Accordingly, an international armed conflict had begun when the two countries' armed forces clashed on 7/8 August 2008. This is regardless of the fact that the Georgian President did not make a declaration of war until 9 August 2008.

From 8 August 2008, Russian armed forces were in belligerent occupation of parts of South Ossetia, extending also to parts of undisputed Georgian territory. In accordance with article 42 of the Hague Regulations (and reflecting the position in

---

[102] By its decision of 2 December 2008 the Council of the European Union established an Independent International Fact-Finding Mission on the Conflict in Georgia (IIFFMCG)—the first time in its history that the EU has decided to intervene actively in a serious armed conflict. It was led by Swiss Ambassador Heidi Tagliavini; see Council Decision 2008/901/CFSP of 2 December 2008 concerning an independent international fact-finding mission on the conflict in Georgia.

[103] IIFFMCG, *Report II*, ch. 7, 298–312.

[104] J-M. Henckaerts and L. Doswald-Beck, *Customary International Humanitarian Law, Volume I: Rules, Volume II: Practice* (2005).

customary international law), territory is considered occupied when it is actually placed under the authority of the hostile army. The occupation extends only to the territory where such authority has been established and can be exercised.[105]

How long the international armed conflict continued, and at what point the law of armed conflict ceased to apply, are more contentious issues. The Fourth Geneva Convention provides that as regards occupied territory, it will cease to apply one year after the 'general close of military operations'. However, the occupying power is bound, for the duration of the occupation, to the extent that it exercises the functions of government in such territory, in relation to specified provisions of the Convention.[106] Additional Protocol I provides that it ceases to apply, in the territory of the parties to the conflict, 'on the general close of military operations' and, in respect of occupied territories, on the termination of the occupation. There is, however, an exception to the effect that Additional Protocol I will continue to apply to detainees until their final release.[107] In the *Tadić* case, the ICTY Appeals Chamber stipulated that '[i]nternational humanitarian law applies from the initiation of such armed conflicts and extends beyond the cessation of hostilities until a general conclusion of peace is reached; or, in the case of internal conflicts, a peaceful settlement is achieved'.[108]

Applying any of these definitions to the situation in South Ossetia would certainly mean that international humanitarian law continued to apply after the conclusion of the ceasefire on 12 August 2008. Furthermore, specific provisions of treaty law expressly continue to apply after the termination of hostilities. For example, as regards international armed conflict, to the extent that Russia was an occupying power in South Ossetia (see further the discussion below) and exercised 'the functions of government' in that territory, it would have been bound by the Fourth Geneva Convention to ensure that detainees enjoyed certain rights (including adequate food, hygiene, medical attention, visits by the ICRC and particular provisions relating to women and minors) for the duration of the occupation.[109] As regards non-international armed conflict, article 2(2) of Additional Protocol II provides that at the end of the armed conflict, those deprived of their liberty will continue to enjoy certain specified rights until the period of their detention ends.

A state of international armed conflict continues during a period of belligerent occupation, and during which period international humanitarian law applies, inter alia, to the conduct of hostilities and the detention of POWs. As noted above, despite an official announcement that Russian forces had ended all combat operations by 13 August 2008[110] it would appear that Russian troops continued to

---

[105] See also *Case concerning armed activities on the territory of the Congo (Democratic Republic of the Congo v Uganda)* ICJ Rep 2005, 168, para 172 *(Congo v Uganda)*.

[106] Geneva Convention IV, art. 6.

[107] Additional Protocol I, art. 3(b).

[108] *Prosecutor v Tadić*, IT-94-1-AR72, Decision on the Defence Motion for Interlocutory Appeal on Jurisdiction (Appeal Chamber), 2 October 1995 *(Tadić)*.

[109] Geneva Convention IV, art. 6 and 76.

[110] HRW, *Up In Flames*, 25; Ministry of Defence of the Russian Federation, 'The Russian Army will not conduct active military activities from 15.00 Tuesday' (13 August 2008), available at: <www.mil.ru/info/1069/details/index.shtml?id=49435> [Russian].

advance into Georgian territory up until 15 August 2008.[111] The Sarkozy-led EU ceasefire plan was signed by Georgia on 15 August and by Russia on 16 August,[112] providing for the withdrawal of Georgian troops to 'their usual bases' and Russian forces to 'the lines they held before the hostilities broke out' pre-6 August.[113] From 15 August onwards, Russian troops began to withdraw from undisputed Georgian territory, leaving Gori on 22 August 2008 but creating a 20-kilometre wide 'buffer zone' north of the city under the control of Russian forces. On 8 September 2008, Russia agreed to withdraw its armed forces deployed outside the boundaries of South Ossetia (and Abkhazia) by 1 October 2008[114] whilst announcing that it intended to keep a total of 7600 troops within Abkhazia and South Ossetia[115] (apparently in violation of the August 2008 ceasefire agreements).[116] As discussed further below, Russian troops, together with South Ossetian forces, continued to exercise control over South Ossetia (and to deny entry to various entities) well into 2009, and continued to do so thereafter.

4.2. A concurrent, non-international armed conflict

Aside from the existence of the international armed conflict, a rather more contentious question is whether the hostilities between Georgia and South Ossetian forces constituted a parallel, simultaneous non-international armed conflict, or whether Russia exercised control over the Ossetian forces, to the extent that they can be considered agents of Russia, in which case such hostilities would be considered to be an aspect of the international armed conflict.

While Common Article 3 of the Geneva Conventions applies to all cases of armed conflict not of an international character which occur in the territory of one of the parties to the Convention, Additional Protocol II to the Geneva Conventions has a more detailed conditionality—and a higher threshold. For Additional Protocol II to come into play, a requisite condition of a non-international armed conflict is that the South Ossetian forces must have constituted an organized armed group. Article 1 of Additional Protocol II states that it applies to 'armed conflicts . . . which take place in the territory of a High Contracting Party between its armed forces and dissident armed forces or other organized armed groups which, under responsible command, exercise such control over a part of its territory as to enable them to carry out sustained and concerted military operations and to implement this Protocol'.[117]

---

[111] HRW, *Up In Flames*, 25.

[112] Ibid. See also I. Traynor, 'Georgia and Russia declare ceasefire' *The Guardian* (16 August 2008).

[113] Embassy of France in Washington, 'Georgia: the 6 Points Plan' (14 August 2008), available at: <http://ambafrance-us.org/spip.php?article1101> [English]; <www.ambafrance-us.org/IMG/pdf/ accord6points.pdf> [French].

[114] President of the Russian Federation, 'Press Conference' (8 September 2008).

[115] HRW, *Up In Flames*, 26. See also 'Russia plans 7,600 force in Georgia rebel regions' *Reuters* (9 September 2008).

[116] HRW, *Up In Flames*, 26.

[117] As opposed to 'situations of internal disturbances ad tensions, such as riots, isolated and sporadic acts of violence and other acts of a similar nature', which are expressly excluded from the scope of the Protocol by art. 1(2).

Therefore, for Additional Protocol II to be applicable, the South Ossetian forces must have been organized, have had a responsible command and exercised control over part of the territory of Georgia.

There is some uncertainty about the nature and identity of the South Ossetian forces.[118] For example, Human Rights Watch reported that they comprised the South Ossetian Ministry of Defence and Emergencies, the South Ossetian Ministry of Internal Affairs, the South Ossetian Committee for State Security, volunteers, and Ossetian peace-keeping forces. The Tagliavini Report concluded that 'the regular armed forces of the *de facto* South Ossetian authorities unquestionably constitute "an organised and hierarchically structured group"'.[119] However, it acknowledged that the situation would be different for other ad hoc fighting groups and individuals. If the South Ossetian authorities did not exercise overall control over such groups and individuals, then this would mean that the fighting between them and the Georgian armed forces could be characterized as a non-international armed conflict to which Common Article 3 of the Geneva Conventions would apply, but not Additional Protocol II. In view of the disparate nature of these forces it might also be arguable that there was therefore a series of separate non-international armed conflicts between Georgia and these various militia and other groups.

International law also distinguishes between non-international armed conflict and 'internal disturbances' on the basis, inter alia, that the former involves *protracted* armed conflict.[120] Other relevant factors include the geographical extent of the conflict, its intensity, the size of the forces involved and the weapons employed.[121] These points raise various questions. What amounts to a 'protracted' conflict? For example, in chapter 11 Michael Schmitt questions the characterization by the Inter-American Commission of Human Rights, in the case of *Abella*, of a 30-hour conflict between Argentinian and dissident forces, as amounting to a non-international armed conflict.[122] Dapo Akande's view in chapter 3 is that while the

---

[118] Amnesty International stated as follows: According to eye-witness testimony collected by Amnesty International, the advancing Russian army was accompanied by both regular South Ossetian forces and an array of paramilitary groups. The latter groups have been widely referred to as 'militias' (*opolchentsy* in Russian, *dajgupebebi* in Georgian), and their exact composition is unclear. Just prior to the conflict there were reports of the arrival of 300 Ossetian volunteers who had been serving in the police in North Ossetia. De facto South Ossetian President Eduard Kokoity reportedly ordered the integration of these volunteers into the de facto South Ossetian Ministry of the Interior forces. There were also reports of representatives of other ethnic groups from the North Caucasus moving into South Ossetia following the onset of hostilities, in order to fight on the South Ossetian side. Amnesty International was also informed in North Ossetia that significant numbers of men who initially fled to North Ossetia from South Ossetia in the first days of the conflict returned to South Ossetia in order to fight. Several South Ossetians interviewed by Amnesty International representatives in both South and North Ossetia stated that they had taken up arms and participated in the hostilities. See Amnesty International (AI), 'Civilians in the Line of Fire—the Georgia-Russia conflict' (2008) 34 (AI, *Civilians in the Line of Fire*).

[119] See e.g. IIFFMCG, *Report II*, 302.

[120] See e.g. *Tadić*, para 70; Statute of the International Criminal Court, art. 8(2)(f).

[121] *Prosecutor v Fatmir Limaj*, IT-03-66-T, Judgment (Trial Chamber), 30 November 2005; *Prosecutor v Haradinaj*, IT-04-84-T, Judgment (Trial Chamber), 3 April 2008, paras 39–49.

[122] See discussion in ch. 11, section 2.3 below. See also Pejic, *Status of Armed* Conflicts, 86; A. Paulus and M. Vashakmadze, 'Asymmetrical war and the notion of armed conflict—a tentative conceptualization' (2009) 91(873) *International Review of the Red Cross* 102.

word 'protracted' suggests that the criterion relates exclusively to the time over which armed conflict takes place, it is accepted that the key requirement here is the intensity of the force.[123]

In South Ossetia, the armed conflict lasted for a minimum of five days, and there is evidence that hostilities continued sporadically after that period. It is suggested that given the long history of tension over the disputed territory of South Ossetia (discussed above), and the length, extent and nature of the hostilities in August 2008, a compelling case can be made that it constituted a non-international armed conflict.

When considering the length of the conflict, it could also be legitimate to treat the situation as an ongoing non-international armed conflict which had continued since the early 1990s, characterized by periodic hostilities in relation to territory that was controlled by the South Ossetian authorities (see the discussion above on the historical context of the South Ossetian conflict). For example, Paulus has argued that 'protractedness' is a broad term that also encompasses recurrent events of violence.[124]

There is substantial evidence of various forms of criminality having been perpetrated by the Ossetian groups, including hostage-taking, arbitrary arrest, ill-treatment, gender-related crime (including rape and assault), the destruction of property, pillaging and looting (see section 4.4 below). Given the disparate groups involved (as noted above), a further question arises as to whether criminal organizations were involved in the conflict, and, if so, whether their actions could be qualified as armed conflict to which the rules of international humanitarian law apply. This will depend upon the level of organization of the groups involved and the intensity of the violence.[125]

4.3. The extent of Russian control over South Ossetia

It is then necessary to establish the extent to which Russia exercised control over the South Ossetian forces, in order to assess whether the South Ossetian forces can be considered to have been acting as de facto agents of Russia, thereby rendering the whole conflict international. If there were no such control, it is suggested that such a conflict (between Georgia and the South Ossetian forces) could be characterized as an 'internationalized non-international armed conflict', but that it would not be an international armed conflict.[126] As we will see, the test of control is not necessarily

---

See discussion in ch. 3, section 6.1 above.

[124] A. Paulus, 'Non International Armed Conflict under Common Article 3' in *Armed Conflicts and Parties to Armed Conflicts under IHL: Confronting Legal Categories to Contemporary Realities* (2010) 40 *Collegium* 31.

[125] See e.g. the discussion of this issue in S. Vité, 'La Lutte Contre La Criminalité organisée: peut-on parler de conflit armé au sens où l'entend le droit international humanitaire?' in *Armed Conflicts and Parties to Armed Conflicts under IHL: Confronting Legal Categories to Contemporary Realities*, (2010) 40 *Collegium*, 69–77.

[126] M.E. O'Connell, 'Saving Lives through a Definition of International Armed Conflict' in *Armed Conflicts and Parties to Armed Conflicts under IHL: Confronting Legal Categories to Contemporary Realities* (2010) 40 *Collegium* 24.

simple to state, let alone apply, and it is of course not unusual for the relationship between a State and militia forces to fluctuate over time.[127]

As Dapo Akande discusses in chapter 3, defining State control over a non-state group is not uncontroversial: there is no single test for the attribution of State responsibility. Akande suggests there are at least two.[128] There is, firstly, a test to determine whether a non-state group is a de facto State organ (under article 4 of the ILC's Articles on State Responsibility). If that test is satisfied then all the acts of the non-state group would be attributable to the State. Secondly, specific acts of a non-state group can be attributable to a State (under article 8 of the ILC's Articles on State Responsibility) where specific acts are carried out under a State's instructions or under its direction or effective control.[129]

Taking the broader test first, in the *Tadić* case, the ICTY Appeals Chamber was required to determine whether an international armed conflict existed in Bosnia and Herzegovina after 19 May 1992, which was found to be the case on the basis that the armed forces of the *Republika Srpska* were under the overall control of the Federal Republic of Yugoslavia (FRY). The Appeals Chamber found that mere financial or military assistance by a State would not be sufficient to engage its responsibility—it applied an 'overall control' test:

> . . . control by a State over subordinate *armed forces or militias or paramilitary units* may be of an overall character (and must comprise more than the mere provision of financial assistance or military equipment or training). This requirement, however, does not go so far as to include the issuing of specific orders by the State, or its direction of each individual operation. Under international law it is by no means necessary that the controlling authorities should plan all the operations of the units dependent on them, choose their targets, or give specific instructions concerning the conduct of military operations and any alleged violations of international humanitarian law. The control required by international law may be deemed to exist when a State (or, in the context of an armed conflict, the Party to the conflict) *has a role in organising, coordinating or planning the military actions* of the military group, in addition to financing, training and equipping or providing operational support to that group. Acts performed by the group or members thereof may be regarded as acts of *de facto* State organs regardless of any specific instruction by the controlling State concerning the commission of each of those acts.
>
> Of course, if, as in *Nicaragua*, the controlling State is *not the territorial State* where the armed clashes occur or where at any rate the armed units perform their acts, more extensive and compelling evidence is required to show that the State is genuinely in control of the units or groups not merely by financing and equipping them, but also by generally directing or helping plan their actions.[130]

---

[127] See e.g. J. Stewart, 'Fragmented Armed Conflicts: 'Internationalised' internal armed conflicts and 'internalised' international armed conflicts' in *Armed Conflicts and Parties to Armed Conflicts under IHL: Confronting Legal Categories to Contemporary Realities* (2010) 40 *Collegium* 54.

[128] See further discussion in ch. 3, section 7.1 above.

[129] *Case Concerning Application of the Convention on the Prevention and Punishment of the Crime of Genocide (Bosnia and Herzegovina v Serbia and Montenegro)* ICJ Rep 2007, 43, paras 396–402.

[130] *Prosecutor v Duško Tadić*, IT-94-1-A, Judgment (Appeals Chamber), 15 July 1999, paras 137–8.

Furthermore, the ICTY Appeals Chamber also found in *Tadić* that 'where the controlling State in question is an adjacent State with territorial ambitions on the State where the conflict is taking place, and the controlling State is attempting to achieve its territorial enlargement through the armed forces which it controls, it may be easier to establish the threshold'.[131]

Russia and the South Ossetian authorities maintained that the latter, not the former, were in control,[132] whereas Georgia argued that Russia was in control of the South Ossetian militia.[133] However, the ICTY Appeals Chamber in *Tadić* rightly warned against an 'undue emphasis upon the ostensible structures and overt declarations of the belligerents', requiring instead a 'nuanced analysis of the reality of their relationship' (para 154).

A historical perspective is important here. Russia had been actively involved in the political mediation of the 1991 South Ossetian conflict and the 1992 ceasefire agreement.[134] In 1996, Georgia and South Ossetia, with the participation of Russia, the Republic of North Ossetia-Alania and the OSCE, signed the Memorandum on Measures to Provide Security and Strengthen Mutual Trust between the Parties to the Georgian-Ossetian Conflict.[135] The Tagliavini Report noted that parallel with this process of Georgian-Ossetian normalization, 'another process was going on: that of the gradual tightening of links between these two territories [South Ossetia and Abkhazia] and the Russian Federation. This second process, more visible after 1999 and accelerated in the spring of 2008, appeared stronger than the first'.[136]

From the late 1990s onwards, Russian citizenship and passports were granted to the vast majority of ethnic Ossetians, thereby also granting them entitlement to Russian pensions and other social benefits.[137] Possession of a Russian passport was

[131] *Prosecutor v Duško Tadić*, IT-94-1-A, Judgment (Appeals Chamber), 15 July 1999, para 140.

[132] IIFFMCG, *Report III*, South Ossetia: Responses to Questions from IIFFMCG (Military Aspects); IIFFMCG, *Report III*, Russia: Responses to Questions from IIFFMCG (Legal Aspects); IIFFMCG, *Report III*, Russia: Responses to Additional Questions from IIFFMCG (Legal Aspects); *Application of the International Convention on the Elimination of All Forms of Racial Discrimination (Georgia v Russian Federation)*, Request for the Indication of Provisional Measures, Order of 15 October 2008 (*Georgia v Russia*, Order of 15 October 2008). See also *Georgia v Russia* Admissibility Decision, para 44.

[133] IIFFMCG, *Report III*, Georgia: Responses to Questions from IIFFMCG (Legal Aspects); *Georgia v Russian Federation*, ECtHR, App No. 38263/08, Application by Georgia; *Application of the International Convention on the Elimination of All Forms of Racial Discrimination (Georgia v Russian Federation)*, Application Initiating Proceedings (12 August 2008); *Georgia v Russia* Admissibility Decision, para 25.

[134] ICG, *Avoiding War*, 6.

[135] Memorandum on Measures to Provide Security and Strengthen Mutual Trust between the Parties to the Georgian-Ossetian Conflict, available at: <www.mtholyoke.edu/acad/intrel/georosse.htm>. See also, United Nations Security Council, Update Report No. 2, Georgia, 12 August 2008, available at: <www.securitycouncilreport.org/site/c.glKWLeMTIsG/b.4423477>.

[136] IIFFMCG, *Report I*, 29, para 31.

[137] Ibid, 8, para 12; PACE, Doc. 9564, para 27. See also M. Danilova, 'Russia launches passport offensive' *Associated Press* (22 February 2009) available at: <http://www.archives.dawn.com/archives/3482>; 'Russian tanks enter South Ossetia' *BBC News* (8 August 2008); C. Levy, 'Russia Backs Independence of Georgian Enclaves' *The New York Times* (26 March 2008); 'Russia Marches into South Ossetia' *Der Spiegel* (8 August 2008).

particularly significant for residents of South Ossetia following the imposition of a visa regime between Russia and Georgia in 2000 and effectively resulted in a visa-free regime for South Ossetia.[138]

In 2002, in a report on the 'Situation in Georgia and the consequences for the stability of the Caucasus region', the Parliamentary Assembly of the Council of Europe called upon the Russian Federation inter alia

i. to refrain from any action or declarations which might interfere in the internal affairs of Georgia or violate the sovereignty and the territorial integrity of Georgia, in particular from launching any military action on Georgian territory as expressed by the President of the Russian Federation on 11 September 2002

ii. to refrain from any unilateral measures affecting Georgia and its citizens, in particular as regards Abkhazia and South Ossetia..... including in the fields of economic assistance and the freedom of movement of persons and goods, in particular, with respect to visas, customs and passport issues...

iii.....

iv. to remove their military bases in Georgia as soon as possible, in accordance with the agreement reached with Georgia.[139]

In addition, PACE further noted in 2002 that 'some statements made in Moscow hinting at a possible unification of South and North Ossetia with the support of Russia, may aggravate the tensions and keep alive unrealistic hopes'.[140]

In 2004, PACE urged the government of Russia, in respect of the secessionist regions '. . . to use its influence with the regimes in Tsinkhvali and Sukhumi to calm down the situation and help the Georgian authorities more actively in the search for a peaceful political way to restore the territorial integrity of Georgia'.[141]

A PACE Report of January 2006 noted that 'Georgia accuses Russia of channelling financial and military aid to the South-Ossetian leadership. Ninety per cent of the population has Russian passports and the key officials are Russian citizens'.[142]

In an interview on 10 June 2006, the de facto president of South Ossetia, Eduard Kokoity stated:

I wish to emphasise that South Ossetia is already de facto an entity of the Russian Federation, because 95% of the citizens of South Ossetia are Russian nationals... Russian laws apply in the Republic of South Ossetia; the currency is the Russian rouble; the RF Criminal Code is in force. South Ossetia is de facto an entity of the Russian Federation. We simply have to consolidate this legally.[143]

---

[138] PACE, Doc. 9564, para 27. See also, PACE, Doc. 919125, 'Honouring of obligations and commitments by Georgia', Report (13 September 2001).

[139] PACE, Doc. 9564, para 10.

[140] Ibid, para 39.

[141] PACE, 'Honouring of obligations and commitments by Georgia', Report, Doc. 10383 (21 December 2004).

[142] PACE, 'Implementation of Resolution 1415 (2005) on the honouring of obligations and commitments by Georgia', Report, Doc. 10779 (5 January 2006) para 36.

[143] 'Eduard Kokoity' *Yuzhnaya Osetiya* (10 June 2006).

The Russian Duma issued a statement on 12 November 2006, inter alia, to the effect that

> inhabitants of South Ossetia ... were forced to create their own independent legislative and executive bodies, law enforcement structure, judiciary and armed forces, providing thus for protection of human rights on this territory and their own security ... Deputies of the State Duma support efforts of the President of the Russian Federation, V. V. Putin and of the Government of the Russian Federation for improvement of the economic situation of South Ossetia and for removal of restrictions of its external economic activities, for providing access of inhabitants of South Ossetia to Russia and world culture, education, for protection of rights of the Russian Federation's citizens, residing on the territory of Ossetia.[144]

Reports of economic assistance provided to South Ossetia include references to an economic, trade, scientific and technical and cultural cooperation agreement between South Ossetia and Karachaevo-Cherkessia[145] and 'donor aid' given by the Russian Federation to South Ossetia.[146]

In April 2008, PACE expressed 'deep concern over the decision of the Russian Federation to establish bilateral legal links with the Georgian regions of Abkhazia and South Ossetia'.[147]

The Tagliavini Report concluded that before the outbreak of the armed conflict in August 2008, Russian officials already had de facto control over South Ossetia's institutions, and especially over the security institutions and security forces.[148]

There is then substantial evidence of the extent of the control and influence of the Russian Federation over the South Ossetian authorities generally, but whether it can be said that the evidence is available to establish the Russian Federation's overall control over the South Ossetian armed forces during the August 2008 hostilities is more questionable.[149] There simply is not yet in the public domain[150]

---

[144] See, inter alia, State Duma of the Russian Federation, 'On the Referendum in South Ossetia on the question of granting it independence and about the results of elections of the president of South Ossetia' (12 November 2006), available at: <www.duma.gov.ru/index.jsp?t=ums_zayavlen/n95.html> [Russian] and <www.rrc.ge/law/gancx_2006_04_12_E.htm?lawid=1600&lng_3=en> [English]. See also, PACE, Doc. 10779, para 32.

[145] Karachaevo-Cherkessia is a republic within the Russian Federation, located in the North Caucasus.

[146] 'Karachaevo-Cherkessia and South Ossetia Signed an Agreement on Trade, Economic, Scientific, Technical and Cultural Cooperation' *Yuzhnaya Osetiya* (18 April 2007), available at: http://ugo-osetia.ru/7.32/7.32-1.html [Russian]; A. Dzhioti, 'Agreement on Announced Projects' *Yuzhnaya Osetiya* (19 May 2007), available at: <http://ugo-osetia.ru/7.42/7.42-4.html> [Russian].

[147] PACE, 'Declaration on unilateral decision by the Russian Federation to legalise ties with the Georgian regions of Abkhazia and South Ossetia', Written Declaration No. 408, Doc. 11584 (17 April 2008) para 1.

[148] IIFFMCG, *Report II*, 132. The Report stated that 'The *de facto* Government and the "Ministries of Defence", "Internal Affairs" and "Civil Defence and Emergency Situations", the "State Security Committee", the "State Border Protection Services", the "Presidential Administration"—among others—have been largely staffed by Russian representatives or South Ossetians with Russian citizenship that have worked previously in equivalent positions in Central Russia or in North Ossetia'.

[149] Amnesty International concluded that: 'It would appear that the majority of these groups answered, if only loosely, to a South Ossetian chain of command and that the South Ossetian forces in turn operated in co-operation with Russian military forces.' See AI, *Civilians in the Line of Fire*, 39.

[150] As to the difficulties of obtaining the requisite evidence in such situations, see e.g. J. Stewart, 'Fragmented Armed Conflicts: "Internationalised" internal armed conflicts and "internalised"

evidence comparable to that in *Tadić*, in which the ICTY Appeals Chamber found, for example, clear evidence of a chain of military command from the Yugoslav army to the Bosnian Serb forces and which were found to have acted in pursuance of military goals formulated in Belgrade (para 152).

As noted above, a second test applicable as regards State attribution is that specific acts of a non-state group can be attributable to a State (under article 8 of the ILC's Articles on State Responsibility) where those specific acts are carried out under a State's instructions or under its direction or effective control. That test may be easier to satisfy, for example, where the Ossetian forces accompanied the Russian armed forces, or because of the presence of Russian troops at, or in the vicinity of, a particular location where the acts in question were carried out by the Ossetians.

In any event, the question of the extent of Russian responsibility for the actions of the Ossetian armed forces is likely to be clarified in the course of the inter-state proceedings at the ICJ and the European Court of Human Rights, brought by Georgia against the Russian Federation.[151] Accordingly, in the meantime, it is suggested that it is correct to classify the hostilities as amounting to two concurrent conflicts, international and non-international.

4.4. Russia's presence in South Ossetia

A further critical question which arises is how to classify Russia's presence on South Ossetian territory after the termination of the period of armed conflict in August 2008.

In October 2008 the Georgian Parliament enacted the 'Law on Occupied Territories' the purpose of which was to define the status of territories 'occupied as a result of the military aggression of the Russian Federation and to establish a special legal regime' for such territories.[152] According to this law, the 'Tskhinvali region' (territory of the former Autonomous Republic of South Ossetia) was classified as occupied territory (as well as the airspace over it).[153] In its pleadings in the inter-state cases before the ICJ and the ECtHR, Georgia characterized South Ossetia as being under Russian occupation. For example:

> At the present time, the whole territory of South Ossetia, in addition to the western part of the former 'buffer zone' (the village of Perevi in the Sachkere District) remains under Russian occupation.
>
> . . .
> . . . after the ceasefire on 12 August 2008, the situation is properly understood as one of occupation, which is also governed within IHL by the provisions pertaining to international armed conflicts. This is because objective evidence illustrates comprehensively that significant portions of Georgia remain occupied by forces of the Russian

---

international armed conflicts' in *Armed Conflicts and Parties to Armed Conflicts under IHL: Confronting Legal Categories to Contemporary Realities* (2010) 40 *Collegium* 54.

[151] The application was declared admissible in 2011, see *Georgia v Russia* Admissibility Decision.

[152] Law on Occupied Territories, 23 October 2008, clause 1. This law is discussed further in section 5.5 below.

[153] Law on Occupied Territories, 23 October 2008, clause 2.

Federation and/or separatist forces acting as *de facto* organs of the Russian Federation.[154]

Georgia's characterization of the situation as being one of occupation by Russia in South Ossetia was flatly denied by Russia:

> ...[T]he Russian Federation submitted that, in any event, the requested provisional measures would not be justified since the Respondent had not in the past, 'does not at present, nor will it in the future, exercise effective control over South Ossetia or Abkhazia'...it explained that the Russian Federation was not an occupying Power in South Ossetia and Abkhazia, that it had never assumed the role of the existing Abkhazian and South Ossetian authorities, 'recognized as such by Georgia itself', which 'have always retained their independence and continue to do so'; and... the Russian Federation added that 'the Russian presence, apart from its participation in limited peace-keeping operations, has been restricted in time and stretches only for a few weeks.'[155]

Russia acknowledged the presence of its armed forces on the territory of Georgia, but denied it was an occupying power, arguing that the determining factor 'is whether the invading State has established effective control over the territory of the country in question and its population'. Relying on the ICTY judgment in *Prosecutor v Naletilic and Martinovic*[156] and the ICJ judgment in *Congo v Uganda*, Russia argued that the two key criteria were that the occupying power must establish a temporary administration to govern the territory and must issue instructions deemed mandatory for the local population. It argued that the Russian armed forces did not replace the lawful governments of Georgia or South Ossetia, and that no regulatory acts aimed at the local population were adopted. Finally, it suggested that the number of troops stationed in South Ossetia (3700) did not allow it to maintain effective control of the region: 'During the active phase of the military conflict the maximum size of the Russian contingent in South Ossetia and Abkhazia reached 12 thousand personnel. However, all of these forces were engaged in a military operation and not in establishing effective control.'[157]

The Tagliavini Report concluded that 'if...Russia's military intervention cannot be justified under international law, and if neither Abkhazia nor South Ossetia is a recognised independent State, IHL—and in particular the rules concerning the protection of the civilian population (mainly Geneva Convention IV) and occupation—was and may still be applicable'.[158]

In its judgment in *Naletilic and Martinovic*,[159] the ICTY drew attention to the difference between the application of the law of occupation to the civilian population according to the Fourth Geneva Convention, as opposed to article 42 of the

[154] *Georgia v Russian Federation*, ECtHR, App No. 38263/08, Application by Georgia, paras 17, 124. See also *Georgia v Russia* Admissibility Decision, para 24.

[155] *Georgia v Russia*, Order of 15 October 2008, 19, para 74. See also *Georgia v Russia* Admissibility Decision, para 44.

[156] *Prosecutor v Naletilic and Martinovic*, IT-98-34-T, Judgment (Trial Chamber), 31 March 2003 (*Naletilic and Martinovic*).

[157] *IIFFMCG, Report III*, Russia: Responses to Questions from IIFFMCG (Legal Aspects).

[158] IIFFMCG, *Report II*, 311.

[159] *Naletilic and Martinovic*, see, in particular, paras 217–21.

Hague Regulations. The commentary to the Fourth Geneva Convention makes it clear that, there, the term 'occupation' has a wider meaning than in the Hague Regulations:

> So far as individuals are concerned, the application of the Fourth Geneva Convention does not depend upon the existence of a state of occupation within the meaning of Article 42 referred to above. The relations between the civilian population of a territory and troops advancing into a territory, whether fighting or not, are governed by the present Convention. There is no intermediate period between what might be termed the invasion phase and the inauguration of a stable regime of occupation.

Accordingly, the ICTY concluded that:

> the application of the law of occupation as it affects 'individuals' as civilians protected under Geneva Convention IV does not require that the occupying power have actual authority. For the purposes of those individuals' rights, a state of occupation exists upon their falling into 'the hands of the occupying power.' Otherwise civilians would be left, during an intermediate period, with less protection than that attached to them once occupation is established.

Therefore, differing legal tests are applicable in determining whether the law of occupation applied, depending on whether the situation concerned individuals or other issues, such as property. As in the ICTY finding in *Naletilic and Martinovic*,[160] any instances of the forcible transfer by the Russian armed forces and the unlawful labour of civilians were prohibited from the moment that they fell into the hands of the opposing power, regardless of the stage of the hostilities; in order to consider such situations, it is not necessary to establish that a state of occupation, as defined by article 42 of the Hague Regulations, was in existence at the particular time.

Subject to the above point about the treatment of civilians, after the conclusion of hostilities in August 2008, it is a moot point whether the presence of Russian armed forces in South Ossetia (and the 'buffer zone') amounted to a state of occupation, as defined by article 42 of the Hague Regulations. The question is whether the available evidence establishes that the Russian Federation exercised its authority as an occupying power in South Ossetia—in a manner that is comparable, for example, to the actions of the Ugandan armed forces in appointing a provincial governor in the Ituri region of the DRC.[161] As at January 2009, Human Rights Watch considered that Russia remained an occupying power in South Ossetia.[162]

The consequence of there being a state of 'occupation' would be that, according to article 43 of the Hague Regulations, the Russian Federation would be under an obligation to take all the measures in its power to restore, and ensure, as far as possible, public order and safety in the occupied area, while respecting, unless absolutely prevented, the laws in force in the territory. Such an obligation would

[160] Ibid, para 222.   [161] *Congo v Uganda*, paras 175–6.
[162] HRW, *Up In Flames*, 35.

comprise the duty to secure respect for the applicable rules of international human rights law and international humanitarian law, to protect the inhabitants of the occupied territory against acts of violence and not to tolerate such violence by any third party. This is discussed further in section 5.4 below.

The Tagliavini Report found that both during the conflict, and even some weeks after the ceasefire, there was a 'campaign of deliberate violence against civilians', including the torching of houses and looting and pillaging. Such acts were primarily carried out in South Ossetia and in the undisputed territory of Georgia, in the areas surrounding the administrative border with South Ossetia. Human Rights Watch suggested that in many cases the perpetrators were the South Ossetian forces 'operating in close cooperation with Russian forces'.[163]

The Tagliavini Report concluded that 'while it appears difficult to conclude that Russian forces systematically participated in or tolerated the conduct of South Ossetian forces, there do seem to be credible and converging reports establishing that in many cases Russian forces did not act to prevent or stop South Ossetian forces'.[164]

Furthermore, Human Rights Watch documented a number of deliberate killings of civilians by Ossetian militia, both during the conflict and its immediate aftermath, in territory and settlements controlled by Russian forces,[165] and two cases of rape in undisputed areas of Georgia under Russian control.[166]

If, however, article 42 is not applicable, then such a wide-ranging obligation as set out in article 43 does not arise. Nevertheless, Russia still remained, and remains, responsible for any actions and omissions of its own military forces in the territory of South Ossetia in breach of its obligations under the applicable rules of international human rights law and international humanitarian law.[167]

5. Use of force and detention

5.1. Domestic law on the use of force, on capture and detention, and other international humanitarian law problems

The domestic laws of both Russia and Georgia include detailed provisions applicable to both international and non-international armed conflict. The Russian domestic law which is discussed below is also being applied on a de facto basis in South Ossetia.[168]

---

[163] HRW, *Up In Flames*, 218.
[164] IIFFMCG, *Report II*, 352.
[165] HRW, *Up In Flames*, 154.
[166] Ibid, 59.
[167] See, *mutatis mutandis*, *Congo v Uganda*, paras 178–80.
[168] According to Georgian domestic law, however, South Ossetia is an integral part of Georgia and accordingly, all the laws of Georgia are applicable in that territory. The laws adopted by the de facto administration of South Ossetia have been regarded by the Georgian government as unlawful and, therefore, as having no legal force. See e.g. art. 1(1) and art. 2 of the Constitution of Georgia (adopted 24 August 1995).

Several provisions of the Russian Criminal Code[169] have application to a situation of armed conflict. The use 'in a military conflict' of 'means and methods of warfare' banned by an international treaty applicable to the Russian Federation is prohibited by article 356 of the Criminal Code. The same provision prohibits the use of weapons of mass destruction, as well as the cruel treatment of prisoners of war or civilians, the deportation of the civilian population and the plunder of national property in occupied territories. Article 359 prohibits mercenarism.

The domestic law also lays down specific provisions establishing the duty of military service personnel to comply with international humanitarian law norms. The 'Law on the Status of Military Servicemen'[170] stipulates that the duties and responsibility of military servicemen include the 'fulfilment of aims in compliance with the international obligations of the Russian Federation' and the observance of 'the generally recognized principles and norms of international law and international treaties of the Russian Federation'. Furthermore, the Internal Service Regulations of the Armed Forces[171] provide that 'military servicemen are obliged to know and observe the norms of international humanitarian law, the rules for the treatment of the wounded, sick, shipwrecked, medical personnel, clergymen, the civilian population in the zone of military operations, as well as prisoners of war...'.

Those regulations also require that commanders must know and apply international humanitarian law norms, and train servicemen under their command in such standards. Commanders are required to instigate disciplinary or criminal proceedings in respect of service personnel who breach these standards.[172]

The international humanitarian law regulations for the Russian Armed Forces provide a concise overview of the applicable law, requiring, inter alia, compliance with the principles of legality, distinction, proportionality, humanity and military necessity.[173] However, the accuracy of the Regulations can be questioned in certain

---

[169] Federal Law of 13 June 1996, No. 63-FZ.

[170] Federal Law of 27 May 1998, No. 76-FZ, art. 26. There is a similar provision in the Internal Service Regulations of the Armed Forces of the Russian Federation (approved by Decree of the President of the Russian Federation of 10 November 2007, No. 1495), art. 16.

[171] Internal Service Regulations of the Armed Forces of the Russian Federation (approved by Decree of the President of the Russian Federation of 10 November 2007, No. 1495), art. 22 and art. 161 (duties of privates).

[172] Articles 77 and 83.

[173] Manual on International Humanitarian Law for the Armed Forces of the Russian Federation (approved by the Minister of Defence of the Russian Federation, 8 August 2001). Article 17 provides: 'While getting military units ready for combat operations and controlling them during hostilities commanders shall be guided by the principles of international humanitarian law: the principles of legality, distinction, proportionality, humanity and military necessity. The principle of *legality* means strict and precise respect of international humanitarian law by all military command bodies, military and civilian personnel. The principle of *distinction* means making distinction, under any circumstances, between the civilian population and servicemen, as well as between civilian objects and military objectives, which helps ensure protection of civilian persons and objects during combat operations and concentrate the force's effort against the enemy military objectives. The principle of *proportionality* means that the belligerents shall not cause damage to civilian objects and losses of civilian life which would be excessive in relation to the military advantage anticipated. The principle of *humanity* means respect and protection of persons not directly taking part in hostilities, including members of the enemy armed groups who have laid down their arms or otherwise ceased to take part in hostilities. The

respects. For example, they characterize the principle of proportionality as consisting 'of the fact that combatants must not cause damage to civilian objects and bring about losses amongst the civilian population, disproportionate to the advantage over the enemy which is expected to be obtained as a result of the military operations'. This formulation does not accurately reflect the principle of proportionality in that it makes its judgment on the basis of the actual result of the military operation. In fact, the test is one of anticipation. Thus, article 51(5)(b) of Additional Protocol I refers to an attack 'which may be expected to cause incidental loss of civilian life, injury to civilians, damage to civilian objects, or a combination thereof, which would be excessive in relation to the concrete and direct military advantage anticipated'. It follows therefore that it is necessary to look at what was foreseen rather than what actually occurred.[174]

The Georgian Criminal Code prohibits calling for, preparing for and waging a war of aggression.[175] Article 411 of the Criminal Code sets out detailed provisions prohibiting violations of international humanitarian law norms in the course of both international and internal armed conflict, including attacks on civilians, indiscriminate attacks on civil objects, attacks on unprotected areas and demilitarized zones, the deportation or illegal expulsion of civilians, unfounded hindrance to the repatriation of POWs or civilians and torture or other inhumane treatment. Other breaches of international humanitarian law norms are prohibited by article 413 of the Criminal Code, including the use of weapons, and the employment of methods of warfare, 'which are of a nature to cause superfluous injury or unnecessary suffering', looting and any other war crime.

Difficulties arising from the provisions of the Georgian law on occupied territories, introduced in October 2008, are discussed in section 5.5 below.

5.2. Treatment of detainees and other significant international humanitarian law problems

The Tagliavini Report found that violations of international humanitarian law and human rights law were committed by Georgia, Russia and the South Ossetian authorities. Particular issues which were considered by the Tagliavini Report, and by other international agencies and NGOs, included allegations of ethnic cleansing (by South Ossetian forces or irregular armed groups), forced displacement, hostage-taking and arbitrary arrest, ill-treatment and gender-related crime (including rape and assault), the destruction of property, pillaging and looting and indiscriminate attacks (both as a result of the nature of weaponry used—which included cluster

---

principle of *military necessity* means a possibility to choose any methods to accomplish the mission, other than those prohibited by the international humanitarian law. When applying the principle of military necessity the commander shall try to minimise incidental losses and destruction.' [unofficial English translation, ICRC].

[174] See also the discussion of the principle of proportionality in ch. 4, section 4.1 above.
[175] Articles 404 and 405.

munitions[176] and GRAD rockets—and their targeting). Much of such conduct is prohibited by international humanitarian law both in time of international and non-international armed conflict, in particular when taking account of customary rules.

However one important point worth flagging here is a consequence which arises if the conflict between Georgia and the Ossetians is to be classified as a non-international armed conflict. In those circumstances, there is legal asymmetry, in that one party, Georgia, was bound by various human rights treaties, but the Ossetian militia groups were not, a problem that Jelena Pejic discusses in chapter 4.[177]

A further issue of legal distinction arising from the South Ossetia conflict is the question of Russia's responsibility for violations arising from aerial attacks in respect of territory in undisputed parts of Georgia over which it did not have effective control on the ground at the time (such as its aerial attacks on Gori city on and after 9 August 2008).[178] There is inconsistency, and therefore continuing uncertainty, as to the extent and nature of the extraterritorial application of human rights law. In its Grand Chamber judgment in *Al-Skeini v United Kingdom*, the European Court of Human Rights reiterated that jurisdictional competence under the European Convention on Human Rights is primarily a territorial matter.[179] However, acts performed, or producing effects, outside a state's territory could, exceptionally, give rise to the exercise of jurisdiction. The Grand Chamber recalled that the Court had previously recognized such exceptional circumstances in two types of situation ('state agent authority and control' and 'effective control over an area'), but it did *not* find that jurisdiction could *only* arise extraterritorially in one or other of those situations. The test is a broader one: 'in each case, the question whether exceptional circumstances exist which require and justify a finding by the Court that the State was exercising jurisdiction extra-territorially must be determined with reference to the particular facts'. Furthermore, the definition of 'effective control' on the ground, as applied by the Grand Chamber of the European Court of Human Rights in the earlier *Bankovic* case,[180] and the definition of 'state agent authority and control', have been considerably refined and expanded (and occasionally conflated) by various recent developments in international law.[181] It is arguable

---

[176] Neither Georgia nor Russia has yet signed the Convention on Cluster Munitions (2008).

[177] See discussion in ch. 4, section 4.3. See also, e.g. A. Paulus and M. Vashakmadze, 'Asymmetrical war and the notion of armed conflict—a tentative conceptualization' (2009) 91(873) *International Review of the Red Cross*, 109.

[178] In relation to Russian aerial attacks on Gori, Amnesty International, for example, reported that: 'The town of Gori was hit in four or five localised areas in the course of a number of separate attacks between 8 and 12 August.' (AI, *Civilians in the Line of Fire*, 29).

[179] *Al-Skeini v United Kingdom* (Judgment) App No. 55721/07 (7 July 2011).

[180] *Bankovic and others v Belgium and others* (Decision) App No. 52207/99 (12 December 2001).

[181] *Ilaşcu and others v Moldova and Russia* (Judgment) App No. 48787/99 (8 July 2004) para 317 ('a State's responsibility may . . . be engaged on account of acts which have sufficiently proximate repercussions on rights guaranteed by the Convention, even if those repercussions occur outside its jurisdiction'); *Issa v Turkey* (Judgment) App No. 31821/96 (16 November 2004) para 74 (reference to the principle that a State can, through military action, be in 'temporary, effective control'); *Pad and others v Turkey* (Decision) App No. 60167/00 (28 June 2007) para 54 (respondent State's responsibility engaged as a result of firing from helicopters); *Andreou v Turkey* (Decision) App No. 45653/99 (3 June 2008); *Armando Alejandre Jr and others v Cuba*, Inter-American Commission on Human Rights, Case No. 11.589, Report No. 86/99 (29 September 1999) para 25; HRC, 'General Comment

that the human rights law jurisprudence has moved on from a territorial preoccu-
pation as exemplified by *Bankovic* (with its focus on 'effective control' and *espace
juridique*) towards more of a 'cause and effect' concept of jurisdiction.[182] These
questions will be decided in due course by the European Court of Human Rights
which has a number of cases pending before it in which applicants complain of the
consequences (including fatalities) of the Russian aerial bombardment of Gori. The
European Court's practice has, to date, not been to refer directly to international
humanitarian law, although it has engaged with humanitarian law concepts such as
the need to carry out military operations in a way that minimizes incidental civilian
losses and the prohibition of the use of indiscriminate weaponry.[183] It is suggested
that it will be increasingly necessary for the European Court, in conflict-related
cases, to assess the legal classification of the conflict in question, before then
applying, for example, the right to life (article 2 of the European Convention on
Human Rights) in the light of applicable provisions of the relevant aspects of
international humanitarian law.

There is however no doubt about the applicability of international humanitarian
law as regards Russia's aerial bombardment of Gori city, in the course of the
international armed conflict with Georgia. Indeed, the emphasis here is on particular issues arising from the characterization of the conflict.[184]

5.3. Detainees

The applicability of international humanitarian law rules relating to detention
depends upon the classification of an armed conflict as being international or

---

31', CCPR/C/21/Rev.1/Add.13, para 10; *Legal Consequences of the Construction of a Wall in the
Occupied Palestinian Territory* (Advisory Opinion) ICJ Rep 2004, 136, paras 109–11; *Congo v Uganda*,
paras 178–80 and 216–17. In the Grand Chamber judgment in *Al-Skeini v United Kingdom*
(Judgment) App No. 55721/07 (7 July 2011), the European Court concluded that the UK, 'through
its soldiers engaged in security operations in Basrah during the period in question, exercised authority
and control over individuals killed in the course of such security operations, so as to establish a
jurisdictional link between the deceased and the United Kingdom for the purposes of Article 1 of the
Convention' (para 149).

[182] See also, e.g. M. Scheinin, 'Extraterritorial effect of the International Covenant on Civil and
Political Rights' in F. Coomans and M.T. Kamminga (eds), *Extraterritorial Application of Human
Rights Treaties* (2004) 73–81, who argued post-*Bankovic* that the question of jurisdiction should be
determined by the relationship between the state and the individual. In *Al-Skeini v United Kingdom*
(Judgment) App No. 55721/07 (7 July 2011) para 142, the Grand Chamber of the European Court
explicitly confirmed that jurisdiction *can* exist outside the territory covered by Council of Europe
member states. See also, *Al-Jedda v United Kingdom* (Judgment) App No. 27021/08 (7 July 2011).

[183] *Isayeva, Yusupova and Bazayeva v Russia* (Judgment) App No. 57947/00, 57948/00, 57949/00
(24 February 2005) paras 177, 195, 197, 199; *Isayeva v Russia* (Judgment) App No. 57950/00
(24 February 2005) paras 176, 187, 189–91. See also C. Droege, 'Elective affinities? Human rights
and humanitarian law' (2008) 90(871) *International Review of the Red Cross* 501.

[184] The commentary and analysis on the South Ossetian conflict to date has tended to focus more
on *ius ad bellum* issues. See e.g. A. Nußberger, 'The War between Russia and Georgia–Consequences
and Unresolved Questions' (2009) 1(2) *Göttingen Journal of International Law* 341–64; N. Petro, 'The
Legal Case for Russian Intervention in Georgia' (2008) 32 *Fordham International Law Journal* 1524;
C. Henderson and J. Green, 'The jus ad bellum and entities short of statehood in the report on the
conflict in Georgia' (2010) 59 *International and Comparative Law Quarterly* 129–39.

non-international. In an international armed conflict detained combatants will have the status of prisoners of war (in certain circumstances).[185] It has been confirmed that the Georgian armed forces captured Ossetians, and vice versa.[186] If the conflict between Georgia and the Ossetian forces is classified as being part of an international armed conflict (because of Russia's overall control of the Ossetian forces) then such detainees would have the status of prisoners of war, but that would not be the case if this aspect of the conflict is to be considered as being non-international—leading to what Pejic has described as 'the uneven protection of humanitarian law'.[187] In that situation, Ossetians detained by the Georgian armed forces would be subject to the domestic laws of Georgia.[188] Thus, what might be regarded as reasonable force in the context of an international armed conflict could be prosecuted as kidnapping, murder or other offences under the domestic law if the conflict is to be classified as being non-international. A further point of (unresolved) contention that arises here is the question whether citizens of the State against which they are fighting can be granted combatant or POW status.[189] The situation is further complicated by the evidence that some detainees held by the Ossetians were then transferred into the custody of the Russian armed forces, and also that Russian forces were present at some of the locations where detainees were held by the Ossetians.[190]

In fact, Georgia distinguished between (the five) 'Russian military personnel held as POWs' and (the 32) 'members of separatist illegal armed formations'.[191] Those entitled to POW status in an international armed conflict include all members of the organized armed forces of a party to a conflict, even if that party is represented by an authority which is not recognized by the adversary, provided that the forces are under a command responsible to a party to the conflict for the conduct of its subordinates, and that they are subject to an internal disciplinary system which enforces compliance with the law of armed conflict.[192] In addition, members of 'any other militias, volunteer corps, or organized resistance movements' would also have POW status provided that they are commanded by a person responsible for subordinates, that they have a 'fixed, distinctive sign recognizable at a distance', that they carry their arms openly and that they comply with the law of armed conflict.[193]

[185] This was formally accepted by Russia, see Russia, 'Responses to Questions Posited by the IIFFMCG (Legal Aspects)' 11.

[186] IIFFMCG, *Report II*, 359–61.

[187] Pejic, *Status of Armed Conflicts*, 93.

[188] Members of the Georgian armed forces captured by the Ossetians would also be subject to the domestic law. As to the applicable domestic law, see section 5.1 above.

[189] See *Public Prosecutor v Koi and others* [1968] AC 829 and e.g. A. Rogers, 'Combatant Status' in E. Wilmshurst and S. Breau (eds), *Perspectives on the ICRC Study on Customary International Humanitarian Law* (2007) 107–8.

[190] IIFFMCG, *Report II*, 359–61.

[191] Georgia, 'Responses to Questions Posited by the IIFFMCG (Humanitarian Aspects)', Question 3, provided to the IIFFMCG on 5 June 2009, 2–3.

[192] Geneva Convention III, art. 4; Additional Protocol I, art. 43.

[193] Article 4(A)(2) Geneva Convention III. Ossetian forces were frequently identified as wearing 'camouflage' or 'paramilitary' uniforms with white armbands. See e.g. IIFFMCG, *Report II*, 352, 363, 387.

Georgia may well be able to make an argument that one or more of these conditions did not apply in respect of their 32 detainees from 'illegal armed formations'.[194] Indeed, Human Rights Watch concluded that the South Ossetian militia did not meet all four of these conditions, and accordingly that the detention of their members should have been carried out in accordance with the Fourth Geneva Convention.[195] However, if that were not the case, to distinguish between the Ossetian detainees and the Russian POWs would appear to be in contradiction to Georgia's classification of the entire conflict as being an international armed conflict. There are differing conditions regulating the release of POWs under the Third Geneva Convention and detainees under the Fourth Geneva Convention. Prisoners of war are required to be released and repatriated without delay after the cessation of active hostilities,[196] whereas the Fourth Geneva Convention provides that detainees are to be released as soon as the reasons which necessitated internment no longer exist (which therefore could be during the conflict).[197]

If the fighting between Georgia and the Ossetian militia is to be classified as a non-international armed conflict, this may also have repercussions as to the legality of the detention of the thirty-two Ossetians. As Jelena Pejic discusses in chapter 4,[198] their 'internment', as such, would have necessitated Georgia's derogation from article 5 of the ECHR. However, Georgia did not make any such measure of derogation. The detention of members of the Georgian armed forces, by the Ossetian militia, would have violated the Georgian domestic law.

5.4. Russia's responsibilities as an occupying power

A further important question is the extent to which Russia was an occupying power over territory in South Ossetia or the 'buffer zone' *after* the termination of hostilities, and therefore the extent to which it had a responsibility to protect residents and other civilians in those regions. As noted above, under the international humanitarian law on military occupation, an occupying power has an obligation to take all the measures in its power to restore, and ensure, as far as possible, public order and safety. Moreover, human rights law requires States to secure the rights of all those 'within their jurisdiction'.[199] As discussed above, a number of international bodies and NGOs, including the UNHCR,[200] the Council of Europe Commissioner for Human Rights,[201] PACE[202] and international

---

[194] Furthermore, there is evidence that Ossetian civilians took part in pillaging and looting—IIFFMCG, *Report*, Vol. 2, 364–5.

[195] HRW, *Up In Flames*, 31, 80.

[196] Article 118, Geneva Convention III.

[197] Article 132, Geneva Convention IV.

[198] For further discussion, see ch. 4, section 3.2 above. She also raises the possibility of the need for derogation from art. 9 of the ICCPR, depending on the content of the domestic law.

[199] See e.g. art. 1 ECHR.

[200] UNHCR, 'UNHCR teams enter Georgia "buffer zone"' (16 September 2008), available at: <www.unhcr.org/news/NEWS/48cfa9b01d.html>.

[201] *CommDH(2008)22*, para 89.

[202] See e.g. PACE, res. 1633 (2008) para 6.

NGOs[203] took the view that Russia occupied and executed de facto control over this region. There is also evidence that there were substantial violations of international humanitarian and human rights law, in both South Ossetia and the 'buffer zone', in particular after August 2008, including assaults, robbery, kidnapping, looting and torching of houses.[204] By way of example, PACE suggested as follows:

> The large-scale looting and destruction of property as well as patterns of ethnic cleansing in South Ossetia are a direct violation of international humanitarian and human rights law. It should be stressed that, even if Russian troops have not been directly involved, Russia, under international law, bears full responsibility for any crimes and human rights violations committed on the territories that are under its effective control.[205]

PACE also stated:

> Russia appears not to have succeeded in its duty, under the 1907 Hague Convention (IV) on the Laws and Customs of War on Land, to prevent looting, maintain law and order and protect property in the areas under the de facto control of its forces. In this respect, the Assembly notes that Russia bears full responsibility for violations of human rights and humanitarian law in the areas under its de facto control. In the light of the case law of the European Court of Human Rights, this also concerns acts committed at the behest of the de facto authorities in Tshkinvali.
>
> The Assembly is especially concerned about credible reports of acts of ethnic cleansing committed in ethnic Georgian villages in South Ossetia and the 'buffer zone' by irregular militia and gangs which the Russian troops failed to stop. It stresses in this respect that such acts were mostly committed after the signing of the ceasefire agreement on 12 August 2008, and continue today.[206]

Russia has denied that it was, or is, an occupying power, but it has stated that it sought to carry out a policing function in the region. Russia acknowledged that in some parts of South Ossetia, and undisputed Georgian territory, there was a 'vacuum of police presence'. The Russian authorities 'tried to maintain law and order and prevent any offences in the areas of their deployment, including Georgia proper, where owing to the flight of Georgian government authorities an apparent vacuum of police presence ensued. The Russian military force could not substitute for the government of South Ossetia'.[207]

They also stated:

> From day one of the operation, the Russian military command undertook exhaustive measures to prevent pillaging, looting and acts of lawlessness with respect to the local Georgian population. All personnel serving in units that took part in the operation was

---

[203] See e.g. HRW, *Up In Flames*, 33–5.

[204] *CommDH(2008)22*, para 87.

[205] PACE, 'The consequences of the war between Georgia and Russia', Doc. 11724 (1 October 2008) Monitoring Committee, co-rapporters: Mr Luc Van den Brande and Mr Mátyás Eörsi, 15, para 54. State responsibility under human rights law may be engaged where a State exercises effective control of an area outside its national territory, or as a result of human rights violations committed against persons considered to be under the State's authority and control through its agents.

[206] PACE, res. 1633 (2008), 2 October 2008, 35th sitting, paras 11–13.

[207] Russia, 'Responses to Questions Posited by the IIFFMCG (Legal Aspects)' 7–8.

familiarised with the Directive issued by the General Staff of the Russian Armed Forces and the order given by the Army Commander-in-Chief 'to maintain public safety and ensure the security and protection of citizens residing in the territory of the South Ossetian Republic'.

Russian troops, jointly with South Ossetian law-enforcement and military units, provided round-the-clock protection of the homes and land allotments that remained undamaged in Georgian villages, at the same time ensuring the safety and security of South Ossetian residents regardless of their ethnic background.

The Tagliavini Report found Russia's reliance upon the South Ossetian authorities to have been flawed, on the basis that they in fact failed to maintain public order or prevent human rights violations, and that as regards the 'buffer zone', the South Ossetian authorities were *not* exercising control. The evidence suggests that Russian forces were aware that violations were being perpetrated, but failed to act. The Tagliavini Report concluded that to a certain extent the Russian authorities were in a position to ensure public order where they were stationed, and that they failed to 'take the necessary measures to prevent or stop the widespread campaign of looting, burning and other serious violations committed after the ceasefire'.[208]

5.5. The Georgian law on occupied territories

In October 2008 the Georgian Parliament enacted the 'Law of Georgia on Occupied Territories' which provided that various territories, including South Ossetia (and the airspace over it), were under occupation by Russia and set out various legal provisions applicable in such areas.[209] A number of its provisions are problematic, as has been highlighted by the Venice Commission.[210] Article 4 places restrictions on free movement into South Ossetia, making it a criminal offence for foreign citizens and persons without citizenship to enter the territory other than from Gori Municipality. Article 6 prohibits various economic activities in the region. With reference to the Fourth Geneva Convention and the preamble to the Hague Convention, the Venice Commission suggested that such laws could impact, inter alia, upon the provision by international organizations of humanitarian aid, and concluded that the laws must not 'contradict the rule of customary international law that the well-being of the population in occupied areas has to be a basic concern of those involved in a conflict'.[211]

Article 5 declares void any real estate transaction concluded in violation of Georgian law. The Venice Commission raised the possibility that such a clause may breach the right to peaceful enjoyment of possessions in article 1 of Protocol

---

[208] IIFFMCG, *Report II*, 375. The Commissioner for Human Rights also argued that the Russian forces had a duty under international humanitarian law to maintain law and order in the zone they controlled, see *CommDH(2008)22*, para 89. See also similar conclusions in AI, *Civilians in the Line of Fire*, 32.

[209] See Law on Occupied Territories, 23 October 2008, clauses 1 and 2.

[210] *Opinion on the Law on Occupied Territories of Georgia*, Venice Commission, Opinion No. 516/2009, 13–14 March 2009 *(Venice Commission Opinion)*.

[211] Ibid, paras 35, 50.

No. 1 to the European Convention, not least because of the retroactive application of the provision as from 1990.[212]

Article 7 of the Law on occupied territories provides that in South Ossetia 'the Russian Federation shall be responsible for violation of internationally recognised human rights stipulated in the Constitution of Georgia', that Russia shall 'reimburse moral and material damages' and shall be responsible for protecting cultural heritage in South Ossetia. However, as the Venice Commission notes, 'questions of international responsibility cannot be regulated on the basis of national law, but are solved on the basis of international law'.[213] The reference to the obligation to protect cultural heritage would apparently explicitly engage Russia's responsibility for acts committed, for example, by Ossetian militia and civilians.

Finally, the Venice Commission expressed its concern about article 8 of the law, the effect of which is to declare invalid any act of the de facto South Ossetian authorities. The Commission noted that if Georgia refused to accept basic documents such as birth or death certificates, this would violate article 8 of the European Convention on Human Rights.[214]

6. Conclusions

6.1. Difficulties of classification

As we have seen, it is far from a straightforward task to define the boundaries of the South Ossetian conflict, in either the temporal or geographical senses. There are also apparently unresolvable questions about the identity of some of the parties involved, and certainly about how, and by whom, they were organized and controlled. As a consequence, it is not simple to classify the conflict or conflicts.

Inevitably the parties themselves did not see eye to eye on classification. Russia sought initially to emphasize its peace-keeping role in a conflict between Georgian and Ossetian forces. It came to acknowledge its role as a part of an international armed conflict, but always maintained that there was also a separate non-international armed conflict as between Georgia and the South Ossetian armed forces. Georgia, however, argued that the totality of the armed conflict was international, and that the Ossetians were properly to be regarded as agents of Russia. The international community (international agencies and individual States) did not give a clear or unambiguous view about classification—indeed it sought to avoid the issue.

---

[212] In accordance with art. 11(2).

[213] *Venice Commission Opinion*, para 37.

[214] Although the Commission stated that it had received assurances from the Georgian authorities that birth and death certificates were 'acknowledged through a simplified procedure', para 43. As to the 'Namibia principle', see *Legal Consequences for States of the Continued Presence of South Africa in Namibia (South West Africa) notwithstanding Security Council Resolution 276 (1970)* (Advisory Opinion) ICJ Rep 1971, 16, and for a recent example of its application by the European Court of Human Rights, see *Demopoulos and others v Turkey* (Decision) App No. 46113/99 et seq (1 March 2010) paras 92–98.

When did the armed conflict begin and end? There is no doubt that the Georgian artillery bombardment of South Ossetia and the Russian counter-attack took place on 7 and 8 August 2008, but given the long-lasting tensions in the region, did this represent simply a more intensive stage of armed hostilities in the course of an enduring conflict? This chapter concludes that the conflict opened with the Georgian artillery attack on South Ossetian armed forces, with Russia then intervening in support of the South Ossetians—a non-international armed conflict very quickly became, at least partially, internationalized. As Jelena Pejic has put it, this therefore meant an 'upward' reclassification of the conflict from non-international armed conflict to international armed conflict,[215] with a broader range of international humanitarian law coming into play as a consequence. Can it be said with confidence when the conflict ended, with the Russian armed forces continuing to occupy South Ossetia and its self-styled 'buffer zone' within undisputed Georgia, long after the termination of the principal period of armed hostilities in the few days after 7 August? This chapter concludes that the 2008 conflict should be considered as an armed conflict distinct from previous hostilities in the region, which commenced on 7 August 2008 and continued at least until 15 August 2008, and which was followed by continuing occupation of Georgian territory by the Russian Federation.

Who was involved in the conflict? The participation of the two States parties, Georgia and Russia, is clear, but the answer to this question is more problematic as regards the armed forces of the de facto authorities of South Ossetia. Comprising both 'regular' forces and paramilitary groups, it does not seem possible to define their composition with any real precision. Moreover, to what extent were the Ossetian forces aligned with, or even controlled by, the Russian armed forces?

As we cannot yet give definitive answers to these critical factual questions, this considerably complicates the legal picture. There can be no doubt about the existence of an international armed conflict between Georgia and Russia; the conflict between Georgia and the South Ossetians, however, raises issues which make its classification rather more difficult. Can that part of the conflict be said to be subsumed into the international armed conflict between the two States?

To answer that question, one needs, firstly, to ascertain to what extent Russia exercised *overall control* over the South Ossetian forces such that it could be said that they were acting as de facto agents of Russia. Although there is a great deal of compelling evidence of Russia's influence over the South Ossetian authorities generally, it cannot yet be definitively concluded that the 'overall control' test was met. Secondly, specific acts of a non-state group can be attributable to a State (under article 8 of the ILC's Articles on State Responsibility) where those acts are carried out under a State's instructions or under its direction or effective control. That test may be easier to satisfy, for example, where the Ossetian forces accompanied the Russian armed forces, or because of the presence of Russian troops at, or in the vicinity of, a particular location where the acts in question were carried out by the Ossetian militia. Nevertheless, this chapter concludes that the better view is that

---

[215] Pejic, *Status of Armed Conflicts*, 95.

there were two parallel conflicts: a non-international armed conflict playing out in tandem with the international armed conflict.

After the termination of hostilities in August 2008, the evidence suggests that the continuing presence of Russian armed forces in South Ossetia, and in the 'buffer zone' around South Ossetia (i.e. in undisputed Georgian territory), constituted a state of occupation, as defined by article 42 of the Hague Regulations.

6.2. Consequences of classification for international humanitarian law

Given the uncertainty as to how long the international armed conflict continued beyond the 12 August ceasefire, the point at which the law of armed conflict ceased to apply is open to question. In certain respects, this will depend upon establishing both the *fact* of Russia's occupation of Georgian territory, and the *nature* of it: for example, as an occupying power Russia would be bound by particular provisions of the Fourth Geneva Convention for the duration of the occupation, to the extent that it exercised the 'functions of government'.

If the hostilities between Georgia and the South Ossetian militia are considered to amount to a non-international armed conflict, as suggested in this chapter, then for Additional Protocol II to the Geneva Conventions to be applicable the South Ossetian forces must have constituted an organized armed group, been subject to responsible command and exercised control over part of the territory of Georgia. That was arguably the case as regards the 'regular' Ossetian forces, but this test presents difficult questions in relation to the other ad hoc fighting groups which also seem to have been involved (to which in any event Common Article 3 of the Geneva Conventions applies).

On the basis that the Russian authorities were in occupation, they were obliged to take all the measures in their power to restore and maintain public order and safety in the occupied area. This they clearly did not do: there is overwhelming evidence of the incidents of assaults, robbery, kidnapping, looting and torching of houses.

This chapter has also considered the implications of the classification of the conflict for the status of detainees. If, as suggested, the fighting between Georgia and the South Ossetian forces amounted to a non-international armed conflict, Ossetians held captive by the Georgian forces would not have had the status of prisoners of war and thus would have been subject to the ordinary Georgian law, and would have been liable to be prosecuted for kidnapping, murder and other criminal offences. Two further issues arise in relation to the position of detainees in the conflict. Firstly, it is still unclear legally whether citizens of the State against which they are fighting can be granted prisoner of war status. Secondly, is the non-international armed conflict classification affected by the fact that some detainees held by the Ossetians were transferred into the custody of the Russian armed forces, or that Russian soldiers were also present in at least some of the places where detainees were held by the Ossetians? That might be the case if this could be construed as further evidence of Russia's overall control of the Ossetian militia.

If, as Georgia contended, its conflict with the South Ossetian forces should be characterized as being a part of an international armed conflict then the South

Ossetian militia would have been entitled to prisoner of war status provided that they met four conditions: responsible command; a recognisable, distinctive sign; carrying arms openly; and compliance with the law of armed conflict. The evidence suggests, however, that they would have failed on at least one of these counts.

6.3. Application of human rights law

The main difficulty as to the application of international human rights law which has been identified in this chapter is the question of Russia's responsibility for its aerial attacks on Gori city. In recent years, there has been inconsistent treatment by international courts as to the nature and extent of the extraterritorial application of human rights law, but it is argued here that the question of extraterritorial jurisdictional competence is not limited solely to 'effective control over an area' or 'state agent authority and control', that both of those concepts have been considerably refined in recent years, and indeed that the appropriate test has moved closer towards a 'cause and effect' concept of jurisdiction. This issue will be decided in due course by the European Court of Human Rights, where there are cases pending against the Russian Federation which raise precisely this question. Nevertheless, this is not an issue that is affected by the legal classification of the South Ossetian conflict.

6.4. Impact of classification for application of the law

This chapter has identified problems as regards both the domestic and international legal regimes that were relevant to the South Ossetian conflict. There certainly were defects in the applicable domestic laws—notably the Russian armed forces' international humanitarian law regulations and the Georgian law on occupied territories. As discussed above, various important questions also arise in relation to the application of the international law of armed conflict. Legal classification does have a considerable impact, for example, on the position of detainees. However, the Tagliavini Report rather played down the practical effects of legal classification, concluding that:

> . . . although the classification of an armed conflict as international or non-international is important in terms of the responsibilities of the various parties involved, when it comes to the effective protection by IHL of the persons and objects affected by the conflict it does not make much difference. Indeed, it is generally recognised that the same IHL customary law rules generally apply to all types of armed conflicts.[216]

Since the South Ossetian conflict was characterized by conduct that was clearly unlawful in the course of either an international or non-international conflict (including, for example, indiscriminate attacks, the deliberate killing of civilians, hostage-taking, the torching of houses, looting and pillaging, and rape) it is difficult to disagree with that conclusion.

---

[216] IIFFMCG, *Report II*, 304.

Chronology

20 September 1990	South Ossetia unilaterally declared independence from Georgian Soviet Socialist Republic (SSR).
11 December 1990	President of Georgia abolished autonomous status of South Ossetia.
5 January 1991	Armed Conflict in South Ossetia.
9 April 1991	Georgian SSR declared independence from USSR.
21 December 1991	South Ossetia voted for independence from Georgia.
19 January 1992	Unrecognized referendum for independence in South Ossetia.
24 June 1992	Russian-brokered ceasefire agreement and Joint Peacekeeping Force established.
2 November 1993	Constitution promulgated in South Ossetia.
27 November 1996	First president of South Ossetia elected.
18 December 2001	Eduard Kokoity became de facto president of South Ossetia.
12 November 2006	Referendum and presidential elections in South Ossetia.
7 August 2008	Georgian troops attacked Tskhinvali, South Ossetia.
8 August 2008	Russian armed forces counter-attacked.
9 August 2008	President Saakashvili of Georgia declared state of war.
15 August 2008	EU ceasefire plan signed by Georgia. Russian troops began to withdraw from undisputed Georgian territory.
16 August 2008	EU ceasefire plan signed by Russian Federation.
22 August 2008	Russian troops withdrew from Gori city.
24 August 2008	Russian Federation recognized South Ossetia as independent sovereign State.
8 September 2008	Russian Federation agreed to withdraw its troops deployed outside the boundaries of South Ossetia by 1 October.
9 September 2008	Russian Federation established diplomatic relations with South Ossetia.

11

Iraq (2003 onwards)

*Michael N. Schmitt**

1. Introduction

Any effort to understand the conflict in Iraq that began in March 2003 must begin by considering events that occurred over a decade earlier. On 2 August 1990, Iraq invaded Kuwait. Following a request for assistance from the Amir of Kuwait, numerous States began deploying military forces into the region pursuant to the law of self-defence, specifically collective defence, enshrined in article 51 of the United Nations Charter.[1] After condemning the invasion as a 'breach of international peace and security' and demanding withdrawal,[2] the Security Council mandated numerous measures under its Chapter VII authority designed to pressure Iraq to do so, including authorization of an embargo on goods into and out of Iraq and occupied Kuwait.[3] When, by November, it became clear that Iraq would not comply with the demands, the Security Council adopted resolution 678, which authorized member States cooperating with Kuwait to employ 'all necessary means' to expel Iraq forces should they not voluntarily leave by 15 January. Two days after the deadline expired, a US-led coalition commenced military operations. Iraqi defeat on the battlefield led to a ceasefire that was formalized in Security Council resolution 687. The terms of the ceasefire required Iraq to, inter alia, destroy its chemical, biological and long-range missile capacity, under international supervision.

In the ensuing years, Iraq repeatedly violated those terms, violations often characterized by the Security Council as serious, sometimes 'material', breaches

---

* The views expressed herein are those of the author in his personal capacity and do not necessarily represent those of any United States government organization.

[1] 'Nothing in the present Charter shall impair the inherent right of individual *or collective self-defence* if an armed attack occurs against a Member of the United Nations, until the Security Council has taken measures necessary to maintain international peace and security' (emphasis added). UN Charter, art. 51. On the affair, see C. Greenwood, 'New World Order or Old? The Invasion of Kuwait and the Rule of Law' (1992) 55 *Modern Law Review* 153.

[2] SC res. 660 (1990).

[3] SC res. 661 (1990); SC res. 662 (1990); SC res. 664 (1990); SC res. 665 (1990); SC res. 666 (1990); SC res. 667 (1990); SC res. 669 (1990); SC res. 670 (1990); SC res. 674 (1990); SC res. 677 (1990); SC res. 678 (1990).

of the ceasefire.[4] Sanctions and occasional military operations to enforce compliance resulted.[5] Faced with continuing Iraqi intransigence, the United States and other Western powers began to consider the use of force. Notably, the US Congress adopted a joint resolution in October 2002 authorizing the use of military force against Iraq.[6] The following month, the Security Council adopted resolution 1441, which afforded Iraq a 'final opportunity' to comply with the disarmament regime, imposed an enhanced inspection regime, and threatened 'severe consequences' in the event of further non-compliance.[7] Despite continuing Iraqi defiance, a proposed resolution mandating the use of force proved elusive. On 19 March 2003, a US-led coalition launched military operations against Iraq.[8]

Since 2003, the conflict in Iraq has been offering unique insights into the issue of classification of conflict, for it has evolved linearly from international armed conflict, through a period of belligerent occupation, to non-international armed conflict.[9] As such, the ongoing hostilities in Iraq constitute a fertile case study into the relationship between the various forms of conflict and how transition occurs between them.

This chapter examines the phases of the hostilities in Iraq with the goal of determining their normative basis and any effect that the transition between them had on operations. It begins with an extended discussion of the various phases and their corresponding classification. The views of the parties to the conflict will also be discussed, although the fact that there was little controversy about classification during the different phases of the hostilities renders this discussion a brief one. As will become apparent, the juridical classification of a conflict may depart significantly from the reality on the ground. The chapter also explores the topic of how classification of the conflict affected operations. The two issues informing companion chapters to this volume—rules on opening fire and detention—will be addressed. Since the case of Iraq also offers a unique example of relatively clear transition through the stages of conflict, other legal issues deriving from classification, such as the activities of occupants, will also be highlighted.

[4] See e.g. SC res. 707 (1991); SC res. 1060 (1996); SC res. 1115 (1997); SC res. 1137 (1997); SC res. 1154 (1998); SC res. 1205 (1998).
[5] For instance, Operation Desert Fox in December 1998, a response to Iraq's refusal to cooperate with the Special Commission arms inspection regime.
[6] Authorization for Use of Military Force against Iraq Resolution of 2002 (Public Law 107–243, 116 Stat. 1497–1502) (Joint Resolution of 2002).
[7] SC res. 1441 (2002).
[8] For a US Army history of the conflict, see G. Fontenot, E.J. Degen and D. Tohn, *On Point: The United States Army in Operation Iraqi Freedom* (2004); D.P. Wright and T.R. Reese, *On Point II: Transition to the New Campaign* (2008).
[9] For an interesting treatment of this issue, see D. Turns, 'International Humanitarian Law Classification of Armed Conflicts in Iraq Since 2003' (2010) 40 *Israel Yearbook on Human Rights* 39 (Turns, *Classification of Armed Conflict in Iraq*).

2. Classification of the conflict

2.1. Phase I: international armed conflict

2.1.1 Views of the parties and others

Legal justifications offered by the various Coalition partners for launching their attack on Iraq varied somewhat.[10] However, in essence they argued that the violations of the ceasefire terms memorialized in resolution 687 constituted a 'material breach' of the agreement. The UK pointed to resolution 1441, in which Iraq's non-compliance with disarmament obligations under previous UN resolutions was characterized as a material breach of the conditions for ceasefire laid down in resolution 687. For the UK, military action was the only option for achieving compliance by Iraq. A variant of this argument adopted by the US centred on the classic law of ceasefire, by which a party to a ceasefire may recommence hostilities in the face of material breach by the other side.[11] These positions proved controversial, with a number of States and commentators arguing that only the Security Council had the authority to mandate military action and that it had not made such a decision.[12]

Regardless of the legality of Operation Iraqi Freedom, there is no question that operations by the States comprising the Coalition against Iraq amounted to an international armed conflict. This appeared to be the view of all of the participants in the Coalition.[13] The International Committee of the Red Cross reminded the

[10] Letter dated 20 March 2003 from the Permanent Representative of the United States of America to the United Nations addressed to the President of the Security Council (S/2003/351). Letter dated 20 March 2003 from the Permanent Representative of the United Kingdom of Great Britain and Northern Ireland to the United Nations addressed to the President of the Security Council (S/2003/350).

[11] This is a matter of customary international law, codified in the context of armistices, in arts 36 and 40 of the 1907 Hague Regulations Respecting the Laws and Customs of War on Land (1907 Hague Regulation IV). The position has been criticized on the basis, *inter alia*, that the law of ceasefire did not survive the UN Charter, at least in situations where the Security Council was dealing with the matter at hand.

[12] France and Germany, traditional US allies, openly opposed the operations. Secretary-General Kofi Annan also harboured doubts as to its legality. P. Tyler and F. Barringer, 'Annan Says U.S. Will Violate Charter If It Acts Without Approval' *New York Times* (11 March 2003). Many academics criticized the operation as illegal in the absence of UN sanction. See e.g. 'The letter from 16 law professors' *The Guardian* (7 March 2003). At the time of the attack, 48 nations were publicly committed to the Coalition. Support ranged from contributions of troops to political actions. 'Operation Iraqi Freedom: Coalition Members' White House Press Release (21 March 2003). On the legality of the conflict, see M. Schmitt, 'The Legality of Operation Iraqi Freedom under International Law,' in T. Sparks and G. Sulmasy (eds), *International Law Challenges: Homeland Security and Combating Terrorism* (2006) 367; S. Murphy, 'Assessing the Legality of Invading Iraq' (2004) 92 *Georgetown Law Journal* 173.

[13] For the US, see e.g. J. Goldsmith, '"Protected Person" Status in Occupied Iraq under the Fourth Geneva Convention', Memorandum Opinion for the Counsel to the President (18 March 2004), available at www.justice.gov/olc/2004/gc4mar18.pdf; for the UK see e.g. UK Ministry of Defence, 'Operation Telic' (the name given to UK operations in Iraq), paper provided to the Foreign Affairs Select Committee, UK Materials on International Law (2004) *British Yearbook of International Law* 884, s. 17/10.

parties of their obligations under the law applicable to international armed conflict, and no State suggested otherwise.[14]

2.1.2 Author's analysis of classification

The touchstone for qualification as an international armed conflict is Common Article 2 to the four 1949 Geneva Conventions, which provides that the Conventions 'apply to all cases of declared war or of any other armed conflict which may arise between two or more of the High Contracting Parties even if the state of war is not recognized by one of them'.[15] The former situation refers to war in the technical sense, the latter to war in the material sense.

In the case of the Iraq conflict, there was no declaration of war and, thus, no war solely in the technical sense. Although the US Constitution grants Congress the power to 'declare war', the Joint Resolution on the Use of Force passed in October 2002 did not qualify as a declaration of war.[16] Rather, it merely authorized the President 'to use the Armed Forces of the United States as he determines to be necessary and appropriate in order to 1) defend the national security of the United States against the continuing threat posed by Iraq; and 2) enforce all relevant United Nations Security Council resolutions regarding Iraq'.[17] Prior to ordering forces into action, the President was required to find that 'diplomatic or other peaceful means alone' had not sufficed to resolve the crisis, nor would they be likely to in the future.[18] A declaration of war, by contrast, must be made in accordance with constitutional requirements, if any, and, by accepted principles of the law of war, be conveyed to the other side as either a declaration of immediate war or a conditional ultimatum.[19]

Instead, Operation Iraqi Freedom exemplified war in the material sense, characterized by Oppenheim's classic definition of war as a 'contention between two or more States through their armed forces, for the purpose of overpowering each other and imposing such conditions as the victor pleases'.[20] The *sine qua non*

---

[14] ICRC, 'Memorandum on the Rules of International Humanitarian Law to be Respected by the States Involved in Military Hostilities' (2003) 850 *International Review of the Red Cross* 423.

[15] The text is identical in each of the four Conventions: Geneva Convention I, art. 2; Geneva Convention II, art. 2; Geneva Convention III, art. 2; Geneva Convention IV, art. 2. Additional Protocol I (AP I) adopts this by standard by reference: art. 1(3). However, it controversially also extends to 'armed conflicts in which people are fighting against colonial domination and alien occupation and against racist regimes in the exercise of their right of self-determination'. Ibid, art. 1(4).

[16] US Constitution, art. I, s. 8; Joint Resolution of 2002.

[17] Joint Resolution of 2002, s. 3(a). The Resolution was characterized by the Congress as an authorization under the War Powers Act, a premise rejected by the Executive branch.

[18] Ibid, s. 3(b).

[19] 'The contracting Powers recognize that hostilities between themselves must not commence without previous and explicit warning, in the form either of a declaration of war, giving reasons, or of an ultimatum with conditional declaration of war.' 1907 Hague Convention relative to the Opening of Hostilities (No. III) art. 1. For instance, on 3 September 1939, the British government notified Germany through its Embassy in Berlin that unless Germany agreed by 11:00 am that its forces would withdraw from Poland, a state of war would exist between the two countries. By this conditional ultimatum, war began that morning.

[20] L. Oppenheim, *International Law, Vol. II* (7th edn, 1952) 202.

of international armed conflict is found in the definition's qualitative first clause—a clash between States that is military in nature. Over time, the quantitative second clause has proven less resilient. For instance, according to the ICRC commentary to the Geneva Conventions, 'any difference arising between two States and leading to the intervention of members of the armed forces' is an armed conflict, a threshold well below that set by Oppenheim.[21] Not all authorities have accepted this narrowing.[22]

Any imaginable threshold of violence for armed conflict was met during the Iraq conflict, with the engaged forces numbering in the hundreds of thousands. Indeed, recall that the first blow of the war was an attempt to decapitate the Iraqi Ba'ath regime by killing Saddam Hussein. There is simply no question but that an international armed conflict was ongoing between Iraq and the States comprising the Coalition, initially the United States, United Kingdom, Australia, and Poland.

The precise date on which the conflict began is, by contrast, the subject of some disagreement. Two possibilities exist. For those who accept the classic breach of ceasefire justification proffered by the United States, it began on 2 August 1990, the day Iraq invaded Kuwait. Ceasefires are merely temporary cessations of hostilities, conditioned on compliance with the material terms of the agreement. International armed conflict continues until such time as: a peace treaty (or equivalent instrument) is signed; the parties act in a fashion that implies agreement; debellatio occurs; or one of the parties makes a unilateral declaration in the absence of hostilities.[23] As the Department of State's Legal Adviser noted in 2003, Operation Iraqi Freedom can be 'viewed as the final episode in a conflict initiated more than a dozen years earlier by Iraq's invasion of Kuwait'.[24]

Reliance on the narrower variant of the ceasefire approach (revival of resolution 678 due to non-compliance with various provisions of 687 and subsequent resolutions) could likewise suggest that the international armed conflict continued through the interim years. But it could also support an argument that a new armed conflict began once Coalition forces acted in response to the repeated breaches of the Security Council resolutions. The United Kingdom took the latter position. Those who reject any ceasefire justification at all typically argue either that the international armed conflict of 1990–1991 ended with the general cessation of hostilities in April 1991 or that it faded away over the dozen-year hiatus between

---

[21] The commentary further notes that 'it makes no difference how long the conflict lasts, how much slaughter takes place, or how numerous are the participating forces'. J. Pictet, *Geneva Convention Relative to the Treatment of Prisoners of War: commentary* (1960) 23 (Pictet, *Commentary*). The ICTY has similarly noted that an armed conflict existed 'whenever there is resort to force between States'. *Prosecutor v Tadić*, IT-94-1-AR72, Decision on Defence Motion for Interlocutory Appeal on Jurisdiction (Appeals Chamber), 2 October 1995, para 70 *(Tadić)*; see also, *Prosecutor v Kunarac*, IT-96-23/1-A, Judgment (Appeals Chamber), 12 June 2002, paras 56–7; *Prosecutor v Milošević*, IT-02-54-T, Decision on Motion for Judgment of Acquittal (Trial Chamber), 16 June 2004, paras 15–17. See also, discussion in ch. 3, section 5 above.

[22] See e.g. Y. Dinstein, *War, Aggression and Self-Defence* (2005) 11–15 (Dinstein, *War*).

[23] Ibid, 34–50.

[24] W. Taft and T. Buchwald, 'Preemption, Iraq and International Law' (2003) 97 *AJIL* 557, 563.

Operations Desert Storm and Iraqi Freedom. For them, a new conflict broke out on 19 March 2003.

Whether military action was a legitimate response to breach of the ceasefire, a response to breaches of Security Council resolutions or naked aggression, the fact is that by March 2003 the forces of one State were engaged in major combat with those of others; war in the material sense had commenced, and it was international in character. That certain justifications for the Coalition action assert the existence of a Security Council Chapter VII use of force mandate is irrelevant, for it is well-settled that Council action does not preclude the existence of a state of international armed conflict between the parties involved in the ensuing hostilities.[25]

2.2. Phase II: belligerent occupation

2.2.1 Views of the parties and others

Coalition operations in Iraq moved with exceptional speed following the 19 March attack. By late March, the south, with the exception of Basra, had been overrun. The regime collapsed on 9 April, and on 14 April Tikrit, the last major Iraqi stronghold, fell. Two weeks later, on 1 May, President Bush proclaimed from the flight deck of the USS Abraham Lincoln that 'major combat operations in Iraq have ended'.[26] In retrospect, he was clearly wrong, for many significant battles remained to be fought. However, by late April the legal status of the conflict in Iraq had been transformed.

There is no question that the United Kingdom deemed the situation one of belligerent occupation.[27] However, certain members of the US administration seemed uncomfortable with applying the term 'occupation' to operations in Iraq, preferring instead to label them 'liberation'.[28] Yet, the former term has no relationship to the *ius ad bellum* issue of the legality of the use of force, and the latter enjoys no legal valence. Semantics aside, it soon became clear that all parties understood that as a matter of law a belligerent occupation of Iraq by the Coalition forces was underway.

---

[25] However, there is a question of whether neutrality can survive Security Council enforcement action involving armed conflict against a State. For an excellent commentary on the legal justification for the conflict and the impact it had on international law, see A. Roberts, 'Law and the Use of Force after Iraq' (2003) 45(2) *Survival* 31.

[26] G.W. Bush, 'Remarks from the USS Abraham Lincoln' (1 May 2003), available at: <www.whitehouse.gov/news/releases/2003/05/iraq/2003501-15.html>.

[27] See e.g. Secretary of State for International Development, 'Reply to Written Question', UKMIL (2003) *British Yearbook of International Law*, s. 17/66; 'FCO Memorandum' UKMIL (2003) *British Yearbook of International Law*, s. 17/92; Solicitor General, 'Reply to Written Question' UKMIL (2003) *British Yearbook of International Law*, s. 17/89.

[28] The term occupation was not used in the letter notifying the Security Council that the Coalition Provisional Authority had been formed; letter dated 8 May 2003 from the Permanent Representatives of the United Kingdom of Great Britain and Northern Ireland and the United States of America to the United Nations addressed to the President of the Security Council (S/2003/538) *(Letter dated 8 May 2003)*. For use of the phrase liberation, see e.g. President George W. Bush, 'Remarks at Carl Harrison High School in Kennesaw, Georgia' (20 February 2003).

On 14 April, Prime Minister Blair, addressing the House of Commons, acknowledged the occupation was about to begin and that the Coalition and the Office of Reconstruction and Humanitarian Aid (ORHA) would exercise 'responsibility under the Geneva and Hague Conventions for ensuring that Iraq's immediate security and humanitarian needs are met'.[29] The next day, Iraqi resistance groups agreed to a reconstruction programme with ORHA. On the 16th, the Coalition Provisional Authority (CPA), as successor to ORHA, 'disestablished' the Ba'ath Party[30] and US General Franks, Commander of Coalition forces, issued the Message of Freedom to the Iraqi People.[31] The CPA used this date as commencement of the occupation.

On 8 May the United States and United Kingdom notified the President of the Security Council that they had established the CPA to exercise temporary governmental powers.[32] CPA Administrator Bremer subsequently issued Regulation 1, which set forth the authority of the occupying forces. According to section 1 thereof:

1) The CPA shall exercise powers of government temporarily in order to provide for the effective administration of Iraq during the period of transitional administration, to restore conditions of security and stability, to create conditions in which the Iraqi people can freely determine their own political future, including by advancing efforts to restore and establish national and local institutions for representative governance and facilitating economic recovery and sustainable reconstruction and development.

2) The CPA is vested with all executive, legislative and judicial authority necessary to achieve its objectives, to be exercised under relevant U.N. Security Council resolutions, including Resolution 1483 (2003), and the laws and usages of war. This authority shall be exercised by the CPA Administrator.[33]

Clearly, the substantive content of the regulation, especially temporary assumption of government powers, contemplated a state of belligerent occupation.

The reference to Security Council resolution 1483 demonstrates that the States comprising the CPA, two of which were permanent members of the Security Council, understood that by mid-May a belligerent occupation was in place.[34] The resolution recognized 'the specific authorities, responsibilities, and obligations under applicable international law of [the United States and United Kingdom] as occupying powers under unified command (the "Authority")' and that 'other States that are not occupying powers are working now or in the future may work under the Authority'. Further, the resolution called 'upon all concerned to comply fully with their obligations under international law including in particular the Geneva Conventions of 1949 and the Hague Regulations of 1907'. That the Hague

[29] Prime Minister Tony Blair, 'Address to the House of Commons' (14 April 2003), available at: <www.iraqcrisis.co.uk/resources.phpidtag=R3E9BC863DOE3C>.
[30] Acknowledged in CPA Order 1, CPA/ORD/16 May 2003/1, De-Baathification of Iraqi Society *(CPA Order 1)*; SC res. 1483 (2003).
[31] Cited in CPA Order 2, CPA/ORD/23 May 2003/2, Dissolution of Entities, preamble.
[32] *Letter dated 8 May 2003.*
[33] CPA Regulation 1, CPA/REG/16 May 2003/1, The Coalition Provisional Authority.
[34] SC res. 1483 (2003).

Regulations and Fourth Geneva Convention contain the vast majority of occupation *lex scripta* is further evidence of a state of occupation. Resolution 1483 also 'called upon' the CPA to exercise 'effective administration of the territory, including in particular working towards the restoration of conditions of security and stability and the creation of conditions in which the Iraqi people can freely determine their own political future', a restatement of an occupier's classic legal duties, as well as occupation law's underlying purpose.

The ICRC did not regard the language of resolution 1483 as conclusive of which States were in occupation; they examined which national contingents had been assigned responsibility for and were exercising effective control over—and thus occupying—a part of Iraqi territory. On that basis they regarded eleven States, including the US and the UK, as occupying powers.[35]

A major question for the UK concerned the geographical extent of its own part of the occupation. Although a member of the Coalition, its forces operated primarily in the southern part of the country and it is only in that area that the UK exercised de facto authority.[36] However, the issue soon became moot, since following the adoption of Security Council resolution 1483, any argument that the UK was only a partial occupier was no longer available.

2.2.2 *Author's analysis of classification*

It might be asserted that a state of 'debellatio' emerged from defeat of the Iraqi Army and collapse of the Iraqi government.[37] Debellatio occurs in the wake of an international armed conflict upon the coincidence of three factors: 1) control over the entire territory of the State by the enemy armed forces; 2) a complete absence of military activities by the State's armed forces, or any other forces acting on its behalf; and 3) the non-existence of any governmental authority. It implies that all sovereignty of the defeated State has been effectively snuffed out. Since only the victorious powers can consequently exercise sovereignty in the resulting void, they are relatively free to take such governmental actions as they desire.[38] Because the State ceases to exist as such, the international armed conflict ends. Debellatio is a controversial notion in modern international law, one not widely embraced.

Regarding debellatio's factual predicates, Coalition forces controlled the entire country and few vestiges of the pre-existing Ba'athist regime remained. No successors to Saddam Hussein or other senior leaders were appointed or otherwise

---

[35] D. Thürer, 'Current challenges to the law of occupation' Speech (21 November 2005), available at: <www.icrc.org/eng/resources/documents/statement/occupation-statement-211105.htm>.

[36] See e.g. *Al-Skeini and others v The United Kingdom* (Judgment) App No. 55721/07 (7 July 2011) paras 21 and 149 (ECHR, *Al-Skeini*); 'The Aitken Report: An Investigation into Cases of Deliberate Abuse and Unlawful Killing in Iraq in 2003 and 2004' (25 January 2008) 6–7.

[37] M. Schmitt, 'Debellatio' in W. Rüdiger (ed.), *Max Planck Encyclopedia of Public International Law* (2010).

[38] At least according to traditional interpretations of the concept, even territorial annexation is permitted. Its provisions on annexation are highly questionable in light of the principle of self-determination.

exercised authority.[39] Only certain elements of local government survived, and the Coalition Provisional Authority, which oversaw the occupation, soon exercised plenary powers.[40] The Iraqi military had fallen apart in the face of the Coalition onslaught, with no major units intact by May, although former regime elements survived in smaller groups.[41]

While the factual circumstances may have resembled debellatio, the international community, as was apparent, universally characterized the situation as one of belligerent occupation. Debellatio is inconsistent with belligerent occupation, for whereas the former implies the extinguishment of the defeated State's sovereignty and total subjugation to the victors, the latter is premised on the principle that an occupier exercises authority only temporarily. Article 55 of the 1907 Regulations annexed to Hague Convention IV, for instance, provides that the 'occupying State shall be regarded *only* as administrator and usufructuary'.[42] The 1949 Fourth Geneva Convention likewise provides for the continuation of the defeated State's government and civil society to the extent feasible in the circumstances.[43] In other words, elements of a State's sovereignty are merely suspended during occupation, to be exercised temporarily by the occupier pending return of full sovereignty.

The defeat of Iraq therefore ushered in a period of belligerent occupation, not debellatio. According to article 42 of the Hague Regulations, which the International Court of Justice has recognized as reflective of customary international law, 'territory is considered occupied when it is actually placed under the authority of the hostile army. The occupation extends only to the territory where such authority has been established and can be exercised'.[44] Hence, occupation is a question of fact; it does not exist in the purely technical sense. An occupier may declare the existence of a state of occupation,[45] but such declarations do not impose an occupation where the purported occupier does not actually control the respective territory; nor does absence of a formal declaration relieve an occupier of its duties towards the population under its control.[46] It must be understood that a state of

---

[39] However, Saddam's sons remained at large until killed on 22 July 2003. Saddam Hussein himself was only captured on 13 December 2003. Arguably, their presence amounted to a threat that an effective resistance could coalesce around their leadership.

[40] Indeed, the CPA disbanded the Ba'ath Party on 16 April and, in its first formal Order, removed all full members of the party holding mid-level and senior positions and prohibited them from further employment in the public sector. *CPA Order 1.*

[41] For an argument that Iraq evidenced debellatio, see M. Patterson, 'Who's Got the Title? or, The Remnants of Debellatio in Post-Invasion Iraq' (2006) 47 *Harvard Journal of International Law* 467.

[42] 1907 Hague Regulation IV, art. 55.

[43] Geneva Convention IV, s. III.

[44] 1907 Hague Regulation IV, art. 42. On the customary nature of the Regulations, *see Legal Consequences of the Construction of a Wall in the Occupied Palestinian Territory* (Advisory Opinion) ICJ Rep 2004, 136, 172; *Legality of the Threat or Use of Nuclear Weapons* (Advisory Opinion) ICJ Rep 1996, 226, 257; International Military Tribunal, Nuremberg, *Trial of the Major War Criminals Before the International Military Tribunal, Vol. I* (1947) 254.

[45] As was done upon the defeat of Germany in 1945. Declaration Regarding the Defeat of Germany and the Assumption of Supreme Authority by Allied Powers, 5 June 1945 (Generals Eisenhower, Zhukov, Montgomery and Lattre de Tassiny), available at: <http://avalon.law.yale.edu/wwii/ger01.asp>.

[46] The concept of occupation is cast more broadly in the Fourth Geneva Convention than in the Hague Regulations, for art. 2 accounts for situations in which the invading forces meet no resistance. Geneva Convention IV, art. 2.

international armed conflict continues during a belligerent occupation. Accordingly, as the *lex specialis,* the law of armed conflict fully governs the conduct of hostilities, detention of prisoners of war and other activities with a direct nexus to the conflict; applicable human rights law (significant controversy exists over the extent of applicability) will generally govern actions taken by the occupying power pursuant to its law-enforcement and governance responsibilities.

The key issue with regard to classification of conflict is identifying the moment at which belligerent occupation begins, such that occupation rights and responsibilities attach.

Occupation may commence without hostilities, a fact recognized in Common Article 2 to the 1949 Geneva Conventions: 'The Convention shall also apply to all cases of partial or total occupation...., even if the said occupation meets with no resistance.'[47] On the other hand, it does not necessarily begin upon the mere presence of enemy forces in the area in question. This scenario presented itself in Baghdad in April 2003. Iraqi forces had retreated from the city and Coalition forces were moving through it in pursuit. Civil disturbances broke out that included widespread looting, most notably of the Iraqi National Museum.[48] Coalition forces were criticized for not quelling the disturbances in accordance with their obligation to do so under the laws of occupation. This duty derives from the Hague Regulations, which require an occupying power to maintain 'public order and safety'.[49] In fact, though, the Coalition forces were in no position to maintain order, as hostilities were ongoing elsewhere and units that might have performed security duties were needed for combat action against the Iraqi military. Rear echelon units had not yet arrived in sufficient numbers and composition to place Baghdad under Coalition authority. In such circumstances, occupation only begins when it is militarily feasible for the advancing forces to actually assume their occupation responsibilities.

The precise date for commencement of the occupation is difficult to fix because an entire State need not be occupied before occupation rights and duties attach.[50] Rather, occupations may be 'rolling', expanding and contracting as the extent of territory controlled by the armed force grows or recedes. In the case of Iraq, it is arguable that a belligerent occupation existed in the southern sectors of the country prior to the final defeat of Iraqi forces further north in mid-April. While that may be accurate, it is of little significance since the Iraqi military and government were collapsing so rapidly. As indicated above, the CPA used the date of 16 April as the commencement of the occupation.

---

[47] Geneva Conventions, Common Article 2. For instance, Germany occupied Denmark during World War II without resistance by Danish forces.

[48] Looting is a form of pillage prohibited in assault and occupation by, respectively, 1907 Hague Regulation IV, art. 28 and art. 47. The duty of occupying forces to protect cultural property from theft is set forth in Convention for the Protection of Cultural Property in the Event of Armed Conflict 1954, art. 4(3).

[49] 1907 Hague Regulation IV, art. 43.

[50] See the Common Article 2 reference to 'partial occupation'.

The situation in Iraq unquestionably constituted an occupation as a matter of the law of belligerent occupation. However, it must equally be understood that once the Security Council recognizes the existence of a state of occupation, as it did in this case, an occupation exists as a matter of law quite aside from whatever is happening on the ground. For instance, if an occupying power loses control of certain territory, it will nevertheless remain legally in occupation of the area if the Security Council so deems it. Such a legal fiction would result from operation of UN Charter article 103, which gives primacy to Charter obligations over those of other treaties. Of course, in such a case, the occupier would not be responsible for duties which it could not factually fulfil as a result of loss of control. Similarly, if the Security Council determines that a State is not an occupier, it will not, as a matter of law, be such even if it would otherwise qualify under the law of belligerent occupation. This was arguably the case of those States referred to in resolution 1483 as 'other States that are not occupying powers' which worked with the Authority.

The following October, in resolution 1511, the Security Council re-affirmed 'the sovereignty and territorial integrity of Iraq, and *underscor[ed]*, in that context, the temporary nature of the exercise by the Coalition Provisional Authority (Authority) of the specific responsibilities, authorities, and obligations under applicable international law recognized and set forth in resolution 1483 (2003), which will cease when an internationally recognized, representative government established by the people of Iraq is sworn in and assumes the responsibilities of the Authority'. Recall that the international law referred to in 1483 was, at least in part, the law of occupation. Interestingly, the resolution further 'authorize[d] a multinational force under unified command to take all necessary measures to contribute to the maintenance of security and stability in Iraq, including for the purpose of ensuring necessary conditions for the implementation of the timetable and programme'. In that the 'international force' consisted primarily of members of the occupying militaries, the Security Council had legitimized the presence of those forces in the country, as well as their use of, as necessary, force.

While the Fourth Geneva Convention ceases to apply in occupied territory one year after the general close of military operations, specified provisions continue to apply 'for the duration of the occupation' to the extent that the occupying power continues to 'exercise the functions of government'.[51] Traditionally, occupation only ends once the occupying power returns authority to the nation's government.

In Iraq, transfer of authority from the CPA occurred in stages. Resolution 1483 'support[ed] the formation, by the people of Iraq with the help of the Authority and working with the Special Representative, of an Iraqi interim administration as a transitional administration run by Iraqis, until an internationally recognized, representative government is established by the people of Iraq and assumes the responsibilities of the Authority'. On 13 July 2003, the Governing Council was established to serve as the 'principal body of the Iraqi interim administration'. The CPA recognized the Council and agreed that it should consult and coordinate the

---

[51] Geneva Convention IV, art. 6.

Council 'on all matters involving temporary governance of Iraq'.[52] The Security Council likewise welcomed the creation of the Council.[53] Various Iraqi ministries were soon established under CPA authority.[54] On 1 September, the Council appointed an Iraqi Council of Ministers with the acquiescence of the CPA.[55] However, real authority, both de facto and de jure, continued to reside with the CPA.

The fact that some limited power was ceded to Iraqi entities did not diminish the status of the situation as one of belligerent occupation. Occupation continues for as long as the territory in question is under the authority of the hostile army. It may be terminated by peace treaty, withdrawal of the occupation forces, or a binding decision of the Security Council.[56] Iraq represents the only case, as will be discussed in the next section, in which the Security Council has exercised that authority.

It must be emphasized that the end of occupation does not necessarily imply the conclusion of armed conflict. For instance, occupying forces may be expelled by hostile action, as was the case with the liberation of Europe by the Allies in World War II. Thus, the demise of the occupation per se did not of itself end the armed conflict in Iraq. Rather, international armed conflicts continue until conclusion of a peace treaty or armistice agreement, debellatio, unilateral declaration, or implied mutual consent.[57] Iraq exemplified the last method. The Interim Government, having been recognized by the Security Council as exercising full sovereignty,[58] was empowered to conclude the conflict on behalf of the State. It impliedly did so when it invited international forces to remain in the country following termination of the occupation.

2.3. Phase III: non-international armed conflict

2.3.1 Views of the parties and others

On 15 November 2003, an Agreement between the Iraqi Governing Council and the CPA set 30 June 2004 as the date of full return of sovereignty to Iraq.[59] Accordingly, on 28 June 2004, the CPA issued Order No. 100, its last.[60] The Order contemplated transfer of 'full governing authority to the Iraqi Interim

---

[52] CPA Regulation 6, CPA/REG/13 July 2003/6, Governing Council of Iraq.

[53] SC res. 1500 (2003).

[54] See discussion in M. Schmitt and C. Garraway, 'Occupation Policy in Iraq and International Law' (2004) 9 *International Peacekeeping: The Yearbook of International Peace Operations* 27, 35.

[55] CPA Memorandum 6, CPA/MEM/3 September 2003/16, Implementation of Regulation on the Governing Council.

[56] Y. Dinstein, *The International Law of Belligerent Occupation* (2009) 270–3. On occupation generally, see also, E. Benvenisti, *The International Law of Occupation* (2004); Y. Arai-Takahashi, *The Law of Occupation* (2009).

[57] Dinstein, *War*, 34–50.

[58] See discussion in section 2.3 below.

[59] Agreement between the Iraqi Governing Council and the Coalition Provisional Authority on the Timeline to a Sovereign, Democratic and Secure Iraq, 15 November 2003, available at: <www.iraqcoalition.org/government/AgreementNov15.pdf>.

[60] CPA Order 100, CPA/ORD/28 June 2004/100, Transition of Laws, Regulations, Orders, and Directives Issued by the Coalition Provisional Authority.

Government'. In fact, transfer occurred that very day. Consistent with the end of the occupation, legal custody of Saddam Hussein was ceded to the Iraqis in June.

As noted earlier, occupation is a question of fact. In post-occupation Iraq, Coalition States maintained a large troop presence and mounted regular combat operations. Indeed, in August 2004 US forces engaged in bloody battles with the supporters of Shia cleric Moqtadar Sadr in Najaf and in November US Marines led a major offensive against insurgents in Fallujah. The situation continued to deteriorate, leading President Bush to announce a new US strategy in January 2007—the 'surge'—which involved sending over 20,000 more US troops to the country.

Nevertheless, the international community clearly embraced the legal fiction that full authority over the country now rested in the hands of the Iraqis. This was envisaged in resolution 1546, which the Security Council adopted earlier in the month. The resolution 'welcome[ed] the beginning of a new phase in Iraq's transition to a democratically elected government, and look[ed] forward to the end of the occupation and the assumption of full responsibility and authority by a fully sovereign and independent Interim Government of Iraq by 30 June 2004'.[61] Iraq may still have been occupied in fact, but as a matter of law the occupation was over.

The views of the international community as to the ending of the occupation can largely be elicited from the Security Council resolutions that are discussed further below. As regards the classification of the hostilities after that time, although neither the United States nor United Kingdom immediately styled their presence in the country as involvement in a non-international armed conflict, it could only have been such. The ICRC correctly so characterized the conflict.

> After the hand-over of power from the Coalition Provisional Authority to the interim Iraqi Government on 28 June 2004, following the United Nations Security Council resolution 1546 stating the end of the foreign occupation, the legal situation has changed.
>
> As stated in the resolution, the presence and the military operations of the Multinational Forces in Iraq are based on the consent of the Interim Government of Iraq. The ICRC therefore no longer considers the situation in Iraq to be that of an international armed conflict between the US-led coalition and the State of Iraq and covered by the Geneva Conventions of 1949 in their entirety. The current hostilities in Iraq between armed fighters on one hand opposing the Multinational Force (MNF-I) and/or the newly established authorities on the other, amount to a non-international armed conflict. This means that all parties including MNF-I are bound by Article 3 common to the four Geneva Conventions, and by customary rules applicable to non-international armed conflicts.[62]

Eventually, the UK government accepted this position, acknowledging in the context of asylum litigation that 'Iraq as a whole is in a state of internal armed conflict for the purpose of IHL'.[63] The United States has not made any formal

---

[61] SC res. 1546 (2004).
[62] ICRC, 'Protecting Persons Deprived of Freedom Remains a Priority' (28 June 2004), available at: <www.icrc.org/eng/resources/documents/misc/63kkj8.htm>.
[63] *KH (Article 15 (c)) Qualification Directive Iraq CG* [2008] UKAIT 00023, para 75.

pronouncement to this effect, but officials generally acknowledged that the conflict was non-international.[64]

In February 2010 US Secretary of Defense Gates decided to change the name of Operation Iraqi Freedom to Operation New Dawn, effective 1 September 2010. According to the memorandum of decision, the change was designed to align the name with the new mission of US forces and to reinforce the US commitment to the Framework Agreement.[65]

2.3.2 *Author's analysis of classification*

When the Security Council speaks pursuant to its Chapter VII authority, it may override contrary norms of international law (except *ius cogens*), such as those of occupation law.[66] The nature of the primacy of UN over other international law during this phase must be distinguished from that which was at play during the belligerent occupation. In the latter case, both UN law and the law of armed conflict led to that same conclusion as to the nature of the conflict. However, UN law supplanted specific contrary rules resident in the law governing belligerent occupation. By contrast, in June 2004 UN law arguably operated to supplant the law of armed conflict as to the very nature of the conflict. Thus, the rules of belligerent occupation no longer applied, not because they conflicted with those imposed by the UN, but instead because they were rendered inapplicable once the Security Council decided to end the occupation as a matter of law.

In the event, once the Security Council had spoken, and, in light of the ongoing hostilities, the nature of the conflict shifted from an international to a non-international armed conflict. The terms of resolution 1546 could have implied nothing else. It provided that 'the presence of the multinational force in Iraq is at the request of the incoming Interim Government of Iraq'. As the Iraqi armed forces remained in a nascent state, the international force (now labelled the MNF-I) was allowed significant leeway. By the resolution, MNF-I enjoyed 'the authority to take all necessary measures to contribute to the maintenance of security and stability in Iraq in accordance with [annexed letters] expressing, inter alia, the Iraqi request for the continued presence of the multinational force and setting out its tasks, including by preventing and deterring terrorism, so that, inter alia, the United Nations can fulfil its role in assisting the Iraqi people . . . and the Iraqi people can implement freely and without intimidation the timetable and programme for the political process and benefit from reconstruction and rehabilitation activities'. Indeed, the resolution provided for assigning Iraqi security forces to MFN-I, and envisioned an agreement over 'sensitive offensive operations'. Despite the wide latitude the multinational forces enjoyed, Iraq controlled the duration of the arrangement.

---

[64] Interviews and correspondence with author.

[65] Secretary of Defense, 'Memorandum for the Commander, U.S. Central Command, Subject: Request to Change the Name of Operation IRAQI FREEDOM to Operation NEW DAWN' (17 February 2010) (Memorandum for the Commander, 2010).

[66] This is clear from the operation of arts 25 and 103 of the UN Charter.

The Security Council mandate was to be reviewed in twelve months or whenever requested by Iraq, could be terminated unilaterally by Iraq, and expired upon formation of a constitutionally elected government.

Two letters to the President of the Security Council annexed to the resolution further emphasized that continued international operations in the country were intended to support the Iraqis in restoring and maintaining security. The first, from Prime Minister Allawi of the Interim Government, noted that 'there continue, however, to be forces in Iraq, including foreign elements, that are opposed to our transition to peace, democracy, and security. . . . Until we are able to provide security for ourselves, including the defence of Iraq's land, sea, and air space, we ask for the support of the Security Council and the international community in this endeavour'.[67]

US Secretary of State Colin Powell issued the second. In it, he confirmed that:

> the MNF under unified command is prepared to continue to contribute to the mainte-
> nance of security in Iraq, including by preventing and deterring terrorism and protecting
> the territory of Iraq. The goal of the MNF will be to help the Iraqi people to complete the
> political transition and will permit the United Nations and the international community
> to work to facilitate Iraq's reconstruction. . . . As recent events have demonstrated,
> continuing attacks by insurgents, including former regime elements, foreign fighters,
> and illegal militias challenge all those who are working for a better Iraq.[68]

In none of the relevant documents is there any suggestion that MNF-I's mission extended beyond the security of Iraq; those threats specifically cited were framed in terms of the Iraqi security context. Moreover, although MNF-I enjoyed substantial freedom of action, the termination of occupation provisions emphasized that ultimate authority resided with the Iraqis and that MNF-I could only operate with the consent of their government.

Despite references to maintaining security, it is clear that the situation was one of armed conflict. At times, distinguishing a non-international armed conflict from internal disturbances can prove difficult. Yet, such a distinction is critical, for the law of armed conflict applies to the former, together with human rights law and domestic norms, but not to the latter.

Common Article 3 to the Geneva Conventions, the only provision in the instruments intended to address non-international armed conflict, offers no assis-tance in making the distinction, merely referring to 'armed conflict not of an international character'.[69] Despite the paucity of express normative criteria, certain

---

[67] Letter of 5 June 2004 from the Prime Minister of the Interim Government of Iraq Dr Ayad Allawi to the President of the Council (Annex to res. 1546).

[68] Letter of 5 June 2004, from the United States Secretary of State Colin L. Powell to the President of the Council (Annex to res. 1546) (Powell Letter of 5 June 2004).

[69] Geneva Conventions, Common Article 3. Additional Protocol II adds the requirement that organized armed groups be under 'responsible command' and 'exercise such control over a part of its territory as to enable them to carry out sustained and concerted military operations and to implement this Protocol'. However, as noted, the Protocol did not apply to the conflict in Iraq, and was, in any event, intended to set a higher threshold of applicability than that of Common Article 3. The ICRC had hoped the threshold would mirror that of Common Article 3. J. Pejic, 'Status of Armed Conflicts'

factors can be identified through State practice, learned commentary and judicial decisions. Based on the text of Common Article 3, 'parties' to the conflict must exist, a term that implies some degree of organization.[70] Additionally, the violence must be more than merely sporadic. As the International Criminal Tribunal for the former Yugoslavia's Appeals Chamber noted in *Tadić*, an internal armed conflict involves '*protracted* armed violence between governmental authorities and organized armed groups or between such groups within a State'.[71] The Statute of the International Criminal Court adopts both of the aforementioned criteria, distinguishing non-international armed conflict from 'situations of internal distur-bances and tensions, such as riots, isolated and sporadic acts of violence or other acts of a similar nature'. It describes the former as 'armed conflicts that take place in the territory of a State when there is protracted armed conflict between govern-mental authorities and organized armed groups or between such groups'.[72] Other factors which have been recognized as relevant include the geographical extent of the fighting, its intensity, the size of the forces involved and the weapons employed by the parties.[73]

Neither Common Article 3 nor Additional Protocol II foresees a non-international armed conflict in which foreign militaries operate in concert with indigenous forces, let alone dominate military operations. It is nonetheless well accepted that State A may assist State B in an internal conflict without transforming it into an interna-tional armed conflict.[74] This presumes that the assistance comes at the request of State B.[75] Only if State A joins the fray in support of the rebels is the conflict internationalized.[76]

There is no question but that the fighting in Iraq was sufficiently widespread and intense to meet the violence threshold or that many of the entities active in the fray amounted to 'organized armed groups'. As to international involvement, MNF-I was present at the request of the Iraqi government, and it is plain that had the Iraqis

---

in E. Wilmshurst and S. Breau (eds), *Perspectives on the ICRC Study on Customary International Humanitarian Law* (2007) 77, 87.

[70] Thus, disorganized violence is excluded, whereas fighting between the State and organized armed groups would qualify.

[71] *Tadić*, para 70. Additional Protocol II does not apply, by its terms, to armed conflict that does not involve a state. Article 1(1) limits the material field of application to conflicts between the armed forces of a Contracting Party and dissident armed forces or other organized armed groups. Somewhat questionably, in *Abella*, the Inter-American Commission on Human Rights characterized a 30-hour conflict between dissident armed forces and the Argentinean military as a non-international armed conflict. See *Abella v Argentina*, Inter-American Commission on Human Rights, Case No. 11.137, Report No. 55/97 (18 November 1997) para 156.

[72] Statute of the International Criminal Court, art. 2(f).

[73] See discussion at *Prosecutor v Haradinaj*, IT-04-84-T, Judgment (Trial Chamber), 3 April 2008, paras 39–49. See also, discussion in ch. 3, section 6.1 above.

[74] But see discussion in Turns, *Classification of Armed Conflict in Iraq*.

[75] Dinstein, *War*, 6–8, 112–16.

[76] Such was the case, for instance, when the Former Federal Republic of Yugoslavia intervened in the non-international armed conflict in the Republic of Bosnia-Herzegovina on behalf of the Bosnian Serb forces. *Prosecutor v Tadić*, IT-94-1-T, Opinion and Judgment (Trial Chamber), 7 May 1997, para 569.

asked them to leave, they would have been obliged to do so. The involvement of the US and the UK can only have been in a non-international armed conflict.

An argument can be fashioned that the non-international conflict actually pre-dated transfer of sovereignty on June 28. The fighting during (and after) the belligerent occupation was extremely complex. Participants included the international forces, the newly formed New Iraqi Army and Iraqi police forces, Kurdish forces, remnants of the Ba'athist regime, Sunni militia groups, Shia militia groups, foreign fighters and terrorist groups loosely affiliated with Al-Qaeda. A number of such groups opposed the predominantly Shia government and in many cases unofficial militia groups targeted each other.

Conflicts may be horizontally mixed in the sense that international armed conflict and non-international armed conflict coexist. An example is Afghanistan in 2001, where the Taliban were battling the Northern Alliance when the US-led Coalition attacked in October. To the extent that the strands of a conflict are demonstrably separate, that is that they have not been internationalized through external State support of the rebel forces, an international armed conflict occurs parallel to the non-international one. This possibility was recognized by the International Court of Justice in the 1986 *Nicaragua* case.[77]

As the government of Iraq was merely embryonic prior to the June 2004 'return of sovereignty', it cannot be characterized as a governmental 'party' to such a conflict. Moreover, in that it functioned under the overall control of the CPA occupation government, armed conflict between its forces and opposing groups is best characterized as international. However, as noted, both the ICTY and the ICC Statutes acknowledge the possibility of a conflict between organized armed groups. Additional Protocol II expressly requires the involvement of a Contracting Party's armed forces,[78] but no such limitation is found in Common Article 3, which is reflective of customary law applicable in all conflicts.[79] Since some of the fighting in Iraq, especially that between Shia and Sunni groups, was essentially unrelated to either the conflict between the Coalition forces and Iraq or the subsequent operation of an occupation regime, it is at least arguable that such conflicts were non-international in character.

On the other hand, might it be argued that elements of international armed conflict survived the end of occupation? In other words, were the United States and certain Coalition partners engaged in a continuing international armed conflict with surviving regime elements or terrorists? After all, the victorious powers that installed the Iraqi Interim Government in 2003 were the driving force the

---

[77] There, the Court held that '[t]he conflict between the Contra forces and those of the Government of Nicaragua is an armed conflict which is "not of an international character". The acts of the Contras towards the Nicaraguan Government are therefore governed by the law applicable to conflicts of that character; whereas the actions of the United States in and against Nicaragua fall under the legal rules relating to international conflicts'. See *Military and Paramilitary Activities in and against Nicaragua (Nicaragua v United States of America)* ICJ Rep 1986, 14, para 219 *(Nicaragua)*.

[78] AP II, art. 1(1).

[79] In *Nicaragua*, the International Court of Justice held that Common Article 3 to the 1949 Geneva Conventions 'constitute[d] a minimum yardstick' in international armed conflict because its rules represent 'elementary considerations of humanity'. *Nicaragua*, para 218. See also, *Tadić*, para 102.

following year behind resolution 1546 (that purported to establish that their continued presence was at the invitation of the Iraqi government). Moreover, colourable arguments have been made that a conflict with transnational terrorists is international in character, a position adopted by the Israeli Supreme Court in the *Targeted Killing* case.[80] Finally, no less an authority than Yoram Dinstein has argued that

> remnants of the Saddamite forces (minus Saddam himself)—strengthened by jihadist foreigners—are still fighting in Iraq, and they have yet to be rooted out. As long as US troops persist in waging combat operations against them, the hostilities constitute an international armed conflict. The belligerent occupation of parts of Iraq by US troops formally ended in 2004, but the war has gone on.[81]

For Professor Dinstein, a separate non-international armed conflict was underway 'in which the Baghdad Government is equally trying to eliminate the last vestiges of the ancient regime'.[82]

There are a number of problems with this approach. Although assertions of the Iraqi government's 'independence' from the occupying forces might be factually suspect, as a matter of law the Security Council had recognized it as legitimate. Both the relevant Security Council resolutions and agreements between Iraq and individual States frame the continuing presence of foreign forces as in support of the Iraqi government efforts to stabilize the country. Additionally, while the letter from Secretary Powell annexed to resolution 1546 specifically cited 'former regime elements', the document framed the presence of US forces as solely related to assisting Iraq in maintaining security.[83] In other words, unanimity existed that the foreign forces remained to aid Iraq in its non-international armed conflict.

Professor Dinstein's position, compelling though it may be as a matter of strict legal analysis, therefore contradicts the general approach taken by States, as well as that of the Security Council. Even if correct, the Security Agreement of December 2008[84] would argue against such a conclusion as of January 2009, particularly in light of withdrawal of US forces from the cities in June 2009. Finally, the position has since become counterfactual, since reports of continued activity by former regime elements have all but disappeared.

The Security Council renewed the MNF-I mandate annually until 2008, when the Iraqi government opposed any further extension.[85] As a result, MNF-I's

---

[80] *Public Committee against Torture in Israel et al v Government of Israel et al* High Court of Justice, Israel, HCJ 769/02 (13 December 2006) para 21. But see *Hamdan v Rumsfeld*, 126 S. Ct. 2749, 2795–6 (2006), where the US Supreme Court finds the conflict with Al-Qaeda to be 'not of an international character' because it is not between States.

[81] Y. Dinstein, 'Concluding Remarks: The Influence of the Conflict in Iraq on International Law' (2010) 40 *Israel Yearbook on Human Rights*.

[82] Ibid.

[83] Additionally, the December 2008 Security Agreement (see text accompanying nn 88–90 below) singles out operations against Al-Qaeda and other terrorist groups.

[84] See discussion in this section below.

[85] Subsequent resolutions included SC res. 1637 (2005); SC res. 1723 (2006); SC res. 1790 (2007).

Chapter VII mandate expired in December of that year. By that point, many States had withdrawn their forces. In July 2009, the United Kingdom and Australia pulled out their remaining troops, leaving only the American as USF-I. An account by one participant in the planning for the transition, which assumed a bilateral agreement would be executed allowing for the continued presence of US forces, illustrates the dilemma incident to the loss of Chapter VII authority.

> We consistently overestimated the degree of latitude the SOFA [Security Agreement] would provide, and kept having to scale back these assumptions. In the contingency of no SOFA at all, we assumed that we could do nothing but withdraw our forces, and take those measures necessary to protect ourselves during the withdrawal. Even this scenario required some legal basis—we relied on Coalition Provisional Authority 17, which authorized the Coalition to protect itself in the absence of other authorities. CPA 17 was adopted as Iraqi law, so we were essentially relying on authority granted by the Iraqis to withdraw. Luckily, this contingency never came to pass.[86]

In light of the mandate's lapse, the United States and Iraq negotiated two instruments, a Strategic Framework Agreement and a Withdrawal Agreement (Status of Forces Agreement—SOFA), which entered into force 1 January 2009.[87] The Framework Agreement signalled that a new phase in the conflict had begun.

> Recognizing the major and positive developments in Iraq that have taken place subsequent to April 9, 2003; the courage of the Iraqi people in establishing a democratically elected government under a new constitution; and welcoming no later than December 31, 2008, the termination of the Chapter VII authorization for and mandate of the multinational forces in UNSCR 1790; noting that the situation in Iraq is fundamentally different than that which existed when the UN Security Council adopted Resolution 661 in 1990, and in particular that the threat to international peace and security posed by the Government of Iraq no longer exists; and affirming in that regard that Iraq should return by December 31, 2008 to the legal and international standing that it enjoyed prior to issuance of UN Security Council Resolution 661;...[88]

US forces were to remain in the country solely at the pleasure of the Iraqi government in order to provide assistance in security matters. Article 4 of the SOFA provided, in part, that

> 1. The Government of Iraq requests the temporary assistance of the United States Forces for the purposes of supporting Iraq in its efforts to maintain security and stability in Iraq, including cooperation in the conduct of operations against al-Qaeda and other terrorist groups, outlaw groups, and remnants of the former regime.

---

[86] E-mail from participant to author, 10 April 2010, on file with author.

[87] Strategic Framework Agreement for a Relationship of Friendship and Cooperation between the United States of America and the republic of Iraq, 27 November 2008, available at <http://usiraq.procon.org/sourcefiles/strategic_framework_agreement.pdf> (Framework Agreement); Agreement between the United States of America and the Republic of Iraq on the Withdrawal of United States Forces from Iraq and the Organization of Their Activities During Their Temporary Presence in Iraq, 27 November 2008, available at <http://usiraq.procon.org/sourcefiles/SOFA-11-19-08.pdf (SOFA)>.

[88] Framework Agreement, preamble.

2. All such military operations that are carried out pursuant to this Agreement shall be conducted with the agreement of the Government of Iraq. Such operations shall be fully coordinated with Iraqi authorities. The coordination of all such military operations shall be overseen by a Joint Military Operations Coordination Committee (JMOCC) to be established pursuant to this Agreement. Issues regarding proposed military operations that cannot be resolved by the JMOCC shall be forwarded to the Joint Ministerial Committee.

3. All such operations shall be conducted with full respect for the Iraqi Constitution and the laws of Iraq. Execution of such operations shall not infringe upon the sovereignty of Iraq and its national interests, as defined by the Government of Iraq. It is the duty of the United States Forces to respect the laws, customs, and traditions of Iraq and applicable international law.[89]

The change was dramatic. Each operation now had to be approved and coordinated with Iraqi forces, at least those not involving the right of 'legitimate self-defense within Iraq, as defined in applicable international law'.[90]

3. Rules on capture and detention

In contrast to the experience in Afghanistan, the handling of detainees in Iraq posed few classification issues, primarily due to recognition that criminals were a distinct category from those involved in hostilities or who represented security threats to the occupying force. From commencement of combat operations through the belligerent occupation, detainees were categorized into three groups: prisoners of war (POWs), which included those captured during hostilities against the Coalition; security detainees, including those who had 'committed a crime against Coalition forces'; and common criminals. The first category was treated in accordance with the 1949 Third Geneva Convention, the remaining two in accordance with the Fourth Geneva Convention, specifically article 78.[91] Once the Iraqi law-enforcement and judicial systems began to function, alleged criminals were turned over to Iraqi authorities based on a finding that there was 'reasonable suspicion that the individual had committed a criminal offense'.[92]

The approach taken by the Coalition partners varied widely. For instance, 'United States forces would detain individuals whereas the UK forces would detain individuals only if really necessary and then they would try to hand them to the Iraqi Police Service. The Italian approach mirrored that of the British'.[93] Differences in approach, however, were driven not by divergent characterizations of the

[89] SOFA, art. 4. The Framework Agreement similarly provided that: 'The temporary presence of the U.S. forces in Iraq is at the request and invitation of the sovereign Government of Iraq and with full respect for the sovereignty of Iraq.' Further: 'The United States shall not use Iraqi land, sea and air as a launching or transit point for attack against other countries; nor seek or request permanent bases or a permanent military presence in Iraq.' Framework Agreement, s. I.
[90] Ibid, art. 4(5).
[91] Geneva Convention IV, art. 78.
[92] US Army Center for Law and Military Operations, 'Legal Lessons Learned from Afghanistan and Iraq: Volume II' 153.
[93] Ibid.

conflict, but differing legal standards. For instance, the European Convention on Human Rights bound British forces when detaining individuals, but not their American partners.[94]

With regard to POWs specifically, the Coalition appeared to have learned from the criticism it faced for failure to conduct tribunals pursuant to article 5 of the Third Geneva Convention in Afghanistan.[95] In Iraq, article 5 Tribunals, which are required in the event of doubt as to whether captured individuals are entitled to POW status, were common. The practical dilemma was that most Iraqi military personnel had shed their uniforms, and upon capture often claimed they were innocent civilians wrongly detained. Judge Advocates conducted a screening of all those captured; if doubt remained as to status, a formal article 5 Tribunal was held.[96]

Since the nature of the conflict remained international, continued detention of prisoners of war as such throughout the occupation was consistent with the law of armed conflict. Article 118 of the Third Geneva Convention only provides that they 'shall be released and repatriated without delay after the cessation of active hostilities'.[97] There is no requirement to release them once an occupation begins, nor any authority to hold them through an occupation if hostilities have ceased. As noted in the ICRC commentary to the provision, 'the internment of captives is justified by a legitimate concern—to prevent military personnel from taking up arms once more against the captor State. That reason no longer exists once the fighting is over'.[98] Hostilities continued throughout the occupation (and years afterwards) and the risk that released prisoners might join insurgents or the remnants of the regime forces was very real.

The detention system was not without flaws. For instance, in November 2003, US forces reportedly seized the wife and daughter of the former vice-Chair of Iraq's revolutionary Command Council in an effort to locate him. Human Rights Watch vigorously protested and they were released.[99] There is no evidence, however, that such practices were widespread. Additionally, US and British forces mistreated a

---

[94] See e.g. *R (Al-Skeini and others) v Secretary of State for Defence* [2008] 1 AC 153, where the House of Lords (then the highest court in the UK) held that the Convention applied to the killing of an Iraqi in a British detention facility. When the case went to the European Court of Human Rights, the Court held that, since the UK assumed the exercise of certain sovereign powers, in particular the maintenance of security in South East Iraq, jurisdiction for the purpose of the Convention went beyond mere detention and extended to its security operations. (*Al-Skeini and others v The United Kingdom* (Judgment) App No. 55721/07 (7 July 2011)). See also, ch. 4, section 2 and 4.3 of this book with regard to the general question of the extraterritorial applicability of international human rights law.

[95] 'Should any doubt arise as to whether persons, having committed a belligerent act and having fallen into the hands of the enemy, belong to any of the categories enumerated in Article 4, such persons shall enjoy the protection of the present Convention until such time as their status has been determined by a competent tribunal.' Geneva Convention III, art. 5.

[96] US Army Center for Law and Military Operations, 'Legal Lessons Learned from Afghanistan and Iraq, Volume I' 43–6.

[97] Geneva Convention III, art. 118.

[98] Pictet, *Commentary*, 546–7.

[99] Human Rights Watch, 'Letter to Defense Secretary Donald Rumsfeld' (12 January 2004), available at: <www.hrw.org/news/2004/01/11/letter-defense-secretary-donald-rumsfeld>.

number of detainees, most famously (as regards the US) at Abu Ghraib prison.[100] Yet, the nature of the conflict has no bearing on such actions, there being no justification for such criminal actions in any form of conflict.

The (presumably) final period of the war in Iraq was, and remains, non-international armed conflict. Although the legal authority to conduct operations during a non-international armed conflict depends primarily on the acquiescence of the host-nation government, action by the Security Council may supplement and even override such consent. During the initial phase of the non-international armed conflict, such authorization loomed large. Security Council resolution 1546 empowered MNF-I to 'to take all necessary measures to contribute to the maintenance of security and stability in Iraq, including offensive operations'.[101] The letter from Secretary Powell annexed to the resolution made clear that the provision provided the legal basis for MNF-I to both mount combat operations and engage in detention.

> Under the agreed arrangement, the MNF stands ready to continue to undertake a broad range of tasks to contribute to the maintenance of security and to ensure force protection. These include activities necessary to counter ongoing security threats posed by forces seeking to influence Iraq's political future through violence. This will include *combat operations* against members of these groups, *internment where this is necessary for imperative reasons of security*, and the continued search for and securing of weapons that threaten Iraqi security.[102]

While it would obviously have been preferable to have the resolution itself explicitly contain such authorization, the direct reference to the Powell letter clearly implied that a Chapter VII mandate had issued since it authorized the use of force for purposes beyond self-defence and defence of the force.

Detention operations were conducted under the authority of resolution 1546, by reference to the Powell letter. Legally, this was a change from the period of belligerent occupation, during which article 78 of the Fourth Geneva Convention governed detention of civilians and the Third Geneva Convention controlled the treatment of captured members of the armed forces. When the occupation ended, these instruments became technically inapplicable.[103] Nevertheless, US forces

---

[100] See e.g. the formal investigations of detainee abuse: US Army, Antonio M. Taguba, Investigating Officer, Article 15–6 Investigation of the 800th Military Police Brigade; US Army, Anthony R. Jones, Investigating Officer, AR 15–6 Investigation of the Abu Ghraib Prison and 205th Military Intelligence Brigade; US Army, George R. Fay, Investigating Officer, AR 15–6 Investigation of the Abu Ghraib Detention Facility and 205th Military Intelligence Brigade.

[101] Although subsequent resolutions did not mention combat operations or detention, they re-affirmed resolution 1546.

[102] Powell Letter of 5 June 2004.

[103] See e.g. ICRC, 'Protecting Persons Deprived of Freedom Remains a Priority' (5 August 2004), available at: <www.icrc.org/eng/resources/documents/misc/63kkj8.htm>: 'Those persons arrested before 28 June and currently interned by the MNF-I should either be released, charged and tried or placed within another legal framework that regulates their continued internment. They remain protected by the Third Geneva Convention (for prisoners of war)or the Fourth Geneva Convention (for interned and detained civilians) until they are released or handed over to Iraqi authorities. Persons arrested prior to 28 June who have been handed over to Iraqi authorities and continue to be detained in connection with the ongoing non-international armed conflict are protected by Article 3 common to

applied article 78 by analogy as a matter of policy, detaining individuals as security internees.

They also applied Department of Defense (DoD) Directive 2310.01E, which sets forth detention guidance for military detainee programs.[104] The directive encompassed the actions of 'DoD contractors assigned to or supporting the DoD Components engaged in, conducting, participating in, or supporting detainee operations; non-DoD personnel as a condition of permitting access to internment facilities or to detainees under DoD control; and all detainee operations conducted by DoD personnel (military and civilian), contract employees under DoD cognizance, and DoD contractors supporting detainee operations'.[105] Detainees were required to 'be treated humanely and in accordance with U.S. law, the law of war, and applicable U.S. policy'.[106] Regardless of either the character of the conflict or a detainee's legal status, anyone subject to the directive had to apply 'at a minimum the standards articulated in Common Article 3 to the Geneva Conventions of 1949 . . . ., in the treatment of all detainees, until their final release, transfer out of DoD control, or repatriation'.[107] Lest this standard be interpreted as the sole requirement, the directive cautioned that 'certain categories of detainees, such as enemy prisoners of war, enjoy protections under the law of war in addition to the minimum standards prescribed in Common Article 3'.[108]

This is not to say that the effect of the shift from international to non-international armed conflict was not considered by US forces. An internal 'thought piece' circulated among Judge Advocates in October 2007 identified a number of possible consequences. Its author suggested that:

> A detainee may be removed from a safe holding area or place of detention and may accompany interrogators to locations in the field as an informant to identify enemy terrorist strongholds and enemy personnel, and may take active part in 'offensive' military operations.
>
>   Private security companies (PSC) may be contracted to: protect US military facilities through screening of personnel/vehicles seeking entry and preventing unauthorized access; protect civilian, contractors and US military personnel within military facilities; protect property (including military property) located within a facility from theft/destruction; protect Class I military convoys, including deadly force authorization for self-defense (including self-defense of personnel in the convoy) against persons seeking to do harm or steal/destroy mission essential property.
>
>   . . .

---

the Geneva Conventions, and customary rules applicable to non-international armed conflicts; other applicable international law and relevant Iraqi law would apply to them as well. The same rules apply to persons arrested since 28 June 2004 by Iraqi authorities or the MNF-I in connection with the ongoing non-international armed conflict.'

[104] Department of Defense, Directive 2310.01E, The Department of Defense Detainee Program (5 September 2006) (DOD Directive 2310.01E). Practice explained in B.J. Bill, 'Detention Operations in Iraq: A View from the Ground' (2010) 40 *Israel Yearbook on Human Rights* 67 (Bill, *Detention Operations in Iraq*).

[105] DoD Directive 2310.01E, para 2(1)2–2(1)4.   [106] Ibid, para 4(1).

[107] Ibid, para 4(2).   [108] Ibid.

> With the approval of the Iraqi…government, U.S. military forces may move detainees from their country of capture since the four Geneva Conventions of 1949 would not be applicable.[109]

Despite such musings, the transition had little practical influence on operational matters for US forces.

One significant point of interest was the Iraqi decision to reintroduce the death penalty following the termination of the belligerent occupation. The British, who were bound by the European Convention on Human Right's prohibition on the death penalty, opposed the reintroduction until such time as they were no longer in belligerent occupation. Further, the Dutch stopped detaining people once the death penalty was in force.

The expiry of MNF I's Chapter VII mandate and the conclusion of the SOFA with the Iraqi government resulted in questions over the issue of detention.[110] Before execution of the agreement, the United States had detained thousands of Iraqis on its own accord consistent with the authority contained in resolution 1546. The SOFA now provided that '[n]o detention or arrest may be carried out by the United States Forces (except with respect to detention or arrest of members of the United States Forces and of the civilian component) except through an Iraqi decision issued in accordance with Iraqi law and pursuant to Article 4'.[111] Although the agreement contemplated Iraqi requests for US assistance in detaining or arresting individuals, those detained had to be turned over to Iraqi authorities within twenty-four hours.[112]

The US working presumption was that transfer of detainees held by its forces to Iraqi authorities would occur pursuant to domestic Iraqi criminal law and be governed by human rights norms, such as those governing preventive detention and prohibiting arbitrary detention. Therefore, US authorities began building criminal cases against the most dangerous detainees, an effort that included the US intelligence community, the FBI and other US law-enforcement agencies, and other Coalition forces. However, by the summer of 2009, not a single criminal case had been fully developed. Instead, the US forces simply transferred their detainees to Iraqi authorities. As the officer involved in the process noted:

> We transferred hundreds of detainees to the Iraqis, but never asked for any criminal evidence to justify the transfer. There was a huge cultural problem in the US military in terms of getting senior commanders to grasp the requirements to build criminally prosecutable cases of detainees. In the end, we just couldn't convince commanders of the validity or urgency of this requirement. The transfers were essentially extra-legal contrivances; it was sordid business.[113]

Be that as it may, no authority existed in international law for continued detention by the United States absent Iraqi consent.

[109] Status of the Current Armed Conflicts (12 September 2007), on file with author.
[110] On detention during this period, see Bill, *Detention Operations in Iraq*.
[111] SOFA, art. 22(1).
[112] Ibid, art. 22(2). Other important provisions established jurisdictional prerogatives over those who committed crimes in Iraq (art. 12) and required withdrawal of US combat forces, first from cities, and ultimately the country (art. 24).
[113] E-mail from participant to author, 10 April 2010, on file with author.

4. Rules on use of force

Despite the complexity of the phase of belligerent occupation, no major issues deriving from classification of the conflict arose with regard to the use of force. In great part this resulted from the existence of an insurgency to which the rules of international armed conflict fully applied.

The transition from an international armed conflict to a non-international one had little impact on the ground, at least as to the applicable law on the conduct of hostilities. While it is true that the treaty law applicable during the former is much more detailed than the latter, most of the conduct of hostilities norms applicable in international armed conflict equally constitute customary norms applicable in non-international conflicts. The ICTY has taken this approach to its limit. In *Tadić*, the Appeals Chamber stated that

> it cannot be denied that customary rules have developed to govern internal strife.
> These rules, as specifically identified in the preceding discussion, cover such areas as
> protection of civilians from hostilities, in particular from indiscriminate attacks,
> protection of civilian objects, in particular cultural property, protection of all those
> who do not (or no longer) take active part in hostilities, as well as prohibition of means
> of warfare proscribed in international armed conflicts and ban of certain methods of
> conducting hostilities.[114]

Although the pronouncement is arguably overbroad in scope, the applicability of most targeting norms to both international and non-international armed conflict has been accepted by such unofficial works as the ICRC's *Customary International Humanitarian Law Study* and the *San Remo Manual on the Law of Non-international Armed Conflict*.[115] Further, while human rights law plays a greater role in non-international than international armed conflict, targeting practices with respect to members of organized armed groups or direct participants in hostilities are relatively constant because of the principle of *lex specialis*. In any event, it is US policy to apply the full gamut of the law of armed conflict protections from attack regardless of state of the conflict, absent an affirmative decision at the appropriate level to do otherwise.[116]

5. Other significant problems of international humanitarian law

During the period of international armed conflict preceding the initiation of the belligerent occupation few problems arose from classification of the conflict. This is

---

[114] *Tadić*, para 127.

[115] J.M. Henckaerts and L. Doswald-Beck, *Customary International Humanitarian Law* (2005); M. Schmitt, C. Garraway, and Y. Dinstein, 'The Manual on the Law of Non-International Armed Conflict with Commentary' (International Institute of Humanitarian Law, 2006), reprinted in 36 *Israel Yearbook on Human Rights* (2006) (Special Supplement).

[116] Department of Defense, Directive 2311.01E, DoD Law of War Program (9 May 2006) para 4(1).

not to suggest that legal problems did not surface.[117] For instance, the wearing of civilian clothes by Iraqi forces, use of human shields, targeting of regime elites, suicide bombings, perfidy and misuse of protected places, such as mosques, presented intricate legal quandaries. However, there was no debate over the character of the conflict, and, in light of the negative experience with novel legal interpretation vis-à-vis Afghanistan and the 'global war on terror', Coalition forces adhered closely to classic applications of the law of armed conflict, including that governing targeting and detention, during the phase of international armed conflict.

The phase of belligerent occupation was far more complex. Activities occurring during the occupation diverged widely from those foreseen by occupation law. Occupation law is premised on the temporary assumption of authority by the occupiers, pending a return of control to the indigenous government. The rights and duties of the occupying power are designed to fill voids in governance, security and provision of basic needs for the population until such time as the defeated State can resume such functions. It is not entitled to enact comprehensive changes to the State's political or economic structures or dramatically modify its judicial system.

Article 43 of the Hague Regulations exemplifies the goal of generally maintaining the status quo *ante bellum*: 'The authority of the legitimate power having in fact passed into the hands of the occupant, the latter shall take all the measures in his power to restore, and ensure, as far as possible, public order and safety, while respecting, unless absolutely prevented, the laws in force in the country.' Similarly, the Hague Regulations require the preservation of the tax system, except as necessary to defray the costs of occupation administration, and designates the occupying power as administrator of public buildings, real estate, etc., belonging to the hostile State in accordance with the rules of usufruct.[118] The Fourth Geneva Convention adopts an analogous approach. For instance, the status of public officials is not to be altered, penal laws remain in effect unless they constitute a threat to the occupier's security or otherwise run contrary to the provisions of the convention, and domestic tribunals are to continue in operation.[119]

Despite these provisions, the CPA purported to exercise all executive, legislative and judicial authority that it deemed necessary to achieve its objectives, which included democratization. It de-Ba'athicized the country, disbanded its military, set up a criminal court system, established ministries and redesigned the economy. Some of these measures can be justified under occupation law on the basis of security concerns. Article 43 of the Hague Regulations requires the occupying power to take measures to 'restore, and ensure, as far as possible, public order and security', while article 54 of the Fourth Geneva Convention allows the removal of public officials from their posts. To the extent that certain individuals represented security threats, had a history of abuse of authority (e.g. by violating human rights

[117] Y. Dinstein, 'Jus in Bello Issues Arising in the Hostilities in Iraq in 2003' (2004) 34 *Israel Yearbook on Human Rights* 1; M. Schmitt, 'The Conduct of Hostilities During Operation Iraqi Freedom: An International Humanitarian Law Assessment' (2003) 6 *Yearbook of International Humanitarian Law* 73.
[118] 1907 Hague Regulation IV, art. 48, 55.
[119] Geneva Convention IV, art. 54, 55.

norms), or otherwise were likely to frustrate compliance by the Coalition with its occupation responsibilities, such actions were lawful.[120] Similarly, it would be incongruous with the foundational premises of occupation laws to allow abusive criminal courts to continue to function.

It is nevertheless undeniable that the CPA's sweeping reforms exceeded its authority under occupation law. For instance, while dissolving certain governmental entities, such as the Iraqi Intelligence Service and presidential bodyguard, and seizing their assets might have been justified by security concerns, the CPA went so far as to disestablish the Iraqi National Olympic Committee.[121] It also created new ministries out of whole cloth, such as the Ministry of Environment and the Ministry of Displacement and Migration.[122] And although reconstruction of the Iraqi economy might have been laudable, there is no basis in occupation law for taking such steps as revising the banking law or replacing the existing foreign investment law.[123]

In August 2003, having earlier disbanded the Iraqi Army, the CPA created the 'New Iraqi Army', over which its Administrator, as civilian Commander in Chief, exercised 'supreme command, control, and administrative authority' pending creation of an Iraqi government. Operational and tactical control over such forces generally rested with a Coalition officer.[124] While occupiers may take measures such as using indigenous military and police forces to maintain order, creation of an entirely new force under their command arguably ran afoul of the Fourth Geneva Convention's prohibition on impressing individuals into an occupier's armed or auxiliary forces for other purposes.[125]

The CPA also engaged in certain activities regarding property that appear inconsistent with occupation law. For instance, in May 2003 it issued Order Number 4, which characterized as State property 'all movable and immovable property, records and data, cash, funds, realizable assets and liquid capital, in whatever form maintained and wherever located, used, possessed, or controlled by the Baath Party, its officials and members, and all residences occupied by Baath officials or members assigned to them by the Party, a member of the Baath Party or other State instrumentality and that were not purchased for full value by those officials or members'.[126] By the order, this property could be seized by the CPA 'on behalf, and for the benefit of the people of Iraq'. Although it might be appropriate

---

[120] For instance, CPA Order 1, which disestablished the Ba'ath Party justified its actions on the basis of 'grave concern of Iraqi society regarding the threat posed by the continuation of Ba'ath Party networks and personnel in the administration of Iraq, and the intimidation of the people of Iraq by Ba'ath Party officials', as well as the 'continuing threat to the security of the Coalition Forces posed by the Iraqi Baath Party'.

[121] CPA Order 2, CPA/ORD/23 May 2003/2/Annex, Dissolution of Entities.

[122] CPA Order 44, CPA/ORD/24 November 2004/44, Ministry of Environment; CPA Order 50, CPA/ORD/11 January 2003 [sic 2004]/50, Ministry of Displacement and Migration.

[123] CPA Order 40, CPA/ORD/19 September 2003/40, Bank Law; CPA Order 39, CPA/ORD/19 September 2003/39, Foreign Investment.

[124] CPA Order 22, CPA ORD/8 August 2003/22, Creation of a New Iraqi Army.

[125] Geneva Convention IV, art. 51.

[126] CPA Order 4, CPA/ORD/25 May 2003/4, Management of Property and Assets of the Iraqi Baath Party.

to characterize party property as State property subject to seizure under the Hague Regulations, private property may only be requisitioned by the occupation commander for the needs of his forces.[127] The property of party officials, as distinct from that of the party itself, would qualify as such protected private property.

Irrespective of occupation law's requirement to generally maintain the existing laws and legal system, the CPA replaced the penal code with that pre-dating Saddam Hussein (with certain modifications), arguing 'the former regime used certain provisions of the penal code as a tool of repression in violation of internationally recognized human rights standards'.[128]

While allowing civil and criminal courts to continue functioning, the CPA also created the Central Criminal Court of Iraq to handle cases of a transnational character, presenting special security concerns, or involving incidents hindering reconstruction, including breach of CPA orders.[129] In December 2003, it established the Iraqi Special Tribunal to address cases concerning 'any Iraqi national or resident of Iraq' accused of genocide, crimes against humanity, war crimes and certain violations of Iraqi law committed during Saddam Hussein's reign. Both Iraqi and non-Iraqi judges were permitted to sit on the bench, and the Tribunal President was required to appoint international advisers/observers to its various subdivisions, such as the Office of the Prosecutor. The Tribunal went on to try former regime members, sentencing a number of them, including Saddam Hussein, to death.[130]

The occupying forces were engaged in what Professor Sir Adam Roberts has perceptively labelled a 'transformative military occupation'.[131] Security Council resolutions provided the legal basis for such expansive activities. Although calling for compliance with occupation law, resolution 1483 'appeal[ed] to Member States and concerned organizations to assist the people of Iraq in their efforts to reform their institutions and rebuild their country, and to contribute to conditions of stability and security in Iraq' and to respond to calls for 'resources necessary for reconstruction and rehabilitation of Iraq's economic infrastructure'. It established the position of Special Representative to work with the CPA and others in establishing 'national and local institutions for representative governance,... facilitating the reconstruction of key infrastructure,... promoting economic reconstruction and the conditions for sustainable development,... promoting the protection of human rights,... and encouraging international efforts to promote legal and judicial reform'. The resolution also authorized a Development Fund, which would be disbursed at the direction of the Authority 'to meet the

---

[127] 1907 Hague Regulation IV, art. 55, 52.

[128] CPA Order 7, CPA/ORD/10 June 2003/7, Penal Code.

[129] CPA Order 13, CPA/ORD/18 June 2003/13, The Central Criminal Court of Iraq (Revised). The CPA Administrator appointed its judges.

[130] CPA Order 48, CPA/ORD/l0 December 2003/48, Delegation of Authority Regarding an Iraqi Special Tribunal.

[131] A. Roberts, 'Transformative Military Occupation: Applying the Laws of War and Human Rights' in M. Schmitt and J. Pejic (eds), *International Law and Armed Conflict: Exploring the Faultlines* (2007).

humanitarian needs of the Iraqi people' and foster 'economic reconstruction and repair of Iraq's infrastructure'.

Resolution 1511 equally aimed towards transformation of Iraq. It tasked the United Nations with 'providing humanitarian relief, promoting the economic reconstruction of and conditions for sustainable development in Iraq, and advancing efforts to restore and establish national and local institutions for representative government' and urged 'Member States and international and regional organizations to support the Iraq reconstruction effort... to help meet the needs of the Iraqi people by providing resources necessary for the rehabilitation and reconstruction of Iraq's economic infrastructure'. And, as noted earlier, the Security Council implicitly and explicitly approved certain of the CPA actions, such as the creation of the Governing Council.[132] In other words, the Security Council resolutions foresaw a State-building effort, not the maintenance of the existing Iraqi governmental, legal, social, and economic systems. As a consequence of the Security Council activism, deviation from the strictures of occupation law was permitted for the purposes set forth in the resolutions. The primacy of 'UN law' over the rights and obligations set forth in other international legal instruments rendered such actions lawful.

6. Conclusions

Some degree of caution is necessary in drawing conclusions from the Iraq experience for application in other times and places. First, the conflict was influenced in part by the experience of the so-called 'global war on terror', which began on 11 September 2001, and continued throughout the conflict in Iraq. Although discussion of that 'conflict' lies beyond the scope of this chapter, it is self-evident that the global war on terror shook several received notions of international law to the core, engendering dramatic global reaction, much of it critical. Second, experiences during the conflict in Afghanistan, launched less than a month after the 9/11 attacks, tempered Coalition operations in Iraq considerably. This is especially so with regard to the characterization and handling of detainees. The negative reaction to US detainee practices and policies impelled a return to traditional understandings and well-advised caution. Third, the conflict fell outside the scope of two of the key treaties of the law of armed conflict, Additional Protocol I, applicable in international armed conflict, and Additional Protocol II, which addresses non-international armed conflict. This was so because Iraq is a party to neither instrument, and, thus, they were inapplicable despite the party status of certain belligerents, such as the United Kingdom. To the extent the Protocols did shape operations, it was either because their provisions were deemed reflective of customary international law or because particular belligerents chose to respect them as a matter of policy, *vice* law. Thus, somewhat different norms will govern future

---

[132] SC res. 1500 (2003).

conflicts to which the agreements apply. Finally, the UN Security Council played a pivotal role in determining the status of the conflict during its various phases, often in the face of contradictory facts on the ground. But for Security Council activism, the legal character of the conflict would have differed appreciably.

As is evident from the discussion above, the conflict(s) in Iraq presented no significant difficulties with regard to classifying the hostilities other than perhaps on the questions of the termination of the occupation and the geographical extent of the responsibilities of the different States in occupation. In particular, classification had no determinative bearing on the treatment of detainees or the use of force. The abuses at, for example, Abu Ghraib would have been contrary to the law applicable in any form of hostilities. Other law of armed conflict problems surfaced during the conflict, but they did not stem from difficulties in classification. For instance, a key difficulty was that of the differing human rights obligations of the Coalition partners, stemming from their different international obligations. It manifested itself particularly with regard to the treatment of detainees and the death penalty.[133] Yet this challenge was not a result of classification of the conflict. Rather, the issues of interest with regard to classification lay instead in the relationship between the various forms of conflict, and the transition between them, as well as the role of the Security Council in changing the law applicable in the phase of belligerent occupation.

Finally, and despite the unique nature of the war, four normative conclusions bear mentioning as potentially applicable in future conflicts.

1) During the conflicts in Iraq, transition between various phases did not significantly impact either the conduct of hostilities or detention practices. In each phase, the law traditionally understood to apply appeared to function as intended. This suggests that the fact of transition is not in itself problematic, at least so long as there is clarity regarding the classification from and to which the conflict is shifting. Of course, there may be practical problems, such as transfer of detainees, but there is little question as to the applicable rules of international humanitarian law.

2) Facts on the ground may not support a de jure classification of a conflict. However, the de jure classification drives the expectations of the international community as to the conduct of belligerents. In 2004, the occupation ended, not because factual circumstances established its demise, but rather because the Security Council counterfactually terminated it.

3) Conduct of hostilities and detention practices can be either enhanced or limited by action of the Security Council. Although operations during a non-international armed conflict are limited to those of which the host State has

---

[133] Cases brought in the European Court of Human Rights subsequent to the termination of the engagement of UK forces indicated that the forces were governed by the European Convention to a greater extent than was apparent at the time: see *Al-Skeini and others v The United Kingdom* (Judgment) App No. 55721/07 (7 July 2011) and *Al-Jedda v The United Kingdom* (Judgment) App No. 27021/08 (7 July 2011).

approved, UN law as expressed in Security Council resolutions addressing the situation in Iraq allowed for deviation from the accepted consent-based scope of foreign force activity during a non-international armed conflict, thereby empowering MNF-I to operate with uncharacteristic autonomy. Expiration of the Chapter VII mandate for MNF-I in December 2008 drastically altered the legal authority for actions by USF-I, and greatly reduced its operational prerogatives.

4) The United Nations Security Council appears to enjoy wide latitude in deviating from the traditional law governing military operations. In Iraq, and although the Council clearly viewed the situation as one of occupation in Phase II, various Security Council resolutions mandated activities that ran counter to both the spirit and letter of the law of belligerent occupation. Despite such dramatic departure from the law, there appeared to be near universal consensus that doing so was appropriate in the circumstances.

Chronology

2 August 1990	Iraq invades Kuwait.
29 November 1990	Security Council resolution 678 authorizes States to use 'all necessary means' to expel Iraqi forces from Kuwait.
3 April 1991	Security Council resolution 687 sets conditions for a formal ceasefire.
16 October 2002	United States Congress passes resolution authorizing the use of military force against Iraq.
8 November 2002	Security Council resolution 1441 affords Iraq a 'final opportunity' to comply with the inspection regime.
19 March 2003	US-led coalition launches military operation against Iraq.
1 May 2003	President Bush proclaims the end of major military operations in Iraq.
8 May 2003	Security Council is notified by the United States and the United Kingdom of the establishment of the Coalition Provisional Authority.
22 May 2003	Security Council resolution 1483 acknowledges the state of belligerent occupation in Iraq.
13 July 2003	Governing Council is established as a principal body of the Iraqi interim administration.
8 June 2004	Security Council resolution 1546 envisages the transfer of governing authority to Iraqis by 30 June 2004.
28 June 2004	Coalition Provisional Authority issues Order No. 100 transferring full governing authority to the Iraqi Interim Government.
January 2007	President Bush announces 'the surge'.
December 2008	MNF-I's mandate under Chapter VII expires.
1 January 2009	Status of Forces Agreement enters into force between United States and Iraq.
July 2009	United Kingdom and Australia withdraw their remaining troops from Iraq.

12

Lebanon 2006

Iain Scobbie*

1. Introduction

1.1. Context

From 1975 to 1990, Lebanon experienced internal communal violence between militias organized along confessional lines. Other States deployed forces in Lebanon during this period, some at the request of the Lebanese government which sought to stabilise the situation. In the 1970s, the Palestine Liberation Organization (PLO) relocated armed units from Jordan to southern Lebanon which it used as a base for operations against Israel. This resulted in Israeli incursions in 1978 (Operation Litani) and 1982 (Operation Peace for Galilee).[1]

Operation Litani resulted in the creation of the UN Interim Force in Lebanon (UNIFIL) by Security Council resolutions 425 (1978) and 426 (1978).[2] The operative paragraphs of resolution 425 called for respect for the territorial integrity, sovereignty and political independence of Lebanon, and called upon Israel immediately to cease its military action against Lebanon and withdraw its forces from all Lebanese territory. At the request of Lebanon, the Security Council established UNIFIL to confirm the withdrawal of Israeli forces, restore international peace and security, and assist the government of Lebanon in ensuring the return of its effective authority in southern Lebanon. UNIFIL forces were in position during the 2006 conflict.[3]

Israel's Operation Peace for Galilee in 1982 resulted in the expulsion of the PLO from Lebanon, but also in the presence of Israeli troops in southern Lebanon until 2000. Although it partially withdrew in 1985, Israel continued to occupy part of southern Lebanon, employing the Israel Defence Forces (IDF) and Lebanese

* As always, a debt which I am pleased to acknowledge is owed to Sarah Hibbin for her assistance with research. I am also grateful to Professor David Kretzmer for his valuable comments on earlier drafts of this chapter. Responsibility for the final text and its deficiencies, however, remains mine.

[1] For an overview, see D. Hirst, *Beware of small States: Lebanon, battleground of the Middle East* (2010) (Hirst, *Small States*).

[2] Security Council resolutions 425 (1978) and 426 (1978) adopted on 19 March 1978: voting 12–0, with 2 abstentions. China did not participate in the vote.

[3] By SC res. 2004 (2011), adopted on 30 August, the mandate of UNIFIL was extended to 31 August 2012.

militia forces (the so-called 'South Lebanon Army') to do so. On 25 May 2000, the government of Israel notified the Secretary-General that Israel had redeployed its forces in compliance with Security Council resolutions 425 and 426. On 16 June 2000, the Secretary-General confirmed to the Security Council that Israel had fulfilled the requirements of resolution 425.[4]

Hezbollah, a Shiite organization, emerged during the period of Israeli occupation, subsuming members of groups which had been known as Islamic Jihad.[5] It has become a political group, active in social services, while maintaining an armed militant wing. In Lebanon, Hezbollah is a recognized political party[6] which, at the time of the 2006 conflict, was represented in both the Lebanese Cabinet and legislature, having two ministers in the former and fourteen members in the 128-seat Parliament.[7] While Hezbollah is funded partly through donations by Lebanese Shiites, it is generally accepted that it also receives financial and political assistance, and also military support in the form of weapons and training, from Iran. It is also claimed that Hezbollah receives military support from Syria.[8]

Syria has a history of interfering in Lebanese politics, and in the past has stationed troops in the Beqa'a Valley in eastern Lebanon. Syria was forced to withdraw these troops as a result of its interference in Lebanese constitutional affairs in the summer of 2004.[9] On 2 September, the Security Council adopted

---

[4] See 'Report of the Secretary-General on the implementation of Security Council resolutions 425 (1978) and 426 (1978)' S/2000/590 (16 June 2000).

[5] For a brief historical overview of Hezbollah, see C. Bloom, 'The classification of Hezbollah in both international and non-international armed conflicts' (2008) 14 *Annual Survey of International and Comparative Law* 64–8 (Bloom, *The classification of Hezbollah*); J. Ching and M. Toiba, 'Hezbollah (a.k.a. Hizbollah, Hizbu'llah)' Council on Foreign Relations (15 July 2010) (Ching and Toiba, *Hezbollah*); L. Deeb, 'Hizballah: a primer' *Middle East Report Online* (31 July 2006) (Deeb, *Hizballah*); Hirst, *Small States,* chs 9 and 10.

[6] See Bloom, *The classification of Hezbollah*, 65–6; Deeb, *Hizballah*; and 'Implementation of General Assembly resolution 60/251 of 15 March 2006 entitled "Human Rights Council": Report of the Commission of Inquiry on Lebanon pursuant to Human Rights Council resolution S-2/1' A/HRC/3/2 (23 November 2006) 22, para 56 (Report of the Commission of Inquiry). Operative para 6 of Human Rights Council resolution S-2/1 (9 August 2006), adopted during its second special session, appointed this 'high-level commission of inquiry' which was given a mandate '(a) to investigate the systematic targeting and killings of civilians by Israel in Lebanon; (b) to examine the types of weapons used by Israel and their conformity with international law; (c) to assess the extent and deadly impact of Israeli attacks on human life, property, critical infrastructure and the environment'. Although the government of Lebanon cooperated with the Commission in its work, the government of Israel refused to do so (see 17, para 19).

[7] Bloom, *The classification of Hezbollah*, 65–6; and Deeb, *Hizballah*. Following the conclusion of the Doha Agreement in March 2008 between Lebanese political factions which aimed to end an 18-month political crisis, Hezbollah was effectively granted a veto power in the Lebanese Parliament. The Doha Agreement led to the formation of a national unity government in which Hezbollah and its allies held 11 of the 30 Cabinet seats. In the June 2009 parliamentary elections, Hezbollah lost to Lebanon's ruling pro-Western 'March 14' coalition. It retained 13 seats in the Parliament but only 2 in the Cabinet: see Ching and Toiba, *Hezbollah*.

[8] See M. Levitt, 'Hezbollah finances: funding the Party of God' in J.K. Giraldo and H.A. Trinkunas (eds), *Terrorism financing and State responses: a comparative perspective* (2007) 134; 'Lebanon: the many hands and faces of Hezbollah' *IRIN News* (29 March 2006); and C. Zambelis, 'Mystery surrounds alleged Hezbollah links to drug arrests in Curacao' VII/18 *Terrorism Monitor* (Jamestown Foundation) 9 (26 June 2009).

[9] See Hirst, *Small States*, ch. 12.

resolution 1559 (2004).[10] Its terms echoed those of the 22 October 1989 Taif Agreement, concluded between Lebanese political factions to end the civil war and re-assert Lebanese authority in Southern Lebanon. The preamble of resolution 1559 noted that the Security Council was '*[g]ravely concerned* at the continued presence of armed militias in Lebanon, which prevent the Lebanese Government from exercising its full sovereignty over all Lebanese territory', and operative paragraphs 1 to 4 re-affirmed its call for the strict respect of the sovereignty, territorial integrity, unity and political independence of Lebanon under the sole and exclusive authority of the government of Lebanon throughout Lebanon; called upon all remaining foreign forces to withdraw from Lebanon, and for the disbanding and disarmament of all Lebanese and non-Lebanese militias; and expressed its support for the control of the government of Lebanon over all Lebanese territory.

On 26 April 2005, Terje Roed-Larsen, the Secretary-General's Special Envoy for the implementation of resolution 1559 (2004), reported to the Security Council that although Syria had claimed that it no longer had a military presence in Lebanon, the Lebanese government did not have full control over all its territory.[11] In particular, Hezbollah had neither disbanded nor disarmed, and the government of Lebanon itself objected to the characterization of Hezbollah as a Lebanese militia in terms of resolution 1159, claiming that it was a 'national resistance group' that had as its goal the defence of Lebanon from Israel and the removal of Israeli forces from Lebanese soil.[12]

On 18 January 2006, a report of the Secretary-General catalogued 'a few serious clashes across the Blue Line' noting that there had been exchanges of fire between Hezbollah and the IDF during November 2005, and that unidentified armed elements had fired rockets towards Israel. Repeated Israeli violations of Lebanese airspace provided 'a continuous source of tension', and there were frequent

---

[10] Adopted 9–0 with 6 abstentions.

[11] See 'First semi-annual report of the Secretary-General to the Security Council on the implementation of resolution 1559 (2004)' S/2005/272 (26 April 2005) and also Report of the Commission of Inquiry, 19, para 36.

[12] See 'Report of the Secretary-General pursuant to Security Council resolution 1559 (2004)' S/2004/777 (1 October 2004) 5, para 19; Report of the Commission of Inquiry, 19, para 35, 20, para 39, and 22–3, para 57; 'Implementation of General Assembly resolution 60/251 of 15 March 2006 entitled "Human Rights Council": Report of the Special Rapporteur on extrajudicial, summary or arbitrary executions, Philip Alston; the Special Rapporteur on the right of everyone to the enjoyment of the highest attainable standard of physical and mental health, Paul Hunt; the Representative of the Secretary-General on human rights of internally displaced persons, Walter Kalin; and the Special Rapporteur on adequate housing as a component of the right to an adequate standard of living, Miloon Kothari' A/HRC/2/7 (2 October 2006) 5, para 6 (Report of the Mission). This mission was undertaken on the initiative of its members in response to a suggestion made by the President of the Human Rights Council, and visited Lebanon and Israel in September 2006 at the invitation of the two governments, where it met with ministers and officials in each. It was independent of the Commission of Inquiry established on the basis of Human Rights Council resolution S-2/1. The main objectives of the mission were (i) to assess, from the perspective of international human rights and humanitarian law, the impact on the civilian populations of the armed conflict that affected Lebanon and Israel in July and August 2006; (ii) to advise the authorities on fulfilling their responsibility to protect and assist affected civilians in accordance with their human rights obligations; and (iii) to make recommendations to United Nations agencies and others on how best to address the protection needs of the people concerned (see 4, paras 1–4). See also, Hirst, *Small States,* 302–3 and 313–15.

incidents of stone throwing from the Lebanese side.[13] The Secretary-General noted that '[m]y senior representatives in the region and I, in addition to a number of concerned Member States, called on numerous occasions on the Government of Lebanon to extend control over all its territory',[14] and, in particular, he observed that the authority and control of the government was limited in the south:[15]

> Control of the Blue Line and its vicinity seems to remain for the most part with Hizbollah. Under such circumstances, Hizbollah has maintained and reinforced a visible presence in the area, with permanent observation posts, temporary checkpoints and patrols. It carried out construction work to fortify and expand some of its fixed positions, demined the adjacent areas, built new access roads and established new positions close to the Blue Line.[16]

This situation had not changed when Hezbollah mounted Operation True Promise on 12 July 2006, so named after a 'promise' by its Secretary General, Hasan Nasrallah, to capture Israeli soldiers in order to exchange them for Lebanese prisoners in Israeli jails,[17] and Israel responded with Operation Change Direction.

1.2. The initiation and conduct of the hostilities

Hezbollah claimed that Israel started the conflict in July 2006 by sending IDF forces into Ayta al-Sha'b, a Lebanese village 60 kilometres north of the Israel/Lebanese border.[18] This claim has few adherents. The general consensus favours the Israeli explanation that the conflict began as the result of a Hezbollah cross-border incursion on 12 July 2006 which attacked an IDF border patrol. This resulted in the death of eight Israeli soldiers and the capture of another two who were carried into Lebanon. Hezbollah also fired rockets at IDF military positions and villages in the north of Israel which caused the death of two civilians.[19]

---

[13] 'Report of the Secretary-General on the United Nations Interim Force in Lebanon (For the period from 22 July 2005 to 20 January 2006)' S/2006/26 (18 January 2006) 1, para 2.

[14] Ibid, 3, para 12.

[15] Ibid, 4, para 18 and 7, para 35.

[16] Ibid, 4, para 21.

[17] See Amnesty International, 'Under fire: Hizbullah's attacks on northern Israel' (September 2006) 1 (AI, *Under Fire*); Bloom, *The classification of Hezbollah*, 62; Hirst, *Small States,* 328–30; and also R. Cohen-Almagor and S. Haleva-Amir, 'The Israel-Hezbollah war and the Winograd Committee' (2008) 2 *Journal of Parliamentary and Political Law* 27 (Cohen-Almagor and Haleva-Amir, *The Winograd Committee*). For discussion of both Hezbollah and Israeli practice on capture and detention see section 5 below.

[18] S. Mahmoudi, 'The second Lebanese war: reflections on the 2006 Israeli military operations against Hezbollah' in O. Engdahl and P. Wrange (eds), *Law at war: the law as it is and the law as it should be. Liber amicorum Ove Bring* (2008) 176 (Mahmoudi, *The second Lebanese war*).

[19] See Israel Ministry of Foreign Affairs, 'Israel's war with Hizbullah: preserving humanitarian principles while combating terrorism' (April 2007) 4 (MFA, *Israel's war with Hizbullah*); UK Foreign Affairs Committee, 'Global Security: the Middle East (Eighth report of session 2006–2007)' (25 July 2007) 44, para 95 (Foreign Affairs Committee, *Global Security*); S/PV.5489, UN Security Council meeting (14 July 2009) (SC 5489th meeting) 2–3, statement of Jean-Marie Guehenno, Under-Secretary for Peacekeeping Operations; US Senate Committee on Foreign Relations hearing, 'Lebanon: securing a permanent cease-fire' (13 September 2006), testimony of C. David Welch, Assistant Secretary of State for Near Eastern Affairs (presenting the views of the US administration) (Welch

Israel initially gave Syria and Hezbollah a 72-hour ultimatum to stop Hezbollah's hostile activity along the border and to release the captured soldiers, but this went unanswered.[20] Hostilities escalated, and military operations lasted for thirty-three days. These were brought to an end following the adoption, under Chapter VII of the UN Charter, of Security Council resolution 1701 (2006).[21] Operative paragraphs 1 to 3 called for a full cessation of hostilities by Hezbollah and Israel, following which the government of Lebanon and UNIFIL should deploy their forces together throughout southern Lebanon, and Israel withdraw all its forces. The Council also emphasized that it was important that the government of Lebanon exercised control over all Lebanese territory in accordance with Security Council resolutions 1559 (2004) and 1680 (2006), and the relevant provisions of the Taif Agreement, so it could ensure that it was the sole authority in the area and that no weapons were held there without its consent. Resolution 1701 was accepted by the Lebanese government and Hezbollah on 12 August 2006, and by the Israeli government on 13 August 2006. The ceasefire took effect at 8:00 a.m., local time, on 14 August 2006.

Although in late July Israel moved land forces into southern Lebanon and on 9 August 2006 launched ground operations which extended far beyond the border, the conflict was primarily conducted through the use of aerial strikes, artillery and rockets.[22] Israel also imposed a maritime and aerial blockade of Lebanon (on 13 and 14 July 2006, respectively).[23] The blockade was lifted on 6–7 September 2006,[24] and on 1 October Israel reported that it had completed its withdrawal from southern Lebanon. This was confirmed by UNIFIL.[25]

testimony of 13 September 2006); Report of the Commission of Inquiry, 20, para 40; Report of the Mission, 5, para 7; Mahmoudi, *The second Lebanese war*,176–7; and M.N. Schmitt, '"Change Direction" 2006: Israeli operations in Lebanon and the international law of self-defense' in M.D. Carsten (ed.), *International law and military operations* (2008) 265, 269–70 (Schmitt, *Change Direction*). The bodies of the two captured Israeli soldiers were returned to Israel on 16 July 2008, see Israel Ministry of Foreign Affairs, 'Behind the headlines: the second Lebanon war—three years later' (12 July 2009) (MFA, *The Second Lebanon War*).

[20] MFA, *Israel's war with Hizbullah*, 7–8.

[21] Adopted unanimously on 11 August 2006. The final preambular paragraph of the resolution determines that the situation in Lebanon constitutes a threat to international peace and security, although it makes no express reference to art. 39 of the Charter. On the classification of resolutions which make an implicit reference to art. 39 as Chapter VII resolutions, see P. Johansson, 'The humdrum use of ultimate authority: defining and analysing Chapter VII resolutions' (2009) 78 *Nordic Journal of International Law* 312–15.

[22] See e.g. M. Norell, 'A victory for Islamism? The second Lebanon war and its repercussions' Washington Institute for Near East Policy, Policy Focus 98 (November 2009) 25–8; and U. Rubin, 'The rocket campaign against Israel during the 2006 Lebanon War' (2007) 71 *Mideast Security and Policy Studies* (Rubin, *Rocket Campaign*).

[23] See Report of the Commission of Inquiry, 20, para 43, 21, para 47, 23, para 58, and 62–4, paras 268–75; Schmitt, *Change Direction,* 270; M.L. Tucker, 'Mitigating collateral damage to the natural environment in naval warfare: an examination of the Israeli naval blockade of 2006' (2009) 57 *Naval Law Review* 161 (Tucker, *Mitigating Collateral Damage*).

[24] See Report of the Commission of Inquiry, 62, para 270; and Israel Ministry of Foreign Affairs, 'Lifting of the Air and Sea Blockade of Lebanon' Press Release (6 September 2006).

[25] Report of the Commission of Inquiry, 21, para 48 and 23, para 58.

2. The views of the relevant States and others on the classification of the conflict

This section sets out the views expressed by States, intergovernmental organizations and UN missions on the nature or classification of the Lebanon 2006 conflict.

2.1. Israel

Identical letters dated 12 July 2006 from Israel's Permanent Representative to the UN (Gillerman) to the President of the Security Council and the Secretary-General invoked Israel's right of self-defence under article 51 of the UN Charter following Hezbollah's barrage of heavy artillery and rockets into Israel; its incursion into Israel; and its kidnapping of two Israeli soldiers. These letters stated:

> Responsibility for this belligerent act of war lies with the Government of Lebanon, from whose territory these acts have been launched into Israel. Responsibility also lies with the Government of the Islamic Republic of Iran and the Syrian Arab Republic, which support and embrace those who carried out this attack.
>
> ...
>
> Today's act is a clear declaration of war, and is in blatant violation of the Blue Line, Security Council resolutions 425 (1978), 1559 (2004) and 1680 (2006) and all other relevant resolutions of the United Nations since Israel withdrew from southern Lebanon in May 2000.[26]

At a press conference on 12 July, Israel's Prime Minister Olmert was reported as saying that this incident represented an 'act of war' by Lebanon, and that 'Lebanon is responsible and Lebanon will bear the consequences of its actions'. He justified his remarks on the basis that Hezbollah had two members in the Lebanese Cabinet.[27]

Similarly, during the 14 July 2006 meeting of the Security Council, Gillerman, Israel's Permanent Representative, stated:

> Let me emphasize this indisputable fact: Israel's actions were in direct response to an act of war from Lebanon. Although Israel holds the Government of Lebanon responsible, it is concentrating its response carefully, mainly on Hizbollah strongholds, positions and infrastructure.
>
> ... It is very important for the international community to understand that while Hizbollah executes this vicious terrorism, it is merely the finger on the blood-stained, long-reaching arms of Syria and Iran ... [28]

Gillerman's 12 July letter and 14 July statement, as well as Prime Minister Olmert's press conference statement, clearly held Lebanon internationally responsible for the

---

[26] Identical letters dated 12 July 2006 from the Permanent Representative of Israel to the United Nations addressed to the Secretary-General and the President of the Security Council, A/60/937-S/2006/515 (12 July 2006).

[27] Reported Foreign Affairs Committee, *Global Security*, 44, para 95.

[28] SC 5489th meeting, 6.

attack(s) on Israel, while Gillerman also implicated Iran and Syria as somehow complicit in Hezbollah's actions. The conclusion must be that Israel, at least initially, considered the situation to be an international armed conflict.

Subsequently, Israel appeared to back-pedal on the question of Lebanese responsibility. Israel claimed that its actions were taken against Hezbollah in order to counter a regional threat, rather than against Lebanon and its population per se. This was first asserted during remarks made during a press conference on 19 July 2006 by Tzipi Livni, then Israel's Foreign Minister. Livni stated:

> Israel is fighting to protect its citizens; Israel is fighting to eliminate the threat posed by the [axis] of terror and hate of the Hizbullah and Hamas, Syria and Iran. Specifically Israel is fighting to end the control of Hizbullah, over the life of both Lebanese and Israelis and to bring an end to its attempt to destabilize the region . . .
>
> . . . Hizbullah and Hasan Nasrallah are threats to the region, not only to Israel. Israel has no conflict with Lebanon. Hizbullah opens a front with Israel to the Iranians, not to Lebanon . . . what we are doing now is an answer to the threat, and not an answer to an incident . . .

She recalled that under Security Council resolution 1559, Hezbollah was to be disarmed, its re-armament prevented, and that the Lebanese army was to operate in southern Lebanon. This, she concluded, meant that there was an understanding between the international community and the Lebanese and Israeli governments that 'Hizbullah is a threat to the region and not only a part of the relationship between Israel and Lebanon'.[29]

Similar remarks were made by Gillerman at the Security Council meetings of 8 and 11 August 2006. During the latter, the ceasefire resolution (resolution 1701) was adopted. Gillerman indicated that Israel's operations had been directed against Hezbollah rather than Lebanon per se:

> . . . The way to avoid the crisis between Israel and Lebanon has been clear: implementation of the unconditional obligations set out in resolutions 1559 (2004) and 1680 (2006), which set out issues for resolution between Lebanon and Syria. The clear path forward required the disarming and disbanding of Hizbollah and other militias, and the exercise by Lebanon, like any sovereign State, of control and authority over all its territory. But the will to implement this way has been lacking, and over the past month the peoples of Israel and Lebanon have paid a heavy price for that inaction.
>
> In the face of the failure to ensure that the obligations set out in those resolutions were implemented, Israel has had no choice but to do what Lebanon has failed to do. As a result, Hizbollah's lethal capabilities have been dealt a major blow . . . [30]

This is a clear break from Gillerman's earlier statements to the Security Council, and from Prime Minister Olmert's remarks of 12 July 2006, which attributed the

---

[29] Remarks to journalists by Javier Solana, EU High Representative for CFSP, and Tzipi Livni, Israeli Foreign Minister, Jerusalem, S214/06 (19 July 2006), available at: <www.consilium.europa.eu/ueDocs/cms_Data/docs/pressdata/en/discours/90615.pdf>.

[30] S/PV.5511, Security Council meeting (11 August 2006) 20–1 (SC 5511th meeting); see also, S/PV.5508, Security Council meeting (8 August 2006) (SC 5508th meeting) 6.

initial incident to Lebanon on the basis that the Cabinet contained two Hezbollah members.

The IDF told the Mission set up under the auspices of the Human Rights Council that its operations were based on the law of international armed conflict, in particular the Fourth Geneva Convention and the provisions of Additional Protocol I that were declaratory of custom.[31] The Ministry of Foreign Affairs' report, *Israel's war with Hizbullah*, cites principally article 52(2) of Additional Protocol I as providing the 'generally accepted definition' of a military objective as well as article 28 of the Fourth Geneva Convention.[32]

Israel's reliance on instruments applicable in an international armed conflict might not be conclusive for purposes of classification. These might have been employed not because the conflict was thought to be an international armed conflict, but simply because, in the absence of conventional rules regarding targeting in a non-international armed conflict, the IDF turned to provisions of the Fourth Geneva Convention and Additional Protocol I as analogies to guide its targeting decisions. Also, according to the 2005 ICRC customary international humanitarian law study, targeting rules in international and non-international armed conflicts are assimilated: in particular, rule 8 repeats the definition of military objective contained in article 52(2) of Additional Protocol I.[33]

2.2. Lebanon

Lebanon denied responsibility for the actions of Hezbollah, but clearly classified the conflict as international. On 13 July 2006, it requested that the Security Council be urgently convened 'to consider the grave situation resulting from the latest Israeli acts of aggression in Lebanon',[34] and during the resulting meeting argued that it was faced with a case of 'widespread and barbaric aggression being waged by Israel . . . against my country, Lebanon [which was] destroying Lebanon's infrastructure and causing the deaths of innocent civilians'. Mahmoud, Lebanon's representative in the Security Council, firmly rejected any imposition of responsibility on Lebanon.[35]

The hostilities effectively only took place between the IDF and Hezbollah, without the participation of the Lebanese armed forces. During Security Council debates, Lebanon consistently maintained that it was the subject of an act of

---

[31] Report of the Mission, 7–8, para 23.

[32] Article 28 of the Fourth Geneva Convention provides: 'The presence of a protected person may not be used to render points or areas immune from military operations.'

[33] See J.M. Henckaerts and L. Doswald-Beck, *Customary international humanitarian law* (2005) (ICRC Customary Law Study) Vol. I, chs 1–6 generally; for rule 8, see 29–32; and for commentary on the formulation of the customary targeting rules, see M.N. Schmitt, 'The law of targeting' in E. Wilmshurst and S. Breau (eds), *Perspectives on the ICRC study on customary international humanitarian law* (2007) 131.

[34] See Letter dated 13 July 2006 from the Chargé d'affaires a.i. of the Permanent Mission of Lebanon to the United Nations addressed to the President of the Security Council, S/2006/517 (13 July 2006).

[35] SC 5489th meeting, 4–5.

aggression by Israel.[36] Thus, on 30 July 2006, it stated, 'It has been clear from the very beginning that it was not Hizbollah that was the target. It was Lebanon that was the target'.[37] On 8 August 2006, it claimed, 'In Israel's wanting to destroy the infrastructure of terrorism . . . it is the infrastructure of Lebanon that is destroyed'.[38] These claims might, in themselves, indicate that Lebanon thought the conflict was international, but it also expressly invoked instruments regulating international armed conflicts. For example, Lebanon specifically invoked article 50 of Additional Protocol I (in relation to Israeli claims that Hezbollah was using civilians as human shields)[39] as well as making the general reference that Israel had 'repeated and wilfully violated' international humanitarian law 'including the Geneva Conventions and its Protocols'.[40] It also made less specific statements, such as 'in international law, there are two principles regarding civilians: the principle of distinction and the principle of proportionality. I am afraid that those two principles have been systematically violated since 12 July'.[41]

2.3. Views expressed by other States in the Security Council and other fora

The views expressed by participants, other than Israel and Lebanon, in Security Council meetings which dwelt on the 2006 conflict in Lebanon were diverse, but principally divided on whether Israel was engaged in action taken in self-defence or in an act of aggression. Thus, for instance, Peru expressly recognized Israel's right to defend itself, as did Argentina, Australia, Denmark, France, Greece, Norway, Turkey and the United Kingdom.[42] This was also the collective position adopted by the European Union, to which other States aligned themselves.[43]

On the other hand, some States took a more critical view of Israel's use of force. Thus the Russian Federation, while condemning Hezbollah's attack, viewed 'Israel's military action as a disproportionate and inappropriate use of force that threatens the sovereignty and territorial integrity of Lebanon and peace and security throughout the region'.[44] While it subsequently recognized that 'Israel has a legitimate right to ensure its security', it expressed disquiet at the extent of force

---

[36] See e.g. ibid, 4.
[37] S/PV.5498, Security Council meeting (30 July 2006) (SC 5498th meeting) 6.
[38] S/PV.5508, Security Council meeting (8 August 2006) (SC 5508th meeting) 7.
[39] S/PV.5503, Security Council meeting (31 July 2006) (SC 5503rd meeting) 3.
[40] SC 5511th meeting, 19.
[41] SC 5508th meeting, 7.
[42] See S/PV.5488, Security Council meeting (13 July 2006) (SC 5488th meeting), remarks by Peru (4); SC 5489th meeting, remarks by Peru (14), Argentina (9), United Kingdom (12), Denmark (15), Greece (17), France (17), Norway (23); S/PV.5493, Security Council meeting (Resumption 1) (21 July 2006) (SC 5493rd meeting (Res. 1), remarks by Greece (3), Peru (4), Argentina (9), Denmark (7), Australia (27), Turkey (28).
[43] SC 5493rd meeting (Res. 1), Finland speaking on behalf of the EU (to which Bulgaria, Romania, Turkey, Croatia, the former Yugoslav Republic of Macedonia, Albania, Bosnia and Herzegovina, Serbia, Iceland, Ukraine, and the Republic of Moldova aligned themselves) 16.
[44] SC 5489th meeting, Russian Federation, 7.

it employed which 'go far beyond a counterterrorist operation'.[45] Concerns that the force employed by Israel might be disproportionate were also expressed by States which endorsed Israel's right to self-defence,[46] with the representative of New Zealand stating 'we cannot accept that Israel has reacted with due proportionality or caution'.[47] Other States, however, were of the opinion that Israel's actions were not taken in self-defence but amounted to acts of aggression.[48] A few took a position which was perhaps intermediate, arguing that the legitimacy of Israel's plea of self-defence was vitiated by the extent of the force it employed.[49]

In short, unless one interprets the statements which described the situation as one of aggression or self-defence as evidence of an armed conflict between Israel and Lebanon as such, which would thus fall to be classified as an international armed conflict, the views expressed by third States during the Security Council debates were not merely inconclusive but completely ignored the issue of how the conflict should be classified.

Statements made in other fora similarly ignored the question of how the conflict should be classified. Concern focused on the resort to force by Israel and the proportionality of its response. Thus, for example, on 13 July 2006, Margaret Beckett, then UK Foreign Secretary, classified the situation as a 'crisis', and expressed disquiet regarding the extent of the Israeli response, 'while Israel is entitled to do what is required to protect its security, it should do so in a way which does not escalate the situation and which is proportionate and measured, conforms to international law, and avoids civilian deaths and suffering'.[50] The House of Commons Foreign Affairs Committee's report, *Global security: the Middle East (Eighth report of session 2006–2007)*, which considered the 2006 Lebanon conflict, affirmed that Israel had an unquestionable right to defend itself against Hezbollah's attacks but that questions had arisen regarding the proportionality of its response, although the UK government had refused to label Israel's actions as disproportionate.[51]

On 16 July 2006, Javier Solana, the EU High Representative for the Common Foreign and Security Policy, stressed that Israel's response should be both lawful and proportionate, and thought it unfair to blame the Lebanese government for the situation.[52] Also on 16 July, the G8 meeting in St Petersburg issued a statement on

[45] SC 5493rd meeting (Res. 1), Russian Federation, 2.
[46] See the statements made by Argentina, Denmark, France, Greece and Peru at the SC 5489th meeting; and by Denmark, Finland (on behalf of the EU and aligned States), Greece, Norway, Peru, and Turkey at its 5493rd meeting (Res. 1).
[47] SC 5493rd meeting (Res. 1), New Zealand, 33.
[48] Ibid, Syrian Arab Republic, 13; Saudi Arabia, 20; Algeria, 21; Jordan, 24; Morocco, 29; Islamic Republic of Iran, 30; Cuba, 37–38; Pakistan, 44; and League of Arab States, 26.
[49] See e.g. S/PV.5493, Security Council meeting (21 July 2006) (SC 5493rd meeting), Qatar, 14; SC 5493rd meeting (Res. 1), Djibouti, 32.
[50] Press statement by Margaret Beckett, UK Foreign Secretary, and Javier Solana, EU High Representative for CFSP, on the Middle East, London, S198/06 (13 July 2006), available at: <www.consilium.europa.eu/ueDocs/cms_Data/docs/pressdata/EN/declarations/90502.pdf>.
[51] Foreign Affairs Committee, *Global security*, 47, para 10.
[52] Press statement of Javier Solana, EU High Representative for the Common Foreign and Security Policy, Beirut, S203/06 (16 July 2006), available at: <www.consilium.europa.eu/ueDocs/cms_Data/

the Middle East which, while endorsing Israel's right to act in self-defence, cautioned it to 'be mindful of the strategic and humanitarian consequences of its actions. We call upon Israel to exercise utmost restraint, seeking to avoid casualties among innocent civilians and damage to civilian infrastructure and to refrain from acts that would destabilize the Lebanese government'.[53]

On the whole, the views expressed on the applicable law by States, other than Israel and Lebanon, which participated in Security Council meetings give little guidance regarding their thoughts on the nature of the Lebanon 2006 conflict. States generally confined themselves to vague references that international human-itarian law[54] or that the principles of distinction and proportionality[55] should be observed. The ICRC customary international humanitarian law study argues that the principles of distinction and proportionality in attack form part of customary international law and are equally applicable in international and non-international armed conflicts.[56] Only a few States expressly referred to specific legal instruments, generally calling upon Israel to abide by the Fourth Geneva Convention,[57] thus indicating a putative view that the conflict should be classified as international.

As in statements made to the Security Council, in other fora States rested content with anodyne affirmations that the parties to the conflict should abide by inter-national humanitarian law[58] or observe the principles of distinction and propor-tionality,[59] without indicating whether they viewed the conflict as international or non-international.

---

docs/pressdata/en/discours/90560.pdf> (Beirut Press Statement of 16 July 2006). On Solana and proportionality, see also, Remarks to journalists by Javier Solana, EU High Representative for CFSP, and Tzipi Livni, Israeli Foreign Minister, Jerusalem, S/214/06 (19 July 2006).

[53] G8 St Petersburg Declaration on the Middle East (16 July 2006).

[54] For statements which refer expressly to international humanitarian law see e.g. SC 5489th meeting, 9, Peru 14, and Greece 17; SC 5493rd meeting (Res.1), Russian Federation 2, Greece 3, Peru 4, Argentina 9, and League of Arab States 27; SC 5511th meeting, Greece 9, and Argentina 15.

[55] For statements which refer, expressly or implicitly, to the principles of distinction and/or proportionality see e.g. SC 5489th meeting, Argentina 9, United Kingdom 12, Denmark 15, Greece 17, and France 17; SC 5493rd meeting (Res. 1), Peru 4, Denmark 7, Norway 23, Jordan 24, Australia 27, and New Zealand 33; SC 5511th meeting, Argentina, 15.

[56] On the principle of distinction, see ICRC Customary Law Study, rules 1, 5 and 6, Vol. I, 3–8 and 17–24; and on the principle of proportionality, rule 14, ibid, 46–50. In contrast, Kretzmer observes that while Additional Protocol II enshrines the principle of distinction in art. 13, it contains no reference to proportionality, see D. Kretzmer, 'Rethinking application of IHL in non-international armed conflict' (2009) 42 *Israel Law Review* 21–2.

[57] See SC 5493rd meeting (Res. 1), Indonesia, 25, and League of Arab States, 26.

[58] See e.g. 'EU action in response to the crisis in Lebanon' EU Joint Press Release (25 July 2006); Letter to the Chairman of the Select Committee on Foreign Affairs from Margaret Beckett the Secretary of State for Foreign and Commonwealth Affairs (7 September 2006), available at: <www.publications.parliament. uk/pa/cm200506/cmselect/cmfaff/1583/6091303.htm> (Beckett Letter of 7 September 2006); EU Council, Press Release after extraordinary meeting (General Affairs and External Relations), 12023/06 (1 August 2006), available at: <www.consilium.europa.eu/ueDocs/cms_Data/docs/pressData/en/gena/ 90739.pdf>.

[59] For statements which refer, expressly or implicitly, to the principles of distinction and/or proportionality see e.g. the views expressed by Beckett (UK Foreign Secretary) and Solana (EU High Representative for CFSP) in their 13 July 2006 Press Statement; Solana's Beirut Press Statement of 16 July 2006; G8 St Petersburg Declaration on the Middle East; The EU Council Conclusions on the Middle East, CL06-138EN (17 July 2006), available at: <www.europa-eu-un.org/articles/en/

2.4. Official UN statements

The two Security Council resolutions adopted in relation to the Lebanon 2006 conflict, resolution 1697 (2006) and resolution 1701 (2006), made no reference to the nature of the conflict or to the law which should regulate it. Resolution 1697 deplored attacks on UNIFIL, called on the parties to the conflict to observe their obligations to respect UNIFIL and other UN personnel, and extended UNIFIL's mandate, while resolution 1701 called for a ceasefire and determined its structure.

During the Security Council meeting on 20 July 2006, the then UN Secretary-General, Kofi Annan, noted that the Lebanese government had no advance knowledge of Hezbollah's attack and acknowledged Israel's right to defend itself under article 51 of the United Nations Charter while condemning its excessive use of force.[60] He made no comment on how the conflict should be classified. On the other hand, subsequent to the conflict and more pertinent for the purposes in hand, the *Report of the Commission of Inquiry* clearly classified the conflict as international, although the *Report of the Mission* took no definitive view on the matter.

Of the two, the *Report of the Commission of Inquiry* contains the more elaborate account of the classification of the conflict. Employing a dual test, namely that the decisive element in determining whether a conflict exists is the factual existence of the use of armed force, while also referring to the *Tadić* test,[61] the Commission of Inquiry found that an armed conflict existed in the territories of Lebanon and Israel between 12 July and 14 August 2006.[62] It noted that Security Council resolution 1701 contained no reference to the classification of the conflict, but also that active hostilities only took place between Israel and Hezbollah fighters. While acknowledging that the Lebanese armed forces did not actively participate in the hostilities, the Commission found that the IDF had attacked Lebanese armed forces and their assets.[63] It further noted that the Lebanese government had denied that it was responsible for, and had no prior knowledge of Hezbollah's 12 July 2006 attack which, moreover, it had expressly disavowed and did not endorse. Also, Lebanese government officials had informed the Commission that they considered that, as Lebanon had been subject to the destructive effect of IDF hostilities, it was a party to the conflict. On the other hand, Israel had stated that responsibility lay with Lebanon, and that the belligerent act was an act attributable to Lebanon. The Commission concluded:

article_6125_en.htm>; Solana's views expressed during his press conference with Livni in Jerusalem on 19 July 2006; and Beckett Letter of 7 September 2006.

[60] S/PV.5492, Security Council meeting (20 July 2006) (SC 5492nd meeting), 3.

[61] *Prosecutor v Tadić*, IT-94-1-AR72, Decision on the defence motion for interlocutory appeal on jurisdiction (Appeals Chamber), 2 October 1995, para 70: 'an armed conflict exists whenever there is a resort to armed force between States or protracted armed violence between governmental authorities and organised armed groups or between such groups within a State'. (*Tadić* Jurisdiction).

[62] Report of the Commission of Inquiry, 21–2, para 51.

[63] Ibid, 22, paras 52 and 53. It is worth noting that a similar conclusion was reached by the House of Commons Foreign Affairs Committee in *Global Security* report where it found that: 'The principal parties to the 2006 conflict in Lebanon were the Israeli military and the Hezbollah militia.' (44, para 95).

It is the view of the Commission that hostilities were in actual fact and in the main only between the IDF and Hezbollah. The fact that the Lebanese Armed Forces did not take an active part in them neither denies the character of the conflict as a legally cognisable international armed conflict, nor does it negate that Israel, Lebanon and Hezbollah were parties to it.[64]

The Commission continued that, under Common Article 2(2) of the Geneva Conventions, the law of armed conflict applied when the armed forces of a High Contracting Party occupied the territory of another, even if this occupation met with no resistance from the latter. Accordingly, the Commission concluded that 'both Lebanon and Israel were parties to the conflict. They remain bound by the Geneva Conventions of 1949, and customary international law existing at the time of the conflict. Hezbollah is equally bound by the same laws'.[65]

In reaching its conclusions, the Commission stressed three factors:

- Hezbollah was a recognized political party in Lebanon, with representatives in Parliament and is part of the government. It thus participated in the constitutional organs of the State;

- essentially relying on the Lebanese government's categorization of Hezbollah as a national resistance group,[66] the behaviour of Hezbollah in south Lebanon suggested an inferred link between the Lebanese government and Hezbollah. Further, Hezbollah was an armed group whose conduct and operations entered into the field of application of article 4(A)(2) of the Third Geneva Convention:[67] 'Seen from inside Lebanon and in the absence of the regular Lebanese Armed Forces in South Lebanon, Hezbollah constituted and is an expression of the resistance ("*mukawamah*") for the defence of the territory partly occupied.' It had assumed de facto State authority and control in south Lebanon despite Security Council resolutions 1559 (2004) and 1680 (2006) which had called for the disarmament of all armed groups in Lebanon,[68] the implication being that Hezbollah was acting as an agent, or organ, of Lebanon; and

- the State of Lebanon was the subject of direct hostilities conducted by Israel, including the temporary occupation of Lebanese territory by the IDF.[69]

The fact that Israel considered Hezbollah to be a terrorist organization did not influence the Commission's classification of the conflict. 'Several official declarations of the Government of Israel addressed Lebanon as assuming responsibility.

---

[64] Report of the Commission of Inquiry, 22, paras 54 and 55: quotation at para 55.

[65] Ibid, 23, paras 59 and 60: quotation at 60.

[66] See above, text to n 12.

[67] For discussion of the argument that Hezbollah fighters fall within the terms of art. 4(A)(1) of Geneva Convention III as members of a militia corps forming part of the armed forces of a party to a conflict, see section 5 below.

[68] See also, Bloom, *The classification of Hezbollah*, 75–85, who concludes that 'Hezbollah is a State actor by implication.'

[69] Report of the Commission of Inquiry, 22–3, paras 56–8.

IDF views its operations in Lebanon as an international armed conflict.'[70] The Commission then proceeded to enumerate the key international instruments it thought potentially applicable to the conflict, noting whether Israel and Lebanon had ratified these instruments or not.[71] While mentioning Additional Protocol II, the instruments listed predominantly regulate international armed conflict.

In contrast, the *Report of the Mission* was less elaborate in its analysis of the classification of the conflict, and essentially took the position that 'the qualification of the conflict as international or non-international is complex' and that the report was 'mainly based on international customary law applicable in both forms of conflict'. Nevertheless, it laid weight on the views expressed by the IDF. 'The mission was informed by representatives of [the] IDF that decisions were taken on the basis of the law on international armed conflicts' in particular the Fourth Geneva Convention and the provisions of Additional Protocol I that are declaratory of custom.[72] The Mission expressly invoked article 52(2) of Additional Protocol I as embodying the current legal rule on the definition of legitimate military objectives, stating that it is accepted as customary.[73] Rule 8 of the ICRC customary international law study repeats the definition contained in article 52(2) and states that it is applicable to both international and non-international armed conflicts.[74] Consequently, the *Report of the Mission* is perhaps best seen as being non-committal in its classification of the Lebanon 2006 conflict.

3. Author's analysis of the classification of the conflict

States do not make claims in a normative vacuum: the reaction of other States can indicate how a particular claim or classification should be gauged, and whether it should be accepted or rejected. Lebanon 2006 illustrates that third States might be unwilling to make this evaluation, or perhaps be unable to do so because they are not clear how the conflict should be classified. While statements made by both Israel and Lebanon could be interpreted to hold that they classified the conflict as international, should this be accepted at face value, bearing in mind that other States were reluctant to classify the conflict clearly?

There are good reasons to argue that the classification placed on a conflict by the opposing parties should not be accepted uncritically. For example, a State cannot circumvent its obligations under the Geneva Conventions by unilaterally claiming that an armed dispute with another does not amount to an armed conflict for the

---

[70] Report of the Commission of Inquiry, 24, para 62.
[71] Ibid, 24–5, paras 65–8. The enumerated instruments were the 1949 Geneva Conventions, to which both Israel and Lebanon are party; Additional Protocols I and II, to which Lebanon is party but not Israel; the Hague Convention on Cultural Property and its First Protocol, to which both are parties; the Conventional Weapons Convention and Protocols I (non-detectable fragments), II (mines and booby-traps) and IV (blinding laser weapons), to which Israel is party, but not Lebanon; and the Biological Weapons Convention, to which Lebanon is party, but not Israel.
[72] Report of the Mission, 7–8, para 23.
[73] Ibid, 12, para 50.
[74] See ICRC Customary Law Study, Vol. I, 29–32.

purposes of their application,[75] although there are examples where some have precisely tried to do this. Thus, in 1989 the United States claimed that its intervention in Panama was not an international armed conflict because General Noriega was not the legitimate leader of Panama, and accordingly its dispute with him was not a dispute with Panama.[76] Although the existence of an international armed conflict is generally self-evident, because it is between States, determining the existence and classification of a conflict where a principal party is a non-state actor can be difficult.[77]

Given the nature of the conflict in Lebanon in 2006, where the main participants were Israel and Hezbollah, although the Lebanese armed forces and infrastructure were also targeted, did different types of conflict occur simultaneously? If so, who were the parties to the(se) conflict(s), and what international status did they possess? Further, is Corn's doctrine of transnational warfare, which he developed using Lebanon 2006 as the paradigm,[78] valid or useful?

The principal issues which appear to be pertinent to the classification of the Lebanon 2006 conflict are: that the principal fighting parties were Hezbollah and the IDF; the Lebanese armed forces took no active part in the conflict, but were the object of attack by the IDF; that Hezbollah was participating in the government of Lebanon, having two Cabinet members and fourteen members of Parliament; that Lebanon saw Hezbollah as a 'national resistance group' that had as its goal the defence of Lebanon from Israel and the removal of Israeli forces from Lebanese soil;[79] that, at the time, Hezbollah was in effective control of southern Lebanon to the exclusion of the Lebanese government and its armed forces, to the extent that the Bush Administration was of the view that 'Hizballah has operated as a "State-within-a-State" in the Lebanese body politic, outside of the control of the central government';[80] and that Israel imposed a maritime and an aerial blockade on Lebanon.

---

[75] See J. Pictet (ed.), *Geneva Convention I for the amelioration of the condition of the wounded and sick in armed forces in the field: commentary* (1952), commentary to Common Article 2, 27–33: Pictet argues that the terms of Common Article 2(1) of the Geneva Conventions, which sets out the conditions for their application, 'deprives the belligerents of the pretexts they might in theory invoke for evasion of their obligations'. (at 32) (Pictet, *Commentary to the First Geneva Convention*).

[76] See G.S. Corn, 'Hamdan, Lebanon, and the regulation of hostilities: the need to recognize a hybrid category of armed conflict' (2007) 40 *Vanderbilt Journal of Transnational Law* 305 (Corn, *Hybrid category*); see also, J. Pejic, 'Status of armed conflicts' in E. Wilmshurst and S. Breau, *Perspectives on the ICRC Study on customary international humanitarian law* (2007) 82–3 regarding claims that the Geneva Conventions were not applicable to the conflict in Afghanistan (Pejic, *Status of armed conflicts*).

[77] See Pejic, *Status of armed conflicts*, 79–80.

[78] See Corn, *Hybrid category*; and also his 'Making the case for conflict bifurcation in Afghanistan: transnational armed conflict, al Qaida and the limits of the associated militia concept' in M.N. Schmitt (ed.), *The war in Afghanistan: a legal analysis* (2009) 181, G.S. Corn and E.T. Jensen, 'Untying the Gordian knot: a proposal for determining applicability of the laws of war to the war on terror' (2008) 81 *Temple Law Review* 787; and their 'Transnational armed conflict: a "principled" approach to the regulation of counter-terror combat operations' (2009) 42 *Israel Law Review* 46.

[79] See 'Report of the Secretary-General pursuant to Security Council resolution 1559 (2004)' S/2004/777 (1 October 2004) 5, para 19; Report of the Commission of Inquiry, 19, para 35, 20, para 39 and 22–23, para 57; and Report of the Mission, 5, para 6.

[80] Welch testimony of 13 September 2006. See also, 'Report of the Secretary-General on the United Nations Interim Force in Lebanon (For the period from 22 July 2005 to 20 January 2006)' S/2006/26 (18 January 2006) 4, paras 18 and 21, and 7, para 35.

Further, in considering how the 2006 Lebanon conflict should be classified, the potential parties must be identified as there are possible overlapping layers of conflict. From the outset, Israel argued that Hezbollah was 'merely the fingers of the bloodstained hands and the executioners of the twisted minds of the leaders of the world's most ominous axis of terror, Syria and Iran'.[81] This allegation is irrelevant for the purposes of classifying the nature of the Lebanon 2006 conflict: whatever indirect involvement Syria and Iran[82] might have had, they were not parties to the conflict as there is no evidence that their relationship with Hezbollah would meet the effective control test laid out in the *Nicaragua* case.[83]

3.1. The conflict between Israel and Lebanon

The factors which appear to be relevant in classifying the conflict between Israel and Lebanon per se are: the status of Hezbollah within the structure of the Lebanese State; the legal effects of the imposition of aerial and maritime blockades on Lebanon by Israel; the range and nature of targets selected by Israel within Lebanon; and the occupation of Lebanese territory by Israel. This list appears to be one-sided, but it must be remembered that Lebanese armed forces effectively did not participate in the conflict.

It may be recalled that Israeli Prime Minister Olmert initially stated that Lebanon was responsible for the border incident that gave rise to the conflict on the ground that Hezbollah was represented in the Lebanese Cabinet;[84] that the *Report of the Commission of Inquiry* found that the conflict was an international armed conflict partly on the basis that Hezbollah was part of the government; and further that it had been categorized as a national resistance group with its behaviour suggesting a link between it and the Lebanese government.[85] If Hezbollah's

---

[81] S/PV.5488, Security Council meeting (13 July 2006), Israel, 7. See also, the letter from the Permanent Representative of Israel to the United Nations to the Secretary-General and the President of the Security Council, A/60/937–S/2006/515 (12 July 2006) which alleged: 'Responsibility also lies with the Government of the Islamic Republic of Iran and the Syrian Arab Republic, which support and embrace those who carried out this attack', and stated 'In this vacuum festers the Axis of Terror: Hezbollah and the terrorist States of Iran and Syria, which have today opened another chapter in their war of terror'; SC 5489th meeting, 6: 'It is very important for the international community to understand that while Hizbollah executes this vicious terrorism, it is merely the finger on the blood-stained, long-reaching arms of Syria and Iran'; and the 19 July 2006 statement by Foreign Minister Livni, quoted in section 2.1 above.
[82] Rubin, *Rocket Campaign*, 6–7 thinks it plausible that Iran distanced itself from the conflict and refused to allow Hezbollah to employ Iranian-supplied rockets. He notes that 'Officially Iran "supported" but did not "participate in" the Hizbullah's cause' (at 7).
[83] *Military and paramilitary activities in and against Nicaragua (Nicaragua v United States of America)* ICJ Rep 1986, 61-5, paras 105–15, at 65, para 115: 'to give rise to legal responsibility of the United States, it would in principle have to be proved that that State had effective control of the military or paramilitary operations.' (*Nicaragua* case); re-affirmed in *Case Concerning Application of the Convention on the Prevention and Punishment of the Crime of Genocide (Bosnia and Herzegovina v Serbia and Montenegro)* ICJ Rep 2007, 43, paras 399–407 (*Genocide Convention* case). For commentary, see A. Cassese, 'The Nicaragua and Tadić tests revisited in the light of the ICJ judgment on Genocide in Bosnia' (2007) 18 *European Journal of International Law* 649 (Cassese, *Nicaragua and Tadić tests*).
[84] See section 2.1 above.
[85] See sections 1.1 and 2.4 above.

conduct could be attributed to Lebanon, whether on the basis that it formed part of the government or because it acted as a State organ or agent, then this would indicate that the conflict between Israel and Lebanon should be classified as an international armed conflict.

At the time of the conflict, Hezbollah was a minority presence in the Lebanese Cabinet, being represented by two ministers.[86] For the purposes of State responsibility, it is difficult to see how an act committed by a minority faction may be attributed to the government as a whole, simply because that faction forms part of the government, in the absence of either collusion, authorization or ratification of that act by the government. The duality of Hezbollah's role as a participant in government and non-state armed group has been recognized by the Israeli judiciary. In a case arising out the 2006 conflict, Justice Rubenstein of the Israeli Supreme Court ruled that:

> the organisation [Hezbollah] is playing a 'double game' in the Lebanese arena. On the one hand, it participated in the Lebanese elections and its representatives serve in the Lebanese government, and on the other hand, the organisation continues to exist and to carry out its independent policies in contravention of Security Council Decision [*sic*] 1559, as well as preserving its existence as a military force. Quotations from the senior ranks of the government of Lebanon, such as the Prime Minister and the Minister of the Interior, pointing to the government of Lebanon's lack of knowledge of the kidnapping of the IDF soldiers were presented [in evidence] . . . it is evident that even after Security Council Decision 1701 and the ceasefire on 14 August 2006, an independent Hezbollah is operating and continues to act like an independent terror organisation that is not subordinate to the government of Lebanon.[87]

Further, Israel subsequently discarded its initial reliance on Hezbollah's participation in government in order to present Hezbollah as a regional threat with which it had to deal as Lebanon had failed to do so, and claimed that 'Israel has no conflict with Lebanon'.[88] This belies the notion that Hezbollah's acts were those of the government.

Accordingly, it must be considered if Hezbollah nevertheless acted as an organ or agent of Lebanon, such that its conduct could be attributable to Lebanon under the law of State responsibility. There is a degree of ambiguity in the status to be accorded to Hezbollah given, on the one hand, its designation as a 'national resistance group' but, on the other, its classification as a 'State within a State'.[89] Cahin cites Hezbollah as an example of the difficulties that arise in subsuming the activities of some non-state armed groups within the established categories of attribution in the law of State responsibility because the Hezbollah-Lebanon

---

[86] See section 1.1 above.

[87] *Srur and others v Israel*, Cr A 8780/06 (20 November 2006), translated in *Oxford Reports on International Law in Domestic Courts* (ILDC) 590 (IL 2006), opinion of Justice Rubenstein, 6, para 12(2) (*Srur and others v Israel*).

[88] See e.g. the 19 July 2006 statement by Foreign Minister Livni, quoted in section 2.1 above.

[89] Welch testimony of 13 September 2006.

relationship cannot be defined in terms of absolute autonomy or strict dependency.[90]

Under the 2001 International Law Commission's Articles on the Responsibility of States for Internationally Wrongful Acts, the attribution of Hezbollah's acts to Lebanon could potentially arise if it were seen as an organ of the State (article 4); as an entity exercising elements of governmental authority (article 5); or as an entity whose conduct is directed or controlled by the State (article 8). Cahin notes that armed groups not acting in the name of or on behalf of a State cannot automatically be deemed to be insurrectional movements[91] whose acts are not in principle attributable to the State.[92] Hezbollah is not an insurrectionist movement as it does not appear to be secessionist or wish to overthrow the government of Lebanon.

In the *Genocide Convention* case, the International Court of Justice ruled that article 4 reflected customary international law,[93] and continued that the application of this rule entailed that the wrongful acts under consideration were committed by '"persons or entities" having the status of organs' of a State under its domestic law[94] as 'the expression "State organ", as used in customary international law and in Article 4 of the ILC Articles, applies to one or other of the individual or collective entities which make up the organization of the State and act on its behalf (cf. ILC Commentary to Art. 4, para. (1))'.[95]

In the *Genocide Convention* case, the ICJ concluded that 'neither the Republika Srpska, nor the VRS [the Army of the Republika Srpska] were de jure organs of the FRY [Federal Republic of Yugoslavia], since none of them had the status of organ of that State under its internal law'. It further ruled that acts of genocide in Srebrenica, perpetrated by the VRS, had not been committed by organs of the Federal Republic of Yugoslavia because it had 'not been shown that the FRY army took part in the massacres, nor that the political leaders of the FRY had a hand in preparing, planning or in any way carrying out the massacres'.[96]

Employing this reasoning, it is submitted that Hezbollah should not be considered as an organ of Lebanon under the terms of article 4(1) as it did not appear to

---

[90] G. Cahin, 'The responsibility of other entities: armed bands and criminal groups' in J. Crawford, A. Pellet and S. Olleson (eds), *The law of international responsibility* (2010) 335 (Cahin, *Armed bands*).
[91] Ibid.
[92] See art. 10 of the International Law Commission's 2001 Articles on the Responsibility of States for Internationally Wrongful Acts; J. Crawford, *The International Law Commission's Articles on State responsibility: introduction, text and commentaries* (2002) (Crawford, *State Responsibility*), commentary to art.10, 116; and G. Cahin, 'Attribution of conduct to the State: insurrectional movements' in J. Crawford, A. Pellet and S. Olleson (eds), *The law of international responsibility* (2010) 247.
[93] *Genocide Convention* case, 202, para 385.
[94] Ibid, 202, para 386.
[95] Ibid, 203, para 388. On the interpretation of art. 4(1) of the Articles on State responsibility, see Crawford, *State Responsibility*, commentary to art. 41, 94–8, paras 1–10; D. Montaz, 'Attribution of conduct to the State: State organs and entities empowered to exercise elements of governmental authority' in J. Crawford, A. Pellet and S. Olleson, *The law of international responsibility* (2010) 239–43 (Montaz, *State Organs*).
[96] *Genocide Convention* case, 202, para 386.

have that formal status under domestic law.[97] During the 2006 conflict, Hezbollah acted independently of the Lebanese government, which moreover expressly repudiated Hezbollah's acts. Accordingly, Hezbollah's designation as a 'national resistance group' might therefore best be seen as rhetorical, rather than indicative of a formal legal status under domestic law.

Similar considerations deny the possibility of attribution on the ground that Hezbollah was acting as an entity exercising governmental authority within the terms of article 5 of the Articles on State Responsibility as this envisages that 'the internal law of the State has conferred on the entity in question the exercise of certain elements of the governmental authority'.[98]

Nevertheless, the question of formal, or de jure, status under Lebanese law does not exhaust the possibility that Hezbollah could be seen as an organ whose conduct might be attributed to Lebanon. The ILC commentary to article 4(2) notes that sometimes domestic law does not comprehensively identify those entities which function as State organs, but that this might be determined by practice. Reliance solely on formal legal provision is accordingly inadequate and 'a State cannot avoid responsibility for the conduct of a body which does in truth act as one of its organs merely by denying it that status under its own law'.[99] Classification of an entity as a de facto State organ is 'exceptional, for it requires proof of a particularly great degree of State control over them'.[100] Following its decision in the *Nicaragua* case, the International Court ruled that a non-state entity could be classified as a de facto State organ only if there were 'dependence on the one side and control on the other':[101]

persons, groups of persons or entities may, for purposes of international responsibility, be equated with State organs even if that status does not follow from internal law, provided that in fact the persons, groups or entities act in 'complete dependence' on the State, of which they are ultimately merely the instrument. In such a case, it is appropriate to look beyond legal status alone, in order to grasp the reality of the relationship between the person taking action, and the State to which he is so closely attached as to appear to be nothing more than its agent.[102]

De facto State organs must be 'mere instruments [of the State] . . . lacking any real autonomy'.[103] As Zimmermann observes, the fact that the Security Council had frequently asked that Lebanon exercise full control over its territory, especially those areas that border Israel, demonstrates that Hezbollah was not under its 'complete control'; nor was it dependent on Lebanon given Israel's repeated claims that it was

---

[97] See also, A. Zimmermann, 'The second Lebanon war: jus ad bellum, jus in bello and the issue of proportionality' (2007) 11 *Max Planck Yearbook of United Nations Law* 110 (Zimmermann, *Second Lebanon War*).

[98] Crawford, *State Responsibility*, commentary to art. 5, 101, para 5; see also, Montaz, *State Organs*, 244–6; and Zimmermann, *Second Lebanon War*, 110–11.

[99] Crawford, *State Responsibility*, commentary to art. 4, 98, para 11.

[100] *Genocide Convention* case, 205, para 393.

[101] Ibid, 204–5, para 391, re-affirming *Nicaragua* case, 62–3, paras 109–10.

[102] *Genocide Convention* case, 205, para 392; see also, Cahin, *Armed bands*, 333–4; Montaz, *State Organs*, 243; and Zimmermann, *Second Lebanon War*, 111.

[103] *Genocide Convention* case, 206, para 394.

supported by Iran and Syria.[104] In determining the relationship between Hezbollah and Lebanon, the Court's finding in the *Genocide Convention* case that 'differences over strategic options emerged at the time between Yugoslav authorities and Bosnian Serb leaders; at the very least, these are evidence that the latter had some qualified, but real, margin of independence'[105] is instructive. The 2006 conflict was initiated and executed by Hezbollah, consequently its conduct cannot be attributed to Lebanon on the basis that it was a de facto State organ.

Even if Hezbollah was not a de facto organ whose conduct as a whole is attributable to the State, it must be considered if *some* of its acts could be attributed to Lebanon under article 8 of the ILC's 2001 Articles regarding the attribution of conduct which is directed or controlled by the State (which the Court also ruled expressed customary international law in the *Genocide Convention* case).[106] Ruling that this article must be interpreted in the light of its jurisprudence, and in particular the *Nicaragua* judgment,[107] the Court rejected the 'overall control' test formulated by the ICTY in *Tadić* as inappropriate for the purposes of determining State responsibility[108] and declared:

> in this context it is not necessary to show that the persons who performed the acts alleged to have violated international law were in general in a relationship of 'complete dependence' on the respondent State; it has to be proved that they acted in accordance with that State's instructions or under its 'effective control'. It must however be shown that this 'effective control' was exercised, or that the State's instructions were given, in respect of each operation in which the alleged violations occurred, not generally in respect of the overall actions taken by the persons or groups of persons having committed the violations.[109]

Given its manifest lack of control over Hezbollah's actions, these cannot be attributed to Lebanon 'in respect of each operation'.

Finally, although the Lebanese government did not control Hezbollah's activities, and indeed disavowed its initiation of hostilities, it is nonetheless possible that it might be responsible for its activities internationally according to article 9 of the International Law Commission's Articles on State Responsibility:

> The conduct of a person or group of persons shall be considered an act of a State under international law if the person or group of persons is in fact exercising elements of the governmental authority in the absence or default of the official authorities and in circumstances such as to call for the exercise of those elements of authority.

The Commission's commentary to this article expressly states that this covers situations in which 'the regular authorities . . . have been suppressed or are for the

---

[104]   Zimmermann, *Second Lebanon War*, 111–12.
[105]   *Genocide Convention* case, 206, para 394.
[106]   Ibid, 207–8, paras 397–8. The ruling that this expresses customary international law is at 209, para 401.
[107]   Ibid, 208, para 399.
[108]   Ibid, 209–11, paras 402–7; see also, Cahin, *Armed bands*, 333; Cassese, *Nicaragua and Tadić tests*; Crawford, *State Responsibility*, commentary to art. 8, 111–12, para 5; and Zimmermann, *Second Lebanon War*, 112–15.
[109]   *Genocide Convention* case, 208, para 400.

time being inoperative'.[110] It is conceivable that Lebanon's factual lack of authority in the areas of southern Lebanon controlled by Hezbollah could potentially fall within the ambit of this article, but its application is restricted to situations which call for an 'agency of necessity'.[111] It is doubtful whether the initiation of a conflict with a neighbouring State falls within this category.

In sum, Hezbollah's acts cannot be attributed to Lebanon under the law of State responsibility and thus, as Hezbollah could not be said to be acting on its behalf, the conflict between Israel and Lebanon cannot be classified as an international armed conflict on the basis that there existed some relationship between Hezbollah and the Lebanese government. Hezbollah operated autonomously—'as a "State-within-a-State" in the Lebanese body politic'[112]—in southern Lebanon, and despite its classification as a 'national resistance movement' by the government, there is no evidence that the latter exercised any control over its activities.

Israel back-pedalled from its initial position that Lebanon was responsible for Hezbollah's armed actions and 'will bear the consequences',[113] and that 'Israel's actions were in direct response to an act of war from Lebanon',[114] and moved to the view that there was no dispute between Israel and Lebanon[115] as Israel was dealing with the regional threat posed by Hezbollah (and Hamas, Syria and Iran);[116] but this was disingenuous. Simply by enforcing its maritime and aerial blockade against Lebanon, Israel engaged in a belligerent act against Lebanon.[117] Under the traditional law of armed conflict, a blockade can only be declared during an international armed conflict as '[b]lockade is a belligerent right, and can only be exercised against a state with which the blockading power is at war'.[118]

The Commission of Inquiry expressly referred to the blockade as evidence that 'the State of Lebanon was the subject of direct hostilities conducted by Israel'.[119] Other States acquiesced in the blockade. For example, the bombing of the Jiyyeh power plant by Israel on 14 and 15 July resulted in a massive oil spill: the French

[110] See Crawford, *State Responsibility*, commentary to art. 9, 114, para 1.
[111] Ibid, 114, para 2.
[112] Welch testimony of 13 September 2006.
[113] Prime Minister Olmert, Press Conference (12 July 2006), reported in Foreign Affairs Committee, *Global Security,* 44, para 95.
[114] SC 5489th meeting, 6.
[115] S/PV.5508, Security Council meeting (8 August 2006) 6.
[116] Remarks to journalists by Tzipi Livni, Israeli Foreign Minister, Jerusalem, S214/06 (19 July 2006).
[117] See e.g. W. Heintschel von Heinegg, 'Blockade' in R. Wolfrum (ed.), *Max Planck Encyclopedia of Public International Law* (2008) para 25 (Von Heinegg, *Blockade*); M. Krauss, 'Internal conflicts and foreign States: in search of the state of law' (1978) 5 *Yale Studies in World Public Order* 186–7; J.B. Moore, *A digest of international law* (1906),Vol. 7, 780–3, 785–6 and 808; S.C. Neff, *The rights and duties of neutrals: a general history* (2000) 22; R.R. Oglesby, *Internal war and the search for normative order* (1971) 40, 42–3; V.A. O'Rourke, 'Recognition of belligerency and the Spanish war' (1937) 31 *AJIL* 402; M.M. Whiteman, *Digest of international law* (1968), Vol. 10, 868–72; G.G. Wilson, 'Insurgency and international maritime law' (1906) 1 *AJIL* 56.
[118] 17 January 1876 letter from the Earl of Derby to Lord Odo Russell, reproduced in J.B. Moore, *A digest of international law* (1906), Vol. 7, 808; see also, e.g. Von Heinegg, *Blockade*, para 25. The use and legal status of blockades imposed not against a State, but rather declared in a conflict which is clearly between a State and a non-state actor alone is considered in ch. 9, section 4.4 above.
[119] Report of the Commission of Inquiry, 23, para 58.

embassy in Lebanon agreed to allow the use of its helicopter to survey the situation, but Israel refused to grant clearance for the flight.[120] Due to the aerial blockade, as no surveillance and assessment of the spill could be undertaken by aircraft, the only possible way to do so was by using satellite remote-sensing imagery.[121]

Further, the extent of damage inflicted on the infrastructure of Lebanon by Israel, which went well beyond the geographic confines of the conflict with Hezbollah, and targeted assets unrelated to Hezbollah's fighting capabilities— such as the Jiyyeh power plant, as well as attacks on Lebanese armed forces and their assets[122]—indicates that an international armed conflict existed between Israel and Lebanon. It should be recalled that Israel claimed that its hostile operations were governed by rules applicable in international armed conflicts, namely, the Fourth Geneva Convention and the provisions of Additional Protocol I that are declaratory of customary international law.[123] Further, the *Report of the Commission of Inquiry* also recorded that the IDF viewed the conflict as an international armed conflict.[124]

During the conflict, Lebanon had claimed that Israel was engaged in an 'all-out war against Lebanon', and 'In Israel's wanting to destroy the infrastructure of terrorism...it is the infrastructure of Lebanon that is destroyed'.[125] Lebanese government officials had also informed the Commission of Inquiry that they considered that, as Lebanon had been subject to the destructive effect of IDF hostilities, it was a party to the conflict.[126]

Finally, in the late stages of the conflict, Israel launched ground operations in southern Lebanon which extended far beyond the border. Under Common Article 2 of the Geneva Conventions, an occupation may come into existence even if this is not resisted; thus an international armed conflict would appear to have existed between Lebanon per se and Israel simply as a consequence of Israel's occupation of areas of southern Lebanon.

Even if the damage inflicted on Lebanon's infrastructure by Israel could be justified on the basis that these constituted legitimate military targets in its conflict with Hezbollah, because of its occupation of Lebanese territory and, a fortiori, the imposition of the maritime and aerial blockades, it must be concluded that an international armed conflict existed between Israel and Lebanon from the time the maritime and aerial blockades were imposed (13 and 14 July 2006, respectively).

3.2. The conflict between Israel and Hezbollah

Undoubtedly, given the extent of lethal force employed, the conflict was not a police enforcement action by Israel against Hezbollah, but rather an armed conflict

---

[120] Tucker, *Mitigating Collateral Damage*, 167.
[121] Report of the Commission of Inquiry, 52, para 212.
[122] Ibid, 22, paras 52–3.
[123] Report of the Mission, 7–8, para 23; see also, section 2.4 above.
[124] Report of the Commission of Inquiry, 24, para 62; see also, section 2.4 above.
[125] S/PV.5508, Security Council meeting (8 August 2006), Lebanon, 7.
[126] Report of the Commission of Inquiry, 23, para 59.

falling within the *Tadić* definition: 'an armed conflict exists whenever there is a resort to armed force between States or protracted armed violence between governmental authorities and organized armed groups or between such groups within a State.'[127]

It is generally accepted that an international armed conflict within the terms of the Geneva Conventions can only exist between States,[128] and Hezbollah is not a State. Despite its cross-border nature, consequently, the hostilities between Hezbollah and Israel should be classified as a non-international armed conflict. Thus for example, in discussing Lebanon 2006, Paulus and Vashakmadze commented:

> Arguably, armed conflicts between a state's armed forces and transnational armed groups operating in the territory of another state without the latter's consent could be treated as international armed conflict because of the cross-border component... It nonetheless appears more appropriate to qualify a transnational armed conflict involving non-state parties not linked to another state as armed conflicts of a non-international character... the geographical element should not determine whether a conflict is qualified as international.[129]

In doing so, Paulus and Vashakmadze dismiss the hypothesis that it could be classified as a transnational conflict which they define as a conflict 'between a state and a non-state group (or between non-state groups) on the territory of more than one state'.[130]

On the other hand, faced with cross-border conflicts between a State and a non-state actor, some authors see the existing paradigm of classifying a conflict as either international or non-international as inadequate.[131] Corn developed his notion of transnational conflict with the conflict in Lebanon in 2006 specifically in mind, arguing that the triggering mechanisms for the application of the law of armed conflict contained in Common Articles 2 and 3 of the Geneva Conventions are inadequate where a State employs its armed forces extraterritorially against a non-state entity.[132] He argues that it is clear when an international armed conflict within the terms of Common Article 2 exists as the armed forces of States are in contention, but Common Article 3 was a response to internal civil wars which occurred during the inter-war period and its text expressly refers to conflict

---

[127] *Tadić* Jurisdiction, para 70.

[128] See e.g. N. Lubell, *Extraterritorial use of force against non-state actors* (2010) 94–6 (Lubell, *Extraterritorial Use of Force*); Pejic, *Status of armed conflicts*, 80–2; Pictet, *Commentary to the First Geneva Convention*, commentary to Common Article 2, 32; and see also, ch. 8, section 2.2 above.

[129] A. Paulus and M. Vashakmadze, 'Asymmetrical war and the notion of armed conflict—a tentative conceptualization' (2009) 873 *International Review of the Red Cross* 111–12, paragraph break and footnote suppressed (Paulus and Vashakmadze, *Asymmetrical war*). See also, Lubell, *Extraterritorial Use of Force*, 250–4; and N. Melzer, *Targeted killing in international law* (2008) 257–61.

[130] Paulus and Vashakmadze, *Asymmetrical war*, 110.

[131] See e.g. Corn, *Hybrid category*; International Law Association, 'Initial report on the meaning of armed conflict in international law' (2008); M.E. O'Connell, 'Defining armed conflict' (2009) 13 *Journal of Conflict and Security Law* 393; and S. Vité, 'Typology of armed conflicts in international humanitarian law: legal concepts and actual situations' (2009) 873 *International Review of the Red Cross* 69.

[132] Corn, *Hybrid category*, 299–301.

'occurring in the territory of one of the High Contracting Parties'.[133] Corn argues that it is accordingly inappropriate to classify the extraterritorial use of force by a State against a non-state entity as a non-international armed conflict.[134]

In relation to the conflict in Lebanon in 2006, he notes that the conduct of this conflict implicated the fundamental principles of distinction, proportionality and necessity: 'This conflict and the international response it evoked indicate an obvious reality: the international community now expects application of these principles to all armed conflicts not merely as a matter of policy but as a matter of law.'[135]

Corn claims that these fundamental principles would not apply as a matter of law if it were claimed that Lebanon 2006 simply constituted a non-international armed conflict regulated by Common Article 3 given the narrow humanitarian scope of the protection it affords.[136] This ignores the convergence of the customary law governing international and non-international armed conflicts.[137] Corn's category of transnational war is neither persuasive, nor legally well-founded, as he posits a binary classification of conflicts, into which he claims an extraterritorial use of force by a State against a non-state entity does not fit. Because the two elements of this paradigm appear inadequate, he assumes that there must exist a third classification, which Corn terms a transnational conflict, and does not consider if rules of customary international law applicable in non-international armed conflicts could provide surer, and more specific, guidance. The latter is to be preferred: the 2006 conflict between Israel and Hezbollah should not be seen as a transnational conflict, but as a cross-border non-international armed conflict.

4. The rules governing the application of force

In the *Report of the Mission* the IDF is recorded as saying that its operations were based on the law of international armed conflict, in particular the Fourth Geneva Convention and the provisions of Additional Protocol I that were declaratory of custom.[138] The *Report of the Mission* noted that in characterizing objects as military objectives, in particular objects that served primarily civilian purposes, Israel also relied on the 'list of categories of military objectives' contained in the 1956 *Draft Rules for the Limitation of the Dangers incurred by the Civilian Population in Time of War* promulgated by the ICRC for use in both international

---

[133] Corn, *Hybrid category*, 306–7, 313, 324.

[134] Compare Paulus and Vashakmadze, *Asymmetrical war*, 117 who argue that, given the International Court of Justice's ruling in the *Nicaragua* case that the provisions of Common Article 3 emanate from elementary considerations of humanity, the territorial requirement of article may be considered obsolete; and also Lubell, *Extraterritorial Use of Force*, 99–104; and Pejic, *Status of armed conflicts*, 87.

[135] Corn, *Hybrid category*, 326–9 and 340.

[136] Ibid, 313–15, 323–9, and 340–1.

[137] See eg ICRC Customary Law Study, *passim*.

[138] Report of the Mission, 7–8, para 23.

and non-international armed conflicts.[139] The Mission criticized Israel's reliance on this list, as it could not definitively classify an object as a legitimate military objective, noting that article 52 of Additional Protocol I imposes both an object- and context-specific assessment of each target, rather than a test based on an object's generic classification.[140]

The Ministry of Foreign Affairs' report, *Israel's war with Hizbullah*, is sparse in its reference to the governing legal instruments, principally citing article 52(2) of Additional Protocol I as providing the 'generally accepted definition' of a military objective and article 28 of the Fourth Geneva Convention[141] as authority for the proposition that a legitimate military objective does not lose this classification if civilians are in its vicinity. It further notes that the principle of proportionality in attack is a legal requirement.[142] It also refers to the 1992 German Military Manual to explain the notion of military advantage, and to the 1994 Australian Defence Force Manual as evidence of State practice demonstrating that the presence of civilians does not prevent a military objective from being a legitimate target.[143]

As alleged by Israel, and confirmed by the *Report of the Mission*, Hezbollah made little attempt to observe the law of armed conflict: most of its rockets fell on civilian areas, although there is some evidence that in the early stages of the conflict attempts were made to focus on military targets.[144] The Mission nonetheless observed that the public statements of the Secretary-General of Hezbollah, Hassan Nasrallah, explicitly rejected the legal requirements for the conduct of hostilities. Although Nasrallah recognized the distinction between civilians and combatants and between civilian and military objects, he argued that Hezbollah had a right to disregard these distinctions in the pursuit of victory. It was claimed that Hezbollah had the right to violate the law of armed conflict in response to Israeli violations, but failed to take account of the point that reprisals against the civilian population are prohibited.[145]

It has repeatedly been alleged that the parties to the conflict engaged in indis- criminate attacks on civilians and civilian objects; that Hezbollah had used the civilian population as human shields and had located military resources in civilian areas and also near UNIFIL positions; that Israel's use of cluster weapons, particu- larly in the final hours of the conflict, was legally questionable;[146] and that Israel

---

[139] ICRC, 'Draft Rules for the limitation of the Dangers incurred by the Civilian Population in Time of War' (1956), available at www.icrc.org/IHL.nsf/INTRO/420?OpenDocument.

[140] Report of the Mission, 12, para 50.

[141] Article 28 of the Fourth Geneva Convention provides: 'The presence of a protected person may not be used to render points or areas immune from military operations.'

[142] See MFA, *Israel's war with Hizbullah*, 9–12.

[143] Ibid, 13–14.

[144] Ibid, 9; Report of the Mission, 16–17, paras 68–75; Rubin, *Rocket Campaign*, 12.

[145] See ICRC Customary Law Study, commentary to rule 146, 520–3; Report of the Mission, 16, paras 68–70: quotation at para 68; and Rubin, *Rocket Campaign*, 12.

[146] See e.g. Report of the Commission of Inquiry, paras 24, 249–56, 337, 343, and see 114–66, Annex XI, List of weapons used—cluster munitions; Report of the Mission, 13–14, paras 52–57; E. Barak, 'Doomed to be violated? The US-Israel clandestine end-used agreement and the Second Lebanon War: lessons for the Convention on Cluster Munitions' (2009) 38 *Denver Journal of International Law and Policy*, and his 'None to be trusted: Israel's use of cluster munitions in the

had unlawfully attacked a UNIFIL post in Khiyam on 25 July 2006 which resulted in the death of four UNIFIL personnel.[147]

The UK House of Commons Foreign Affairs Committee's report, *Global security: the Middle East* highlighted these issues, and concluded:

> We accept that Israel has an inalienable right to defend itself from terrorist threats. However, we conclude that elements of Israel's military action in Lebanon were indiscriminate and disproportionate. In particular, the numerous attacks on UN observers and the dropping of over three and a half million cluster bombs (90 per cent of the total) in the 72 hours after the Security Council passed Resolution 1701 were not acceptable.[148]

Further, the Commission of Inquiry found that a number of UNIFIL positions had been either directly hit by IDF fire or were the subject of firing close to their positions, with a dramatic increase in direct attacks on 13–14 August after the ceasefire had been announced. The UNIFIL positions were clearly marked and had been notified to the IDF in twelve figure grid references. It further observed that while Hezbollah had breached the law of armed conflict by using the vicinity of UNIFIL positions to launch their rockets, '"the vicinity" does not mean from within the bases ... The direct targeting by IDF, when they have the advantage of modern precision weapons, remains inexcusable'. The Commission of Inquiry also found that the direct firing on UNIFIL posts by Hezbollah was equally illegal.[149] Thus a principal failure to respect the law of armed conflict during Lebanon 2006 was the disregard, by both sides, of the principle of distinction in targeting matters.

Attacks were also seen to be disproportionate, particularly Israel's devastation of Lebanese infrastructure. This appears to have been a conscious policy choice by Israel as, on 4 February 2008, in responding to the Winograd Committee's Final Report before the Knesset, then Prime Minister Olmert stated: 'The unequivocal opinion of the defense establishment before the Second Lebanon War was that in the case of an abduction attempt or rocket attacks, Israel must respond harshly in the entire area in a disproportionate fashion.'[150]

Subsequently, at the beginning of October 2008, the Commanding Officer of the IDF's Northern Command, Major General Gadi Eisenkott, gave an interview to a newspaper, *Yedioth Ahronoth*, in which he unveiled what has come to be known as the *Dahiya doctrine*:

> What happened in the Dahiya Quarter of Beirut in 2006, will happen in every village from which shots are fired on Israel. We will use disproportionate force against it and

---

Second Lebanon War and the case for the Convention on Cluster Munitions' (2009) 25 *American University International Law Review* 423; J.B. Bottoms, 'When close doesn't count: an analysis of Israel's jus ad bellum and jus in bello in the 2006 Israel-Lebanon war' (2009) 23 *Army Lawyer* 52–3; M.L. Gross, 'The Second Lebanon War: the question of proportionality and the prospect of non-lethal warfare' (2008) 7 *Journal of Military Ethics* 10–12.

[147] For a summary, see Mahmoudi, *Second Lebanese War*, 180–6; and also Report of the Commission of Inquiry, 26–64; and Report of the Mission, 9–18.

[148] Foreign Affairs Committee, *Global Security*, 49, para 108.

[149] See Report of the Commission of Inquiry, 56–8, paras 233–46: quotation at 58, para 245.

[150] Quoted in Cohen-Almagor and Haleva-Amir, *The Winograd Committee*, 41.

we will cause immense damage and destruction. From our point of view these are not civilian villages but military bases... This is not a recommendation, this is the plan, and it has already been authorized.[151]

Moreover, the Commission of Inquiry concluded that the impact of the blockade on human life, the environment and the Lebanese economy seemed to outweigh any military advantage Israel wished to obtain by imposing it.[152]

Further, arguably, Israel's bombing of the Jiyyeh power plant breached international humanitarian law, as evidenced in rules 43 and 44 of the ICRC Study, regarding the protection of the natural environment.[153] The environmental effects of the resultant oil pollution were exacerbated as the Mediterranean is an enclosed or semi-enclosed sea, and thus particularly susceptible to pollution which is not readily discharged into oceanic waters.[154] Further, this could be seen as a breach of neutrality given the impact of the resultant oil spill on neighbouring littoral States.

Hezbollah's rocket campaign was indiscriminate. It was also alleged that Hezbollah had used the civilian population as human shields and had located military resources in civilian areas and also near UNIFIL positions. The *Report of the Commission of Inquiry* found that there was some evidence that Hezbollah used towns and villages as 'shields' for their firings; however, it seemed that this occurred when most of the civilian population had departed. It found no evidence regarding the use of 'human shields' by Hezbollah, but there was evidence of Hezbollah using UNIFIL and Observer Group Lebanon posts as deliberate shields for the firing of their rockets.[155]

5. Rules on capture and detention

During the Lebanon 2006 conflict, it is fair to assume that Hezbollah did not observe international legal requirements on the treatment of prisoners. This is indicated by its general repudiation of the law of armed conflict and the fact that Hezbollah refused the ICRC access to the two soldiers captured during the 12 July 2006 incursion. Their bodies were returned to Israel on 16 July 2008[156] in an exchange, but the circumstances surrounding their deaths are unknown. It might be that they died during or as a result of the initial Hezbollah incursion as there is

---

[151] See Hirst, *Small States*, 396; Public Committee against Torture in Israel, 'No second thoughts: the changes in the Israeli Defense Forces' combat doctrine in the light of "Operation Cast Lead"' (November 2009) 20; and D. Travers, 'Operation Cast Lead: legal and doctrinal asymmetries in a military operation' (2010) *Defence Forces Review* 98–9.

[152] Report of the Commission of Inquiry, 64, para 275, see 62–4, paras 268–75 generally.

[153] See ICRC Customary Law Study, 143–51; rule 43 is said to apply during both international and non-international conflicts, while rule 44, on the need to take all feasible precautions to avoid or minimize incidental damage to the natural environment, is said to apply in international armed conflicts and, 'arguably', also in non-international armed conflicts.

[154] For an outline of the environmental damage caused, see Tucker, *Mitigating Collateral Damage*, 162–3.

[155] Report of the Commission of Inquiry, 6, para 26.

[156] See MFA, *The Second Lebanon War*.

evidence that both were seriously wounded.[157] In return for their bodies, Israel released five Lebanese prisoners, four of whom were Hezbollah fighters captured during the 2006 conflict, and handed over the bodies of Hezbollah fighters killed during the conflict, as well as the bodies of some Palestinian militants.[158]

Israeli human rights organizations claim that eleven Lebanese nationals were detained by Israel during the 2006 conflict: five were released shortly after their detention; one in October 2007; and two in July 2008. The remaining three were not merely interned but prosecuted on criminal charges, but also released in July 2008.[159] The *Report of the Commission of Inquiry* contains a brief section on *Abduction, transfer and unlawful imprisonment of civilians*, but does not indicate whether the individuals concerned were detained because they were, or were suspected to be, members of Hezbollah. It does, however, allege that they were subjected to cruel, degrading and inhuman treatment during their detention.[160]

Israel did not consider that the captured Hezbollah fighters were entitled to prisoner of war (POW) status. Bearing in mind that Israel considered the Lebanon 2006 conflict to be an international armed conflict, and if it may be assumed that active hostilities ceased with the implementation of Security Council resolution 1701 and the withdrawal of Israeli forces from Lebanese territory on 1 October 2006, these fighters should have been 'released and repatriated without delay' if Israel had considered them to be entitled to POW status under article 118 of the Third Geneva Convention. This is also a requirement of customary international law, and an obligation re-affirmed in Israel's *Manual on the laws of war*.[161]

On the contrary, Israel justified its detention of Lebanese nationals captured during the 2006 conflict on the basis of its Internment of Unlawful Combatants Law which was first enacted in 2002.[162] This defines an unlawful combatant as anyone who is not entitled to POW status under article 4 of the Third Geneva Convention and who has taken part, directly or indirectly, in hostilities against Israel. Internment is based on the decision of the Chief of General Staff of the IDF on grounds of State security, is subject to judicial review by civilian courts, and is

---

[157] 'Lebanon welcomes "heroes" after Israel swap' *MSNBC News* (16 July 2008); 'Yielding Prisoners, Israel Receives 2 Dead Soldiers' *New York Times* (17 July 2008).

[158] See 'Who are the Mid-East Prisoners?' *BBC News* (26 November 2009).

[159] B'Tselem/Hamoked, 'Without trial: administrative detention of Palestinians by Israel and the Internment of Unlawful Combatants Law' (2009) 54 (B'Tselem, *Without Trial*).

[160] Report of the Commission of Inquiry, 48–9, paras 193–8.

[161] See ICRC Customary Law Study, rule 128, 451–3; for the rule set out in the Israeli *Manual*, see ibid, Vol. II.2, 2866, s. 648.

[162] B'Tselem, *Without Trial*, 53. Dinstein employs a slightly different translation of the title of this legislation, namely the Detention of Unlawful Combatants Law, see Y. Dinstein, *The conduct of hostilities under the law of international armed conflict* (2004) 31 (Dinstein, *Conduct of Hostilities*). Israel had followed a policy of holding captured militants as bargaining chips until this was prohibited by the Israel Supreme Court in the *Anonymous (Lebanese citizens) v Minister of Defence, final decision judgment*, FCrA 7048/97 (12 April 2000), translated in *Oxford Reports on International Law in Domestic Courts*, *ILDC* 12 (IL 2000). For a critical account of the legal position of Lebanese detainees in Israel before the Supreme Court delivered this decision, see O. Ben-Naftali and S. Gleichgevitch, 'Missing in legal action: Lebanese hostages in Israel' (2000) 41 *Harvard International Law Journal* 185. As a response to this judgment the Israeli government adopted the 2002 law. The background to the legislation, and its application in relation to individuals detained in Gaza, is discussed in ch. 9, section 6 above.

not limited in time as an unlawful combatant may be held in detention for as long as hostilities continue to be waged by the force to which he belongs.[163]

Some of those detained under this legislation during the Lebanon 2006 conflict were indicted before the Nazareth District Court for murder and attempted murder of IDF soldiers and for other terrorist-related offences under Israeli criminal law. This court ruled that, prima facie, they were not entitled to combat immunity under the Third Geneva Convention: this decision was appealed to the Israeli Supreme Court, sitting as a Court of Criminal Appeals. The appellants argued that, as Hezbollah acted as the sole military force in southern Lebanon with the express permission of the Lebanese government, it constituted part of Lebanon's armed forces. Accordingly, by virtue of article 4(A)(1) of the Third Geneva Convention, they should be classified as POWs, and thus be immune from criminal proceedings. The appellants further argued that, by virtue of article 5 of the Third Geneva Convention, in case of doubt regarding a prisoner's status, he enjoyed the Convention's protections until that status was determined by a competent tribunal. Accordingly, the appellants claimed that a preliminary proceeding by a competent tribunal should be undertaken before they could be detained and tried under Israeli criminal law.[164]

Justice Rubenstein of the Supreme Court rejected this appeal. He held that article 5 was not intended to determine whether a particular organization fell within article 4, but rather whether a given individual fulfilled the article 4 requirements, and ruled that the individual appellants did not:[165]

> given the complexity of the tragic situation in Lebanon, there is great uncertainty whether it is possible to join together the Lebanese Army and Hezbollah and in any event much persuasion would be needed in order to make a determination on this complexity and to view Hezbollah as 'members of the armed forces of a Party to the conflict' (this under the assumption, for the sake of discussion, that Lebanon at present is 'a Party to the conflict') or as members of militias or volunteer corps forming part of such armed forces, as required pursuant to Article 4(a)(1). Under the circumstances, the fundamental legal situation is . . . that they are not prisoners of war by virtue of their belonging to a terror organisation operating in violation of the laws of war and its customs. On the face of the matter, we are dealing with illegal combatants . . . to whom the Imprisonment of Illegal Combatants Law applies . . .[166]

Justice Rubenstein, however, noted that this did not dispose of the appellants' plea regarding determination of their status by a competent tribunal. He found that this function could be discharged, as a preliminary plea, by the trial court—in this case, the Nazareth District Court.[167] When the case was referred back to it, the District Court followed the jurisprudence of the Israeli Supreme Court and affirmed that

---

[163] B'Tselem, *Without Trial*, 51–2; Dinstein, *Conduct of Hostilities*, 31–2.
[164] *Srur and others v Israel*, fact summary at 1–2, paras F1–F7.
[165] Ibid, opinion of Justice Rubenstein, para 11.
[166] Ibid, para 12(4).
[167] Ibid, paras 12(5) and 13–14.

Hezbollah fighters were not to be classified as POWs because Hezbollah, as an organization, acted contrary to the law of armed conflict.[168]

The *Oxford Reports on International Law in Domestic Courts* commentary on both these cases notes that neither court discussed the preliminary question whether the Lebanon 2006 conflict should be classified as an international armed conflict.[169] Further, it notes that the Supreme Court disregarded the argument made before it by the Israeli government that a terrorist group may never be considered as part of a State's regular armed forces under article 4(A)(1) of the Third Geneva Convention. In fact, as it based its decision on an examination of the relationship between Hezbollah and the Lebanese government, the Supreme Court rejected that argument, although it agreed that Hezbollah was a terrorist organization.[170] Finally, the commentary notes that in its analysis of article 4(A)(1) of the Third Geneva Convention, the District Court ruled that Hezbollah's operations were in violation of the law of armed conflict. The commentary observes that, according to the plain text of article 4(A)(1), its applicability is not affected by a breach of the law of armed conflict: that condition is enumerated in article 4(A)(2) 'which formally constituted a separate ground for protection'. Although the Court did not explain this interpretation, the commentary speculates that 'the incorporation into Article 4(A)(1) of the qualification concerning compliance with the law of armed conflict seemed consistent with customary international law (see *Mohamed Ali v Public Prosecutor*, 1 AC 430, 21 May 1968)'.[171]

This view is consonant with that propounded by Dinstein—'regular forces are not absolved from meeting the cumulative conditions binding irregular forces'— who, in addition to *Mohamed Ali*, cites *Ex parte Quirin* in support.[172] This is not the place for an extended discussion of whether regular forces must meet the irregular forces requirements to qualify as combatants and thus as prisoners of war, but Rogers' view appears to have more merit, namely that these cases are, at best, only of persuasive value and are not conclusive.[173] This is perhaps a point of particular force with regard to the *Quirin* decision which is hardly a model of an independent judicial process.[174]

---

[168] See *Israel v Srur and others*, Decision on Jurisdiction, Nazareth District Court 548/06, 549/06, 550/06 (4 December 2007), translated summary *ILDC* 845 (IL 2007) 2, para H2 *(Israel v Srur and others (Jurisdiction))*.

[169] The reporter, and commentator, on both cases was Elad Peled, see *Srur and others v Israel*, para A4, and *Israel v Srur and others (Jurisdiction)* para A4.

[170] *Srur and others v Israel* para A1.

[171] *Israel v Srur and others (Jurisdiction)* para A1.

[172] Dinstein, *Conduct of Hostilities*, 36: *Ex parte Quirin*, 317 US 1 (1942).

[173] A.P.V. Rogers, 'Combatant status' in E. Wilmshurst and S. Breau, *Perspectives on the ICRC Study on customary international humanitarian law* (2007) 114; see also, 107–8, 112–15 and 116–19.

[174] See M. Dobbs, *Saboteurs: the Nazi raid on America* (2004); L. Fisher, *Nazi saboteurs on trial: a military tribunal and American law* (2003); and I. Scobbie, 'The last refuge of the tyrant?: judicial deference to executive actions in time of "terror"' in A. Bianchi and A. Keller (eds), *Counterterrorism: democracy's challenge* (2008) 277–9.

6. Conclusions

6.1. Difficulties of classification

In the first instance, the difficulties arising in the classification of the conflicts in Lebanon 2006 lay in the States parties' unwillingness to classify the conflict expressly, and the ambiguity of the positions they adopted. The views held by States not party to the conflict were too elusive to pin down. There are no indications that Hezbollah even thought about questions of classification.

On the Israeli side, the problem arose from the mixed messages it gave out. The initial reaction of holding Lebanon responsible for the activities of Hezbollah mutated into claims that there was no quarrel between Israel and Lebanon per se, but rather that Israel was engaged in some form of regional security operation against Hezbollah and the forces of Iran and Syria, despite the absence of any evidence that Iran and Syria were directly involved in the conflict or in control of, or the instigators of, Hezbollah's actions. On the other hand, Israel's declaration of a maritime and aerial blockade of Lebanon as such, as well as the widespread nature and location of its attacks, clearly pointed to the existence of an international armed conflict being prosecuted against Lebanon.

As for Lebanon, the principal difficulty lay in its ambiguous attitude towards Hezbollah, namely, whether Hezbollah was a militia, a 'national resistance movement', which effectively acted as an agent for the Lebanese government in southern Lebanon, or whether it was an autonomous entity for whose actions Lebanon was not responsible. Given the Lebanese government's absence of any control over the actions of Hezbollah, and the latter's autonomy in southern Lebanon, the better view appears to be that the claim that it acted as a 'national resistance movement' was one made for internal political reasons rather than as a true designation of its legal status. The presence of two Hezbollah members in the Lebanese Cabinet is irrelevant in this matter: to argue that the actions of a faction or party which has a minority representation in a government may be taken as the action of the government itself is to invert responsibility and claim that the dissident view trumps that of the majority.

6.2. Whether classification had practical consequences

It is submitted that the conflict had a dual character: that there existed an international armed conflict between Israel and Lebanon, and a parallel extraterritorial non-international armed conflict between Israel and Hezbollah. Whether the consequences would have been different had the conflict been thus classified at the time raises issues regarding the claimed assimilation of the rules applicable in international and non-international conflict. As Sassòli notes, although the ICRC customary international law study claims that there are many rules common to international and non-international conflicts, it does not clarify the distinction between the two—in particular where a conflict with a non-state actor extends beyond the borders of a State.[175] The ICRC study neither leads to a complete convergence of substantive norms nor eradicates the need to define the different categories of conflict.

Practical problems may arise in relation to targeting when a conflict has a dual character. While planned targeting should not give rise to problems, as the timescale involved allows for additional information to be sought in order to fulfil the attacker's duties regarding precautions in attack, difficulties might arise, perhaps particularly for ground forces, in relation to opportunistic targets. In an international armed conflict, ground forces should generally be able to identify individuals as legitimate targets according to their status as combatants, with the question of targeting civilians taking a direct part in hostilities being a secondary matter. In a non-international armed conflict the problems, and debates, surrounding the targeting of individuals who are alleged to belong to non-state armed groups on the basis of their behaviour come to the fore. For some armed forces, these difficulties might be ameliorated if their State interprets the doctrine of direct participation in hostilities to encompass individuals undertaking a continuous combat function. This appears to be the position adopted by Israel.[176] Nevertheless, the identification of specific opportunistic targets as legitimate could be problematic and give rise to controversy.

Given the predominantly aerial nature of the 2006 conflict in Lebanon, discussion of the applicable law has largely focused on targeting decisions. Israeli targeting decisions were claimed to conform with the provisions of Additional Protocol I which have passed into custom. It is doubtful, however, whether classification would have had a practical consequence in this regard, as rule 8 of the ICRC customary international law study argues that the definition of military objective contained in article 52(2) is applicable to both international and non-international armed conflicts.[177] Concerns were also expressed regarding the proportionality of attacks, but again, as noted in rule 14 of the ICRC Study, the principle is applicable to both international and non-international armed conflicts, so classification in this respect was immaterial.

Possibly the principal practical consequence attendant on classification during the Lebanon 2006 conflict was the status of Hezbollah operatives upon capture by the IDF. Had there existed a unified international armed conflict in which Hezbollah was legally an agent of Lebanon, with its forces recognized as a militia forming part of the Lebanese armed forces, then on capture they should have been entitled to POW status under article 4(A)(1) of the Third Geneva Convention (leaving to one side Dinstein's claim that forces falling within article 4(A)(1) should observe the conditions specified in article 4(A)(2)). As the conflict was bifurcated, and the Israel-Hezbollah conflict was an extraterritorial non-international armed

---

[175] M. Sassòli, 'Transnational armed groups and international humanitarian law' Harvard Program on Humanitarian Policy and Conflict Research, Occasional Paper 6 (Winter 2006) 3.

[176] *Public Committee against Torture in Israel et al v Government of Israel et al* High Court of Justice, Israel, HCJ 769/02 (13 December 2006) paras 11–12 and 39.

[177] ICRC Customary Law Study, 29–32.

conflict, the question whether POW status should be accorded to Hezbollah fighters was irrelevant, and Israel dealt with them under its Detention of Unlawful Combatants law.

The adoption of some position on classification by Hezbollah would probably have had no effect on its conduct of hostilities as it did not see itself as bound by law of armed conflict requirements.[178]

Whatever the classification of the hostilities, there was a failure to implement the law of armed conflict during the Lebanon 2006 conflict. It has also been alleged that there was a failure to observe international human rights law.[179] While Hezbollah made no effort to comply with the law of armed conflict, Israel's observance was the subject of extensive criticism, particularly in relation to the protection of the civilian population and civilian objects and the inviolability to be accorded to UNIFIL forces. Both engaged in methods of warfare which were legally questionable if not flatly unlawful. Neither comes out of this conflict well.

Chronology

14 March 1978	Israel commenced Operation Litani on Lebanese territory.
19 March 1978	Security Council adopted resolutions 425 and 426 which established the UN Interim Force in Lebanon (UNIFIL).
6 June 1982	Israel commenced Operation Peace for Galilee on Lebanese territory.
February–June 1985	Israel partially withdrew from Lebanon.
22 October 1989	The Taif Agreement was concluded between Lebanese political factions to end the civil war.
16 June 2000	UN Secretary-General confirmed to the Security Council that Israel had redeployed its forces in compliance with resolution 425.
2 September 2004	The Security Council adopted resolution 1559.

[178] See section 4 above.

[179] The Report of the Mission observed that Israel claimed that buildings were targeted in the 'air war' primarily because they served as launching or storage sites for rockets or other war materiel, and secondarily on the basis that they contained Hezbollah fighters. It concluded, however, that this could not justify the destruction of hundreds of civilian houses in South Lebanon, nor other distant houses or infrastructure (11, para 46). The Report found that the demolition of homes in violation of the law of armed conflict and subsequent displacement amounted to forcible eviction, and noted that the Commission on Human Rights in resolution 1993/77 stated that forced evictions constitute 'gross violations of human rights, in particular the right to adequate housing' (15, para 61). According to official Lebanese figures, 974,184 persons were displaced by the conflict (15, para 65), while it was estimated that 300,000 individuals fled or were evacuated from the dangers of Hezbollah rocket attacks on northern Israel (17, para 76). The Report recalled that international human rights law prohibits arbitrary displacement—which includes displacement in situations of armed conflict—which is not warranted by the need to ensure the security of the civilians involved or imperative military reasons (15, para 66). Further, isolated communities of especially vulnerable people suffered from a lack of elements of the right to the highest attainable standard of health as well as from severe problems arising from the denial of the right to adequate housing, such as access to potable water, sanitation and electricity (15, paras 63–64).

November 2005	Reported exchanges of fire between Hezbollah and the IDF, unidentified armed elements had fired rockets towards Israel. Repeated Israeli violations of Lebanese airspace.
12 July 2006	Hezbollah mounted Operation True Promise, and captured Israeli soldiers in order to exchange them for Lebanese prisoners in Israeli jails. Israel responded with Operation Change Direction.
13 and 14 July 2006	Israel imposed a maritime and aerial blockade on Lebanon. Lebanon urged the Security Council to consider the situation.
11 August 2006	The Security Council adopted resolution 1701.
14 August 2006	The ceasefire called for in resolution 1701 took effect.
6 and 7 September 2006	The maritime and aerial blockades were lifted.
1 October 2006	Israel reported that it had completed its withdrawal from southern Lebanon

13

The War (?) against Al-Qaeda

Noam Lubell

1. Introduction

This chapter examines the legal ambiguities surrounding a war that might not be a war, against an elusive enemy whose existence as an organized entity is sometimes cast in doubt. Military operations are carried out under the mantle of this war and casualties and destruction have followed, rendering the analysis and classification a crucial matter. The very use of the phrase 'war against Al-Qaeda' or the more general 'war on terror' can cause controversy. The former is a more plausible option, as at the very least it denotes the existence of parties to the conflict. The latter phrase will, however, rear its nebulous head at certain points in the chapter, since the conflict with Al-Qaeda has at times been described as part of a war on terror.[1] While the term war will feature repeatedly, this is a result of its inescapable and frequent occurrence in the surrounding debates. Nonetheless, when the actual classification of the situation is to be examined, the analysis will rest upon the term of armed conflict as the more accurate legal categorization. It must also be stressed at the outset of the chapter that although this conflict encompasses numerous—if not endless—challenges in the area of international law, the focus therein is on those issues that have direct bearing upon the classification of the conflict.[2]

2. Background to the hostilities

The majority of the combat operations by the US and its allies against Al-Qaeda in its various forms have occurred in Afghanistan. The armed conflict in Afghanistan is, however, the subject of chapter 8 in this book and is not at the focus of the current analysis. Rather, this chapter has at its core operations conducted against

---

[1] The inverted commas surrounding these phrases are a pertinent reminder of the controversy surrounding them; the rest of the chapter will avoid using them but their existence is assumed.

[2] For further detailed analysis of a number of issues raised in this chapter, see N. Lubell, *Extraterritorial Use of Force Against Non-State Actors* (2010) (Lubell, *Extraterritorial Use of Force*). The current chapter builds upon the previous analysis, further developing the arguments and examining the issue within new contexts.

Al-Qaeda outside the Afghan battlefields. These include operations carried out in Yemen, Somalia and Pakistan. Since the US is the fulcrum upon which this declared war turns, it will also be the State at the focus of the current chapter.

The temporal background to the hostilities presents a preliminary challenge to any analysis. Some 'benchmark the war on terrorism as beginning in March 1973 when Yassir Arafat ordered the murder of two United States diplomats in Khartoum',[3] and references to Al-Qaeda's attacks against the US in this context mention incidents such as the bombing of US embassies in East Africa and of the USS Cole.[4] Certain US administration officials have taken a position which appears to be more restrictive, if not altogether unambiguous, noting that the war with Al-Qaeda is 'since at least that day'—referring to 11 September 2001.[5] If there is to be considered an armed conflict with Al-Qaeda, this date would appear to be less controversial than the earlier ones, and shall be the temporal starting point for the current analysis.

The geographical scope of this conflict is a further challenge to be addressed. Afghanistan has clearly been the epicentre of operations against Al-Qaeda, although it might be argued that Pakistan now occupies an equally central position. A recent media article points to operations against Al-Qaeda spanning across an area stretching from Algeria to Somalia, and Yemen to Tajikistan.[6] Whilst some of these operations are primarily in the realm of intelligence gathering and support for the efforts of other governments, a number of the situations concern direct use of US forces against Al-Qaeda bases and operatives.[7] Of these, the most active of areas is Pakistan. According to the May 2010 US National Security Strategy, 'Al Qa'ida's core in Pakistan remains the most dangerous component of the larger network, but we also face a growing threat from the group's allies worldwide'.[8] The most publicized operation in recent time is, of course, the killing of Osama bin Laden in Abbottabad, Pakistan.[9] The other and more frequent type of operation is the use of unmanned aerial vehicles (drones) to carry out strikes against militants. Since 2004 until the first half of 2011, there have been over 250 strikes by the US against Al-Qaeda/Taliban/related targets, mainly in the

---

[3] A.N. Pratt, '9/11 and Future Terrorism: Same Nature, Different Face' in M. Schmitt and G. Beruto (eds), *Terrorism and International Law: Challenges and Responses* (2002), 155–62, 156.

[4] R. Wedgwood, 'Military Commissions: Al Qaeda, Terrorism, and Military Commissions' (2002) 96 *AJIL* 328, 330.

[5] Remarks by Alberto R. Gonzales, Counsel to the President, before the American Bar Association Standing Committee on Law and National Security, Washington, DC (24 February 2004) 5, available at: <www.fas.org/irp/news/2004/02/gonzales.pdf> (Remarks by Alberto Gonzales), see also discussion below on threshold of violence.

[6] 'Secret Assault on Terrorism Widens on Two Continents' *New York Times* (14 August 2010) (*Secret Assault on Terrorism*).

[7] Ibid.

[8] The White House, 'The National Security Strategy of the United States of America' (May 2010) 20 (US National Security Strategy).

[9] Press Briefing by Senior Administration Officials on the Killing of Osama bin Laden, Office of the Press Secretary, The White House (2 May 2011). See further discussion of the operation in the section on rules on application of force.

areas of North and South Waziristan.[10] The number of strikes has been rising, with large jumps in 2008 and since 2010. The estimate of casualties from these strikes ranges between 1500 to 2500, and the ratio between militants to non-militants is disputed—some place non-militant casualties at around 7 per cent, while others have arrived at a far higher number, comprising approximately 20 per cent of the fatalities, and even more.[11] The question of fatalities amongst the US forces carrying out these strikes is virtually a non-issue, since unmanned aerial drones are regularly employed. Notwithstanding, the use of drones raises other questions of international law which will be addressed at a later point in this chapter.

Yemen has been an additional staging ground for operations against Al-Qaeda. The most well-known of strikes occurred in 2002, when a US Predator drone launched a Hellfire missile at a vehicle travelling on a desert road in Yemen. In the vehicle, were Qaed Salim Sinan al-Harethi, an alleged Al-Qaeda leader, and five of his associates.[12] This particular strike received significant attention as it was one of the first publicized incidents of its kind. It was not, however, the last. In the nine months since December 2009, there have been at least four strikes by the US in Yemen, and dozens of casualties have been reported. Most of these were said to be targeting Al-Qaeda operatives.[13] Attacks have also been carried out against Al-Qaeda targets in Somalia using missiles and, in September 2009, a helicopter raid by special forces in which they attacked trucks carrying militants—including an alleged Al-Qaeda cell ringleader—and then carried away the bodies of some of these militants for identification.[14] Allegations have also been made of US involvement in a military operation which led to the death of Al-Qaeda operatives in Syria.[15]

The geographical scope of detention operations is as wide, if not more so. Many individuals have been detained in this war against Al-Qaeda. As noted at the outset, the conflict in Afghanistan is the subject of a separate chapter and, accordingly, the current section does not cover the issues surrounding those detained in Afghanistan. Detentions said to be part of a war against Al-Qaeda do, however, go beyond the Afghan battlefields. Individuals from countries such as Pakistan, Somalia and

[10] The link between Al-Qaeda and Taliban and the unclear affiliation of individuals will be revisited below when examining the nature of the parties, and later in the classification of the situation in Pakistan in the context of the connection to the conflict in Afghanistan.

[11] Formal and verifiable information is virtually impossible to find, but a number of organizations present information said to be based on reliable sources. See e.g. The New America Foundation, 'The Year of the Drone: An Analysis of U.S. Drone Strikes in Pakistan, 2004–2010' available at: <http://counterterrorism.newamerica.net/drones#2010chart> (NAF, *The Year of Drone*); an additional source of statistics is 'The Long War Journal', available at: <www.longwarjournal.org/pakistan-strikes.php>; however these statistics, especially in relation to the civilian fatalities, are called into question by other organizations. See M. Ahmad, 'The magical realism of body counts' *Al Jazeera* (13 June 2011).

[12] 'U.S. Strike Kills Six in Al Qaeda' *Washington Post* (5 November 2002).

[13] *Secret Assault on Terrorism*, civilians have also been killed in these attacks, although precise figures are unclear. Ibid.

[14] 'US bombs Islamist town in Somalia' *BBC News* (3 March 2008); 'U.S. Kills Top Qaeda Militant in Southern Somalia' *New York Times* (14 September 2009).

[15] 'Syria Halts Diplomacy After U.S. Military Strike' *The Wall Street Journal* (28 October 2008) (*Syria Halts Diplomacy*).

Yemen have ended up in US detention, as have others from European States. In some cases they have been transferred as part of a formal process between the US government and the authorities of the State which detained them, whether under a pre-existing extradition agreement or a formal similar ad hoc agreement. In other cases, however, individuals have been transferred to US hands—and beyond— outside of a formal and judicially supervised process as part of what has become known as 'extraordinary rendition'. There is no single method or pattern to this practice and it varies on a number of aspects, for example: individuals might be initially detained formally by the security forces of the State they are in before being handed over;[16] they might be 'captured' and then handed to the US by a non-state armed group, or even by other individuals with hidden personal agendas;[17] they may even be abducted directly by covert US agents.[18] Once captured, they could find themselves in a known US-controlled facility such as in Guantánamo Bay; they might be held by the US in a secret location; and they may find themselves transferred by the US to a third State.[19] Secret CIA detention facilities, known as 'black sites', are alleged to have existed in Thailand, Romania, Poland and Lithuania, amongst other countries.[20] Individuals have also been transferred to or detained by other States where they have allegedly been held on behalf of the CIA for the purposes of interrogation or detention without trial, with concerns arising over such cases in relation to Jordan, Egypt, Morocco, Syria, Pakistan, Ethiopia, Djibouti and Uzbekistan.[21]

2.1. Al-Qaeda

While the targets of these military strikes, operations and detentions are often described as Al-Qaeda operatives, their precise affiliation and the nature of Al-Qaeda itself raises a number of questions. First and foremost is the need for an examination of Al-Qaeda as a party to a conflict. Who and what is Al-Qaeda?

Most notable is the fact that its description ranges from being a distinct group, to a network of groups, or even a network of networks, and in some cases an ideology

---

[16] See e.g. the case of Murat Kurnaz and other alleged cases mentioned in 'Joint Study on Global Practices in Relation To Secret Detention in The Context of Countering Terrorism' of The Special Rapporteur on The Promotion and Protection of Human Rights and Fundamental Freedoms While Countering Terrorism, Martin Scheinin; The Special Rapporteur on Torture and Other Cruel, Inhuman or Degrading Treatment or Punishment, Manfred Nowak; The Working Group on Arbitrary Detention represented by its Vice-Chair, Shaheen Sardar Ali; and The Working Group on Enforced or Involuntary Disappearances represented by its Chair, Jeremy Sarkin, UN Doc.A/HRC/13/42 (19 February 2010) paras 127, 133 (UN, *Study on Secret Detention*).

[17] See allegations of capture and transfer for money in Georgia. Ibid, para 134.

[18] 'CIA agents guilty of Italy kidnap' *BBC News* (4 November 2009).

[19] See detailed reports and examples in UN, *Study on Secret Detention*; see also Committee on Legal Affairs and Human Rights, 'Secret detentions and illegal transfers of detainees involving Council of Europe member states: second report', Rapporteur: Mr Dick Marty (11 June 2007) (CoE, *Second Report*).

[20] UN, *Study on Secret Detention*, paras 108–11, 120–2; CoE, *Second Report*.

[21] UN, *Study on Secret Detention*, paras 141–58.

rather than an entity.[22] Al-Qaeda has been described as an organized entity with 'central direction, training, and financing',[23] and up until 2001 it appears that it could be identified as an organized group with a clear leadership and even a fixed location, including training camps and headquarters.[24] The US invasion of Afghanistan precipitated the physical dispersal of the group and the transition towards a decentralized network of many groups and individuals operating on the basis of a shared ideology and, in some cases, past training in the Afghan camps.[25] However, there may still be loose connections to the leadership of a 'mother Al-Qaeda (*Al Qaeda al Oum*)',[26] or, as the US has referred to it, 'The Al Qa'ida Associated Movement (AQAM), comprised of al Qa'ida and affiliated extremists', which displays 'decentralizing control in the network and franchising its extremist efforts within the movement'.[27] The Australian government, which at times has been supportive of the US position in the war on terror, sets forth a similar assessment, going so far as to point out that '[f]or many Muslim extremists, Al Qaeda has become more an idea or ideology than a physical entity'.[28]

According to a 2010 Report to the US Senate Foreign Relations Committee:

> Over the past eight years, Al Qaeda has evolved into a significantly different terrorist organization than the one that perpetrated the September 11 attacks. At the time, Al Qaeda was composed mostly of a core of veterans of the Afghan insurgency against the Soviets, with a leadership structure made up mostly of Egyptians and bin Laden, a Saudi of Yemeni descent. Most of the organization's plots either emanated from—or were approved by—the leadership. The Al Qaeda of that period no longer exists. Due to pressures from U.S. and international intelligence and security organizations, it has transformed into a diffuse global network and philosophical movement composed of dispersed nodes with varying degrees of independence. [...] The Al Qaeda network today also is made up of semi-autonomous cells which often have only peripheral ties to either the leadership in Pakistan or affiliated groups elsewhere. Sometimes these individuals never leave their home country but are radicalized with the assistance of others who have travelled abroad for training and indoctrination.[29]

---

[22] 'US National Military Strategic Plan for the War on Terrorism', Chairman of the Joint Chiefs of Staff, Washington, DC 20318 (1 February 2006) 13 (US National Military Strategic Plan); 'Transnational Terrorism: The Threat to Australia', Publication of the Government of Australia (2004) 31, available at: www.dfat.gov.au/publications/terrorism(*The Threat to Australia*). For a detailed study of Al-Qaeda in the past, see J. Burke, *Al-Qaeda: Casting a Shadow of Terror* (2003); for a recent study see J. Rollins, 'Al Qaeda and Affiliates: Historical Perspective, Global Presence, and Implications for U.S. Policy', Congressional Research Service Report (5 February 2010) (Rollins, *Al Qaeda and Affiliates*).

[23] Remarks by Alberto Gonzales, 3; see also D. Jinks, 'September 11 and the Laws of War' (2003) 28 *Yale Journal of International Law* 1, 38.

[24] M. Mohamedou, 'Non-Linearity of Engagement: Transnational Armed Groups, International Law, and the Conflict between Al Qaeda and the United States'. Program on Humanitarian Policy and Conflict Research, Harvard University (July 2005) 13 (Mohamedou, *Non-Linearity of Engagement*).

[25] It is said that the number of people trained in the camps ranges between 10–20,000. Ibid.

[26] Ibid, 14.

[27] US National Military Strategic Plan, 13.

[28] *The Threat to Australia*, 31.

[29] US Senate Foreign Relations Committee, 'Al Qaeda in Yemen and Somalia: A Ticking Time Bomb: Report to the Senate Committee on Foreign Relations', S. Rep. No. 111, 111th Congress, 2nd Session (21 January 2010) 5 (SFRC, *A Ticking Time Bomb*).

At best, it appears that if Al-Qaeda is to be described as a distinct entity, perhaps the most appropriate depiction that has been offered is of a structure that is 'murky' with a loosely organized but highly focused network.[30] Indeed, even the Director of the FBI spoke of a three-tiered threat, with the core Al-Qaeda organization as the first tier, a second tier of 'small groups who have some ties to an established terrorist organization, but are largely self-directed. Think of them as Al Qaeda franchises—hybrids of homegrown radicals and more sophisticated operatives', and a third tier of 'homegrown extremists. They are self-radicalizing, self-financing, and self-executing. They meet up on the Internet instead of in foreign training camps. They have no formal affiliation with al Qaeda, but they are inspired by its message of violence'.[31] Regional groups operating under the Al-Qaeda name operate in a number of places, including 'Al Qaeda in the Arabian Peninsula' (AQAP, who are a merger of the Saudi and Yemeni Al-Qaeda groups),[32] Al-Qaeda in the Islamic Maghreb,[33] and Al-Qaeda in Iraq (sometimes referred to as Al Qaeda in Mesopotamia).[34]

Members of Al-Qaeda, together with members of other militant groups and parties to more than one conflict, appear to be moving and regrouping in different formats. As noted in the Foreign Relations Committee Report:

> The U.S. military has largely pushed Al Qaeda out of Afghanistan and Iraq. While the military efforts should be praised, they have not eliminated the threat. Many fighters affiliated with Al Qaeda and other militant groups have taken refuge across the Afghan border in Pakistan's Federally Administered Tribal Authority, which remains a major safe haven. At the same time, intelligence and counter-terrorism officials said hundreds and perhaps thousands of veterans of the wars in Iraq and Afghanistan have relocated to other places, primarily Yemen and Somalia.[35]

In addition to the difficulty of describing Al-Qaeda as a distinct organization, it is therefore apparent that many of the Al-Qaeda operatives targeted by the US operations may have links or be directly affiliated with other groups. In particular, the strikes in Pakistan are often aimed at a mixture of Al-Qaeda and Taliban militants. In fact, a significant proportion of the targets of these strikes are described as members of Taliban, rather than Al-Qaeda. The differentiation between the groups and individuals runs along numerous lines, from ideological aims to tribal

---

[30] 'Transnationality, War and the Law, A Report on a Roundtable on the Transformation of Warfare, International Law, and the Role of Transnational Armed Groups', Program on Humanitarian Policy and Conflict Research, Harvard University (April 2006) 9 (Transnationality Roundtable).

[31] R. Mueller, Director, Federal Bureau of Investigation, 'From 9/11 to 7/7: Global Terrorism Today and the Challenges of Tomorrow' Transcript of Chatham House event (7 April 2008), available at: <www.chathamhouse.org/events/view/154891>. See also Rollins, *Al Qaeda and Affiliates*: 'Al Qaeda network today also comprises semi-autonomous or self radicalized actors, who often have only peripheral or ephemeral ties to either the core cadre in Pakistan or affiliated groups elsewhere.'

[32] SFRC, *A Ticking Time Bomb*, 9.

[33] Rollins, *Al Qaeda and Affiliates*, 14–18; 'Profile: Al-Qaeda in North Africa' *BBC News* (3 June 2009).

[34] Rollins, *Al Qaeda and Affiliates*, 13–14; E. Schmitt, 'Iraqi Qaeda Group Shifts to Remain a Threat' *New York Times* (20 December 2009).

[35] SFRC, *A Ticking Time Bomb*, 2.

affiliations. Indeed, under the heading 'Taliban' there are a number of different groups operating in both Afghanistan and Pakistan. There are additional groups and networks, such as the Haqqani network, who are described as being affiliated with both Taliban and Al-Qaeda.[36] Groups based in Pakistan have been engaged in fighting against the Pakistani government, as well as against NATO forces in Afghanistan. The government of Pakistan is said to view some of them as a threat, while others are 'good Taliban' who do not carry out their attacks inside Pakistan.[37] Al-Qaeda operatives appear to be embedded within Taliban strongholds in Pakistan. Moreover, the identity of the group does not necessarily clarify their scope of operations—Pakistani Taliban do not restrict their operations to Pakistan, but also cross into Afghanistan and have been accused of being behind the attempted bombing in New York's Times Square in May 2010.[38] Attempts to neatly categorize the militant groups are further compounded by the presence of militants belonging to groups active in additional countries. For example, it appears that one of the targets of a strike in Pakistan was the head of the Islamic Movement of Uzbekistan.[39] Pakistan has developed into a major recruiting ground and operational base for widespread militant activity, and it has been estimated that '[i]n just over half of the serious plots against the West since 2004, alleged militants received training at camps in Pakistan'.[40] Based on the above, it is clear that Al-Qaeda plays an important role in this setting, but the precise nature and involvement is hard to determine. The connections between the groups and their activities revolve around various factors, ranging from tribal affiliations to shifting political alignments amongst factions within Al-Qaeda and the Taliban. A study into the relationship between Al-Qaeda and the Taliban, notes that '[t]here is no single way to characterize the al-Qaeda-Taliban relationship after 2001, because neither al-Qaeda nor the Taliban is a homogeneous and centrally controlled organization. Rather, they consist of networks of like-minded groups and individuals that answer, to some degree or other, to a centralized leadership, but at the same time have autonomy to act on their own'.[41]

Other areas of operations in the war against Al-Qaeda raise similar questions about the nature and identities of the parties involved. Thus, in Somalia there appear to be ties between Al-Qaeda and one of the local Islamist insurgent groups engaged in the Somali conflict.[42] Connections exist not only with the fighting in

---

[36] B. Woodward, *Obama's Wars* (2010) 11 (Woodward, *Obama's Wars*); 'Pakistan Fight Stalls for U.S.' *The Wall Street Journal* (13 August 2010).

[37] B. Roggio, 'US airstrikes targets Haqqani Network, kill 17 in North Waziristan' *The Long War Journal* (23 August 2010).

[38] Woodward, *Obama's Wars,* 361–3; 'Holder Backs a Miranda Limit for Terror Suspects' *New York Times* (9 May 2010).

[39] 'Uzbek rebel "killed" in Pakistan' *BBC News* (2 October 2009).

[40] The New America Foundation, 'The Battle for Pakistan: Militancy and Conflict in Pakistan's Tribal Regions', available at: <http://counterterrorism.newamerica.net/the_battle_for_pakistan>.

[41] A. Stenersen, 'Al-Qaeda's Allies: Explaining the Relationship Between Al-Qaeda and Taliban Factions After 2001', Policy Paper by The New America Foundation (April 2010), available at: <http://counterterrorism.newamerica.net/publications/policy/al_qaeda_s_allies>.

[42] Rollins, *Al Qaeda and Associates,* 19–22; 'Somali Islamists al-Shabab "join al-Qaeda fight"' *BBC News* (1 February 2010); 'U.S. Kills Top Qaeda Militant in Southern Somalia' *New York Times* (14 September 2009).

Afghanistan, but also to Iraq. The operation against Al-Qaeda operatives in Syria targeted an 'al Qaeda-linked head of a Syrian network that smuggled fighters, weapons and cash into Iraq', and was said to be aimed at preventing the flow of Al-Qaeda fighters through Syria into Iraq.[43]

In light of the above, and unlike many other conflict situations, the case of Al-Qaeda presents a unique challenge of identifying who, in fact, are the parties to the conflict. This amorphous identity of the groups and their individual affiliation will be of direct relevance to the classification analysis and returned to in later sections.

3. Views of the parties and of others on conflict classification

The complexities and lack of clear answers in the factual background to this situation are reflected in the views of States and others as to the classification. Not only is it virtually impossible to find an agreement on the classification, it is in fact difficult to find any coherent opinion on the matter by States, whether or not they are directly involved.

3.1. The United States

The primary findings are a collection of statements made by various officials and in policy papers, all of which differ in time and by speaker. In the early years following September 2001, there were numerous statements asserting that the US was engaged in war with Al-Qaeda, and on occasion with a wider group of terrorists. Examples include:

> The nation is at war with terrorist organizations that pose a threat to its security and that of other societies that cherish the principle of self-government[44]
> The United States has been at war with al Qaeda.[45]
> The enemy includes al-Qaeda and other international terrorists around the world, and those who support such terrorists [...] and certainly terrorists who can strike not only within the United States but who can threaten our forces abroad and our friends and allies.[46]

The US administration under President Obama is reported to have sought to distance itself from the previous administration's rhetoric of a 'war on terror' and some of the more controversial policies that accompanied it.[47] The 2010 National

---

[43] *Syria Halts Diplomacy*; see also 'U.S. says raid in Syria targeted smuggler' *Reuters* (27 October 2008).
[44] US National Military Strategic Plan.
[45] Remarks by Alberto Gonzales, 3.
[46] Excerpts from interview with Charles Allen, Deputy General Counsel for International Affairs, US Department of Defense, By Anthony Dworkin (16 December 2002), on file with the author.
[47] 'Under Obama, "War on Terror" Phrase Fading' *Associated Press* (1 February 2009); 'Obama Administration Says Goodbye to "War On Terror": US Defence Department Seems to Confirm use of the Bureaucratic Phrase "Overseas Contingency Operations"' *The Guardian* (25 March 2009).

Security Strategy uses terms such as 'global campaign', but does not do away with the rhetoric of war. Rather, the change is in the attempt to better define the enemy: '[T]his is not a global war against a tactic—terrorism or a religion—Islam. We are at war with a specific network, al-Qa'ida, and its terrorist affiliates who support efforts to attack the United States, our allies, and partners.'[48]

The notion of being at war with Al-Qaeda has therefore been retained by the US.[49] The question of precise classification is, perhaps deliberately, most often avoided. Notwithstanding, there have been references to it in certain statements and cases which may shed light on the matter.

In a speech given at the Annual Meeting of the American Society of International Law, the Legal Adviser of the US Department of State took the unequivocal view that 'the United States is in an armed conflict with al Qaeda'. Although in his presentation of the legal framework there was no clear statement of classification, reference was made to reliance on Common Article 3 of the Geneva Conventions, and Additional Protocol II, whose subject matter is non-international armed conflicts. Furthermore, the current conflict was differentiated from 'traditional *international* conflicts'.[50] It should, however, be noted that this speech covered a number of situations together: the US operations with consent of the Afghan government, ISAF forces in Afghanistan and the wider conflict with Al-Qaeda. It is therefore left open whether the inference on classification was intended to cover all situations or just some of them. The clearest evidence of thought being given to the issue of classification arose in the context of the *Hamdan* case before the US Supreme Court. Although the individual was captured in Afghanistan, the Court's reasoning is relevant to all operations against members of Al-Qaeda. The government was resistant to a categorization as international armed conflict, in particular owing to the ramifications this might have on entitling individuals to status of prisoner of war. Simultaneously, the idea of a non-international conflict was portrayed as meeting the obstacle of not being an internal situation. In the context of applying Common Article 3 of the Geneva Conventions, the Court accepted that the conflict could potentially be classified as non-international armed conflict.[51] The US government appears to have since accepted this classification of non-international as applying to its self-declared war against Al-Qaeda.[52] The debate over the possibility of extraterritorial non-international armed conflict will be returned to in the next section.

---

[48] US National Security Strategy, 20.

[49] See also 'The United States is currently at war with Al Qaeda and its associated forces' in HRC, 'National report submitted in accordance with paragraph 15 (a) of the annex to Human Rights Council resolution 5/1—United States of America' (Universal Periodic Review), UN Doc. A/HRC/WG.6/9/USA/1 (23 August 2010) para 82 (US Periodic Review Report).

[50] H. Koh, 'The Obama Administration and International Law' Remarks at the Annual Meeting of the American Society of International Law, Washington, DC (25 March 2010).

[51] *Hamdan v Rumsfeld*, 548 U.S. 557, 126 S.Ct. 2749 (29 June 2006) 65–9 (*Hamdan*).

[52] US Periodic Review Report, para 84.

3.2. Al-Qaeda and territorial States

Al-Qaeda itself does not engage in legal classifications of armed conflict, although it has in the past adopted the war rhetoric in the form of a Fatwa declaring war.[53] As for the governments in whose territory the US operations against Al-Qaeda have taken place, their views have largely been concerned with the issues relating to the resort to force within their territories, rather than its classification. In Pakistan, the debate has been whether or not Pakistan and the US are acting in cooperation, based on a contradicting mixture of public statements and back-room dealings.[54] The strikes in Yemen appear to have been approved by the country's leaders,[55] while the chaos that is Somalia renders questions of approval a matter of legal theory. There may also be internal situations within these countries that are to be classified as non-international armed conflicts regardless of US involvement, and which may, as will be seen in the later analysis, affect the classification of US operations.

3.3. Other States and entities

The views of other States cannot be readily discerned since they do not usually differentiate between a war against Al-Qaeda, and the wider context which includes Afghanistan and often Iraq. In debates at the Security Council, the most common approach is a general call for adherence to international law, including human rights law and humanitarian law. This does little to clarify the existence of an armed conflict situation, let alone its classification. Of the UN human rights bodies, the Special Rapporteur on extrajudicial, summary or arbitrary executions has noted the difficulty of claiming the existence of a conflict with Al-Qaeda outside Afghanistan and Iraq.[56]

4. Author's analysis of the classification (or existence) of the conflict

There are five possible outcomes to the classification analysis in this case:

1) This is an international armed conflict between the US and Al-Qaeda.
2) This is a non-international armed conflict between the US and Al-Qaeda.

[53] Declaration of War against the Americans Occupying the Land of the Two Holy Places: A Message from Osama Ben Mohammad Ben Laden (August 1996), translation available at: <www.pbs.org/newshour/terrorism/international/fatwa_1996.html>.
[54] Woodward, *Obama's Wars*, 26, 52, 117, 286, 367; 'A Quiet Deal With Pakistan' *The Washington Post* (4 November 2008); B. Ghosh and M. Thompson, 'The CIA's Silent War in Pakistan' *Time* (1 June 2009).
[55] *Secret Assault on Terrorism*.
[56] HRC, 'Report of the Special Rapporteur on extrajudicial, summary or arbitrary executions, Philip Alston' UN Doc. A/HRC/14/24/Add.6 (28 May 2010) para 53.

3) This is not a separate armed conflict, but is part of other existing conflicts such as the one in Afghanistan.

4) This is an armed conflict between the US and Al-Qaeda that requires a new classification since it is neither international nor non-international.

5) This is not an armed conflict at all, and none of the discussed operations should be classified as such.

4.1. International armed conflict

The short answer to this proposition would be that international armed conflict must be between two (or more) States, and since Al-Qaeda is not a State, we do not have an international armed conflict. This conclusion is based on the fact that according to article 2 of the Hague Regulations[57] and article 2 common to the 1949 Geneva Conventions, the conventions apply to armed conflicts between contracting parties.[58] Since Al-Qaeda, as a non-state actor, cannot be a contracting party to these treaties,[59] it follows that these treaty rules will not apply to armed conflicts between it and the US.[60] As for customary international law, it tends to focus on the substantive elements of international humanitarian law rather than conditions for applicability. Furthermore, the content of the rules for international armed conflict are obviously predicated on inter-state conflicts, as is clear from the detailed rules on prisoners of war, and in the rules of the Fourth Geneva Convention on civilians which rely heavily on the notions of countries operating in sovereign territories (or occupying each other's territory).[61] Applying the rules of international conflicts would place, in most cases, impossible burdens on the non-state actor to comply with a myriad of detailed provisions such as those of the Third Geneva Convention.

Two caveats require mention. First, there is the possibility that Al-Qaeda might be considered as part of State forces. The clearest potential for this interpretation would be in the first stages of the war in Afghanistan, when the Taliban was the de facto government, and Al-Qaeda and Taliban were fighting alongside each other.[62]

---

[57] Regulations Annexed to the Hague Convention (IV) Respecting the Laws and Customs of War on Land, 1907.

[58] Unlike the Geneva Conventions, the 1907 Hague treaties only apply if all the parties to the conflict are parties to the treaties. The Hague Regulations are recognized as reflecting customary international law.

[59] Though they can declare an intent to abide by treaties, or enter into specific agreements with states on adherence to rules of international humanitarian law, see discussion of the possibilities in M. Sassoli, 'Transnational Armed Groups and International Humanitarian Law', Program on Humanitarian Policy and Conflict Research, Harvard University, Occasional Paper Series, No. 6 (Winter 2006) 28–30 (Sassoli, *Transnational Armed Groups*).

[60] With the exception of Common Article 3 to the Geneva Conventions, which will be dealt with in the next section.

[61] S. Murphy, 'Evolving Geneva Convention Paradigms in the "War on Terrorism": Applying the Core Rules to the Release of Persons Deemed "Unprivileged Combatants"' The George Washington University Law School Public Law and Legal Theory Working Paper No. 239 (2007) 8 (Murphy, *Evolving Paradigms*).

[62] See discussion of that conflict in ch. 8 on Afghanistan above.

This is largely a factual question as to the nature of their relationship, and is of relevance to chapter 8 on Afghanistan. Outside of Afghanistan, there does not appear to be evidence that would support an assessment of Al-Qaeda as State forces. The second issue concerns the possibility of an international armed conflict being triggered by virtue of military operations by one State taking place in the territory of another State, for example the US in Pakistan.[63] This goes to the question of whether there might be an international armed conflict between the US and Pakistan (or Yemen or Somalia), but does not necessarily transform the conflict with Al-Qaeda into an international one—two conflicts can exist alongside each other. This matter will be returned to later.

Lastly, a separate matter arises in the context of the *ius ad bellum*. The fact that these operations take place against a non-state actor located on the territory of another State gives rise to legal issues of the *ius ad bellum* and how the relevance of the laws on the resort to force might affect the classification. Issues beyond classification and therefore not dealt with under the current scope include questions such as responsibility for harbouring alleged terrorist groups; attribution of group acts to a State; and the right to self-defence against non-state actors.[64] Much of the debate over classification will rest upon the question of consent by the territorial State. If the latter consents to the operation, then the focus turns to classifying the existing situation within the State. If, however, the territorial State does not consent, there arises the question of whether the use of force on its territory is a violation of the *ius ad bellum* which, in turn, might lead to the finding of an international armed conflict. There are two reasons that such an automatic conclusion is not supported in this chapter. First, the separation between the *ius ad bellum* and the *ius in bello* lies at the heart of the need to remember that we are faced with two separate questions: 1) whether the resort to force on the territory of another State violated the *ius ad bellum*; and 2) how to classify the hostilities taking place in this territory under the *ius in bello*. These are separate matters and must not be confused. The lack of consent may or may not lead to the determination that the rules on resort to force have been violated; much of this will rest on issues such as a possible right to self-defence against non-state actors and whether a particular case meets the legal requirements mandated by such a right.[65] The question of classification rests not on this, but on a factual determination of hostilities, and if these are between the foreign State and the non-state actor, with both the foreign State and territorial State not engaging in fighting between them and not claiming to be at war with each other, then there may be little support for the argument that there is

---

[63] See discussion of the possibility in ch. 3, section 9 and in ch. 12 on Lebanon above.

[64] See arts 4–11 of International Law Commission's Draft Articles on Responsibility of States for Internationally Wrongful Acts (2001), and the commentaries thereto, 80–122; *Military and Paramilitary Activities in and against Nicaragua (Nicaragua v United States of America)* ICJ Rep 1986, 14, paras 93–116; *Prosecutor v Tadić*, IT-94-1-A, Judgment (Appeals Chamber), 15 July 1999, paras 146–62; *Case Concerning Application of the Convention on the Prevention and Punishment of the Crime of Genocide (Bosnia and Herzegovina v Serbia and Montenegro)* ICJ Rep 2007, 43, paras 379–415; SC res. 1373 (2001); for detailed analysis of self-defence against non-state actors see Lubell, *Extraterritorial Use of Force*.

[65] Ibid.

an international armed conflict. Although some may argue that 'any use of force by a State on the territory of another without the consent of the latter brings into effect an international armed conflict between the two States',[66] it is submitted that such a position unnecessarily mixes the *ius ad bellum* and the *ius in bello* and can lead to problematic results. The underlying question for classification must be that of identifying the parties to the conflict, rather than consent. For example, when US forces apparently crossed the border into Syria and killed members of the Al-Qaeda in Iraq group,[67] this was not claimed to be an armed conflict between the US and Syria, despite the lack of Syrian consent and a possible violation of the *ius ad bellum*. Moreover, if one were to accept the view that violations of the prohibition on the use of force in article 2(4) of the UN Charter necessarily trigger an international armed conflict between the two States involved, it should be recalled that such violations are not limited to large-scale military operations. Indeed, Israel's abduction of Eichmann was an illegal use of force on Argentinian territory. Surely nobody would argue that Israel and Argentina were then engaged in an international armed conflict? The determination and classification of an armed conflict must remain separate from possible violations of the *ius ad bellum*.

Nonetheless, the view may exist that extraterritorial operations against non-state actors in certain circumstances do trigger an international armed conflict, especially if consisting of large-scale attacks that damage national infrastructure and cause widespread harm. If that is the case, this would still not necessarily affect the classification of the conflict we are examining; it could bring about an international armed conflict between the two States, but this would take place alongside the separate non-international armed conflict with the non-state actor. This picture could of course change if the non-state actor became aligned with a State.[68]

The second reason the classification of the conflict currently examined is unlikely to be affected, is that apparently, at least in the case of Pakistan, some form of consent does exist. Public displays of dissatisfaction are likely to be the result of domestic politics, and cannot hide the fact that there appears to be cooperation at the highest level. On balance, politicians' statements cannot overcome the factual reality of Pakistani approval for drones to take off from within Pakistan and involvement of Pakistani intelligence officers in the choice of targets.[69] There have also been reports of a 'fusion cell' in a jointly operated command centre across the Afghan border, and possible Pakistani involvement in operational matters such

---

[66] See discussion in ch. 3, section 9 above. The same chapter also recognizes that this appears to be a minority opinion at least in this volume if not also in the literature.

[67] *Syria Halts Diplomacy*.

[68] A similar discussion may be had in the context of the 2006 conflict between Israel and Hezbollah in Lebanon. As long as Hezbollah was not a State agent and could be said to be a non-state actor, it is submitted that the conflict between it and Israel should be classified as non-international. It might be argued that there was an international armed conflict between Israel and Lebanon on account of some of the targets chosen by Israel, or occupation of Lebanese land in the final days of the conflict, but this would be separate to the non-international conflict between the State of Israel and the non-state actor Hezbollah. See debate over the classification of this conflict in ch. 12 on Lebanon.

[69] Woodward, *Obama's Wars*; 'The drones of war' (2009) 15(4) *Strategic Comments* 1–2; 'Secrecy and denial as Pakistan lets CIA use airbase to strike militants' *The Times* (17 February 2009).

as routes and targets,[70] although the amount of information and control given to Pakistan may be limited to video feeds and communications intercepts.[71]

4.2. Non-international armed conflict

The possibility of the US and Al-Qaeda being engaged in a non-international armed conflict must be addressed in two stages. The first is whether this is conceptually possible, as a matter of legal classification. If the answer to this question is positive, the second question is whether the facts of the case match the required criteria. At first glance there may appear to be two instinctive and contradictory responses to the initial question. On the one hand, seeing as the conflict involves a State fighting a non-state actor, it would seem that classification as a non-international armed conflict is the most obvious route. On the other hand, since the operations by the US are taking place in the territory of other States, there might also be an inclination to classify the situation as international. The possibility of non-international armed conflicts including extraterritorial situations is not a new idea, for example when one State sends forces into another State to assist, by request, in the conflict against a rebel group, or spill-over conflicts.[72] While a detailed theoretical analysis of extraterritorial non-international armed conflict is not possible here,[73] the following points serve to show that the non-international armed conflict model can be both applicable and suitable to cases such as the one at hand.

The notion that extraterritorial hostilities between a State and a non-state actor can be regulated by the rules of non-international armed conflict finds support in the views of numerous commentators.[74] The essence of this claim rests primarily on viewing the category of non-international armed conflict as *non-international*, i.e. a conflict that is not between States, whether or not it is purely *internal*. As noted earlier, this approach is supported by the fact that the substantive differentiation between the rules of international armed conflict and non-international armed conflict is linked to the nature of the parties engaged in the fighting. Non-state actors would be unable to comply with many of the international armed conflict provisions, and States would be unwilling to grant non-state actors immunities from prosecution granted to prisoners of war in conflicts of this type. The rules of non-international armed conflict are precisely designed for conflicts in which one of the parties is a non-state actor.

---

[70] J. Barnes and G. Miller, 'Pakistan Gets a Say in Drone Attacks on Militants' *Los Angeles Times* (13 May 2009).

[71] E. Schmitt and M. Mazzetti, 'In a First, U.S. Provides Pakistan With Drone Data' *The New York Times* (13 May 2009).

[72] See discussion in ch. 4, section 2 on applicable law.

[73] For further analysis see Lubell, *Extraterritorial Use of Force*.

[74] Sassoli, *Transnational Armed Groups*, 8–9; Murphy, *Evolving Paradigms*, 14–32; D. Jinks, 'The Applicability of the Geneva Conventions to the "Global War on Terrorism"' (2005) 46 *Virginia Journal of International Law* 165, 189; Human Rights First, 'Memorandum to the Human Rights Committee' (18 January 2006) 3 fn 7.

As for the textual interpretation of the treaties, Additional Protocol II would not apply extraterritorially, as it requires that the non-state actor control territory of the State it is fighting.[75] Common Article 3 requires that the conflict be taking place 'in the territory of one of the High Contracting Parties'. However, this provision does not mention that it need be the territorial State which is engaged in the fighting. Insofar as the Geneva Conventions have achieved global recognition with 194 States parties,[76] virtually any territory would be that of a High Contracting Party.[77] Indeed, it is not altogether preposterous to advance an interpretation of this type, and it appears to nest comfortably with the original intention of Common Article 3, as explained by Sassoli:

> Does this imply that conflicts between a High Contracting Party and an armed group, which do not occur on the territory of that High Contracting Party, but on the territory of another State, are not non-international armed conflicts? Or, does it simply recall that according to the principle of the relative force of treaties, those treaty rules apply only on the territories of States that have accepted them? From the perspective of the aim and purpose of IHL, the latter interpretation must be correct, as there would otherwise be a gap in protection, which could not be explained by States' concerns about their sovereignty.[78]

Indeed, although most of the Common Article 3 situations might be internal, the provision uses the term 'non-international' rather than internal and, as supported by the commentaries, 'the Article should be applied as widely as possible'.[79] The question of whether the role played by the territorial State may or may not affect classification will be dealt with in a separate section later in this chapter.

The position taken here is that regardless of the extraterritorial element, the fighting between the US and Al-Qaeda could potentially be classified as non-international armed conflict. This may solve the conceptual possibility, but transforming potential applicability into an agreement on classification will necessitate further examinations of the actual facts at hand, in light of the required criteria for non-international armed conflicts.

---

[75] Moreover, the US has not ratified this Protocol.

[76] See ICRC database at: <www.cicr.org/ihl.nsf/Pays?ReadForm>; see also view of the ICRC that '[a]s the four Geneva Conventions have universally been ratified now, the requirement that the armed conflict must occur "in the territory of one of the High Contracting Parties" has lost its importance in practice. Indeed, any armed conflict between governmental armed forces and armed groups or between such groups cannot but take place on the territory of one of the Parties to the Convention'. ICRC, 'How is the Term "Armed Conflict" Defined in International Humanitarian Law?' Opinion Paper (March 2008).

[77] Exceptions might be conflicts taking place on the high seas, or in a new State which did not become party to the Conventions.

[78] M. Sassoli, 'Use and Abuse of the Laws of War in the "War on Terrorism"' (2004) 22 *Law and Inequality: A Journal of Theory and Practice* 200–1.

[79] J. Pictet (ed.), *Geneva Convention for the Amelioration or the Condition of the Wounded and Sick in Armed Forces in the Field: commentary* (1952) 50; See also ibid, 43: 'In the end the draft text submitted by the International Committee of the Red Cross was approved with the exception of the words "especially cases of civil war, colonial conflicts, or wars of religion" which were omitted. The omission of these words, far from weakening the text, enlarged its scope.'

The existence of a non-international armed conflict rests primarily on two elements: identifying the existence of organized parties to the conflict, and moving beyond a certain intensity of violence.[80]

An obstacle to classification as a non-international armed conflict arises from the need to determine the nature of Al-Qaeda as an organized armed group capable of being a party to the conflict. As noted earlier, there are serious concerns about describing Al-Qaeda as a distinct and organized armed group, rather than a network of loosely affiliated groups sometimes reduced to little more than similar ideologies. The bomb attacks on public transport in Madrid in 2004[81] and London in 2005[82] underscore the difficulty in connecting the dots to reveal any clear image of a single group behind all the attacks. In these and other cases, although the perpetrators appear to have been inspired by and share the Al-Qaeda ideology, questions were raised over the existence of sufficient concrete evidence to attribute directly the attacks to the same Al-Qaeda group responsible for the September 2001 attacks.[83] Moreover, an attack on Spanish soil is not an armed conflict involving the US, unless, arguably, the target was associated with the US (e.g. an embassy) or if the Spanish government considered itself at war with the perpetrators and asked the US to assist. Should additional groups engage in hostilities with the US at an intensity to qualify as armed conflict, then such a conflict might be said to exist with them as parties, possibly even a few separate conflicts, but unless these hostilities are actually taking place, one cannot speak of them as being a party to the conflict. There is therefore great difficulty in credibly claiming that all incidents are part of a single armed conflict with Al-Qaeda, unless being inspired by the same ideology would suffice.

Excluding the conflict in Afghanistan, there is also genuine reason to question whether the intensity of violence between the US and Al-Qaeda crosses the required threshold. There is the view that: 'Since 11th September 2001, there have been further brutal terrorist attacks in Bali (twice), Madrid, London, and Jordan. It is quite clear that the conflict with al Qaeda is not an internal disturbance, nor is it isolated or sporadic.'[84]

To others, however, six or so attacks in the same number of years is precisely what might be termed as 'sporadic'.[85] A further, and significant, query that arises in relation to the aforementioned incidents is whether they can all in fact be attributed to a single organization. This problem was evident in the earlier examination, and it should be noted that if the said violence cannot in fact be attributed to Al-Qaeda, it

---

[80] See further the discussion in ch. 3, section 6.1 above.

[81] 'Scores die in Madrid bomb carnage' *BBC News* (11 March 2004).

[82] 'In depth—London attacks' *BBC News* (8 July 2008).

[83] J. Bennetto and I. Herbert, 'London bombings: the truth emerges' *The Independent* (13 August 2005); P. Hamilos, 'The worst Islamist attack in European history' *The Guardian* (31 October 2007); see also Sassoli, *Transnational Armed Groups,* 9–11; J. Pejic, 'Terrorist Acts and Groups: a Role for International Law?' (2004) 75 *British Year Book of International Law* 86–7.

[84] J. Dalton, 'What is War?: Terrorism as War after 9/11' (2006) 12 *ILSA Journal of International and Comparative Law* 527–8.

[85] M.E. O'Connell, 'When Is a War Not a War? The Myth of the Global War on Terror' (2006) 12 *ILSA Journal of International and Comparative Law* 538.

raises serious questions over whether these incidents can be construed as evidence of an existing high level of violence between the group and the US. Adding the more recent operations by the US in Pakistan would raise the death toll by a thousand or more, which may lend credibility to the argument that the threshold for non-international armed conflict has been crossed.[86]

The threshold of violence and the identity of the party to the conflict are linked: if numerous incidents round the world classified as terrorism could be attributed to the same entity then one could argue that the threshold for conflict has been crossed; if however these incidents are perpetrated by separate groups with no unified and organized command and control structure, it becomes difficult to add them all up together as evidence of an existing conflict. This reasoning applies not only to the London and Madrid incidents, but also to the operations by the US in Pakistan, Syria, Somalia and Yemen. There would need to be a connection between the militant groups that fulfils the organizational requirements, such as a unified command and control structure and hierarchy. Even within Pakistan there appears to be a lack of clarity as to whether the targets of the strike can all be said to belong to one organized group, and based on the existing reports it appears that the drone strikes are targeting a number of different militant groups.[87]

From the above, it appears that while there is no conceptual obstacle to classifying the US fight against Al-Qaeda as a non-international armed conflict, it is highly questionable whether the facts merit this classification, although this will remain a question of further factual evidence and differing interpretations of the threshold.

4.3. Part of pre-existing armed conflict

Notwithstanding the above difficulties in claiming a stand-alone global war against Al-Qaeda outside Afghanistan, that would not be the only way in which some of these operations might be part of an armed conflict. There remains the possibility that some of the military operations conducted by the US might be considered part of an already existing armed conflict. Focusing on the operations in Pakistan, there are in fact two possibilities for an analysis of this type. The first of these options links some of the strikes by the US in Pakistan to the current conflict in Afghanistan. The essence of the argument is that militants belonging to parties to the conflict in Afghanistan (be they Taliban or Al-Qaeda) are also operating from across the border in Pakistan. It must be stressed that this requires not just that individuals may have had a link with the forces in Afghanistan or have participated in the Afghan conflict in the past and have now disengaged, but that they are actively continuing to engage in hostilities from Pakistan. Accordingly, it could be argued that US operations against these militants is a 'spill-over' from the Afghan conflict, and part of the ongoing non-international armed conflict in Afghanistan. From the earlier background discussion it is, however, apparent that not all of the militants operating in Pakistan can be tied in to the parties fighting in Afghanistan.

---

[86] See discussion in next section on the relation to the conflict in Pakistan.
[87] NAF, *The Year of Drone.*

A second possibility must be also examined, that of a non-international armed conflict within Pakistan itself. The scale of hostilities—including air, artillery and ground operations of 30,000 troops in South Waziristan—clearly indicates the existence of a non-international armed conflict in Pakistan between the government of Pakistan and militant groups.[88] Some of the targets of US operations appear to have been members of armed groups opposing the Pakistani government. In fact, it appears that strikes against certain targets are requested by the Pakistani government.[89] The question then arises whether the US might be operating against these militants in assistance of the Pakistani government as part of the Pakistani armed conflict. The media reports provide a mixed picture of the level of cooperation, pointing to a difference between public condemnation of the attacks which may be necessary for internal political reasons, and the simultaneous approval given behind closed doors.[90] Notwithstanding, there appears to be a growing level of cooperation between the governments in the coordination of operations.[91] It could, therefore, be argued that when the US is targeting Pakistani militants as part of a joint operation with the Pakistani government, such operations could come within the scope of the non-international armed conflict between Pakistan and these groups. Lastly, it should be stressed that the dividing line between the two conflicts is blurred, and there are many crossovers. Pakistani Taliban leader Baitullah Mehsud, for example, was a desirable target for both the Pakistani government, and for the US on account of his alleged responsibility for deadly attacks in Pakistan (including the bombing of the Marriot Hotel and the assassination of Benazir Bhutto), and for involvement in attacks against US forces in Afghanistan.[92]

The above two possibilities would not necessarily cover all the US strikes in Pakistan, and would exclude circumstances in which the targeted militants were neither directly involved in the Afghan conflict, nor being targeted in accordance with Pakistani interests. Moreover, this analysis would not automatically include other operations against Al-Qaeda in other geographical locations. A similar reasoning may, arguably, apply in the cases of Al-Qaeda in Iraq and possibly in Yemen,[93] but is unlikely to cover strikes in Somalia—assuming the Somali militants are not participating in the Afghan conflict and since the chaos that is Somalia does not leave much room for cooperation by invitation from the government. Moreover, while there appears to be some form of cooperation between Al-Qaeda militants and members of Somali groups, whether or not the Somali militants

---

[88] 'Pakistan launches Taliban assault' *BBC News* (17 October 2009).
[89] Woodward, *Obama's Wars*, 117; J. Mayer, 'The Predator War' *The New Yorker* (26 October 2009) (Mayer, *The Predator War*); S. Shane, 'CIA to Expand Use of Drones in Pakistan' *The New York Times* (4 December 2009) (Shane, *Drones in Pakistan*).
[90] Woodward, *Obama's Wars*; D. Ignatius, 'A Quiet Deal With Pakistan' *The Washington Post* (4 November 2008); B. Ghosh and M. Thompson, 'The CIA's Silent War in Pakistan' *Time* (1 June 2009).
[91] See discussion in section 4.1 above on *ius ad bellum*.
[92] Mayer, *The Predator War*.
[93] On cooperation between the US and Yemen, see D. Priest, 'US Military Teams, Intelligence Deeply Involved in Aiding Yemen on Strikes' *The Washington Post* (27 January 2010).

desire to engage in attacks against the US, or are focused purely on internal matters, is a subject for debate.[94]

4.4. New type of conflict

Claims have been made in the past that the US is engaged in a new type of war, one which cannot readily be classified and in which existing rules of international humanitarian law are outdated, to the point of being rendered obsolete and quaint.[95] There have also been suggestions of new methods of classification to better suit current conflicts.[96] These positions are not endorsed in the current chapter, and suggestions of new categories of armed conflict are rejected for two reasons.

First, it is arguable whether in fact we are faced with a new situation. Various elements are mentioned as being new, including: the blurring of the combatant-civilian divide; the means and methods used for attacks; the divergence from traditional State-centred models of conflict; and the multi- and extraterritorial scope.[97] These are, however, not entirely new faces of conflict. Other than the extraterritorial element, most of these are a regular challenge in the context of traditional non-international conflicts, and have been so for decades.[98] As for the geographical dimension, threats from groups operating in multiple territories are not new, as was seen in the attacks on European airports and elsewhere, allegedly attributed to the Abu Nidal group in the 1980s.[99] States acting extraterritorially against non-state actors is also not a new phenomenon, and has occurred in the context of 'spill-over' conflicts, or in assistance of other governments.

Secondly, it is unclear why the existing rules would be unsuitable for regulating these conflicts. A new factual situation does not automatically call for new laws to regulate it; the question that must first be answered is whether existing laws can adequately handle a new situation. The distinction between maintaining that a factual situation is new, to that of calling for new laws to regulate it, is an important one. It might well be appropriate to analyse and examine the novelty of a new set of

---

[94] SFRC, *A Ticking Timebomb*, 15.

[95] Memorandum From Alberto R. Gonzales, Counsel to the President, to President Bush (25 January 2002) in K. Greenberg and J. Dratel, *The Torture Papers: The Road to Abu Ghraib* (2005) 118–21.

[96] R. Schondorf, 'Extra-State Armed Conflicts: Is There a Need for a New Legal Regime?' (2004) 37 *New York University Journal of International Law and Politics* 1 (Schondorf, *Extra-State Armed Conflicts*); G. Corn, 'Hamdan, Lebanon, and the Regulation of Hostilities: the Need to Recognize a Hybrid Category of Armed Conflict' (2007) 40 *Vanderbilt Journal of Transnational Law* 295.

[97] Mohamedou, *Non-Linearity of Engagement*, 2, 5; Schondorf, *Extra-State Armed Conflicts*, 8–9; Transnationality Roundtable, 8.

[98] In fact, even the claims of inadequacy of the law are not new in the context of fighting non-state groups, with situations half a century ago leading to the following remarks by Thompson in a 1966 publication: 'There is a very strong temptation in dealing with both terrorism and with guerrilla actions for government forces to act outside the law, the excuses being that the processes of law are too cumbersome, that the normal safeguards in the law for the individual are not designed for an insurgency and that a terrorist deserves to be treated as an outlaw anyway.' R. Thompson, *Defeating Communist Insurgency: Experiences from Malaysia and Vietnam* (1966) 52.

[99] 'Abu Nidal' in J. Thackrah, *Dictionary of Terrorism* (2004) 1–3.

circumstances, and perhaps even to come up with new theoretical models and names designed to describe this situation.[100] These new names should relate however to differing approaches to describing a *factual* situation, and not automatically become new *legal* categories which would then call for new substantive rules applying to them. The existing legal categories may well be able to withstand and encompass a host of new factual circumstances, without the need for new laws. For example, the concerns of States over granting legitimacy to armed groups through the immunity from prosecution that is given to combatants would be a non-issue if the rules of non-international armed conflict applied, as these do not grant any such status. The rules of non-international armed conflict are precisely designed for conflicts with non-state actors. The greater challenge in the conflict at hand relates to matters of inter-state relationships, and questions of using force in the territory of another State. These are questions of the *ius ad bellum* and separate to the classification of the fighting between the State and the non-state actor.[101]

If it is nevertheless insisted that this is an armed conflict which is not a 'traditional' international or non-international conflict, it is submitted here that any such conflict would ultimately be analogous to non-international conflicts. This is based upon the notion that to prove the existence of a conflict one would need to point to the occurrence of hostilities and identify distinct parties to the conflict, similarly to the minimum requirements for non-international armed conflict. As for the substantive rules for any such conflict with non-state actors, there is growing recognition that a core set of international humanitarian law rules should apply to any armed conflict.[102] These are likely to include the rules considered as customary international law in non-international armed conflict.[103] Finally, should there nonetheless be a claim that this does not fit the mould of non-international armed conflict, this may be because—as was seen in the previous section—it may not be a conflict at all, having failed to pass necessary threshold requirements.

---

[100] See e.g. Schondorf, *Extra-State Armed Conflicts*.

[101] See section 4.1 above on international armed conflict.

[102] The reasoning presented in *Tadić* is equally applicable to any notion of armed conflict: 'Why protect civilians from belligerent violence, or ban rape, torture or the wanton destruction of hospitals, churches, museums or private property, as well as proscribe weapons causing unnecessary suffering when two sovereign States are engaged in war, and yet refrain from enacting the same bans or providing the same protection when armed violence has erupted "only" within the territory of a sovereign State?' *Prosecutor v Tadić*, IT-94-1-T, Decision on the Defence Motion for Interlocutory Appeal on Jurisdiction (Appeals Chamber), 2 October 1995, para 97. The US promotes as policy, even if perhaps not as law, that '[m]embers of the DoD Components comply with the law of war during all armed conflicts, however such conflicts are characterized, and in all other military operations'. DoD Law of War Program, Department of Defense Directive No 2311.01E (9 May 2006) para 4.1. See also J. Rawcliffe and J. Smith (eds), *The US Operational Law Handbook* (2006) 418; C. Garraway. 'The 'War on Terror': Do the Rules Need Changing?' Chatham House Briefing Paper (September 2006) 10; S. Ratner, 'Revising the Geneva Conventions to Regulate Force by and Against Terrorists: Four Fallacies' (2003) 1 *IDF Law Review* 8–9.

[103] For a detailed analysis of all the points in the above section, see Lubell, *Extraterritorial Use of Force*, ch. 5.

4.5. No armed conflict

The fifth option for classification is the determination that there is, in fact, no armed conflict between the US and Al-Qaeda. The position taken here is that, while the concept of extraterritorial non-international armed conflict does exist, the circumstances at hand support the contention that there is no stand-alone armed conflict between the US and all Al-Qaeda manifestations around the globe. Nonetheless, it does appear that some of the military operations against Al-Qaeda can be said to occur as part of existing armed conflicts in Afghanistan, Pakistan and Iraq. A number of questions that have arisen in the above examination of classification will be returned to in the final sections.

5. Rules on application of force

The striking feature of this conflict is that the majority of operations under discussion involve direct recourse to lethal force, often in the form of missiles fired by unmanned aerial drones. In these types of operations there is little room to examine a sliding scale of force or rules of engagement of the kind that would be used by soldiers on the ground. The questions here are of a different nature, and include the matter of how the targets are determined, verified and precautions taken during the strikes. There is scant information on the process used to decide who is targeted in these strikes, but it does appear that the strikes are based upon lists of targets, naming 'high value individuals/targets'. It should also be noted that while the drones themselves are owned by the military, a significant amount of the drone strikes are operated by the CIA. Much of the use of drones by the military occurs in the Afghanistan and Iraq conflicts, while the CIA focus is in areas in which US troops are not stationed. Although a small amount of information about the practice of the air force can be gleaned from public information, there is very little transparency with regard to the CIA operations,[104] and the process by which individuals are placed on the target list has been the subject of a legal case brought before the US courts.[105] Most of the information currently available relies upon media sources who, in turn, often gather their facts from anonymous insider sources.

It seems that the process for adding names to the CIA list includes a two- or three-page memo detailing the activities of the individual and why they should be added to the list. The primary question asked is whether this individual is 'deemed to be a continuing threat to US persons or interests'.[106] The list is approved at a high level within the CIA, and actual strikes may have to go through

---

[104] When asked about the lists, the White House Press Secretary responded that '[t]here's a process in place that I'm not at liberty to discuss'. See Robert Gibbs, Press Briefing (3 August 2010).
[105] *Al-Aulaqi v Obama,* 727 F.Supp.2d 1 (7 December 2010) (*Al-Aulaqi v Obama*).
[106] G. Miller, 'From Memo to Missile' *Los Angeles Times* (31 January 2010) (Miller, *From Memo to Missile*).

the authorization of the CIA Director, who requests details on various aspects of the strike.[107] It is the policy-makers that decide who can be targeted, rather than the operators of the drones. Although it is envisaged that the targets would be leaders,[108] it appears that in practice low-level militants are also targeted.[109] The list is examined every six months, and names of individuals can be removed 'if the intelligence on them has grown stale'.[110]

Prior to carrying out attacks, a 'pattern of life' analysis is undertaken, in which the individual and the area are monitored to determine the activities taking place and whether the surroundings are civilian or primarily a militant area. Identification relies on video, mobile phone interceptions, Pakistani intelligence and tips from locals (which can come from resentful neighbours).[111] On occasion, 'locator chips' are employed, which can be used (with the help of locals) to signal which individuals should be followed and kept under surveillance for suspect militant activity.

When a decision is taken to launch a strike, the circumstances at the time are taken into account in order to calculate whether the attack will remain within the confines of proportionality. The military uses a computer algorithm to calculate proportionality,[112] and lawyers are usually on hand for the air force strikes. The video feed from the drone provides detailed imagery. For example, in the strike that killed Pakistani Taliban leader Baitullah Mehsud, he was clearly identified sitting on his rooftop, hooked to a medical drip (he suffered from a kidney ailment). Others, including his wife, were also seen to be in the vicinity. After already authorizing the strike earlier that day, CIA Director Panetta was contacted again for authorization to go ahead in the knowledge that there would be additional casualties.[113] Mehsud and eleven others were killed, including family and body-guards.[114]

The operation in which Osama bin Laden was killed was a rare deviance from the use of drones in favour of sending ground troops into Pakistan. This may have been due to both a desire to avoid civilian casualties in a central Pakistani area, as well as the wish to gather positive and concrete identification of the target's identity. There has been much controversy over the legality of this operation, sometimes confusing a number of separate legal issues that must be considered independently. Crucially, one must unpack the question into two primary components: 1) whether the use of force on Pakistani soil violated the UN Charter and rules on resort to force in other States; 2) whether the manner in which the operation was conducted and force was employed, was in accordance with the international rules regulating the actual use of force. Additional concerns not dealt

---

[107] '"He asks a lot of questions about the target, the intelligence picture, potential collateral damage, women and children in the vicinity," said the senior intelligence official.' P. Finn and J. Warrick, 'Under Panetta, a More Aggressive CIA' *The Washington Post* (21 March 2010) (Finn, Warrick, *A More Aggressive CIA*).

[108] Miller, *From Memo to Missile.*   [109] Mayer, *The Predator War.*
[110] Miller, *From Memo to Missile.*   [111] Shane, *Drones in Pakistan.*
[112] Mayer, *The Predator War.*   [113] Finn, Warrick, *A More Aggressive CIA.*
[114] Mayer, *The Predator War.*

with here, can be raised on other aspects of the operation such as the disposal of the body, which must also be examined in light of international law.[115]

The first question takes us back to the earlier discussion of the *ius ad bellum*,[116] and rests upon two elements: if there was consent—and, as mentioned earlier, it is difficult to ascertain the truth in the context of public denials combined with back-room agreements—then the resort to force may have been lawful. Without consent, the legality will largely rest on the viability of a legitimate claim to self-defence: whether bin Laden was actively engaged in ongoing armed attacks in such a way as to give rise to self-defence under the UN Charter, and whether there was necessity to exercise this self-defence.[117]

The answer to the second question may depend upon the determination of the correct applicable legal framework. The law of armed conflict can allow the killing of individuals not entitled to civilian protection, while the law-enforcement paradigm demands a more restrictive sliding scale approach to force.[118] The applicability of the international humanitarian law framework to this operation requires the existence of an armed conflict. As noted in the earlier sections, the position taken in this chapter raises serious doubts over the existence of an amorphous global armed conflict between the US and Al-Qaeda. However, if bin Laden was taking a direct part in the specific Afghan conflict, ordering and directing hostilities from his location in Pakistan, this may, arguably, place him in the category of individuals not entitled to civilian protection.[119] Conversely, if bin Laden was not an active participant in an existing armed conflict, the only remaining applicable legal framework governing force in this operation, would be the law-enforcement paradigm, as found in international human rights law. While assessment of legality of the killing may differ in accordance with the legal framework applied—and be affected by the interplay between the two frameworks—both frameworks make room for situations in which killing of an individual might not violate international law, and other situations in which it would be unlawful. Ultimately, for a full and accurate assessment of the operation, the exact details must first come to light; everything from the nature of the order given and on to what exactly transpired in the seconds before he was killed (e.g. did he attempt to surrender), can all affect the legality.[120] Perhaps one day, when the video footage of the operation surreptitiously makes its way onto the internet, we might at last know the details of what occurred, and be able to definitively determine the legality of the operation.

---

[115] See e.g. discussion of the rules regarding return of the deceased or burial, in J. Henckaerts and L. Doswald-Beck, *Customary International Humanitarian Law Vol. 1: Rules* (2005) 411–20.

[116] See section above on international armed conflict.

[117] For analysis of self-defence against non-state actors, see see Lubell, *Extraterritorial Use of Force*, chs 1–3.

[118] See discussion in ch. 4, section 4 above.

[119] See also section 7.2 below on individual status.

[120] More than one version of events has appeared in the media. 'White House Fixes Record, Says Target Wasn't Armed' *The Wall Street Journal* (4 May 2011).

As for rules on use of force used by Al-Qaeda, there is very little deserving of meaningful assessment in light of relevant international law. While there is room for detailed and fruitful comparison of Islamic Law and international humanitarian law,[121] these rules do not appear to have been followed or be manifested in the conduct of Al-Qaeda. Statements have been made supporting the deliberate killing of civilians,[122] and subsequent lip-service to the principle of distinction carries little weight in contrast when it is simply designed to categorize all enemy civilians as non-civilians who may be targeted.[123] This is not so much a set of rules that can be examined, but rather a blank cheque to kill whomever they wish in whatever manner available.

6. Rules on detention

The detainees in the operations against Al-Qaeda can be divided into distinct groups, depending on the purpose of the examination. In the current context of identifying rules for detention it may be useful to divide them as follows: 1) detainees held directly by the US in Guantánamo and other formally recognized detention facilities; 2) detainees held by the US in secret 'black sites', and detainees held by other States allegedly on behalf of the US; 3) detainees held in Afghanistan and Iraq.[124] In general, the rules, practices, and rights afforded to the detainees vary between groups. A full and detailed examination of all the legal issues surrounding the Guantánamo and other detainees cannot be covered in the confines of this single section of a chapter. While a number of significant issues will be briefly pointed out, the focus here is limited to identifying which matters are linked to the classification of conflict, in accordance with the objective of this work.

---

[121] See N. Shah, *Islamic Law and the Law of Armed Conflict: the Armed Conflict in Pakistan* (2011).

[122] 'We do not have to differentiate between military or civilian. As far as we are concerned, they are all targets.' ABC John Miller interview with Osama bin Laden (May 1998), available at: <www.pbs.org/wgbh/pages/frontline/shows/binladen/who/interview.html#video>.

[123] 'Our retaliation is directed primarily against the soldiers only *and against those standing by them.* Our religion forbids us from killing innocent people such as women and children.' (emphasis added), ibid; see also the following: In the video, bin Laden says: 'The Twin Towers were legitimate targets, they were supporting US economic power. These events were great by all measurement. What was destroyed were not only the towers, but the towers of morale in that country.' The hijackers were 'blessed by Allah to destroy America's economic and military landmarks'. He freely admits to being behind the attacks: 'If avenging the killing of our people is terrorism then history should be a witness that we are terrorists. Yes, we kill their innocents and this is legal religiously and logically.' In a contradictory section, however, bin Laden justifies killing the occupants of the Twin Towers because they were not civilians—Islam forbids the killing of innocent civilians even in a holy war. He says: 'The towers were supposed to be filled with supporters of the economical powers of the United States who are abusing the world. Those who talk about civilians should change their stand and reconsider their position. We are treating them like they treated us.' In 'Bin Laden: Yes, I did it' *The Telegraph* (11 November 2001).

[124] The last of these groups are outside the scope of this chapter: see ch. 8 and ch. 11 on Afghanistan and Iraq respectively.

6.1. Guantánamo and formal detention

The precise grounds upon which individuals associated with Al-Qaeda were formally detained has varied over the years, with differing and new definitions and interpretations arising from a long succession of executive orders, internal memorandums, congressional acts and legal cases. In the early days of this conflict, two months after the attacks in September 2001, President Bush issued a military order which contained authorization for detention. The individuals subject to such detention were those defined as being either members of Al-Qaeda, persons engaged (or aided) in acts of terrorism against the US, or who harboured one of the above.[125]

The term 'enemy combatant' later became a central element of this process, and was seen as the status justifying the grounds and continuation of detention. In 2004, The Department of Defense defined enemy combatant as an: 'individual who was part of or supporting Taliban or al Qaeda forces, or associated forces that are engaged in hostilities against the U.S. or its coalition partners. This includes any person who has committed a belligerent act or has directly supported hostilities in aid of enemy armed forces.'[126] The term was again defined—with some alterations which included differentiating between lawful and unlawful enemy combatants—in the Military Commissions Act of 2006.[127] Later amendments and memorandums moved away from reliance on the term enemy combatant, together with a policy decision to refrain from using the phrase.[128] In a March 2009 memoranda filed with the federal District Court for the District of Columbia, the government asserted that:

> The President has the authority to detain persons that the President determines planned, authorized, committed, or aided the terrorist attacks that occurred on September 11, 2001, and persons who harbored those responsible for those attacks. The President also has the authority to detain persons who were part of, or substantially supported, Taliban or al-Qaeda forces or associated forces that are engaged in hostilities against the United States or its coalition partners, including any person who has committed a belligerent act, or has directly supported hostilities, in aid of such enemy armed forces.[129]

This matter of defining the individuals whom the US can lawfully detain is one of the detention-related issues that is directly linked to classification. First, there is the

---

[125] Military Order of 13 November 2001, Detention, Treatment, and Trial of Certain Non-Citizens in the War Against Terrorism, Federal Register, 16 November 2001.

[126] Department of Defense, 'Order Establishing Combatant Status Review Tribunals' (7 July 2004); see also definition in *Hamdi v Rumsfeld*, 542 U.S. 507 (28 June 2004).

[127] Senate Bill 3930 Military Commissions Act of 2006, S.3930 (22 September 2006).

[128] 'Department of Justice Withdraws "Enemy Combatant" Definition for Guantanamo Detainees', Department of Justice, Office of Public Affairs (13 March 2009); see also Military Commissions Act of 2009, National Defense Authorization Act for Fiscal Year 2010, which refers instead to 'alien unprivileged enemy belligerents'.

[129] Respondents' Memorandum Regarding the Government's Detention Authority Relative to Detainees Held at Guantanamo Bay (13 March 2009).

obvious question of prisoner of war status and whether it should be afforded to any of the detainees. Such status only exists in international armed conflicts, and in the current context is likely to have been potentially applicable only to members of the Taliban forces at the early stages of the war in Afghanistan, when this was an international armed conflict between the two States.[130] The remaining detainees, not entitled to prisoner of war status, would need to be detained in accordance with other rules of international law, primarily those dealing with internment of civilians. The term 'unlawful enemy combatant' is not recognized in international humanitarian law, and while States may choose to employ it in domestic laws and policies, their actual practice must rely upon existing international law.[131] Second, the classification of the conflict may have further effect on the authority to detain since there is debate on the grounds for detention in non-international armed conflict, and in particular when the conflict is extraterritorial.[132] In the current case, views of the conflict have been inconsistent, and more recently the US position appears to have settled on the position of it being a non-international armed conflict.[133]

Numerous further concerns have arisen with regard to the Guantánamo detainees, far more than can be detailed here. These include allegations of ill-treatment; de facto indefinite detention without charge; the use of military commissions in light of fair trial rights; the right to habeas corpus, and more.[134] Many legal cases have arisen from these circumstances, and a number of them have influenced subsequent changes in policy.[135] Insofar as classification is concerned, other than the rules regarding prisoners of war and questions over grounds for detention under the laws of non-international armed conflict, these other issues would be likely to raise similar concerns regardless of the classification of the conflict as international or non-international. An additional classification concern is with regard to individuals whose link to armed conflict is tenuous—as noted in the earlier discussion, not all elements of the war against Al-Qaeda are in fact an armed conflict,[136] and individuals detained not as part of an existing conflict cannot be held under the rules of international humanitarian law.

6.2. Secret detention and detention by proxy[137]

The former US President acknowledged the existence of a secret detention programme run by the CIA, which included the holding of detainees in the territory of other countries. The exact number of detainees held in these sites

---

[130] See further discussion in ch. 8 on Afghanistan.
[131] See section on 'unlawful combatant' in Lubell, *Extraterritorial Use of Force*, ch. 6.
[132] See discussion in ch. 4, section 3.2 above.
[133] See sections 2 and 3 above on background and on views of parties to the conflict.
[134] 'Situation of detainees at Guantánamo Bay' Report, UN Doc. E/CN.4/2006/120 (15 February 2006).
[135] See e.g. *Hamdan*, on military commissions, and *Boumediene v Bush*, 476 F. 3d 981 (20 February 2007), on habeas corpus.
[136] See discussion in section 4 above on classification.
[137] See discussion in ch. 4, section 3 above.

remains unknown, although it was reported at the time that there were 'fewer than 100' between 2001 and 2006.[138] The alleged mastermind of the September 11th attacks, Khalid Shaikh Mohammed, was one of a number of detainees held in these facilities in the past.[139] Although President Bush's statement appeared to indicate that the detainees were being transferred out of the secret sites which were then left empty, concerns persisted that the secret detention facilities remained in use and detainees were still being held in such sites.[140] More recently, President Obama's administration is said to have '[i]nstructed the CIA to close as expeditiously as possible any detention facilities that it currently operated as of 22 January 2009 and ordered that the CIA shall not operate any such detention facility in the future'.[141] It should be noted that secret detention can also occur in a formal and recognized place of detention, on the basis of the detention being incommunicado and lack of information given about the detainee's location and fate.[142]

Secret detention and renditions risk violating a number of human rights, including the right to liberty, the right to a fair trial, the prohibition of enforced disappearance, the prohibition of torture and other ill-treatment.[143] In the case of transfer of an individual from one State for the purpose of secret detention in another State, both the sending State and the State of detention may be in violation of international law.[144] The practice of 'extraordinary renditions' also raises concerns about the complicity of other States in a myriad of ways, including the requesting of an act of secret detention; the use of information passed on to them from secret detention sites; the direct participation in the arrest or transfer; allowing passage in the process of transfer to secret detention.[145]

7. Rules on other significant problems of international humanitarian law

7.1. Drones

The frequent use of unmanned aerial drones has drawn much attention and raises numerous questions about their regulation under international humanitarian law. On the one hand, drones could allow for wider precautions to be taken prior to attack, gathering information in advance, and with the video feed allowing more

---

[138] 'President Moves 14 Held in Secret to Guantanamo' *The New York Times* (7 September 2006).
[139] Ibid.
[140] 'Off the Record: U.S. Responsibility for Enforced Disappearances in the "War on Terror"', Joint report by six human rights organizations (7 June 2007), available at: <www.hrw.org/en/reports/2007/06/07/record>.
[141] UN, *Study on Secret Detention*, para 160; certain concerns remain, see ibid, para 161.
[142] Ibid, para 9.
[143] Ibid, paras 18–35. In addition, for a legal study of transfer of individuals, see M. Satterthwaite, 'The Legal Regime Governing Transfer of Persons in the Fight Against Terrorism' New York University Public Law and Legal Theory Working Papers, No. 192 (2010); see also CoE, *Second Report*.
[144] UN, *Study on Secret Detention,* paras 36–43.
[145] Ibid, para 159.

involvement of headquarters (and lawyers) in the decisions at the moment of actual attack. It has been claimed that the track record of drones is in fact more accurate than that of fighter jets.[146] On the other hand, reports of high numbers of civilian casualties and concerns over remote control warfare, amongst many other issues, have led to criticism of the use of drones.[147]

The fact that many of the strikes are carried out by the CIA raises further questions. Once again, some of these—such as whether the operatives involved become members of the armed forces or civilians directly participating in hostilities, and all the ensuing implications—are beyond the scope of this chapter. However, the CIA involvement might also have bearing upon the classification of the conflict. In particular, if the CIA operatives are not members of the armed forces, one might ask whether a situation could be classified as an armed conflict if those taking part are not members of the armed forces. However, if these operations are taken in the context of other existing conflicts such as in Afghanistan in which the military is involved, then this question does not arise, although other questions of international law do remain.[148]

7.2. Individual status

One of the crucial and most debatable aspects of this conflict is whether or not the individuals being targeted should be categorized as having a status that deprives them of civilian protection. If this is not an international armed conflict, then combatant status cannot exist.[149] In non-international armed conflicts, civilians could lose their protection under the rule of direct participation in hostilities, or—if the controversial ICRC position is accepted—through the engagement in a continuous combat function.[150] Either way, there must, as a minimum, be some form of direct engagement in hostilities, and it is unclear whether the actions of the targeted individuals always meet this requirement. Although the initial intent appears to have been the targeting of Al-Qaeda leadership, in practice many low-level militants are targeted, not just leaders.[151] This is difficult to assess, as the tendency of States is to aggrandize their targets after the attack, promoting the success of the strike by emphasizing the value of the target. While targeting the leadership may, prima facie, seem to be more warranted, and the planning of attacks by militant leaders could constitute direct participation in hostilities, the low-level militants actually

---

[146] Mayer, *The Predator War*.

[147] M.E. O'Connell, 'Unlawful Killing with Combat Drones: A Case Study of Pakistan, 2004–2009' Notre Dame Legal Studies Paper No. 09-43; see also analysis of possible concerns in HRC, 'Report of the Special Rapporteur on extrajudicial, summary or arbitrary executions, Philip Alston' UN Doc. A/HRC/14/24/Add.6 (28 May 2010) paras 79–86.

[148] As mentioned earlier, there is the issue of the individual status of the CIA operatives. See section 8 below for analysis of the question of transparency and accountability.

[149] Even were it an international conflict, it is unlikely the militants would satisfy the criteria for such status.

[150] N. Melzer, 'Interpretive Guidance on the Notion of Direct Participation in Hostilities under International Humanitarian Law' (2009) (Interpretive Guidance).

[151] Mayer, *The Predator War*.

engaged in the fighting would in fact provide for an even clearer case of loss of protection through direct participation. It has also been said that individuals involved in training might be targeted, although not those whose involvement is limited to financing.[152] This would conform to certain interpretations of the rules on loss of protection.[153] Finally, it has emerged from a US Senate Foreign Relations Committee Report that around fifty drug traffickers said to link drugs and insurgency, have also been included on the target list, although it is unclear whether these targets are only within Afghanistan or beyond.[154] Notably, the drug link is said to play a large role in the workings of the Taliban, but is of little or no relevance to Al-Qaeda.[155]

As mentioned earlier, a 'pattern of life analysis' can be conducted through prior drone surveillance. This analysis may indeed point to an individual being engaged in militant activities on a regular basis. However, this cannot be deemed sufficient to determine whether the person is a legitimate target, since, as noted in the background of this chapter, there may be a wide array of militant groups operating in the same area (this is especially true of Pakistan), and not every gun-carrying militant is necessarily involved in the conflicts to which the US is party.

Another related question, also linked to the earlier debate of the *ius ad bellum*, is whether any militant who crosses over from Afghanistan into Pakistan, or goes further to Yemen and elsewhere, automatically remains a legitimate target. It is submitted here that individuals do not carry the battlefield away with them whenever they relocate to a different territory, otherwise there would be no possibility to disengage from an armed conflict. Rather, it is a question of whether the conflict activities themselves have also relocated. In other words, only if the individual or group are continuing to engage in the armed conflict from their new location could operations taken against them be considered to be part of the armed conflict. The test here could be similar to the determination of direct participation in hostilities: if the actions of the individual in their new location satisfy the criteria for direct participation in hostilities, then it would be difficult to argue that hostilities are not taking place in that same location. Clearly, there will remain debatable aspects, such as the temporal element and how to classify the situation when the individual is in between carrying out attacks—but these are the same questions that have arisen over the years with regard to the notion of direct participation in hostilities, and similar interpreta-

---

[152] Miller, *From Memo to Missile*.

[153] For detailed discussion and debates on the interpretation of the rule on direct participation, see ICRC/TMC Asser Institute, 'Third Expert Meeting on the Notion of Direct Participation in Hostilities' (2005); ICRC/TMC Asser Institute, 'Fourth Expert Meeting on the Notion of Direct Participation in Hostilities' (November 2006); ICRC/TMC Asser Institute, 'Fifth Expert Meeting on the Notion of Direct Participation in Hostilities' (2008); Interpretive Guidance.

[154] US Senate Foreign Relations Committee, 'Afghanistan's Narco War: Breaking the Link Between Drug Traffickers and Insurgents: Report to the Senate Committee on Foreign Relations' S. Rep. No. 111, 111th Congress, 1st Session (10 August 2009) 16.

[155] Ibid, 10.

tions and views could apply in our case.[156] Notwithstanding, the test for the question before us is based on the hostilities rather than the individual, but the actions of the latter may be the evidence of the existence of the former. This does not, however, lead to a *carte blanche* to strike at any individual in any country, and will also depend on the laws of the *ius ad bellum* and its rules on necessity, self-defence and more. In most cases these rules may prevent the extension of resorting to operations in new areas, unless there is consent by the territorial State or a case for self-defence can be made.[157]

There is also a question here regarding the recourse to lethal force: under international human rights law it is expected to be the last option and only in extreme circumstances of protecting life, whereas the use of lethal force under international humanitarian law can also be linked to the status of the individual (e.g. targeting a combatant).[158] A measure of debate has recently emerged on the latter rules, primarily as a result of the ICRC's guidance on the notion of direct participation in hostilities.[159] Whether there should be a prior attempt to detain rather than opting for use of force loses much of its relevance to many of the drone strikes, as these occur in areas in which such a possibility is virtually non-existent. Carrying out detention operations in the tribal hills of Waziristan, if not impossible, would likely cause many more casualties and mass displacement of civilians. There may however have been a detention option in some of the cases. For example, in the Yemen strike in 2002, there were reports that the Yemeni authorities had been tracking the men for months and relaying the information to the US,[160] which raises the question of whether there might in fact have been many chances to attempt to detain, rather than using a lethal strike. If the Yemen strike is not classified as within an armed conflict (as discussed earlier), then the need to attempt a detention becomes clearer, through human rights standards.

The use of a list of targets has generated controversy, and even a legal challenge.[161] Clearly, under a law-enforcement paradigm creating a list of names who can be targeted with lethal force is unlikely to pass the sliding scale of force approach. Conversely, under international humanitarian law such a list might be argued as not only legitimate, but even required. The determination of direct participation in hostilities (or the continuous combat function) is an individual test, examining whether a specific person meets the threshold and thereby loses protection. If this is said to be the purpose of the list, then it may be allowed under international humanitarian law. Notwithstanding, the lack of transparency in the process raises further difficulties, and will be returned to later.

---

[156] Interpretive Guidance.

[157] See section 4.1 above on the *ius ad bellum*, and for detailed analysis see Lubell, *Extraterritorial Use of Force.*

[158] See discussion in ch. 4, sections 4.1 and 4.3 above.

[159] Interpretive Guidance; see also discussion in ch. 4, section 4.1 above.

[160] B. Whitaker, 'Killing probes the frontiers of robotics and legality' *The Guardian* (6 November 2002). In fact, the US may have been jointly tracking Al-Harethi, as part of a joint intelligence team with the Yemenis. S. Hersh, 'Manhunt' *The New Yorker* (23 December 2002).

[161] *Al-Aulaqi v Obama.*

8. Conclusions

8.1. Difficulties of classification

One of the greatest challenges in the analysis of this conflict stems from the lack of available information about virtually every aspect under examination. The information obstacle thus affects the ability to reach a definitive analysis of classification. The identity of the militant groups is one of the questions in determining whether they are part of a conflict and if so which one; without knowledge of their identity and affiliation, the classification is hindered. This deficit of known facts stretches across the spectrum of stages of the conflict. There is little information on how the lists of targets are compiled, and the CIA process for placing names on the list is particularly notable for its lack of transparency. This creates great difficulty in assessing the legality of the attacks. Moreover, it makes the possibility of demanding accountability and redress a daunting prospect, and this itself may be a violation of international law.[162] The actual situation on the ground in Pakistan (and other places) can itself be far from simple to describe, with the numerous different militant groups operating alongside each other in an ever-changing environment of shifting alliances and overlapping conflicts. Even the facts on the results of the strikes themselves are often unclear. Without regular access for media or independent organizations, it becomes extremely difficult to assess who and what was actually hit by the attack, and there are wide differences between some of the assessments of the ratio of civilian to militant casualties. Information deficit is also a concern in relation to matters of detention, and assessing some of the legal issues in the context of renditions to uncooperative third States or secret locations is a hard task. Not only does it become difficult to monitor issues such as risk of ill-treatment and procedural guarantees in detention and trial, it can even be difficult to ascertain whether and where a particular individual is being detained.

Classification of hostilities which occur over multiple territories not even sharing a border raises the difficulty of whether they can be said to be part of a single conflict. The suggested answer is that they can in theory, but only if in all these territories it is possible to identify the same entities as being the parties to the same conflict. In relation to a 'global war against Al-Qaeda' such a determination would appear to be largely untenable.

Classification of an extraterritorial conflict against a non-state actor does not, prima facie, fit the traditional understandings of international or non-international armed conflict. This chapter takes the position that these are the only two existing classifications, and that they are capable of encompassing new situations of this type. The classification rests primarily on the nature of the parties, and thus a conflict between a State and a non-state actor is a non-international armed conflict, even if it occurs extraterritorially.

---

[162] HRC, 'Report of the Special Rapporteur on extrajudicial, summary or arbitrary executions, Philip Alston' UN Doc. A/HRC/14/24/Add.6 (28 May 2010) paras 87–92.

The primary classification question therefore examined in this chapter was whether the current situation passed the test for non-international armed conflict. Difficulties in this regard related to the assessment of the threshold for non-international armed conflict: determining the organization of a party said to be made up of multiple dispersed groups with a joint agenda and calculating the intensity claimed to be based on incidents that may or may not be connected to each other. The global US operations against Al-Qaeda in territories other than Afghanistan are concluded to be unlikely to pass the threshold for non-international armed conflict. This is due to a combination of issues surrounding the nature of Al-Qaeda and the question whether one single party can be said to be involved in all the different violent acts that are said to be proof of the existence of the conflict. Nonetheless, it is also concluded that some of the actions in the 'war against Al-Qaeda'—especially those in Pakistan—could be considered to be part of an already existing non-international armed conflict, either as spill-over from the Afghan conflict, or an existing conflict in Pakistan.

A separate classification dilemma is raised by the links between *ius ad bellum* and *ius in bello* and whether these can affect classification. This relates particularly to the question of the implications of non-consent by the territorial State. In this chapter it is noted that in some instances there may actually be consent (e.g. Pakistan). However, when consent does not exist, the position taken here is that it does not in most cases affect the classification of the conflict between the foreign State and the non-state actor, which would remain a non-international armed conflict. Violations of the *ius ad bellum* are a separate matter between the two States. If, in the context of the operations there appears to also develop a conflict between the two States, then this would be an international armed conflict alongside the non-international one.

8.2. Consequences of classification for international humanitarian law

The controversy as to whether there was an international or a non-international armed conflict would have had little consequence to most of the issues raised in this chapter, since the greatest difference between the two categories relates to individual status and in the present case the individuals would have been unlikely to meet the requirements for combatant status even had it been international.

The debate over whether the situation is to be classified as a non-international armed conflict, as opposed to not being an armed conflict at all does, however, have serious consequences. These are, above all, in relation to the mode of use of force, which currently includes missile strikes against individuals based on their status—many of these strikes (but not necessarily all) might be considered unlawful if the rules of armed conflict do not apply. In addition, if the grounds given for detention are based on the armed conflict model, then, if there is no armed conflict, many of the detentions—particularly, but not only, outside the Afghan (and possibly Pakistani) battlefields—may become highly questionable. Where there is a non-international armed conflict, however, the problems discussed in earlier chapters with regard to the grounds for detention are relevant.[163]

There is also the problem of determining individual status and loss of protection for members of militant groups, in a context of multiple groups crossing borders and engaging in more than one conflict. Does an individual who crosses a border continue to have lost protection and be a legitimate target in the new location? The conclusion suggested here is that loss of protection is primarily linked to activities and participation in the conflict, rather than the location. However, the new location will also bring questions of *ius ad bellum* into play which may affect the legality of resorting to these operations.

8.3. Application of human rights law

International human rights law becomes of crucial importance for regulation of conduct if some of the operations are taking place not within existing armed conflicts as analysed earlier, but as part of an amorphous global war on Al-Qaeda that does not satisfy the criteria for classification as armed conflict. In the absence of armed conflict international humanitarian law is not applicable, and human rights law should be the sole authority for regulating the use of force. Even if international humanitarian law does apply, the relationship with human rights law may affect the rules on use of force.

Consequently, the question of extraterritorial applicability of international human rights law is paramount to the situation. While there is growing support for the position that human rights obligations can extend to operations beyond a State's own borders, there is no clarified and uniform agreement.[164] The case at hand involves two of the greatest obstacles in this debate: the use of air power to strike at individuals from a distance, and the fact that the State in question is the US. Although it can be argued that killing from a distance must not be excluded from the sphere of extraterritorial human rights obligations (and that in fact such a conclusion would provide an incentive to such killings),[165] the *Banković* case prevents an automatic assumption of this type.[166] Additionally, the US has been amongst the most resistant of all States to the notion of extraterritorial human rights obligations.[167] Finally, operations taken in Pakistan raise a further issue of the human rights obligations of Pakistan, and whether these also bind the US if it is operating in coordination with Pakistani authorities.

---

[163] See discussion in ch. 4, section 3 above.
[164] See examination of the issue in Lubell, *Extraterritorial Use of Force*, ch. 8. For the application of the European Convention on Human Rights see also *Al-Skeini and others v the United Kingdom* (Judgment) App No. 55721/07 (7 July 2011) (*Al-Skeini v the United Kingdom*).
[165] Lubell, *Extraterritorial Use of Force*, ch. 8.
[166] *Banković et al v Belgium et al* (Decision) App No. 52207/99 (12 December 2001) (*Banković*). See also *Al-Skeini v the United Kingdom*.
[167] 'Third periodic reports of States parties due in 2003: United States', CCPR/C/USA/3 (28 November 2005) 109; see also the remarks by Waxman and Harris in HRC, 'Consideration Of Reports Under Article 40 Of The Covenant (Continued), Second And Third Periodic Reports Of The United States Of America (Continued)', CCPR/C/SR.2380 (27 July 2006) paras 3 and 8.

When it comes to detention, the controversy does not disappear, but is significantly reduced. There is considerable support for the contention that human rights law obligations are attached to the operation of a detention facility even if the location is outside the borders of the State.[168] Even in the *Banković* case, despite aiming to limit extraterritorial applicability in other circumstances, there appeared to be acceptance of it in the context of detention.[169]

If, on the other hand, the situation is to be classified as an armed conflict, the ongoing debates of concurrent applicability of human rights and international humanitarian law are the main issue to be resolved and are not unique to this case study.

8.4. Impact of classification for application of the law

Classification and in particular the difficulties of classifying extraterritorial operations against non-state actors involving multiple territories and groups is at the heart of the problem of determining whether an armed conflict exists at all and, consequently, whether the laws of armed conflict govern the operations in question.

Overall, it has been clear throughout this chapter that the situation between the US and Al-Qaeda encompasses numerous controversial areas of international law relating to the classification of the conflict and beyond. However, even were these to be resolved and agreement to be reached on the issues of law, the paucity of information on the operations will remain a major obstacle in applying the law to the facts.

Reaching agreement on classification of extraterritorial conflicts against non-state actors would clarify some of the debates. It is suggested that these be accepted as constituting non-international armed conflicts, but only if meeting the required threshold. This also necessitates differentiating between the matters of *ius ad bellum* and *ius in bello*.

There is need to recognize the role to be played by international human rights law in the use of force (not only in detention), especially in those extraterritorial situations which might not meet the threshold to be classified as armed conflict.

The huge difficulties raised by the lack of facts necessitates greater emphasis on the need to gather more information—whether through research or by demanding information through legal and accountability mechanisms. Without more facts, many of these matters will remain as continuous academic debates based on hypothesis, without being able to apply them to actual situations.

---

[168] See e.g. *Hess v United Kingdom* (1975) 2 D&R 72; *Coard et al v United States*, Inter-American Commission on Human Rights, Case No. 10.951, Report No. 109/99 (29 September 1999) para 37; IACHR, 'Request for Precautionary Measures Concerning the Detainees at Guantanamo Bay, Cuba' (12 March 2002) 41 ILM 532; see also *R (on the application of Al-Skeini) v Secretary of State for Defence* [2004] EWHC 2911 (14 December 2004) paras 286–8 and, in the European Court of Human Rights, *Al-Skeini v the United Kingdom*.

[169] Verbatim Record of the hearing 24 October 2001, cited in M. O'Boyle, 'The European Convention on Human Rights and Extraterritorial Jurisdiction: A Comment on "Life After Bankovic"' in F. Coomans and M. Kamminga (eds), *Extraterritorial Application of Human Rights Treaties* (2004) 138; see also 'The submissions of the respondent Governments' in *Banković*, para 37.

14

Classification in Future Conflict

Michael N. Schmitt

1. Introduction: understanding future conflict

Anticipating the future is an inherently imprecise endeavour. It typically relies on preconceptions shaped by past events out of a sense that history evolves directionally. Therefore, the past offers clues as to the future's likely vector. Nowhere is this truer than in efforts to craft visions of future conflict. We assume that conflict will evolve in an evolutionary, rather than revolutionary, manner.

Such assumptions underpin the development of national security and defence strategies, as well as the force planning and military doctrine which they engender. In fact, assumptions based on careful deconstruction of security trends often prove valid. But sometimes they do not. Two dynamics skew the predictive process.

First, any deviation from the anticipated evolutionary direction grows as time goes by. In much the same way that a bullet which is slightly misaimed will miss its intended target by an ever greater distance the further it travels, so too with strategic miscalculation. Consider transnational terror. Although it pre-dated 9/11 by decades, the failure to identify it as a core future national security threat until the attacks hit left the international community woefully unprepared—militarily, normatively and psychologically—to address conflict with a globalized networked organization like Al-Qaeda. The result has been frenzied strategic 'catch-up' ball.

Second, the predictive process may fall prey to the 'big bang' of the unanticipated event or phenomenon. For instance, a new technology or method of warfare may disrupt the prevailing vision of future conflict. Cyber warfare offers an excellent example. While it came to the attention of military thinkers in the 1990s,[1] cyber lost its place of prominence in the aftermath of the attacks of 9/11. Thus, when massive cyber attacks were mounted against NATO member Estonia in 2006 from, inter alia, sites in Russia, and when cyber attacks peppered Georgia during its 2008

---

[1] For a discussion of events in Estonia and Georgia, see E. Tikk, K. Kaska and L. Vihul, *International Cyber Incidents: Legal Considerations* (2010) 14–33. For early consideration of the normative issues raised by cyber, see M.N. Schmitt and B.T. O'Donnell (eds), *Computer Network Attack and International Law* (2002).

war with Russia, a frantic scramble ensued to understand the implications of such attacks, practical and normative, for extant national security strategies.[2]

Daunting obstacles clearly lie in the way of accurate forecasts as to the future security environment. However, tomorrow's conflicts will be fought by the militaries currently being built, and will do so based on doctrine, training and tactics attuned to today's vision of tomorrow's wars. Imprecise and unreliable as the predictive process may be, there is simply no other choice but to make the attempt to foresee the future of warfare.

The likely nature of future war also bears on the normative architecture governing armed conflict. Law and war exist in a symbiotic relationship. International law, particularly the *ius ad bellum* and the *ius in bello*,[3] shape the options available to States in meeting security threats. Conflict responds to law. At the same time, law responds to changes in the nature of warfare. Occasionally, law anticipates future forms of warfare.[4] More often, law emerges as a reaction to events that have occurred during armed conflict. Indeed, the birth of the modern law of armed conflict was a direct result of Henri Dunant's graphic account of suffering at the Battle of Solferino.[5]

In light of this symbiotic relationship, it is useful to contemplate how future visions of conflict may intersect with the contemporary law of armed conflict. Three possibilities exist. First, a norm may fall into desuetude when it no longer comports with the extant practices in warfare. The rules regarding balloon warfare exemplify this possibility.[6] Second, law may be reinterpreted in light of developments in conflict. The 1949 Second Geneva Convention provides that 'hospital ships may not possess or use a secret code for their wireless or other means of communication',[7] a requirement designed to ensure they not be used for intelligence purposes. Yet, because failure to use encrypted communications risks

---

[2] See e.g. White House, 'The Comprehensive National Cyber Security Initiative' (May 2009), available at <www.whitehouse.gov/sites/default/files/cybersecurity.pdf>.

[3] The *ius ad bellum* governs when it is that States may resort to force. It addresses such issues as the actions under Chapter VII of the UN Charter and the law of self-defence. By contrast, the *ius in bello* (referred to below as the law of armed conflict and also known as international humanitarian law) deals with how force may be employed once an armed conflict exists.

[4] The paradigmatic example is the ban on permanently blinding lasers found in the 1980 Convention on Certain Conventional Weapons, which was adopted in advance of any such weapons being fielded on the battlefield. See Additional Protocol IV to the Convention on the Prohibitions or Restrictions on the Use of Certain Conventional Weapons which may be Deemed to be Excessively Injurious or to Have Indiscriminate Effects, Protocol on Blinding Laser Weapons.

[5] H. Dunant, *Souvenir de Solferino* (1862). The book famously led to the creation of the International Committee of the Red Cross and, eventually, the adoption of a series of treaties designed to alleviate the suffering of wounded combatants, including the first 'Geneva Convention' in 1864. Similarly, victimization of occupied populations during the Second World War motivated the first convention expressly designed to protect such individuals, the 1949 Fourth Geneva Convention. And more recently, incidental harm to civilians as a result of anti-personnel mines and unexploded cluster munitions bomblets has led to the adoption, respectively, of the Convention on the Prohibition of the Use, Stockpiling, Production and Transfer of Antipersonnel Mines and on Their Destruction (1997 Ottawa Convention) and the Convention on Cluster Munitions (2008 Dublin Convention).

[6] 1899 Declaration to Prohibit for the Term of Five Years the Launching of Projectiles and Explosives from Balloons, and Other Methods of a Similar Nature (Hague IV, 1).

[7] Geneva Convention II, art. 34(2).

revealing the location of the military forces that hospital ships serve, the 1995 *San Remo Manual on International Law Applicable to Armed Conflicts at Sea* interpreted the provision in context by allowing the use of cryptographic equipment, albeit 'not in any circumstances to transmit intelligence data nor in any other way to acquire military advantage'.[8] Third, changing conflict may reveal real or purported lacunae in the law. Debates over the detention of so-called 'unlawful combatants', with some commentators arguing that they nether qualified as prisoners of war under the 1949 Third Geneva Convention nor as civilians under the Fourth, illustrate this possibility.[9]

This chapter examines the legal issue of classification of conflict in light of one vision of future warfare, that of the United Kingdom.[10] The British vision is the result of a sophisticated and systematic process of assessment conducted by experts affiliated with the Ministry of Defence's Development, Concepts and Doctrine Centre (DCDC). Like any strategic prediction, it will eventually prove less than completely prescient. Nevertheless, DCDC's works are as reliable a template as is presently available.

The Ministry of Defence (MoD) has perceptively noted that '[c]onflict classification, and the legal envelope for operations, *will* contribute to the complexity of future conflict, creating major challenges for those engaged in the planning and conduct of operations'.[11] This chapter seeks to pinpoint those aspects of future conflict that are most likely to pose challenges for those charged with classifying a particular conflict. Three occupy centre stage: cyber warfare, transnational terrorism and the complexity of the battlespace. Anticipation of such challenges will surely enhance the quality of legal input into strategic decision-making. Since the relationship between war and law is synergistic, the chapter will conclude by highlighting likely normative trends in classification which may influence conflict.

2. Cyber warfare

The United Kingdom has identified cyberspace as a likely medium of conflict, one standing on equal footing with such traditional media as land, sea and airspace. In its 2010 *National Security Strategy*, the UK characterized 'cyber attack, including by other States, and by organised crime and terrorists' as one of four 'Tier One' threats

---

[8] L. Doswald-Beck (ed.), *San Remo Manual on International Law Applicable to Armed Conflicts at Sea* (1995) rule 171, reprinted in A. Roberts and R. Guelff (eds), *Documents on the Laws of War* (2000) 573.

[9] See e.g. Y. Dinstein, *The Conduct of Hostilities under the Law of International Armed Conflict* (2010) ch. 2 (Dinstein, *International Armed Conflict*).

[10] Of course, other visions exist and are not necessarily less reliable. See e.g. NATO, 'Strategic Concept for the Defence and Security of the Members of the North Atlantic Treaty Organisation: Active Engagement, Modern Defence' (2010) (NATO, *Strategic Concept*); United States, 'National Security Strategy' (May 2010) (US, *National Security Strategy*); United States Department of Defense, 'Quadrennial Defense Review' (February 2010)

[11] Ministry of Defence (Development, Concepts and Doctrine Centre), 'Global Strategic Trends—Out to 2040' (2010) 83 (DCDC, *Global Strategic Trends*).

to British national security, the others being international terrorism, international military crisis between States and a major accident or natural hazard.[12]

Cyber attacks represent a particularly attractive means—and one which is both cheap and accessible—of striking at a State. The global cyber system is expanding at an exponential pace, with ever greater dependence of, inter alia, the energy, transportation, economic, financial and military critical infrastructures on networking. Additionally, as illustrated by activities ranging from interpersonal communications and social networking to on-line medical services and education, computer technology will continue to redefine the way in which society itself evolves. As dependence grows, so too does the risk of cascading failure due to the complex interrelatedness of the system. The potential consequences of a serious cyber attack could include such catastrophic consequences as meltdown of the economy, total disruption of the transportation system, and widespread property destruction and death. In the twenty-first century, the MetaWeb will constitute a, perhaps 'the', key vulnerability of modern States.

In *Global Strategic Trends—Out to 2040*, the MoD predicts that 'some actors *will* identify the cyber vulnerability of potential adversaries and recognise that exploiting such vulnerabilities in times of conflict is less expensive than conventional warfare, and more difficult to detect, attribute and prove'.[13] Accordingly, it suggests that 'denial of service' attacks such as those seen in Estonia in 2006 and Georgia in 2008, which targeted the civilian infrastructure, '*will* become routine' aspects of the unitary approach to conflict.[14] Attackers will not be limited to States, but also include terrorists, criminal organizations and malicious hackers.

If conducted as a component of an ongoing armed conflict, cyber attacks pose no particular difficulties as to *classification* of conflict. True, cyber warfare presents unique challenges to the *application* of the law of armed conflict. For instance, when does a cyber operation constitute an 'attack' as that term of art is employed in the rules on targeting? Is it necessary that the operation result in death of or injury to individuals or damage or destruction of property? Or is some other form of harm a more suitable standard?[15] And when do malicious civilian hackers qualify as direct participants in hostilities such that they lose their immunity from attack? But with regard to classifying conflict, cyber warfare takes on the classification of the conflict already underway.

---

[12] HM Government, 'A Strong Britain in an Age of Uncertainty: The National Security Strategy' (2010) 11.

[13] DCDC, *Global Strategic Trends*, 150.

[14] Ibid. NATO shares this vision. According to its new Strategic Concept, 'Cyber attacks are becoming more frequent, more organised and more costly in the damage that they inflict on government administrations, businesses, economies and potentially also transportation and supply networks and other critical infrastructure; they can reach a threshold that threatens national and Euro-Atlantic prosperity, security and stability. Foreign militaries and intelligence services, organised criminals, terrorist and/or extremist groups can each be the source of such attacks'. NATO, *Strategic Concept*, para 12.

[15] On this issue, see M.N. Schmitt, 'Wired Warfare: Computer Network Attack and International Law' (2002) 846(84) *International Review of the Red Cross* 365, 375–8 (Schmitt, *Wired Warfare*).

However, if cyber attacks occur in the absence of ongoing kinetic hostilities, how should they be classified?[16] Along the same lines, how are they to be classified when they take place during a more traditional conflict, but without any nexus to that conflict? The threshold question is whether cyber operations, without more, can amount to armed conflict at all.

The law of armed conflict treaties unfortunately contain no definition of the phrase 'armed conflict', instead referring to its two subcategories, international and non-international armed conflict. Although it is not the place here to revisit the technical analysis of each contained in the preceding chapters, it is useful to briefly recall their core elements.

As to international armed conflict, Article 2 Common to the four 1949 Geneva Conventions sets forth the traditional formula: 'all cases of declared war or to any other armed conflict which may arise between two or more of the High Contracting parties.'[17] In the official commentary to the article, the International Committee of the Red Cross (ICRC) notes that 'any difference arising between two States and leading to the intervention of members of the armed forces is an armed conflict within the meaning of Article 2, even if one of the Parties denies the existence of a state of war. It makes no difference how long the conflict lasts, how much slaughter takes place, or how numerous are the participating forces'.[18] Along the same lines, the International Criminal Tribunal for the Former Yugoslavia (ICTY) has suggested that 'an armed conflict exists whenever there is resort to force between States'.[19]

This is a low threshold, one which must not be confused with the *ius ad bellum* condition precedent for the use of force in self-defence—'armed attack'.[20] In the *Nicaragua* case, the International Court of Justice (ICJ) set a higher threshold for armed attacks by requiring certain 'scale and effects' and excluding, for instance, 'a mere frontier incident'.[21] Similarly, the traditional legal concept of 'war' excludes minor armed incidents from its ambit.[22] Despite these limitations, under the law of armed conflict any armed exchange between the militaries of States initiates an

---

[16] E.g. the Pentagon has recently concluded that computer sabotage coming from another country can constitute an act of war. See e.g. 'Cyber Combat: Act of War' *The Wall Street Journal* (31 May 2011). For further discussion of the question of classification see M. Schmitt 'Cyber Operations and the *Jus in Bello*: Key Issues' in R. Pedrozo and D. Wollschlaeger (eds), *International Law and the Changing Character of War* (2011) 88.

[17] Geneva Convention I, art. 2; Geneva Convention II, art. 2; Geneva Convention III, art. 2; Geneva Convention IV, art. 2.

[18] J. Pictet (ed.), *Geneva Convention Relative to the Treatment of Prisoners of War: commentary* (1960) 23 (Pictet, *Geneva Convention III Commentary*).

[19] *Prosecutor v Tadić*, IT-94-1-AR72, Decision on Defence Motion for Interlocutory Appeal on Jurisdiction (Appeals Chamber), 2 October 1995, para 70 *(Tadić)*.

[20] UN Charter, art. 51.

[21] *Military and Paramilitary Activities in and against Nicaragua (Nicaragua v United States of America)* ICJ Rep 1986, 14, para 219 *(Nicaragua)*. This standard has been subject to careful parsing (see e.g. *Oil Platforms (Islamic Republic of Iran v United States of America)* ICJ Rep 2003, 161, para 72), and criticized by commentators (see e.g. Y. Dinstein, *War, Aggression and Self-Defence* (2005) 194–6; W. Taft, 'Self-defense and the Oil Platforms Decision' (2004) 29 *Yale Journal of International Law* 295, 300).

[22] Dinstein, *International Armed Conflict*, 11–13.

'international armed conflict' to which its rules apply. In fact, the law imposes no requirement for hostilities at all. Article 2 of the Geneva Conventions extends to cases of 'partial or total occupation..., even if said occupation meets with no armed resistance'.[23] Similarly, when the forces of a State detain individuals protected by the law of armed conflict (especially members of the opponent's armed forces), an armed conflict exists.[24]

If a cyber operation attributable to a State results in damage or destruction of objects or injury to or death of individuals of another State, an international armed conflict undoubtedly occurs. Such actions are universally accepted as 'attacks' under the law of armed conflict, and as such would always meet the threshold for armed conflict. The question remains, however, of how to treat cyber operations falling below this level. Some may merely cause the target State inconvenience or irritation. Others could involve taking control of its national cyber systems or causing severe disruption to the economy, transportation system or other critical infrastructure. Obviously, not every cyber operation by one State against another should amount to an armed conflict. But where should the line be drawn?

The first possibility is at those operations constituting an 'attack', that is, ones which result in death, injury, damage or destruction (or severe suffering). In that attacks are defined as 'acts of violence',[25] doing so would reflect textual fidelity to the use of the adjective 'armed' in connection with 'armed conflict'. It would also seem consistent with the ICRC Commentary's reference to intervention by members of the armed forces. While occupation and detention qualify actions as an armed conflict but do not necessarily harm persons or objects, the prospect of the having to use force (to maintain order or custody) is implicit in both.

On the one hand, this approach would be the simplest means of classifying a cyber operation. By it, non-destructive computer network exploitation, espionage, denial of service attacks and other similar actions would not constitute armed conflict. On the other, the approach is arguably under-inclusive. Cyber operations could prove non-physically devastating without rising to this level. A State suffering such a strike would likely treat it, the technical parameters of the law aside, as an 'armed attack' under the *ius ad bellum*. Should it do so, it would also probably characterize the operation as the initiation of an armed conflict.

The ongoing debate over the meaning of the term 'attack' in the law of armed conflict raises a second possibility, one based on the argument that the essence of the legal restrictions on attacks is a desire to afford certain persons, places and objects protection under the law.[26] Applying this construct to cyber, directing

---

[23] 1949 Geneva Conventions, art. 2(1).

[24] Pictet, *Geneva Convention III Commentary*, 23.

[25] Additional Protocol I, art. 49 (definition of attack). On relationship to non-kinetic operations, see Schmitt, *Wired Warfare*; Program on Humanitarian Policy and Conflict Research at Harvard University, 'Commentary on the HPCR Manual on International Law Applicable to Air and Missile Warfare' (2010) 28.

[26] K. Dörmann, 'Applicability of Additional Protocols to Computer Network Attack', Paper delivered at the International Expert Conference on Computer Network Attacks and the Applicability of International Humanitarian Law, Stockholm, 17–19 November 2004, available at <www.icrc.org/web/eng/siteeng0.nsf/htmlall/68lg92?opendocument>.

operations against protected persons or objects would amount to an attack. By extension, an international armed conflict would commence once a State or those under its control launched them.

This approach suffers from the opposite weakness of the first, over-inclusivity. By focusing on the object of an operation, it fails to distinguish non-destructive 'attacks' from non-destructive military operations that clearly do not qualify as attacks, such as lawful psychological operations 'targeting' a civilian population. Analogously, the distinction between non-destructive operations which meet the armed conflict threshold and those which should not is missing in the approach.

Intuitively, it seems that the determinative criterion must be consequence severity. Death, injury, damage or destruction clearly qualify an action as armed conflict, while inconvenience and irritation do not. But beyond that, the law is uncertain. Such uncertainty is problematic, for it must be remembered that armed conflict renders hostile actions by combatants lawful absent breach of a particular legal norm. It is entirely possible that a third interpretation of armed conflict in the purely cyber context may emerge, one which lowers the bar by articulating a standard of significant non-destructive harm to the target State. The precise height of the bar can only be set over time through State practice combined with expressions of *opinio iuris*.

A further complication with respect to cyber operations is the fact that they will often be conducted by non-state actors ranging from terrorists to 'patriotic hackers'. In neither the Estonian nor Georgian cases did dispositive evidence of actions by Russia exist; rather the attacks were conducted by 'hactivists'. Can the actions of such individuals launch an international armed conflict between States?

The issue of attribution has been addressed elsewhere in this volume and need only be summarized here.[27] In *Nicaragua*, the ICJ set forth the 'effective control' test, one twice re-affirmed by the Court.[28] It must be cautioned that the issue there was State responsibility for alleged actions of the non-state group in question (the Contras), not conflict classification. In *Tadić*, the ICTY Appeals Chamber addressed the issue of classification head on. It held that the authority of the Federal Republic of Yugoslavia over the Bosnia Serb armed groups 'required by international law for considering the armed conflict to be international was *overall control* going beyond the mere financing and equipping of such forces and involving also participation in the planning and supervision of military operations'.[29] In doing so, the Chamber expressly rejected the higher *Nicaragua* threshold of effective control. Based on this jurisprudence, when a State directs a particular cyber attacks by non-state actors (*Nicaragua*) or (perhaps) participates in general planning and supervision (*Tadić*), an international armed conflict will exist between the victim State and the State sponsor.

---

[27] For further discussion, see ch. 3, section 7 above.

[28] *Nicaragua*, para 115. See also, discussion at para 109. Re-affirmed in *Armed Activities on the Territory of the Congo (Democratic Republic of the Congo v Uganda)* ICJ Rep 2005, 168, para 53 (*Congo v Uganda*); *Application of the Convention on the Prevention and Punishment of the Crime of Genocide (Bosnia and Herzegovina v Serbia and Montenegro)* ICJ Rep 2007, paras 391–2.

[29] *Prosecutor v Tadić*, IT-94-1-A, Judgment (Appeals Chamber) 15 July 1999, para 145.

There is no reason to limit these standards to actions by non-state organized groups. In the cyber context, a single individual may launch a devastating attack. Alternatively, the attacks may come from hundreds of individuals who operate independently. So long as the requisite relationship between them and the State exists, the threshold is satisfied. As an example, during the Georgia conflict a website, StopGeorgia.ru, was created which urged attacks and contained both a list of potential targets and hacker tools. Assume an armed conflict had not already been underway. If the Russian government had created the website, and had the attacks caused the requisite level of harm (whatever that might be), the cyber strikes would have started an international armed conflict between Russia and Georgia. On the other hand, a State which merely tolerates (or even sympathizes with) cyber attacks from its territory may be in breach of its international legal obligation to 'police' its territory to ensure it is not used to the detriment of other States,[30] but the inaction does not set off an international armed conflict.

Assessment of whether cyber attacks constitute *non*-international armed conflict is more problematic still. Common Article 3 to the Geneva Conventions defines non-international armed conflicts as those which are 'not of an international character'.[31] As discussed in other chapters of this book, two criteria exist.

The first derives from the phrase 'each Party to the conflict' in Common Article 3. Parties are generally understood to be States or groups which exhibit a certain degree of organization and command structure. Non-international armed conflict therefore occurs between a State and organized armed groups or between such groups. The requirement of organization rules out attacks conducted by either individual 'hackers' or multiple hackers operating without the necessary degree of organization, regardless of the consequences of the attacks. Instead, such attacks are governed by domestic criminal law.

This raises the question of virtual organization. On-line groups are common-place. Although they may never physically meet each other, the groups often act in concert, whether in finance, education or even military affairs. Unfortunately, the issue of the nature of the required organization is not well-developed in the law of armed conflict. The ICRC commentary to Common Article 3 suggests that 'the Party in revolt against the de jure Government possesses an organized military force, an authority responsible for its acts, act[s] within a determinate territory and [has] the means of respecting and ensuring respect for the Convention'.[32] Yet, it further notes that compliance with these criteria is merely indicative, not necessarily required.

---

[30] The ICJ affirmed this principle in its first case, *Corfu Channel*. The Court held that every State has an 'obligation to not allow knowingly its territory to be used for acts contrary to the rights of other States'. *Corfu Channel case (Merits)* ICJ Rep 1949, 4, 22.

[31] 1949 Geneva Conventions, Common Article 3 ('In the case of armed conflict not of an international character occurring in the territory of one of the High Contracting Parties, each Party to the conflict shall be bound to apply, as a minimum, the following provisions . . .'). Only States may be High Contracting Parties.

[32] Pictet, *Geneva Convention III Commentary*, 36.

At one extreme are hackers who operate wholly autonomously. As noted, the mere fact that many hackers are attacking a State would not render them 'organized'. At the other is a distinct on-line group with a leadership structure which coordinates its activities, for instance by allocating specified cyber targets amongst themselves, providing each other with tools or vulnerability assessments, and doing cyber damage assessment to determine whether 're-attack' is required. They are operating cooperatively. That the group members may never actually meet should be no obstacle to attributing the required degree of organization to the group. But since its members only interact virtually, there would appear to be no means to enforce compliance with the law of armed conflict. Whether this would bar qualification as an organized group is uncertain. By a strict traditionalist interpretation, it would; by one sensitive to the changing face of warfare it should not.

The more difficult case is that of an informal grouping of individuals who operate not cooperatively, but rather collectively. For instance, acting with shared purpose, they access a common website which contains tools and targets, but do not coordinate their attacks in any fashion. Whether such a group meets the organization criterion should depend on the nature of their collective action. Is there an identifiable 'leader' responsible for setting up and maintaining the site? Do they only attack targets found on the site? In most cases, such groupings would likely not qualify as a party to a non-international armed conflict. That said, the content of the organization criterion in the cyber context is decidedly vague.

Non-international armed conflicts also require a certain level of intensity, higher than that for the initiation of an international armed conflict. 'Internal disturbances and tensions, such as riots, isolated and sporadic acts of violence and other acts of a similar nature' fall short of the threshold.[33] In *Tadić*, the ICTY described non-international armed conflicts as 'protracted armed violence between governmental authorities and organized armed groups or between such groups within a State'.[34] This definition is reflected in the jurisprudence of the International Criminal Tribunal for Rwanda and in the Statute of the International Criminal Court.[35]

Few cyber attacks standing alone would rise to this level, for they would have to be protracted, that is, occur over a period of time. The criterion would therefore exclude individual or sporadic attacks no matter how destructive. Additionally, recall the discussion of whether non-destructive cyber operations even qualify as actions constituting armed conflict. In light of the intensity criterion, an argument that they do not would be even stronger in the context of non-international armed conflict. While future State practice may add clarity to the issue, it is likely that only regular cyber operations mounted by a specific group and which are destructive in nature will be classified as a non-international armed conflict.

---

[33] Additional Protocol II, art. 1(2). The limitation is generally deemed to reflect the standard applicable to Common Article 3 and in customary international law. See e.g. Statute of the International Criminal Court, art. 8(2)(f) (ICC Statute).

[34] *Tadić*, para 70.

[35] *Prosecutor v Akayesu*, ICTR-96-4-T, Judgment (Trial Chamber), 2 September 1998, para 619; ICC Statute, art. 8(2)(f).

Additional Protocol II sets, for States parties thereto, an even higher threshold for non-international armed conflict, one which excludes conflicts between organized groups and requires rebel groups to 'exercise such control over a part of' a State's territory that it can 'carry out sustained and concerted military operations'.[36] The territorial control requirement precludes any independent operation of Additional Protocol II in the cyber context, for the exercise of control would require resort to classic armed force and thus any cyber operations conducted by the group in control would assume the classification of the ongoing kinetic conflict irrespective of the cyber operations.

Finally, one of the major concerns expressed in the various UK visions of future conflict is that of cyber terrorism.[37] There is no reason to distinguish a terrorist group's cyber activities from those conducted by States or other non-state actors. For instance, before cyber terrorism can be classified as an international armed conflict, it must meet the threshold of armed conflict. Similarly, in the case of domestic cyber terrorism, the actions will have to satisfy the organization and intensity criteria before qualifying as a non-international armed conflict. That said, the very classification of transnational terrorism is a subject of much contention.

3. Transnational terrorism

As highlighted earlier, the UK *National Security Strategy* cites terrorism as one of the four Tier 1 threats.[38] This reality is unlikely to change in the foreseeable future. Additionally, '[t]here is likely to be an increased sponsorship of irregular activity by states, seeking to utilise and exploit, through proxies, gaps in the international system, either to assert themselves or to secure advantage without exposing themselves to state-on-state risks. Acts of extreme violence, including mass casualty attacks, *will* continue to be used by groups with sophisticated networks and the ability to exploit the media in order to maximise the impact of the "theatre of violence"'.[39] In other words, there will be more terrorists, they will employ a wider array of techniques, they will be harder to identify, and State sponsorship is likely to grow.

There are various options for classifying a conflict involving transnational terrorists.[40] If transnational terrorists are acting in concert with a State during an

---

[36] Additional Protocol II, art. 1(1). It must also be able to implement the provisions of the Protocol.

[37] For instance, DCDC notes that '[m]any extreme political groups *will* have a transnational following, and *may* increasingly employ sophisticated methods of coercion, including cyber attack and Weapons of Mass Destruction (WMD)'. DCDC, *Global Strategic Trends*, 130.

[38] UK, *National Security Strategy*, 11. So too does the new NATO Strategic Concept, which notes that '[t]errorism poses a direct threat to the security of the citizens of NATO countries, and to international stability and prosperity more broadly. Extremist groups continue to spread to, and in, areas of strategic importance to the Alliance, and modern technology increases the threat and potential impact of terrorist attacks, in particular if terrorists were to acquire nuclear, chemical, biological or radiological capabilities'. NATO, *Strategic Concept*, para 10.

[39] DCDC, *Global Strategic* Trends, 130.

[40] The classification of transnational terrorism has been addressed in ch. 13 above; this author generally accepts the taxonomy set forth therein.

armed conflict with another State, then their activities will assume the international character of the armed conflict underway between the States. Should they operate against a State, but under the control of another State, the conflict will likewise be classified as international. The determining factor will be the degree of control the latter State exercises and whether the *Nicaragua* effective control or the *Tadić* overall control standard applies. If the State-terrorist relationship falls below these levels, as in the case of mere financing or the provision of sanctuary, the transnational terrorism cannot qualify as international armed conflict solely on the basis of its nexus to a 'State sponsor'.

More problematic from a classification point of view is the situation of transnational terrorism with no, or an insufficient, relationship to a State. Significant controversy surrounds the question of how to classify such conflicts. The debate derives from the fact that non-international armed conflicts are typically seen as conflicts between a State and 'rebels', in other words, civil wars within a country. Additional Protocol II appears to make this requirement explicit in its reference to conflicts taking place 'in the territory of a State . . . between its armed forces and dissident armed forces or other organized armed groups'.[41] Common Article 3 contains no such restriction, but its mention of conflicts 'occurring in the territory' of a party to the 1949 Geneva Conventions can be interpreted as excluding conflicts that cross national borders. If the transnational terrorism is not international because it crosses borders, then it must be non-international.

The Israeli Supreme Court adopted this in the *Targeted Killings* case.

> [T]he fact that the terrorist organizations and their members do not act in the name of a state does not turn the struggle against them into a purely internal state conflict. Indeed, in today's reality, a terrorist organization is likely to have considerable military capabilities. At times they have military capabilities that exceed those of states. Confrontation with those dangers cannot be restricted within the state and its penal law. Confronting the dangers of terrorism constitutes a part of the international law dealing with armed conflicts of international character.[42]

Even if transnational terrorism qualifies as international in character, the question remains as to the requisite level of violence (as distinct from the nature of that violence, the central issue in cyber warfare). Recall that in the context of State-on-State hostilities, the armed conflict threshold is low—basically any resort to force qualifies. There is no reason to depart from this principle when a transnational terrorist group acts under the control of a State. However, the logic underpinning the low threshold does not transfer easily into a situation in which a terrorist group is acting autonomously, for violence between a State and non-state actors can also be characterized as crime to which a law-enforcement paradigm should apply.

Since the same holds true in non-international armed conflict, one logical approach would be to apply the non-international threshold—protracted armed

---

[41] Additional Protocol II, art. 1(1).
[42] *Public Committee against Torture in Israel et al v Government of Israel et al* High Court of Justice, Israel, HCJ 769/02 (13 December 2006) para 21.

violence. By this criterion, only attacks which signalled the start of a 'campaign' of violence against the State would reach the threshold. Single or otherwise isolated attacks would not. They would instead be subject to domestic criminal law and human rights norms, but not the law of armed conflict. The point is that some line must be drawn between acts committed by transnational terrorists that rise to the level of international armed conflict, assuming for the sake of analysis that it is the proper classification, and those which are mere criminality.

An alternative interpretation is that international armed conflicts are strictly limited to those between States. Therefore, to the extent that an armed conflict with transnational terrorists exists, it is 'not of an international character'. The US Supreme Court adopted this approach in *Hamdan v Rumsfeld*.

> The Court of Appeals thought, and the Government asserts, that Common Article 3 does not apply to Hamdan because the conflict with al Qaeda, being 'international in scope', does not qualify as a 'conflict not of an international character'. That reasoning is erroneous. The term 'conflict not of an international character' is used here in contradistinction to a conflict between nations. So much is demonstrated by the 'fundamental logic [of] the Convention's provisions on its application'. Common Article 2 provides that 'the present Convention shall apply to all cases of declared war or of any other armed conflict which may arise between two or more of the High Contracting Parties.' ... Common Article 3, by contrast, affords some minimal protection, falling short of full protection under the Conventions, to individuals associated with neither a signatory nor even a non-signatory 'Power' who are involved in a conflict 'in the territory of' a signatory. The latter kind of conflict is distinguishable from the conflict described in Common Article 2 chiefly because it does not involve a clash between nations (whether signatories or not). In context, then, the phrase 'nor of an international character' bears its literal meaning.
>
> Although the official commentaries accompanying Common Article 3 indicate that an important purpose of the provision was to furnish minimal protection to rebels involved in one kind of 'conflict not of an international character,' *i.e.*, a civil war, ... the commentaries also make clear 'that the scope of the Article must be as wide as possible,' ... In fact, limiting language that would have rendered Common Article 3 applicable 'especially [to] cases of civil war, colonial conflicts, or wars of religion,' was omitted from the final version of the Article, which coupled broader scope of application with a narrower range of rights than did earlier proposed iterations.[43]

Classifying transnational terrorism as non-international would have the benefit of avoiding the threshold of violence issue, for there is no reason to discard the

---

[43] *Hamdan v Rumsfeld*, 548 U.S. 557, 631 (2006). Although the Court did not mention it, the 1907 Hague Convention IV Respecting the Laws and Customs of War on Land, the annexed Regulations to which have been deemed reflective of customary law, was also framed solely in terms of States: 'do not apply except between contracting Powers, and then only if all the belligerents are parties to the Conventions'. See also, 1899 Convention with Respect to the Laws and Customs of War on Land annex, art. 2. On the Convention's customary status, see *Legal Consequences of the Construction of a Wall in the Occupied Palestinian Territory* (Advisory Opinion) ICJ Rep 2004, 136, 172 *(Palestinian Wall)*; *Legality of the Threat or Use of Nuclear Weapons* (Advisory Opinion) ICJ Rep 1996, 226, 257 *(Nuclear Weapons)*. The rules were also found to be customary by the Nuremberg Tribunal. International Military Tribunal, Nuremberg, *Trial of the Major War Criminals Before the International Military Tribunal, Vol. I* (1947) 254.

'protracted' requirement simply because the violence is not confined to a single State. Of course, this approach depends on a flexible interpretation of the territorial references in Common Article 3.

A particularly difficult case would involve a transnational terrorism campaign against multiple States in which the violence was not protracted as to one or more of the victim States. Two classification options present themselves. First, a State-by-State analysis could be used to determine with which States a non-international armed conflict was underway, with the domestic criminality model applying as to the others. Second, the violence could be amalgamated across States such that once a group had engaged in protracted armed violence, wherever located, it would be involved in a non-international armed conflict with all States against which it was acting. The former has the benefit of containing the geographical scope of armed conflict, whereas the latter would facilitate joint military action against a common threat.

A unique, and controversial, approach suggests that because transnational terrorism meets neither the traditional requirements of international nor non-international armed conflict (since it does not involve conflict between States, but transcends border), it comprises a new form of conflict—a hybrid armed conflict. This approach has been championed by Professor Geoffrey Corn.

> [T]he time has come for states to reject any interpretation of the Common Article 2/3 paradigm that results in denial of applicability of these principles to situations of armed conflict where the regulatory effect of the law is essential to ensure this mitigation of suffering and the disciplined application of combat power. Therefore, the ongoing evolution in the nature of warfare requires acknowledgment that any armed conflict triggers the foundational principles of the laws of war. If this outcome is achieved by characterizing such military operations as Common Article 3 conflicts that trigger the humane treatment obligation plus additional customary law of war principles, the regulatory purpose of the law can be achieved. Given that Common Article 3 conflicts have become generally synonymous with internal conflicts, however, it is more pragmatic to expressly endorse a hybrid category of armed conflict: transnational armed conflict.
>
> The recognition of this hybrid category would not render Common Articles 2 or 3 irrelevant. Instead, these Articles would continue to serve as triggers for application of the treaty provisions to which they relate. But this new category would be responsive to the rapidly changing nature of warfare, a change that creates an increased likelihood that states will resort to the use of combat power to respond to threats posed by non-state armed entities operating outside their territory. Such armed conflicts justify a more precise interpretation of the de facto conditions that trigger the foundational principles of the laws of war, supporting the conclusion that any de facto armed conflict serves as such a trigger. Common Articles 2 and 3 would then serve to trigger layers of more defined regulation in some ways redundant to and in other ways augmenting these principles. This layered methodology will ensure no conflict falls outside the scope of essential baseline regulation while preserving the technical triggers for more detailed regulation required by application of specific treaty provisions.[44]

---

[44] See e.g. G. Corn, 'Hamdan, Lebanon, and the Regulation of Armed Conflict: The Need to Recognize a Hybrid Category of Armed Conflict' (2006) 40 *Vanderbilt Transnational Law Journal* 330–1. See also, G. Corn and E. Talbot Jensen, 'Untying the Gordian Knot: A Proposal for

Compelling though the proposition may be in theory, it has not been widely embraced by scholars and practitioners. As Corn noted in a later piece co-authored with Professor Eric Jensen, '[t]he notion of transnational armed conflict represents an evolution of the law, more properly characterized as *lex ferenda* than *lex lata*'.[45] They are correct.

Finally, it might be argued that there is no armed conflict at all; transnational terrorism is simply egregious international criminality. By reference to the express terms of the *lex scripta*, this would appear to be the correct result. There are two possible variants of the position. The ICRC has advanced the 'strictest' strand:

> International humanitarian law (the law of armed conflict) recognizes two categories of armed conflict: international and non-international. International armed conflict involves the use of armed force by one State against another. Non-international armed conflict involves hostilities between government armed forces and organized armed groups or between such groups within a state. When and where the 'global war on terror' manifests itself in either of these forms of armed conflict, international humanitarian law applies, as do aspects of international human rights and domestic law. For example, the armed hostilities that started in Afghanistan in October 2001 or in Iraq in March 2003 are armed conflicts.
>
> When armed violence is used outside the context of an armed conflict in the legal sense or when a person suspected of terrorist activities is not detained in connection with any armed conflict, humanitarian law does not apply. Instead, domestic laws, as well as international criminal law and human rights govern.[46]

A more relaxed version of the 'no armed conflict' position acknowledges the inadequacy of treating large-scale terrorist attacks as mere criminality. By this interpretation, a robust response beyond that which would be permitted in a purely law-enforcement paradigm is permissible pursuant to the *ius ad bellum* principle of self-defence. Since the terrorism and resulting counter-terrorist actions do not amount to an armed conflict, the law of armed conflict would not apply. Roy Schondorf has suggested that for advocates of this approach, 'in accordance with the literature and jurisprudence regarding the use of force in self-defense during peacetime, the laws that would govern military actions taken in self-defense would be the same laws as apply in times of formal armed conflict'.[47] But assuming this is so, the question is which laws? General principles applicable in all armed conflicts, such as distinction? The law of non-international armed conflict? That of international armed conflict?

Determining Applicability of the Laws of War to the War on Terror' (2008) 81 *Temple Law Review* 787; G. Corn, 'Making the Case for Conflict Bifurcation in Afghanistan' in M. Schmitt (ed.), *The War in Afghanistan: A Legal Analysis* (2009) 181. For a well-structured and argued piece suggesting a category of 'extra-state armed conflict', see R. Schondorf, 'Extra-State Armed Conflict: Is There a Need for a New Legal Regime?' (2004) 37 *New York University Journal of International Law and Politics* 1 (Schondorf, *Extra-State Armed Conflict*).

[45] G. Corn and E. Talbot Jensen, 'Transnational Armed Conflict: A "Principled" Approach to the Regulation of Counter-Terror Combat Operations' (2009) 42 *Israeli Law Review* 46, 50.

[46] ICRC, 'Statement: The Relevance of IHL in the Context of Terrorism' (21 July 2005), available at: <www.icrc.org/eng/resources/documents/misc/terrorism-ihl-210705.htm>.

[47] Schondorf, *Extra-State Armed Conflict*, 30.

Professor Yoram Dinstein has raised an interesting side note as to the normative consequence of actions by a State outside its borders against terrorists. Explaining his notion of 'extra-territorial law enforcement' in situations in which the State where the terrorists are located does not consent to counter-terrorist operations on its territory, Dinstein suggests that

> [a]lthough acting beyond the limits of Arcadian consent, Utopia – in taking these measures – does what Arcadia itself should have done, had it possessed the means and disposition to perform its duty. The situation amounts to an international armed conflict since Utopia resorts to forcible measures on Arcadian soil in the absence of Arcadian consent, and thus two States are involved in the use of force without being on the same side. But there is no war between Utopia and Arcadia: the international armed conflict is 'short of war'.

This is an interesting take on the issue. However, if Utopian and Arcadian forces do not engage in hostilities, the fact that they may be technically engaged in an international armed conflict is of little practical import. Rather, as noted, the key issue is what law governs Utopia's actions against the terrorists.

At present, the issue of how to classify transnational conflict remains unresolved. Only State practice, either physical or verbal, will eventually resolve the issue.

4. Complex battlespaces

A central feature of the British vision of future warfare is complexity. The battle-space will be congested, cluttered, contested and connected and combat actions will be constrained by Western legal and societal norms.[48] Britain's enemies will engage in hybrid warfare by combining conventional, irregular and high-end asymmetric actions.[49] In this environment, application of the law of armed conflict, especially its core principle of distinction, will prove especially difficult.

In terms of conflict classification, the most challenging aspect of this complexity is the coincidence of conflicts. 'Conflict could involve a range of trans-national, state, group and individual participants who will concentrate and operate both globally and locally'.[50] Indeed, '[a] single adversary *may* constitute an amalgam of regular, insurgents, terrorists, irregulars, and criminals'.[51] The classification predicament is that one's forces may be involved in different forms of conflict in the same battle-space. Such conflicts are 'horizontally mixed', that is, two or more conflicts which are distinct in terms of classification are underway in the same area of operations.[52]

---

[48] See MoD, DCDC, 'Future Character of Conflict' (2010) 20–5 (DCDC, *Future Character of Conflict*); DCDC, *Global Strategic Trends*, 88–90.
[49] DCDC, *Future Character of Conflict*, 13.
[50] Ibid. DCDC, *Global Strategic Trends*, 84.
[51] DCDC, *Global Strategic Trends*.
[52] The ICJ acknowledged horizontally mixed conflicts in the 1986 *Nicaragua* case. There, the Court held that '[t]he conflict between the Contra forces and those of the Government of Nicaragua is an armed conflict which is "not of an international character". The acts of the Contras towards the

A glimpse of this future was apparent in Iraq, where Coalition forces performing occupation duties or conducting counter-terrorism missions, remnants of the Iraqi armed forces, the New Iraqi Army, Iraqi police, militia groups opposed to the Coalition forces and/or the emergent Iraqi government, transnational terrorists, jihadis, tribal groups involved in the Sunni Awakening, private security companies and foreign intelligence operatives, inter alia, operated in the same battlespace at one time or another.[53] Similarly, in Afghanistan, the United States and its allies launched an international armed conflict against Afghanistan in October 2001 which, for a period, took place alongside an ongoing non-international armed conflict between the Taliban and the forces comprising the Northern Alliance.[54] And in the Great Lakes conflicts, non-international armed conflicts that spilled over into neighbouring territory at times generated international armed conflicts between the territorial State and the State fighting insurgents, as well as non-international armed conflicts between the insurgents and the forces of the territorial State.[55] Complicating matters, and as perceptively noted in British future conflict scenarios, States which are exercising a degree of control over an organized armed group are likely to mask their activities, thereby frustrating the already difficult task of assessing whether sufficient control exists to qualify as an armed conflict between the State sponsor and the target State.[56]

The nature of a conflict, or conflicts, may also shift over time, as illustrated again by both the cases of Iraq and Afghanistan, where international armed conflicts morphed into non-international ones once the Baathist and Taliban governments were respectively ousted from power. In the *Tadić* case, the ICTY's Appeals Chamber accepted the premise that an intra-state armed conflict can become international through the participation of other States.[57] A conflict which shifts from international to non-international, or vice versa, is 'vertically mixed'.[58] The complexity of classification is dramatically exacerbated when conflicts in a particular area are both vertically and horizontally mixed.

Beyond the intricacy of classifying the various strands of conflict lies the challenge of making practical sense of the law which applies. Militaries employ rules of engagement (ROE) to transform legal requirements into action. To be effective, the ROE must both be understandable to fielded forces and reflect policy and operational concerns. Optimally, the ROE should normatively track the type of conflict in which they are to be applied, lest they prove either unnecessarily restrictive or overly permissive.

Nicaraguan Government are therefore governed by the law applicable to conflicts of that character; whereas the actions of the United States in and against Nicaragua fall under the legal rules relating to international conflicts'. *Nicaragua*, para 219.

[53] See ch. 11 on classification of conflict in Iraq.
[54] See ch. 8 on classification of conflict in Afghanistan.
[55] See ch. 6 on classification of conflict in the DRC.
[56] 'In order to confuse the international community both state and non-state adversaries may seek to obscure their involvement.' DCDC, *Future Character of Conflict*, 10.
[57] *Tadić*, para 84.
[58] On horizontally and vertically mixed conflicts, see Dinstein, *International Armed Conflict*, 26–8.

In a vertically mixed conflict, the difficulty lies in determining when the classification of conflict has changed such that the ROE can be modified accordingly. Experience in contemporary conflicts demonstrates that this is no easy task.[59] Even more problematic is the horizontally mixed conflict, for combat forces cannot be expected to shift back and forth between ROE depending on the force against which they are engaged. In practice, this sometimes necessitates a single set of ROE based on the most restrictive form of conflict. When this occurs operational flexibility in dealing with those forces involved in the type of conflict to which more permissive norms would otherwise apply is sacrificed.

As noted, the MoD has identified a further factor complicating the future battlespace—the growing prevalence of criminal organized armed groups. '[P]olitical violence *will* often be indistinguishable from criminal violence. Criminal elements *will* become more sophisticated; they *may* have access to military hardware and *will* be comfortable operating in cyberspace.'[60] For instance, both Mexico and Columbia have had to resort to robust military force in order to combat well-armed and trained criminal drug cartels.

It is uncertain how such hostilities should be treated with respect to classification. At first blush, it would seem a law-enforcement paradigm should attach. However, in light of the size, organization and fighting wherewithal of many criminal groups, as a practical matter a State will only be able to deal with them by employing its armed forces in classic combat operations. Are high order counter-criminal operations armed conflict and, if so, of what classification?

Some purely domestic criminal groups will meet the organization and protracted armed violence criteria applicable to non-international armed conflict. In such cases, the hurdle is underlying motivation, specifically whether some form of political motivation is a condition precedent to armed conflict.

The Commentaries to Common Article 3 suggest that the drafters of the 1949 Geneva Conventions intended to exclude mere criminality. An early proposal of text for the article provided that the conventions would apply '[i]n all cases of armed conflict which are not of an international character, especially cases of civil war, colonial conflicts, or wars of religion, which may occur in the territory of one or more of the High Contracting Parties'.[61] Numerous delegations expressed concern the wording would

> cover in advance all forms of insurrection, rebellion, anarchy, and the break-up of States, and even plain brigandage.... To compel the Government of a State in the throes of internal conflict to apply to such a conflict the whole of the provisions of a Convention expressly concluded to cover the case of war would mean giving its enemies, who might be no more than a handful of rebels or common brigands the

---

[59] M.N. Schmitt, 'Targeting and International Humanitarian Law in Afghanistan' in M.N. Schmitt (ed.), *The War in Afghanistan: A Legal Analysis* (2009) 307.

[60] DCDC, *Global Strategic Trends*, 84.

[61] Pictet, *Geneva Convention III* Commentary. 31; J. Pictet (ed.), *Geneva Convention Relative to the Protection of Civilian Persons in Time of War: commentary* (1958) 30 (Pictet, *Geneva Convention IV Commentary*).

status of belligerents, and possibly even a certain degree of legal recognition. There was also a risk of ordinary criminals being encouraged to give themselves a semblance of organization as a pretext for claiming the benefit of the Convention, representing their crimes as 'acts of war' in order to escape punishment for them.[62]

Although the core objection was application of the Conventions in their entirety to non-international armed conflict, a desire to exclude criminality from their reach was also apparent. For many delegations, '[t]he expression [not of an international character] was so general, so vague, that . . . it might be taken to cover any act committed by force of arms—any form of anarchy, rebellion, or even plain banditry'.[63] The response to the concerns also reflected a sense that criminal motivation did not suffice. 'Insurgents . . . are not all brigands' and 'the behaviour of the insurgents in the field would show whether they were in fact mere felons, or, on the contrary, real combatants who deserved to receive protection under the Conventions'.[64] That the delegates generally understood conflict not of an international character to contain some form of political motivation was likewise evident in the ICRC's non-binding and non-exclusive list of sample criteria, which refers to 'the Party in revolt against the de jure Government' and 'insurgents'.[65] Elsewhere, the Commentary adopts the denominator 'rebel Party'.[66]

The problem is that the 'criminals' the drafters had in mind were brigands and bandits, those who roamed areas of hostilities taking advantage of the disorder for criminal ends. In future conflict, as suggested by the present activities of Mexican and Columbian drug gangs, the issue is not banditry and brigandage, but rather armed violence resembling that envisaged by the drafters with respect to Common Article 3. The Commentary notes that '[s]peaking generally, it must be recognized that the conflicts referred to in Article 3 are armed conflicts, with armed forces on either side engaged in hostilities—conflicts, in short, which are in many respects similar to an international war, but take place within the confines of a single country. In many cases, each of the parties is in possession of a portion of the national territory, and there is often some sort of front'.[67] This description accurately depicts what is occurring in Mexico, Columbia and elsewhere with regard to counter-criminal operations.

This being so, and assuming their activities meet the criteria of organization and protracted armed violence, two classification options are reasonable. It can be plausibly asserted that the activities of criminal organized armed groups do not comprise armed conflict because their motivation is financial, rather than political. They are not fighting the State out of any sense of opposition to the government, but rather because the government stands in the way of fulfilment of their criminal designs. The legal regime applicable to law-enforcement activities should accord-

---

[62] Pictet, *Geneva Convention III Commentary*, 32.

[63] Pictet, *Geneva Convention IV Commentary*, 35. The Commentary to the Second Convention uses the term 'brigandage'. J. Pictet (ed.), *Geneva Convention for the Amelioration of the Condition of Wounded, Sick and Shipwrecked Members of the Armed Forces at Sea: commentary* (1960) 32.

[64] Pictet, *Geneva Convention III Commentary*, 32.

[65] See e.g. Pictet, *Geneva Convention IV Commentary*, 35, 36.

[66] See e.g. ibid, 34.   [67] Ibid, 36.

ingly apply irrespective of the level of violence. This interpretation seems to adhere most closely to the drafters' original intent.

Alternatively, it is arguable that the hostilities between the State and the criminal groups amount to a non-international armed conflict when they are indistinguishable in practice from more traditional non-international armed conflicts. The State must resort to military force to combat the organizations, civilians are placed at equal (arguably greater) risk during such conflicts and in many cases the criminal gangs control territory. In particular, the threat to the State is as grave as that posed by politically motivated rebels and insurgents. Since the prescriptive regime must remain responsive to the context in which they operate, it makes sense to classify these conflicts as non-international.

The dilemma of classifying trans-border criminality is equally acute. Reduced to basics, international armed conflict is a conflict between one State and either another State (including non-state forces under its control), or, more controversially, external organized armed groups acting against the State. Since the activities of transnational criminal groups are not infused with a desire to strike at the State itself, it would appear overbroad to classify such conflicts as international. This is especially so in light of the lower threshold of violence necessary to qualify as an international armed conflict, for it is already questionable whether criminal violence can even constitute non-international armed conflict (which requires a higher level of violence). Such conflict would accordingly be more appropriately styled non-international, although the obstacles outlined above to this classification would be compounded by the fact that the conflict transcends borders.

Finally, it must be noted that the growing permeability of State borders will further aggravate classification difficulties. This is certainly true in the context of technological innovation. For instance, advances in global communications and transportation increase the likelihood of conflict, even purely intra-state conflict, having international features. They also enhance the ease (and stealth) with which external States can exert control over organized armed groups in, or targeting, another State. The continued existence of un- or poorly-governed territory will also prove attractive to transnational armed groups seeking bases beyond the reach of their enemies. And as States are attacked from abroad, military technology has made it possible for them to strike back quickly thousands of miles away. These and similar factors will complicate classification issues such as attribution of the actions of non-state actors to States and the classification of non-state transnational terrorist and criminal activity, cyber warfare and spill-over conflicts.

5. Law's influence on future conflict

The topics addressed above reflect those aspects of future conflict cited by the MoD that bear most directly on classifying conflict. But evolving legal norms will also affect conflict, for, as pointed out at the beginning of this chapter, law and war exist in a symbiotic relationship.

Three trends emerge from the studies contained in this volume. First, human rights are increasingly making their weight felt in the battlespace. The fit is not an easy one. Human rights law responds to the disproportionate power States wield over individuals, and therefore seeks to safeguard them from the abuse of that power through the granting of 'rights'. The law of armed conflict, by contrast, reflects a delicate balance between two competing State interests, that of effectively using force during an armed conflict (military necessity) and the protection of those for whom the State is responsible (humanity).[68] Moreover, the effective application of the law of armed conflict depends to an extent on the dynamic of reciprocity between parties to a conflict, a factor generally absent with regard to the implementation of human rights norms.

In the past, some experts argued that human rights law was inapplicable during armed conflict.[69] This view has generally been rejected (although debates over the scope and manner of application in armed conflict remain highly nuanced).[70] The ICJ has on numerous occasions confirmed that human rights apply in armed conflict. For instance, in the *Nuclear Weapons* Advisory Opinion it found the International Covenant on Civil and Political Rights applicable during armed conflict. Importantly, it opined that the determination of when a killing during armed conflict violates the prohibition on arbitrary deprivation of life is made by reference to the *lex specialis* of the law of armed conflict.[71] The Court further developed its view on the relationship between human rights law and the law of armed conflict in the *Wall* Advisory Opinion. There it highlighted three possibilities: 'some rights may be exclusively matters of international humanitarian law; others may be exclusively matters of human rights law; yet others may be matters of both these branches of international law'.[72] It then applied the principle of *lex specialis*. Regional and domestic courts have likewise been active in imposing human rights obligations on States involved in armed conflicts.[73]

The trend can only be expected to continue. This is particularly so whenever 1) the nature of the conflict departs from the traditional paradigm of armed conflict, as

---

[68] See M.N. Schmitt, 'Military Necessity and Humanity in International Humanitarian Law: Preserving the Delicate Balance' (2010) 50 *Virginia Journal of International Law* 795 (Schmitt, *Military Necessity*).

[69] Contemporary arguments against applicability tend to be more sophisticated. For instance, applying human rights law in particular armed conflicts may be objected to on the basis that a relevant treaty norm was not intended to apply in armed conflicts or that human rights law has no extraterritorial effect, positions that have been advanced most notably by the United States. See generally, M. Dennis, 'Application of Human Rights Treaties Extraterritorially in Times of Armed Conflict and Military Occupation' (2005) 99 *AJIL* 119.

[70] On the relationship between human rights law and the law of armed conflict, see F. Hampson, 'The Relationship between International Humanitarian Law and Human Rights Law from the Perspective of a Human Rights Treaty Body' (2008) 871(90) *International Review of the Red Cross* 549 (Hampson, *Human Rights Law*). An interesting, albeit somewhat controversial, discussion of the relationship is R.J. Delahunty and J. Yoo, 'What is the Role of International Human Rights Law in the War on Terror?' (2010) 59 *DePaul Law Review* 803.

[71] *Nuclear Weapons*, para 25; International Covenant on Civil and Political Rights (ICCPR), art. 6(1).

[72] *Palestinian Wall*, para 106. See also, *Congo v Uganda*, paras 216–20.

[73] See Hampson, *Human Rights Law*.

in terrorism and criminality; 2) the State is involved in hostilities with those over whom it exercises a degree of control, as in non-international armed conflict and occupation; or 3) robust regional or domestic human rights architectures exist that can be extended to the battlespace by activist judiciaries.[74]

A second tendency that will impact future classification efforts is a bleeding together of the norms applicable to the various genres of conflict. To the extent this occurs, the need to differentiate between categories of conflict becomes less pressing. For good or bad, the ICTY has been a leader in breaking down the barriers between non-international and international armed conflict. Although professing fidelity to the distinction, it has watered down its impact by extending norms governing the latter into the former in the guise of customary law of armed conflict. According to the Tribunal,

> it cannot be denied that customary rules have developed to govern internal strife. These rules ... cover such areas as protection of civilians from hostilities, in particular from indiscriminate attacks, protection of civilian objects, in particular cultural property, protection of all those who do not (or no longer) take active part in hostilities, as well as prohibition of means of warfare proscribed in international armed conflicts and ban of certain methods of conducting hostilities.[75]

The Tribunal adopted an array of international armed conflict rules into the law of non-international armed conflict.[76] It took a similar tack in the *Čelebići* case: 'In light of the fact that the majority of the conflicts in the contemporary world are internal, to maintain a distinction between the two legal regimes and their criminal consequences in respect of similarly egregious acts because of the difference in nature of the conflicts would ignore the very purpose of the Geneva Conventions, which is to protect the dignity of the human person.'[77]

To justify its position, the ICTY implicitly cited an attitudinal shift regarding conflict.

> A State-sovereignty-oriented approach has been gradually supplanted by a human-being-oriented approach. Gradually the maxim of Roman law *hominum causa omne jus constitutum est* (all law is created for the benefit of human beings) has gained a firm foothold in the international community as well. It follows that in the area of armed conflict the distinction between interstate wars and civil wars is losing its value as far as

---

[74] K. Watkin, 'Controlling the Use of Force: A Role for Human Rights Norms in Contemporary Armed Conflict' (2004) 98 *AJIL* 1, 2.

[75] *Tadić*, paras 111–12, 127.

[76] The ICTY's cautionary note in this regard provides little guidance in making the distinction.

> The emergence of the aforementioned general rules on internal armed conflicts does not imply that internal strife is regulated by general international law in all its aspects. Two particular limitations may be noted: (i) only a number of rules and principles governing international aremd conflicts have gradually been extended to apply to internal conflicts; and (ii) this extension has not taken place in the form of a full and mechanical transplant of those rules to internal conflicts; rather, the general essence of those rules, and not the detailed regulation they may contain, has become applicable to internal conflicts. (*Tadić*, para 126.)

[77] *Prosecutor v Delalić et al (Čelebići)*, IT-96-21-A, Judgment (Appeals Chamber), 20 February 2001, para 172.

human beings are concerned. . . . If international law, while of course duly safeguarding the legitimate interests of States, must gradually turn to the protection of human beings, it is only natural that the aforementioned dichotomy should gradually lose its weight.[78]

The ICRC's *Customary International Humanitarian Law* study evidences the same tendency to blur the lines between international and non-international armed conflict.[79] This drew a sharp rebuke from the United States, which argued that two general errors permeated the study: 1) assertion that 'a significant number of rules contained in the Additional Protocols . . . have achieved the status of customary international law', and 2) the lack of evidence to support the customary status of many of the purported rules for non-international armed conflict.[80]

Despite US protestations, the erosion of the barriers between these two forms of conflict is undeniable. This is certainly the case with regard to treaties. Prominent post-Additional Protocol II examples include the Ottawa Convention on Anti-Personnel Mines (1997),[81] the Second Protocol to the Hague Cultural Property Convention (1999)[82] and the Dublin Convention on Cluster Munitions (2008).[83] In 2001, an amendment to the Convention on Certain Conventional Weapons was adopted that extended the coverage of its protocols into non-international armed conflict.[84] As these examples illustrate, the tide appears to be moving ineluctably in the direction of prophylactic legal regimes which govern both international and non-international armed conflict.

Lastly, there is a growing propensity to craft rules of engagement that are far more restrictive than would otherwise be the case under the law of armed conflict. In great part, this tendency is the product of two forces. First, non-governmental organizations such as Human Rights Watch and Amnesty International are increasingly active in monitoring the application of law on the battlefield. Unsurprisingly, they tend to tilt their assessments in the direction of limitations on the use of force, arguably skewing the delicate balance between military necessity and humanitarian concerns undergirding the law of armed conflict.[85] In the face of real-time globalized media coverage of war, such propensities cannot be ignored by the warfighters.

---

[78] *Tadić,* para 97.

[79] J.M. Henkaerts and L. Doswald-Beck, *Customary International Humanitarian Law* (2005).

[80] Letter from Mr John Bellinger, Legal Counsel of the Department of State, and Mr William Haynes, General Counsel of the Department of Defense, to Dr Jakob Kellenberger (3 November 2006), available at: <www.defense.gov/home/pdf/Customary_International_Humanitiarian_Law.pdf>.

[81] 1997 Ottawa Convention, art. 1.

[82] Second Protocol to the Hague Convention for the Protection of Cultural Property in the Event of Armed Conflicts, art. 2.

[83] 2008 Dublin Convention, art. 1(1).

[84] Amendment to the Convention on Prohibitions or Restrictions on the Use of Certain Conventional Weapons which may be deemed to be Excessively Injurious or to have Indiscriminate Effect, Doc. No. CCW/CONF/II/2 (21 December, 2001).

[85] See e.g. Amnesty International, 'NATO/Federal Republic of Yugoslavia: "Collateral Damage" or Unlawful Killings? Violations of the Laws of War by NATO During Operation Allied Force' (2000), available at: <www.amnesty.org/en/library/info/EUR70/018/2000>; Human Rights Watch, 'Off Target: The Conduct of the War and Civilian Casualties in Iraq' (2003), available at: <www.hrw.org/en/reports/2003/12/11/target>. For comments thereon, see Schmitt, *Military Necessity*, 822–5.

Second, military forces engaged in counter-insurgency campaigns and stability operations, such as those in Afghanistan and Iraq, have ratcheted down their use of force through restrictive ROE designed to avoid alienating the civilian population.[86] The practical result is that for fielded forces, classification of conflict matters less than it has in the past. Of course, ROE are not law. Rather they constitute guidance to the armed forces engaged in a conflict as to how and when they may use force based on law, policy and operational concerns. Nevertheless, it must be acknowledged that they exert subtle influence on the attitudes of those on and off the battlefield as to appropriate behaviour.

6. Conclusions

The British vision of future conflict presents legal analysts with complex problems that admit of no easy solution. This is understandable, for the extant regime of classification was based on the twentieth century proposition that only two forms of armed conflict existed, hostilities between States or conflict between a State and those in rebellion. Moreover, conflict was carried out kinetically—dropping bombs, firing artillery, shooting weapons and so forth—and only one conflict dominated a particular space.

In the context of likely twenty-first century conflict, this regime is placed under significant stress by new means and methods of warfare, organized armed terrorist and criminal groups that operate both transnationally and employ high levels of violence and conflicts which are mixed horizontally and vertically. It will be some time before a consensus understanding of how the present norms regarding classification will evolve to deal with these phenomena. As those understanding emerge, they will be influenced by trends in the law, such as the growing weight of human rights norms and the blurring of the boundaries between international and non-international armed conflict.

The impact on classification of conflict is likely to reflect all three possibilities set forth at the beginning of this chapter as to how law and conflict adjust to changes in each other. Some aspects of conflict classification are likely to fall into desuetude. For instance, over time the distinction between conflict under Common Article 3 and conflict under Additional Protocol II, which occupied a *de minimis* role in the analysis of future warfare set forth above, may fade away. Other aspects will likely be reinterpreted to fit emerging contexts of armed conflict that were unanticipated. This is probable as to cyber operations. Finally, new norms will emerge to address phenomena that have so fundamentally changed that the existing classification architecture is no longer acceptable or which reveal classificatory lacuna. This can be expected with regard to criminality approaching what is today understood as war. Ultimately, though, the foundational questions will remain the same: 1) What is armed conflict? 2) Where do the boundaries lie between the various forms of conflict? and 3) What law applies in each?

[86] See eg the approach taken in the US 'COIN Manual'. Headquarters, Department of the Army & Headquarters, Marine Corps Combat Development Command, FM 3-24/MCWP 3-33.5, Counter-insurgency (2006).

PART III

15

Conclusions

Elizabeth Wilmshurst

1. Introduction

The purpose of this chapter is to draw together themes which emerge from the case studies and to consider the challenges they leave with us.[1] The chapter is in three parts. It begins by summarizing many of the difficulties in classifying the situations of armed violence covered by the case studies,[2] difficulties which relate both to the process of classification and its outcome. The chapter then discusses the legal and practical consequences of classification, in particular with regard to issues of detention and the application of force. The final section reaches conclusions.

2. Case studies: problems of classification

In classifying the various situations of armed violence, whether in accordance with the views of the participants or with their own, the authors of the case studies met with significant practical difficulties. The first lay in establishing the facts. The problem of finding objective, verifiable information was particularly acute in the cases of the DRC,[3] Al-Qaeda[4] and Colombia,[5] not only for outside analysts but also for the parties to the hostilities. For example in the DRC and in Colombia, it would not always have been clear to the parties themselves in every phase of armed

---

[1] Although the issues in this chapter have been discussed by the contributors to this volume, the views expressed here are not necessarily shared by all contributors.

[2] The hostilities in Libya and Mexico are included in this discussion where appropriate, as explained in ch. 1 above. Some classification difficulties are not summarized here, e.g. effect of blockade.

[3] Chapter 6, section 6.1: 'Congo's vast territory coupled with its porous borders and its history of perpetual cross-border migrant flows and associated violence makes reliable evidence-gathering an almost impenetrable task and even allegations of the active deployment of foreign troops on its territory have been difficult to confirm.'

[4] Chapter 13, section 8.1.

[5] Chapter 7, section 8.

violence whether the threshold of an armed conflict had been reached or whether there was still 'merely' a breakdown of law and order. The author of the Al-Qaeda case study concluded that:

> The huge difficulties raised by the lack of facts necessitates greater emphasis on the need to gather more information—whether through research or by demanding information through legal and accountability mechanisms. Without more facts, many of these matters will remain as continuous academic debates based on hypothesis, without being able to apply them to actual situations.[6]

Linked to this was the persistent problem of changing circumstances which made it difficult to assess the nature of the armed violence at any one moment.[7]

A further difficulty lay in identifying the parties to the conflict. The theoretical problem, discussed in section 2.7 below, was to decide on the legal criteria for ascertaining control by one State or group over another. The factual problem lay in determining the nature of the relationship. In South Ossetia, for example, ascertaining whether or not there was a separate non-international armed conflict, in addition to an international one, depended upon whether Russia in fact controlled the South Ossetian forces.[8]

The authors of the case studies set out to identify how the participants in armed violence classified the situation, but in doing so discovered that the participants often failed to classify clearly, if at all. Sometimes there were political reasons for this failure or for the choice of an obviously 'wrong' classification. In the DRC case study, where there was overwhelming factual evidence to support a particular legal assessment, the author concluded that political rhetoric and State interests appeared to prevail over fact.[9] In Northern Ireland, the British government did not classify the hostilities as an armed conflict even during the most violent period of the Troubles; its application of the law-enforcement paradigm throughout was done for political and practical reasons, not because of difficulties in understanding the nature of a conflict.[10] This exemplifies a reluctance of States to acknowledge that internal violence has reached the level of armed conflict and that the opposition must therefore be regarded as an 'equal' party to a conflict rather than a group of common criminals. In different circumstances, however, there is increasingly the opposite tendency of classifying as armed conflict what might more appropriately be termed a law-enforcement situation.[11]

---

[6] Chapter 13, section 8.4.

[7] In the DRC, the changing allegiances of armed groups made analysis difficult: 'as the armed groups splintered, reconstituted, and realigned themselves with the different belligerent States over the course of the conflict, gauging the element of control becomes even more testing'; ch. 6 , section 4.2. In Colombia 'the longer an armed conflict continues, the more fluctuations are likely to occur, both in the intensity of the hostilities, and in the organizational structure of groups involved, [which] makes it difficult to assess when a situation reaches, or falls below, the thresholds for Common Article 3 and Additional Protocol II'; ch. 7, section 8.

[8] Chapter 10, section 4.2; see also, the difficulty in establishing the relationship between Taliban and Al-Qaeda (ch. 8 (Afghanistan), section 2.1).

[9] Chapter 6, section 6.1.

[10] Chapter 5. See also, the varying statements made by the Colombian government as to the existence or not of an armed conflict in relation to FARC and in relation to the illegal armed groups; ch. 7, section 3.1.

[11] See ch. 13 (Al-Qaeda).

In other cases the parties to the conflict made contradictory statements[12] or disagreed with each other about classification. There were cases when parties on the same side of the conflict could not agree as to the type of conflict in which they were engaged.[13]

Further complicating matters was the fact that States not parties to a conflict rarely expressed clear views as to classification, even when condemning breaches of international humanitarian law. The Security Council regularly made vague references to the law.[14] The ICRC is another international actor which does not usually make public its analyses of classification until after the event.

In addition to these difficulties of a factual nature, the authors of the case studies faced legal problems familiar to all those attempting classification of hostilities. Many of those arising in the studies are outlined below.

2.1. Non-international armed conflict

One of the more difficult issues in classification is establishing the distinction between armed violence not reaching the threshold of an armed conflict, for which the law-enforcement paradigm is appropriate, and violence constituting a non-international armed conflict. The case studies had to address various issues regarding the protracted nature or intensity of armed violence[15] and the organization of a non-state armed group,[16] criteria which together need to be met before categorizing a situation of violence as a non-international armed conflict. These difficulties were however ones of application of the law, not of the law itself.

While the omission of a definition of non-international armed conflict in Common Article 3 was not identified as a difficulty by any of the authors of

---

[12] In Libya, for example, the Libyan Interim National Council referred to the 2011 hostilities as the February 17 revolution or liberation, leading to the conclusion (as must clearly have been the case) that the 'rebels' were engaged in a non-international armed conflict, but the Council also stated 'that its policies strictly adhere to the Geneva Convention relative to the Treatment of Prisoners of War', a treaty which is applicable only in international armed conflict. See The Libyan Interim National Council, 'The treatment of Detainees and Prisoners' Press Release (25 March 2011), available at: <www.ntclibya.org/english/prisoners/>.

[13] E.g. the differing views of NATO parties as to the nature of the hostilities in which ISAF was engaged in Afghanistan; see ch. 8, section 3.1.

[14] In the case of Libya, an example among very many, the Council condemned 'all violations of applicable human rights and international humanitarian law, including violations that involve unlawful killings, other uses of violence against civilians, or arbitrary arrests and detentions' without specifying which body of international humanitarian law was applicable. SC res. 2009 (2011).

[15] E.g. the conflict in South Ossetia lasted for five or six days, giving rise to discussion of the issue whether it was of a sufficiently protracted nature to be a non-international armed conflict and the meaning of intensity of violence for this purpose; ch. 10, section 4.2. In the Al-Qaeda study the threshold of violence and the identity of the party to the conflict were linked. 'If numerous incidents round the world classified as terrorism could be attributed to the same entity then one could argue that the threshold for conflict has been crossed; if however these incidents are perpetrated by separate groups with no unified and organized command and control structure, it becomes difficult to add them all up together as evidence of an existing conflict.'; ch. 13, section 4.2.

[16] See ch. 13, section 4.2; the writer identified 'serious concerns about describing Al-Qaeda as a distinct and organized armed group, rather than a network of loosely affiliated groups sometimes reduced to little more than similar ideologies'. The situation in Libya in February 2011, where violence arose from political protests, also illustrated the difficulty of identifying the point at which there developed the necessary level of organization of an armed group for the purpose of assessing whether the violence amounted to a non-international armed conflict.

the case studies,[17] a problem met by some of the authors in distinguishing the law-enforcement paradigm from that of armed conflict related to whether the purpose or motive of the hostilities had any relevance to their classification. Are organized crime and the responses to it to be regarded as an armed conflict; are armed groups engaged in organized crime parties to an armed conflict? The question was addressed in the case studies on Colombia[18] and on the DRC.[19] The situation in Mexico is another case in point: the scale of armed criminal activity is well in excess of the threshold level of violence that would normally qualify it as armed conflict, and combating it requires a security response exceeding that normally associated with law enforcement.[20]

In considering a future where 'political violence will often be indistinguishable from criminal violence', the author of chapter 14 discussed the problem of classification as follows:

> ...assuming their [criminal groups'] activities meet the criteria of organization and protracted armed violence, two classification options are reasonable. It can be plausibly asserted that the activities of criminal organized armed groups do not comprise armed conflict because their motivation is financial, rather than political. They are not fighting the State out of any sense of opposition to the government, but rather because the government stands in the way of fulfilment of their criminal designs. The legal regime applicable to law-enforcement activities should accordingly apply irrespective of the level of violence. . . .
>
> Alternatively, it is arguable that the hostilities between the State and the criminal groups amount to a non-international armed conflict when they are indistinguishable in practice from more traditional non-international armed conflicts. The State must resort to military force to combat the organizations, civilians are placed at equal (arguably greater) risk during such conflicts and in many cases the criminal gangs control territory. In particular, the threat to the State is as grave as that posed by politically motivated rebels and insurgents. Since the prescriptive regime must remain responsive to the context in which they operate, it makes sense to classify these conflicts as non-international.[21]

It is the latter approach which is taken in this book, with the conclusion that motivation is not a criterion for determining the existence of an armed conflict.[22]

---

[17] See ch. 3, section 6.1; ch. 5 (Northern Ireland), section 3.2; ch. 10 (South Ossetia), section 4.2. As Pejic states: 'no definition would be capable of capturing the factual situations that reality throws up and . . . a definition would thus risk undermining the protective ambit of humanitarian law.' J. Pejic, 'Status of Armed Conflicts' in E. Wilmshurst and S. Breau (eds), *Perspectives on the ICRC Study on Customary International Humanitarian Law* (2007) 85 (Pejic, *Status of Armed Conflicts*); see also, D. Schindler 'The Different Types of Armed Conflicts According to the Geneva Conventions and Protocols' (1979) 163 *Recueil des Cours* 147; and L. Moir, *The Law of Internal Armed Conflict* (2002) 32.

[18] Chapter 7, section 4.4.

[19] Particularly in the period following the Second Congo War, much of the violence in the resource-rich provinces was directly linked to the control over resources for personal financial gain; ch. 6, section 5.2.

[20] See ch. 2, section 3.2 for a brief description of the violence in Mexico.

[21] Chapter 14, section 4.

[22] See ch. 2, section 3.2 and ch. 3, section 6.1. The author of ch. 2 notes, however, that the motives behind this kind of conflict 'differ from those traditionally ascribed to war by Clausewitz and his followers' and 'the view that the actions of criminal gangs can be regarded as being those of an

As the author of the Colombia case study pointed out, it would anyway be very difficult in practice to determine the motivation of all armed groups.[23] Similarly, none of the case studies regarded a terrorist motivation as significant for classification purposes.[24]

As to the two thresholds for non-international armed conflict—those of Common Article 3 and Additional Protocol II—none of the case studies revealed evidence of any practical impact of the division. The case study on Colombia for example referred to the government's acceptance on policy grounds of Additional Protocol II standards (as well as those of Common Article 3), in relation to at least some of the conflicts, and its authors carefully categorized the various hostilities as non-international armed conflict either under Common Article 3 or Additional Protocol II.[25] It was clear however that the distinction between the two thresholds had no impact in practice in any of those hostilities.[26] Similarly, in the Afghanistan case study, the author discussed the criteria for both forms of non-international armed conflict in treaty and customary law, as well as the question whether the conflict crossed the threshold of applicability of Additional Protocol II, either at all or in relation to different areas of Afghanistan, and the legal consequences for the rules on the use of force, but reached the conclusion that the issues seemed to have had no importance in practice.[27]

The fact is that there is no agreement on what the threshold is for non-international armed conflict in respect of the application of all of the rules of customary international law. It is difficult to show that there are two thresholds of non-international armed conflict *as a matter of customary law* and to establish the law that is applicable in each of them. The ICRC Customary Law Study, which did not examine the issue, does not distinguish between the different thresholds 'because it was found that in general States did not make this distinction in practice'.[28] The ICC Statute does not make a distinction;[29] nor does the ICRC Interpretive Guidance on Direct Participation in Hostilities. Chapter 14 concludes

---

"organised armed group", resulting in violent circumstances being categorized as armed conflict, is not uncontroversial'. (Section 3.2.)

[23] Chapter 7, section 4.4: 'How is the determination as to whether fighting is taking place for criminal or political reasons to be made? If non-state armed groups were to claim a political agenda or aim, would this suffice? Or would States demand the right to determine whether an armed group it opposes has a political motive or not?'

[24] See in particular ch. 13 (Al-Qaeda). This coincides with the ICRC's approach: 'the ICRC has taken a case by case approach to legally analyzing and classifying the various situations of violence that have occurred in the fight against terrorism. Some situations have been classified as an IAC, other contexts have been deemed to be NIACs, while various acts of terrorism taking place in the world have been assessed as being outside any armed conflict.' ICRC, 'International Humanitarian Law and the challenges of contemporary armed conflicts' Report (October 2011) 10 (ICRC, *Challenges of Contemporary Armed Conflicts*).

[25] Chapter 7, section 4.5.

[26] Ibid, section 8.

[27] Chapter 8, sections 3.2 and 4; and section 7.1.

[28] Pejic, *Status of Armed Conflicts*, 88.

[29] Akande dismissed the notion that art. 8(2)(f) of the ICC Statute introduces a third threshold; ch. 3, section 6.3. See also, A. Cullen, 'The Definition of Non-International Armed Conflict in the Rome Statute of the International Criminal Court: An Analysis of the Threshold of Application Contained in Article 8(2)(f)' (2007) *Journal of Conflict and Security Law* 419. For discussion of whether the ICC Statute has lowered the Protocol II threshold and suggestions that there should be a similar extension of the scope of applicability of customary rules in the Protocol see A. Paulus and

that 'over time the distinction between conflict under Common Article 3 and conflict under Additional Protocol II . . . may fade away';[30] this must be so at least with regard to the protective provisions of international humanitarian law.

2.2. Issues of recognition

The extent to which recognition of a new government[31] may change the classification of a conflict was a question that was addressed in the case of Afghanistan. The author of that case study considered that since the recognition of the Massoud government was never withdrawn, the US may have regarded at least a part of the Northern Alliance as the forces of Afghanistan; this could have been of direct significance to classification of the conflict if recognition plays a determinative role, in contrast to priority being given to the facts on the ground.[32] The issue also arose in the case of Libya. Beginning with the intervention of the NATO coalition under the authority of Security Council resolution 1973 (2011), there was an international armed conflict between the individual forces of the Coalition and Libya, in parallel with the non-international armed conflict between the 'rebels' and the Gaddafi regime. The recognition of the National Transitional Council as the government of Libya by some member States of the coalition did not, it is submitted, alter the classification of the conflict between those States and Gaddafi's forces. In other words, it is the facts rather than a subjective act of recognition alone which determines the category of armed violence.

2.3. Extraterritorial operations against non-state groups

Military operations conducted by one or more States against non-state armed groups on the territory of another State have given rise to problems of classification that were examined in the case studies. Examples include force used by Uganda and Rwanda in the Democratic Republic of the Congo, Colombian attacks on the FARC in Ecuador in 2008, and Israel's intervention in Lebanon in 2006; the counter-terrorism operations of the so-called 'war against Al-Qaeda' or 'global war on terror' conducted by the US provide another obvious example, with the targeting of persons connected with Al-Qaeda in countries such as Yemen, Somalia, and Pakistan.

M. Vashakmadze 'Asymmetrical war and the notion of armed conflict—a tentative conceptualization' (2009) 91 (873) *International Review of the Red Cross* 123.

[30] Chapter 14, section 6, see also, ch. 6, section 5.2 where the author concluded of Protocol II that: 'Although the Protocol advances the basic set of rules provided in Common Article 3 by strengthening the protections due to civilians and developing the rules pertaining to the conduct of hostilities, the evolution of customary international humanitarian law rules for non-international conflict has rendered the treaty rules almost redundant.' See further discussion in section 3.2 below (application of force).

[31] The fact that the UK has since 1980 not extended formal acts of recognition to governments (although the 2011 recognition of the Libyan TNC seemed to have been an exception to the practice) does not affect the question; some States do still accord recognition to governments, and the UK practice of 'dealing' with new administrations as though they were governments raises the same issue.

[32] See ch. 8, section 2.1.

The author of chapter 3 characterized as international armed conflict such uses of force as are carried out without the consent of the territorial State,

> because the use of force by the intervening foreign State on the territory of the territorial State, without the consent of the latter, is a use of force *against* the territorial State. This is so even if the use of force is not directed against the governmental structures of the territorial State, or the purpose of the use of force is not to coerce the territorial State in any particular way.[33]

But the more common view (and that accepted by most other contributors to this book) was that since the conflict is between the attacking State and the non-state actor, it is not one between two or more States (as in Common Article 2) and it is therefore a non-international armed conflict (unless of course it constitutes extra-territorial law enforcement). In the study on Al-Qaeda, for example, the author stated that 'classification rests primarily on the nature of the parties, and thus a conflict between a State and a non-state actor is a non-international armed conflict, even if it occurs extraterritorially',[34] with the proviso that the acts of force concerned meet the required threshold of armed conflict. The question of the consent—or not—of the territorial State is an issue for the *ius ad bellum* and not relevant to classification. The debate between these two views is likely to continue.

Whatever the differences in their views on this point, the contributors to this book showed no appetite for the creation of a new category of armed conflict to address the issue. While the author of the Al-Qaeda study took the position that an extraterritorial conflict against a non-state actor does not, prima facie, fit the traditional understandings of international and non-international armed conflict, he considered that they are nevertheless capable of encompassing new situations of this kind.[35] No new category was recommended for any of the forms of conflict which have a transnational element.[36]

2.4. Occupation and hostilities within an occupation

Contemporary forms of foreign military presence on a State's territory have given rise to a number of questions regarding the existence of occupation and the applicable law, and some of these were raised in the case studies.[37] International humanitarian law does not provide clear answers to questions as to the

---

[33] Chapter 3, section 9.

[34] Chapter 13, section 8.1. The author of ch. 14, in the context of a discussion on combating transnational terrorism, is more cautious: 'At present, the issue of how to classify transnational conflict remains unresolved.' (section 3.)

[35] Chapter 13, section 4.4.

[36] See discussion (and rejection) of proposals for a new category of armed conflict in ch. 3, section 9; ch. 12 (Lebanon), section 3.2; ch. 13 (Al-Qaeda), section 4.4; ch. 14 (the Future), section 3.

[37] The case study on Gaza (ch. 9), for example, as was to be expected, had to address controversial questions regarding both the classification of occupation and the laws applicable to it. See also, ch. 10 (South Ossetia): 'differing legal tests are applicable in determining whether the law of occupation applied, depending on whether the situation concerned individuals or other issues, such as property.' (section 4.4.) The occupation of Iraq which began in 2003 showed that the Security Council itself can interpose its own view of classification. (ch. 11, section 2.2; see also, section 6: 'although the Council

beginning and end of an occupation and as to the law applicable in prolonged occupations.[38]

A particular issue of difficulty was whether a conflict between the occupying State and non-state armed groups within the occupied State constituted an international or a non-international conflict.[39] On this point the views of the contributors to this book were divided. While a state of international armed conflict continues during a belligerent occupation, and the law of international armed conflict governs the conduct of hostilities, detention of prisoners of war and civilians, and other activities with a direct nexus to the original inter-state conflict,[40] a more complicated situation arises where the violence is not connected with the international conflict between the occupying and occupied States but concerns the occupying State and non-state armed groups.

In the DRC case study the question arose in the context of Uganda's occupation of Ituri, where Ugandan armed forces were already fighting armed groups. The author's view was that occupation per se did not transform the classification of the conflicts.[41]

The author of chapter 3 differed, and relied on the *Armed Activities* case[42] to support the view that in such circumstances, the actions of the occupying State in hostilities against non-state groups during the period of occupation will be governed by the law of occupation and other rules relating to international armed conflicts.[43] This is the view that was also taken by the Pre-Trial Chambers of the ICC in the *Lubanga* and *Katanga* cases,[44] the Chambers remarking that for the period between September 2002 and June 2003 the classification of the conflict must be international, due to the Ugandan occupation. The decisions of the Court were much criticized by those who point out that occupation does not internationalize the entire situation that exists in a territory; whilst the laws of international

---

clearly viewed the situation as one of occupation in Phase II, various Security Council resolutions mandated activities that ran counter to both the spirit and letter of the law of belligerent occupation.').

[38] See e.g. discussion in ICRC, *Challenges of Contemporary Armed Conflicts*, 26, 27.

[39] This is in addition to the sometimes difficult distinction between law enforcement by the occupying power and hostilities amounting to armed conflict, as to which the ICRC has noted that 'there is a need to clarify how the rules governing law enforcement and those regulating the conduct of hostilities interact in practice in the context of an occupation'. ICRC, *Challenges to Contemporary Armed Conflicts*, 28. The matter is touched on at the end of ch. 8 (Afghanistan), section 4.

[40] See ch. 11, section 2.2.

[41] See ch. 6, section 4.2. See also, ch. 9, section 4.4 at n 112.

[42] *Case Concerning Armed Activities on the Territory of the Congo (Democratic Republic of the Congo v Uganda)* ICJ Rep 2005, 168 and see also, ch. 3, section 5.1.

[43] See ch. 3, section 5.1: 'The conclusion follows from the fact that the Geneva Conventions, and other rules concerning international armed conflicts (including Additional Protocol I, where applicable), apply to the acts of the occupying power and regulate the relationship between the occupying power and the people in the occupied territory.'

[44] *Prosecutor v Thomas Lubanga Dyilo*, ICC-01/04-01/06-803, Decision on the Confirmation of Charges (Pre-Trial Chamber I), 29 January 2007, paras 216 and 220 (*Lubanga* Confirmation of Charges).

armed conflict are applicable to the occupation, the laws of non-international armed conflict can govern a particular armed conflict.[45] The judgment of the Trial Chamber in *Lubanga* effectively agreed with the critics and found that:

> although there is evidence of direct intervention on the part of Uganda, this intervention would only have internationalised the conflict between the two states concerned (viz. the DRC and Uganda).[46]

2.5. Operations established or authorized by the UN Security Council

It is well-accepted that international humanitarian law can apply to constrain the actions of peacekeepers and other mandated multinational forces;[47] the view that that body of law applies differently or not at all to such forces is now heard less often.[48] The mandate given to a multinational force does not preclude it from becoming a party to an armed conflict and the fact that it has an international mandate or authorization should not affect the general rules of classification, leading to the application of the ordinary rules of international humanitarian law. Although the UN as such is not bound by the relevant treaties, it is bound by customary international humanitarian law, by relevant Status of Forces Agreements with host States and agreements with troop-contributing countries.[49] But there remain controversies as to the point at which the armed violence in which the multinational forces are involved becomes an armed conflict to which they are a party, and as to the classification of such a conflict.

The author of chapter 3 gave the view that when peacekeepers act in personal self-defence they will generally not be participating directly in hostilities and thus are not to be regarded as parties to a conflict, a view supported by the case law.[50] On the other hand 'where the force used by UN forces is of a nature and intensity as would otherwise bring into effect an armed conflict, it ought to be recognized that they are involved in one, despite the fact that they act lawfully (in terms of the *ius ad*

---

[45] See e.g. T. Hoffman, 'Squaring the Circle?—International Humanitarian Law and Transnational Armed Conflicts' in M.J. Matheson and D. Momtaz (eds), *Rules and Institutions of International Humanitarian Law put to the Test of Recent Armed Conflicts* (2010) 217 (Hoffman, *Squaring the Circle*). For further discussion see T. Ferraro (ed.), 'Report on Occupation and other Forms of Administration of Foreign Territory' ICRC (2012).

[46] *Prosecutor v Thomas Lubanga Dyilo,* ICC-01/04-01/06-2842, Judgment pursuant to Article 74 of the Statute, 14 March 2012, para. 563 (*Lubanga,* trial judgment).

[47] See C. Greenwood, 'International Humanitarian Law and United Nations Military Operations' (1998) 1 *Yearbook of International Humanitarian Law* 3; Institut de Droit International, 'Resolution on the Conditions of Application of Humanitarian Rules of Armed Conflict to Hostilities in which United Nations Forces may be Engaged, adopted at Zagreb in 1971 ('the Zagreb Resolution')' (1971) 54 (II) *Annuaire de l'institut de droit international* 465.

[48] But the governments of some national contingents in the NATO force authorized by resolution 1973 (2011) in 2011 by the UN Security Council to undertake the humanitarian operation in Libya were not willing to declare that the conflict in which they were involved was an international armed conflict to which international humanitarian law applied as a matter of law, not merely of policy; this shows that the 'old' view is not completely dead.

[49] See ch. 3, section 8.

[50] See cases referred to in ch. 3, section 8.

bellum) in using such force'.[51] The DRC study addressed the question whether MONUC and MONUSCO were engaged as combatants in an armed conflict, and reached the view that at different periods they were, although it had initially been assumed in the normal way that the personnel of MONUC were 'civilians' and entitled to civilian protection.[52] The situation must be assessed at any one time in relation to the level and nature of the involvement of the forces in support of one of the parties to the conflict. This may lead to constant change.

> To accept that the status of peacekeepers in armed conflict is potentially a fluid one is to recognize the need to respond to the realities on the ground. But such a position is not without its problems. The consequence of adaptability is uncertainty, since the lawfulness of the use of force is inextricably tied to and contingent on the specific role of the peacekeeper at any given moment in time.[53]

As regards the classification of the conflict if a multinational force is under the command of the UN (or of some other organization such as NATO) and the hostilities are against the armed forces of a State, normal classification rules would point to an international armed conflict; the conflict would be between either the State and the troop-contributing countries or, where the force is a UN (or NATO) operation with the acts of its individual forces attributable to the organization, between the State and the international organization.[54] International forces may also be involved in non-international armed conflict, where they are fighting alongside the armed forces of a State within its territory against one or more organized armed groups.[55] Although not without controversy,[56] the better view is that such a conflict is indeed non-international, regardless of the international components of the multinational force. Thus in the DRC, 'putting to one side the difficulties faced in determining whether or not MONUC was a party to the conflicts, there is no question that the conflicts remained non-international in character since all the military operations were conducted either with the support of the DRC or in close collaboration with the FARDC [*Forces Armées de la République Démocratique du Congo*].'[57]

Thinking on this issue seems to have shifted over the years, and the existence of earlier instruments such as the 1994 Convention on the Safety of UN Personnel,[58]

---

[51] Ibid.
[52] Chapter 6, sections 5.2 and 5.3.
[53] Ibid, section 5.3.
[54] For the first alternative see ch. 3, section 8; the second requires that customary law has developed to broaden international armed conflicts to include those involving international organizations and States.
[55] See typology of non-international armed conflict in ch. 4, section 3.2.
[56] As pointed out in ch. 3, section 8.
[57] Chapter 6, section 5.2.
[58] The Convention does not apply to 'a United Nations operation authorized by the Security Council as an enforcement action under Chapter VII of the Charter of the United Nations in which any of the personnel are engaged as combatants against organized armed forces and *to which the law of international armed conflict applies*'. Kirsch notes that this clause was specifically accepted by the negotiators, for whom 'it was widely recognised that it is impossible for the Organization to be involved in an internal armed conflict, because once the UN or associated personnel intervene in a conflict against local forces, by definition, the conflict takes on an "international" scope'. P. Kirsch, 'La Convention sur la sécurité du personnel des Nations Unies et du personnel associé' in C. Emanuelli

which is limited to international armed conflict, and the 1999 Secretary-General's Bulletin, which also refers only to international armed conflicts, leaves the position with regard to the applicability of the correct body of law a little more uncertain than is quite comfortable. That correct classification in this area is essential is emphasized by the introduction in the ICC Statute of the war crimes of intentionally directing attacks against personnel involved in a peace-keeping mission, 'so long as they are entitled to the protection given to civilians or civilian objects under the international law of armed conflict'.[59]

2.6. Attribution

In determining the identity of the parties to a conflict, many of the case studies had to discuss the legal rules on attribution; this was relevant for example to their determination of whether acts of an armed group are attributable to a party to an international armed conflict such that hostilities with the group constitute part of that conflict, or are not so attributable, in which case the law of non-international armed conflict will apply.[60] The problem of the two different tests of 'effective' and 'overall' control, established by the rulings of the ICJ and the ICTY respectively, had to be addressed. While that problem has been resolved, according to the ICJ, by affirming that the tests are for different purposes—one to determine State responsibility and one for classification of a conflict—this two-test solution is not a universal view.[61] Various points of view are reflected in this volume. The author of chapter 3, for example, considered that the question of which test is to be used for classification of a conflict—whether support by a foreign State for a non-state group transforms a conflict into an international armed conflict—should be answered by whether the foreign State 'can be said to have used force' against the other State.[62] A similar conclusion, though by a different route, was reached by

---

(ed.), *Les casques bleus: policiers ou combattants?* (1997) 56 as cited by G. Porretto and S. Vité, *The application of international humanitarian law and human rights law to international organizations* (2006) 36.

[59] Article 8(2)(b)(iii) and (e)(iii).

[60] The issue is discussed in ch. 3, section 7.1; ch. 6 (DRC), sections 2.2 and 4.2; ch. 7 (Colombia), section 4.3; ch. 10 (South Ossetia), section 4.3; ch. 12 (Lebanon), section 3.1; ch. 14 (the Future), section 2.

[61] This view is expressed in the judgment of the ICJ in the *Genocide Convention* case: 'logic does not require the same test to be adopted in resolving the two issues, which are very different in nature', with the consequence that the degree of a State's involvement in an armed conflict may well differ from that required for State responsibility to arise, see *Case Concerning the Application of the Convention on the Prevention and Punishment of the Crime of Genocide (Bosnia and Herzegovina v Serbia and Montenegro)* ICJ Rep 2007, para 405. Cassese however declared that the ICJ put forward the two-test theory only 'as a gracious concession to the ICTY: it concedes that probably the Tribunal was right when dealing with issues concerning the nature of armed conflicts, but warns that it should not suggest solutions for more general international law problems. It bears recalling that the ICTY instead took the contrary view, holding that although the two questions differed, the test was to be the same'; A. Cassese, 'The *Nicaragua* and *Tadić* Tests Revisited in Light of the ICJ Judgment on Genocide in Bosnia' (2007) 18 *EJIL* 651.

[62] Although indirectly, by supporting the non-state actor; ch. 3, section 7.1. The author points out that a prior question is whether the non-state actor is a de facto organ of the foreign state.

the case study on Colombia in discussing the attribution of acts of an armed group operating on the territory of the State concerned; the authors regarded the correct test as one of agency, as outlined in the *La Rochela Massacre Case* by the Inter-American Court of Human Rights.[63] On the other hand, in assessing whether the acts of Hezbollah could be attributed to Lebanon for the purpose of classifying the conflict with Israel, the case study used exclusively the rules of State responsibility, adopting the test of effective control to make the determination.[64] The test of overall control, however, was used in the DRC case study.[65] This is clearly a debate that will have to continue.

2.7. Mixed or parallel conflicts

The possibility of international and non-international armed conflicts being carried out concurrently in the same territory was recognized by the International Court of Justice in the 1986 *Nicaragua* case.[66] There is still some support for taking a global view of such conflicts occurring in one territory when one party is the same in each case, and regarding them all as international.[67] But what is perhaps the more common view, and the view espoused by the contributors to this book, is that the only acceptable way of classifying mixed conflicts is to split them up into their component parts.[68]

The case studies which had to consider mixed conflicts in this volume were those on Afghanistan, the DRC, South Ossetia and Lebanon.[69] The consequences for the application of two bodies of international humanitarian law in the same space may be problematic,[70] and in some circumstances the only practical course may be to treat the hostilities as a single conflict. Thus the author of the Afghanistan case study commented with regard to the hostilities in which the US-led Coalition was involved in 2001:

> It may...be doubted whether it is feasible in this context to distinguish between operations of and against Al-Qaeda and the Taliban. Even if it is possible to make the legal distinction, for all practical purposes this was a single international armed conflict.[71]

[63] See discussion in ch. 7, section 4.3.

[64] See ch. 12, section 3.

[65] Chapter 6, section 4.2. And in the Afghanistan study, no choice was made between the two tests; ch. 8, section 2.1.

[66] *Military and Paramilitary Activities in and against Nicaragua (Nicaragua v United States of America)* ICJ Rep 1986, 14, para 219 *(Nicaragua).*

[67] See discussion in ch. 3, section 7.3, where the author cites Meron's reference to 'a crazy quilt of norms' applicable to the same conflict.

[68] See ch. 3, section 7.3, ch. 6 (DRC), section 6.1, ch. 10 (South Ossetia), section 6.1. See also, e.g. Hoffman, *Squaring the Circle*, 217.

[69] Chapter 8, section 2.2; ch. 6, sections 3.4, 4.2 and 6.1; ch. 10, sections 4.2 and 6.1; ch. 12, section 3.

[70] According to Stewart 'the relative strengths and weaknesses of the "mixed" and "global" views as to whether there can be two conflicts on the same territory indicate that reaching any sort of agreement within the present framework will inevitably involve choosing between a theory that cannot work and a practice that is not justified'. J. Stewart, 'Towards a single definition of armed conflict in international humanitarian law: A critique of internationalized armed conflict' (2003) 85 *International Review of the Red Cross* 335.

[71] Chapter 8, section 2.2.

In short, the rules on classification must not produce a result which is impossible of application in practice.

2.8. Geography

Finally, some of the case studies had the difficulty of ascertaining the geographical scope of the hostilities in question. In the case of Al-Qaeda, the controversy related to whether individuals 'carry the battlefield away with them whenever they relocate to a different territory', thus remaining a legitimate target.[72]

A related question concerns the classification of various forms of armed violence occurring in different parts of the same country. The Afghanistan case study asked whether it was possible to have, in different parts of one country, internal disturbances, a Common Article 3 non-international armed conflict and a conflict within Protocol II; and whether the criterion of protracted nature continues to apply once the situation is characterized as an armed conflict or whether the classification varies from week to week.[73] The question also arose in relation to UN troops: where one of their contingents is engaged for a time in armed conflict with a group in one part of the country does that mean that all contingents elsewhere in the country also lose their civilian immunity? The author of the case study on the DRC concluded that a positive answer 'is not only counter-intuitive but, clearly, hugely problematic for troop-contributing States'.[74] These questions remain unresolved.[75]

3. Case studies: the legal and practical consequences of classification

The choice of the case studies examined in this volume has dictated which difficulties of classification law should be discussed; they include a large number of the problems of classifying contemporary forms of armed violence. The issues are familiar to all international humanitarian lawyers, and they reflect problems both in

---

[72] Chapter 13, section 7.2.

[73] Chapter 8, section 3.2 . See also, discussion in relation to South Ossetia and Northern Ireland (ch. 10, section 6.1; ch. 5, section 3.2).

[74] Chapter 6, section 6.1. The author of ch. 3 believes that it is difficult to see why the answer should not be a positive one, although the outcome would 'deprive all UN peacekeepers of the protected status they ordinarily enjoy'; questions are also raised in that chapter with regard to the temporal element: 'May peacekeepers move from armed conflict to non-conflict depending on whether they are using force? Or once an armed conflict kicks in does it continue until there is some general conclusion of peace?': ch. 3, section 8.

[75] See L. Arimatsu, who criticizes 'territorialised legal reasoning' and suggests that recognizing that international humanitarian law 'is framed by spatial demarcations constituted by the emergence of the state, prompts us to inquire whether the apparent failure of the law to capture contemporary armed conflicts within its ambit can be partially explained by our inability to respond to de-territorialised armed conflicts within the territorialised framework' of the law; 'Territory, Boundaries And The Law Of Armed Conflict' 12 *Yearbook of International Humanitarian Law* (2009) 157 at 190. See also, F. Hampson 'Direct Participation in Hostilities and the Interoperability of the Law of Armed Conflict and Human Rights Law' in R. Pedrozo and D. Wollschlaeger (eds), *International Law and the Changing Character of War* (2011) 187, 190–2.

identifying the law and in applying it to the facts. The question discussed in this section is whether the problems of classification identified by the contributors created difficulties in the application of the *substantive* law and whether the classification decisions made by the participants in the armed violence had an impact in practice. What, in short, were the consequences of classification?

At first sight, classification 'must' have consequences, since it determines the law which is applicable to those responsible for and affected by any military operation, including the legal prohibitions and permissions relevant to the conduct of operations, and the level of protection for civilians. Governments involved in conflicts rely on classification in order to train their forces to ensure compliance with the applicable law, to avoid complicity with the forces of others which are not complying with the law and to confront those others with the need to comply with the law. Classification affects the relationship with a foreign sovereign on whose territory a conflict is being fought, in that it may determine the relevance of the local law; and it decides the applicability of such concepts as neutrality.

On the classification of the conflict may depend the appropriate standards of responsibility and liability for governments and for non-state groups. Classification also leads, in the present state of the law, to the determination of criminal responsibility for the individual soldier or commander. Prosecution before national courts or before an international tribunal will require the appropriate selection of charges, dependent in part on the category of the armed violence in question.

Such should be the legal consequences of classification. In this section we consider to what extent the case studies found that it had consequences in practice.

3.1. Few or no consequences

Many of the case studies showed that there were either few or no consequences of classification. In some cases classification did not matter in practice since one or more of the participants did not follow the law applicable to *any* kind of armed violence. Thus, the author of the case study on the DRC noted that, with the exception of the part played by the UN missions, there were systematic violations of fundamental treaty and customary rules on the conduct of hostilities, and the classification of many of the different conflicts concerned was therefore 'simply not a consideration'.[76] As regards the South Ossetian conflict, it 'was characterized by conduct that was clearly unlawful in the course of either an international or non-international conflict (including, for example, indiscriminate attacks, the deliberate killing of civilians, hostage-taking, the torching of houses, looting and pillaging, and rape)'; classification was therefore immaterial.[77] Few of the non-state

[76] Chapter 6, section 6.2; see also, section 4.3.
[77] Chapter 10, section 6.4. It should, however, be pointed out that classification may here be relevant in respect of the determination of individual criminal responsibility by the ICC; note that Georgia is a party to the ICC Statute. Under art. 8 of the Statute, attacking civilian objects is a war crime in international armed conflict but not in non-international conflict.

participants made any coherent classification.[78] Where the participants did not categorize the relevant hostilities at all this was merely a part of the wider fact that international humanitarian law was not sufficiently adhered to. It is unfortunately true that the main problem in almost all of the case studies was failure to follow the law, whether by States or by non-state armed groups.

In some instances, the participants, State or non-state, did not use classification as a significant basis for the application of the appropriate body of law, but adopted ROE or practices which followed policy directives for political, operational or other reasons. ISAF forces, engaged in counter-insurgency campaigns and stability operations in Afghanistan, had at times restrictive ROE designed to avoid alienating the civilian population (whether or not they succeeded in that task).[79] NATO forces in the 2011 Libyan intervention adopted targeting decisions well within the range of what international humanitarian law would have allowed and governments concerned were largely silent as to the classification of the conflict in which they were involved.[80] For policy reasons Israel applied to its military operations in Gaza 'the rules of armed conflict governing both international and non-international armed conflicts' because the rules on international armed conflict were clearer.[81] In Colombia, the decision by the government to apply Additional Protocol II as a matter of policy meant that some of the problems that could have arisen in relation to classification were rendered moot.[82] The author of chapter 14 concluded that: 'The practical result is that for fielded forces, classification of conflict matters less than it has in the past.'[83]

Some States are continuing to honour the classification rules in theory but adopting solutions on the ground with the aim either of avoiding the theoretical difficulties or of meeting some other goal. The US military apply the law relating to international armed conflict to all conflicts of whatever kind, unless they are directed otherwise.[84] As for the UK, David Turns of the UK Defence Academy

---

[78] See e.g. ch. 5 (Northern Ireland), section 3.1 ; ch. 9 (Gaza), section 3.1 ; ch. 12 (Lebanon) section 6.1; ch. 8 (Afghanistan), section 2.1.

[79] Chapter 8, section 4.

[80] See ch. 2, section 3.3 in relation to the operation in Libya: NATO 'did not apply force to the limits permitted under international humanitarian law. In this operation . . . NATO's targeting restrictions were significant. Only precision-guided munitions were used and, if an attack on any target was likely to result in any civilian casualties at all, the attack was not mounted or was called off. For this operation, therefore, no proportionality arguments were permitted when targets were being selected'. Indeed the main constraints on the targeting were the limitations of the mandate from the Security Council rather than the classification of the conflict.

[81] Official Israeli report on Operation Cast Lead, Gaza; ch. 9, section 5. At an earlier period, Israel's position, as argued in the *Targeted Killings* case, was that 'the question of the classification of the conflict between Israel and the Palestinians is a complicated question, with characteristics that point in different directions'. Ibid, section 3.2.

[82] Chapter 7, section 8.

[83] Chapter 14, section 5.

[84] The reference that is always given for such statements as this is DOD Directive 2311.01E, DOD Law of War Program. E.g. *The Commander's Handbook On The Law Of Naval Operations* (edition July 2007) states: '5.2 The Law Of Armed Conflict And its Application: DOD Directive 2311.01E, DOD Law of War Program, defines the law of war (synonymous with the term law of armed conflict) as that part of international law that regulates the conduct of armed hostilities. . . . It is DOD policy to comply with the law of armed conflict during all armed conflict, however such conflicts are characterized, and

has written: 'Generally the approach of the United Kingdom is to be as vague as possible concerning the legal classification of military operations in which British forces are engaged and to concentrate instead on the legal basis for such operations.'[85]

In other cases the reason why classifying the hostilities had few consequences was that there was little difference between the applicable bodies of law. Where the rules on the conduct of hostilities were concerned, classification in some of the studies was mentioned as being of no significance in practice because of the similarity of the rules in international and non-international conflict, as was noted in chapter 4. The consequences of classification for this and other areas of the law are considered in the next section.

3.2. The consequences of classification for the application of force, detention, and other issues of international humanitarian law and international criminal law

A question raised when the project for this book was conceived was whether difficulties in classifying armed violence and other hostilities had any impact on the many problems in implementing or ascertaining the applicable substantive law. While recognizing that, for the reasons given above, it might be difficult to show practical consequences of classification in some areas, there were thought to be two sets of legal issues which would be particularly affected by the classification of hostilities: the application or exercise of force and rules pertaining to detention of captured personnel. The authors of the case studies discussed whether difficulties in classification made any difference to these two issues; the question is also raised below in relation to the application of international human rights law and international criminal law.

3.2.1 Application of force

The distinction between international and non-international armed conflict was not regarded as significant in practice in most of the case studies, because of the similarity of the applicable rules. Thus, the DRC case study noted that 'for those

in all other military operations (see DOD Directive 2311.01 (series). Consistent with this policy, this manual will apply the law of armed conflict to all three of the types of armed conflicts discussed above.' This text does not however make clear to the reader whether what is being applied is the law of armed conflict applicable to international or to non-international armed conflict; Michael Schmitt, chairman of the International Law Department, US Naval War College, confirmed in conversation with the author that the text is intended as meaning that it is the law of international armed conflict that will be applied as a matter of policy to all armed conflicts (unless directed otherwise); June 2007 at 447.

[85] Quoted in D. Turns '*Jus ad Pacem in Bello*? Afghanistan, Stability Operations and the International Laws Relating to Armed Conflict' in M. Schmitt (ed.), *The War in Afghanistan: a legal analysis* (2009) at 403. This policy was indeed reflected in their involvement in the 2011 Libyan conflict. At one time the UK appeared to be of the view that international humanitarian law was being applied only as a matter of policy and that the 'proactive humanitarian action' did not amount to an armed conflict. (Unattributable conversation with the author.)

parties that did comply with the rules, the classification of the conflict was immaterial. This is best illustrated by the example of MONUC which in its *military operations* has, by and large, complied with the laws pertaining to the conduct of hostilities as provided in the Secretary-General's Bulletin'[86] (which does not distinguish between one form of conflict and the other). The Iraq case study concluded that because of the similarity of the rules, the transition from international to non-international conflict had little impact on the ground so far as the conduct of hostilities was concerned.[87] The author of the Gaza case study agreed with the official Israeli view that 'classification of the armed conflict between Hamas and Israel as international or non-international in the current context is largely of theoretical concern, as many similar norms and principles govern both types of conflicts'.[88] The same was true of the Lebanon study, where the author doubted whether classification would have had a practical consequence on targeting decisions, since even States which are not parties to Additional Protocol I accept the definition of military objectives set out in article 52(2) as accurately reflecting customary international law applicable in both international and non-international armed conflict; the same is true for the rule of proportionality codified in articles 51 and 57 of that Protocol.[89] The South Ossetia case study quoted the passage in the *Tagliavini* Report, which went even further (probably too far) in claiming an identity of rules:

> although the classification of an armed conflict as international or non-international is important in terms of the responsibilities of the various parties involved, when it comes to the effective protection by IHL of the persons and objects affected by the conflict it does not make much difference. Indeed, it is generally recognised that the same IHL customary law rules generally apply to all types of armed conflicts.[90]

There was however some controversy among the contributors with regard to the application of the same rules of international humanitarian law governing the conduct of hostilities in *all* circumstances of non-international armed conflict. A minority view among the contributors was that at the level of a Common Article 3 conflict the rules on the conduct of hostilities may differ in that it may not be permissible to target, by reason of membership, a member of an organized armed group exercising a continuous combat function.[91] It is here too that the interplay of human rights law and international humanitarian law becomes problematic. A further difficulty is raised in circumstances of prolonged occupation, where the relevant area is not in a conflict zone, there is no sustained violence and troops are engaged in merely law-enforcement activities: at this point, although the rules of international humanitarian conflict may apply to the situation overall,

---

[86] Chapter 6, section 6.2.   [87] Chapter 11, section 4.
[88] Chapter 9, section 8.
[89] Chapter 12. See however section 6.2 noting that as regards ground troops, a distinction might be made between the law applicable in the two kinds of armed conflict.
[90] Chapter 10, section 6.4.
[91] This view is discussed in ch. 8 (Afghanistan), section 4.

international human rights law would seem to be applicable to the law-enforcement activities.[92] These difficulties do not stem from the classification of hostilities but illustrate the extent to which classification itself is not solving the problems of determining the applicable law.

The distinction between armed conflict on the one hand and armed violence not amounting to armed conflict is of course of major relevance to the rules on application of force. The distinction was particularly relevant to the discussion of Al-Qaeda; the US regards the 'war against Al-Qaeda' as a global armed conflict, but others consider that in respect of many of the component hostilities it may be more appropriate to apply the law-enforcement paradigm. The author of the case study noted that the consequences of classifying as armed conflict 'are, above all, in relation to the mode of use of force, which currently includes missile strikes against individuals based on their status—many of these strikes (but not necessarily all) might be considered unlawful if the rules of armed conflict do not apply'. The same goes for the use of listed names of persons who can be targeted.[93]

3.2.2 Detention

The case studies confirmed the expected impact of classification on the determination of the law relating to detention.[94] In this context, classification of the armed violence had a direct relevance in the case studies. The distinction between the rules in international and non-international conflict was noted as relevant to the practice on detention followed by Israel in Lebanon 2008,[95] during the Second Congo War by the States parties in the DRC[96] and in the South Ossetian conflict.[97] The case studies confirmed the difficulty which arises from the lack of clear rules in non-international armed conflict, particularly regarding the grounds for detention and procedural safeguards.[98] In mixed conflicts the application of the two bodies of law can be difficult:

---

[92] See discussion of the controversy regarding the applicability of international human rights to checkpoints during the occupation of Iraq in C. Garraway 'To Kill or Not to Kill?—Dilemmas on the Use of Force' (2009) 14(3) *Journal of Conflict and Security Law* 499; and discussion of the regulation of checkpoints during the non-international armed conflict in Afghanistan in ch. 8, section 4 (last paragraph) and in R. Geiss and M. Siegrist, 'Has the armed conflict in Afghanistan affected the rules on the conduct of hostilities?' (2011) 93 *International Review of the Red Cross* 40–4.

[93] Chapter 13, section 8.2.

[94] The law on detention is set out in ch. 4, section 3.

[95] Chapter 12, section 5.

[96] '[B]y contrast with the rules on opening fire, classification obviously mattered to the States parties in respect of internment. There is ample evidence to show that during the Second Congo War each of the States parties distinguished between lawful combatants and other armed groups by according the former POW status when detained'; ch. 6, section 6.2.

[97] Chapter 10, section 5.3.

[98] See e.g. ch. 6 (DRC), section 6.2; ch. 8 (Afghanistan), section 5. See also, ch. 4, sections 3.2 and 3.3. A related problem was identified in the DRC case study as the absence of an express prohibition on *refoulement* in non-international armed conflict, which resulted in many Rwandan and Burundian refugees being forcibly returned to their respective States.

Questions relating to the standards for detention will sometimes depend solely on who happened to capture or to detain a particular person since the Third Geneva Convention dealing with POWs and the Fourth Geneva Convention, which includes provisions on internment, are only applicable if the person is interned by State forces in an international armed conflict, but are not applicable if the conflict in question is non-international.[99]

The problem is also apparent in relation to the transfer of detainees.[100]

In non-international armed conflict, where international humanitarian law is incomplete, the identification of customary law rules and the application of international human rights law have significantly improved the situation, but there are still gaps. The applicability of international human rights law to detainees in conflicts outside a State's own territory is controversial for some States and, in the current state of the law, its applicability to non-state armed groups is highly debatable. The efforts which have been made to agree guidelines to supplement international humanitarian law[101] have improved but not resolved the situation. According to the ICRC, States have identified the area as one where further work is urgently needed.[102]

In the event that there is no armed conflict but armed violence below that threshold, the rules of international humanitarian law will not of course apply. In the Al-Qaeda case study, for example, it was pointed out that if, contrary to the view of the US, there is not a global armed conflict with Al-Qaeda, 'many of the detentions—particularly, but not only, outside the Afghan (and possibly Pakistan) battlefields—may become highly questionable'.[103]

3.2.3 *International human rights law*

Actions taken in armed conflict are increasingly being assessed by human rights law as well as international humanitarian law; examples of the sometimes casual way in which the two separate bodies of law are thrown together are given in the case studies. The DRC case study gives an example of what is a frequent practice:

> [T]he UN bodies treated human rights law as applying concurrently with international humanitarian law. The targeting of the civilian population and the failure to distinguish were repeatedly condemned as both gross human rights violations and violations

---

[99] Chapter 3, section 7.3.

[100] See ch. 4, section 3.2, ch. 13 (Al-Qaeda), section 6.2 and ch. 8 (Afghanistan), section 5.3.

[101] The ICRC issued institutional guidelines in 2005 entitled 'Procedural Principles and Safeguards for Internment/Administrative Detention in Armed Conflict and Other Situations of Violence'. And the intergovernmental 'Copenhagen Process' was established in response to concerns that Danish troops were involved in a range of situations involving the potential detention of non-state enemy fighters without sufficient guidance on applicable rules; the goal was 'to establish a common framework for all troop-contributing States' on detention questions in UN-approved multilateral operations. See ch. 4, section 3.2.

[102] J. Kellenberger, 'Strengthening legal protection for victims of armed conflicts—States' consultations and way forward' Statement addressed to the permanent missions in Geneva by Dr Jakob Kellenberger, President of the ICRC (12 May 2011).

[103] Chapter 13, section 8.2; see also, discussion of detention in Guantánamo Bay in section 6.1.

of the laws of war. Moreover, in his regular reports to the Security Council the Secretary-General continued to draw attention to the failure of both the Government and the rebels to uphold human rights norms in the territories under their control. While on one level, UN reports might be explained as rhetorical gestures in part, it is unsatisfactory that the ICJ found Uganda in breach of its obligations to secure respect for the applicable rules of international human rights law, without clarifying the basis upon which such obligations accrue. It remains unclear whether the Court's finding was based on the extra-territorial applicability of the treaties in question or whether those obligations arose out of the requirement for the occupying power to respect the laws in force in the DRC.[104]

The applicability of international human rights law was mentioned in many of the other chapters in this volume. Numerous questions were raised in this context, including: the continued applicability of international human rights law during armed conflict;[105] the extraterritorial applicability of human rights law;[106] the applicability of human rights obligations to non-state actors party to a conflict;[107] the mandate of human rights bodies to assess violations during armed conflict;[108] the method for resolving perceived disparities between human rights and humanitarian law in situations of concurrent applicability;[109] the lack of uniformity in this regard of the case law of international human rights bodies and regional courts.[110] These issues have been the subject of extensive attention and debate in the literature over many years.[111] The case studies in this volume do not, and were not intended to, delve into these matters substantively. The brief mention of them, however,

---

[104] Chapter 6, section 4.5.
[105] See ch. 4, section 2; ch. 6, section 2.5; ch. 7, sections 5 and 8; ch. 14, section 5.
[106] See ch. 4, sections 2 and 3.2; ch. 6, sections 3.5 and 4.5; ch. 9, section 7; ch. 10, sections 5.2 and 6.3; ch. 13, section 8.3.
[107] See ch. 4, section 2; ch. 6, sections 2.4, 4.5 and 6.2.
[108] See ch. 6, section 4.5; ch. 12, sections 1 and 6.
[109] See ch. 4, section 4.3; ch. 6, sections 2.5, 3.5 and 4.5; ch. 13, section 8.3.
[110] Chapter 4, section 4.3. See also, the discussion of the jurisprudence of the European Court of Human Rights in ch. 10 (South Ossetia), section 5.2.
[111] G.I.A.D. Draper, 'The relationship between the human rights regime and the law of armed conflicts' (1971) 1 *Israel Yearbook on Human Rights* 191; K. Suter, 'An Inquiry into the Meaning of the Phrase "Human Rights in Armed Conflicts"' (1976) 15 *Revue de Droit Pénal Militaire et de Droit de la Guerre* 393; L. Doswald-Beck and S. Vité, 'International Humanitarian Law and Human Rights Law' (1993) 293 *International Review of the Red Cross* 94; R.E. Vinuesa, 'Interface, Correspondence and Convergence of Human Rights and International Humanitarian Law' (1998) 1 *Yearbook of International Humanitarian Law* 69–110; C. Droege, 'The Interplay Between International Humanitarian Law and International Human Rights Law in Situations of Armed Conflict' (2007) 40 *Israel Law Review* 310; N. Prud'homme, 'Lex Specialis: Oversimplifying a More Complex and Multifaceted Relationship?' (2007) 40 *Israel Law Review* 356; F. Hampson, 'Is Human Rights Law of Any Relevance to Military Operations in Afghanistan?' in M. Schmitt (ed.), *The War in Afghanistan: A Legal Analysis* (2009); N. Lubell, *Extraterritorial Use of Force Against Non-State Actors* (2010) chs 8–9; R. Provost, *International Human Rights and Humanitarian Law* (2002); UN Sub-Commission on the Promotion and Protection of Human Rights, 'Working paper on the relationship between human rights law and international humanitarian law by Françoise Hampson and Ibrahim Salama' E/CN.4/Sub.2/2005/14 (21 June 2005); Expert Meeting on the Right to Life in Armed Conflicts and Situations of Occupation, Convened at International Conference Centre, Geneva: The University Centre for International Humanitarian Law, Geneva (September 2005); L. Doswald-Beck, 'The Right to Life in Armed Conflict: Does International Humanitarian Law Provide all the Answers?' (2006) 864 *International Review of the Red Cross* 881; M. Sassòli and L. Olson, 'The Relationship between International

draws attention to the fact that while classification has as its purpose the signposting of the relevant body of international humanitarian law, this by no means resolves the question of the applicability of other bodies of law.

3.2.4 International criminal law

The classification of hostilities can be relevant to the trial of persons accused of committing war crimes, and thus also to the normative function of international criminal law. Upon correct classification depend the choice of the appropriate charge or indictment and the application of the appropriate body of law. The courts rely on the existing classifications, experience the same problems in categorizing as are described in this book, contribute to developing the interpretation of the law but also, because they are bound by their own statutes, ossify the existing categorizations. Classification too answers the question whether universal jurisdiction in national courts is required (as it is for those war crimes termed grave breaches, committed in international armed conflict)[112] or is merely permitted (in respect of war crimes committed in non-international armed conflict).

The ICC Statute has entrenched the separate categories of international and non-international conflict into the definitions of war crimes, even while the different wording of the statutes of the ad hoc tribunals gave the judges more latitude to merge the differences.[113] In those cases where the ICC Statute criminalizes the same substantive conduct in both categories of conflict, the same definition of crimes is generally adopted for both and so the need to determine the nature of the armed conflict in which they occurred is less acute.[114] The criminalization of the conscription and enlistment of child soldiers, however, has a slight but crucial difference in the terminology between the two respective crimes,[115] which may render the classification of the conflict necessary in order to choose the correct charge.

Humanitarian and Human Rights Law where it Matters: Admissible Killing and Internment of Fighters in Non-International Armed Conflicts' (2008) 871 *International Review of the Red Cross* 599.

[112] Geneva Convention I, art. 49; Geneva Convention II, art. 50; Geneva Convention III, art. 129; Geneva Convention IV, art. 146; Additional Protocol I, art. 85(1).

[113] In the *Tadić* interlocutory appeal on jurisdiction, the broad statement was made that '[w]hat is inhumane, and consequently proscribed, in international wars, cannot but be inhumane and inadmissible in civil strife' (*Prosecutor v Tadić*, IT-94-1-AR72, Decision on the Defence Motion for Interlocutory Appeal on Jurisdiction (Appeal Chamber), 2 October 1995, para 119) but later in the decision it is made clear that customary law has not equated non-international with international armed conflict; para 126. See brief discussion of the relevant cases in ch. 14, section 5. See also *Lubanga*, trial judgment, para 539, where the ICC Trial Chamber emphasized that the distinction between the two forms of conflict was enshrined in the Rome Statute and stated that it did not have the power 'to reformulate the Court's statutory framework'.

[114] *Prosecutor v Germain Katanga and Mathieu Ngudjolo Chui*, ICC-01/04-01/07-717, Decision on the Confirmation of Charges (Pre-Trial Chamber I), 30 September 2008, para 38; *Lubanga* Confirmation of Charges, 29 January 2007, para 204; *Prosecutor v Jean-Pierre Bemba Gombo*, ICC-01/05-01/08-295-Anx3, Decision on the Confirmation of Charges (Pre-Trial Chamber II), 15 June 2009, para 44.

[115] ICC Statute, art. 8(2)(b)(xxvi) and 8(2)(e)(vii).

This difficulty came to a head in *Lubanga,*[116] the first case before the ICC, where the accused was charged with the war crime of conscripting and enlisting child soldiers between July 2002 and December 2003 in the context of the conflicts occurring in the Ituri region of the DRC. The Prosecutor characterized the conflict in the context of which the alleged war crimes were committed as being of a non-international character[117] but, when confirming the charges, the Pre-Trial Chamber ruled that in the later part of the period—that between June 2003 and December 2003—the conflict was international, thereby requiring an amendment of the charge. The ruling of that Chamber, which was much criticized,[118] illustrates the difficulty in reaching views on classification even by tribunals who are examining a situation in the calm of retrospective analysis. The Trial Chamber has put the matter right.

Difficulties of classification may have the result of encouraging the Prosecutor to select charges for crimes against humanity rather than war crimes. The situation in Libya may provide an example. In February 2011, the UN Security Council referred the ongoing situation of violence in Libya to the ICC. If the Prosecutor had chosen to investigate allegations of war crimes, he would have had to address questions about the point at which the situation descended from a state of 'internal disturbance and tensions, such as riots, isolated and sporadic acts of violence or other acts of a similar nature'[119] to a non-international armed conflict.

4. Conclusions

None of the case studies in this volume reaches conclusions as to the classification of the relevant situation of armed violence which are entirely free from controversy. In most cases the decision of an author as to the relevant classification is either different from that arrived at by the parties themselves, or different from others to be found in the literature, illustrating the complexities of the law and the extent to which classification in practice is often a subjective matter for the participants rather than an objective analysis of facts and law.[120] The law is disputed on some matters; indeed, as we have seen, the authors of this book were themselves in disagreement

---

[116] *Lubanga* Confirmation of Charges.

[117] Thus charging him under art. 8(2)(e)(vii). *Prosecutor v Thomas Lubanga Dyilo,* ICC- 01/04-01/06-356, Submission of the Document Containing the Charges Pursuant to Article 61(3)(a) and of the List of Evidence Pursuant to Rule 121(3) (Pre-Trial Chamber I), 28 August 2006, para 12, and *Prosecutor v Thomas Lubanga Dyilo,* ICC-01/04-06/356-Anx2, Document Containing the Charges (Pre-Trial Chamber I).

[118] See e.g. Hoffman, *Squaring the Circle,* 217. See now, to the contrary, *Lubanga,* trial judgment. Since the Trial Chamber characterized the armed conflict in question as non-international, it did not need to consider the difference in wording of the two war crimes.

[119] ICC Statute, art. 8(2)(d) and (f).

[120] See e.g. ch. 5, Northern Ireland (classification different from the UK's view); ch. 9, Gaza (different from Israel's view); ch. 7, Colombia (almost certainly different in part from the government's view and that of the other participants); ch. 10 , South Ossetia (different from Georgia's view as regards non-international armed conflict); ch. 12, Lebanon (different from the parties and from some commentators); ch. 13, Al-Qaeda (different from the US view).

about two or three major aspects of classification law. Some of the arguments about classification reach a high degree of abstraction, so that even the most legally sophisticated of governments do not engage with them in practice. Sometimes indeed it has appeared that classification is possible only retrospectively, when all the evidence is available, with the result that it can only be criminal courts, trying combatants who could not know the 'right' classification, which are able to come to a considered view.[121]

What then are the conclusions to be drawn from the picture of rather poor practice on classification which has been presented by the case studies? None of the authors of the preceding chapters has recommended major changes in the classification system; they have concluded that the existing categories of international and non-international armed conflict are sufficient to encompass all existing forms of conflict. Nor has there been any support from the authors for the creation of new categories of conflict to follow military or operational distinctions. The current classification system is likely to remain. While an assimilation of the two main forms of armed conflict has been proposed elsewhere,[122] the division into non-international and international armed conflict is inevitable so long as the post-Westphalian paradigm of sovereign States remains and so long as the Geneva Conventions and Protocols are the main body of applicable law, whether as treaties or as customary law. But the rules of international humanitarian law applicable in the two forms of armed conflict will continue to merge,[123] though that is unlikely to happen by way of amending treaty, and the more closely the law coincides, the less need there will be for engaging in the complexities of division between the two forms.

As the law now stands, however, the existence of the difficulties of classification discussed in this volume encourages a search for improvements, with regard both to the law and its implementation. In the first place, the difficulties of classification deserve more attention and more work by practitioners and commentators so as to lead to clearer classification in those instances where the distinction between different forms of armed violence continues to be significant for the choice of the applicable law. It has to be possible to reach a view on classification at the time of the violence, not only afterwards, and the appropriate rules of international humanitarian law have to be capable of being identified. Legal complexities about

---

[121] And the conclusions of the tribunals may themselves be controversial; see discussion of Pre-Trial Chamber decision in *Lubanga* at section 3 above.

[122] See discussion of such proposals in ch. 3, section 4. In the view of some writers 'we would appear to be moving tentatively towards the position whereby the legal distinction between international and non-international armed conflict is becoming outmoded. What will matter as regards legal regulation will not be whether an armed conflict is international or internal, but simply whether an armed conflict exists per se'. L. Moir, *The law of internal armed conflict* (2002) 51. And see W.M. Reisman and J. Silk, 'Which law applies to the Afghan conflict?' (1988) 82 *AJIL* 465: 'Paying lip service to the alleged distinction [between international and non-international armed conflict] simply frustrates the humanitarian purpose of the law of war in most of the instances in which war now occurs.'

[123] Chapter 14 (The Future) predicts a 'bleeding together of the norms applicable to the various genres of conflict'; section 5.

the distinctions between categories of hostilities should not be allowed to get in the way of the objectives of international humanitarian law, either by making the application of the legal protections more difficult or by rendering the law so complex that none but the most sophisticated of armed forces can realistically apply it. The case studies have illustrated the difficulty of classifying hostilities in rapidly changing situations, or where the facts or the law are otherwise complex. One element that is lacking in the corpus of international humanitarian law is an independent authority with the role of giving guidance to participants as to which law is applicable. Is there a role for the creation of a process or mechanism which could issue, after consultation with the participants, opinions as to classification and its legal consequences?[124]

Secondly, where controversies as to classification remain, it may be feasible to encourage the making of unilateral commitments by States participating in hostilities with regard to the law they will apply; the proviso of course is that the law specified must give the highest relevant rights and protection. A unilateral statement by a government, accepting much of the law on international armed conflict for the purpose of non-international conflict, would make clear what law was being applied, carving out certain areas of the law and modifying others to fit the situation of non-international conflict. Such declarations would not solve the problem of the interplay with other obligations (in particular under international human rights law); but even here they may be helpful in those countries where the courts are more inclined to apply human rights law simply because of the perceived absence of any other applicable law. A declaration would be binding on the government concerned[125] and, if it were implemented in national law, could lay the basis for individual accountability.

But, as the UN Secretary-General has said: '[I]mproved compliance with international humanitarian law and human rights law will always remain a distant prospect in the absence of, and absent acceptance of the need for, systematic and consistent engagement with non-state armed groups.'[126] Here too unilateral declarations may possibly be a way forward. Many groups have pledged compliance with the principles of the Anti-personnel Mine Treaty by signing the deed of

---

[124] Resolution 1 of the 31st International Conference of the Red Cross and Red Crescent 1 December 2011) recognized 'the importance of exploring ways of enhancing and ensuring the effectiveness of mechanisms of compliance with international humanitarian law, with a view to strengthening legal protection for all victims of armed conflict'; it is suggested by this author that any new compliance process or mechanism should be mandated to examine issues related to classification. See also, The Rule of Law in Armed Conflicts Project at The Geneva Academy of International Humanitarian Law and Human Rights which usefully assesses the classification of hostilities around the world, although not always in a timely manner; at available <www.adh-geneva.ch/policy-studies/ongoing/rule-of-law-of-armed-conflicts-project>.

[125] *Nuclear Tests (Australia v France)* ICJ Rep 1974, 253, para 43. In the case of multilateral operations, the members of a coalition would have to work on their respective declarations together to avoid the situation where allied parties use different rules in the same conflict because of different perceptions of classification.

[126] Security Council, 'Report of the UN Secretary-General on the Protection of Civilians in Armed Conflict' S/2010/579 (11 November 2010) para 56.

commitment drawn up by the non-governmental organization Geneva Call.[127] Some groups have incorporated the principles of international humanitarian law in their military doctrines, formulating a set of directives governing the conduct of hostilities.[128] The forms of non-international armed conflicts are increasing; so are the varieties of non-state armed groups. Unilateral declarations could deal with the differences and take into account the specificities of the conflict, including the abilities of non-state armed groups, tailoring the appropriate rules and principles to the particular circumstances without departing from the general law.[129] But work needs to be done on what would provide an incentive to such groups to obey the law, particularly for those whose purpose it is specifically to terrorize a population, or to foment a breakdown of law and order.[130]

Thirdly, the case studies in this volume have illustrated that problems of classification are frequently not themselves the cause of difficulties in determining and complying with the applicable law; those problems arise from gaps in the law applicable to non-international armed conflict, uncertainties arising from the interplay between international human rights law and international humanitarian law, and practical problems. A further conclusion of this volume must be therefore that where the substantive law is insufficient or uncertain, appropriate ways to supplement it should continue to be examined;[131] and if courts and human rights mechanisms are not able adequately to remove the existing uncertainty in the relationship between international humanitarian law and human rights law, governments and other actors should seek to agree on appropriate principles.

Finally, classification needs to be taken more seriously. States engaged in conflict should categorize objectively and in reliance on ascertainable facts and should make explicit their decisions as to classification. Courts and other authorities enforcing criminal law and the law of State responsibility will make objective determinations as to the categories of hostilities after the fact; it will be to the detriment of individual soldiers if subjective classification decisions have led to actions beyond what is permitted by the appropriate body of international law. On classification

---

[127] For current participants see <www.genevacall.org/Themes/Landmines/landmines.htm>. In the past, national liberation movements made unilateral declarations agreeing to be bound by international humanitarian law, many of these being made explicitly under Protocol I; see e.g. the list of declarations made by African liberation movements in C. Ewumbue-Monono, 'Respect for international humanitarian law by armed non-state actors in Africa' (2006) 864 (88) *International Review of the Red Cross* 908–9 (Ewumbue-Monono, *Non-state actors in Africa*).

[128] Ewumbue-Monono, *Non-state actors in Africa*, 920. More recently, the Libyan National Transitional Council made a statement about the application of the third Geneva Convention, National Transitional Council, 'The treatment of detainees and prisoners' (25 March 2011), available at: <www.ntclibya.org/english/prisoners/>.

[129] See The Geneva Academy of International Humanitarian Law and Human Rights, 'Rules of Engagement: Protecting Civilians through Dialogue with Armed Non-State Actors' (October 2011) (ADH, *ROE: Protecting Civilians*). See also, discussion in S. Sivakumaran, 'Re-envisaging the International Law of Internal Armed Conflict' (2011) 22 *EJIL* 235–6.

[130] See e.g. ADH, *ROE: Protecting Civilians*.

[131] See ch. 4, sections 3.2 and 3.3 for discussion of ways in which the law on detention and transfer of detainees should be further developed. Soft law instruments incorporating standards which are likely to become more concrete as they continue to be adopted in practice are one possibility, since the conclusion of new treaties is unlikely.

depends the rule of law and, finally, accountability. Governments also owe it to their citizens to explain matters properly, because of their responsibility to educate about the law.[132] Where they are not using correct classifications under the impression that the general public will not accept the term 'conflict' they may be misjudging the likely response; but the effect of continuous such misinterpretations may be that people will indeed not understand. The protection of victims of war depends upon the proper application of international humanitarian law and that depends upon the appropriate classification.

---

[132] Geneva Convention I, art. 47; Geneva Convention II, art. 48; Geneva Convention III, art. 127; Geneva Convention IV, art. 144.

Index